Introduction to Computers and Information Processing

Apple® is a registered trademark of Apple Computer, Inc., Sunnyvale, California.
ATARI® is a registered trademark of Atari, Inc.
ADABAS™ is a trademark of Software AG of North America.
Burroughs® is a registered trademark of Burroughs Corp., Detroit, Michigan.
Compaq™ is a trademark of Compaq Computer Corporation.
Commodore™ is a trademark of Commodore Business Machines.
Commodore 64® is a registered trademark of Commodore Business Machines.
CP/M® is a registered trademark of Digital Research Corp., Pacific Grove, California.
Coke® is a registered trademark of the Coca-Cola Company.
CompuServe® is a registered trademark of CompuServe, Inc.
DEC® is a registered trademark of Digital Equipment Corporation.
DEC Rainbow® is a registered trademark of Digital Equipment Corporation.
DB MASTER™ is a trademark of Barney Stone and Alpine Software, Inc.
dBASE II™ is a trademark of Ashton-Tate, Inc.
Hewlett-Packard® is a registered trademark of Hewlett-Packard Company.
IBM® is a registered trademark of IBM Corp.
Intel® is a registered trademark of Intel Corporation.
IBM® PC*jr* is a registered trademark of IBM Corporation.
Kaypro® is a registered trademark of the Kaypro Corporation.
Lisa™ is a trademark of Apple Computer, Inc.
LOTUS 1-2-3™ is a trademark of Lotus Development Company.
Macintosh™ is a trademark licensed to Apple Computer, Inc.
Microsoft® is a registered trademark of Microsoft Corporation.
MS-DOS™ is a trademark of Digital Research Corp.
The Manager Series™ is a trademark of DATAMENSION CORPORATION.
MEDLARS® is a registered trademark of the National Library of Medicine, National Institutes of Health, Department of Health and Human Services.
North Star™ is a trademark of North Star Computers, Berkeley, California.
Osborne™ is a trademark of Osborne Corporation.
PET® is a registered trademark of Commodore Business Machines.
PC-DOS™ is a trademark of IBM Corporation.
Pascal™ is a trademark of the Regents of the University of California at San Diego.
Radio Shack® is a registered trademark of Radio Shack, a division of the Tandy Corporation.
RAMIS II® is a registered trademark of Mathematica Products Group, Inc.
Sony® is a registered trademark of Sony Corp., 1 Sony Dr., Park Ridge, NJ.
The Source^{SM} is a service mark of Source Telecomputing Corporation, a subsidiary of The Reader's Digest Association.
System 2000® is a registered trademark of Intel Corporation.
Texas Instruments™ is a trademark of Texas Instruments.
TIS™ is a trademark of Software Arts, Inc.
UNIVAC® is a registered trademark of Sperry.
UNIX™ is a trademark of Bell Laboratories (AT&T).
UPI™ is a trademark of Intel Corporation.
VAX™ is a trademark of Digital Equipment Corporation.
Visi On™ is a trademark of VisiCorp.
VisiCorp™ is a trademark of VisiCorp.
VisiCalc® is a registered trademark of VisiCorp.
VIC® is a registered trademark of Commodore Business Machines.
WANG® is a registered trademark of Wang Laboratories, Inc.
Xerox® is a registered trademark of Xerox Corporation.
Z-80™ is a trademark of Zilog Corp.

SECOND EDITION

Introduction to Computers and Information Processing

DON CASSEL
MARTIN JACKSON

Reston Publishing Company, Inc.
A Prentice-Hall Company
Reston, Virginia

To Lindsay

Ginger will always be my spice of life.

Martin Jackson

Library of Congress Cataloging in Publication Data

Cassel, Don,
    Introduction to computers and information processing.

    1. Computers. 2. Electronic data processing.
3. Programming languages (Electronic computers)
I. Jackson, Martin. II. Title.
QA76.C365   1985   001.64   84-13422
ISBN 0-8359-3148-X

© 1980, 1981, 1985 by Reston Publishing Company, Inc.
A Prentice-Hall Company
Reston, Virginia 22090

All rights reserved. No part of this book may be reproduced in any way or by any means, without permission in writing from the publisher.

10 9 8 7 6 5 4 3 2 1

PRINTED IN THE UNITED STATES OF AMERICA

Contents

Preface, xi

Section A: A GUIDE TO COMPUTERS, 1

1 Introduction, 3
  Influence in Our Daily Lives, 4
  The Computer Impact, 6
  What is a Computer? 10
  The Need for Computers, 11

2 Historical Development—Tools of Man, 15
  Inventions and Their Inventors, 15
  The First Computers, 23
  Unit Record Systems, 26
  Modern Computer Generations, 30

3 Number Systems, 39
  Mathematical Number Systems, 40
  Computer Number Systems, 54

Section B: COMPUTER HARDWARE, 65

4 Computer Data Processing Systems, 67
  Data Processing Terminology, 67

The Computer and Its Components, 71
Processing Concepts, 79

5 Data Entry, 93
Punched Cards, 94
Key Entry Devices, 102
Central Collection System, 111
Point of Sale Terminals (POS), 115
A Practical Application of Data Entry, 119

6 Computer Output, 121
Types of Printers, 121
Digital Display Screens, 133

7 Magnetic Tape, 145
Physical Structure of Tape, 145
Applications for Magnetic Tape, 156

8 Direct Access Storage Devices, 163
Magnetic Disk, 163
File Organization and Access Methods, 171

9 Other I/O Devices, 187
Optical Character Recognition (OCR), 187
Optical Mark Recognition (OMR), 191
Magnetic Ink Character Recognition (MICR), 192
Graphic Display, 195
Mass Storage, 198
Computer Output Microfilm (COM), 199
Drum Plotter, 202

10 Central Processing Unit, 205
Physical Structure, 205
Principles of Storage Technology, 213
Channels, 221
Control Units, 223

11 Minicomputers and Microcomputers, 227
Minicomputers, 227
Microcomputers, 232
Breakdown of Main Microcomputer Components, 236
Markets—Or Who is Buying Microcomputers? 245
Future Trends, 251

Section C: COMPUTER PROGRAMMING, 255

12 Problem Solving, 257
Problem Analysis, 257
Programmer Productivity. 271

13 Introduction to Programming, 283
Translators, 283
Programming Languages, 285
Fourth Generation Languages, 295
Low-Level Languages, 296
Characteristics of a Good Program, 298
Program Coding, 302
Program Test and Debug, 303

14 Basic, 307
BASIC Programming Fundamentals, 307
Arithmetic Operations, 312
Alphanumeric Operations, 317
Simple Interest Program, 317
Input and Output, 320
Labelled Output Program, 327
Program Control Statements, 330
Sales Commission Program, 332
Lists and Tables, 337
Subroutines, 343

Section D: SYSTEMS ANALYSIS AND DESIGN, 345

15 Concepts of a System, 347
Deriving a Definition, 347
The Four Stages of a System, 350

16: Analysis, 355
Stage 1: Analysis, 355
Part 1: Data Gathering Techniques, 355
Part 2: Constraints, Policies, and Requirements, 363
Part 3: Determining What the Problem Is!, 366

17 Design, 371
Introduction, 371
Coding, 372
Forms Design, 378

Data Control, 387
Design of a Payroll System, 394
Making More Use of a Terminal, 403

18 Implementation, Operation, and Modification, 409
Part 1: Implementation Techniques, 410
Part 2: Dealing with Computer Manufacturers, 412
Part 3: We're Up and Running, 414

19 Tools of the Trade, 417
Systems Flowcharting, 417
Decision Tables, 420
Structured Systems Analysis, 422
Presentation Abilities, 425
Summary, 426

20 Applications, 429
Accounts Receivable, 430
Inventory, 433
Accounts Payable, 436
Word Processing, 444

Section E: ADVANCED CONCEPTS, 449

21 Operating Systems, 451
Functions of an Operating System, 451
Operating System Components, 460

22 Data Communication Systems, 473
Types of Systems, 473
Types of Terminals, 476
Files, 485
Distributed Processing Systems, 487

23 Data-Base, 491
Data-Base Concepts, 492
Data Structures, 494
Data-Base Files, 498
Data-Base Languages, 501
Language Attributes, 501
Data-Base Perspectives, 502
CODASYL Data Description Language, 502
Data Language/1, 504
Other Data-Base Languages, 506

24 Computers in Society, 511
Privacy, 512
Electronic Funds Transfer, 513
Unemployment, 514
Electronic Mail, 515
Education, 515
Hospital Information Systems (HIS), 518
Transportation, 519
Law Enforcement, 521
Public Information Utilities, 522
Careers in Computers, 523

25 The Future is Now, 531

Appendixes, 535
Appendix A: Metric Measurement, 535
Appendix B: Careers in Computers, 538
Appendix C: Periodicals of Interest, 541

Language Supplement, 545
COBOL, 547
FORTRAN, 585
Pascal™, 609

GLOSSARY, 643

INDEX, 667

Preface

Since this book was first published in 1980 immense changes have occurred in the computer industry. Probably the most obvious of these changes has been the emergence of the personal computer from a curiosity in the late 1970s to a driving force in the industry as we approach the mid-1980s. The personal computer has already been well established as a mainstay in the offices of the Fortune 500 companies as well as many smaller organizations who have recognized the computer's potential.

A second trend which was well underway in the early 80's was a move toward transaction oriented mainframe systems. This movement was evident in many ways but was signalled by the installation of display terminals and the software needed to support them.

As vast and far reaching as theses changes are, many of the older systems are still in widespread use. Transaction oriented systems are often backed-up by batch systems and many applications simply do not lend themselves to effective interactive processing.

THE APPROACH TAKEN IN THIS BOOK

In this book we have attempted to create a blend of the old and the new. Clearly our students should be exposed to the current concepts and directions being taken in the computer industry. But we also recognize that there are many 5 to 10 year old (and older) systems in operation and many of our students will also leave college to work in that environment. So a balance is needed for an effective academic program.

The book is composed of five sections. The first section is a guide to the computer and presents a multifarious array of computer concepts and terminology. Section B covers the hardware, ranging from data entry devices and methods, to a variety of storage and I/O devices. Although we look at hardware in depth we also examine the application of these devices to everyday problems in business.

Section C gives an overview of programming from problem solving concepts to languages, including those of third and fourth generation. A complete chapter is devoted to introductory programming concepts using the BASIC language. Section D concentrates on systems analysis and design while the final section of the book covers the advanced concepts of data communciations networks and data-bases. Recognizing that not everyone wants to teach BASIC in this course, the book ends with language supplements for COBOL, FORTRAN, and Pascal™.

TEACHING AND LEARNING AIDS

Over the last 16 years we have taught numerous introductory courses to first year college students. One major concern in the learning process that students have is the understanding of the numerous terms that are important to a fundamental grasp of the computer industry.

Naturally this book is filled with terms many of which will be new to the first time student whose only exposure to the computer may have come from a home computer, video game, or POS terminals in a retail store. Of course none of this truly creates much in the way of computer literacy to say nothing of going on to become a computer professional.

To address this need we have included the "key concept" where new terms are presented. Other terminology is discussed throughout each chapter as they are needed. Each chapter ends with a list of the important terms that have been covered in the chapter. Terms are also addressed in the glossary at the end of the book.

Each chapter also includes questions and exercises to help the student acquire a working knowledge of the material and to prepare for tests and examinations. As a further aid to study and to generate appreciation for the vastness of the subject, most chapters, have a section at the end with problems for research and discussion. Some of these problems can be used for independent study or assignments. In other cases, they would make an excellent team project or could be used for classroom discussion. Because of the ever changing nature of our topic these problems can also serve as a guide to new topics which are of current interest to your class.

CHAPTER CONTENT

The book is divided into five sections with a general theme running through each section. The book can be used from beginning to end or there can be selective concentration on several of the sections that are appropriate to the needs of your course. Here is a brief summary of the five sections.

Section A—A Guide to Computers

This section presents the basic foundation for the chapters that follow. We look at the impact the computer has had on our daily lives, its growth since the first computer in the 1950s and the four generations of computers we have seen in our lifetime. Basic computer concepts are examined with artwork, graphics, and photographs to show how these concepts work.

Section B—Computer Hardware

This section covers the never-ending variety of computer input/output and processing devices. The chapter proceed from punched cards (yes, cards are still in use by many companies) through data entry terminals to tape, disk, central processing units and other I/O devices.

However, we do not stop at discussing how the devices function. Rather each chapter discusses the application and implications of using the various devices. The section ends with a chapter on mini- and microcomputers. This is no doubt where the most exciting changes have occurred in the computer industry in the last few years. We have addressed the effect of personal computer hardware, and software such as spreadsheets, word processors, and data-bases on the industry.

Section C—Computer Programming

Any course on the computer should expose the student to some programming, if for no other reason than to break down some of the barriers between humans and the computer. Of course, BASIC has been the main language emerging for this purpose. So in this section we look at the evolution of programming languages, discuss some of the more prominent languages like BASIC, COBOL, FORTRAN, Pascal, PL/1, and RPG and go on to consider what is meant by a fourth generation language.

A chapter is devoted to structured problem solving techniques and a final chapter on BASIC programming. In our courses about 20% of the semester is devoted to problem solving and programming and BASIC is the language used for this activity. For those schools that prefer other languages the end of the book contains supplements for COBOL, FORTRAN, and Pascal. These are also suitable for a programming component in the course.

Section D—Systems Analysis and Design

The ability to understand and design systems is emerging as a need in the computer industry where a flood of programmers has changed the needs of industry. A well-rounded education in information processing requires a strength in the understanding of systems: their design, implementation, and operation. We feel a book on the computer must address the importance of the systems analyst and the systems process.

Section E—Advanced Concepts

The final section of the book leads to concepts such as data communications networks for mainframe systems and local area networks for the personal computer. Another emerging force has been the data-base. It covers the range of the corporate data-base where both hierarchical and relational systems are used, the public data-bases such as The Source^{SM} or Telidon, and private data-bases such as those used on personal computers.

This section ends with chapters on the use of computers in our society and career paths that may be taken within the computer industry.

We hope you will find this book a useful ally in your course on computers and information processing. We would like to thank all the faculty at Humber College who have used the first edition over the last few years for their helpful comments and suggestions for improving the content. A special thanks is also due those who responded to the questionaire sent to them and the feedback they so graciously provided. We also appreciate the direction and support given by our editors at Reston. **Ben Wentzell, John Sulzycki, Nanette Edwards,** and **Carolyn Ormes** each deserve our thanks for their contribution to this project.

A Guide to Computers

1

Introduction

We are in the midst of a revolution: the Computer Revolution. It is destined to overshadow even the Industrial Revolution, which gave us electricity, global communication, the automobile, and the airplane. It has immensely affected the lives of every person, not only in the industrialized nations but even in the Third World countries, around our globe. What kind of future this is leading to is starting to unfold, but the long term future is at best the speculation of futurists and science fiction writers.

Since the mid-1950s, the prices of computers have decreased dramatically, and the performance in terms of speed and data capacity has increased spectacularly. James Martin in *The Computerized Society* shows these factors to be expanding at a logarithmic rate. Speed has increased 10 fold every five years from 1955 to 1980. If this continues, we can expect another order of magnitude increase by 1985. What does this mean in everyday terminology? If the population of the United States grew at this rate and we assumed a population of 160 million people in 1955, then by 1975 there would have been 1.6 trillion people and by 1985 the population would grow to 160 trillion. The capacity for storing data in the computer system has increased at a similar rate. Whether computer performance will continue to improve at such a rate is anyone's guess, but the impact of what has already occurred will have a lasting influence on this planet.

INFLUENCE IN OUR DAILY LIVES

The computer influences your life to a far greater extent than might be imagined. You may be awakened in the morning by music from the digital alarm clock/radio, the circuitry of which was designed with the aid of a computer and uses computer technology for the miniaturization of its components. The music heard may have been selected and organized into the morning program using a computer.

The morning paper delivered to the door was produced while you slept and used computer typesetting to bring the most recent news events to you with a minimum delay and at the lowest cost. However, the computer did not write the stories, nor did it deliver the paper to your door. Creative activity is not something the computer does very well. And Johnny still does a better job of delivery than any computerized robot.

During breakfast you may look through various bills received by mail. The electric, gas, oil, telephone, and magazine companies all send bills produced by computer. The company computer scans its customer records, determines who owes money and the amount, prints an appropriate bill, and addresses it. In some cases, the computer even stuffs the mailing envelopes. When you return the bill or its stub with a check, the stub becomes input to the computer, which updates your record showing the bill has been paid.

Your car's design has been influenced by the computer. Most major automobile manufacturers use computers to design their cars and components. Engineers with the assistance of computer programs develop style, economy, comfort, ride, handling, and cost. During assembly of a car, the computer schedules parts and labor to ensure that everything is ready at the right time.

Many modern cars are being assembled with the help of computerized robots. If you drive a car with fuel injection, there may be a small computer built into the car to measure road speed and driving conditions; and from this, the computer determines the air/fuel mixture supplied to the engine. As you drive through the city, traffic lights are computer controlled to optimize traffic flow. If this system fails, it will take much longer to arrive at your destination than usual. Your driver's license and ownership papers have likely been printed by computer, and your driving record is maintained by the government on a computer file.

Arriving at school, you attend classes scheduled by a computer. Grades received in your courses are tabulated by computer, which generates reports for you and your professors. If you have applied for a student loan, scholarship, or financial assistance, a computer will likely assist in the analysis of your request. When you receive your loan, this information will be recorded on the computer with the repayment terms,

"It can't actually think, but when it makes a mistake, it puts the blame on some other computer."

This cartoon and the ones on pages 118, 230, 248, 284, 309, 367, 413, and 471 are reprinted with permission of *CREATIVE COMPUTING*. Copyright 1979 by Creative Computing, P.O. Box 789-M, Morristown, NJ 07960.

and periodic checks will be made to ensure repayment at the appropriate time.

When you go to the library to do research for an assignment, the books there have been ordered and catalogued with computer assistance. If your library belongs to an association of libraries, computer listings of books available at other branches are used to assist in finding exactly what you need.

For lunch you might go to a local McDonald's for a Big Mac. The computer has even come here. In many retail outlets such as this, a computerized cash register is used to speed up checkouts as well as record all sales and update inventory records. This type of system keeps prices down for the consumer and profits up for the retailer.

During the afternoon, you and a few friends may decide to spend the long weekend at the beach. You phone a travel agent for reservations. The airline tickets and motel reservation systems are all computerized. These computers check available openings suitable to your needs. If a given flight is filled, the computer can suggest an alternative. You receive an immediate response saying your reservations are confirmed for a specific date, time, and cost.

That night you sit down to read a book for your course in computer programming. You notice that the type appears slightly different from that in most books. It appears that the author is a professor of computer studies and has used a word processing computer to help write the book.

While all of these experiences may not affect each of us every day, they are all quite common uses of the computer today. Not all cities use computer controlled traffic lights, and not all books are written using computers (this one was only typeset by computer), but in many diverse ways, we are all affected by the Computer Revolution and will be increasingly so in the future.

THE COMPUTER IMPACT

The term computer is used so casually today that we seldom stop to consider what is meant by the word. Businesses use computers for payroll, accounting, billing, inventory, sales analysis, and, in general, information systems. Hotels, motels, airlines, and even some restaurants use computers for reservation systems. The U.S. space program would never have reached the pinnacle of success it did without the massive computer installations used by NASA. Computers are also used in such diverse applications as weather forecasting, medicine, security systems, library systems, language translation, and classroom instruction.

Large scale improvements have placed computer power within reach of large and small businesses, offices, schools, factories, and even the home. With the increase of computing speeds, more powerful computers were developed. These computers had the capacity for more work than one organization could provide. As a result, time-sharing systems were developed that allowed many users to share the time available on a single computer. Users could be found in a variety of places. Some might be in the same building, others across the city, and even others across the country. By attaching various terminal devices by telephone line, many people could have simultaneous access to the same computer.

Another impact came in the area of the mini- and microcomputer. The development of small, low-cost computer systems permitted each user to have his own computer without reliance upon a larger system. The minicomputer moved quite rapidly into small business and did such basic chores as payroll, accounting, record keeping, and inventory.

Computers cover a very broad span of prices. For example, the Commodore 64, which sold for under $200 in 1984, is a sophisticated computer with color, sound, and graphic capabilities designed for personal use. At the other extreme is Cray Research Inc.'s Cray-1, which costs several million to purchase the central processor.

THE COMPUTER IMPACT 7

Figure 1-1. Sperry-Univac BC/7 business computer system. (*Courtesy of Sperry-Univac*)

Figure 1-2. Commodore 64.

Figure 1-3. Cray-1.

Some Computer Terms

Computer machinery is known as hardware. The hardware consists of all the physical components of the computer such as the central processing unit, display screens, printers, tape drives, and disk drives.

Instructions that tell the computer to perform certain operations are called software. The software or programs consist of a series of commands or statements that direct the operation of the computer. It is the software that supplies instructions for payroll or accounts receivable applications to be processed by the computer. A large part of this book explains in detail what hardware and software are and how they are used.

Computer Occupations and Growth

Another area of consideration is the human role in the use of the computer. This role represents a large and significant component in the successful use of computers. Areas such as analysis, design, programming, and operating are occupations that require human proficiency for effective computer use.

The widespread application of computers has sometimes resulted in the criticism that computers are taking jobs and creating unemployment. This was a strong argument against the use of computers in the 1960s

THE COMPUTER IMPACT 9

Figure 1-4. The Sperry-Univac 1100/60. (*Courtesy of Sperry-Univac*)

and, to a certain degree, even today. However, the computer has become a major industry in itself and is now the creator of hundreds of thousands of skilled and professional jobs.

In the U.S., the computer industry growth rate has been 15 percent per year. In Canada, growth is 17 percent per year. In Europe, 20 percent and in Japan, 25 percent. The revenues from the sale of hardware, services and other products in 1975 was $22 billion in the U.S., $7.2 billion in Europe, $2.4 billion in Japan, and $1.1 billion in Canada. U.S. based companies supply the world market with about 53 percent of the world's computers. So we can see that the computer has been fully accepted as a necessary tool in today's world.

WHAT IS A COMPUTER?

What then is a computer? How can it be so flexible in its application and cover so broad a range in price? A computer is a device with the following characteristics.

1. It is constructed from electronic components.
2. It contains a storage device for data and programs.
3. It receives instructions from a stored program, which controls all operations and calculations automatically.
4. It has provision for input and output of data.

Although each computer may include these characteristics in a broad variety of ways, they each will be included in the design of the computer. These are the primary features distinguishing computers from other machines. There are also some secondary features by which computers are known. One of these is the ability to perform calculations and decisions at very high speed. Some very high-speed computers can do well in excess of 1,000,000 operations per second. Related to this is the ability to perform a sequence of repetitive operations effectively. This is one basic advantage over the human. A computer does not become bored by repetition, nor is it as error prone as people are.

The types of computers discussed in this book are digital. This means that they work with digits (i.e., 0, 1) and in many cases with characters.

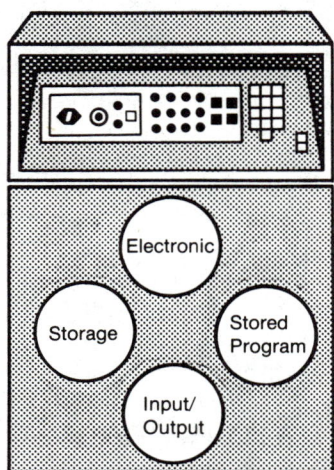

Figure 1-5. Characteristics of a computer.

THE NEED FOR COMPUTERS 11

Figure 1-6. The Control Data CYBER 205 is the world's most powerful computing system.

The vast majority of computers are digital. There are some computers used in industry that are analog. These computers function by measuring a continuous process such as the flow of electrical current or the temperature change of a liquid.

Another important characteristic of digital computers is that they are (with few exceptions) general-purpose machines. This characteristic permits them to be used for a variety of applications without changes to the computer hardware. All that is needed to change from a payroll to an accounting system, for example, is to load another program into the computer. This action takes only a few seconds, and the computer is ready to do a completely different job. However, it may have taken months or years to write the programs.

THE NEED FOR COMPUTERS

As industrialized society became more advanced in its technology, competition became more intense. One of the ways of dealing with this development was to apply the computer to areas that would improve business performance. Figure 1-7 shows some of the advantages realized by using the computer and related techniques.

```
INCREASES ACCURACY
REDUCES PAPERWORK
REDUCES TEDIOUS JOBS
PROVIDES EFFICIENT STORAGE
IMPROVES CUSTOMER SERVICE
GIVES FAST ACCESS TO INFORMATION
```

Figure 1-7. Advantages of using a computer.

When the high-speed computer system is applied to business applications, its improved turnaround of information results in improved customer service. Turnaround refers to the time it takes to receive data, process it, and provide the results. In non-computer applications, a sales order might take several weeks to process completely because of the manual operations required. With a computer system that can add 15-digit numbers in a few millionths of a second, the process might take less than a second to complete. Of course, there may still be some manual work that would be far more time consuming. The point is the enormous improvement in the time needed—and customer satisfaction.

Another aspect of this improvement is the reduction of errors made. In a manual system, humans are error prone especially when jobs are boring and tedious. The computer can easily be applied to these tedious tasks, and the error rate substantially reduced. By removing the tedious tasks, people are freed to perform more creative and meaningful jobs.

The computer also has the potential to reduce paper work and paper itself. This fact is particularly true of on-line systems where terminal devices such as CRT (cathode ray tube—a visual device) displays eliminate the necessity for hard copy (paper).

Most companies accumulate massive quantities of information relating to employees, accounts, sales, inventory, customers, and produc-

tion. Although each company has different needs, large files tend to accumulate over the years until access to specific items of data can become very time consuming. The computer provides devices that can store large amounts of data in considerably less space than paper files and can retrieve information at speeds approaching one million characters per second. This storage is primarily on magnetic files such as tapes or disks. For example, a typical disk pack can store all the data printed in a stack of invoices 30 meters (100 feet) high.

In the following chapter, we will look at where computers came from. They have a relatively short but dynamic history, which is compressed primarily into the 20th century.

A LARGE PIECE OF PI

William Shanks, an English mathematician in the 19th century, spent 15 years of his life calculating the value of pi. He was able to develop pi to 707 decimal places before his death. However, modern day computers have determined that the last one hundred or so decimal places were incorrect. Pi can now be calculated accurately to thousands of places in only a few minutes.

TERMS TO STUDY

Analog
Computer
Computer Revolution
Computer System
Digital

Hardware
Manual System
Microcomputer
Software
Time-sharing

QUESTIONS FOR REVIEW

1. What areas of the business world are using the computer?
2. What is the advantage of a time-sharing system?
3. What is a major characteristic of the minicomputer?
4. Two terms frequently used are hardware and software. What do these mean?

5. What role does the human play in the use of computers?
6. Name the four characteristics of a computer.
7. In what ways are computers superior to a human?
8. In what ways are humans superior to the computer?
9. What are some advantages to businesses that use computers?

PROBLEMS FOR RESEARCH AND DISCUSSION

1. Between now and your next class, make a list of the ways your life is affected by the computer. Compare notes with your classmates.
2. Using the definition of the characteristics of a computer, discuss whether any of the following could be classified as a computer: an electronic calculator, a programmable calculator, an adding machine, a typewriter, an electronic TV game, and a digital clock radio.

2

Historical Development— Tools of Man

How far back do you think the computer goes? 20 years? 30 years? This would seem to be the case since the computer is widely acclaimed today as an invention of modern science. This notion is partly due to the highly advanced use of electronic technology in the computer industry. However the needs that brought us the computer are not new. Indeed, the many concepts used in computer design are not of modern origin but date back several hundred years.

The need for efficient and accurate counting has been with us from the beginning of civilized man. In essence, all of the computer's vast ability comes from its capability for counting faster than any previous invention. Originally man used his fingers for counting. But as his needs became more complex, this method was soon replaced by a variety of increasingly more sophisticated devices. Figure 2-1 shows some of these, beginning with the abacus. The following pages discuss the development of these tools of man up to the modern day computer.

INVENTIONS AND THEIR INVENTORS

Abacus

The abacus is an ancient calculating device originating about 2000 B.C. It is still widely used in Japan, China, and other Asian countries as well as in European Russia. The abacus in use in 1200 A.D. consisted of a

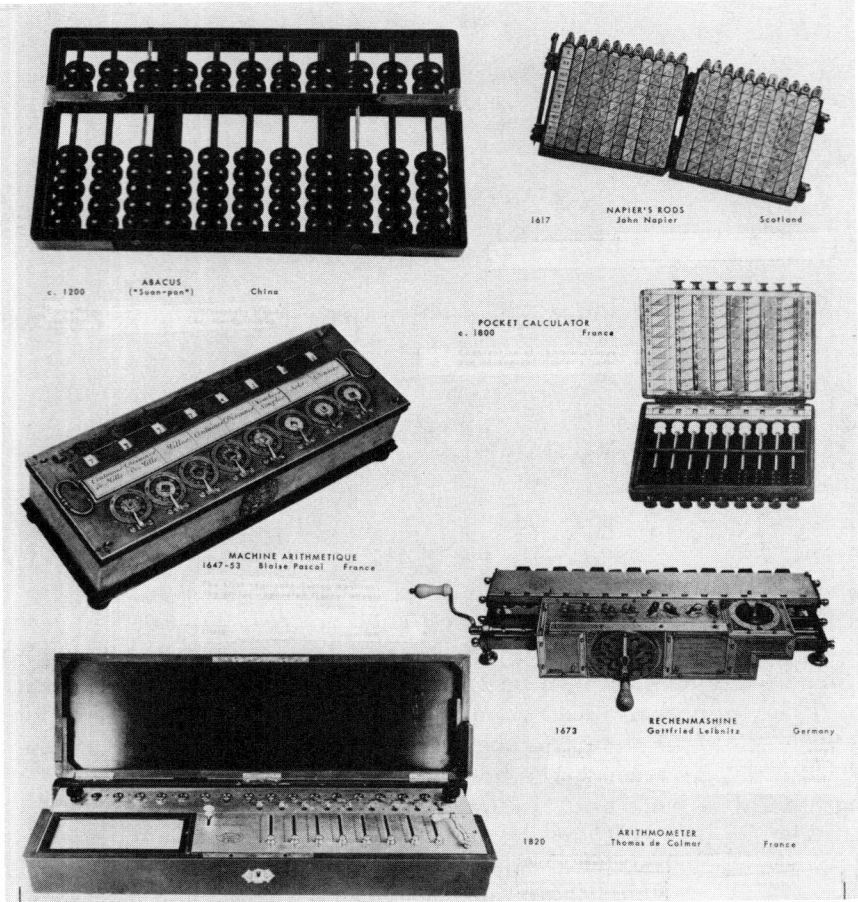

Figure 2-1. Highlights in the story of the calculator. (*Courtesy of IBM Corporation*)

rectangular frame that could be hand held. In the frame were several fixed rods strung with moveable beads (Figure 2-2).

This is the way it works: There are seven beads on each rod—two on one side of the crossbar and five on the other. The beads on the rod at the right represent units, the next rod to the left represents tens, then hundreds, and so on. Each bead above the crossbar represents five times the value of a bead below the crossbar. Numbers are recorded by moving beads to the crossbar.

A skilled abacus operator can easily keep pace with a person using an office calculating machine.

INVENTIONS AND THEIR INVENTORS   17

Figure 2-2. The abacus. (*Courtesy of IBM Corporation*)

Napier's Bones

John Napier (1617), a Scottish politician and mathematician, created an ingenious device for multiplying, dividing, and extracting roots. The Napier's Bones (Figure 2-3) are made of strips of bones or wood each divided into nine small squares. Across the top are digits 1 to 9 and 0. Down the side are digits 1 to 9. At the intersection each row and column is the result of multiplying these digits. If the result is a two-digit number, the tens digit is written above the broken line and the units digit below.

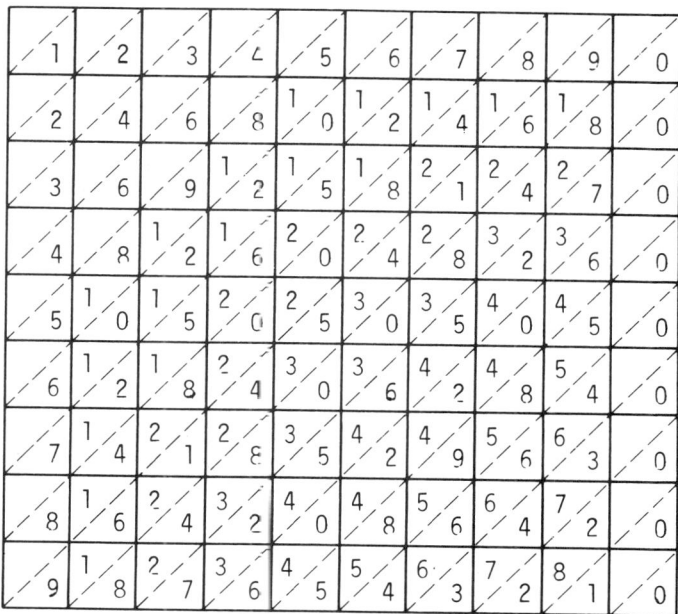

Figure 2-3. Napier's bones.

How to multiply 5 times 148

```
Top diagonal    24
Digits below   500
               ---
               740
```

To multiply 5 times 148, we take the 5 bone and lay it alongside the 1, 4, and 8 bones. Looking down to the fifth row, we select the digits 2 and 4 at the top of the diagonal lines. To these digits add the digits 5, 0, and 0, which are on the same diagonal. The sum of these is 740, which is the product of 5 × 148.

While the abacus worked well for adding and subtracting, the operations of multiplying or dividing were very time consuming. Napier's method simplified these operations and made them relatively efficient.

Blaise Pascal

Pascal was a French philosopher, scientist, and mathematician born in 1623. In 1647 he invented the first calculating machine using pin-wheel gearing and numbered disks for addition and subtraction (Figure 2-4).

His invention was instigated by the drudgery of adding long columns of numbers in his father's tax office in Rouen, France. This design was the basis for most mechanical calculators to be built over the next 300 years.

The pin wheel registered decimal values by using a cog to represent each decimal digit. Also included on the wheel was a carry lever to cause the next higher digit wheel to register an overflow. Reversing the rotation would allow the machine to subtract. The automotive odometer continues to work on this same principle today.

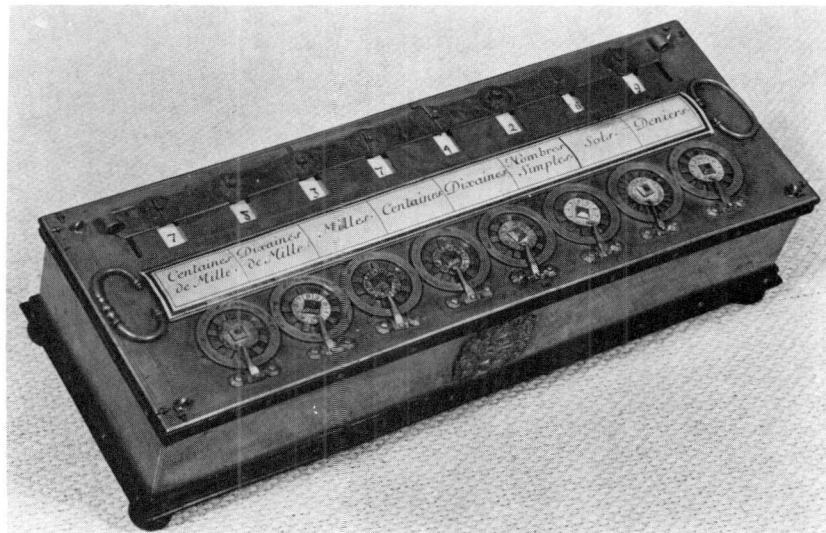

Figure 2-4. Pascal's calculator. (*Courtesy of IBM Corporation*)

Joseph Marie Jacquard

Born in 1752 in Lyons, France, Jacquard worked in a Lyons factory and in his spare time constructed an improved loom. His invention had an automatic selection device, which used perforated (punched) cards to represent the designer's pattern. The punched card concept is still in use today in the computer industry. His loom was fiercely opposed by silk weavers, who feared its introduction would deprive them of their livelihood. However, progress won, and by 1834 there were 30,000 Jacquard looms in use in Lyons alone.

In 1806, Napoleon Bonaparte made the loom public property and gave Jacquard a pension and royalty payments for his lifetime.

Charles P. Babbage

A move toward a machine that could go beyond addition and subtraction was conceived by Charles P. Babbage in 1812. Babbage was an English mathematician born in 1792 in Devonshire, England. When working with logarithmic tables that contained an excessive number of errors, he built the Difference Engine (Figure 2-5) to produce these tables mechanically with an accuracy of 20 digits. The first experimental model had 96 computing wheels mounted on 24 shafts. Unfortunately the precision necessary in its components made wide scale production impossible.

Figure 2-5. Babbage's difference engine. (*Courtesy of IBM Corporation*)

Babbage went on in 1833 to develop what he called the Analytical Engine. Except for being mechanical, Babbage's machine had all the components of a modern computer including memory, control, arithmetic unit, and input/output capabilities. The design would enable the machine to express each number to 50 places. In one minute the machine would be able to do 60 additions or subtractions.

Unfortunately, Babbage was before his time. Although he had great intellectual brilliance and creativity, he was unable to get the necessary support from his people and the government to continue his project. He died in 1871 a frustrated and unhappy man. However, his achievements and foresight have won him a recognition he never lived to see.

> ### THE FIRST WOMAN PROGRAMMER
>
> Ada, the Countess of Lovelace, was the daughter of the noted poet Lord Byron. Ada was a gifted child who was deeply involved with linguistics, music, and mathematics. By age fifteen she had mastered geometry and wanted to continue in that field. But her tutor discouraged her because he believed that, although she had a real genius for mathematics, it would require greater stamina and concentration than a woman could handle.
>
> But then she met Babbage. He was amazed at her understanding of his machine and urged her to continue her studies in mathematics. Ada worked with Babbage to translate an account into Italian of the Analytical Engine. In her translation, Ada used terms that were closely related to modern computer terminology.
>
> In 1983, the U.S. Department of Defense began to use a single programming language for most of their computer applications. The language is called Ada.

James Ritty

In 1878 James Ritty developed the first cash register. The first model had two rows of keys and a large clocklike dial containing two rows of figures showing dollars and cents. When the machines sold poorly, Ritty sold the business to Jacob H. Eckert, who organized the National Cash Register Company (NCR).

NCR is still in the cash register business today and is one of the leading computer, business machine, and terminal manufacturers in North America.

William S. Burroughs

William S. Burroughs was born in 1857 in Rochester, New York. He worked in a bank for five years until, tired of routine adding and checking of figures, he quit to work in a machine shop. He and Thomas Metcalf got together to build an adding machine that would record entries on paper showing a running total as entries were made.

After many failures and partial successes, the American Arithmometer Company was formed in 1886. Soon banks became a major customer, and the company built up world-wide facilities for manufacturing and marketing.

Burroughs continued with adding and accounting machines, and after World War II, the company moved to computers. In 1953, the company became Burroughs Corporation. A ground guidance computer system for Atlas missiles was delivered to SAGE in 1957. Burroughs computers guided the Gemini flights into space in the sixties. Today Burroughs is a major commercial computer manufacturer.

Herman Hollerith

Hollerith is widely known as the person who originated the punched card. Although he adopted the original idea from Jacquard, the modern punched card closely resembles Hollerith's invention.

In 1879, he was employed by the U.S. Census Bureau. He started work on a machine for mechanically tabulating population statistics. His machinery used electrical contacts for the sensing of holes and provided a method for sorting punched cards (Figure 2-6).

Figure 2-6. Hollerith's sorter. (*Courtesy of IBM Corporation*)

His first card was 16.8 cm. (6⅝") by 8.25 cm. (3¼") and had 24 columns each containing 12 punching positions. The standard IBM card used today is 19.68 cm. (7⅜") by 8.25 cm. (3¼") with 80 columns of 12 punch positions.

The census committee in 1889 estimated Hollerith's system would save about $600,000 to tabulate the results of the 1890 census with a population of 65,000,000.

In 1896, Hollerith formed the Tabulating Machine Company and began to sell equipment to the railroads and insurance companies. In 1911, Hollerith merged with the International Time Recording Company, the Dayton Scale Company, and Bundy Manufacturing to form the Computing-Tabulating-Recording Company (CTR). In 1924, CTR was renamed International Business Machines Corporation (IBM).

James Powers

James Powers worked with the U.S. Census Bureau in 1910 developing tabulating equipment so that the bureau could save the expense of renting Hollerith's equipment. In 1911, Powers left the Census Bureau and formed the Powers Accounting Machine Company which became the major supplier of equipment to the Census Bureau.

In 1927, the Powers Accounting Machine Company became the Tabulating Machine Division of the Remington Rand Corporation. This Corporation merged with Sperry Gyroscope in 1955 to form the Sperry-Rand Corporation.

THE FIRST COMPUTERS

Mark I

In 1937, Howard Aiken, professor of applied mathematics at Harvard, was working on a digital computer that could be used to solve mathematical and other problems. He received financial backing from Thomas J. Watson, president of IBM in 1939. By 1944, the Mark I, or Automatic Sequence Controlled Calculator, was built. The ASCC used many of Babbage's ideas and even went beyond them.

The Mark I was 15.5 meters (51 feet) long and 2.4 meters (8 feet) high, containing more than 760,000 parts. It used 23-digit numbers, had 60 registers for constants, and 72 storage registers. Input was in the form of punched cards. Output was typed or recorded on punched cards. Multiplication of two numbers took about 3 seconds.

The Mark I was followed by the Mark II in 1947. It was three times the size of Mark I and had 12 times the speed. Both computers were electromechanical, consisting of wiring, switches, relays, and panels.

ENIAC

John W. Mauchly and T. Presper Eckert were professors at the Moore School at the University of Pennsylvania. In 1942 they submitted a proposal to the United States Army to develop an electronic computer for calculating firing tables. The machine came to be called ENIAC for Electronic Numerical Integrator and Computer.

A major difference from previous devices was the use of the electronic vacuum tube. It was used as an on-off binary device and contributed to a large increase in speed. Addition required 0.2 thousandth of a second (0.2 millisecond), and multiplication used 2.8 milliseconds of computer time. ENIAC consisted of 30 separate units weighing over 30 tons. It contained 18,000 vacuum tubes, 70,000 resistors, and 10,000 capacitors.

ENIAC's real value became obvious when it was used to compute a 60-second trajectory. Manually this calculation took 20 hours; ENIAC was able to do it in 30 seconds.

EDVAC

Between 1947 and 1950, the EDVAC computer was built at the Moore School. EDVAC or Electronic Discrete Variable Automatic Computer used 5900 vacuum tubes and 12,000 diodes, thus establishing a trend toward the use of solid state devices in the computer.

A major contributor to EDVAC was John von Neumann. He devised the stored program concept used by all of today's computers. This innovation made changing programs a simple matter and made the computer a truly general purpose machine.

The use of delay lines for the storing of data was also introduced, which allowed the storing of binary digits at one hundredth of the cost of a vacuum tube.

EDVAC's addition time was 864 microseconds (millionths of a second). Input and output consisted of paper tape, typewriters, and punched cards.

KEY CONCEPT

STORED PROGRAM

Early computers were wired to solve a specific problem. If a different problem needed to be solved, the machine was rewired to instruct it to solve the new problem. This process required many hours and even days of work. Unit record machines were also instructed through a wired panel. Modern computers, beginning with those built by von Neumann, stored a program in an internal magnetic memory, or storage unit. The program, or set of instructions, was punched into cards and read into the computer when needed. This procedure required only several seconds to change from one program to another.

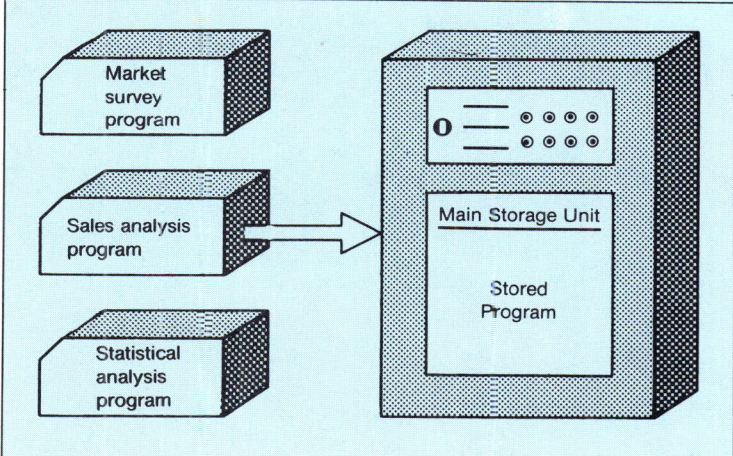

UNIVAC I

In the 1950s, Mauchly and Eckert developed the UNIVAC I (Universal Automatic Computer) with Remington Rand. It became one of the first commercially available computers that could be used for both numeric and alphabetic data. UNIVAC I was an electronic computer consisting of mostly vacuum tubes and solid state diodes. It could read data from magnetic tape and print results on a line printer. Addition took 0.5 millisecond and multiplication, 2.5 milliseconds.

Soon after UNIVAC I was developed, automatic programming techniques came into use. These techniques were the forerunner of today's programming languages, which simplify the technical complexity of the computer's internal language.

KEY CONCEPT

UNIT RECORD

The punched card has also been called a unit record. This term refers to the way in which the card is generally used. On a single card, all of the information relating to a given transaction or record is stored as a unit. In the case of cost accounting, a transaction may contain an item number, quantity, and dollar value. Combining these data items produces a unit record.

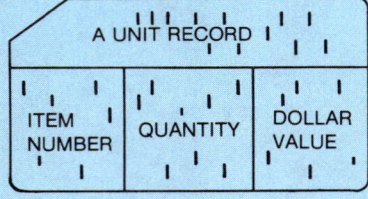

UNIT RECORD SYSTEMS

Hollerith's invention of the punched card led to the production of punched card equipment called unit record devices. These machines used the punched card to perform a variety of operations such as sorting, merging, calculating, and printing. Unit record was the typical method of introducing data processing to a company in the 1950s. The success of these machines is evident from their continued use through several generations of computers into the 1970s.

Initially, cards were punched with a keypunch by pressing keys in a manner similar to that of the typewriter. Once cards were punched, they were processed by the unit record machine to give the desired reports and summaries.

Figure 2-7. A card sorter. (*Courtesy of IBM Corporation*)

Sorter

The card sorter (Figure 2-7) rearranges a file of punched cards into a desired sequence. For instance, an accounts payable file may need to be in account number sequence. The sorter takes these cards and organizes them so that the lowest account number is first, followed by consecutively higher numbers.

A numeric sort requires one pass through the file for each digit in the number. If the account number were seven digits in length, the file would have to be passed through the sorter seven times in order to be sorted.

Alphabetic sorts may also be done. This requires two passes for each character. A description field consisting of 12 characters would require 24 passes through the sorter.

Collator

Some applications require that two files of cards be merged together. After each file has been sorted, they may be merged by a collator (Figure 2-8). One card file is placed in the primary stacker and the other in a secondary stacker. The collator matches a field in each card electrically, then merges them into a hopper.

The collator can be used to perform four operations. These are (1) merging, (2) matching and selecting cards that do not match, (3) checking

Figure 2-8. IBM 188 collator. (*Courtesy of IBM Corporation*)

the sequence of a card file to verify the accuracy of a previous sort, and (4) selecting cards containing specific information from a file of cards.

Reproducer

The reproducer (Figure 2-9) can be used to duplicate information from a file of cards to create an identical copy of the file. Another use is to take information, such as a date, from a header card and punch it into the following card. This process is called gang punching.

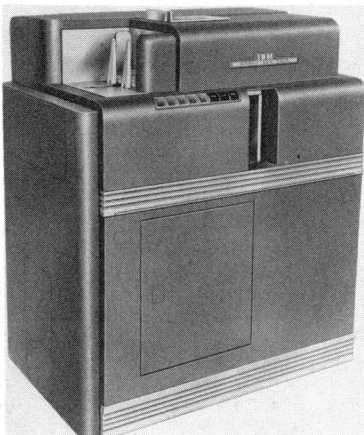

Figure 2-9. Reproducer and summary punch. (*Courtesy of IBM Corporation*)

A reproducer can also be used as a summary punch to punch summarized information accumulated by an accounting machine during the printing of a detail report. The detail printed by an accounting machine may consist of all employee records for a company, while the reproducer punches a single summarize record showing totals for each department.

Interpreter

Often when cards are keypunched, the data punched are *printed* along the top edge of the card. However, in some cases it may be preferable to print the data in a position other than along the top edge. In other cases it is desirable to print on cards produced by some other process such as with a reproducer. This printing may be done by an interpreter (Figure 2-10).

An interpreter reads cards containing data that have not been printed. This data may be printed anywhere on the surface with spaces between fields and improved clarity of the printed characters.

Calculator

The calculator can be used to read cards containing data that may then be used in any of the four arithmetic operations: addition, subtraction, multiplication, and division The results of the calculation are then punched on the card.

For example, an invoice card may show the quantity and unit cost of an item. The calculator can multiply these values and punch the extended cost into the card.

Figure 2-10. Alphabetic interpreter. (*Courtesy of IBM Corporation*)

Figure 2-11. 407 Accounting machine. (*Courtesy of IBM Corporation*)

Accounting Machine

The accounting machine (Figure 2-11), or tabulator as it was sometimes called, is used to produce reports from files of cards. This machine reads the cards, accumulates necessary totals, prints headings and details, and summarizes the information processed.

The machine consists of a device to read punched cards, a section to do arithmetic calculations and make decisions, and a printer to produce the report. These components are electromechanical and are usually housed in one cabinet.

MODERN COMPUTER GENERATIONS

First Generation (1950–1959)

Like families, computers also trace their roots back several generations. The first generation of commercially available computers in the 1950s were based on vacuum tube design. These devices had the characteristic of rather gigantic size relative to the performance characteristics. Speeds were measured in the millisecond range.

Because of the use of vacuum tubes, the computers developed enormous amounts of heat, which had to be controlled by large air conditioning units. Tubes also used a great deal of electrical power to operate and were notoriously unreliable.

Figure 2-12. IBM 705 first generation computer. (*Courtesy of IBM Corporation*)

The IBM 650 was a first generation computer—there were over 1000 built. This machine was followed by the IBM 702, 704, 705, and 709 computers (Figure 2-12). The 702 had 5000 vacuum tubes and weighed 11 tons. Other competitive machines were the UNIVAC I (the first commercial computer), UNIVAC II, and the Burroughs E101. Programming was generally done in machine language rather than in the easier symbolic languages used by today's programmers.

Second Generation (1960–1965)

The next generation of computers (Figure 2-13) used the solid state transistor invented by John Bardeen, William Shockley, and Walter Brattain

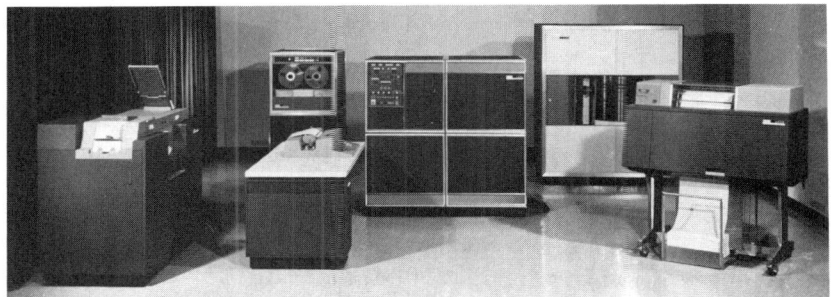

Figure 2-13. IBM 1401 second generation computer. (*Courtesy of IBM Corporation*)

KEY CONCEPT

WHAT IS COMPUTER TIME?

Humans think of time in terms of days, hours, minutes, or seconds. Occasionally we might refer to a split second, which is not precisely defined. However, the computer measures time in fractions of a second. These times are as follows:

millisecond (ms)—$1/1{,}000$—one thousandth of a second
microsecond (μs)—$1/1{,}000{,}000$—one millionth of a second
nanosecond (ns)—$1/1{,}000{,}000{,}000$—one billionth of a second
picosecond (ps)—$1/1{,}000{,}000{,}000{,}000$—one trillionth of a second

What does this mean in human terms? Suppose you required one minute to multiply two numbers together giving a product. A first generation computer might be able to do the same operation in say 25 milliseconds. This means that while you are doing your calculation in one minute, the computer could do 2400 similar calculations. A second generation computer might take 25 microseconds and could therefore do 2,400,000 calculations while you do your one.

---

at the Bell Telephone Laboratories in 1948. The transistor was many times smaller than the vacuum tube; and it consumed less power, generated less heat, and had improved reliability. The use of transistors resulted in physically smaller computers that operated in the microsecond range. The increased speed was primarily due to the use of transistors but was also influenced by the use of magnetic core for main storage. The introduction of core allowed storage of larger capacity, and this greater capacity in turn permitted the use of more input and output devices.

Computers in this generation began to proliferate as many companies came into the market. Some of these were the IBM 1400 and 7000 series computers, the Burroughs B5000, UNIVAC III, NCR 304, and the Control Data Corporation 1604 computer.

Programming was done in symbolic languages, and some compilers became available for higher level languages such as COBOL and FORTRAN. Programmers were relieved of many programming tasks such as input/output control, which was now handled by a monitor program or operating system.

Third Generation (1965–1975)

A new breed of technology gave rise to major changes in computation during these years. This was the solid logic technology, or integrated circuits. These components were again smaller, faster, less power hungry, and cooler operating than the transistor. A new speed called the nanosecond was born.

Main storage technology also began to change as plated wire, thin film, and monolithic storage replaced core. All of these developments in hardware caused the software to lag behind for some time. Gradually, however, software underwent a change and computers showed new potential. Multiprogramming, which allowed several programs to execute simultaneously on one computer, was introduced. This technique had not been possible before. On-line systems with remote terminals became popular so that the user could access the computer from a remote location. Languages improved, in some cases becoming much more sophisticated for the professional. In other cases, languages were simplified for the casual user.

If ever there was a revolution in the computer industry, it would have to be third generation. Computers included in this generation were the IBM 360 series, which started it all; the Burroughs 6500, 7500, 8500 computers; UNIVAC 9000 series; and the NCR Century series.

KEY CONCEPT

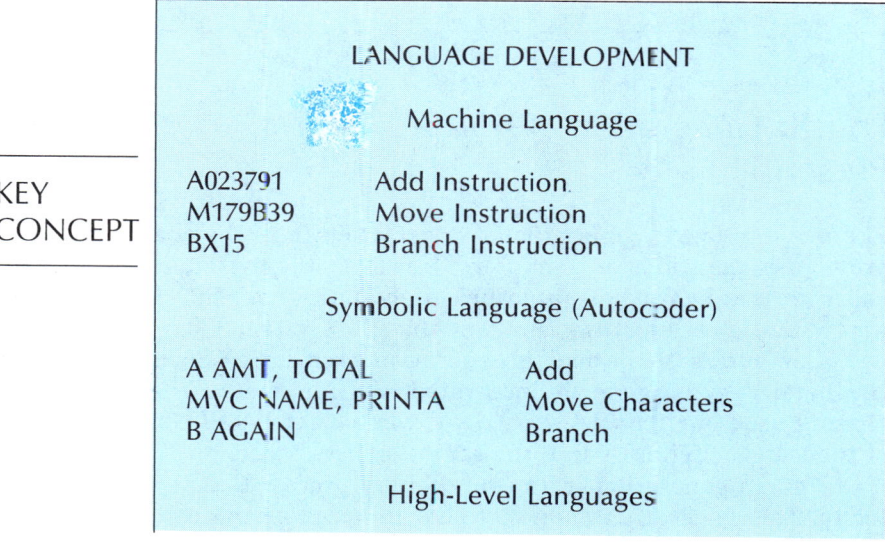

LANGUAGE DEVELOPMENT

Machine Language

A023791	Add Instruction
M179B39	Move Instruction
BX15	Branch Instruction

Symbolic Language (Autocoder)

A AMT, TOTAL	Add
MVC NAME, PRINTA	Move Characters
B AGAIN	Branch

High-Level Languages

FORTRAN (Formula Translator) 1954

T = T + A	Add
P = N	Move (Assignment)
GO TO 20	Branch or GO TO
DO 10 I = 1,100	
N = N + I	Iterative DO
10 CONTINUE	

COBOL (Common Business Oriented Language) 1959

ADD AMOUNT TO TOTAL.	Add
MOVE NAME TO PRINT-AREA.	Move
IF AMOUNT IS GREATER THAN LIMIT THEN ADD 1 TO OVER-WEIGHT.	Decision
GO TO COMPUTE-INCOME-TAX.	GO TO

PL/1 1964

DEMO:PROCEDURE;	
TOTAL = TOTAL + AMOUNT;	Add
PRINT_AREA = NAME;	Assign
DO I = 1 TO 100;	Iterative
NUM = NUM + I;	DO
END;	
END DEMO;	

Fourth Generation (1975–Present)

The move to fourth generation was not as clear as the change between previous generations of computers. However, these systems were again characterized by further miniaturization and refinement of semiconductor technology. One of the first was the IBM System/370.

Computers of the fourth generation used Large Scale Integration (LSI) and Very Large Scale Integrated (VLSI) circuits. Where transistor circuits used one transistor per logic component, VLSI could pack tens of thousands of circuits into the same compact space.

Fourth generation is an evolutionary process that is still going on today. This generation is further characterized by the use of microelec-

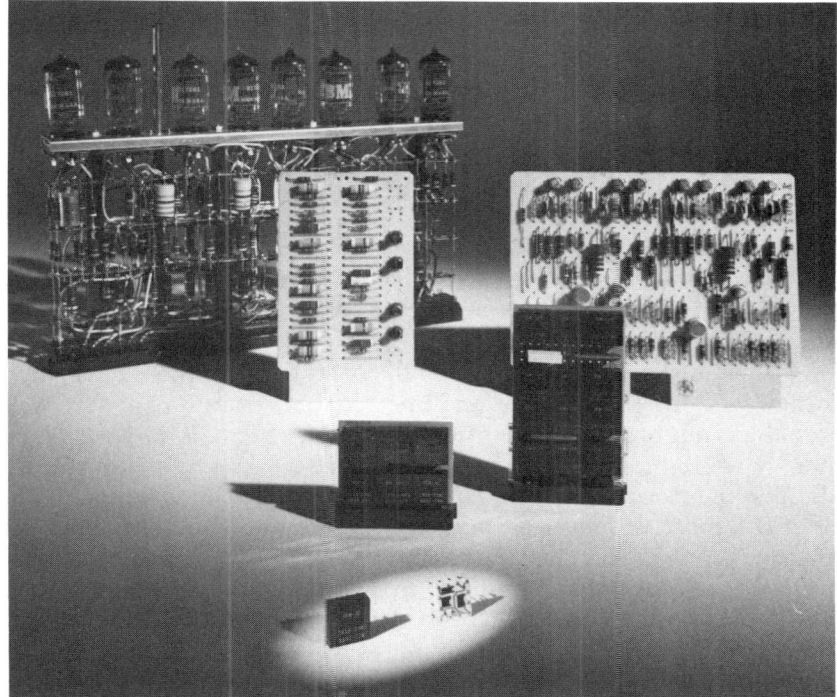

Figure 2-14. Three generations of technology. (*Courtesy of IBM Corporation*)

tronic technology that has permitted computer manufacturers to place into hardware what was formerly program code in the software.

Software developments have allowed concepts such as virtual storage to be used. Virtual storage expands main storage capacity to millions of characters by utilizing a disk drive as an extension of main storage.

The Micro Generation (1974–Present)

While many strides were being made in the large scale computer systems, another parallel development was occurring. Robert Noyce, who had worked with William Shockley on the transistor, formed a new company with Andrew Grove and Gordon Moore. The company, Intel Corporation, invented a new integrated circuit, the microprocessor, resulting in the birth of the microcomputer.

In 1974, Intel produced the first widely used microprocessor, the 8080, which incorporated 4500 transistors into a single integrated circuit in a space two-tenths of an inch square. By 1979, RCA was producing chips containing 32,000 circuits and the race was on. These chips were comparable in complexity to the IBM 704. But the 704's processor occupied about fifty cubic feet of space.

The microcomputer was characterized by its small size. Most were desktop units and were easily portable. They had no special power requirements (just plug them in like a TV) and no special air conditioning requirements like the larger machines. And as they developed they became very easy to use. "User friendly" was the term the manufacturers liked to use to describe their products because almost anyone could use these computers.

Other successes grew from humble beginnings in the microcomputer world. Two chums, Steve Jobs and Steve Wozniak built a homebrew computer that caught the imagination of their friends. So they raised some funds by selling an old Volkswagen van and a programmable calculator to launch their own company. The company, Apple Corporation, produces one of the most widely used microcomputers today, the Apple II+; the company is one of the most successful in the microcomputer business.

Nolan Bushnell, an engineer, invented a game for his own amusement to play on his home television. The game, Pong, was the beginning of Atari, which started into the computer business with electronic games. Atari is now owned by Warner Communications and makes several microcomputers for the personal and educational markets.

Of course, there have been a number of companies that have had their own successes in a variety of endeavors, who are now strong forces in the microcomputer marketplace. Some of these companies who are now producing microcomputers are Commodore, Radio Shack, IBM, Hewlett-Packard, and Digital Equipment Corporation.

TERMS TO STUDY

Abacus
Accounting Machine
Calculator
Collator
Difference Engine
EDVAC
ENIAC
First Generation
Fourth Generation

Microsecond
Millisecond
Nanosecond
Napier's Bones
Picosecond
Reproducer
Second Generation
Sorter
Stored Program Concept

Hollerith	Third Generation
Interpreter	Unit Record
Jacquard	Unit Record Concept
Mark I	UNIVAC I

QUESTIONS FOR REVIEW

1. Explain the function of the abacus.
2. Show how 4 is multiplied by 135 using Napier's Bones.
3. What specific contribution did Blaise Pascal make to the field of computation?
4. Who invented the first mechanical computer? Describe this device briefly.
5. What invention of Jacquard is still in use by the computer industry today?
6. Trace the beginnings of the computer giants: NCR, Burroughs, IBM, and Sperry-Rand.
7. Describe the contribution made by John von Neumann and the significance of this advanced concept.
8. Compare the early electronic computers for capacity, size, speed, and application.
9. Describe the Unit Record Concept.
10. Name six unit record devices. Describe briefly the function of each.
11. Explain the difference between a mechanical, electromechanical, and electronic device.
12. A given sorter can process cards at 600 cards per minute. We have a file of 9000 cards and wish to sequence the cards on a 5-digit employee number. How long will it take to sort these cards? How long would it take for a 12-character name?
13. Describe what is meant by a computer generation.
14. What major changes are reflected in each of the computer generations?
15. If Roland Solinsky drives his dragster down the quarter mile in 6.23 seconds, how many milliseconds does it take him?
16. A computer can add two numbers in 250 nanoseconds. How many pairs of numbers can it add in one second?
17. Why might some people claim we now have fourth generation computers while others say we are still in third generation?

PROBLEMS FOR RESEARCH AND DISCUSSION

1. There have been literally hundreds of high-level languages developed over the past 20 years. What are some of these languages, and what applications are they used for?
2. Who are some of the currently outstanding people in the computer field? What are some of the contributions made by these people?

3
Number Systems

Numbers have been used by mankind down through the ages. In early days a shepherd may have needed a simple system to count his sheep or his children. This may have been a method as simple as using sticks or pebbles to represent each sheep. As trade and commerce grew, this method was inadequate for dealing with larger quantities. So more sophisticated methods were developed.

The decimal number system we know so well today was used as far back as 3400 B.C. in Egypt. This system based on the number 10 is thought to have developed because counting began on man's ten fingers.

Although the base ten system is widely used, it is not the only method of counting used. The Papuan language tribes of the Torres Strait of Australia and parts of New Guinea use a base two numbering system. The base 3 and 4 number systems are used by tribes in Terra del Fuego, and a South American language called Saraveca uses the base 5 system. Interestingly, all of these systems use bases of less than 10. This may be a result of rather simple needs for counting in relatively simpler civilizations. Conversely, there are tribes in Central America and Mexico whose interest in astronomy led them to develop a base 20 system.

MATHEMATICAL NUMBER SYSTEMS

Decimal Numbers 0 1 2 3 4 5 6 7 8 9

The number system commonly used today for counting is the base ten, or decimal system. This system consists of the digits 0, 1, 2, 3, 4, 5, 6, 7, 8, 9. Each of these digits has a specific value. However, when two or more decimal digits are used together, the value of each digit depends upon its position in the number as well as its digit value.

For example, the number 868 may be broken down as follows:

8	6	8
↑	↑	↑
8 Hundreds	6 Tens	8 Units
8 × 100 +	6 × 10 +	8 × 1

Because the rightmost 8 is in the units position, it represents that digit value. The 6 is in the tens position and it represents 6 times 10, or 60. The next 8 is in the hundreds position and gives the value 8 times 100,

Counting to 16 in Decimal

1
2
3
4
5
6
7
8
9
10
11
12
13
14
15
16

Powers of 10

$10^0 =$	1
$10^1 =$	10
$10^2 =$	100
$10^3 =$	1,000
$10^4 =$	10,000
$10^5 =$	100,000
$10^6 =$	1,000,000

which is 800. Although this has the same digit value as the first 8, its position assigns it a greater value.

All number systems follow a basic principle of digit values and positional notation. In base ten, numbers are represented in each position by powers of ten. The number 3025 would be represented in the following positional notation.

$$3 \times 10^3 + 0 \times 10^2 + 2 \times 10^1 + 5 \times 10^0$$

The tens used in this expression are called the base or radix. Values 0, 1, 2, 3 are exponents, or powers. The powers of ten are multiplied by the digit to give the positional value. These values are:

$$3 \times 1000 + 0 \times 100 + 2 \times 10 + 5 \times 1$$

If these expressions are multiplied, we get

$$3000 + 0 + 20 + 5$$

The sum of this expression gives the value 3025, which is the original number.

Numbers used by computers are often referenced by their high order or low order digit. In the previous example of 3025, the digit 3 is the high order, or most significant digit, since it contributes the greatest value to the number. The digit 5 in the units position is the low order, or least significant digit.

```
            3        0    2    5
            ↑                  ↑
    High Order Digit    Low Order Digit
           or                  or
    Most Significant    Low Significant
```

Binary Numbers   0 1

It was discovered in the early stages of development that binary numbers were better suited to computer usage (Figure 3-1) because of the electronic nature of computers. Binary numbers are base two numbers, which use the digits 0 and 1. The advantage of base two in a computer may be seen from Figure 3-1, which shows a number of electronic components. A light bulb is either off or on, and these states may be used to represent the binary values 0 and 1. Similarly an electrical switch is either off or on. A transistor either conducts electricity or not, and a magnetic core may be magnetized in either of two directions to represent a 0 or 1 digit. Since computers are constructed from solid state devices similar to transistors, the binary system is well suited to computer usage.

Counting to 16 in Binary

0
1
10
11
100
101
110
111
1000
1001
1010
1011
1100
1101
1110
1111
10000

Powers of 2

$2^0 = 1$
$2^1 = 2$
$2^2 = 4$
$2^3 = 8$
$2^4 = 16$
$2^5 = 32$
$2^6 = 64$
$2^7 = 128$
$2^8 = 256$
$2^9 = 512$
$2^{10} = 1024$

Converting Binary to Decimal. Binary numbers may be represented by the same positional notation used for decimal numbers except that a base of two (i.e., base two) is used. The binary number 1101 in positional notation would be

$$1 \times 2^3 + 1 \times 2^2 + 0 \times 2^1 + 1 \times 2^0$$

Applying the powers of two to this expression gives

$$1 \times 8 + 1 \times 4 + 0 \times 2 + 1 \times 1$$

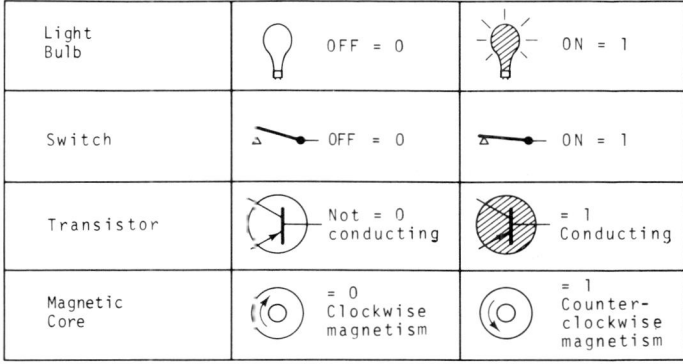

Figure 3-1. Advantage of base two in a computer.

Which simplifies to

$$8 + 4 + 0 + 1 = 13$$

The result 13 is a base ten number. By applying positional notation to a binary number, we get its decimal equivalent. This scheme gives us a method for converting binary numbers to decimal. For example, convert 1100001 to decimal.

$1 \times 2^6 + 1 \times 2^5 + 0 \times 2^4 - 0 \times 2^3 + 0 \times 2^2 + 0 \times 2^1 + 1 \times 2^0 =$
$1 \times 64 + 1 \times 32 + 0 \times 16 + 0 \times 8 + 0 \times 4 + 0 \times 2 + 1 \times 1 =$
$64 + 32 + 0 + 0 + 0 + 0 + 1 = 97$

Another method for changing binary numbers to decimal numbers applies the sum of the positional values to the binary digits. The binary number 1101011 would have the following positional values.

64	32	16	8	4	2	1	*Positional Values*
1	1	0	1	0	1	1	*Binary Number*

To convert to decimal, simply find the sum of each positional value that has an associated binary digit of 1. Values with a 0 binary digit are ignored. In this case we have

$$64 + 32 + 8 + 2 + 1 = 107$$

The sum 107 is the decimal equivalent of the binary number 1101011.

When we are using several number systems, confusion is often possible when writing a number. For instance, is 101 the decimal number one hundred and one, or is it the binary number one zero one? To avoid confusion, the number may be written with a subscript indicating the base of the number. If 101 were a decimal number, it would be written

$$101_{10}$$

whereas if it were binary, a subscript of 2 would be used.

$$101_2$$

Converting Decimal to Binary. Decimal numbers may be converted to binary using the method of successive division. This is done by dividing the decimal number by the base of two and recording the remainder. The quotient is then divided by 2, and the next remainder is recorded. This is repeated until a quotient of zero is derived. The example shows how 13 is converted to binary.

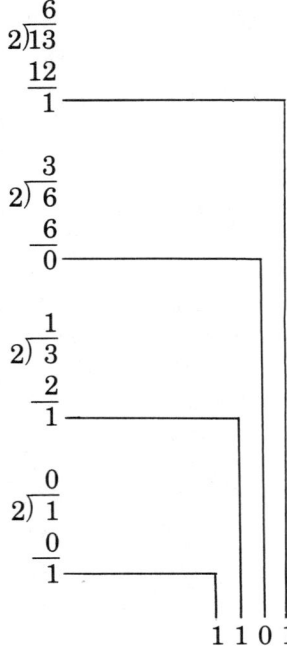

MATHEMATICAL NUMBER SYSTEMS   45

This cartoon, and the one on page 201 are reprinted with permission of *DATAMATION* magazine Copyright by Technical Publishing Company, a division of Dun-Donnelley Publishing Corporation, a Dun & Bradstreet Company, 1978—all rights reserved.

When 13 is divided by 2, the quotient is 6. The remainder is 1, which is recorded as the least significant digit of the binary number. The quotient 6 is then divided by 2 giving 3 with a remainder of 0. The 0 is recorded as the next binary digit. Next, the 3 is divided by 2 giving a 1 quotient and a 1 remainder. In the final step, the 1 cannot be divided by 2. Therefore the quotient is 0 and the remainder becomes the most significant digit of the new binary number.

The binary equivalent of 13 is 1101. To check our work, we can apply the sum of positional values method. This gives:

8	4	2	1	*Positional Values*
1	1	0	1	*Binary Number*

The sum of 8 + 4 + 1 is 13, the original base ten number.

Octal
Numbers   0 1 2 3 4 5 6 7

When larger numbers are used, which is typical of many computer applications, representing them in binary is rather difficult for the human. For instance, a number such as 1692 would be 11010011101 in binary. Although the computer uses binary code internally, this code is usually represented in an external form that is easier for human understanding. One of these representations is the octal, or base eight, number system consisting of the digits 0, 1, 2, 3, 4, 5, 6, 7.

Counting to 16 in Octal

0
1
2
3
4
5
6
7
10
11
12
13
14
15
16
17
20

Converting Octal to Decimal. The system of positional notation used to convert binary to decimal may also be used when converting any number system to decimal. Only the base is changed—in this case to base eight.

To convert 476_8 to decimal, we write

$$4 \times 8^2 + 7 \times 8^1 + 6 \times 8^0 =$$
$$4 \times 64 + 7 \times 8 + 6 \times 1 =$$
$$256 + 56 + 6 = 318_{10}$$

Convert 57216_8 to decimal.

$$5 \times 8^4 + 7 \times 8^3 + 2 \times 8^2 + 1 \times 8^1 + 6 \times 8^0 =$$
$$5 \times 4096 + 7 \times 512 + 2 \times 64 + 1 \times 8 + 6 \times 1 =$$
$$20480 + 3584 + 128 + 8 + 6 = 24206_{10}$$

Powers of 8

8^0	=	1
8^1	=	8
8^2	=	64
8^3	=	512
8^4	=	4,096
8^5	=	32,768
8^6	=	262,144
8^7	=	2,097,152
8^8	=	16,777,216

Converting Decimal to Octal. The method of successive division may also be applied when converting to octal. In this case, the base used as a divisor is eight. Each remainder then becomes an octal digit, and the quotient is again divided by eight. This procedure is repeated until a zero quotient is reached.

To convert 92_{10} to octal we take the following steps.

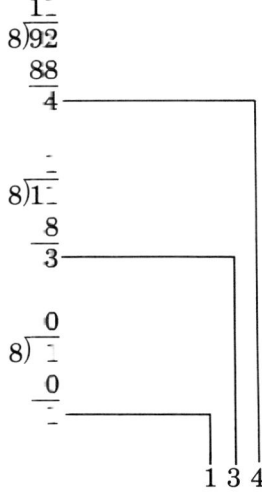

The result of 134_8 is the equivalent to 92_{10}.
Convert 1000_{10} to octal.

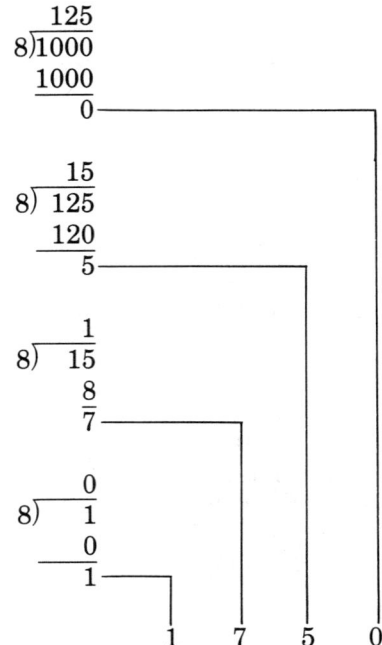

This shows 1000_{10} to be equal to 1750_8. Observe that in both cases, the octal equivalent gives somewhat larger digit position values although the actual values are the same. Octal is simply a different number system. The fact that octal values are larger than their corresponding decimal values can be used to do a quick check to see if a solution is reasonable.

Octal Numbers with Binary Equivalents

Octal	Binary		
	4	2	1
0	0	0	0
1	0	0	1
2	0	1	0
3	0	1	1
4	1	0	0
5	1	0	1
6	1	1	0
7	1	1	1

For instance, if the answer in the second example was 750_8, we would be certain that something was wrong with our calculations since this number is smaller than the original value. However, the only certain way of checking the accuracy of 1750_8 is to convert it back to decimal.

$$1 \times 8^3 + 7 \times 8^2 + 5 \times 8^1 + 0 \times 8^0 =$$
$$512 + 448 + 40 + 0 = 1000_{10}$$

The sum of the terms above confirms that 1000_{10} is 1750_8.

Converting Binary to Octal. Binary numbers may be easily converted to octal by assigning the sum of the digit positions to groups of these binary digits. A three-digit binary number has position values of 4, 2, 1. The sum of these positions is seven, which is the largest possible digit in base eight. The binary number 101 is

4	2	1	*Digit Positions*
1	0	1	*Binary Number*

This configuration gives $4 + 1 = 5$, which is the base eight equivalent of binary 101. It is also the decimal equivalent. However, when the binary number exceeds three digits, things begin to change. In this case, each group of three binary digits are assigned the positional values of 4, 2, 1. The number 110010 would be converted in this way

4	2	1	4	2	1
1	1	0	0	1	0
$4 + 2 = 6$			2		

This arrangement gives digits 62, which is the base eight number. The 6 is derived from the first three binary digits, and the 2 from the last three.

A number that cannot be broken equally into 3-digit groups is extended with high order zeroes. This technique is demonstrated with the number 11101111.

4	2	1	4	2	1	4	2	1
0	1	1	1	0	1	1	1	1
	3			5			7	

These bits give the octal number 357. Appending the high-order zero gives each group three digits but does not affect the value of the number. Once some experience is gained, converting from binary to octal can be done mentally. Simply take each group of three digits and write down the octal equivalent.

Converting Octal to Binary. Once the above technique is mastered, it is equally simple to convert an octal number to binary. In this case, take each octal digit and write the equivalent binary sequence. For example, the number 240_8 gives the following binary configuration.

2			4			0		
4	2	1	4	2	1	4	2	1
0	1	0	1	0	0	0	0	0

This value is 010100000_2, or 10100000_2, since the leading zero is not necessary. Each digit is given the corresponding value in binary according to the 4, 2, 1 sequence.

Change 57216_8 to binary.

5			7			2			1			6		
4	2	1	4	2	1	4	2	1	4	2	1	4	2	1
1	0	1	1	1	1	0	1	0	0	0	1	1	1	0

The answer is 101111010001110_2.

Hexadecimal
Numbers 0 1 2 3 4 5 6 7 8 9 A B C D E F

The architecture of some computers requires that internal binary codes be represented in a hexadecimal format. Hexadecimal is a number system based on 16. This system would require the use of digits 0 to 15. However, the digits 10 through 15 create a problem because they require two digit positions each. To solve this problem, the letters A, B, C, D, E, F are used to represent 10 through 15.

Decimal	10	11	12	13	14	15
Hexadecimal	A	B	C	D	E	F

Counting to 16 in Hexadecimal

0
1
2
3
4
5
6
7
8
9
A
B
C
D
E
F
10

Converting Hexadecimal to Decimal. The positional method applied to binary and octal numbers is again used when converting hexadecimal numbers to decimal. The basic method works here except we must convert any of the letters A through F to their numeric equivalents. To change $1A5_{16}$ to decimal write

$$1 \times 16^2 + 10 \times 16^1 + 5 \times 16^0 =$$
$$256 + 160 + 5 = 421_{10}$$

In this example, the letter A in the second digit position is given the numeric equivalent of 10.

A hexadecimal number may, in some cases, consist of all alphabetic characters. For instance, $CADF_{16}$ is a legitimate hexadecimal number. It is converted as follows:

$$12 \times 16^3 + 10 \times 16^2 + 13 \times 16^1 + 15 \times 16^0 =$$
$$49152 + 2560 + 208 + 15 = 51935_{10}$$

Converting Decimal to Hexadecimal. Again, successive division may be used as applied to other number systems. In this case, the divisor is sixteen. Care must be taken when the remainder found is a two-digit number because the equivalent hexadecimal letter must be written.

Convert 2620_{10} to hexadecimal.

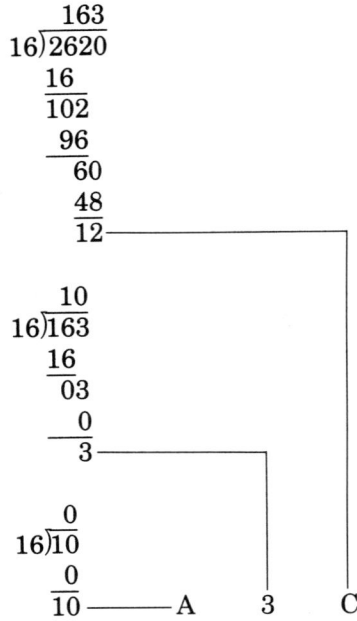

The result is $A3C_{16}$. When a remainder of 12 was found in the first division, the equivalent letter C was substituted. A common mistake is to write 12 directly in the hexadecimal number. If this had been done above, the result 10312 would have been quite incorrect and much different from the correct number.

Converting Binary to Hexadecimal. In the section on octal numbers, a method was presented for changing binary numbers directly to octal. This required taking groups of 3 digits and writing the octal equivalent.

Power of 16

$16^0 =$	1
$16^1 =$	16
$16^2 =$	256
$16^3 =$	4,096
$16^4 =$	65,536
$16^5 =$	1,048,576
$16^6 =$	16,777,216

Hexadecimal Numbers with Binary Equivalents

Hexadecimal	Binary			
0	0	0	0	0
1	0	0	0	1
2	0	0	1	0
3	0	0	1	1
4	0	1	0	0
5	0	1	0	1
6	0	1	1	0
7	0	1	1	1
8	1	0	0	0
9	1	0	0	1
A	1	0	1	0
B	1	0	1	1
C	1	1	0	0
D	1	1	0	1
E	1	1	1	0
F	1	1	1	1

Similarly, to convert binary to hexadecimal, groups of 4 binary digits are written according to their digit position values. The binary number 1001 would translate as follows.

8	4	2	1	*Digit Positions*
1	0	0	1	*Binary Number*

The result is 8 + 1 = 9. The hexadecimal equivalent, therefore, of 1001_2 is 9.

Binary 1101 would convert as follows

8	4	2	1	*Digit Positions*
1	1	0	1	*Binary Number*

The result is 8 + 4 + 1 = 13 = D. D, therefore, is the hexadecimal equivalent of 1101_2.

Larger binary numbers are converted by separating the number into groups of 4 digits from right to left. Convert 110101100100.

8	4	2	1	8	4	2	1	8	4	2	1
1	1	0	1	0	1	1	0	0	1	0	0

$$8 + 4 + 1 \qquad\qquad 4 + 2 \qquad\qquad 4$$
$$D \qquad\qquad\qquad 6$$

This value is D64 in hexadecimal.

Converting Hexadecimal to Binary. The reverse process is simply a matter of taking each hexadecimal digit and writing the equivalent 4-digit binary number. Convert 7BF to binary.

	7				B				F		
8	4	2	1	8	4	2	1	8	4	2	1
0	1	1	1	1	0	1	1	1	1	1	1

Putting these digits together gives 011110111111, the binary equivalent of 7BF.

COMPUTER NUMBER SYSTEMS

Pure mathematical number systems are rarely used directly in computer design and operation. Because of the varied needs of computer users ranging from scientific to business applications, these types of numbers are not suitable for everyone. Of course, there is also the problem of hardware design. The only type of number conveniently stored in today's hardware is the binary number. But neither business nor scientific programmers wish to write their numbers in binary. Decimal is the preferred method.

Relationship Between Mathematical and Computer Coding Systems

In an attempt to solve these problems, a variety of computer number systems have been devised. These number systems generally bridge a gap between the computer and human needs. Internally, computers store data in a type of binary code. This is not necessarily a binary number but rather a sequence of ones and zeroes, which represent certain data. These data could be a number, an alphabetic character, or some special character. Three of the most common computer number systems are described here.

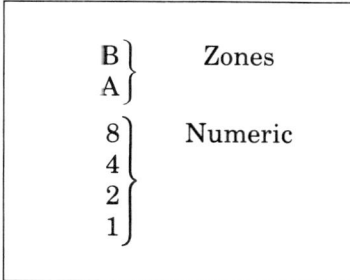

Figure 3-2. BCD bit positions.

Binary Coded Decimal

The Binary Coded Decimal system, abbreviated BCD, is used in computers where 6 binary digits or bits represent a single character of information. The appropriate combination of ones and zeroes in these bits represent a number, letter, or special character such as a dollar sign ($) or comma (,).

Figure 3-2 shows the bit positions used in the BCD system. There are two zone bits (BA) and four numeric bits (8421). Each bit represents a storage position that can record a 0 or 1. The combined 6-bit code represents an addressable storage location called a character or byte. Several of these storage positions combined may represent a field containing a unique item of data such as a quantity or a name.

The chart in Figure 3-3 shows the BCD code for numeric data. In this case, the zone bits are both zero, while the numeric bits give the equivalent binary value for the digit. A single exception is the number

	B A 8 4 2 1
0	0 0 1 0 1 0
1	0 0 0 0 0 1
2	0 0 0 0 1 0
3	0 0 0 0 1 1
4	0 0 0 1 0 0
5	0 0 0 1 0 1
6	0 0 0 1 1 0
7	0 0 0 1 1 1
8	0 0 1 0 0 0
9	0 0 1 0 0 1

Figure 3-3. Numeric BCD codes.

	B	A	8	4	2	1
A	1	1	0	0	0	1
B	1	1	0	0	1	0
C	1	1	0	0	1	1
D	1	1	0	1	0	0
E	1	1	0	1	0	1
F	1	1	0	1	1	0
G	1	1	0	1	1	1
H	1	1	1	0	0	0
I	1	1	1	0	0	1
J	1	0	0	0	0	1
K	1	0	0	0	1	0
L	1	0	0	0	1	1
M	1	0	0	1	0	0
N	1	0	0	1	0	1
O	1	0	0	1	1	0
P	1	0	0	1	1	1
Q	1	0	1	0	0	0
R	1	0	1	0	0	1
S	0	1	0	0	1	0
T	0	1	0	0	1	1
U	0	1	0	1	0	0
V	0	1	0	1	0	1
W	0	1	0	1	1	0
X	0	1	0	1	1	1
Y	0	1	1	0	0	0
Z	0	1	1	0	0	1

Figure 3-4. Alphabetic BCD code.

zero, which uses both the 8 and 2 bits. The configuration gives a decimal equivalent of 10, but if the overflow digit is ignored, only the zero remains.

Alphabetic characters coded in BCD are shown in Figure 3-4. For letters A–I, the zone bits A and B contain ones. Each letter is numbered according to its position in the alphabetic sequence. A is 1, B is 2, and so on. Letters J–R use a 1 in the B zone, and S–Z use a 1 in the A zone. In the case of the last group, S starts counting at 2.

The recording of a word or number in BCD requires the complete 6-bit code for each letter or digit. A word like RECORD would appear as follows in BCD:

101001	110101	110011	100110	101001	110100
R	E	C	O	R	D

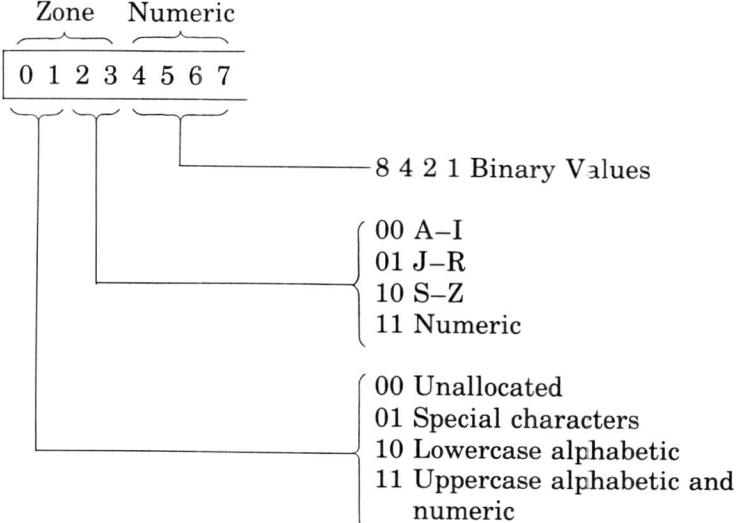

Figure 3-5. EBCDIC bit configuration.

Extended Binary Coded Decimal Interchange Code

One of the most common computer codes in use today is the 8-bit Extended Binary Coded Decimal Interchange Code (EBCDIC). Using eight bits per byte allows a possible maximum of 256 different characters. Although fewer characters are in actual use, this system allows for possible future expansion. Figure 3-5 shows how the eight bits are organized to represent various characters. The first four bits, numbered 0–3, represent the zone portion and bits 4–7, the numeric portion.

The zone is divided into two parts. Bits 0 and 1 identify special characters (01), lowercase alphabetic (10), and uppercase alphabetic or numeric (11). For alphabetic characters and for numbers, zone bits 2 and 3 indicate the letter groupings using values 00, 01, and 10 and numbers using the value 11.

The numeric bits 4–7 are used to indicate the relative position of the letter in the alphabetic sequence. In the case of numbers, these bits give the binary value of the number.

For example, the *number* 5 uses 11 in bits 0 and 1, 11 in bits 2 and 3, and 0101 in bits 4 through 7.

5 in EBCDIC

0	1	2	3	4	5	6	7	*Bit Positions*
1	1	1	1	0	1	0	1	
				8	4	2	1	*Binary Value*

Character	EBCDIC	Character	EBCDIC
a	1000 0001	A	1100 0001
b	1000 0010	B	1100 0010
c	1000 0011	C	1100 0011
d	1000 0100	D	1100 0100
e	1000 0101	E	1100 0101
f	1000 0110	F	1100 0110
g	1000 0111	G	1100 0111
h	1000 1000	H	1100 1000
i	1000 1001	I	1100 1001
j	1001 0001	J	1101 0001
k	1001 0010	K	1101 0010
l	1001 0011	L	1101 0011
m	1001 0100	M	1101 0100
n	1001 0101	N	1101 0101
o	1001 0110	O	1101 0110
p	1001 0111	P	1101 0111
q	1001 1000	Q	1101 1000
r	1001 1001	R	1101 1001
s	1010 0010	S	1110 0010
t	1010 0011	T	1110 0011
u	1010 0100	U	1110 0100
v	1010 0101	V	1110 0101
w	1010 0110	W	1110 0110
x	1010 0111	X	1110 0111
y	1010 1000	Y	1110 1000
z	1010 1001	Z	1110 1001
		0	1111 0000
		1	1111 0001
		2	1111 0010
		3	1111 0011
		4	1111 0100
		5	1111 0101
		6	1111 0110
		7	1111 0111
		8	1111 1000
		9	1111 1001

Figure 3-6. EBCDIC bit configuration.

The *letter* K uses 11 in bits 0 and 1, since it is uppercase; 01 in bits 2 and 3, since it is in the sequence J through R; and 0010 in bits 4 to 7, since it is the second letter in the sequence J through R.

K in EBCDIC

0	1	2	3	4	5	6	7	Bit Positions
1	1	0	1	0	0	1	0	
				8	4	2	1	Binary Value

To represent the lowercase k, bits 0 and 1 contain 10. The other bits are the same as uppercase.

k in EBCDIC

0	1	2	3	4	5	6	7	Bit Positions
1	0	0	1	0	0	1	0	
				8	4	2	1	Binary Value

Figure 3-6 contains upper- and lowercase alphabetic and numeric characters with their associated EBCDIC codes.

The *word* DATA would appear as follows in EBCDIC:

1100 0100	1100 0001	1110 0011	1100 0001
D	A	T	A

American Standard Code for Information Interchange

The ASCII code (Figure 3-7) is an 8-bit code similar in construction to EBCDIC, although it does have its own unique coding structure. ASCII is used primarily for data communication in telecommunications systems.

Numeric values are recorded in ASCII using the zone 0011 with the corresponding binary value in the numeric portion. The number 7 would be the following configuration of ones and zeroes:

7 in ASCII

0	1	2	3	4	5	6	7	Bit Positions
0	0	1	1	0	1	1	1	
			8	4	2	1		Binary Value

60 NUMBER SYSTEMS

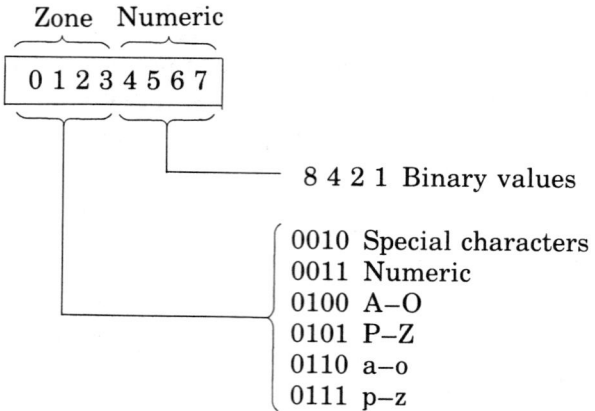

Figure 3-7. ASCII bit configuration.

An alphabetic character uses the appropriate zone depending upon the letter recorded and whether it is upper- or lowercase. The letter sequence is recorded in binary in the numeric part of the byte. This binary value runs from 0 to 15 (F in hexadecimal). Uppercase J would be recorded

```
                  J in ASCII
   0   1   2   3    4   5   6   7   Bit Positions
 | 0   1   0   0    1   0   1   0 |
                    8   4   2   1   Binary Value
```

Notice that the numeric portion for J is 1010, or ten in decimal, since J is the tenth letter in the alphabet. The letter O is the 15th letter and has the code 0100 1111. The 15 is recorded in the numeric portion of the byte. Lower case j is recorded as

```
                  j in ASCII
   0   1   2   3    4   5   6   7   Bit Positions
 | 0   1   1   0    1   0   1   0 |
                    8   4   2   1   Binary Value
```

Figure 3-8 shows the complete ASCII code for numeric digits and for uppercase alphabetic characters.

Numeric	ASCII	Alphabetic	ASCII
0	0011 0000	A	0100 0001
1	0011 0001	B	0100 0010
2	0011 0010	C	0100 0011
3	0011 0011	D	0100 0100
4	0011 0100	E	0100 0101
5	0011 0101	F	0100 0110
6	0011 0110	G	0100 0111
7	0011 0111	H	0100 1000
8	0011 1000	I	0100 1001
9	0011 1001	J	0100 1010
		K	0100 1011
		L	0100 1100
		M	0100 1101
		N	0100 1110
		O	0100 1111
		P	0101 0000
		Q	0101 0001
		R	0101 0010
		S	0101 0011
		T	0101 0100
		U	0101 0101
		V	0101 0110
		W	0101 0111
		X	0101 1000
		Y	0101 1001
		Z	0101 1010

Figure 3-8. American Standard Code for Information Interchange (ASCII).

TERMS TO STUDY

ASCII	High Order
Base	Least Significant Digit
BCD	Low Order
Bit	Most Significant Digit
Binary	Octal
Byte	Positional Notation
EBCDIC	Subscript
Hexadecimal	Successive Division

EXERCISES

1. Convert the following binary numbers to decimal.
   - a. 1101
   - b. 10000
   - c. 11111
   - d. 11101
   - e. 1100110
   - f. 101010
   - g. 1000001
   - h. 1100001
   - i. 10101111
   - j. 11111111

2. Convert the following decimal numbers to binary.
   - a. 10
   - b. 32
   - c. 31
   - d. 28
   - e. 101
   - f. 255
   - g. 257
   - h. 4000
   - i. 4200
   - j. 4096

3. Convert the following octal numbers to decimal.
   - a. 16
   - b. 21
   - c. 17
   - d. 23
   - e. 10
   - f. 103
   - g. 12
   - h. 77
   - i. 777
   - j. 100

4. Convert the decimal numbers in exercise 2 to octal.
5. Convert the binary numbers in exercise 1 to octal.
6. Convert the following hexadecimal numbers to decimal.
   - a. 1A
   - b. 100
   - c. 3B0
   - d. B7
   - e. ABC
   - f. FACE
   - g. 9F
   - h. FADE
   - i. 1D3C7
   - j. DEAF

7. Convert the decimal numbers in exercise 2 to hexadecimal.
8. Convert the binary numbers of exercise 1 to hexadecimal.
9. Convert the hexadecimal numbers of exercise 6 to binary.
10. Record the title of this book in EBCDIC.
11. Record the name of your college in ASCII.
12. Record your name and address in BCD.

QUESTIONS FOR REVIEW

1. Describe a method for converting from base ten to any other number system.

2. Describe a method for converting from any number system to base ten.
3. Devise a method for converting from octal to hexadecimal without using decimal numbers.
4. Describe the BCD coding system.
5. Describe the EBCDIC coding system.
6. What is the difference between a hexadecimal number system and an 8-bit computer code based on hexadecimal?
7. What coding system is used in your local computer?
8. Try to get a storage dump from your computer center. See if you can interpret some of the code.
9. What is a bit? A byte?

Computer Hardware

4

Computer Data Processing Systems

Chapter 1 discussed some of the reasons why business organizations use a computer. Their motivations included improved efficiency in the storage, processing, and access of data as well as a reduction of manual effort and the number of errors introduced. These advantages led to an improvement in the quality of information supplied to both management and operational personnel.

DATA PROCESSING TERMINOLOGY

However, what exactly is meant by such terms as data and information? The word *data* is used to indicate a representation of facts necessary for communicating items of specific meaning. These facts can be represented as numeric, alphabetic, or alphanumeric data. Figure 4-1 shows various data items that might be used in a data processing system. These are the basic components that are processed by the computer to produce information.

Although the term *information* is sometimes used to mean data, it also has a more specific meaning. Information refers to data that has been organized into some coherent pattern and processed to provide some specific format. Although each of the data items in Figure 4-1 has some specific meaning, these items do not really tell us much as they stand.

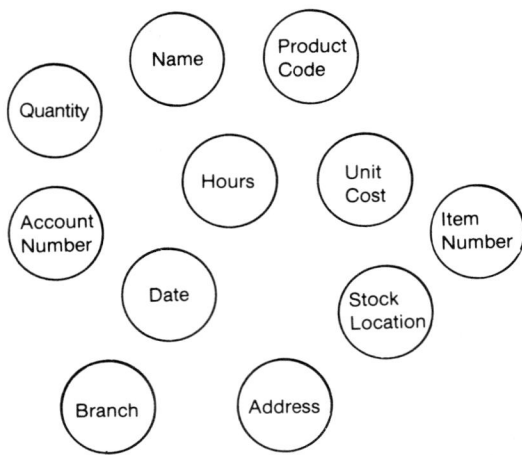

Figure 4-1. Data items.

If some of these data are organized to give Figure 4-2, we now have information. This data now gives us information about some kind of transaction involving an item number, name, address, and so on. This diagram also shows total cost, which was not in Figure 4-1. This data has been generated or computed as a result of some kind of processing.

The term *data processing* essentially refers to the systematic operations involving data. Organizing the data from Figure 4-1 into the orderly presentation in Figure 4-2 and the computing of the total cost were data processing operations. The expression *information processing* is synonymous with *data processing* and is sometimes considered to be a more modern term. The illustrations in Figures 4-3 and 4-4 give a practical example of the relationship between data and information.

For data to be useful to a computer, it must be recorded on a machine-readable medium. For many years, the punched card was the traditional object for the recording of data. More recently, data has been recorded on a magnetic medium such as tape or disk. This data is recorded in a logical format known as a record. A record is a set of related items of

Figure 4-2. Information.

DATA PROCESSING TERMINOLOGY   69

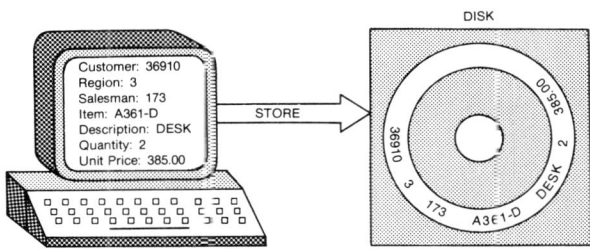

Figure 4-3. One way of entering "data" into the computer is through the keyboard. A program in the computer then instructs the computer to store the data on disk for later processing.

data in a machine-readable format. The example in Figure 4-5 could be an accounts receivable record. Other types of records could be a payroll record, inventory record, or student record. Each of these records contains related items of data. A student record would contain a student number, name, address, and course number; but it would not contain an inventory number because an inventory number has nothing to do with student records.

The component of a record that contains a specific unit of information is called a *field*. The first five positions of the record in Figure 4-5 contain the item number field. This is followed by the description field and so on. Fields may contain numeric data (such as a quantity), alphabetic (such as a person's name), or alphanumeric (such as a street address),

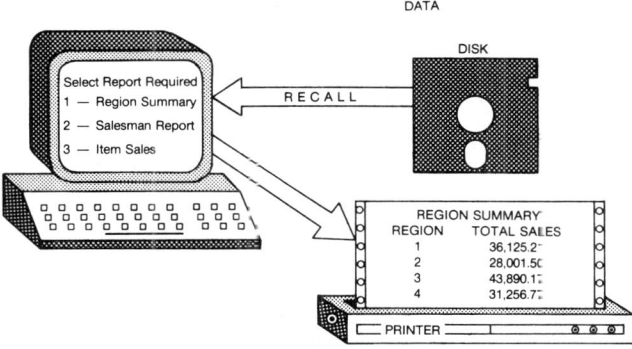

Figure 4-4. Producing "information" from data is done when the user selects an option from the screen display. When the user asks for a region summary, the computer will recall the data from the disk where it was previously stored. After sorting and summarizing, the computer produces the information here in the form of a region summary report.

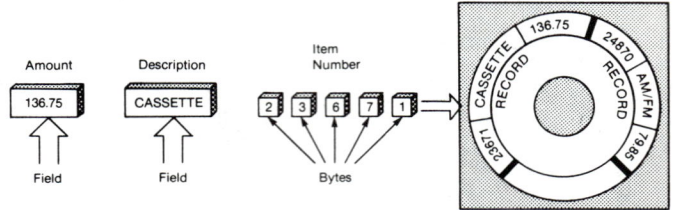

Figure 4-5. A file is composed of a series of records, which in turn is a collection of fields. Each field contains one or more bytes that are either letters, numbers, or special characters.

depending on the requirements of the application. An account number may be numeric or alphanumeric, but an amount would always be numeric and a name would always be alphabetic.

A set of related records is a *file*. Figure 4-5 contains a product file. This file is a collection of product records.

There are several different types of files used in computer systems. Two commonly used files are the *master file* and the *transaction file*. These are general terms and may apply to an application area such as payroll, inventory, or accounting.

A master file contains permanent records for a specific application. If Figure 4-5 represented a master file, these would be permanent records for items 23671 and 24870.

A transaction file represents changes to be applied to a master file. A transaction record may provide for a change to item 23671. The processing of this transaction would change the amount in the master record for this item from 136.75 to 142.15 as a result of the update.

KEY CONCEPT

BYTE, FIELD, RECORD, AND FILE

BYTE: A byte, another term for character, is a unit of computer storage. It is the smallest unit of data that a programmer normally accesses. A byte of computer memory can store any one of the ten digits 0 to 9, twenty-six letters A to Z, and a variety of special characters such as ,.;:"#$%()*+ −/ etc. Many computers can also store the lowercase letters a to z and special graphic

EXAMPLE

characters. Each of these characters requires one byte of storage space.

FIELD: A field is a component of a record that contains a specific unit of information. Common fields in information processing are account number, description, amount, date, code, name, and address. A field will consist of one or more bytes. For instance, a code could be a single digit to represent sex and therefore require only one byte, but a name field might need 15 bytes.

RECORD: A record contains a set of related fields. For example, when a student registers in school a record could be created containing a student number, name, address, phone number, program, and semester. Records for different applications will contain different fields and will be of different lengths.

FILE: A set of related records is a file. A set of records for all students registered in a school would be a registration file. Like records, different files can also be of different lengths. The length of a file determines how much space will be required for it on a disk.

THE COMPUTER AND ITS COMPONENTS

The word *computer* is often used with a variety of meanings. Sometimes it refers to a single machine, and at other times it can be used to mean a large number of devices. Although the term may be used correctly in both instances, more precise terminology is required if we wish to communicate effectively in this area. A large scale computer may have literally hundreds of components varying from circuit boards to magnetic tape drives. A number of these components will be discussed in depth in the following chapters. For now, a general picture will be developed to place these components in certain categories.

Figure 4-6 shows the basic components of any computer system. These are:

1. Central processing unit
2. Input devices
3. Output devices

KEY CONCEPT

TYPES OF PROCESSORS

Not all central processing units are the same. They are designed and built on the basis of their intended use. In fact, computers fall into a variety of categories, which are quite different from each other.

Digital Computers

This type of computer is the most common in use today. It operates on the basis of counting numbers or digits. These digits are used to express quantities or amounts, which are then processed arithmetically. It functions on the principle of precise quantitative processing.

Analog Computers

An analog computer works on the basis of analogy. It measures changes in current, temperature, or pressure and translates these into electrical current for processing. No counting is done. An example of this type of operation is the thermostat, which translates air temperature into electrical current to control the operation of a furnace.

Hybrid Computers

A computer that combines the characteristics of both the digital and analog computer is a hybrid computer. Its use is in specialized applications where both kinds of information need to be processed.

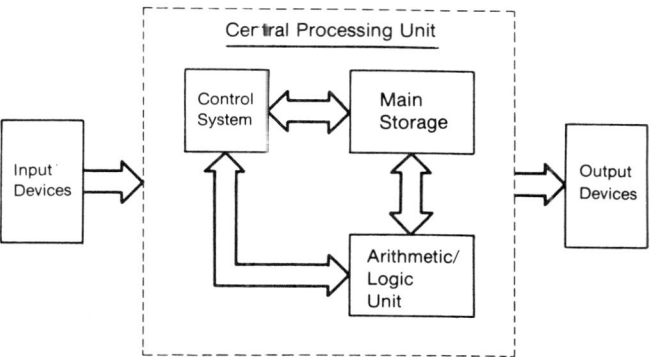

Figure 4-6. Computer components.

Regardless of whether a computer is very small, costing a few hundred dollars (Figure 4-7), or a multimillion dollar large scale system, it will have these three basic components. However, the type of computer system determines to a large degree the elements making up these components.

Central Processing Unit

It can be seen from Figure 4-6 that at the center of a computer system is the *central processing unit* or *CPU*. This processor consists of three elements:

> Main Storage
> Arithmetic and Logic Unit (ALU)
> Control System

Main Storage. The storage part of the CPU is a magnetic or electronic device. It provides for the temporary storage of data in the form of records or tables. The result of a processing step is stored here, and a program that is to be executed by the CPU is also resident in main storage. Both data and program statements are referenced at particular storage locations by addresses. Often the size of a CPU is expressed in terms of the number of storage locations. A 2M CPU means that its storage unit contains approximately 2,000,000 storage locations. CPUs will be discussed more fully in Chapter 10.

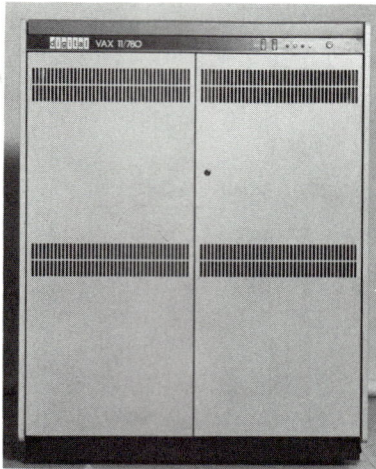

Figure 4-7. The Digital VAX-11/780-A 32-bit central processor unit. This VAX computer is one of a series of minicomputers suitable for educational and business applications. (*Courtesy of Digital Equipment Corporation*)

KEY CONCEPT

SPECIAL PURPOSE AND GENERAL PURPOSE COMPUTERS

In addition to the three types of processors, there are the ways in which the computer is used. There are special purpose computers that are designed to perform a single function. These are quite efficient and economical but lack versatility. Uses might be in the areas of air traffic control, military decisions, and automotive fuel injection.

A general purpose computer is used for a wide variety of applications such as inventory, payroll accounting, market research, and sales analysis. These computers use a stored program to change from one application to another. They sacrifice some efficiency and economy to gain versatility. In this book, we are primarily concerned with general purpose digital computers.

Arithmetic and Logic Unit. The ALU is the section of the CPU that does arithmetic and logical operations. Arithmetic involves addition, subtraction, multiplication, and division of numbers. Logical operations relate to the comparison of two values to determine their relationship. For instance, one number may be less than, greater than, or equal to another. Based upon the relationship found, the program may choose between one of several actions. This kind of logical decision is necessary when, for example, selecting a tax percentage for a given income in a payroll program.

Control System. The control system directs the flow of data between main storage and the ALU and also between storage and the input or output devices. It also accesses program statements from main storage and interprets their meaning. Since it then executes the program, the control system is actually under program control.

Input Devices

All computers require a minimum of one input device. Most use a number of input devices of various kinds. The purpose of an input device is to supply data records to the CPU for processing. Some input devices are shown in Figure 4-8. Data recorded for these devices may be in a number of different codes depending upon the medium used such as disk or tape.

Magnetically recorded data, such as tape and disk, generally use either EBCDIC or ASCII as the coding method. Other devices such as the Magnetic Ink Character Reader (MICR) and the Optical Scanner use unique coding methods, which will be described in a later chapter.

Because a computer may have a variety of devices using different coding arrangements, each code must be translated into a common code for use by the CPU, which recognizes only one code. This translation is accomplished by another device called a control unit, not to be confused with the control system discussed earlier, which is situated between the input device and the CPU.

Source Data. Data supplied for use as input to a computer system may come from a variety of origins. Some of these sources are listed in Figure 4-9, which shows the differences between direct inputs and source documents.

Source documents are in the form of handwritten or typed paper forms. These are generated as a result of a transaction between the user and the system. A customer may phone to place an order for an item, which is then written on the customer order form. This form is then taken to a terminal or key entry device and recorded for computer input.

Direct inputs are data that become immediate input to the computer at their source. An example of direct input is the use of bar codes in a retail supermarket application. As items are checked by the cashier, a bar code on the package is read by a wand. The code is translated into

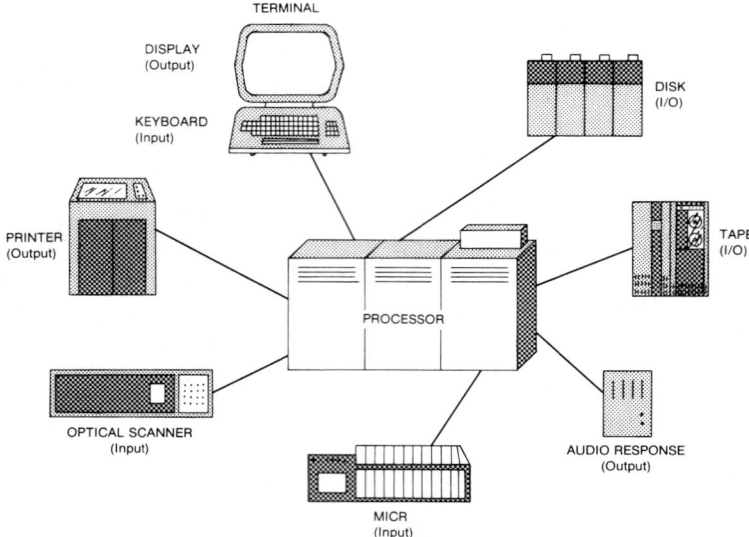

Figure 4-8. Input/output devices.

digital information giving product identification. This becomes input to the computer, which supplies the price and description for the customer's bill. It also updates the inventory records to show that the item has been purchased and reduces the shelf quantity field by the quantity of the item purchased. Data supplied for processing must be error free and complete. Lacking accuracy, the computer is supplied with "garbage," which in turn produces "garbage" as output; hence the term GIGO meaning Garbage In Garbage Out.

Source Documents	Direct Inputs
Invoices	Optical Read Documents
Sales Slips	Teller Terminal
Shipping Forms	Retail Bar Codes
Coding Sheets	Reservation Terminal
Customer Orders	Touch Sensitive Terminal

Figure 4-9. Source data.

Output Devices

The output from a computer consists of records, which are produced in either human- or machine-readable format. Output devices are also shown in Figure 4-8. Examples of human-readable outputs are hard copy from the printer and display screen. The printer records information, produced as a result of processing, on paper in a manner similar to typing. This printed information (known as hard copy) may be payroll checks, accounting statements, personalized letters, inventory reports, and so on. A display shows similar information except that it is displayed on a TV-like screen. The display is temporary, allowing sufficient time for the information to be read visually. This information may then be replaced on the screen by other displayed data as required.

Machine-readable devices record data to be stored and then read again as input to the computer. For this reason, devices like magnetic tape and disk may be used as either input or output devices. These devices may store the data for periods of time ranging from a few minutes to many months.

Other types of output devices are essentially for human use but are specialized in nature. Examples of these are microfilm output and audio response output devices. A more detailed discussion on all input and output devices will be found in Chapters 5 through 9.

Destination of Data. Following processing, data must be generated in a form suitable for human reference and action. This data may be used in the daily operations of a business organization. Computer-generated information for human use comes in a variety of forms as shown in Figure 4-10 but in only two basic categories. These categories are hard copy and soft copy.

Hard copy refers to reports or documents that are permanent in nature. They can be picked up and read or, in the case of computer output microfilm (COM), may be placed in a microfilm reader. Documents are

Hard Copy	**Soft Copy**
Documents	CRT Display
Reports	Graphic Display
Summary Reports	Audio
COM	

Figure 4-10. Output data for human use.

items such as paychecks and customer billing forms. These are usually produced on preprinted forms with the computer inserting specific information such as name and address, amount, and date.

Reports are generally for internal use by departmental personnel. Included are inventory, production, and sales reports. These reports are in detail and show every activity. For instance, a sales report would have a record of each individual sale indicating the product sold, the salesman who sold it, the quantity of the sale, and the dollar amount represented. Detail reports can be very bulky and awkward to use for some applications. In this case, summary reports are prepared summarizing the detail into a compact form. The sales report in this case might only show total sales per salesman rather than including details about each sale.

Soft copy reports appear on a medium that is not permanent. The sales report mentioned above could be displayed on a CRT display screen (Figure 4-11). The information displayed would be read and analyzed by the sales manager. When the required information is found, the screen may be blanked out and other information displayed. Graphic display and audio response systems also produce information to be visually or audibly sensed.

Magnetic recordings use disk or tape for storage of the data. This data may be retained indefinitely and then used as input to the computer. It is not a human-readable format but only machine-readable.

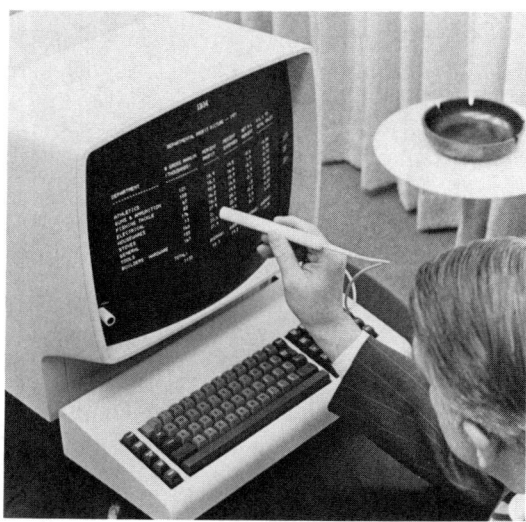

Figure 4-11. Soft copy report on a CRT display. (*Courtesy of IBM Corporation*)

PROCESSING CONCEPTS

As we have just seen, the program controls the processing steps that occur between the input and output of the data. The program defines the need to read input data, to perform arithmetic and logical operations on that data, and produces the desired output. While the detailed steps taken by the program can be many and varied, there are a few general categories of operations that are done by the computer under program control. These steps can be summarized in a menu (Figure 4-12).

Storage

One of the most basic types of processing a computer can do is the storing of data. When source data is first entered into the computer though the keyboard, it will be stored on a secondary device so that it may be referenced later by other programs.

The devices commonly used for storage are the tape and disk. When the data is first read, it may be checked for validity to ensure its correctness. Then it is stored on a device such as the disk where other programs may access the data as required.

Figure 4-13 shows a job reporting record for an employee; it indicates the number of hours worked by that employee and the rate per hour. This data is first entered on the keyboard. After the program has verified the correctness of the data, a record is created and stored on the disk file along with other similar records for other employees. The record is now available for reference by other programs when additional processing is needed.

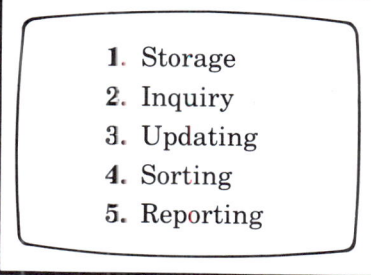

Figure 4-12. Operations a computer can do.

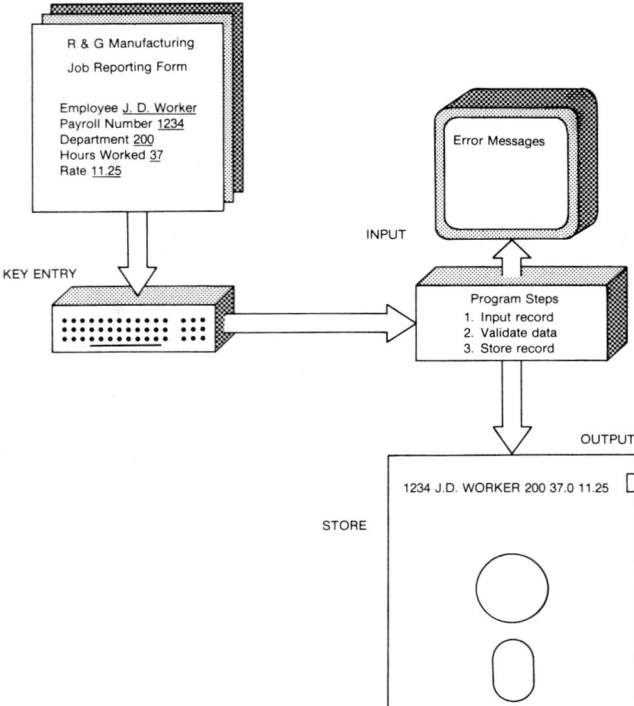

Figure 4-13. The process of "storing" data begins with a source document. Data from this document is entered into the computer from the keyboard under program control. The program then checks the data for correctness, and if the data is found to be valid, the program will then store the data on a disk file.

Inquiry

Another basic operation the computer can do is to retrieve data that was previously stored. This operation comes in the form of an inquiry since the computer user generally asks for specific information from the computer.

Figure 4-14 shows an operation where the computer user requests a display of the record for employee number 1234. The program locates the disk record for this employee and displays it on the screen for reference purposes. Optionally, the computer can create a hard copy of this inquiry on the printer.

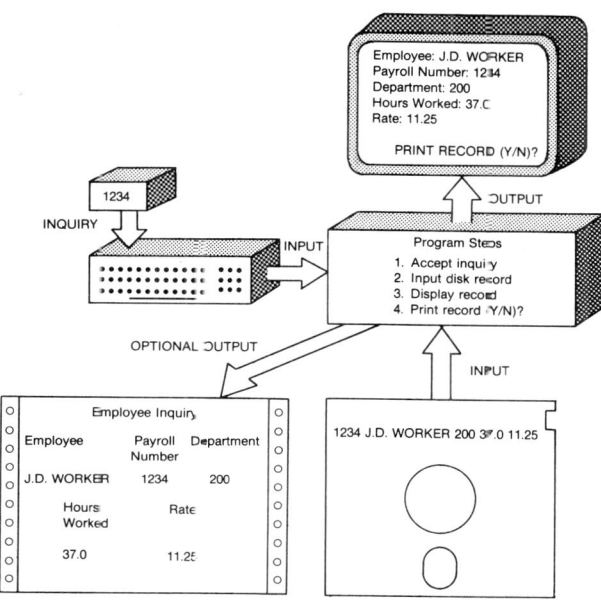

Figure 4-14. An "inquiry" is made by the computer user about employee number 1234. The program reads the disk record for employee 1234 and creates an output on the display screen. The user making the inquiry then has the option to select a hard copy of the record.

Updating

In addition to making inquiries possible, records are frequently stored so that they may be used to update data retained on other files called master files. An example of this might be a bank account that is updated by deposits and withdrawals—or an inventory file that is updated to reflect items moving into and out of stock.

Updating generally falls into three types of activities against a master file. An update may

1. Add a new record to the file. This would be done when a new customer opens an account in a banking application.
2. Revise an existing record on the master file. This is the most frequent type of update. It applies to activities like deposits and withdrawals, which change the balance on existing accounts.

82 COMPUTER DATA PROCESSING SYSTEMS

3. Delete a record from the file. In a banking application, this update occurs when a customer closes an account and it is removed from the file.

The example we used earlier of recording an employee's hours worked is used again in Figure 4-15. The data that had been previously stored on a disk is now processed by an update program against a Year to Date Payroll File. The purpose of this update is to revise the year-to-date gross salary by adding to it the current gross. To do this update, the program first calculates the current gross and then it is added to the year-to-date gross from the master file. The record is then written back to the master (not shown in the diagram) so that the master now reflects current year-to-date data.

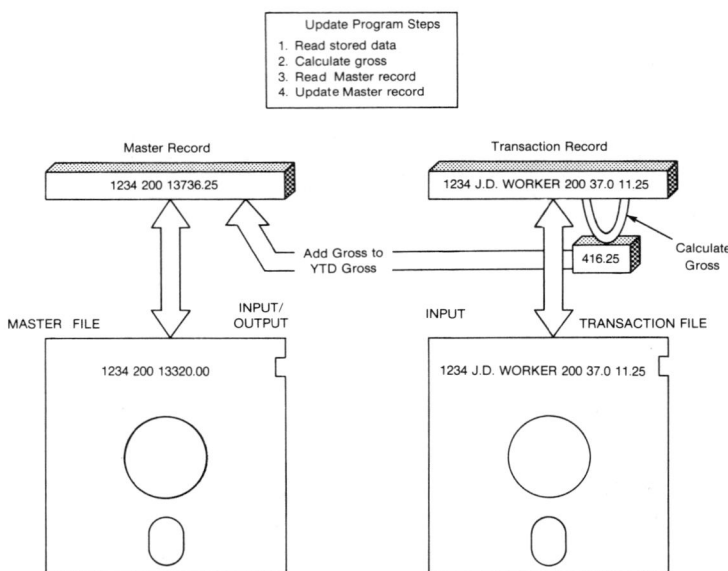

Figure 4-15. This is an example of an "Update" that revises an existing record. The program reads the transaction record representing the employee's weekly data. A master record with a matching employee number is read into the program to be updated. After the gross for the transaction has been calculated, it is then added to the year-to-date gross in the master, thus changing it from 13320.00 to 13736.25. The revised master is now rewritten back on the master file (not shown).

Sorting

The process of sorting is needed in many applications to reorganize data into a specific sequence. This is a particularly important process to be applied after the entry of source data when the data is not in any particular sequence but is simply stored as it arrives at the computer.

Data often needs sorting before reports are generated. It is quite common for the same data to be sorted into different sequences for use on different reports.

Figure 4-16 shows an unsorted file of payroll data which had been recorded as it was received. The program in this diagram is a sort that sequences the data by employee number and creates an output file in employee number sequence.

Usually, generalized utility programs are used to sort files of data. By specifying the field or fields to be sorted, the program then takes care of efficiently resequencing the file according to the specifications.

KEY CONCEPT

ASCENDING AND DESCENDING SEQUENCE

Data may be sorted into either ascending sequence or descending sequence. Ascending means the data is in order beginning with the lowest number and proceeding to the highest. Descending sequence is just the reverse: the data begins with the highest value and goes to the lowest.

ASCENDING (Account Number)		*DESCENDING* (Grade)	
Account	Amount	Student	Grade
123	12.56	2345	4.0
145	15.47	1574	3.4
166	243.01	1847	3.0
171	85.44	1601	3.0
172	9.89	2107	2.5
180	47.74	1939	1.8

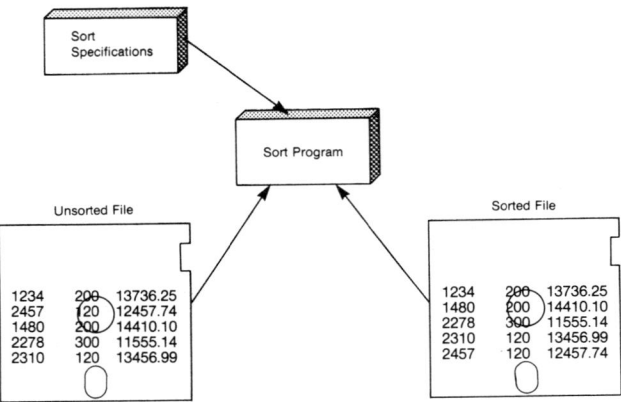

Figure 4-16. A "Sort" program reads as input an unsequenced file and sorts it according to the specs supplied. In this case, the sort program sequences the input records and creates an output file in employee number sequence.

Reporting

Reporting is perhaps the most important operation the computer can do. Programs that produce reports are communicating to the user the information available in the computer's data files. Usually, reporting also includes other processing of the data, both arithmetic and logical. It is not unusual for a program to use a combination of both for even relatively simple reports.

Arithmetic processing may involve calculations, totals and summarizing of numerical data. Logical processing may also be applied to the arithmetic process by deciding which data is to be included in the operation. For example, an income tax preparation program may select certain fields as deductions and others as taxable income.

Logical processing can also include sorting the data to prepare it for the reporting process. For instance, a summary report of sales by region would require the data to be sorted into region sequence before the summary report could be developed.

A detail report, shown in Figure 4-17, contains all of the detail information present on the file. Each record is read by the program and printed almost without change, except for field editing such as inserting decimal points or commas for readability. Additional headings and totals may also be included in the detail report.

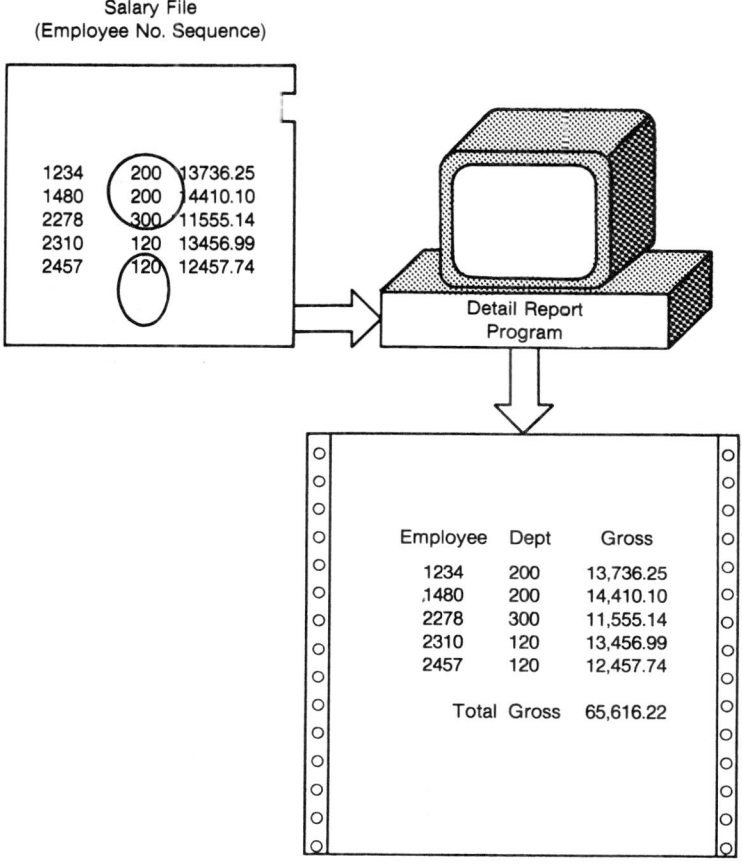

Figure 4-17. A "Detail Report" is produced by the program when each record read from the input file is printed or displayed in detail. Headings and totals are often used to provide additional information.

A second type of report is the group report as shown in Figure 4-18. The group report uses control breaks on a certain field or fields where totals are given for that group of data. In the example, control breaks occur whenever a department change takes place and a total is generated for the gross amounts in that department. This total is called a minor total.

At the end of a group report is a final total, which is the same as in the detail report. This total is called a major total when it appears on a group report.

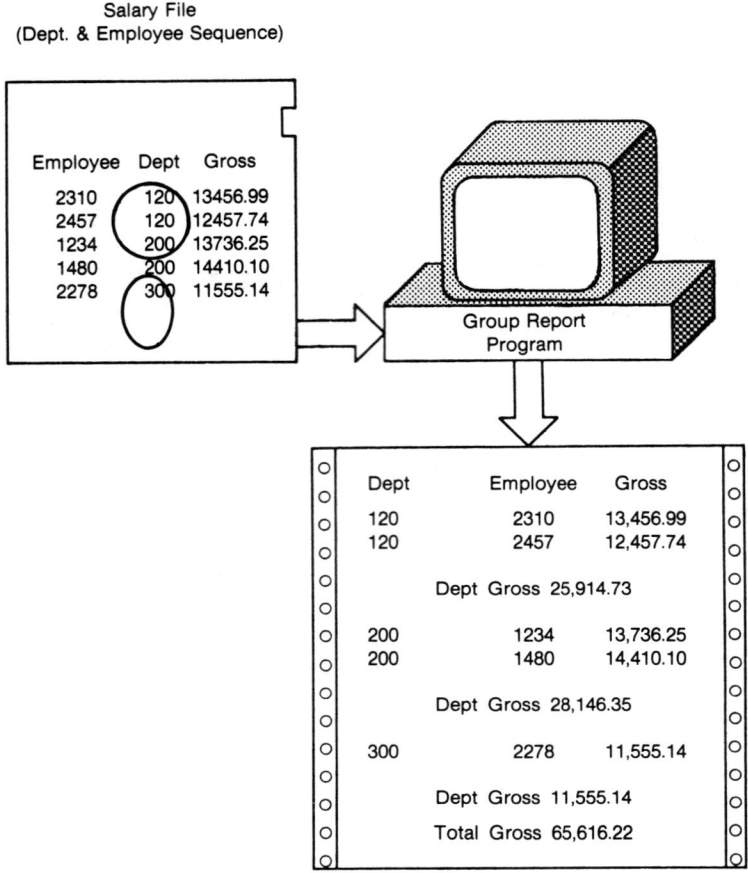

Figure 4-18. A "Group Report" shows totals on control breaks within the data. In this case, control breaks occur by department number, causing a department gross to be printed at the end of each department.

Summary reporting is a third form of output. It is very similar to group reporting except that in summary reports the detail data within a group is not printed, only the group totals are.

Figure 4-19 shows a summary report produced from the salary file, which is in department and employee number sequence. To produce a summary report, each detail record from the input must be read, but the program only accumulates totals for these records and does not print them. In this example, each employee record is read, but instead of printing or displaying the data, a total of the gross salary for each employee is accumulated.

When a control break occurs on the department number, the total that has accumulated is printed for the preceding department. This approach results in only one line of summarized output for each department.

Another type of report is called exception reporting. Frequently, in data processing applications, large quantities of data are accumulated on a file—much more than anyone would care to read By permitting the user to supply selection criteria, the program then selects only some records from the file. Records selected for exception reporting are those that have satisfied the selection criteria.

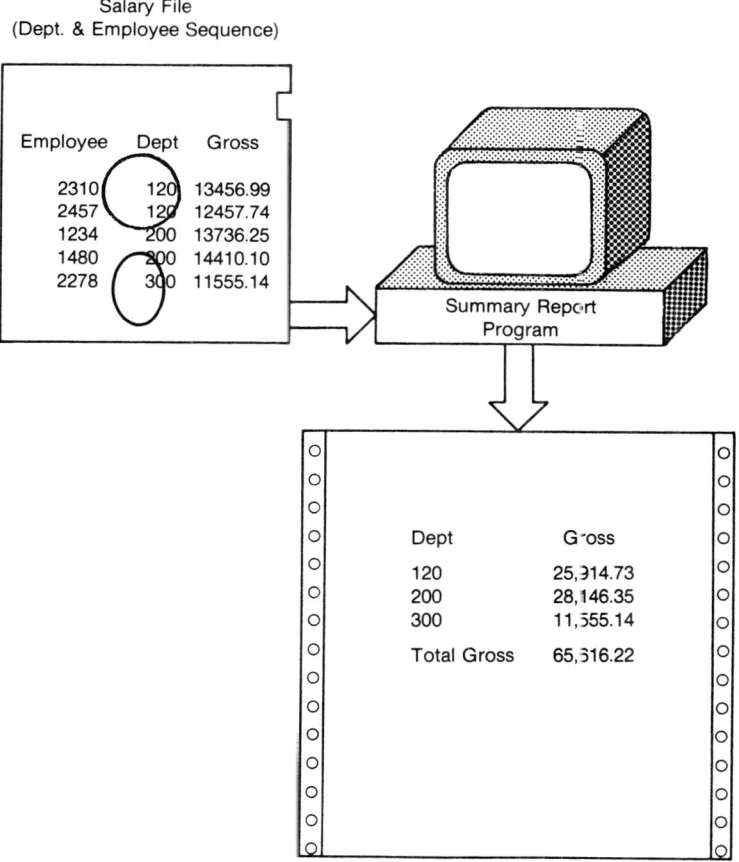

Figure 4-19. A "Summary Report" accumulates data for a group of records and then prints a summary of those records. In this example, department forms the group and the summary is the total of gross salaries within each department.

Examples of exception reporting can vary from selecting source data records containing data errors to selecting records from a master file of permanent data. For instance, an inventory file may be used for a selection report of all items that are out of stock. In another application, an accounts receivable file may be used to generate an exception report of all past due accounts.

In Figure 4-20, the salary file is used to produce a report of employees having gross incomes under $13,000.00. In this file, two records meet this selection criteria and are printed. All other records are simply ignored by the program.

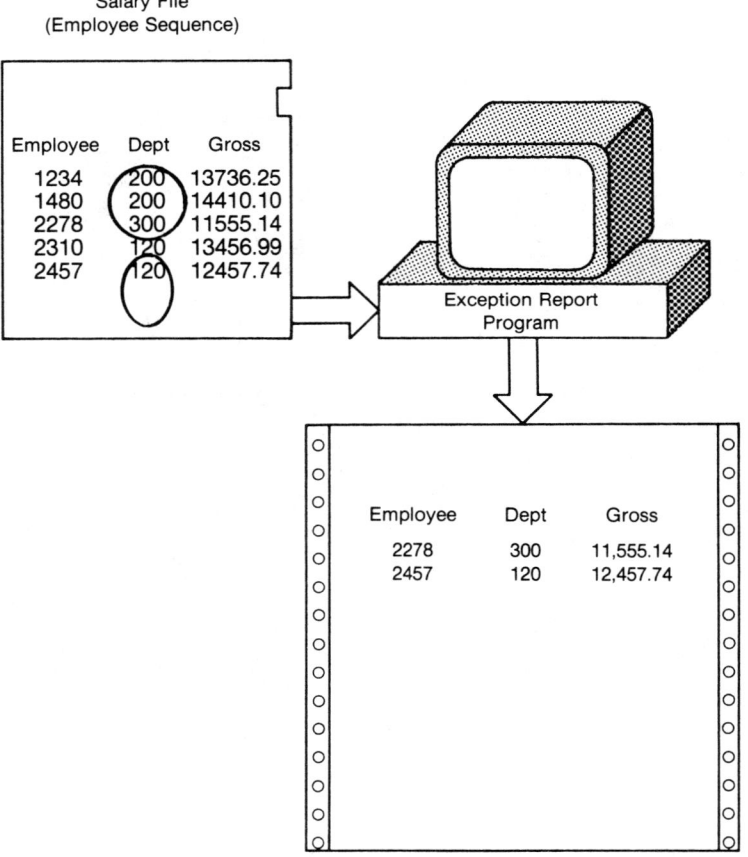

Figure 4-20. The "Exception Report" is produced by specifying certain conditions for selecting a record. In this example, records with a gross of less than $13,000.00 are selected for the exception report.

Many types of data manipulation are possible, such as reporting, selecting, and updating. Each of these forms, as discussed under the section on Processing Concepts, may be implemented under one of several possible processing methods.

Batch Processing

This processing method requires that all transactions or records, such as invoices, sales slips, route cards, etc., be accumulated prior to processing. These records are organized to represent groups of data. A batch may be records received over a given time period (day or week), or it may represent a category of data, such as a sales region. The batch of data is then processed at a scheduled time by the computer. Outputs are made available after the processing. However, there may be a considerable time delay from the time an original transaction occurs until the computer output is made available.

Although time delays are significant, they may not present a serious problem in applications such as monthly billing. The batch method does permit the processing of large amounts of data at one time and in so doing makes the most efficient use of computer hardware.

Remote Batch Processing

This method is essentially like batch processing. Transactions are accumulated in groups and processed at one time. Time delays offset by efficient use of the hardware also apply here. The major difference in the two methods is that batch processing requires the data, in the form of cards, tape, etc., to be taken physically to the computer. In remote batch, data is entered into a terminal at a physically remote location. The terminal could be a card reader, tape drive, minicomputer, etc., and is attached by telephone lines, or the equivalent, to the remote computer. The terminal may be located in the same building as the computer, across town, or across the country. Using this method, data does not need to be physically transported to the computer. Instead, it is transmitted by digital signals over communication lines. Where long distances are involved, remote batch does improve the time delay factor of batch processing.

Real-Time Processing

Like remote batch, this method of processing uses remote terminals for data entry. Terminals such as teletype keyboards or display screens are often suitable for human use. The primary feature of real-time processing is the immediate processing of a transaction as it is entered. Each transaction is considered individually, not in a batch. Essentially, there is no delay between input, processing, and output.

A common use for real-time processing is the reservation system used by hotel chains and airlines. In these systems, a customer may request a reservation for a hotel room in a distant city. The transaction is entered into a terminal. The central computer immediately evaluates the reservation and responds directly—indicating the reservation has been made, or if not, suggests an alternative.

The use of hardware in real time is less efficient than in batch, but the faster processing of transactions gives much greater customer satisfaction.

Time Sharing

Time sharing is a technique similar in concept to real time in that terminals are attached to the computer by communication lines. In time sharing, the processing power of the computer is shared among many users. This processing time is divided into small slices and each terminal user gets a slice of time. Applications here include computer assisted instruction (CAI), interactive programming in languages like BASIC and APL, and data processing required by small businesses who need some computer time but not enough to require their own computer.

TERMS TO STUDY

ALU
Batch Processing
Control Unit
CPU
Data
Field
File
Hard Copy
Information
Input
Inquiry

Output
Real Time
Record
Remote Batch
Reporting
Soft Copy
Sorting
Storage
Time Sharing
Updating

QUESTIONS FOR REVIEW

1. What is the difference between the terms *data* and *information*? Give specific examples of each.
2. What is meant by data processing? In what way is data prepared for processing?
3. In what way do the terms *data* and *information* relate to records and fields?
4. What is the purpose of a master file? A transaction file? How are they related?
5. Briefly define a computer. What are its components?
6. What is the difference between input and output? Give practical examples of computer input and output devices.
7. What methods are used for processing data? Give some examples of these from your experience. They do not need to be computer related.
8. Evaluate the benefits of batch versus remote batch versus real-time processing. Do this in chart form for easy comparison.

PROBLEMS FOR RESEARCH AND DISCUSSION

1. Design a file containing information about the people in your class. Be sure to define records and fields and show how these might be organized. How long must each field be? Does it contain numeric, alphabetic, or alphanumeric data? How long is each record? Are they all the same fields?
2. Find some examples of computer inputs and outputs used in your school or community. Hard copy would be best because it can be brought to the classroom and discussed.
3. What kind of computer is used by your school? What is its size? What input and output devices are used? What processing method(s) is/are used?

5

Data Entry

In the business world, data originates from many sources. Invoices, sales orders, purchase orders, and so on, are documents that provide data to be processed by the computer. However, since these are usually hand prepared, they are not in a form that is easily and efficiently read by a computer input device. Therefore, methods and machines are needed to transcribe this information into machine-readable form.

Since data entry can cost up to one-half of the data handling dollar, it is important that a data entry method be selected with care. A poor choice can lead to inefficient operation because of:

1. An increase in personnel requirements
2. An increase in the number of errors created
3. A longer time than necessary from source data to computer input.

The earliest unit record and computer systems used punched cards as the only form of input. Documents were read by a keypunch operator, who keyed in the data and produced the punched cards. The cards were then read into the computer by a card reader (Figure 5-1). However, cards were bulky to store and subject to wear. They were also limited to record size and were a relatively slow computer input. As a result, new and improved forms of data entry emerged around 1965. There has been a strong movement since then toward magnetic recording devices such as the keytape and key disk and to more direct forms of data entry using the display screen with a keyboard.

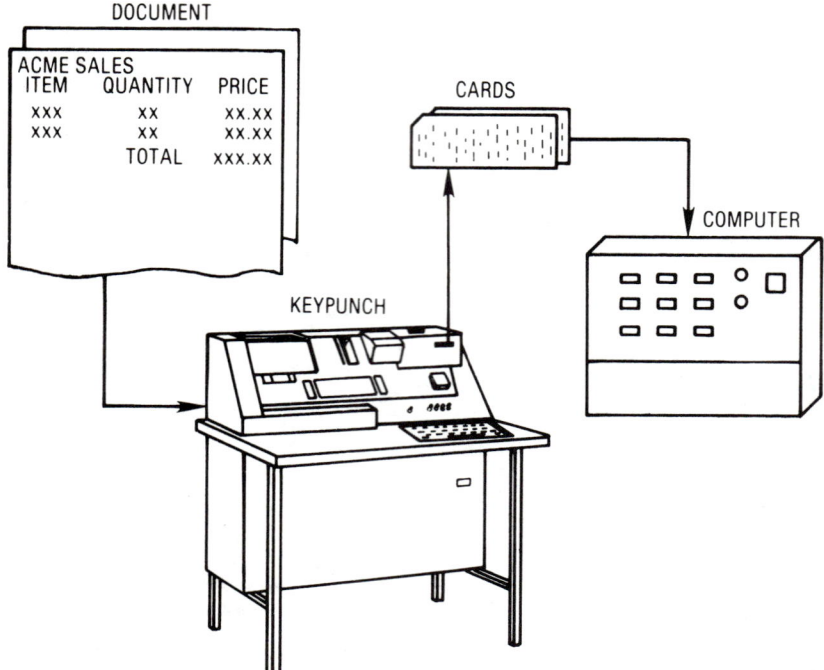

Figure 5-1. In a card-oriented system, cards are keypunched from the original document by typing the data into the keypunch machine. The resulting punched cards are then read into the computer, where the data is processed or stored.

These devices eliminate (or reduce to an insignificant level) the problems with the punched card. Although these devices generally cost more than the keypunch, their faster operating characteristics, fewer errors, and decreased operator requirements generally result in a lower overall cost.

PUNCHED CARDS

The punched card was developed in the 1880s by Herman Hollerith and over the years has become a standard method of initial recording of information for use in data processing equipment. This card, rectangular in shape, contains 80 characters of information in the form of punched rectangular holes. Before the computer began to dominate the business world to satisfy its data processing needs, unit record machines were widely used. Data was supplied to these machines in the form of the punched card, known as a unit record.

The term *unit record* indicated that a card contained one unit of information. For example, a card might contain all the data relating to the sale of an item, the account information for a single customer, or the payroll data for an employee.

Since the Hollerith card was produced, it has gained an unequalled position of respect among data processors. The only serious contender was the 90-character Powers card, which was discontinued in 1966. In 1969, IBM announced a new 96-character punched card for use with their new small computer, the System/3. This card has also virtually disappeared from use.

Hollerith Card

Commonly called the IBM card because of its widespread adoption by this company, it is made from paper about 178 microns ($7/10000$ of an inch) in thickness and is rectangular with dimensions of 8.25 cm. by 18.73 cm. (3¼ inches by 7⅜ inches).

This card is shown in Figure 5-2. The front of the card, which is normally printed, is called the face. The corners may be either rounded or square. Rounded corners are generally preferred because they are less susceptible to damage, which would interfere with the reading. A corner cut is employed on one of the four corners. When this is used, a card that is upside down or backwards in a deck of cards may be readily seen and corrected.

The card is divided into 80 vertical columns and 12 horizontal rows. Each column may contain a single character of punched information. A character may be a digit, a letter of the alphabet, or a special character such as a comma or a dollar sign.

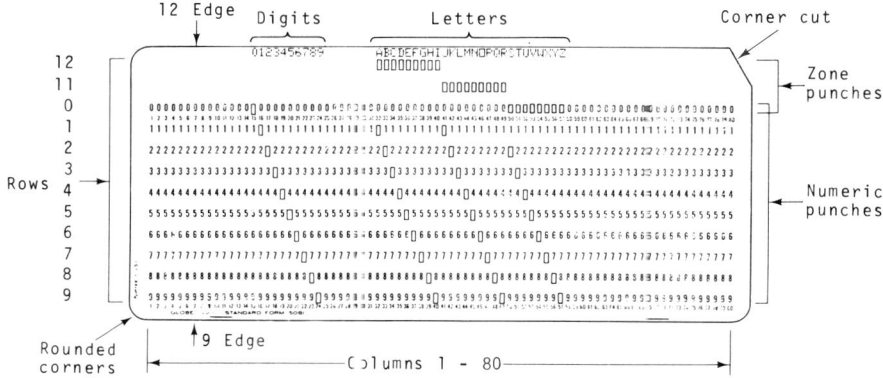

Figure 5-2. The 80-column Hollerith punched card.

Digit	Punches Used	Letter	Punches Used	Letter	Punches Used	Letter	Punches Used
0	0						
1	1	A	12 1	J	11 1		
2	2	B	12 2	K	11 2	S	0 2
3	3	C	12 3	L	11 3	T	0 3
4	4	D	12 4	M	11 4	U	0 4
5	5	E	12 5	N	11 5	V	0 5
6	6	F	12 6	O	11 6	W	0 6
7	7	G	12 7	P	11 7	X	0 7
8	8	H	12 8	Q	11 8	Y	0 8
9	9	I	12 9	R	11 9	Z	0 9

Figure 5-3. Hollerith punched card codes.

Characters are punched into the card with a keypunch machine, which has a keyboard similar to a typewriter. By pressing the appropriate key, the correct combination of punches is entered into the card column.
Numeric Coding. Numeric information consisting of the digits 0–9 requires only a single punch in a card column. The digit 1 is represented by the presence of a punch in row 1 of the card. The digit 2 by a punch in row 2, and so on. In Figure 5-2, the digit 1 is punched in column 16, and the digit 2, in card column 17. Numeric digits are listed in Figure 5-3.

Alphabetic Coding

Alphabetic data uses two punches to represent each letter. For example, the letter A uses a 12 punch and a 1 punch as shown in column 32 of Figure 5-2. The 12 punch is called a zone punch while, of course, the 1 is a numeric punch. Other zone punches are 11 and 0 as shown in the chart of Figure 5-3. With this combination of zone and numeric, all 26 alphabetic characters are represented.

Although the punched card is frequently being replaced by more advanced forms of data entry, it is still in widespread use. Many organizations such as department stores and oil companies find the punched card useful for customer billing. After punching the amount owed into the card, the card is then mailed to the customer. When payment is made, the customer returns the card—which is immediately machine readable. This quality of machine readability continues to attract users of the punched card.

Keypunch and Verifier

Data is recorded in a punched card by several possible methods. The most commonly used method is the keypunch machine, followed by mark sensing and manual punching. The keypunch is by far the fastest method and the most accurate. Figure 5-4 shows several keypunch models and their related functions. These are a selection of some of the popular keypunch machine types. The operating characteristics of each manufacturer's machine are similar although some of the facilities vary somewhat.

Figure 5-1 showed a keypunch as part of the data entry process. This device punches and prints standard 80-column Hollerith cards. Unpunched cards are placed in the card hopper and fed through to the punching station. As data is keyed into the keyboard, it is punched one column at a time into the card. Following punching, the card is passed through to the card stacker.

Information that is to be duplicated on each card, such as today's date, can be read from the first card at the read station and punched into the second card at the punch station. Each subsequent card may also receive data from the preceding card.

Once the cards have been punched from a source document, a second operation is employed to ensure the accuracy of the punched data. When the keypunch used is a non-buffered device, a second machine called a verifier is used. The verifier is virtually identical in appearance to the keypunch. The verifier operator takes the punched cards and places them in the hopper. The data from the source document is then reentered on the verifier keyboard. The verifier reads the punches in the card and compares them to the keyed data. If each character in the card corresponds to each character entered on the keyboard, the verifier places a notch at the end of the card.

Any character entered on the keyboard that does not compare with the punched character in the card causes an error notch to be made above the card column in error. This card must then be repunched with the correct data.

Keypunch Make/Model	Punch	Printing	Buffered
IBM 29	√	√	
IBM 129	√	√	√
Univac 1700	√	√	√
Decision Data 8001	√	√	√
Decision Data 8010	√		√

Figure 5-4. Keypunches and buffered keypunches.

Buffered Keypunch

Due to many advances in the data preparation and entry field, the keypunch and verifier were quickly replaced by more advanced and efficient devices. One of these was the buffered keypunch. The outstanding characteristic of this machine is that it performs the functions of both a keypunch and verifier in the one unit. One of the earliest entries in the field was the Univac 1710 shown in Figure 5-5.

The buffered card punch contains a storage area used to store the entire contents of a card. During the punching operation, the data is entered into this storage rather than being physically punched in the card. As data is being entered, corrections may be made. When the data for one complete card has been entered, it is released from storage and punched into the card. While punching is happening, the operator may enter data for the next card.

KEY CONCEPT

BATCH PROCESSING

When cards are used for input, data such as sales documents is collected into a batch. This group of documents is then keypunched, and the resulting cards are read into the computer by the card reader. Processing data such as a set of cards is called batch processing.

Figure 5-5. Univac 1710 buffered keypunch. (*Courtesy of Sperry-Univac*)

Figure 5-6. Card reader. (*Courtesy of NCR Corporation*)

Card Readers and Punches

Data that originates from some source document, such as an invoice, is first punched into cards and then read through a card reader into the computer Figure 5-6.

Reading Methods. The card reader is a device that senses holes in the punched card and converts them to electrical impulses. These impulses are transmitted via a channel to the central processing unit. Here the data is processed, calculations may be done, analysis of the data performed, files updated, and reports produced. The exact steps taken depends upon the program in the CPU and the requirements of the system.

The converting of holes into electrical impulses is accomplished in one of two ways: reading brushes (Figure 5-7) and photoelectric light cells (Figure 5-8).

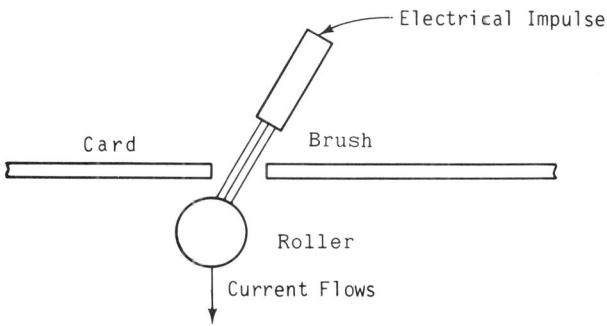

Figure 5-7. Card reading brush.

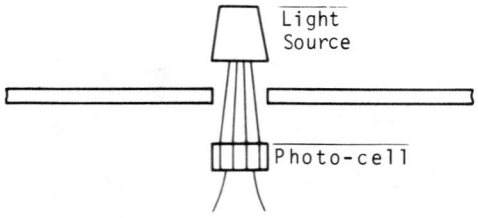

Figure 5-8. Card reading photoelectric light cell.

The reading brush, which is fast becoming obsolete, is a conductor of electricity. As the card passes between the brush and a metal roller, the card acts as an insulator and does not allow current to flow in the circuit. When a punched hole comes under the brush, the brush makes contact through the hole with the roller, and current flows. This indicates the presence of a hole and converts it to an electrical impulse that is sent to the CPU.

The photoelectric light cell operates on much the same principle. A light source replaces the brush and shines on the card. Beneath the card is a photocell (similar to that used for measuring light in a camera) that senses the presence of light. When the card is between the light and the cell, current is inhibited in the circuit. When a hole passes the light source, the beam shines through the hole and is detected by the photocell. This causes an electrical current to flow, indicating the presence of a punch.

The photocell is the superior method of the two. Since there is no direct contact on the card, wear of the sensor is almost nonexistent. A crease or slightly damaged card can sometimes cause the brush to skip a hole but the light cell (photocell) is not affected this way. Generally the light-cell reader can be designed to operate faster than the brush.

Error Checking. To reduce the possibility of machine errors, card readers have two read stations (Figure 5-9). The card is read at the first station, and the data is stored in a buffer. At the second read station, the data read are compared to the buffer. If all data read are the same as in

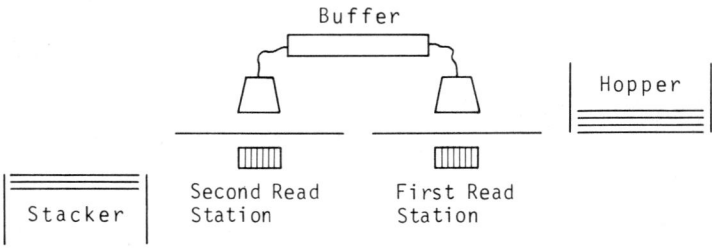

Figure 5-9. Read stations.

Figure 5-10. Card punch. (*Courtesy of Honeywell Information Systems*)

the buffer, the card is passed through to the stacker. When the data are not equal, the reader stops and the operator then identifies and corrects the errors.

Card readers vary in speed from 200 to 2,200 cards per minute, depending upon the type and model of device used.

Card Punches. A card punch (Figure 5-10) is similar in appearance to a reader and may be used to produce output from the CPU. Data that has been processed may be punched into cards and then used for storage or other processing. The punch is a very slow output device and as a result not commonly used, except when the quantity of data is rather low. Speeds vary up to 500 cards per minute.

Card Reader/Punch. When both card reading and punching are required by a computer system, a combined unit (Figure 5-11) called a Multiple Function Card Unit (MFCU) may be used; it both reads and punches cards. Basically, the reader unit has the characteristics of a separate reader and the punching unit of a separate punch. Speeds and op-

Figure 5-11. Card reader/punch. (*Courtesy of IBM Corporation*)

erations are comparable. The advantage of a combined unit is that one housing contains both devices and usually requires less floor space than two stand-alone units.

A second advantage is the use of stackers, which in some machines may be shared between the reader and punch. In this situation, a card may be read and merged with a card that has been punched. This was a popular technique with second generation computers. Today, with the large multiprogrammed system, this advantage of the combined unit is seldom used.

KEY ENTRY DEVICES

Keytape

One of the most significant changes in data entry came when the technology of computer hardware became compact and inexpensive enough to be used for key entry devices. Some of these devices used magnetic tape rather than punched cards as the storage medium.

The key tape device Figure 5-12 essentially consists of a keyboard and a magnetic tape unit (see Chapter 8 for details on magnetic tape). Data is entered via the keyboard in a manner similar to typing and is recorded magnetically on the tape. Operation is similar to that described for the buffered keypunch. Data, upon entry, may be corrected, edited, accumulated, and duplicated and fields skipped, numeric fields zero-filled,

Figure 5-12. Mohawk Series 21. (*Courtesy of Mohawk Data Sciences*)

and check digits developed. Because of these features, keytape is a direct contender for the buffered keypunch market. It can also replace the keypunch and verifier.
Advantages. The three prime advantages over punched cards are:

1. No cards are used.
2. Record lengths are not limited to 80 characters.
3. The computer reads tape much faster than it reads cards.

The first point is obvious. The second is important because data records seldom work out to exactly 80 characters. Either the record is shorter and space on the card is wasted, or it exceeds 80 characters and two or more cards are required for each record. Neither of these situations is particularly convenient for the systems analyst or the programmer. They have just lived with the problem over the years. Record lengths of 400 characters are available on some machines (see Figure 5-17). Others allow a smaller record size. In any case, records need occupy only the amount of space needed. Nothing is wasted. Thirdly, magnetic tape has been a common form of computer input/output device and has been used because of its speed. This advantage is now applied to data entry.

Another area of consideration is in the efficiency of operation. Because of the improved technology, the operator performs more keystrokes per hour than a typical keypunch operator. Most keytape manufacturers suggest three units will replace four keypunches and give the same through-put.
Kinds of Tape. Tape may be one of three types: (1) cassette, (2) cartridge, or (3) reel.

The cassette has the same physical characteristics as a home cassette recording. The plastic enclosure is 6.35 cm. by 10.16 cm. (2½″ × 4″) and contains a length of 0.64-cm. (¼″) wide magnetic tape. Cassettes may store up to 200,000 characters of data (Figure 5-13).

Figure 5-13. NCR key cassette. (*Courtesy of NCR Corporation*)

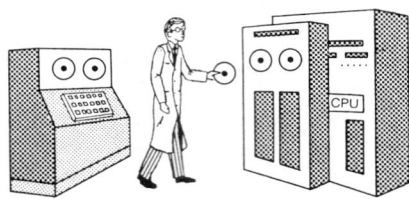

Figure 5-14. Tape carried to the computer center.

The cartridge is larger than cassette and contains about 30 meters (100 feet) of tape with holes for a sprocket drive. Cartridges contain about 28,000 characters. Both cassettes and cartridges are economical, easy to handle, and simple to load into the drive mechanism. In addition, the plastic housing provides protection from damage and dust. The reel uses a computer-compatible magnetic tape. The tape mechanisms is usually ordered so that tape is recorded exactly as it will be read by the computer. Therefore, options are available for 7-track, 9-track, even or odd parity, and various densities.

Tape Transmitted to Computer. When a tape has been recorded with data, the tape may be sent to the computer in a number of ways.

1. Tape is carried physically to the computer and mounted on the computer's tape drive (Figure 5-14).
2. The keytape device is attached directly to a computer channel and read by the computer as input (Figure 5-15). In this case the keytape device is situated very close to the computer, usually in the same room or in an adjacent room.
3. The keytape device is connected to the computer through a communication channel (Figure 5-16). In this case the channel, which could simply be a telephone line, connects the two. There is essentially no limit to the distance separating the keytape from the computer using this method.

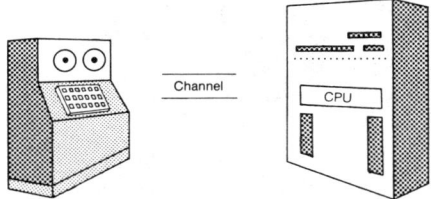

Figure 5-15. Keytape on a computer channel.

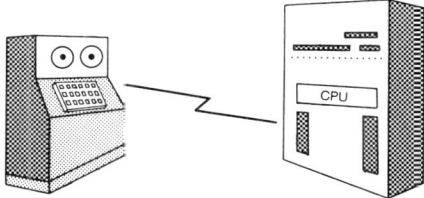

Figure 5-16. Keytape on a communication channel.

When several keytapes are used in an installation, each operator produces a tape containing data. An operator can usually create about 92 meters (300 feet) of tape a day. However, the length of most units is 732 meters (2400 feet). As a result, a pooling operation may be done that combines the data from several tapes onto a single tape. This one tape is then sent to the computer using one of the above methods. See Figure 5-17 for additional keytape specifications.

Some Additional Advantages of the Keytape. These include the auxiliary devices available. These devices may be attached to the tape unit to give added flexibility to the user's operation. Depending on the make and model, printers, card readers, and papertape readers are optional equipment. These allow existing cards or cards from a system not yet converted to keytape to be read and recorded on tape. This technique also applies to paper tape.

Data stored on the tape may be selected and printed for reference purposes. The primary advantage here is that the computer itself is not needed. Thus the operation of printing is accomplished off-line without using valuable computer time.

For an organization presently using keypunches as a major source of data entry, keytape is relatively easy to install. Existing operators can be retrained with a minimum of time and effort. Time and cost advantages vary with the application but are considered to be around 25 percent savings over a typical keypunch installation.

Key Disk

The key disk data entry device can be compared quite favorably with keytape. Its operation is similar in terms of recording data, program control, record size, and speed. Where key to tape uses a magnetic tape for data recording, this device uses a magnetic disk called a diskette, or floppy disk. Some key disk hardware permits a keyboard and disk recorder to be used alone. However, the trend is for a number of key disk work stations to be linked together to a minicomputer. The use of a computer in

106 DATA ENTRY

Make and Model	Type of Tape	Max. Density Bytes/cm. (in.)	Max. Record Size Bytes	Data Communications Rate
Honeywell 701	Reel	315(800)	400	1200 to 4800 bits/sec
Burroughs N	Reel	315(800)	160	1200 to 1800
IBM	Cartridge	7.87(20)	720	NA
Mohawk 6400	Reel	315(800)	180	1200 to 4800
NCR 7200	Cassette	315(800)	256	1200 to 4800
Sycor 340	Cassette	315(800)	256	1200 to 4800
Intelligent Terminal Olivetti DE521	Cassette	315(800)	216	NA

Figure 5-17. Keytape specifications.

a data entry system has some very significant advantages, which will be discussed in the next section.

One key disk that can be used alone or in a system is the IBM 3740 (Figure 5-18). This data entry station is characterized by the use of the diskette. The diskette, which resembles a 45-rpm record, is made of Mylar and is coated with a magnetic material on one side (Figure 5-19).

Each diskette is 20.32 cm. (8") in diameter and 635 microns ($^{25}/_{1000}$") thick. The surface is divided into 26 pie-shaped sectors and 77

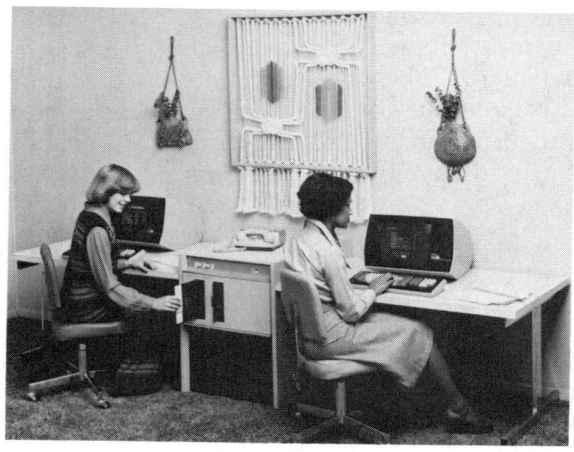

Figure 5-18. Key to diskette system. (*Courtesy of Mohawk Data Sciences*)

KEY ENTRY DEVICES   107

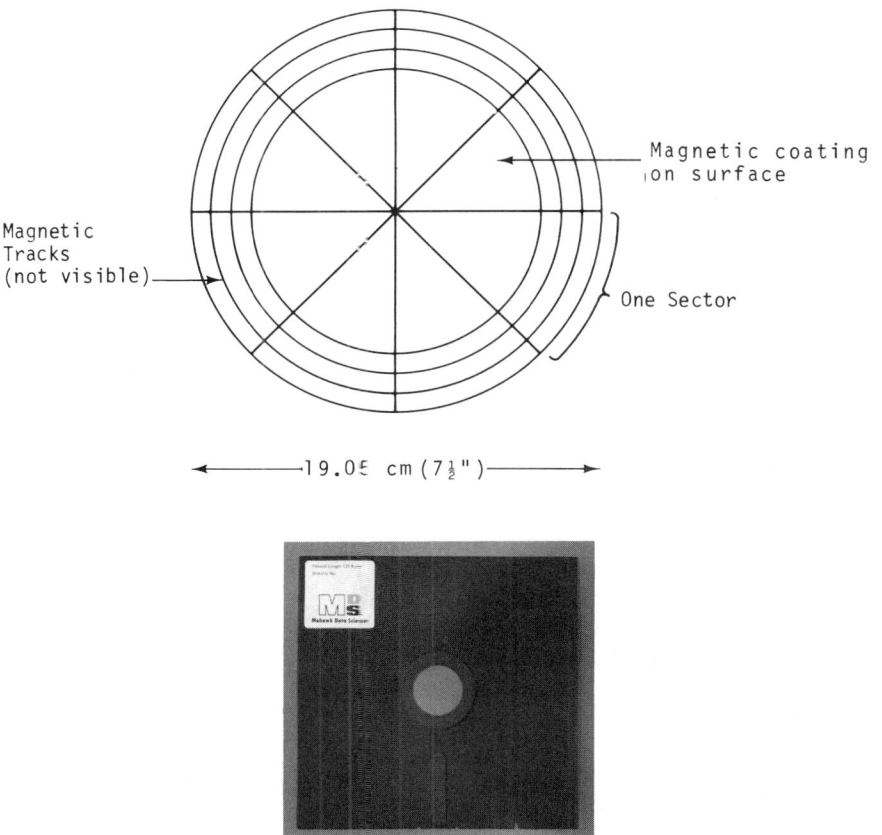

Figure 5-19. A diskette. (*Courtesy of Mohawk Data Sciences*)

tracks. The tracks are concentric—unlike the 45-rpm record, which has spiral tracks. One diskette can record approximately 250,000 characters of 128-byte records. Like tape, the floppy disk can be reused, is easy to store, and is relatively inexpensive (about $8.00).

The 5¼" floppy disk is also popular on key to disk systems. This disk is similar to that used on microcomputer systems. Capacity ranges from 150,000 to over 500,000 bytes per diskette.

There are several significant advantages for diskette; among them are the fast access time to retrieve data (300–400 times faster than tape) and superior reliability. The improved reliability is particularly important when comparing it to cassette. Machine errors are significantly less on floppy disk than on tape.

The diskette can supply data to the computer in three basic ways:

1. A diskette reader can be attached directly to the computer channel as an input device. This is a separate device from the key disk unit.
2. A diskette-to-tape converter can be used off-line to produce a magnetic tape, which is then read by the computer.
3. The key disk may be a part of a data communication system and the data can be transmitted to the central computer.

Peripheral devices are also available to increase the flexibility of key disk. Devices like printers, display screens, card readers, and magnetic tape may be attached depending upon the make and model of the machine. Key-to-disk really comes into its own when used as a complete data entry system with a minicomputer. This is also known as a central collection system and is an area we will examine shortly.

Transaction Processing

Data that is entered directly into the computer from its source is called a transaction. With faster and larger computers, this approach to data entry is now one of the most widely used forms of data entry. Figure 5-20 shows some typical applications for transaction processing.

Point of sale terminals in retail stores are probably the most easily recognized form of transaction processing. When a customer makes a purchase, the item is entered on a cash register either by reading a bar code or a magnetically coded tag, or by keying in the item's number. The cash register is attached to a computer that supplies the price and description of the item for the sales slip. The computer then updates the store's inventory records as a result of this transaction.

Display Terminals

The mainstay of the transaction processing oriented system is the visual display terminal (Figure 5-21). This popular terminal consists of a CRT ("TV-like" Cathode Ray Tube) and a keyboard packaged into a container. Figure 5-22 shows the CRT screen as an output device that displays data transmitted from the computer and the keyboard an input device. Characters entered on the keyboard are displayed on the screen for direct visual feedback. The data are also immediately transmitted to the computer.

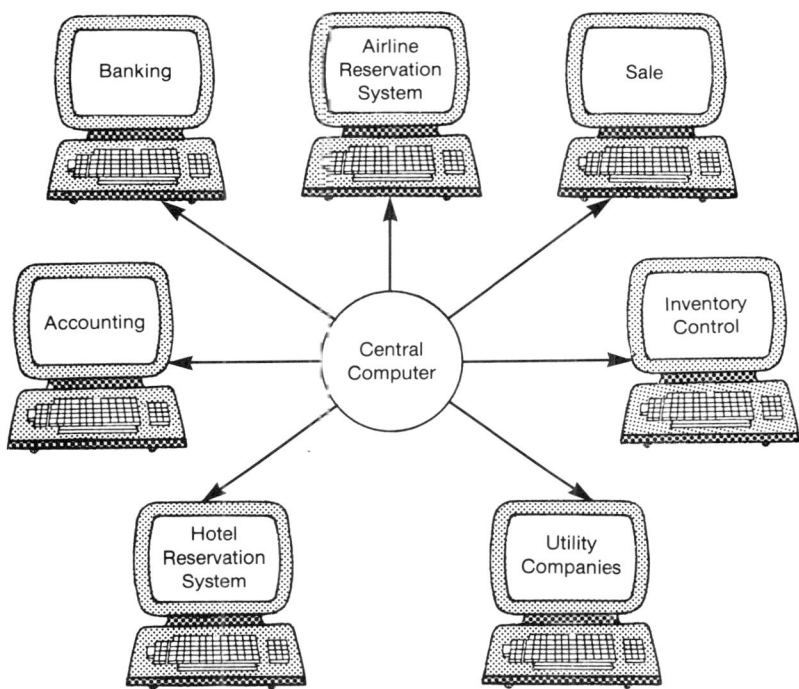

Figure 5-20. Transaction processing applications. Although a single computer is unlikely to handle all of these applications, these are some ways that transaction processing is used.

Figure 5-21. A Visual Display Terminal (VDT) used for input and output of data, word processing, personal computing, and electronic mail. (*Courtesy of Sperry-Univac*)

110 DATA ENTRY

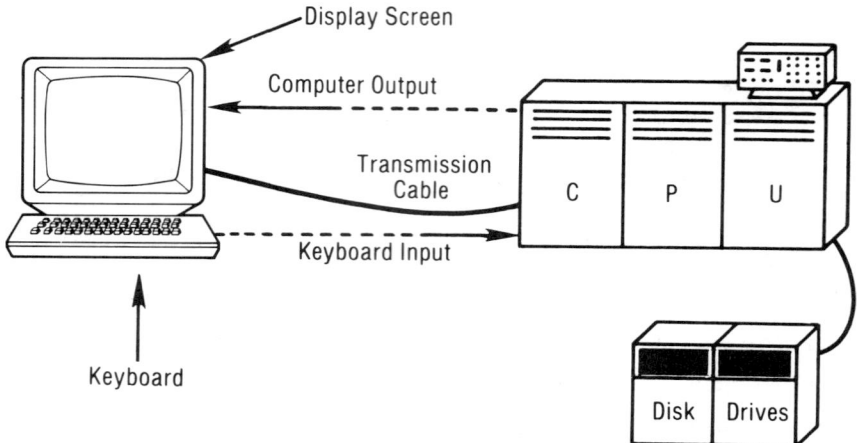

Figure 5-22. The digital display terminal is used both as an input and as an output device to the computer.

Display terminals are both input and output devices. The most common terminal is a digital display that displays alphanumeric digits and characters. Less common is the graphic terminal that can display lines and drawings as well as character data. Both types of displays will be considered in the chapter on output devices.

Keyboards

Display terminals use several types of keyboards for entering the input data. The most widely used is the alphanumeric keyboard, shown in Fig-

Figure 5-23. Terminal with an alphanumeric keyboard. (*Courtesy of Digital Equipment Corporation*)

Figure 5-24. Terminal using a specialized function keyboard. (*Courtesy of Hewlett-Packard Company*)

ure 5-23. It is used in offices for accounting, payroll, word processing, and general information retrieval. The alphanumeric keyboard closely resembles the office typewriter keyboard with numbers, letters, and special characters. Additional keys for controlling the cursor on the screen are often included.

A second kind of keyboard is the function keyboard (Figure 5-24). This keyboard is usually special purpose because it is designed for a specific application. Some uses of the function keyboard are for restaurants, bars, and reservation systems.

CENTRAL COLLECTION SYSTEM

The use of a central collection data entry system is another step up from a keytape or disk. Central collection is of interest to the larger user with substantial quantities of data. A basic system consists of a number of key entry terminals (Figure 5-25) attached to a minicomputer. The minicomputer has a number of devices attached for the collection of data. Figure 5-26 shows a typical data collection system that permits from 4 to 24 data entry stations, depending on the needs of the user. Disk and tape are used to capture the data supplied by the operator of the key station. A console is used by a supervisor to coordinate the various activities of the system. A central collection system may also have a communication line to transmit data to a central computer.

The basic operation at the keyboard is not very different from keytape or disk. Data entry is accompanied by the standard features of field control, zero insertion, and verifying of source data. However, the real advantage comes as a result of the minicomputer. By means of a stored

112   DATA ENTRY

Figure 5-25. Key entry terminals. (*Courtesy of Sperry-Univac*)

program, a complete range of data editing is possible as a by-product of data entry. Because of the sophistication involved, the name *intelligent terminal* is often being applied to the data entry station. The station itself is still a basic keyboard, but the computer supplies the "intelligence" to significantly improve the accuracy and efficiency of data entry.

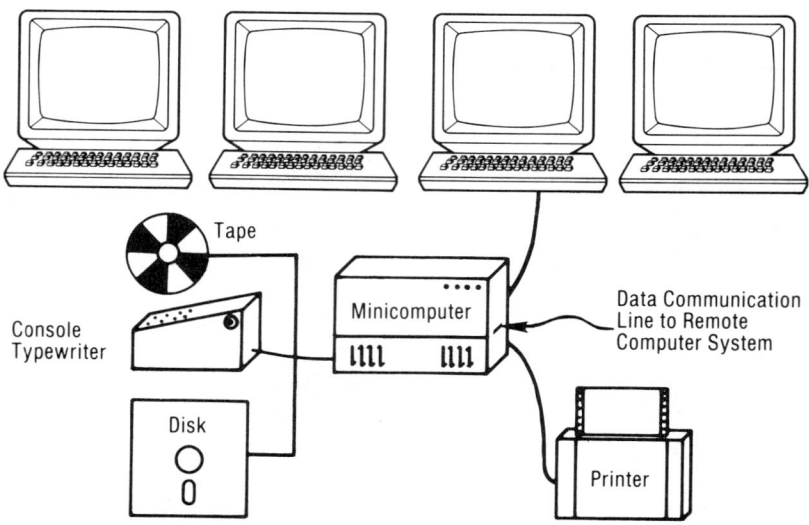

Figure 5-26. Data collection system.

There are two times when the program acts upon the data:

1. Input time—used during keyboard entry.
2. Output time—used when data is placed on a storage device.

At input time, the program interacts with the terminal operator. Depending upon the make and model of the equipment and the type of program used, the following activities may occur:

Input Edits.

1. Definition of record length
2. Definition of field length and type
3. Checking for alphabetic or numeric data
4. Left zero insert
5. Calculation of check digits
6. Selection of several record formats
7. Arithmetic calculations
8. Display of program messages to the operator to assist in data entry
9. Inserting of constant data, such as a date

These facilities reduce the possibility of errors in transcribing data from the source document and lead to increased operator productivity. Users give figures of up to 50 percent cost reduction over keypunching and 80 percent reduction in errors using this kind of system. Of course, not every user will experience the same improvements. If the above checks are not sufficient, then additional checking is possible at output time when the operator releases the data to be stored. Usually storage is on a magnetic disk. Possible output editing is shown below.

Output Edits.

1. Checking of arithmetic
2. Checking the range of a field
3. Checking for alphabetic or numeric data
4. Computing batch totals
5. Inserting missing data by table look-up
6. Inserting of constant data
7. Reorganizing data
8. Producing of reports

114 DATA ENTRY

Figure 5-27. A data collection system. (*Courtesy of Honeywell Information Systems*)

A comparison of the input and output edits shows some duplication of functions. This allows the user to decide when a particular kind of task is most suitable. For instance, inserting constant data such as a tax rate may not be important at input time, and furthermore, it would slow down the data entry operation. Therefore, this constant could be included at output time so the operator is unaffected by the insert operation.

Figure 5-27 shows a Honeywell system with 4 key entry stations. Included in the system are a disk, tape, central processor, and supervisor console. As data is entered by each operator, it is verified and edited and then placed on disk storage. The supervisor then selects data through the supervisor console and transfers it to tape. Other supervisor functions are:

1. Produce system operating statistics
2. Maintain and load programs
3. Allocate disk space
4. Assign batches of data for entry

Figure 5-28 shows the basic specifications for some popular central collection systems. This is by no means inclusive. Many manufacturers

Make and Model	Number of Stations	CPU Size	Tape Density	Disk Capacity	Data Communications Rate (bits/sec)
Key-Edit 60	24	64K	1600	5.6M	9600
Honeywell 5500	64	32K	800	7.5M	NA
IBM 3740	24	128K	1600	243K per station	2400
Univac 1900	32	131K	1600	4.4M	NA
Sycor 250	32	remote		computer	7200

Figure 5-28. Central collection systems.

have several model lines with different capacities. In some cases, additional disks may be added to increase storage capacity. In the case of IBM, diskettes are used at each station so total storage depends on the number of stations. One rather unusual system here is the Sycor model. It functions basically as a data communication system. As such, it does not have a minicomputer with disk and tape. Rather, all entry stations are attached by communication lines to a remote computer that supplies all the "intelligence."

CanFarm, the Canada Farm Management Data System, uses a central collection system for data entry. Located in Guelph, Ontario, it provides bookkeeping and accounting services for more than 10,000 farmers across Canada. Farmers mail in their journal entries each month to CanFarm. The data is recorded on a KEY-EDIT system with two minicomputers with a total of 32 stations. Data is then processed to produce monthly and annual statements to assist in the accounting and financial management of farms. CanFarm had moved from keytape units to KEY-EDIT and found an increase of 20 percent in operator productivity.

POINT OF SALE TERMINALS (POS)

Another alternative for data entry is the POS terminal. This is used by an increasing number of retail and food stores, restaurants, and banks. In most cases, the POS terminal is similar to a cash register but much more sophisticated. Depending upon the type of system used, the POS terminal may record all transactions on a cassette (Figure 5-29) and transmit this data daily to a central computer. Prices and product categories are entered on the keyboard. Special keys are provided to calculate quantities, partial quantities, taxable items, trading stamp totals, and coupon refunds.

116　DATA ENTRY

Figure 5-29. NCR 250 electronic cash register with cassette tape. (*Courtesy of NCR Corporation*)

Universal Product Code (UPC)

The bar code (Figure 5-30), or UPC, has been developed by the grocery industry for use in computerized checkout systems. It is based on a 10-

Figure 5-30. Cash register tape and Universal Product Code. (*Courtesy of Oshawa Group*)

POINT OF SALE TERMINALS (POS)

Figure 5-31. Supermarket checkout. (*Courtesy of IBM Corporation*)

digit code. The first 5 digits represent the manufacturer. The second group of 5 digits represent the specific product. Each item in the store has the bar code printed on the container. The equivalent code is stored in the store's computer with a description and price. When the customer checks out the groceries, a cashier passes each item face down over a bar code sensor (Figure 5-31) in the scanning window. The computer then reads the code and supplies the price and description, which is printed on the sales slip. Reading the code is instantaneous and therefore much faster than keying in prices and codes. A keyboard is available for items not containing the UPC such as fresh fruit, vegetables, and meat.

Wand Readers

Figure 5-32 shows a cash register with a wand reader. The wand captures data from a magnetically encoded price tag. The terminal automatically records the product identification and price. This is printed on the sales slip with any applicable taxes. From this data, inventory records are updated to show current in-stock information.

Advantages

Advantages of using POS terminals are the following:

1. Reduced time to handle each customer
2. Reduction in operating staff and the time needed to train an operator
3. Direct updating of inventory records in the computer system
4. Automatic credit checks and identification of credit risks

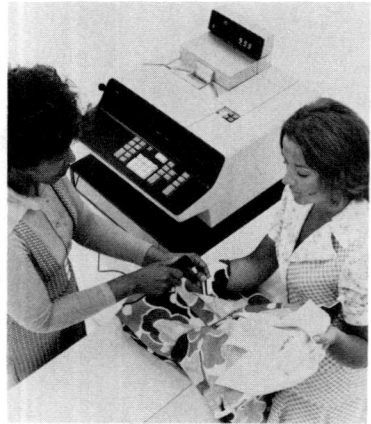
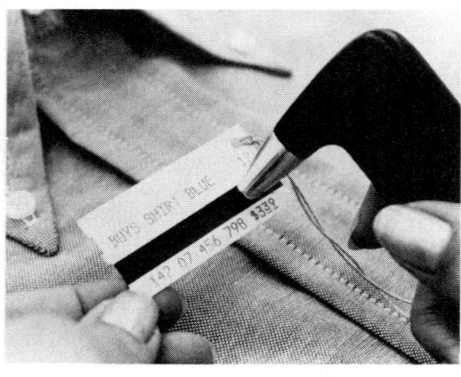

Figure 5-32. Cash register with a wand reader.

In addition to these advantages, the data collected may be used by the retailer to provide reports of the store's sales activities. This may include accounting, inventory, cashier, and department reports. Prior to POS, these reports were available only if the data were prepared manually and entered into the computer system with punched cards or paper tape. With POS, this data is recorded automatically when a sale is made—without additional data preparation.

© *Creative Computing*

A PRACTICAL APPLICATION OF DATA ENTRY

Medical Plan Services (MPS) is an independent insurance company that processes hospital claims for over 300,000 people and medical benefits for over 650,000 people per year. To handle these transactions, the company used as many as 45 keypunches, which punched up to 12 million cards per year. Because of this large and ever increasing quantity, which lead to errors and inefficiencies, MPS recently replaced most of the keypunches with 12 data entry stations. This action reduced the annual number of cards to one million.

    Each data entry station has a keyboard, display screen, and diskette. As data is keyed, it is stored magnetically on the diskette. Errors, which are detected automatically by the system, are displayed on the screen; and the operator may correct them immediately by re-keying the data. The new machines are quieter, easier to operate, give improved control over errors, and lead to greater operator satisfaction.

    At the end of a day, the data is transferred by data communication lines from the diskette to a central computer for processing. Using a data entry system resulted in a large reduction in computer time because the diskettes are read at a much higher speed than cards. Storage problems are also reduced due to the compact nature of the diskette. In general, MPS has saved money and increased the efficiency of the operation by upgrading from a keypunch system of data entry to the key to diskette data entry system.

TERMS TO STUDY

Alphabetic Code	Key Punch
Batch Processing	Keytape
Buffered Keypunch	Numeric Punch
Card Reader	POS Terminal
Card Punch	Punched Card
Cartridge	Read Station
Cassette	Record
Central Collection	Reel
Character	Transaction Processing
Display Terminal	Universal Product Code
Floppy Disk	Unit Record
Hollerith	Verifier
Intelligent Terminal	Zone Punch
Key Disk	

QUESTIONS FOR REVIEW

1. What are the negative results of a poor choice of data entry methods?
2. Describe fully the Hollerith punched card, naming each part of the card.
3. Outline the Hollerith code used for numeric and alphabetic characters.
4. Discuss the concept of batch processing.
5. Compare the functions of a keypunch and a verifier.
6. What are the advantages of a buffered keypunch over the regular keypunch machine?
7. Describe the most common method used for reading punched cards.
8. What is keytape, and what are its advantages over the punched card?
9. Describe key diskette and the ways in which it is used for data entry.
10. What is meant by transaction processing? How does this method differ from batch processing?
11. A typical device used for transaction processing is the display terminal, or VDT. How would you characterize this device? Input? Output?
12. What is a central collection system, and why is it superior to keytape or disk?
13. What is meant by the term POS? Who uses POS? How does it work? What is UPC?

PROBLEMS FOR RESEARCH AND DISCUSSION

1. Who are the leading suppliers of data entry devices in your community? What devices do they market?
2. What form of data entry primarily is used in your school for programming courses? What are the advantages and disadvantages of this method? How might the system for data entry be improved?

6

Computer Output

One of the most common types of computer output for human use is the printed page. Printed material is produced by a printer in the form of reports, summaries, bills, invoices, and tables. Although there is a progression to other forms of human-readable output, such as the display screen and microfiche, printed paper is still the most common and widely used medium.

Paper is relatively easy to handle and transport to where information is needed. It can be filed easily in a desk or filing cabinet and just as easily retrieved. Various qualities and colors of paper may be used to improve durability and increase the aesthetics of the document.

On the negative side, paper tends to accumulate and, in the case of large computer installations, it can cause disposal problems because of the great volume produced. When paper is used for reference purposes, large reports may be necessary to supply adequate information. This is true even when a small portion of this information is referenced at any one time. Although display screens and microfiche can solve some of these problems, paper is still widely used by the business community.

TYPES OF PRINTERS

Printers are available in a great range of speeds varying from 10 characters per second to 21,000 lines per minute (Figure 6-1). The lower speed units are generally like typewriters and use single character printers known as serial printers. These operate at up to 300 characters per second.

Type of Printer	Impact/ Non-Impact	Printing Positions	Speed Lines per Minute
Chain	I	132	600–1200
Band	I	132	2000
Daisy Wheel	I	120	150
Drum	I	120	1000
Wire Matrix	I	120	500–1000
Daisy Wheel	I	132	45 char. per sec. max.
Typewriter	I	100	600 char. per minute
Laser	N	136–204	7890–21,000
Thermal	N	80	10–30 char. per sec.

Figure 6-1. Types of printers.

Medium speed printers function at up to 2000 lines per minute. These are the chain and band printers (Figure 6-2), which print a line at a time. In the high-speed category are printers that range up to 21,000 lines per minute. This includes the laser and electrostatic printers.

Printers are grouped into two functional categories: impact and non-impact printers. The most widely used is the impact printer, which requires that the print mechanism strike the paper through an ink ribbon, which makes the character impression on the page.

Non-impact printers use photographic or Xerographic means to print on either regular paper or specially treated dielectric paper. This method does not require physical contact with the page and generally results in very high speeds.

Figure 6-2. A Honeywell chain printer. (*Courtesy of Honeywell Information Systems*)

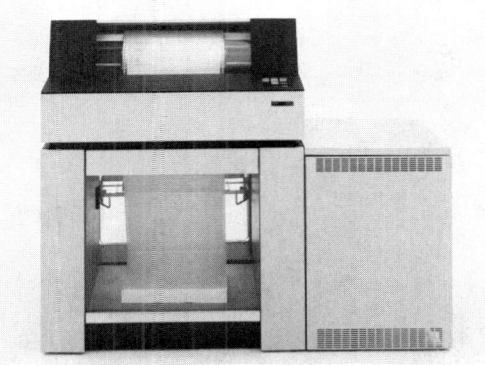

Figure 6-3. The IBM 3203 chain printer. (*Courtesy of IBM Corporation*)

Chain and Band Printers

The chain and band printers (Figure 6-3) are electromechanical impact printers using a continuous chain (Figure 6-4) (which can be visualized as a bicycle chain) composed of 5 sections of 48 characters per section. The 48 characters are a composite of numeric, alphabetic, and special characters. This chain rotates at a high speed behind continuous form paper. In front of the page is an ink ribbon and a set of 132 magnetically activated hammers. As the character to be printed comes to the print position, the hammer is activated, driving the paper against the ribbon and character on the chain, and the character is printed. Several characters may print simultaneously, substantially increasing the speed of the printer.

Type chains are also interchangeable to allow for different type styles and character selection, which are customized to suit the needs of the user.

Daisy Wheel Printer

The daisy wheel printer is also a line impact printer; it consists of a single plastic or metal printwheel (Figure 6-5). The wheel contains 88 characters that are positioned on the outer surface. Printing occurs when the wheel is positioned to the correct character and print position. The daisy wheel is used mainly on terminals and word processing equipment. Speeds can range up to 55 characters per second.

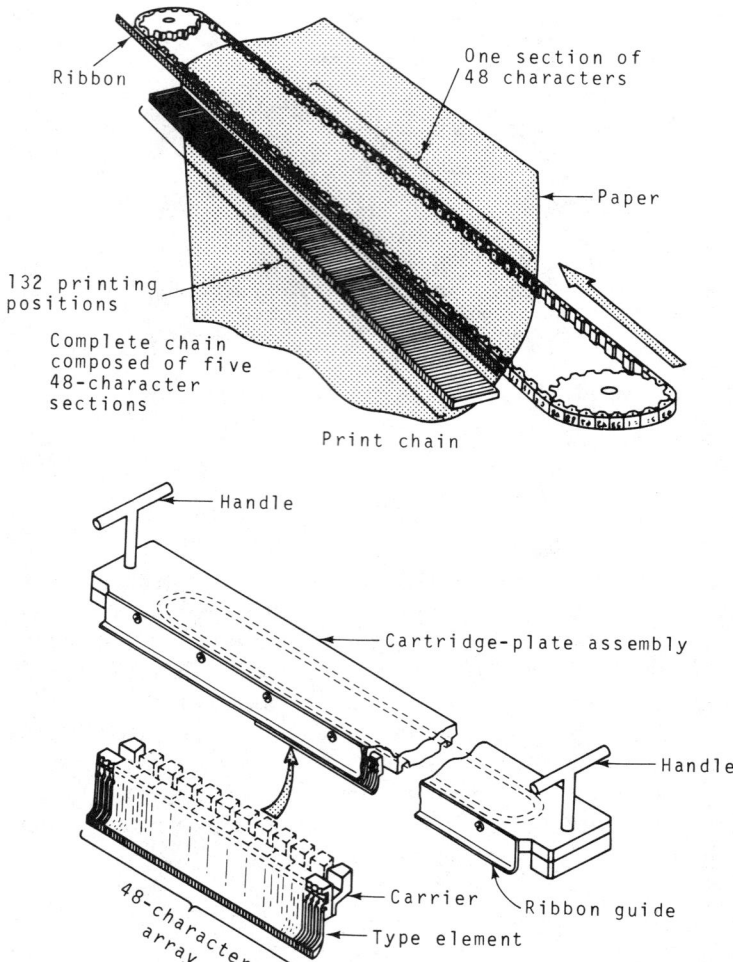

Figure 6-4. Print train.

Drum Printer

The drum printer uses a cylindrical drum containing rows of characters on its outer surface (Figure 6-6). As the drum revolves, the print hammer is fired when the appropriate character appears in the print position. All A's are printed simultaneously on a line, then all B's and so on. A complete revolution is required to print a full line.

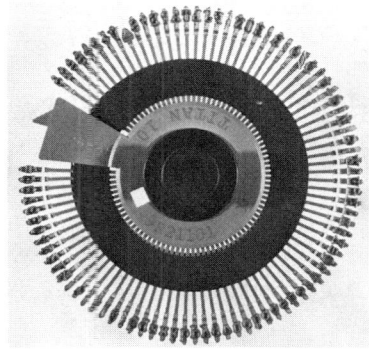

Figure 6-5. A metal daisy wheel. (*Courtesy of AHearn and Soper*)

Wire Matrix Printer

In the wire matrix printer, characters are formed by the selection of a series of small wires formed in a 5 × 7 matrix (Figure 6-7). By selecting certain wires and pressing them against an inked fabric ribbon, different characters may be formed (Figure 6-8).

The matrix mechanism is passed from left to right in front of the paper, and characters are printed serially on the line. Faster models also print when the matrix is returning from the right to the left.

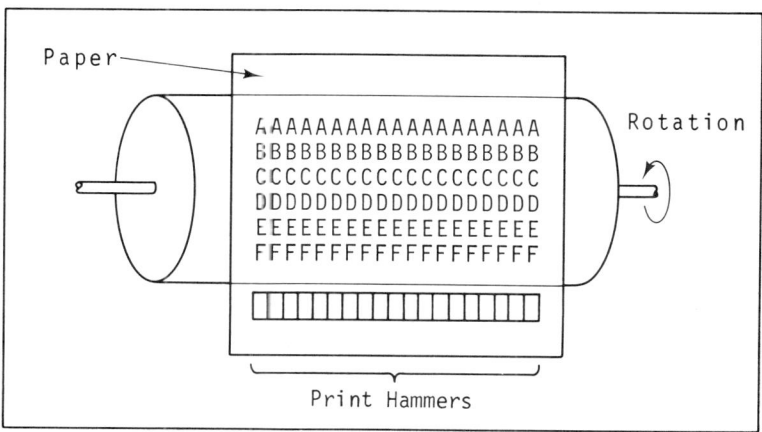

Figure 6-6. Drum printer.

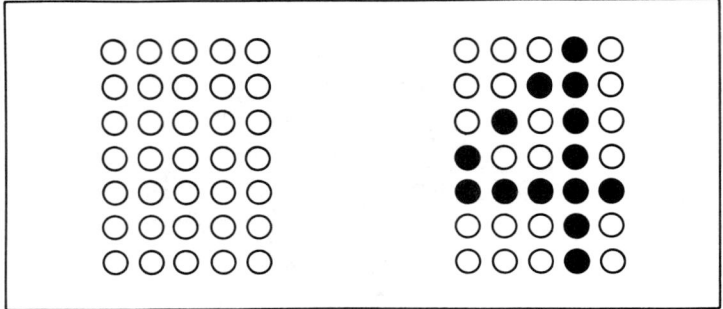

Figure 6-7. Wire matrix dot pattern.

Figure 6-8. Wire matrix character set.

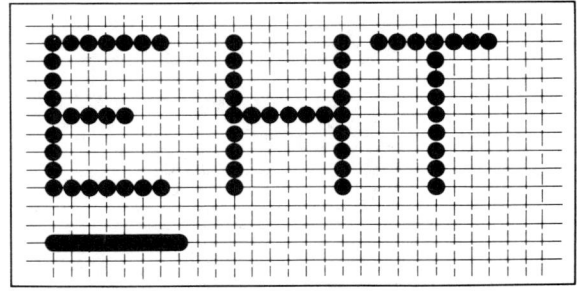

Figure 6-9. 7 × 9 Dot matrix.

Figure 6-10. IBM 2741 typewriter printer. (*Courtesy of IBM Corporation*)

For even greater character resolution, a 7 × 9 dot matrix is available (Figure 6-9). The effect of more dots is a clearer, more precise character pattern, which improves the readability of the printed character. Some matrix printers overlap the dots or use several passes of the print head to create higher quality printout.

Typewriter Printer

This printer resembles an office typewriter. The difference is that it is wired to the computer like any output device and is under control of the CPU. A wide variety of devices similar to the one shown in Figure 6-10 are available. The printer mechanism is often the golf ball as used in the IBM Selectric or a wire matrix unit.

The typewriter keyboard is often used by the computer operator for communicating with the supervisor program resident in the CPU. Another common use is as a terminal in teleprocessing activities.

Laser (Electrographic) Printers

One of the common problems with all printers is that of speed. Compared to devices like magnetic tape or disk, the printer is extremely slow. This has been partially solved through the use of electrophotographic and laser technology. This is a non-impact system that can operate at speeds up to about 68,000 characters per second (Figure 6-11).

With this system, preprinted forms may be used or the printer can print its own forms through the use of an overlay insert and graphic

Figure 6-11. IBM 3800 laser printer. (*Courtesy of IBM Corporation*)

```
THIS IS 10 CHARACTERS PER INCH PRINTING.
THIS IS 12 CHARACTERS PER INCH PRINTING.
THIS IS 15 CHARACTERS PER INCH PRINTING.
```

Figure 6-12. 10, 12, or 15 characters per inch.

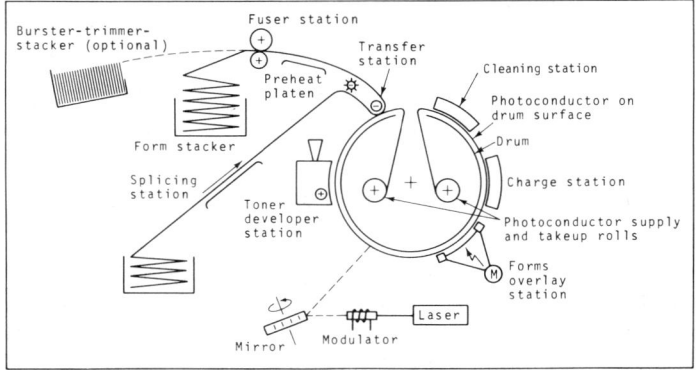

Figure 6-13. Laser electrographic printing. (*Courtesy of IBM Corporation*)

TYPES OF PRINTERS 129

Figure 6-14. Honeywell page printer. (*Courtesy of Honeywell Information Systems*)

characters to draw lines and produce headings. Print sizes of 10, 12, or 15 characters per inch may also be selected as shown in Figure 6-12.

The method of printing is similar to the way a cathode-ray gun scans a TV screen to produce a picture. As shown in Figure 6-13, the image is produced by horizontal scanning of the line by a laser beam. The image is developed with a toner and transferred to paper. The photoconductor surface of the drum is cleaned after each exposure.

The Honeywell Page Printing System (Figure 6-14) also uses a dielectric paper upon which the image of a report is exposed. This system uses continuous roll paper. The system prints graphics for page layout, thus eliminating the need for preprinted forms. After being printed at 600 pages per minute, the pages are cut to size, holes may be punched for insertion in a binder, and the pages are collated into as many as 32 different pockets. This automatic assembly of reports increases the cost effectiveness and efficiency of high volume printer applications.

Ink-Jet Printer

In the continuing search for low-cost quality printing, researchers have developed the ink-jet printer This device uses a matrix of ink dots to form a character. Unlike the dot matrix printer, the ink-jet is a non-impact printer which uses ink drops much smaller than the dots in the impact matrix. Because of the smaller drops, more dots are used to form a character and therefore the resolution of the character is greater than the impact dot matrix printer. This resolution produces a quality of print comparable to a typewriter using a fabric ribbon. Being non-impact, it is also a quiet printer.

In addition to the resolution and quietness of the ink-jet printer is the ability to change the size and style of type almost instantaneously. This change can be achieved because character formats are produced electronically. By changing the electrical impulses to the print mechanism, the style of type can be changed. Figure 6-15 shows how the characters are formed in the ink-jet printer. Ink is stored in the drop generator and expelled in a stream through an opening about 35 micrometers in diameter. The ink is given an electrostatic charge by the charge electrode. Because of the small size of the ink stream, the ink separates into a stream of dots. The dots then pass through a pair of deflection plates that control the amount of deflection of each dot prior to reaching the paper. Excess ink is deflected to a gutter that collects the ink and sends it back to the drop generator. The ink-jet principle is used in the IBM 6640 printer.

Forms Control of Printers

Carriage Control. Printers that are used for computer output use continuous form paper to provide for continuity and speed while printing. The paper has sprocket holes, which are used to move the forms through the printer. Each page of the continuous form is joined together at a perforation. After printing, the pages may be separated at the perforation

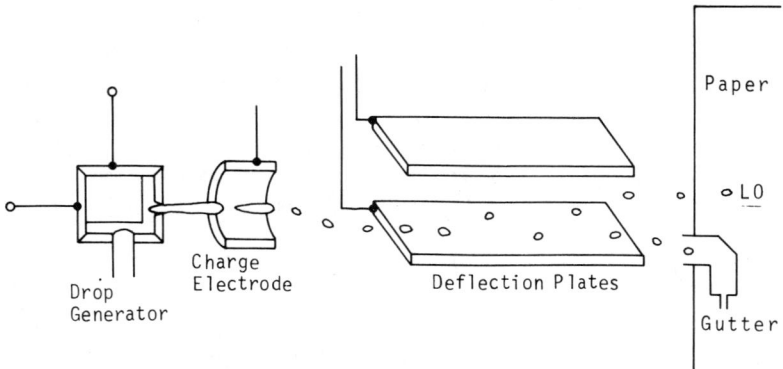

Figure 6-15. Ink-jet character formation.

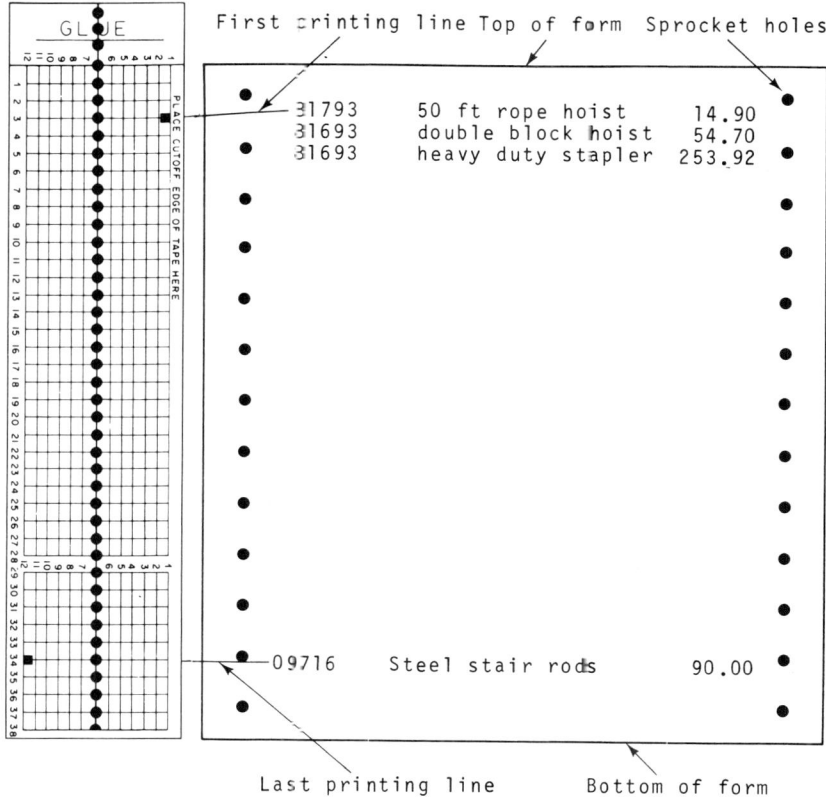

Figure 6-16. Printer carriage control. (*Courtesy of IBM Corporation*)

to form individual pages. To define the size of a page and control skipping of the paper, a carriage control tape is used. The control tape (which is made of a durable paper) is cut to the length of the page (Figure 6-16). The ends of the tape are glued together to form a continuous loop. This loop is placed in a carriage control mechanism in the printer.

Carriage tapes have 12 channels that may contain a punched hole to define a particular location on the page. A punch in channel 1 defines the first printing line on the page. A channel 12 punch defines the last printing line on a page. These controls prevent printing over the perforation. The instructions to skip to channel 1 prior to printing the first line and to sense the channel 12 punch are a function of the program producing the report.

Figure 6-17 shows how the control tape is used for an invoice containing a variety of outputs such as headings, details, and totals at dif-

132   COMPUTER OUTPUT

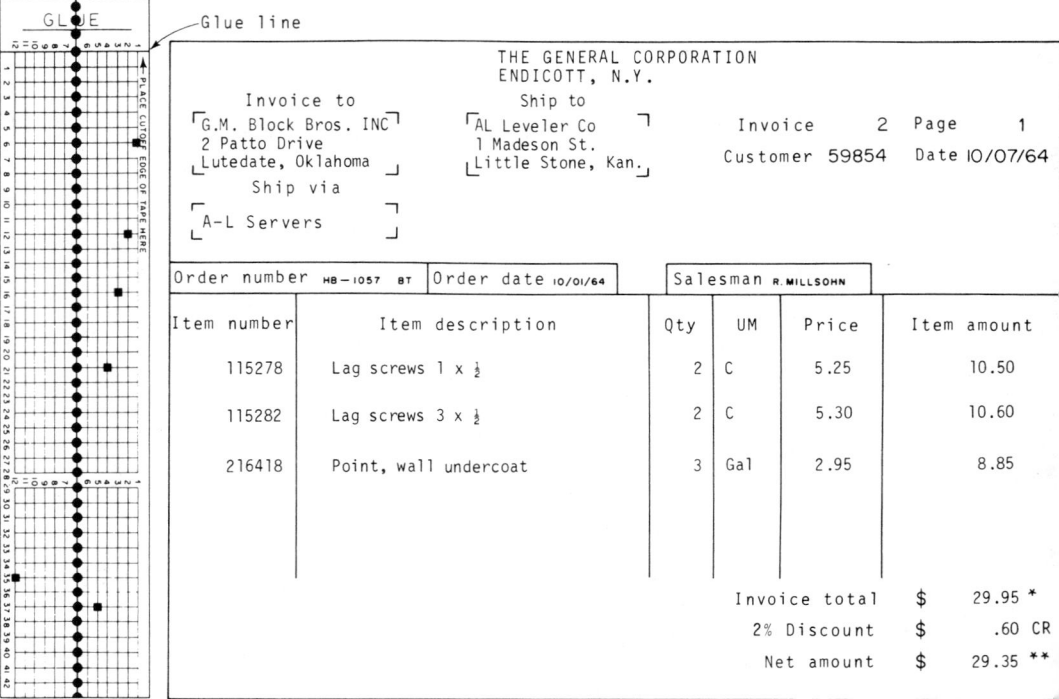

Figure 6-17. Example of control tape used for an invoice with a variety of outputs. (*Courtesy of IBM Corporation*)

ferent locations on the page. Channel 1 is used to indicate the beginning line of the Invoice To and Ship To Address. Invoice and Page Number are also on this line. The next two lines of this information are spaced a line at a time by the program. This does not require control by the carriage tape.

Additional channels may be used to show where secondary information is to print. Channel 2 is used to identify the location for printing Ship Via data. The Order Number and Salesman line is identified by a punch in channel 3. Next the printer skips to channel 4, which is the first line of the detail information. Subsequent details are printed on every two lines. If there were a large number of detail lines for one invoice, channel 12 would be detected and the program would cause the printer to skip to a new page and printing would continue.

When all of the detail for an invoice has been printed, the carriage skips to channel 5 and the totals are printed. Notice that channel 12 does not necessarily indicate the end of a page but rather the last line of detail information. Figure 6-18 shows the anatomy of a report.

		DREAM MANUFACTURING		
		MONTHLY EXPENDITURES REPORT		
		April Expenditures		
MONTH	DAY	DEPT	CATEGORY	AMOUNT
APRIL	01	12	3	12.00
		14	2	17.00
		15	3	10.00
	TOTAL	APRIL 01		39.00*
APRIL	13	12	4	27.00
		14	3	15.00
	TOTAL	APRIL 13		42.00*
APRIL	27	14	1	12.00
		15	2	18.00
				30.00*
	TOTAL APRIL EXPENDITURES			111.00**
RUNDATE 05-12-84				PAGE—01

Figure 6-18. The anatomy of a report.

Forms Control Buffer. Some printers use a stored program in a forms control buffer to control the printer carriage instead of a carriage control tape. In this case, the program defines the beginning of the page as well as where any secondary information is to print. Detail and total lines may also be defined in the program. The stored program is faster and easier to change when different reports are produced. Wear and tear, which can be a problem with carriage tapes, are eliminated with a programmable carriage.

DIGITAL DISPLAY SCREENS

With the advent of data communications, the display screen and typewriter keyboard combination became an increasingly popular device. It consists of a CRT (Cathode Ray Tube) similar to a TV screen and a keyboard usually packaged into one container (Figure 6-19).

Figure 6-19. An HP-2626W CRT display screen and keyboard. (*Courtesy of Hewlett-Packard Company*)

The keyboard is used for entering data or making inquiries. Responses from the computer are displayed as alphanumeric characters on the screen. Character size is similar to a character on a printed page. Display screen characters are white on a black background although many now display green characters, which are easier on the eyes if the screen is used for a long time. Reverse characters can sometimes be selected by program control to draw the user's attention to a specific field on the screen.

As you look at the screen, a bright underline symbol or rectangular character will be seen. This is called the *cursor*; its purpose is to indicate where the next character will be entered. In some cases, a blinking cursor is used to heighten visibility.

A cursor will also go past an existing character on the line without the character being erased. This is useful for correcting characters on the line without erasing those that are correctly entered. The more sophisticated the display and the program that controls it, the more control the user has over cursor movement. Some units will permit both vertical and horizontal movement either forward or backward on the screen.

Other considerations in selecting a CRT are the brightness of the characters, the size of the character, and whether individual characters can be highlighted separately from the rest of the screen (Figure 6-20).

Screen specifications give the number of lines and number of characters per line. A typical size is 24 lines by 80 characters per line, which is somewhat smaller than a typical report. Displayed data on the screen

DIGITAL DISPLAY SCREENS

Figure 6-20. This Digital VT101 screen shows standard upper- and lowercase letters and numbers, reverse characters, graphics, double width and double height characters. The bright rectangular symbol in the bottom left corner is the cursor. Other screens can also show underlining and highlighting. (*Courtesy of Digital Equipment Corporation*)

may be scrolled a line at a time or displayed by page. A key on the keyboard flips a page as needed.

Another important characteristic of display screens is the data transmission rate. This refers to the number of bits per second (baud) the screen can transmit or receive data. A typical rate is 9600 baud.

The use of a CRT display allows the system designer to develop systems oriented to the needs of a particular application. Output for human use is no longer limited to the printer and printed page. Lengthy reports containing redundant and obsolete information are no longer necessary. With the display, programs may be written to directly access information stored in the computer and immediately update that information. Inquiries to files on direct access storage devices may be made as needed without delays of hours or days to get a printed report.

On the negative side, the CRT does not produce a permanent record. Information is only presented on the screen when requested. A new request will cause the previously displayed information to be replaced on the screen with the new. For this reason, many applications still use a printer to produce a hard copy of the displayed information when it is needed. In recognition of this need, several varieties of display terminals provide a Screen Print Key. By simply pressing this key, a hard copy of the contents of the screen is generated on the printer.

Essentially, any information that can be printed can be displayed. The limitation is screen size, which determines the amount of data available at one time for viewing. This means that detail or summary reports can be displayed a page at a time and read by the user.

136 COMPUTER OUTPUT

Figure 6-21. An inquiry about a customer's order may be made by responding to a prompt on the screen with the customer's number.

Inquiries

A major use of the terminal is for making an inquiry or query into the current status of a customer's record. For instance, a customer may call regarding an order that was not received. The person handling the customer's request would respond to a prompt on the screen (Figure 6-21) that asks for the customer's number.

When the customer number has been typed and the ENTER key pressed, the computer then looks up the record for that customer. The first page of the order record is then displayed on the screen shown in Figure 6-22.

The customer may then be advised that items 220, 231, and 243 have been sent but that item 233 is on backorder because it is temporarily out of stock. Notice that the backorder indicator is highlighted to draw attention to backordered items.

Also highlighted is the MORE indicator. This tells the operator that another page of information is available. At the press of a key, the page is flipped and the next screen (Figure 6-23) is displayed, which shows that item 310 is also on backorder. This time there is no MORE indicator so we know that all pages for customer 1234 have been displayed.

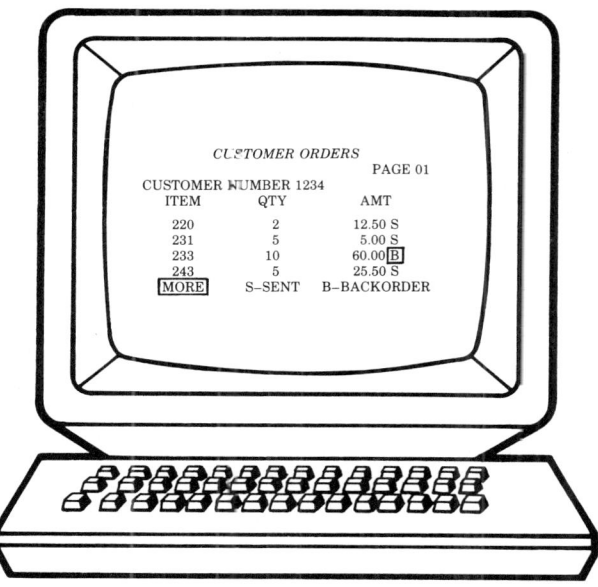

Figure 6-22. The program accesses the customer's record and displays the first page on the screen. The MORE indicator tells the user that additional data is available by pressing a key.

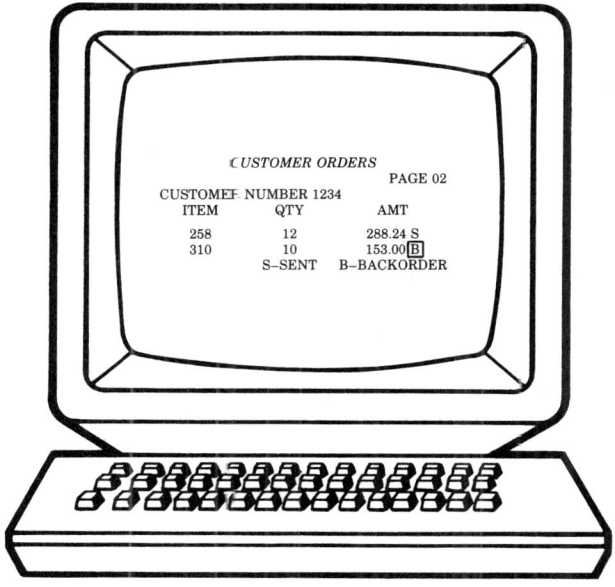

Figure 6-23. By pressing a key on the terminal keyboard, a second page of data for customer 1234 is displayed.

Figure 6-24. A prompt is a message on the screen indicating that the program is waiting for the terminal user to respond to the prompt. When a response is given, such as the name, the next prompt appears on the screen.

Prompts

New data may be entered directly on a terminal, transmitted to the computer, and stored on a disk file. Data may be entered as the result of a prompt on the screen such as shown in Figure 6-24.

The program displays a prompt and then waits for the data to be entered. When the name has been entered, the next prompt (street address) appears and so on until all the data has been supplied.

The program that accepts and processes the data may also analyze it for correctness. For instance, it would not accept a number as part of a name, or a letter as part of a phone number. Phone numbers that are not seven digits would also be rejected.

Form Filling

Another form of screen organization is the form filling technique. In this approach, the program presents a screen layout that looks like a form. As in a paper form or document where the applicant fills in the blanks, the displayed form has blanks that are filled in by the terminal's user.

Figure 6-25 shows a screen using the form filling technique. To use the form, the blank is filled in at the position of the cursor. To begin, the surname would be typed and the ENTER key pressed. The cursor would then move to the FIRST NAME blank indicating that is the next entry to be made. In some cases, when data is not available, the ENTER key is pressed without entering other data. This creates a null entry that may be filled in at a later time or simply left empty.

Menus

In many applications, the terminal user has a choice of a variety of activities. For example, in an Accounts Receivable System you may want to choose to handle Receipts, Print Billing, do Month End, or check a Past Due Report. Instead of requiring the user to respond to a series of prompts asking what activity is required, the terminal could display a menu of the available activities.

A menu is a list of activities available at the terminal. Figure 6-26 shows a menu for Accounts Receivable. Each item has a number that is used to select that activity. If the user presses the 5 key, the Past Due Report data will be displayed.

Multi-level Menus. In larger systems, the number of activities available may be much greater than the size of the screen. Thus the Accounts Receivable menu in Figure 6-26 may only be one of several including Accounts Payable and General Ledger. In this case a hierarchy of menus may exist as shown in Figure 6-27.

The main menu is shown in Figure 6-28. Some of the other menus are in Figure 6-29. Each lower level menu provides an exit to return back to the main manu, which provides the means to get to any other menu.

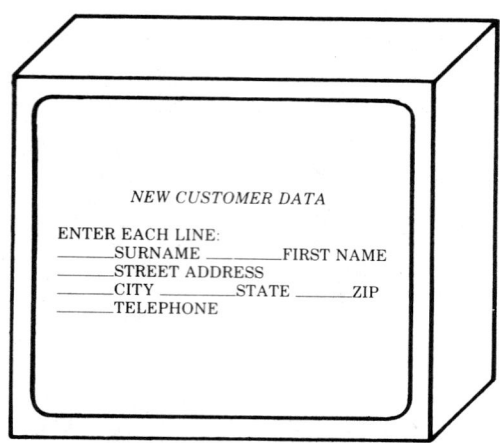

Figure 6-25. Some screen layouts use a form filling technique. With this method, all of the required items are displayed with blanks appearing where the data is to be entered. As each item is typed, the cursor moves to the next blank entry on the screen.

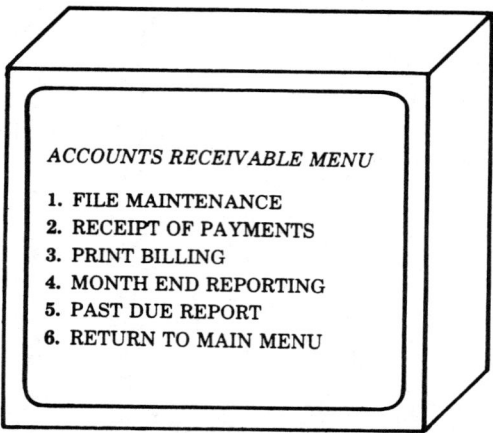

Figure 6-26. A menu for Accounts Receivable. An activity such as print billing is activated by keying the number (in this case 3) associated with the entry.

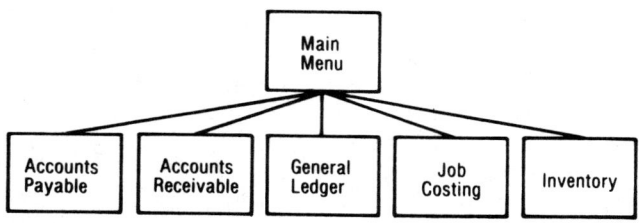

Figure 6-27. Hierarchy of menus.

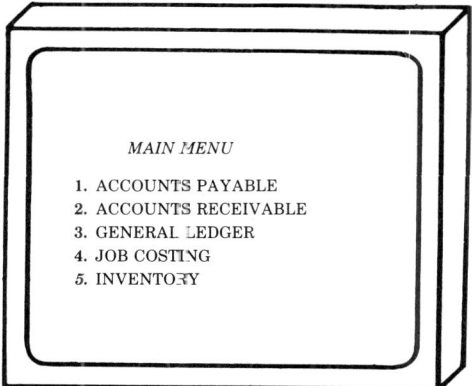

Figure 6-28. Main menu in general business system.

```
        MAIN MENU
    1. ACCOUNTS PAYABLE
    2. ACCOUNTS RECEIVABLE
    3. GENERAL LEDGER
    4. JOB COSTING
    5. INVENTORY
```

```
  ACCOUNTS PAYABLE MENU
    1. FILE MAINTENANCE
    2. SELECT PAYMENT
    3. PRINT CHECKS
    4. MONTH END REPORTING
    5. RETURN TO MAIN MENU
```

```
      JOB COSTING MENU
    1. JOB COST MAINTENANCE
    2. TASK TABLE MAINTENANCE
    3. JOB COST REPORTING
    4. EMPLOYEE TABLE MAINTENANCE
    5. RETURN TO MAIN MENU
```

```
    GENERAL LEDGER MENU
    1. FILE MAINTENANCE
    2. BALANCE SHEET INCOME
    3. YEAR END
    4. PLANNING
    5. RETURN TO MAIN MENU
```

```
       INVENTORY MENU
    1. FILE MAINTENANCE
    2. REORDER POINT
    3. POINT OF SALES
    4. INVENTORY REPORT
    5. RETURN TO MAIN MENU
```

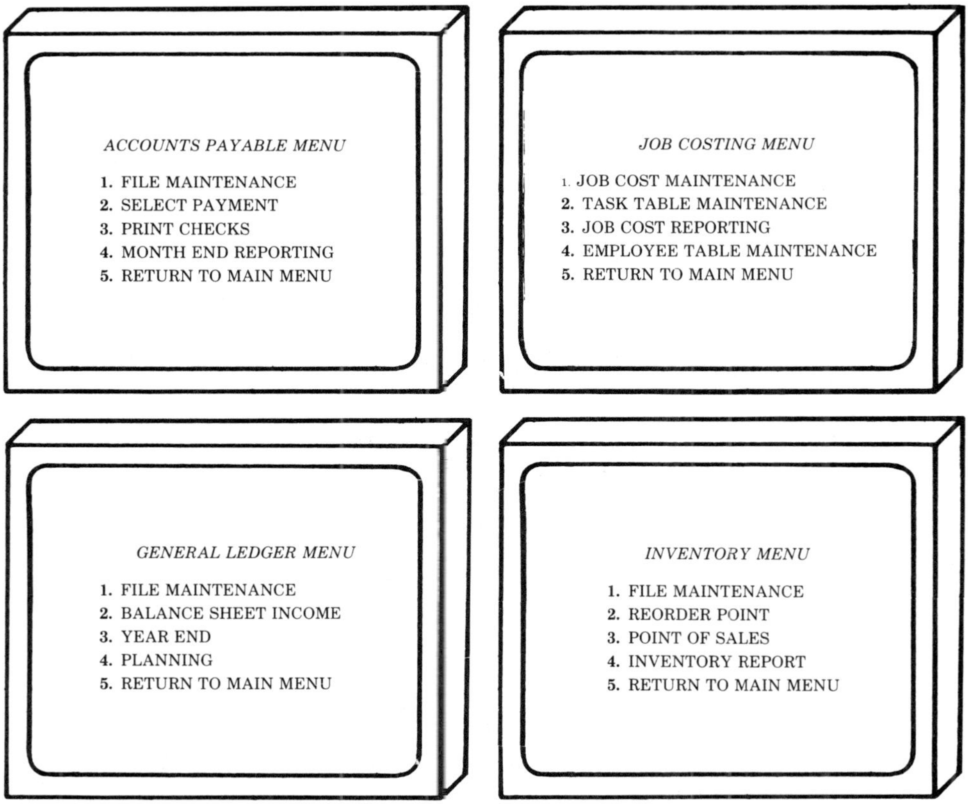

Figure 6-29. Four menus from the general business system. Depending on the choice made in the main menu, one of these screens will be displayed.

TERMS TO STUDY

Band Printer
Carriage Control Tape
Chain Printer
Continuous Form
CRT
Cursor
Daisy Wheel Printer
Display
Drum Printer
Electrographic Printer
Forms Control Buffer

Impact Printer
Ink-jet Printer
Inquiry
Laser Printer
Line Printer
Menu
Non-Impact Printer
Prompt
Train Printer
Wire Printer

QUESTIONS FOR REVIEW

1. What are the two functional categories of printers? What are the two most common numbers of print positions? What is the typical speed range of printers?
2. Describe the function of a chain printer.
3. In what ways do the daisy wheel printer and dot matrix printer differ?
4. Describe how a dot matrix printer forms the character to be printed.
5. A basic difference between a typewriter printer and other printers is that it has a keyboard. What is the advantage of this? What other output device has this characteristic?
6. Why was the development of the electrographic laser printer essential? Describe how this system functions.
7. Discuss two methods of page control used by printers.
8. Discuss the advantages and disadvantages of the CRT display as an output device.
9. What is the function of the cursor on the display screen?
10. What factors should be considered when selecting a display screen?
11. Compare the pros and cons of prompts versus menus.

PROBLEMS FOR RESEARCH AND DISCUSSION

1. Find out the type of output devices for human use used by your school's computer system. Don't include tape and disk, which are not human readable. Determine the specifications for these devices such as speed, line length, page size, and so on.
2. An inventory report is printed weekly consisting of 25,000 entries. Each page printed contains 5 heading lines, 30 detail lines, and 1 total line. Each page also contains 4 lines of spaces to improve readability. How much printer time is needed to produce this report using an 800 line per minute printer?
3. Search the publications for articles and advertisements on display screens. Write a report on the various types of displays available and the ways in which they are applied to the use of the computer in business.

7
Magnetic Tape

Magnetic tape is a compact and efficient means of recording large quantities of data at high speed. An average tape can store 315 bytes per centimeter (800 per inch) and read this data at a rate of 120,000 bytes per second. Data processing applications use this medium for input and output files intended for computer use (Figure 7-1). The program processes these files sequentially by beginning at the first record on the tape and reading each subsequent record until the last record has been processed.

PHYSICAL STRUCTURE OF TAPE

Magnetic Tape

Magnetic tape (Figure 7-2) is composed of a magnetic oxide coating (dull side) on a Mylar plastic base (shiny side). The tape is 1.27 cm. (½ in.) wide, 0.0038 cm. (0.0015 in.) thick, and up to 732 m (2400 ft.) long.

Reels. Tape comes on a plastic reel (Figure 7-3), which can be a maximum of 26.7 cm. (10.5 in.) in diameter, depending upon the length of the tape. An external adhesive backed paper label is placed on the reel to identify the contents of the tape.

File Protection. Data is recorded on the surface of the tape in a series of magnetic spots in a manner roughly comparable to a home tape re-

Figure 7-1. IBM 3420 magnetic tape drive. (*Courtesy of IBM Corporation*)

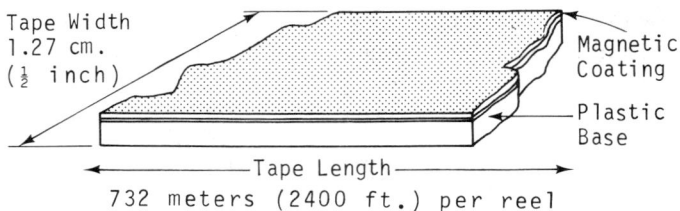

Figure 7-2. Magnetic tape composition.

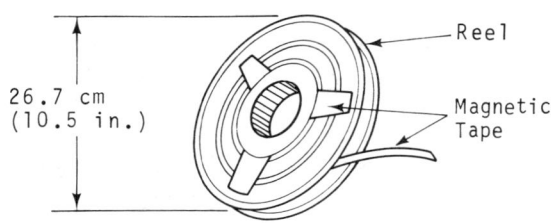

Figure 7-3. Magnetic tape on plastic reel.

PHYSICAL STRUCTURE OF TAPE

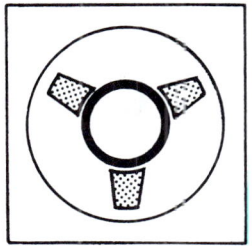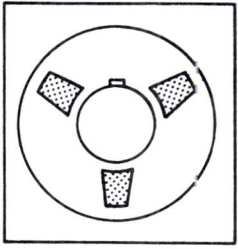

Figure 7-4. File protection ring.

corder. For file protection, a plastic ring is provided that fits into a groove in the back of the reel as shown in Figure 7-4. When the ring is positioned in the back of the reel, it is sensed by the drive mechanism and data may be written on the tape. If the ring is removed, the file is protected and data cannot be written on the tape. "No Ring No Write" is a phrase worth remembering.

Loadpoint Marker. To load the tape onto a tape drive, a length of unused tape, called a leader, is provided at the beginning of the tape. The position of the first record on the tape is then identified by a reflective marker called a loadpoint marker (Figure 7-5). This marker is sensed by a photocell when a beam of light is reflected from its surface. This reflection signals the beginning of data. At the other end of the tape is a similar marker called the end-of-reel marker whose presence prevents data from being written past the end of the reel of tape.

Tape Drives

A tape drive (Figure 7-6) is used to read and write data on a reel of tape. A full reel of tape is placed on the drive mechanism as shown in Figure 7-7. The tape leader is passed through the drive capstan past the read/

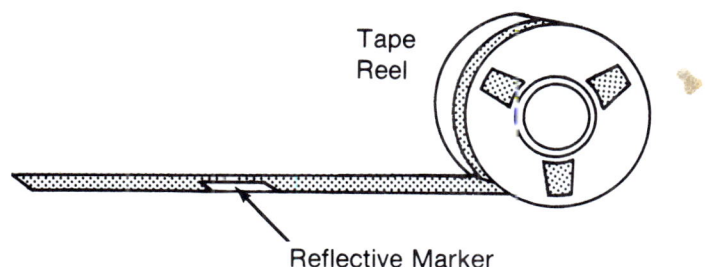

Figure 7-5. Loadpoint marker.

Figure 7-6. Tape reel mounting. (*Courtesy of NCR Corporation*)

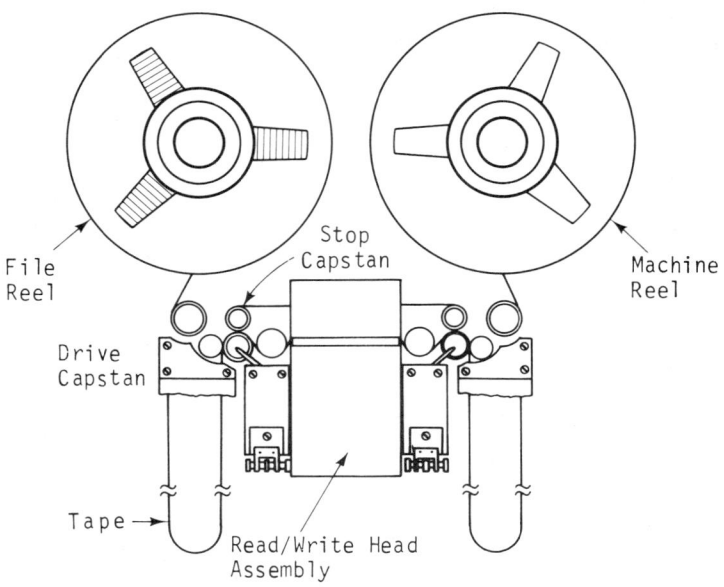

Figure 7-7. Tape drive head assembly and drive mechanism.

PHYSICAL STRUCTURE OF TAPE

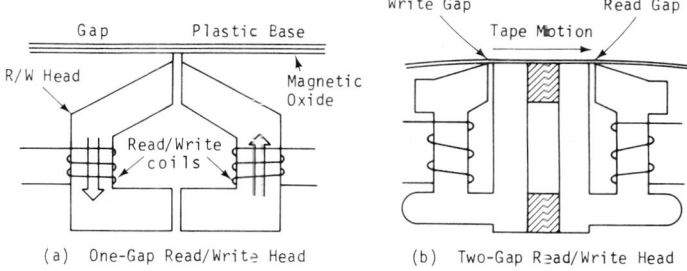

Figure 7-8. Read/write head assembly.

write head assembly and onto the machine or take-up reel. The drive capstan moves the tape past the read/write heads during the read or write operation. On each side, a loop of tape acts as a buffer to prevent pulling or snapping of the tape as it starts and stops at the head. After a tape has been processed, it is rewound back onto the original reel at high speed. (Figure 7-11 gives some rewind times for several different tape drives.) These times assume a full reel of tape is used for a file. In many cases, a file requires less than a full reel and, therefore, rewind time will be relative to the length of the tape used.

Reading and Writing

Figure 7-8 shows the read/write head assembly. When data is being written, electrical current is passed through the write coil while the tape is moving past the write gap. This current causes a magnetic field to appear temporarily at the gap, which then leaves a magnetic spot on the surface of the tape. Old data, which may have been on the tape, is automatically erased, and the new data is retained. This is called destructive writing and allows tape to be used over again when a file is no longer needed.

When a tape is read, the magnetic spots on the tape surface move past the read gap of the head, and the magnetic flux causes a current to flow in the read coil. This is done without any change in the data magnetically encoded on the tape, and the data remains intact. This is nondestructive reading.

Tracks

Most tape drives are 9-track devices for recording either EBCDIC or ASCII code. To create tracks of nine bits (Figure 7-9), the tape drive has an assembly of nine read/write heads that are mounted together.

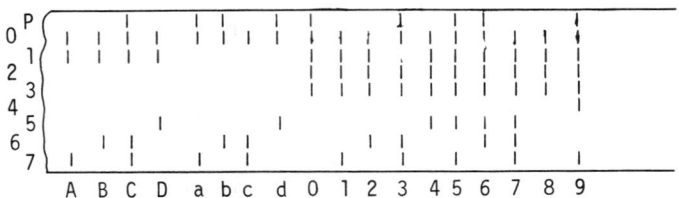

Figure 7-9. Nine-track tape.

Parity Checking. Nine-track tape uses eight tracks for the bits of the EBCDIC or ASCII coding system. These represent the bits discussed in Chapter 3. The presence of a magnetic spot represents the 1 bit, and the absence of a magnetic spot, the 0 bit. A 9th bit is used as a check or parity bit. This bit is used for error checking and can be designed for either even or odd parity.

When odd parity is used (as in Figure 7-9), there must always be an odd number of bits for each character. In the case of a character like the letter C, which has four bits, the parity bit is also magnetized to ensure odd parity.

To ensure even greater accuracy in the recording and reading of data, an additional check bit is used at the end of the physical record. This is called the longitudinal check bit. It appears on each track and provides for parity checking along the track.

Figure 7-10. This Digital Equipment Corporation tape drive stores data magnetically on a removable magnetic tape. (*Courtesy of Digital Equipment Corporation*)

Density

The amount of data a tape can store is affected by a characteristic called density. This refers to the number of bytes that can be stored in a centimeter or inch of the tape surface. An average tape drive records data at a density 315 bytes per centimeter (BPC), i.e., 800 bytes per inch (BPI). At this density, the data from an 80-column punched card can be stored in 0.25 cm. (0.1 in.) of magnetic tape. Both lower and higher densities are available for different storage requirements. In some cases, tape drives are dual density and may operate at 315 and 630 BPC (800 and 1600 BPI). This allows for greater flexibility when several different computer systems are used by a company.

Tape Speed

Another factor affecting the performance of magnetic tape is the tape speed. This refers to the number of centimeters or inches per second the tape travels past the read/write head. A common tape speed is 508 centimeters per second (CPS) (200 inches per second). Tape drives are available with a wide variety of tape speeds suitable for many applications and budgets.

When density and tape speed are multiplied together, a new measurement is derived—*data rate*. This measurement is the number of bytes per second a tape drive can read or write. Depending on density and tape speed, data rates may range from 60,000 to 780,000 bytes per second (BPS). Some sample tape drive specifications are given in Figure 7-11. Tape drives are shown in Figure 7-12.

Organization of the Tape

Blocking Concepts. As a tape record is being written, the tape must be moved past the read/write head at a constant rate of speed. When the operation is finished, the tape stops until the next instruction to write is received from the CPU. At this time, the tape is accelerated up to speed, and the next record is written. Since starting and stopping the tape requires space for accelerating (.75 cm.) and decelerating (.75 cm.), a gap is left between records on the tape (Figure 7-13). This gap is called an inter-record gap (IRG), or inter-block gap (IBG). A common size for the gap is 1.5 cm. (0.6 in.) in length. As we have seen, an 80-byte record requires only 0.25 cm. when stored at 315 BPC (800 BPI). This means the record uses only one sixth the length of a gap. In other words, six times as much space is used for gaps as compared to records. This leads to rather inefficient use of the tape.

	IBM			UNIVAC		BURROUGHS	
	3420-3	3420-6	3420-7	UNISERVO-12	UNISERVO-20	B-9392	B9495-6
Density (BPI)	1600	6250	1600	1600	1600	800	1600
(BPC)	(630)	(2450)	(630)	(630)	(630)	(315)	(630)
Data Rate (BPS)	120K	780K	320K	68K	320K	72K	400K
Tape Speed (IPS)	75	125	200	42.7	200	90	250
(CPS)	(190)	(318)	(508)	(108)	(508)	(228)	(635)
IBG (in.)	0.6	0.6	0.6	0.6	0.6	0.6	0.6
(cm.)	(1.524)	(1.524)	(1.524)	(1.524)	(1.524)	(1.524)	(1.524)
Rewind Time (sec.)	60	60	45	108	60	NA	45

Figure 7-11. Selected tape drive specifications.

PHYSICAL STRUCTURE OF TAPE

Figure 7-12. IBM 3510 tape drives. (*Courtesy of IBM Corporation*)

This problem is reduced by applying the principle of blocking as shown in Figure 7-14. If six of these 80-byte records are grouped together and written on tape as one block, only one gap is needed for each block of 6 records. In this case, the gap is still 1.5 cm. (0.6 in.), but the physical record is now $6 \times 0.25 = 1.5$ cm. (0.6 in.). Now data occupies the same amount of space as the IBG.

This can be improved further by using a blocking factor of 12. Now the block is $12 \times 0.25 = 3.0$ cm. (1.2 in.), and the gap is unchanged. In this case, gaps use only one-half the space of data. This is far superior to the case when records were unblocked. There are, however, limitations to the size a block may be depending upon the channel and CPU capacities of the computer being used.

Fixed Length Records. The most commonly used tape record is a fixed length record (Figure 7-15). For a specific file, each record is a constant length. A file containing records to be printed might have a fixed length of 133 bytes. This means each record on the tape file consists of 133 bytes of data. There is no limit on the size of each record except that imposed by the hardware. Therefore a record may be 30 bytes, 80 bytes, or 500 bytes, depending upon the needs of the application. However, each file will have a specific length, and all records in that file will be that length.

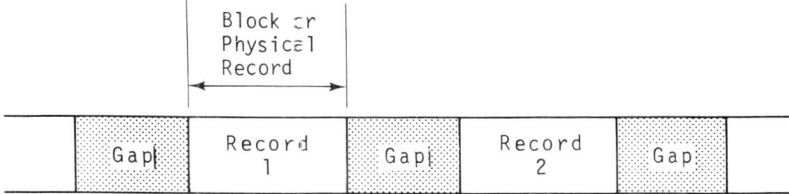

Figure 7-13. Inter-block gap.

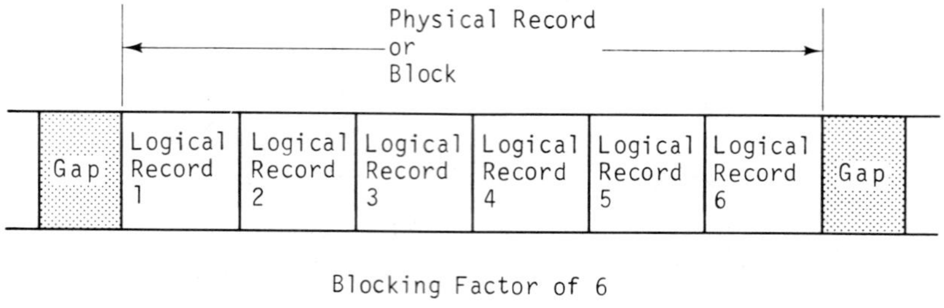

```
|Gap| Logical | Logical | Logical | Logical | Logical | Logical |Gap|
|   | Record  | Record  | Record  | Record  | Record  | Record  |   |
|   |   1     |   2     |   3     |   4     |   5     |   6     |   |
```

←—————— Physical Record or Block ——————→

Blocking Factor of 6

Figure 7-14. Blocked records.

When a fixed length record is blocked, the blocking factor is also fixed (Figure 7-16). In this example, a blocking factor of 4 is used. Every block in the file will then contain 4 logical records. Again, a variety of blocking factors may be chosen, but when one is selected, that is used for the entire file.

Variable Length Records. A variable length record (Figure 7-17) is used for files requiring records of differing length. A purchase order file may have a record identifying a particular customer by account number, name, address, order number, order date, and so on. This record may require 100 bytes of data. Following this record are a number of records that give item number, quantity, and the cost of items purchased. These records may only require 40 bytes. Following all of the detail for one customer would be another 100-byte customer identification record and further details.

Variable records may also be blocked. The important difference here is that specific blocking factors are not given. This is because record lengths do not always occur in predictable patterns. Instead of a blocking factor, a maximum blocksize is specified, and the maximum number of records possible are placed in a block. If we chose a maximum block of 180 bytes, then a file could appear as shown in Figure 7-18. In the first block, a total of 180 bytes are used. However, in the second block only 120 bytes are required. If the next record of 100 bytes were included, the blocksize would be exceeded. Therefore a shorter block is used and no space is wasted on the tape.

Header and Trailer Labels. In addition to the external paper label on the tape reel, an internal label is recorded magnetically on the surface of the tape. A header label precedes the file contents, and a trailer label follows the file. The exact information and the size of the label vary from one computer manufacturer to another, but Figure 7-19 gives an outline of possible contents. Identification gives unique information to identify

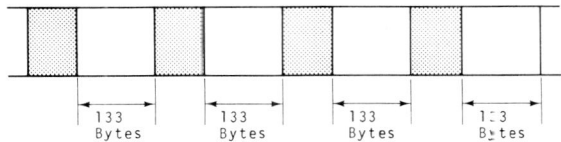

Figure 7-15. Fixed length records.

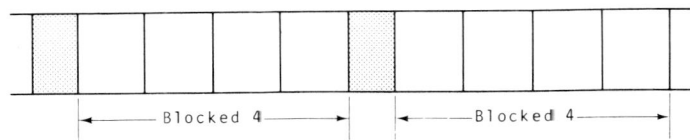

Figure 7-16. Fixed length blocked records.

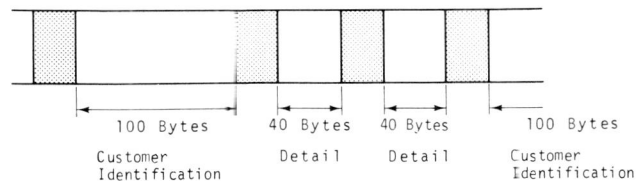

Figure 7-17. Variable length records.

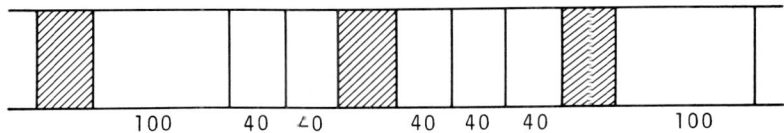

Figure 7-18. Variable length blocked records.

```
IDENTIFICATION
VOLUME NUMBER
FILE NUMBER
CREATION DATE
EXPIRY DATE
BLOCK COUNT
```

Figure 7-19. Header and trailer label contents.

a specific file. This may be alphanumeric, such as ACTREC meaning Accounts Receivable File, or a strictly numeric code like a serial number. In some cases both types of identifications are used.

Volume number is sometimes called reel number. A volume number is necessary when a file exceeds the length of one reel of tape. In this case, each reel is numbered consecutively as shown in Figure 7-20. A multi-volume file is needed in applications that handle large quantities of data. For instance, an on-line banking system may wish to record on tape a record of each transaction for back-up purposes. In a large city, this may mean hundreds of thousands of records to represent the transactions against the accounts master file. As a result, several tape files may be needed to record this activity.

APPLICATIONS FOR MAGNETIC TAPE

Magnetic tape is suitable for any sequential file application requiring compact storage and high speed read and write operations. As discussed, tape is a very reliable method of storage and has a wide variety of densities and speeds suitable for many applications. The following discussion describes some of the most common uses of magnetic tape.

```
DATA ENTRY   MASTER FILES   WORK FILES
             REPORT              LOG
               OFFLINE STORAGE
```

Data Entry Files

This approach to recording source data stores the records sequentially on magnetic tape. Three types of tape used are cassette, cartridge, and open

ACCOUNTS ACTIVITY FILE

Figure 7-20. Tape volumes.

reel. This form of recording is discussed in more depth in the data entry chapter.

Master Files

A master file (Figure 7-21) is a file containing records that rarely change relating to a specific application. For example, a payroll master file would contain a collection of all current payroll records. Each record would provide data such as payroll number, name, department, hourly rate, salary (if not paid hourly), tax category, and year-to-date totals.

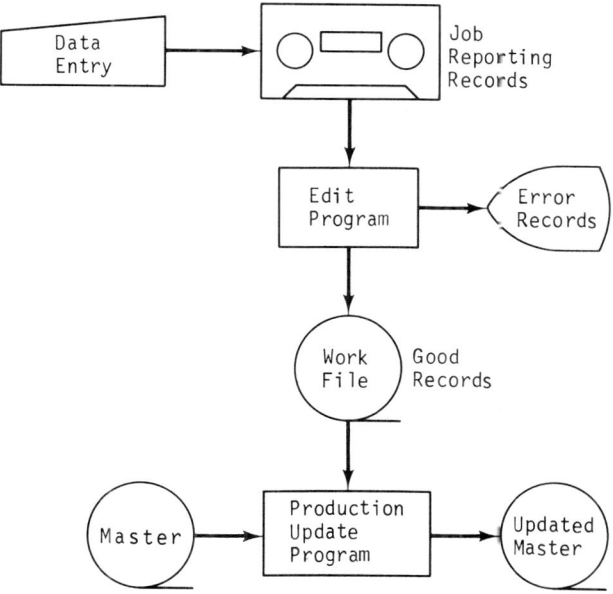

Figure 7-21. Master and work files.

Work Files

Tape files also provide a convenient means for producing data in one program and reading it in another program. These files are intermediate files and are not permanent. They are used simply to provide a link between two or more programs.

Figure 7-21 shows a work file that transfers valid records from an edit program to an update program. The edit program processes the job reporting records and selects only the correct records for output on the work file. Records containing errors are printed or displayed and will need to be corrected and resubmitted on a future computer run. The work file provides for input to the Production Update program. Here the good records are read as transactions and update the master file.

Report Files

Report files (Figure 7-22) are similar to work files except that they contain records destined to be printed on reports. This is quite useful when a

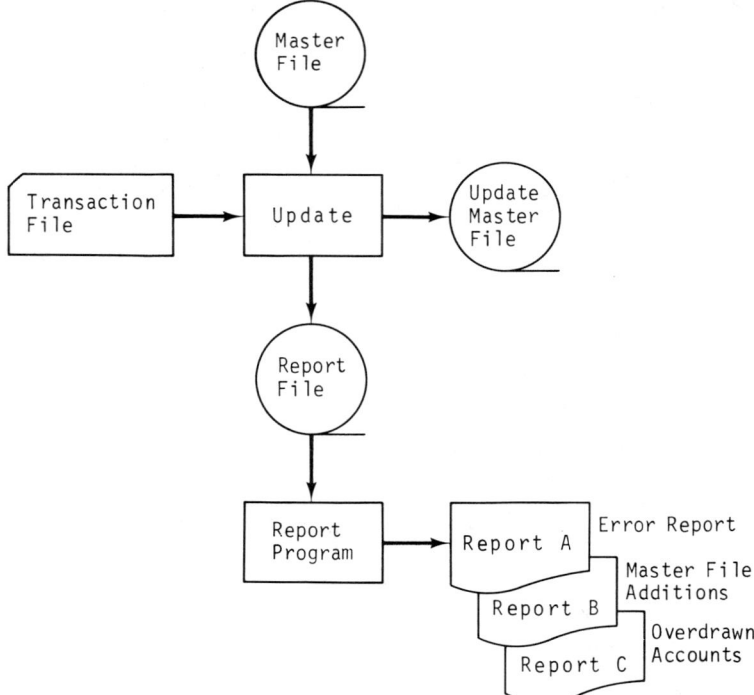

Figure 7-22. Report files.

single program needs to produce several reports. These can all be placed on one tape and then printed from this tape by a report program. In some cases the records need to be sorted prior to printing.

This method is also useful when a large scale computer does the processing. Instead of taking time to print reports on a high-speed computer, they are written on tape. The report tape is then taken to a small computer, which does the printing.

Logging Files

In on-line systems, data comes from many sources. Some of these sources, such as a CRT display screen and keyboard, do not provide a permanent record of data entered. One method of recording these real-time transactions is to write them onto magnetic tape. This provides a log of all entries made at each terminal. If a system failure occurs, the log tape may be used to retrieve the source data entered at the terminal without the necessity for manual re-entry. This can be a great time saver as well as cost reduction (Figure 7-23).

Off-line Storage

Files that are being processed by the computer are called on-line files. In many cases, a file is on-line only for a few minutes and then is no

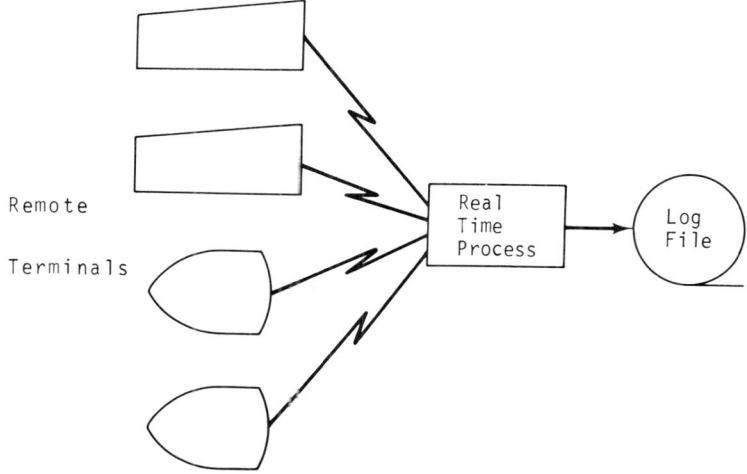

Figure 7-23. Logging tape.

longer needed by the program. For sequential applications, a payroll master file may only need to be read once a week; an inventory master file once a day; and monthly sales report data once a month. During the interval, the files are not needed. In these situations, tape is a convenient and inexpensive way of storing the data. Usually the tapes are externally labelled and placed on racks in a tape library. The library is situated close to the computer center for easy access to the tapes when they are needed.

For security reasons, duplicate files are often stored at a remote location from the main computer center. This may be at another location in the same city or even in a different city. This method is used to provide backup data in the event of disaster such as fire, hurricanes, flooding, or war.

TERMS TO STUDY

Block
Blocking Factor
Data Rate
Density
Fixed Length Record
Header Label
IBG
Loadpoint Marker
Log
Logical Record
Longitudinal Check Bit

Master File
Off-line
Parity
Physical Record
Read/Write Head
Tape Drive
Tape Speed
Track
Trailer Label
Variable Length Record
Work File

QUESTIONS FOR REVIEW

1. Describe the physical characteristics of magnetic tape.
2. What is the difference between an external and an internal tape label?
3. Describe the difference between a reflective marker and an end-of-file marker.
4. What is meant by non-destructive reading of tape?
5. What are the different codes used on 9-track tape?
6. Describe the various means of ensuring the correct recording of data on tape.

7. What factors determine the amount of data that can be stored on a reel of tape? What factors affect the rate at which data is read or written?
8. Why is it necessary to start and stop tape when it is being read or written?
9. Blocking is one of the most effective methods of using tape efficiently. Why is this so?
10. What is the difference between fixed and variable length records? Give an application for each type of record.
11. Identify the application areas for magnetic tape and describe each briefly.

PROBLEMS FOR RESEARCH AND DISCUSSION

1. Develop a formula to determine the amount of space (in inches or centimeters) a given file requires on tape. Develop a second formula to determine the amount of time necessary to read the file.
2. Using the formulas developed in problem 1, calculate the length of tape and time required for the following file.

    200000 records   100 bytes per record

    Density 1600 BPI   Blocking Factor 15
    (630 BPC)

    Tape Speed 112.5 IPS   Inter-Block Gap 0.6 in.
    (286 CPS)   (1.524 cm.)

    Gap Time 5.3 ms.

    Note: Not all of these values will be needed to solve problems 1 and 2.

3. Compare the space requirements for the file in problem 2 if it were stored on Hollerith cards. Note that a 100-byte record will require two cards per record. What time would be necessary to read this file using an 800-card-per-minute card reader?

8

Direct Access Storage Devices

MAGNETIC DISK

The most popular magnetic storage device used by computers is the magnetic disk. Its wide usage may be attributed to high speed, large storage capacity, and variety of access methods (Figures 8-1 and 8-2). Disk is generally much faster than magnetic tape. A disk can store more data than a reel of tape and permits both sequential and direct access to the data stored on it. Although disk is more expensive, these advantages far outweigh the cost difference.

Physical Structure

Disks are constructed of a number of metal platters 35.5 cm. in diameter (14 in.) coated with a magnetic material on both surfaces. These platters are mounted above each other on a central hub to form a disk pack (Figure 8-3), which weighs about 9 kg. (20 lb.). In most cases, the disk pack is removable from the drive mechanism; however, some are permanently mounted. Each magnetic surface is divided into a series of concentric tracks (Figure 8-4) along which data is recorded. Unlike the stereo LP recording, the tracks do not spiral to the center. Rather, each track is independent of the other. A track may contain up to approximately 15,000 bytes of data, depending on the device type.

Data is read and written by a series of read/write heads (Figure 8-5). These heads are mounted on access arms that permit the heads to be

164 DIRECT ACCESS STORAGE DEVICES

Figure 8-1. IBM 3370 disk drives. Various models of these disk drives range from 300 million to over 2 billion bytes of storage capacity. (*Courtesy of IBM Corporation*)

moved to any track desired. Usually there is one head per disk surface with the exception of the outer surfaces which do not record data.

The disk is mounted on a drive (Figure 8-6) and rotated at a constant speed—unlike magnetic tape, which starts and stops.

KEY CONCEPT

Sectors

Some types of disk drives divide their tracks in sectors. Each sector has a length from 100 to several thousand characters, depending on the type of disk. A sector may hold one or more records. Records that exceed the sector length may overflow into the following sector.

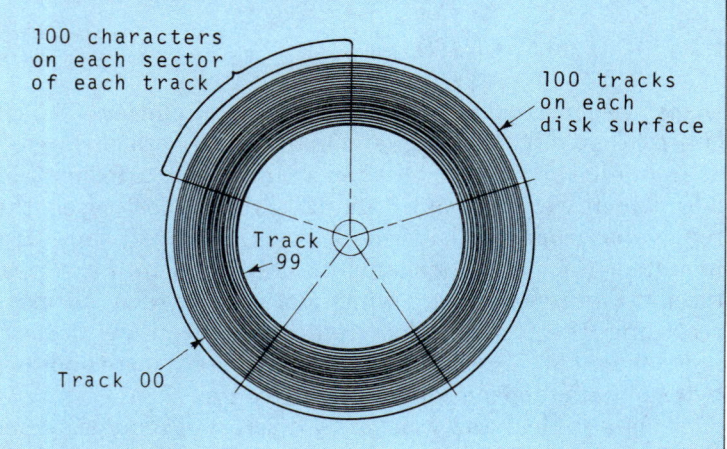

Figure 8-2. IBM 3340 disk drives. (*Courtesy of IBM Corporation*)

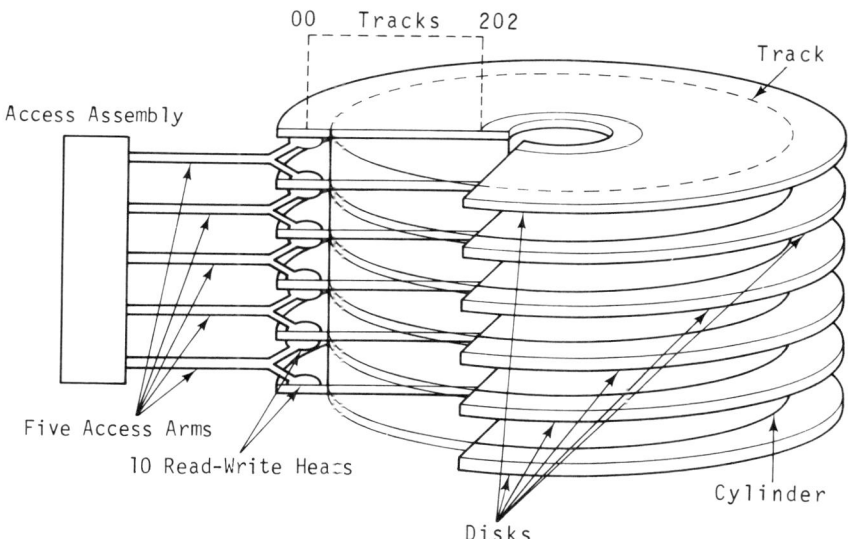

Figure 8-3. IBM 3348 disk pack. (*Courtesy of IBM Corporation*)

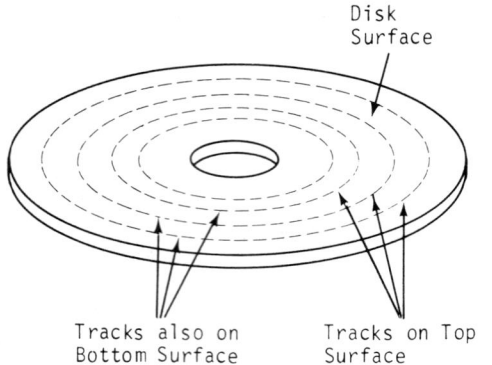

Figure 8-4. Magnetic disk tracks.

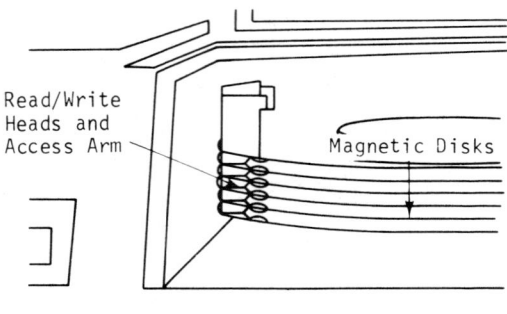

Figure 8-5. Read/write access arms.

Figure 8-6. Mounting a disk pack in the drive. (*Courtesy of Sperry-Univac*)

Reading and Writing on Disk

As the disk turns, the heads are situated over a track, and data may be read or written on the track. Since there is no starting and stopping, some other method must be used to indicate where data begins on the track. This is achieved through a magnetic marker recorded on the track (Figure 8-7). During rotation, the marker is sensed, and data may be written following it. The time taken for the marker to rotate to the head is called the rotational delay. For computational purposes, a time called the average rotational delay is used. This is equivalent to half a rotation.

KEY CONCEPT

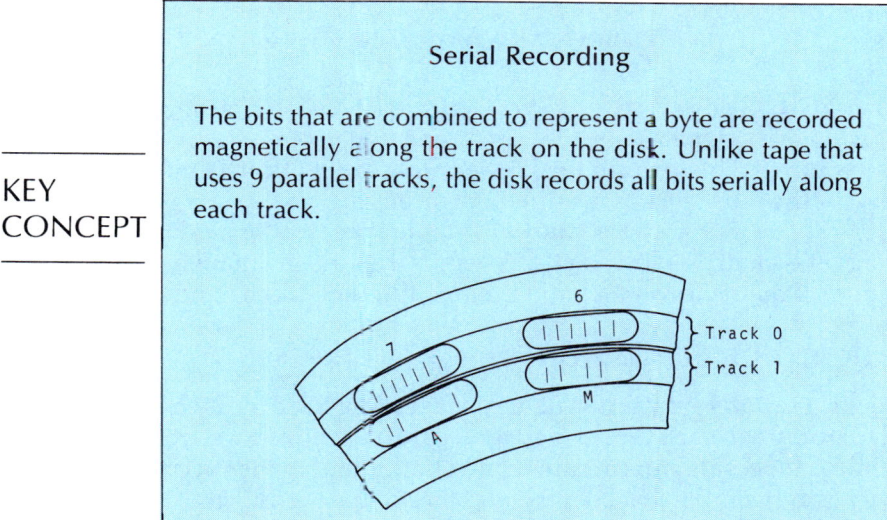

Serial Recording

The bits that are combined to represent a byte are recorded magnetically along the track on the disk. Unlike tape that uses 9 parallel tracks, the disk records all bits serially along each track.

As the head is moved from one track to another, a time factor called seek time is required. If the head is moved to an adjacent track, say from 136 to 137, the time is track-to-track seek time. If more than two tracks are involved, for example from 63 to 128, the time used is average seek time.

To minimize this seek time on sequential files, data is read from all surfaces while the heads are in one position (Figure 8-3). This means that data is read from the first track on surface one followed by the first track on surface two and so on for each surface. This method gives the appearance of a cylinder and is called the cylinder concept as shown in Figure 8-3 at the beginning of the chapter. If there are 10 read/write heads, then 10 tracks are read before a seek is necessary to the next track. This reduces seek time to the smallest time possible.

One way to eliminate seek time entirely is to provide a head for each track. The head per track disk has permanently mounted access

168 DIRECT ACCESS STORAGE DEVICES

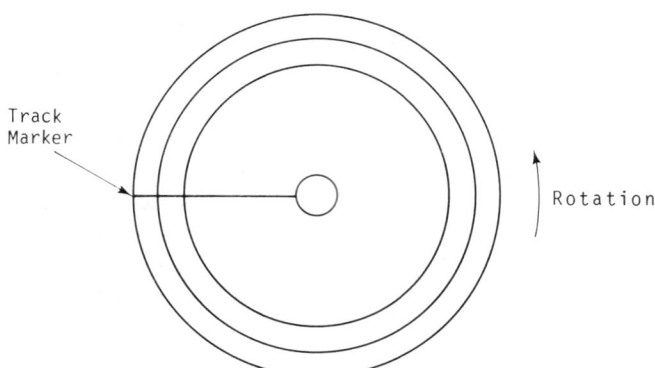

Figure 8-7. Magnetic track marker.

arms with heads positioned over every track on each surface. Since each track has its own head, no head movement is necessary, and no seek time is required. This results in a faster disk, although it is more expensive due to the many heads required (Figure 8-8).

Figure 8-9 shows a chart of sample specifications taken from a variety of disk drives and packs. A wide variety is available to suit a broad range of applications including many different speeds and capacities.

Record Organization

Logical records are written along each track of the disk as shown in Figure 8-10. Between each record is a gap separating the records from each other. Unlike tape, this gap contains control information identifying the record, its position on the track, and error-checking data. Since the gap requires space, it reduces the number of bytes available for recording data. For instance, the IBM 3340 has a track capacity of 8368 bytes. If the logical records were 100 bytes in length, it would seem that we could store 83 records on the track (8368/100). In fact, because of the gaps, fewer records

Figure 8-8. NCR 6590 data modules with head in pack. (*Courtesy of NCR Corporation*)

	IBM 3330	IBM 3340	IBM 2305 Fixed Head	IBM 3375	BURROUGHS 9484-4	UNIVAC 8440
Disks Per Pack	12	4	6	6	11	11
Recording Surfaces	19	6	12	12	20	20
Pack Capacity (bytes)	100M	69.8M	11.2M	819.7M	121M	119M
Track Capacity (bytes)	13,030	8,368	14,660	35,616		14,910
No. of Cylinders	404	696	1	959		400
Tracks Per Cylinder	19	12	768	12		20
Tracks Per Pack	7,676	8,352	768			8120
Average Seek Time	30 ms.	25 ms.	5 ms.	19 ms.	30 ms.	30 ms.
Track-to-Track Seek Time	10 ms.	10 ms.	0			
Rotation Speed (rpm)	3600	2964	6000			2400
Average Rotational Delay	8.3 ms.	10.1 ms.	5 ms.	10.1 ms.	12.5 ms.	12.5 ms.
Data Transfer Rate	806K	885K	1.5M	1.859MB	625K	624K

Figure 8-9. Disk specifications.

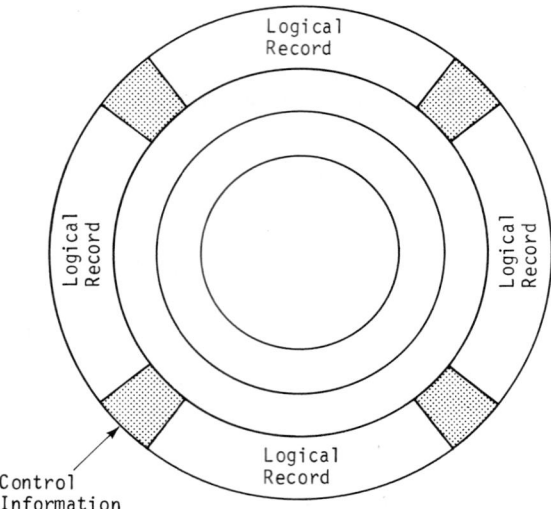

Figure 8-10. Logical records on disk.

may be recorded. The exact number of records is determined by a formula provided by the manufacturer. In the case of the IBM 3340, the formula used is

$$\frac{8535}{\text{Physical Record Length} + 167} = \text{No. of physical records per track}$$

In our example this gives

$$\frac{8535}{100 + 167} = 31 \text{ physical records}$$

This is considerably less than the 83 records expected on the track. However, this can be improved by blocking the records. Figure 8-11 shows what happens when a blocking factor of 2 is used. When records are blocked, control information is required for each physical record, not for each logical record. Therefore, only half as many control records are used in the file when a blocking factor of 2 is used.

Using a 200-byte physical record in the formula gives

$$\frac{8535}{200 + 167} = 23 \text{ physical records}$$

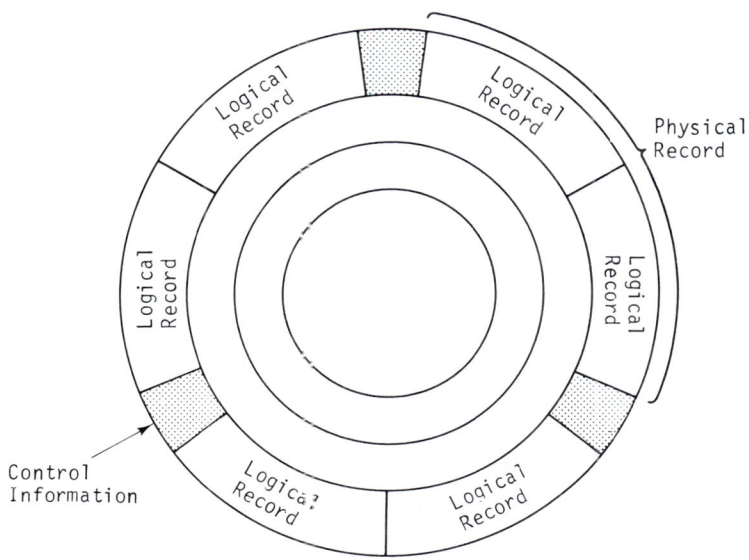

Figure 8-11. Blocking records on disk.

Since the blocking factor was 2, this gives 2 × 23 = 46 logical records, which is significantly better than an unblocked file.

This process is continued in Figure 8-12 showing the effect of choosing a variety of blocking factors. In general, the larger the blocking factor, the more records per track. However, there are some exceptions. A blocking factor of 12 gives 72 records per track, whereas 13 gives only 65 records. As the physical record length approaches the track capacity, the choice becomes critical. However, blocks of this length are seldom used because of their extreme size.

FILE ORGANIZATION AND ACCESS METHODS

Direct access devices are the most versatile input and output mediums available on today's computer systems. This is not only a result of their high speed and large storage capacity, but also because they offer several methods for accessing data. The most commonly used methods are sequential, direct, indexed sequential, and virtual.

Blocking Factor	Physical Record Length	Number of Physical Records	Number of Logical Records
1	100	31	31
2	200	23	46
3	300	18	54
4	400	15	60
5	500	12	60
6	600	11	66
7	700	9	63
8	800	8	64
9	900	7	63
10	1000	7	70
11	1100	6	66
12	1200	6	72
13	1300	5	65
14	1400	5	70
15	1500	5	75

Figure 8-12. Optimum blocking factors for 100-byte logical records on the IBM 3340 disk.

Sequential Files

Sequential processing of disk records is the same as magnetic tape record processing. In both tape and disk, processing begins at the first logical record and proceeds through each record in the file until the final record has been read or written. The major difference with sequential disk files is that the records are located on different tracks and surfaces on the disk. In Figure 8-14, the file shown begins on the first track (cylinder) of surface one. This consists of records 123, 125, 127, 130, and 131. These records are in sequential order on the track. The next group of records are on track (cylinder) 1 of surface 2. They are records 133, 135, 136, 138, and 140. As reading continues, each surface is referenced, and the data read and processed. Since track 1 of each surface is read first, this eliminates head movement. This is the cylinder concept defined earlier in the chapter.

When all records from cylinder 1 have been read, processing continues from the track on cylinder 2. A small file may consist of only a few cylinders—in which case, several files may be stored on one disk. Larger files may use all of the cylinders of a disk pack and even extend to several packs where necessary.

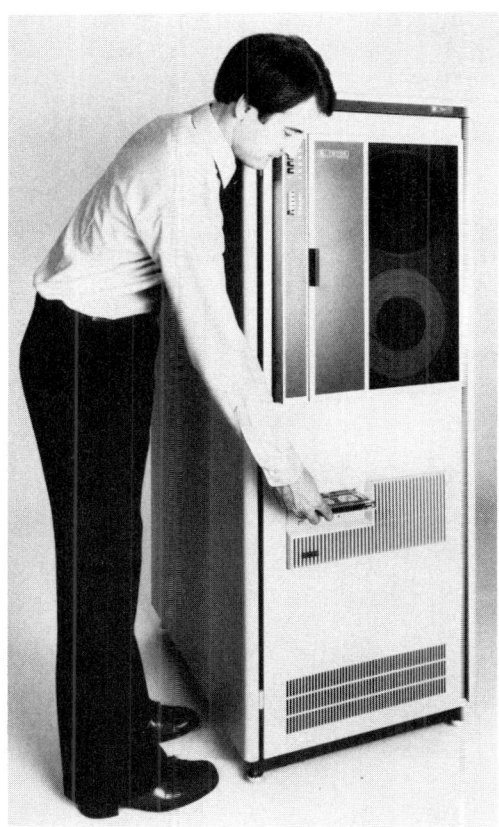

Figure 8-13. This Hewlett-Packard mass storage subsystem combines a magnetic tape drive with a 132-million-byte disk drive.

Surface	Cylinder 1		Cylinder 2	
1	123 125 127 130 131	Records 1–5	352 354 357 360 362	Records 51–55
2	133 135 136 138 140		367 370 371 377 378	
3	142 143 147 151 152			
4	153 158 163 170 175			
5	198 208 209 231 244			
6	250 251 252 253 258			
7	262 265 267 270 271			
8	278 281 285 286 296			
9	303 307 319 327 330	Records 46–50		
10	344 346 347 348 351			

Figure 8-14. Sequential access files.

KEY CONCEPT

SEQUENTIAL DISK APPLICATIONS

Although disk is physically quite different from tape, sequential files are logically very much the same. With some minor modifications, the following are the sequential applications as they relate to disk.

1. **Data Entry**—Usually floppy disk is used for key entry.
2. **Work Files**—Part or all of a disk file may be reserved for this use. One disk pack may contain several smaller work files.
3. **Logging File**—Disk may be used to log activity on a telecommunications system.
4. **Sort/Merge**—Files on direct access devices may be sorted or merged sequentially in a manner similar to tape.
5. **Off-line Storage**—Disk packs may be used to store data off-line in a disk library. However, a disk pack is bulkier and more expensive than a reel of tape.

Figure 8-15. The Hewlett-Packard 7925 disk drive uses a removable disk pack that stores a maximum of 120 million bytes of data.

Direct Access Files

A major disadvantage of sequential files is the necessity to process all records of the file when only a single record or a small number of records require processing. In many applications, only a small percentage of the file needs to be processed in any given computer run. An inventory file containing 30,000 items may require processing of only 4 percent of these records each day. This means that only 1200 records need to be accessed. If a sequential file were used, all 30,000 records would be read, 96 percent of them unnecessarily. For this reason, direct file organization may be used because it permits access to any record without the necessity to read other records in the file. If 1200 records are required, only 1200 records are read. To accomplish this, each record is uniquely identified with a key. The key is usually a component or field in the record, such as a part number or account number, depending on the type of file. Using this key, the record is placed randomly on the file as shown in Figure 8-16. The exact location of the record is determined by applying a randomizing formula to the key. The result of this formula is a track number, which is used to locate the record on the disk. Applying this formula at any time to the key will result in the same track number, and therefore the location of the record is found. The file in Figure 8-16 consists of 20 tracks numbered 0 to 19. To locate a record, the key is divided by the number

Track	Cylinder 1	Track	Cylinder 2
0	20 40	10	70 110 330 950
1	41 61 161 801	11	71 211 771 791
2	62 102 202 242	12	92 112 212 272
3	43 83 183 203	13	53 73
4	24 64 84	14	14 54 94 114
5	5 25 105 185	15	15 35 75 115
6	86 106 166 406	16	76
7	87 107	17	97 117 157 197
8	28 48 108 188	18	78 98 158 218
9	9 209 229 609	19	359 479 699 739

Figure 8-16. Direct access file organization.

of tracks in the file, and the remainder is used as the track number for that record. This method is called randomizing.

For instance, if the record key is 771, the calculation is as follows:

$$\frac{771}{20} = 36 \text{ with a remainder of } 11$$

> **KEY CONCEPT**
>
> **KEY**
>
> A key is a field that uniquely identifies a record in much the same way as a name identifies a person. Fields that may serve as keys are: Part Number, Account Number, Payroll Number, Product Code, Policy Number, Authorization, Social Security Number.

Since the remainder for key 771 is 11, this record will be located on track 11 of the disk file.

A record containing the key 40 would be located on track 0.

$$\frac{40}{20} = 2 \text{ with a remainder of } 0$$

Using this randomizing formula gives no guarantee that each track will be completely filled with records. Some tracks may contain less than their full capacity. This may require a more complex randomizing formula to improve record allocation. Even so, direct files will not have equal record distribution and therefore use space less efficiently than other file organization methods.

In some cases, it is possible that more records than the track capacity randomize to the same track. If a track can hold only 20 records then the 21st record that randomizes to that track exceeds the track's capacity. For instance, if record 201 were to be added to the file, it would randomize to track 1. However, track 1 is at its full capacity and cannot store additional records. This may be resolved by creating an overflow track to store records that will not fit elsewhere.

KEY CONCEPT

Uniquely Identified Records

Files used for data processing must consist of records with unique identification. This is necessary since identifiers like names or descriptions are often duplicated for several different people or items. For this reason unique keys are allocated to each record.

Key (Acct. No.)	Name	Amount Payable	Balance
16738	Smith K	12.75	127.50
16875	Boyd D	17.95	179.50
17456	Jones A	7.75	77.50
18563	Smith K	25.34	253.40

Because of the direct access capabilities of disk, it is often used for on-line storage of data. This makes data instantly available for reference purposes, updating, and inquiry for both batch and real time systems.

Direct Access Files	
Master Files	Tables
Libraries	Operating Systems
Data Base	Virtual Storage

Indexed Sequential

As we have seen from the previous discussion, there are two quite different ways of accessing disk files: sequential or direct. When one of these methods is used, the other is not possible. If a sequential file is created, then records may only be accessed sequentially from that file. No direct accessing is possible. However there are times when both sequential and direct access capabilities are desirable. This can be accomplished with indexed sequential file organization.

A payroll is a good example of the need for this type of access method. When the weekly paychecks are produced, all employee records need to be accessed to provide salary and deduction information and to maintain

Figure 8-17. Three different models of disk drives provide on-line storage for digital computer systems.

year-to-date totals. In this case, sequential access would be the most suitable method. However, when new employees are hired or existing employees make a change, such as transferring to a new department, then direct access is the most effective. This is because only very few employee records change at any one time, and hiring usually represents a small percentage of existing staff. Therefore there are two quite different access methods required for the same file.

The indexed file in Figure 8-18 shows how data may be organized to achieve both sequential and direct accessing. Individual records are stored sequentially on the disk. Each record has a unique key. In this case, a name is used as the key. This facilitates sequential reading of the file in a way similar to a sequential file organization. Reading may start at the beginning of the file and progress record by record from AAPRO to ZEOLI at the end of the file.

For direct accessing, an index is used. This is really a series of indexes provided to allow for efficient accessing of any record in the file. First, each cylinder has a track index. The track index contains the highest key for each track in that cylinder. Track Index 1 contains ABEX,

FILE ORGANIZATION AND ACCESS METHODS 179

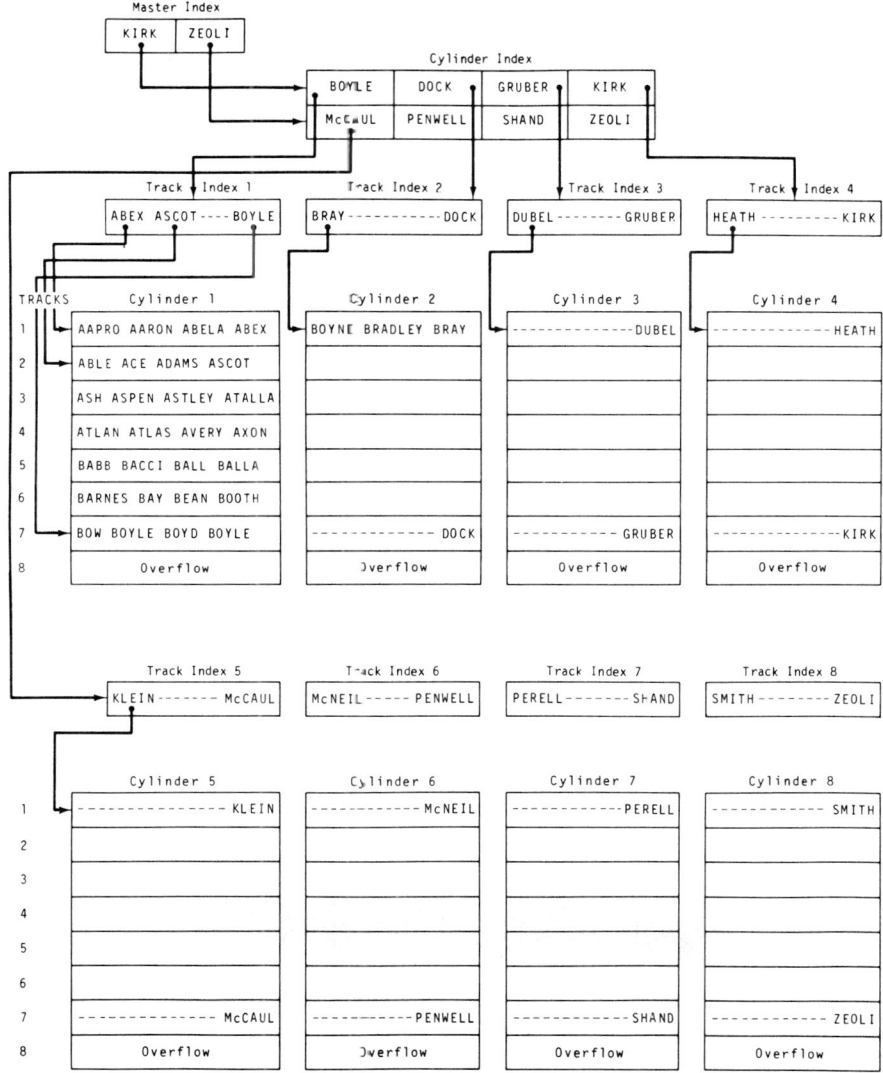

Figure 8-18. Indexed sequential file organization (IBM's ISAM).

the highest key on Track 1; ASCOT, the highest key on track 2; and so on down to BOYLE, the highest key on the last track of the first cylinder. Notice that the index contains only a key and a pointer, not the record itself.

Above the track index in Figure 8-18 is a cylinder index that contains the highest key of each cylinder. This is equivalent to the highest key on each track index. Since the diagram has 8 cylinders, the cylinder index has only 8 entries. A disk pack using all 200 cylinders for an indexed sequential file would have 200 entries in the cylinder index.

Finally, there is a master index that reduces the number of searches in the cylinder index. In the example, the highest key in the first half of the cylinder index is KIRK. This is the first master index entry. The second half has the highest key of ZEOLI.

To find a record directly, a search is made through the indexes. To find BRADLEY's record, a comparison is made to the master index. Since BRADLEY is less than KIRK, this determines that BRADLEY's record is in the first half of the file. Next a search is made in the first section of the cylinder index. BRADLEY is greater than BOYLE but less than DOCK. Therefore the record is in the second cylinder. The pointer here directs us to track index 2. The search in this index shows BRADLEY to be less than BRAY. This pointer goes to the first track of data, and the record we are looking for is located.

Although this search is not as fast as accessing a direct file, the record may still be found quite quickly using the index. This method is much faster than a sequential search.

Additions of new records may also be made to an indexed file. This requires the use of overflow tracks in each cylinder (Figure 8-19). For instance, if ARNOLD were to be added to the file, it would go between ADAMS and ASCOT. Since this track is full, ASCOT is placed on the overflow track and ARNOLD goes on track 2. A pointer is used to reference ASCOT on the overflow track.

As additional records are placed on the overflow track, the efficiency of the file is degraded. After a period of time, it becomes necessary to do file maintenance and remove the records from the overflow area and place them in the primary data area.

Updating of an indexed file may be done without a second file. Records may be read directly into the program. Changes are made to the record as required, and then the new version of the record is rewritten on the file to replace the original. Since the original record no longer exists, a copy is often made on a logging file as back-up in the event of an error or a system failure.

Virtual Files

Virtual file organization has many similarities to indexed sequential. It provides for both sequential and direct accessing of records; it is accomplished through indexes and pointers. There are, however, two main differences in a virtual file. These are device independence and the method used for inserting new records on the file.

Device independence refers to the capability of the virtual file to be used on any direct access device without regard for the physical construction of the device. Therefore disk, drum, and mass storage devices can be used equally well with the exception of differences in access time. This is possible since virtual files are not organized by tracks and cylinders but are independent of these.

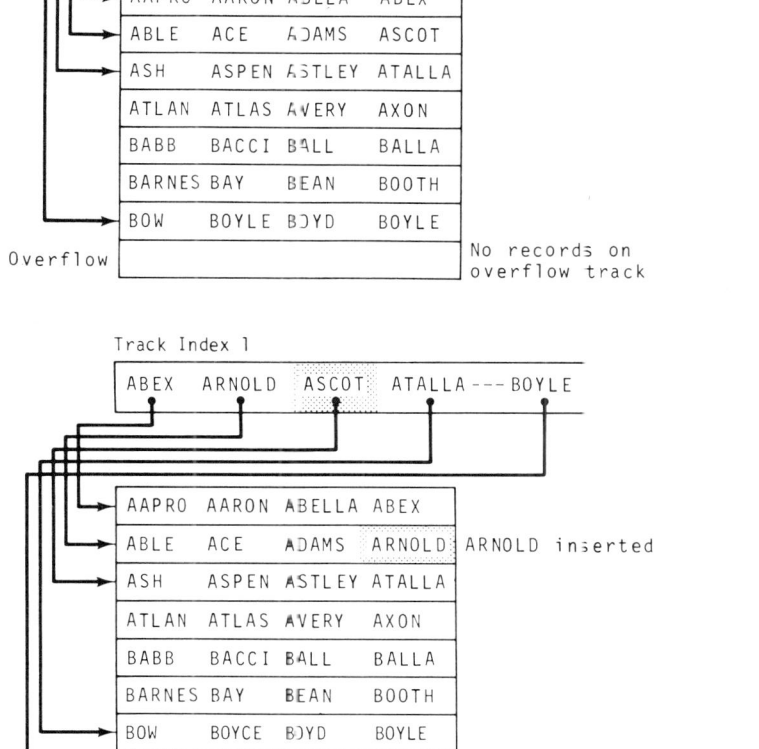

Figure 8-19. Adding new records to an indexed sequential file.

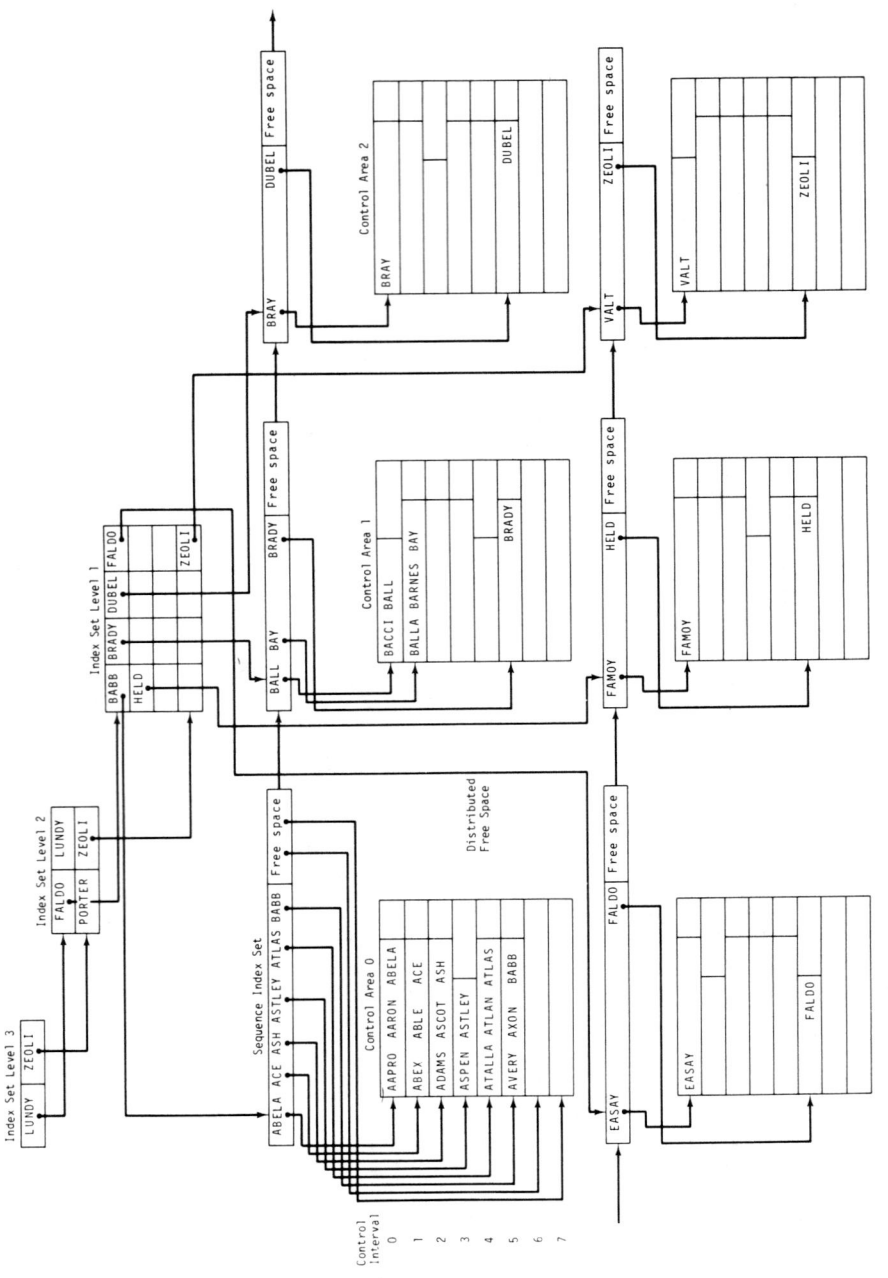

Figure 8-20. Virtual file organization

FILE ORGANIZATION AND ACCESS METHODS   183

The second difference between virtual and indexed files is the provision of space for inserting new records on the virtual file. An indexed file does this by providing an overflow area at the end of each cylinder. A virtual file distributes free space among the records in the file. New records may be added to this free space.

Figure 8-20 shows a virtual file organization. Data records are stored in sections of the file called Control Intervals. Each Control Interval contains some data and some free space for the addition of new records. Records in each Control Interval are sequenced by a key that can be numeric, alphabetic, or alphanumeric.

A set of Control Intervals are grouped together into a Control Area. The Control Area may also use several Control Intervals for free space as shown in the diagram. Associated with each Control Area is a Sequence Index Set, which points to the data contained in the Control Area. The Index Set also shows where free space is available in the Control Area.

The high key of each Index Set is referenced by an Index Set Level 1. This reduces the number of searches for a record and makes direct access of data more efficient. Larger files may also have an Index Set Level 2 and Level 3 as shown for greater referencing efficiency.

Because of the use of free space, new records may be added to the file without the need for an overflow area. In most cases, new records are inserted directly into the file. This is shown in Figure 8-21 with the insertion of ACCO into the file. Since Control Interval 1 has adequate free space, ACE is simply shifted to the right and ACCO is inserted.

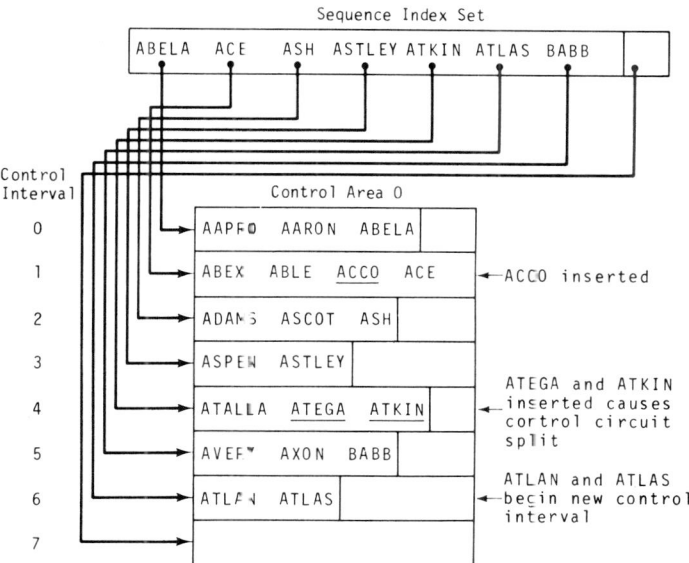

Figure 8-21. Adding new records to a virtual file.

When ATEGA is added to Control Interval 4, there is also room due to free space in the interval. When ATKIN is to be inserted, a minor reorganization occurs. This involves shifting ATLAN and ATLAS to the free space in Control Interval 6. This leaves room for ATKIN and some additional free space in interval 4. This use of free space leads to a low frequency of file maintenance on virtual files compared to an indexed file.

Because of the effectiveness of the virtual method, this type of organization is often used for data base files, which will be discussed more fully in the chapter on data base.

TERMS TO STUDY

Access Arm
Average Rotational Delay
Average Seek Time
Concentric Track
Control Area
Control Interval
Cylinder
Cylinder Index
Direct Access
Disk Pack
Free Space
Head Per Track

Indexed Sequential
Master Index
Optimum Blocking
Overflow
Randomize
Rotational Delay
Seek Time
Sequence Index Set
Track Capacity
Track Index
Track-To-Track Seek Time
Virtual Access Method

QUESTIONS FOR REVIEW

1. Describe the components (and their function) of a magnetic disk drive.
2. Discuss the operations necessary to read or write on disk.
3. What is meant by a cylinder on disk?
4. What are the differences between seek time, average seek time, and track-to-track seek time?
5. Describe the organization of records along a disk track.
6. What optimum blocking factor could be used on an IBM 3340 disk with records of 400 bytes in length and a maximum block size of 4000 bytes?
7. What factors contribute to the head per track disk's higher speed than most disks?

9. Discuss why it is more efficient to read a sequential file sequentially than an indexed file sequentially.
10. Why don't records use 100 percent of the space available on a direct access file?
11. What relationships exist between the master, cylinder, and track indexes on an Indexed Sequential file?
12. What are the advantages of a virtual file over an indexed file?
13. What is the function of free space in a virtual file? How does it differ from the overflow area in an indexed file?

QUESTIONS FOR DISCUSSION AND RESEARCH

1. Develop a file for storing personnel data for college employees. Describe fields used in each record. Choose an appropriate direct access storage device for the file. What file organization and access method(s) would you use?
2. Assume your file in problem 1 was sequential and stored on an IBM 3340. How many tracks of disk space will you use? What percentage of the disk pack is this? How much time would it take to read this file? (Ignore any processing or printing time.)
3. Discuss what you think are necessary timing considerations for an Indexed Sequential file. What are the effects of blocking, rotational delay, and seek time?

9

Other I/O Devices

OPTICAL CHARACTER RECOGNITION (OCR)

The use of Optical Character Recognition (OCR) equipment (Figure 9-1) goes back as far as 1955 although it rose to popularity only recently. The main argument for its use is that it reduces the manual keying of data and thereby decreases the time of data entry and the number of errors produced. OCR in a broad sense includes Optical Mark Recognition and Bar Code Recognition. In this section we will look at the character aspect of the optical systems.

OCR Fonts

Optically read characters can be found on a wide variety of documents. These range from continuous adding machine tapes to embossed credit cards. The fonts used depend upon the type of document and hardware in use and generally include imprinted, typed, and handwritten characters. Figure 9-2 shows some of the most commonly used fonts. The OCR-A font is the standard approved by the American National Standards Institute. It comes in three sizes: one for high speed printers and typewriters, a second for cash register and adding machine tapes, and a third for embossed plastic credit cards. The Farrington 7 B is used for plastic credit cards and the Farrington 12 F for typewriters and high speed printers. The E13B is an MICR (Magnetic Ink Character Recognition) code, which can also be read by some optical scanners. Finally, the Hand Print

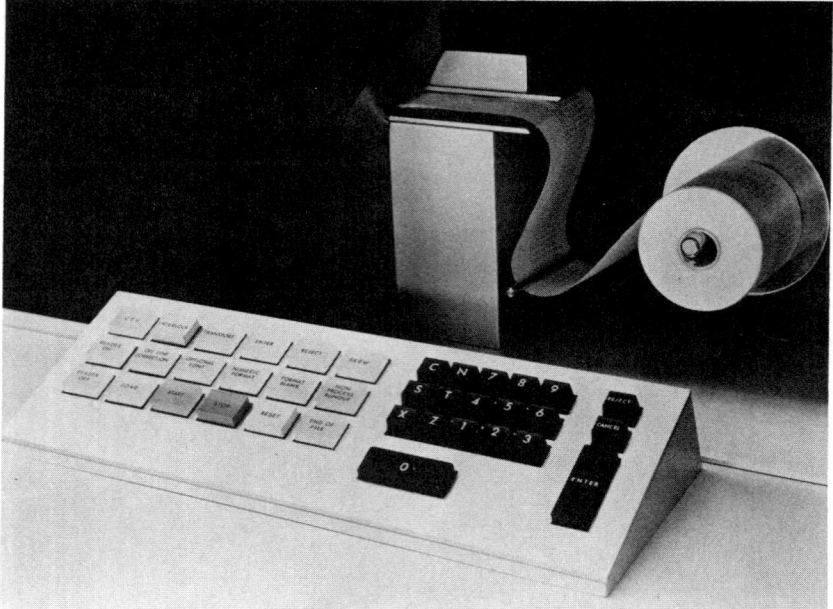

Figure 9-1. IBM 1285 optical reader. (*Courtesy of IBM Corporation*)

is the form used for handwriting the OCR code. These characters must be written as illustrated in Figure 9-2 with the character nearly filling the box on the form.

OCR Scanning Techniques

All optical scanning is accomplished by the ability of a scanner to sense varying degrees of reflected light. Whenever there is a contrast between the reflected light from a character and the reflected light from the background, the scanner can detect the shape of the character. Three techniques for scanning are discussed here; one uses a mechanical disk, and the other two use photocells.

Mechanical Disk Scanner. Figure 9-3 shows how a character and the background around it are flooded with light. The light is reflected from the document through a lens, a perforated rotating disk, and a fixed aperture to a photomultiplier tube. As the disk rotates, the photomultiplier sees more of the character until its entire shape is evident.

Single Column of Photocells. A single line of characters is moved beneath a row of photocells aligned at right angles to the line of characters

OPTICAL CHARACTER RECOGNITION (OCR)

OCR-A NUMERIC	0123456789 +-.$
OCR-A ALPHA	ABCDEFGHIJKLMNOPQRSTUVWXYZ
OCR-B Numeric	1234567890+-/<>
Farrington 7 B	0123456789 EPH+
Farrington 12F	0123456789-H
407	0123456789+.$-□
E13B	0123456789⑊⑈⑉⑊
1428 Numeric	0123456789 ./-+
Hand Print	0 1 2 3 4 5 6 7 8 9 X

Figure 9-2. Some of the most common OCR fonts. (*Courtesy of Canadian Datasystems*)

(Figure 9-4). At each position, the photocells sample the character until sufficient samples have been taken to identify the character. This method speeds up the sampling process and results in a higher speed reader.

Array of Photocells. The third and fastest method of character recognition uses an array of photocells that completely cover the character to be read (Figure 9-5). This permits the entire character to be read without scanning.

OCR Applications

Since OCR documents include a wide range of sizes, from 2¼ in. to 12 in. (5.7 cm. to 30.5 cm.) wide and 2½ in. to 14 in. (6.4 cm. to 35.6 cm.) long, as well as continuous forms, this makes OCR applicable to many application areas. A traditional use has been payment processing for utilities, oil companies, and retail stores. These companies often use OCR equipment to read payment stubs returned by the customer when remitting a payment.

Some banks use OCR to process checks and credit card sales drafts. The U.S. Federal Reserve Bank also uses OCR to verify, count, and sort bills.

Other uses include hospital registration, doctors' claim forms, attendance reporting, driver's license issuance, and word processing.

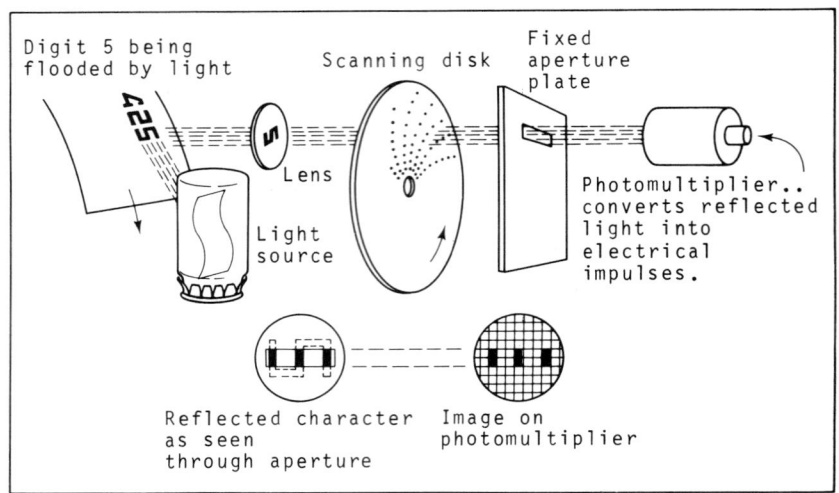

Figure 9-3. Mechanical disk scanner. (*Courtesy of Moore Business Forms*)

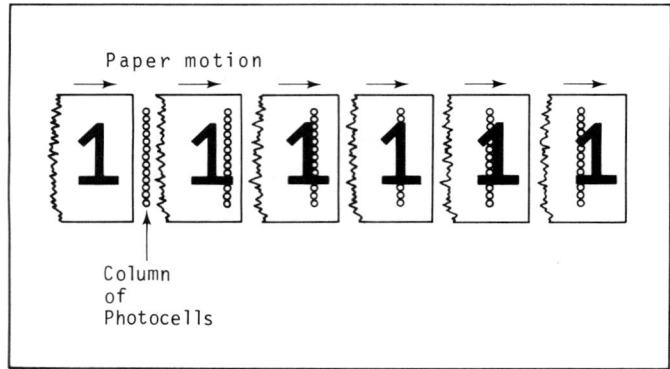

Figure 9-4. Single column of photocells. (*Courtesy of Moore Business Forms*)

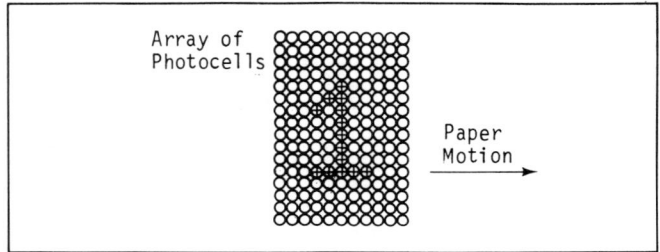

Figure 9-5. Array of photocells. (*Courtesy of Moore Business Forms*)

OPTICAL MARK RECOGNITION (OMR)

The use of Optical Mark Recognition has been with us as long as OCR. OMR is automatic machine reading of handwritten marks on cards or forms. The cards may be standard size Hollerith cards, or in some cases, such as the Hewlett-Packard system, a long card of 96 columns is used. An 80-column card may have up to 40 columns for OMR coding. Punched holes may coexist in the card with OMR coding. To code an OMR card, all that is required is a simple pencil stroke to represent a number or character. Errors are corrected by erasing the mark and entering the correct mark (see Figure 9-6).

Forms are also a popular vehicle for OMR. They may be up to 11⅛ in. (28.26 cm.) in length, although the ultimate size depends upon the machine used to read the document. Printing on forms or cards is done in reflective ink, which is quite visible to the eye but invisible to the Optical Mark Reader.

Mark reading does not require the complex scanning of OCR. Instead, the scanning head looks for the presence of marks (Figure 9-8). When a mark and its location are recognized, an impulse is emitted, which becomes input to a program The program then converts the impulse to a character. The value of a mark can be separately determined for each application because the program finally decodes the mark.

Applications for OMR are widespread. It has been quite popular in education for grading tests and examinations of the true/false and multiple-choice variety. In business, they may be used for payroll time recording, call reports for salesman or physicians, inventory control, and student grade reporting. In every case, a card or form is designed for the

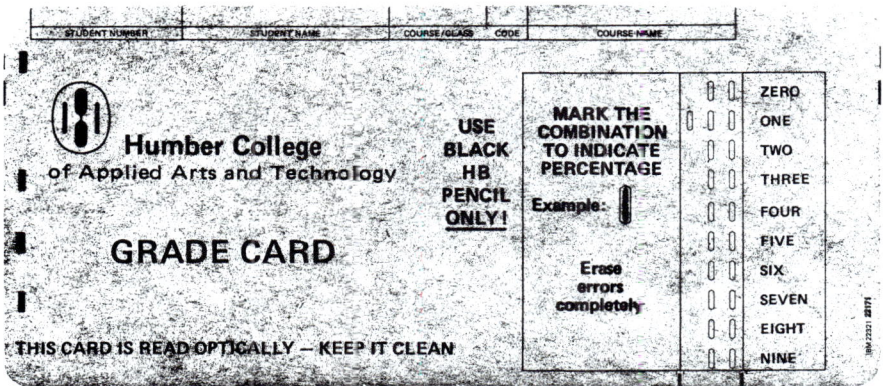

Figure 9-6. OMR grade reporting card. (*Courtesy of Humber College*)

192 OTHER I/O DEVICES

Figure 9-7. HP Model 7260A optical card reader. (*Courtesy of Hewlett-Packard*)

specific application. To use the document, the appropriate marks are entered. For instance, in the case of payroll time recording, the employee would mark the employee and department numbers and the number of hours worked. No keypunching is necessary because the marked card may be used immediately for computer input.

MAGNETIC INK CHARACTER RECOGNITION (MICR)

The use of magnetic ink characters is predominately found in the processing of checks by the banking industry. A check such as in Figure 9-9 is precoded on the lower left bottom edge with the branch and customer

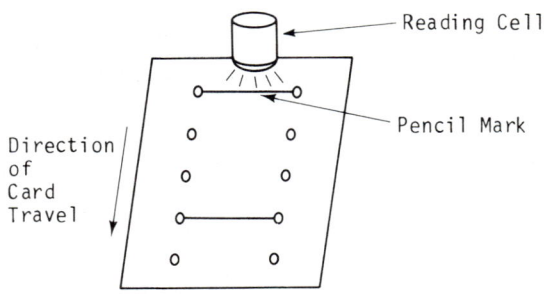

Figure 9-8. Mark sensing.

MAGNETIC INK CHARACTER RECOGNITION (MICR)

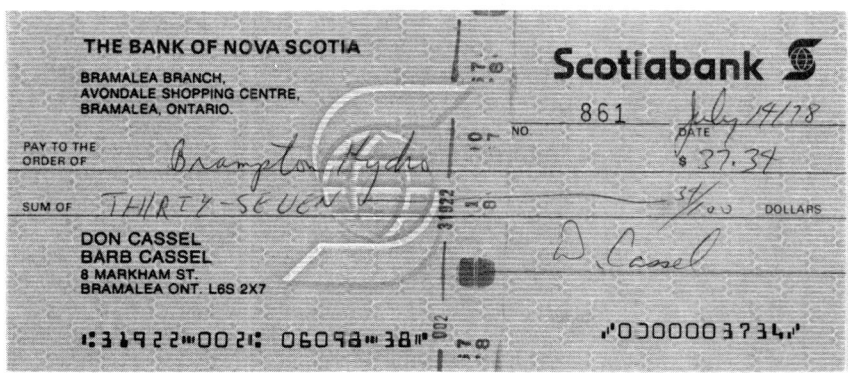

Figure 9-9. An MICR coded check.

account number in magnetic ink. When a check is written by the customer, it is sent to the bank's data processing center. Here the amount for which the check was written is encoded on the lower right bottom edge of the check. This check is then processed with thousands of other similar checks through a magnetic ink character reader/sorter (Figure 9-10). This device senses the magnetic codes and sorts the checks by branch and account number. Following sorting, the checks are returned to the respective branches, which process each check and send the cancelled checks to the customer.

MICR offers several advantages to banking. First the magnetic coding is both machine- and human-readable. The original document may be used as computer input since the reader/sorter may be used as a computer input device for direct processing of the checks. Finally, the encoding of branch, account, and amount on the check minimizes the possibility of error and speeds processing.

On the other side, MICR has a limited character set—as shown in Figure 9-11. It cannot read alphabetic or special characters. This tends to limit its flexibility and restrict the number of applications. Documents that have been damaged or improperly coded must be manually processed, thus delaying the operation.

Figure 9-11 shows the standard fourteen characters used in MICR. The first two rows are the numbers from one to nine and zero, which is quite evident to the reader. The last row of four characters are symbols used in the processing of the checks. These are from left to right, the "amount" symbol; "On-Us" symbol, indicating the commencing of the account number; the "transit" symbol; and the "dash" symbol, used as a hyphen or divider. Each of these symbols must be produced with a high degree of accuracy to be read correctly by the reader/sorter.

Figure 9-10. IBM 3890 magnetic ink character reader/sorter. (*Courtesy of IBM Corporation*)

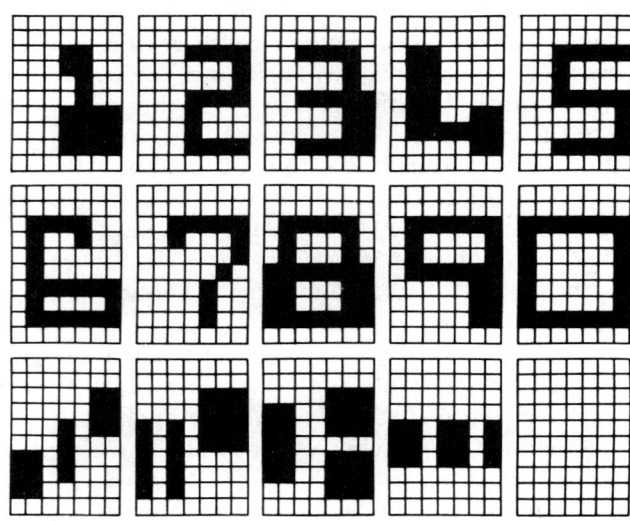

Figure 9-11. Magnetic ink character recognition code.

GRAPHIC DISPLAY

The old adage, "A picture is worth a thousand words," might well be changed as a result of computer graphics to read, "A picture is worth a thousand pages." The use of graphic display devices such as that shown in Figure 9-12 permits the graphic representation of data in picture form. Data shown in this form is easier to read and understand than the traditional report. Although many data are not suitable for graphic display, applications have been found in mapping, computer-assisted engineering design, computer-assisted instruction, earth resources management by NASA, aircraft flight simulation, and subdivision planning.

The most common use of graphics in business is graphs for displaying financial data. These graphs conveniently illustrate economic trends and show profit and loss statistics. Although graphs may also be produced on drum plotters, the CRT offers a valuable alternative. With graphic CRT and a keyboard or light pen, interaction with the data is possible. By changing portions of the data, the user may observe the effect this has on the overall trend. This is an invaluable tool for management and researchers.

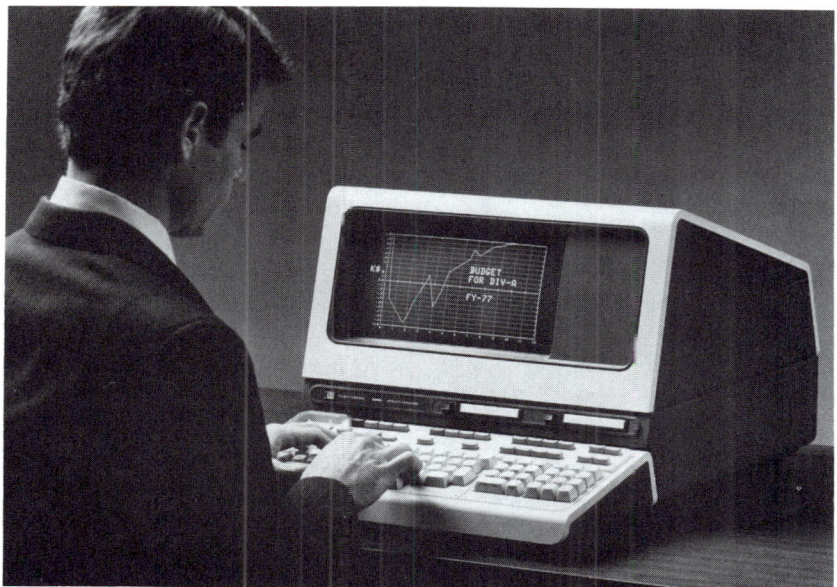

Figure 9-12. HP 2648A graphics terminal. (*Courtesy of Hewlett-Packard*)

Graphic displays are available with a black and white screen or in color (Figure 9-13). The Tektronix 4027 has a 64-color palette to choose from with up to 8 colors on the screen simultaneously. Although color is more expensive, it offers more creativity in the display of information and therefore has a greater potential effectiveness. However, color graphics are in their infancy, and much development in their use is needed.

The majority of graphic displays in use are the refresh tube variety. In this type, the image to be displayed is stored in the CRT memory and displayed on the screen from the memory. Since the screen cannot retain an image, the memory is constantly refreshed and displayed. Refresh technology provides the capability for rotation, zooming, blinking, and animation of the image.

Graphic displays also require special software for their support. Some of the common packages are VIVIDATA, designed for producing plots, charts, and illustrations for business and engineering; DISSPLA, a package that produces bar charts, pie charts, and graphs (DISSPLA is written in FORTRAN and can display three-dimensional graphics); and PLOT 10, which is an English language program supporting both black and white and color graphics.

Graphic presentation for business management should use a form appropriate for the type of data represented. The most common formats are:

1. Graphs—For the comparison of items over time
2. Bar Charts—Displays one amount over several time periods
3. Pie Charts—Breaks amounts into component parts

Figure 9-13. This HP 2627A color-graphics terminal may be used for business, engineering, process control, and industrial graphics applications.

GRAPHIC DISPLAY 197

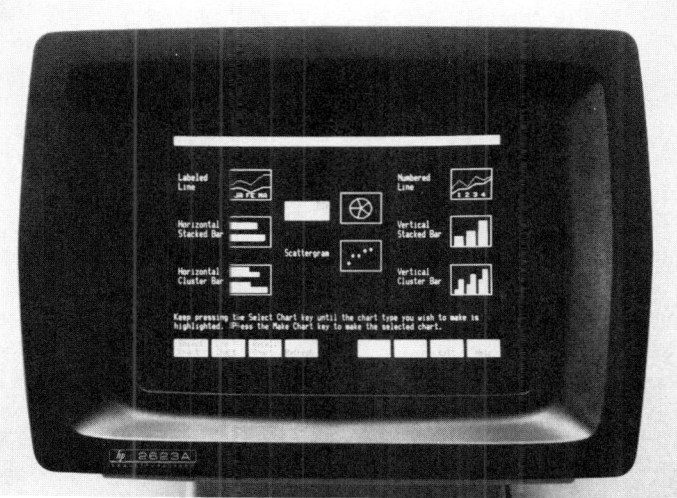

Figure 9-14. The HP 2623A graphics terminal operates with the Hewlett-Packard Business Graphics software package to create business charts.

Because of the concise and efficient representation of data in graphic form, we can expect real growth to continue in this form of computer output.

Figure 9-15. Tektronix 4051 graphic system. (*Courtesy of Tektronix*)

MASS STORAGE

According to Control Data, 70 percent of all magnetic tape data sets use less than 2 million bytes and 90 percent use less than 16 million bytes of data. One of the goals of Mass Storage is to replace large libraries of tape files and place them on line in a Mass Storage System (MSS). Not only will this reduce the size and cost of the library, but it eliminates a lot of mounting and dismounting of tape and disk. This is possible since MSS is a high capacity, low cost, on-line storage device.

The IBM 3850 Mass Storage System uses a roll of magnetic tape in a cartridge (Figure 9-16). Control Data's Mass Storage uses the same principles. In the IBM system, a cartridge can hold up to 50 million bytes of data. Cartridges are stored in cells in a storage unit, which has a honeycomb appearance (Figure 9-17). An arm mechanism extracts or inserts the cartridges as needed. If the tape is to be read or be written on, it is mechanically passed under a read/write head similar to a typical magnetic tape unit. The complete IBM 3850 can store 472 billion bytes of data.

In addition to providing for increased data storage, Mass Storage may also expand the way Virtual Storage is used. Data that is needed for processing goes to a high-speed direct access device. The program only

Figure 9-16. IBM 3850 mass storage cartridges. (*Courtesy of IBM Corporation*)

Figure 9-17. Mass storage cells. (*Courtesy of IBM Corporation*)

sees the data on the high-speed disk. The software takes care of all other data handling. After processing, the data, which may have been changed, is sent back to the MSS to replace the original. The data on the MSS is now in the most recent form and available again for immediate access.

COMPUTER OUTPUT MICROFILM (COM)

Microfilm and microfiche have been used in non-computer applications where large quantities of data requiring fast look-up is needed. These records were prepared from hard copy by means of a photographic reduction process. Since the development of COM, the microfilm has been produced as either a by-product of computer output or a direct computer output.

Microfilm is 16-mm roll film, something like the negative used in a camera. More popular is microfiche (Figure 9-18), which is a rectangular film 4 in. × 6 in. (10.16 cm. × 15.24 cm.) in size.

To produce microfiche from a computer, a COM recorder (Figure 9-19) is required. This can be either an on-line or off-line device. With an on-line COM recorder, the microfiche is a direct result of computer output. The more popular off-line recorder uses a magnetic tape for input that has been prepared by a computer. In the COM recorder, computer data is displayed a page at a time on a display tube. The recorder then photographs the page producing a 42× or 48× reduction in size. The negative produced is developed by the COM recorder resulting in the microfiche.

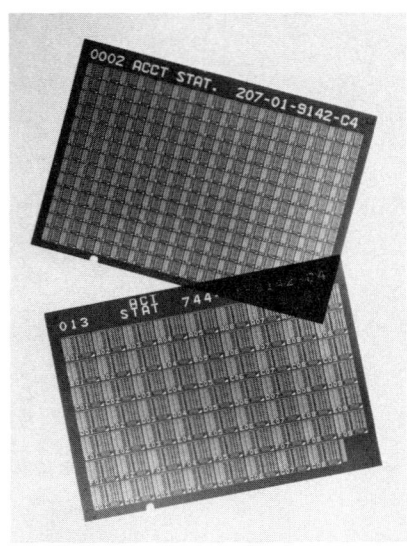

Figure 9-18. Microfiche card. (*Courtesy of Kodak*)

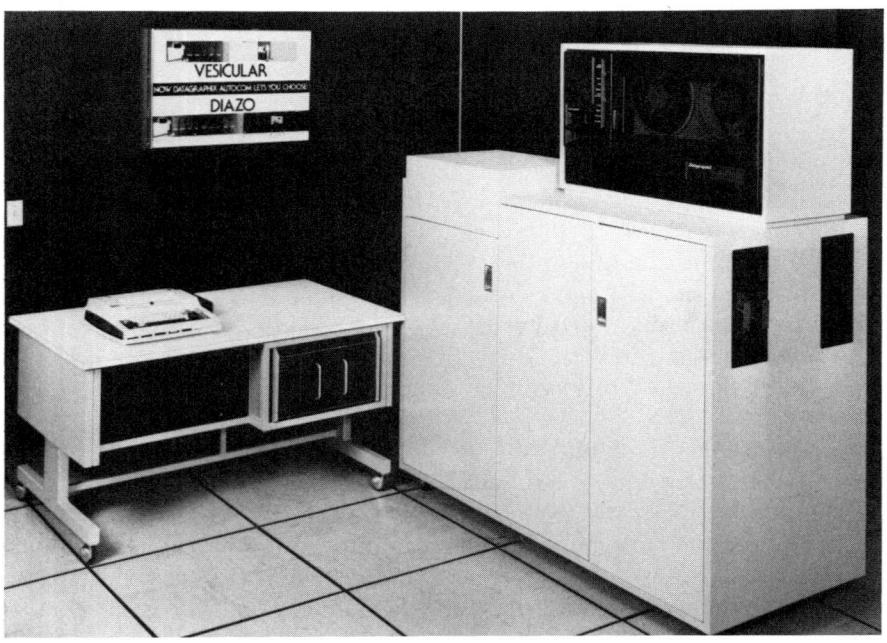

Figure 9-19. DatagraphiX COM recorder. (*Courtesy of DatagraphiX, Inc., a General Dynamics subsidiary*)

Benefits from using COM are many but, by its very nature, it must be limited to very high volumes of documents. Some of the advantages of COM produced microfiche are:

1. Compact—At 48× reduction, a microfiche can contain up to 269 pages (11 in. × 14 in.) of computer output.
2. Speed—While printers rarely exceed 2000 lines per minute, speed ranges for COM recorders vary from 10,000 to 60,000 lines per minute.
3. Multiple copies—Printers generally can print six-part forms on a single computer run. Additional copies require a second relatively slow computer run. Microfiche can be duplicated at up to 1000 copies per hour. The preparation of each new fiche is about one-third the cost of the original.
4. Ease of distribution—Because microfiche is lightweight and compact, distribution is simpler and less costly than paper. This is particularly valuable when documents must be mailed. In this case, microfiche reduces postage costs considerably.

COM is suitable to any application that produces high volumes of computer printout. Some analysts consider a volume as low as 200,000 pages per month to be a prime candidate for COM. As a result, users are to be found in banking, insurance, government, publishing, sales, and public utilities.

© *Datamation*

DRUM PLOTTER

The drum plotter (Figure 9-20) provides a hard copy of computer graphics. Engineering designs, maps, suburban planning, and charts may be drawn on paper as a computer output. These application drawings are produced by drawing lines relative to an X- and Y-axis by moving a pen and paper under program control. Plotters use ballpoint or felt-tipped pens as well as liquid ink pens for high quality work. Some plotters will even select pens of different colors for multicolored graphics.

As the pen and paper are moved, the point is set down on the paper to produce a line. A gap in the line or a new line is produced by the machine raising the pen and moving it to a new position before setting it down again.

Curves, arcs, and circles are plotted with about .05 mm. (.002 in.) resolution. This means that individual increments of the pen's position are not discernible to the naked eye, thus resulting in smooth curves. Typical axial plotting speed is 25.4 cm. (10 in.) per second.

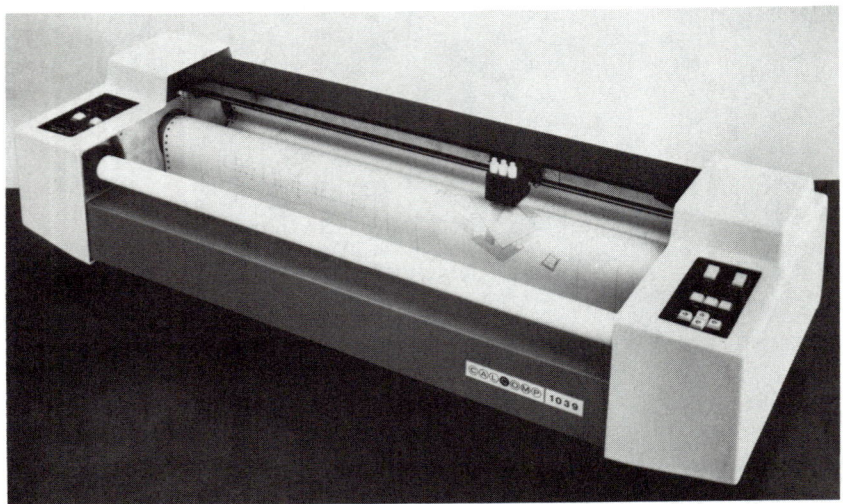

Figure 9-20. Drum plotter. (*Courtesy of Calcomp*)

TERMS TO STUDY

COM
Font
Graphic Display
Mass Storage System
MICR

Microfiche
Microfilm
OCR
OMR
Plotter

QUESTIONS FOR REVIEW

1. What is meant by CCR? What fonts are used for printers, typewriters, credit cards, and handwriting?
2. How does OCR read the character from a document?
3. What is OMR? How does it differ from OCR? What applications use OMR documents?
4. Describe the use of MICR in the banking industry.
5. What are the benefits of graphic display over the digital display?
6. What types of files are likely to be replaced by a Mass Storage System?
7. What is the difference between microfilm and microfiche?
8. How does a COM recorder produce microfiche?
9. Describe the advantages of COM over printed reports.
10. In what way is the plotter different from most other output devices? What device is it most like?

PROBLEMS FOR RESEARCH AND DISCUSSION

1. There are many other devices, not discussed in this chapter, available on today's market. Some of these are audio response, voice recognition, automated tape library, security devices, array processors, and intelligent terminals. Find out what several of these devices are and discuss their function and application.

2. Very likely the general availability of mass storage will increase and/or disk storage will grow in capacity and decrease in price—the trend in recent years. If these events occur, what will be the impact on main storage devices? What will be the impact if main storage prices drop with a comparable increase in capacity?

10

Central Processing Unit

The CPU, or Central Processing Unit (Figure 10-2), is the heart, or more accurately, the brain of the computer system. All activity from input to output is under its control. The CPU is essentially an electronic device and is the fastest of all hardware devices. Within the CPU resides the program that supplies all of its instructions. Depending on the instructions given, the CPU can do payroll calculations or satellite orbital trajectory calculations. In other words, CPUs are general purpose devices and can be used for any application determined by the program used. Most computers are of this type. Special purpose computers are designed to perform only one application and can only be used for that purpose. For instance, the computer used to control the fuel injection system in a Volkswagen Rabbit is special purpose.

PHYSICAL STRUCTURE

Components of a CPU

A CPU consists of the three basic components: the arithmetic-logic unit (ALU), control section, and main storage (Figure 10-3). The first two are composed of miniaturized solid state components, while main storage may

Figure 10-1. IBM System/370 model 3032 processor. (*Courtesy of IBM Corporation*)

be one of a number of different technologies ranging from magnetic core to laser holographic storage.

These three units are interconnected by wiring to form a completely integrated unit. Even the simplest operations such as adding two numbers bring all three units into play.

Figure 10-2. IBM 4341 central processor. (*Courtesy of IBM Corporation*)

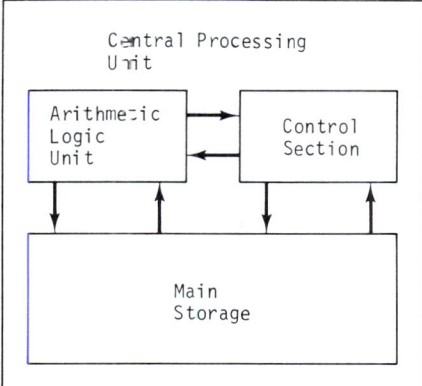

Figure 10-3. Components of a CPU.

KEY CONCEPT

Instructions

An instruction is the element of a program that directs the operation of the computer. It may command the CPU to add or move data, to set an indicator on or off, to specify the location of the next instruction, or to set an input/output operation into action.

The instruction consists of two parts: an operation and an operand:

1. The operation specifies to add, move, read, or branch.
2. The operand specifies the address or addresses of the data to be acted upon during the operation.

A	0005 0025
Operation	Operand

The A means this is an add operation. The data in address 0025 is to be added to the data in address 0005. This is a two-address operand.

Figure 10-4. NCR Century 300 System. (*Courtesy of NCR Corporation*)

When any program instruction is to be executed, the CPU goes through a number of cycles called machine cycles. A machine cycle is the basic unit of time in the CPU and is the basis upon which CPU speed is measured. For instance, the NCR Century 300 has a memory cycle time of 650 nanoseconds.

Each instruction requires a given number of cycles to complete its operation (Figure 10-4). The number of cycles required depends upon the type of instruction and the design of the CPU. An add would take two machine cycles, while a multiply or divide would require three or more cycles. The number of cycles determines how fast an instruction can be executed and the ultimate speed of the CPU.

The two cycles for adding are the instruction cycle and execution cycle (Figure 10-5). The instruction cycle is the time needed to get the program instruction from main storage and place it into an instruction register. During this process, the control section interprets the instruction and determines the action to be taken.

Next, the execution cycle gets the data from main storage and performs the addition. This involves the arithmetic portion of the ALU. The result of the add could be placed in an accumulator or in main storage, depending on the type of add operation.

Arithmetic and Logic Unit. The ALU contains the circuitry to perform arithmetic and logical operations. For arithmetic operations, the ALU

PHYSICAL STRUCTURE 209

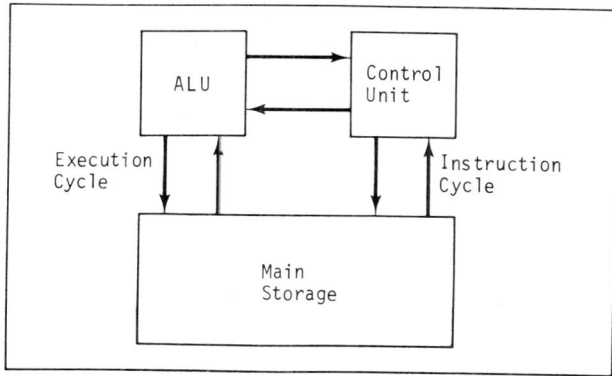

Figure 10-5. Machine cycles.

provides for addition, subtraction, multiplication, and division. All operations are based on the principle of addition. Subtraction uses the complement method of addition. Multiplication uses repetitive addition, and division, repetitive subtraction (Figure 10-6).

An example in Figure 10-7 shows a series of steps using the arithmetic portion of the ALU. As each step proceeds, the ALU uses its own storage device to do the calculation. Intermediate results such as Extended Cost and Sales Tax use either main storage or a register, depending on the program in use.

The logic portion of the ALU performs decision or comparison operations, comparing two data items and finding the logical relationship between them. An item may be either equal to, less than, or greater than another item. The result of this comparison sets on an indicator in the ALU that may be tested by the program. On the basis of this test, branching may occur in the program.

Figure 10-8 shows an example of decision making. In this case, a Sales Code is compared to a constant of 2. If it is equal, the program proceeds to the next step. If it is not equal, the program branches to another part labelled A.

In the second decision, if Sales Amount is greater than 2000, then a branch occurs to the 5 percent commission calculation. Otherwise, the program will branch to the 3 percent calculation.

Control Section. The control section coordinates all operations occurring in the central processing unit. It determines when program instructions are to be read and executed, when to use the arithmetic or logic portion of the ALU, when to read input data, or when to write output.

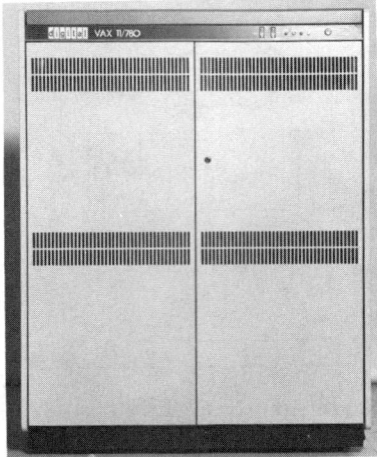

Figure 10-6. The Digital VAX-11/750 is a 32-bit minicomputer central processing unit. This VAX computer is one of a series of minicomputers suitable for educational applications. (*Courtesy of Digital Equipment Corporation*)

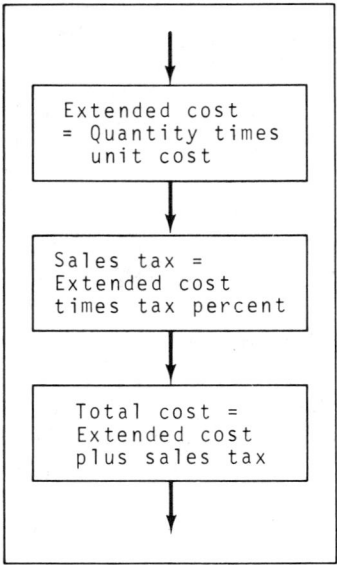

Figure 10-7. Arithmetic operations.

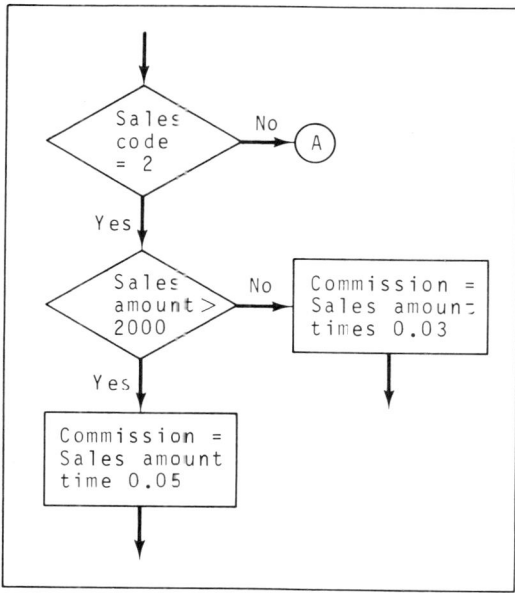

Figure 10-8. Logical operations.

In short, it administers all of the activity needed to run a program successfully.

When a program instruction is to be executed, the control section first retrieves it from storage. Next, the instruction is interpreted to determine the necessary action. This could mean an arithmetic operation is needed—or a compare or a data move, or a branch. After this is determined, the appropriate part of the control section or ALU is used to execute the instruction. Often this process will require the use of registers.

A register is a separate storage area used by the control section and ALU. It is usually one or two words in length and can be used for a variety of purposes as outlined in Figure 10-9. Registers are only used for temporary storage, and therefore most computers have a rather small number of them. For instance, the IBM mainframe computers have only 16 general purpose registers used for accumulators/storage and index registers.

Main Storage Unit. In addition to the ALU and control section, the CPU also has a main storage unit. Sometimes called memory, internal storage, or primary storage, it is the device containing the program and some data during execution. This is direct access high-speed storage, which has a limited capacity in contrast to auxiliary or secondary storage,

212   CENTRAL PROCESSING UNIT

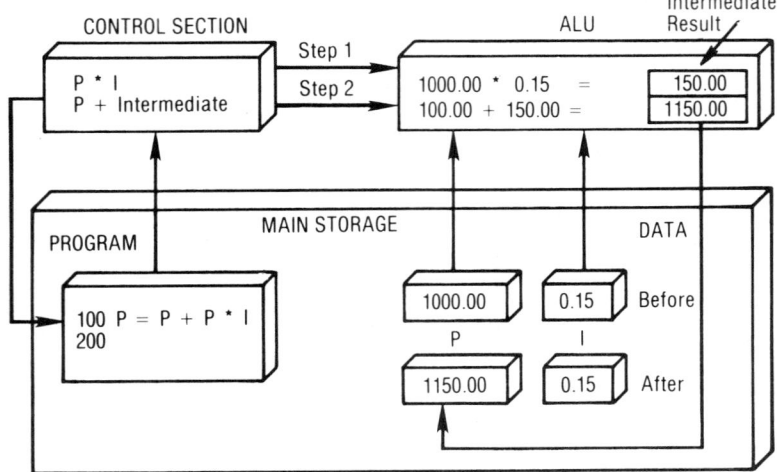

Figure 10-9. This demonstrates how a calculation for simple interest is done by the CPU. The program takes the principle (P) and interest (I) and calculates the value of the investment after 1 year with simple interest. After the instruction has been executed by the ALU, the result is replaced into memory location P as defined by the program. The control unit then gets the next instruction from the program.

Figure 10-10. Univac 1110 processor. (*Courtesy of Sperry-Univac*)

Registers

1. Address register—Used for addressing main storage.
2. Accumulator—Used for arithmetic operations.
3. Instruction register—Program instructions are stored here while they are executed.
4. Storage register—used to reference storage addresses.
5. Index register—Addresses tables or arrays.

Figure 10-11. Types of registers.

which is somewhat slower but has a relatively high capacity. Figure 10-12 shows some of the types of main and auxiliary storage.

PRINCIPLES OF STORAGE TECHNOLOGY

Main storage began with magnetic core, which had been the most widely used method since the 1950s. However, the search for smaller, more compact, and faster technologies led to thin film and plated wire, which are also magnetic in nature. The development of solid state components led to the use of MOS (metal-oxide semiconductor) and integrated circuit memory devices. These are even more compact and operate at higher speeds than previous technologies.

Although the physical characteristics of storage devices vary considerably, the principle of storage is similar in each case. Data is stored as a series of 0 and 1 bits. These bits are grouped to form characters using codes such as ASCII or EBCDIC.

Main Storage Types	*Auxiliary Storage Types*
Core Thin Film Plated Wire MOS Magnetic Bubble CCD	Magnetic Disk Magnetic Tape Mass Storage

Figure 10-12. Types of main and auxiliary storage.

Storage size is measured in terms of the number of bytes or, in some cases, words available in main memory where 1K = 1024. A 64K CPU will hold 65,536 bytes of data where each byte consists of 8 bits or binary digits plus a parity bit. One million bytes of storage is represented by 1M.

Some computers measure storage size in words rather than bytes. A word may be 4, 8, 12, or 16 bits in length, depending on the type of computer, so size comparisons with byte memory must be made with due caution. For instance, a 128K computer using 16-bit words is equivalent in size to a 256K-byte computer.

Data may be accessed from these bytes or words based on the address of the storage location where the data is stored. Each storage location has a unique address, which contains a unit of information such as a number or character. A field of data, such as a 5-byte quantity, will require five storage addresses. The time taken to access the data from storage is called access time. Higher speed storage units measure their access time in nanoseconds.

Magnetic Core

The first highly efficient method of storing data in the CPU used magnetic core (Figure 10-13). Core was developed early in the first generation of computers. A core is a ferromagnetic ring with a center hole. In appearance it is doughnut-shaped, but it is only about the size of a pinhead.

Core is a low cost device for main storage. It has very low power consumption, is durable, and generates very little heat. It is also non-

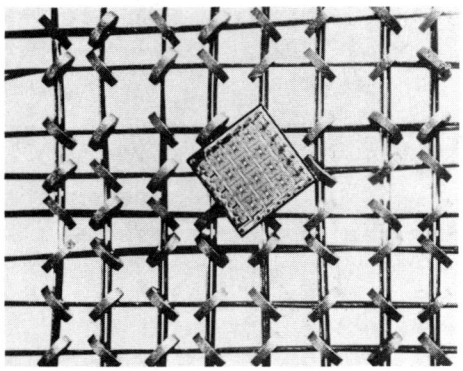

Figure 10-13. Magnetic core and MOS storage comparison. (*Courtesy of IBM Corporation*)

Figure 10-14. An Intel microprocessor chip. This silicon chip contains the entire central processing unit for a typical microcomputer. (*Courtesy of Intel Corporation*)

Figure 10-15. The Intel microprocessor photographically enlarged. The lines on this picture are the circuits for data flow through the central processor as logical and arithmetic operations are executed. (*Courtesy of Intel Corporation*)

volatile, meaning it will not lose data when a power interruption occurs although other processing failures usually override the advantage of non-volatility.

KEY CONCEPT

Fixed and Variable Length Words

Data can be organized and addressed in either fixed or variable length words. When fixed word lengths are used, all data are of a predefined length such as 31 bits plus a sign bit. All processing is done using parallel operations for efficiency. Registers, accumulators, storage, and files are designed to accommodate the fixed word length.

Variable length words permit data to vary in length from one to a predefined number of bytes. On the IBM 4300 and 3000 series, the limit is 32,767 bytes. Operations on data use serial methods. Since fields can be almost any length, it is necessary for the instruction to contain a length code, which defines the length of each field involved in an operation. Some computers combine both fixed and variable length words in one system (see Chapter 7).

Thin Film

The first computer to use thin film for main storage was the Univac 1107 in 1961. This method of storage was more compact and used less power than magnetic core. A sheet of plastic or glass is printed with an array of copper wires. At the intersection of these wires is a small metal dot. The dot acts much like a magnetic core and can be magnetized in one of two directions (Figure 10-16) to represent a 1 or 0 state.

Plated Wire

Another storage technique uses a method similar to thin film except that a metallic coating is placed around a wire or rod as shown in Figure 10-17. Around this coated wire are wrapped two small wires carrying the writing current. When current flows, a small amount of magnetism is recorded on the surface of the plated wire to represent a 0 or 1.

Plated wire has all the speed, size, and power advantages of thin film. Manufacturing is fully automated—leading to a low cost storage device.

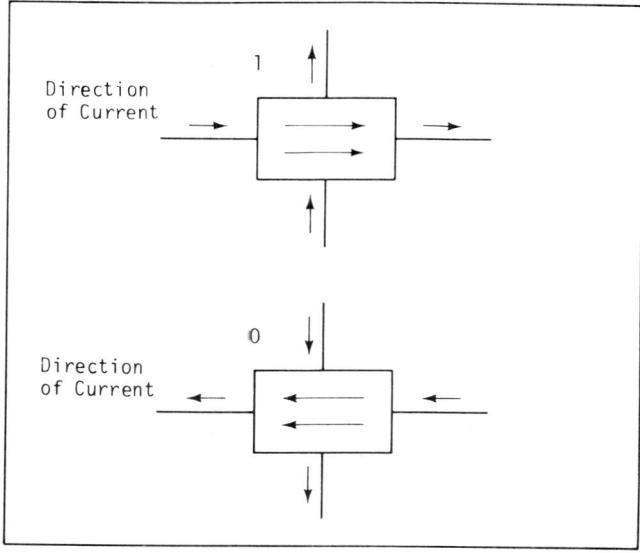

Figure 10-16. Recording on thin film.

Metal Oxide Semiconductor (MOS)—Integrated Circuit

Several solid state storage techniques are in use that are based on the principle of storing data electronically on small chips of silicon. A typical memory chip is about half a centimeter square (Figure 10-18) and can

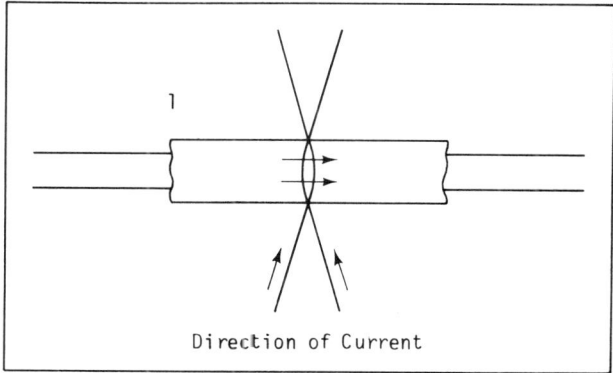

Figure 10-17. Plated wire recording.

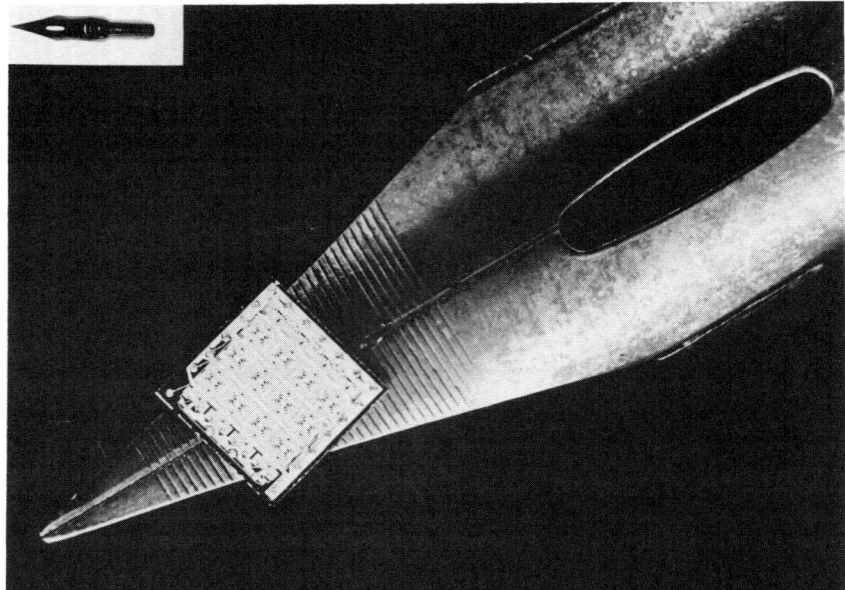

Figure 10-18. IBM's monolithic storage chip. (*Courtesy of IBM Corporation*)

store 64,000 bits of data. The technology has developed to the stage of what is called large scale integration (LSI) and very large scale integration (VLSI). Integrated circuits (ICs) are used in the majority of computers where it is called monolithic storage. Semiconductor memory is volatile, meaning that it loses data when the power to the device is interrupted or turned off.

Charged Coupled Devices (CCD)

These devices were invented by the Bell Labs in the early seventies. CCDs (Figure 10-19) store data as packets of charge within a semiconductor chip. The circuitry to store, move, and access the packets also resides on the same chip.

A chip can store up to 65,000 bits and is about ten times faster than magnetic bubble storage. It is also a volatile storage method like MOS.

Magnetic Bubble

This device uses bubbles, which are tiny magnetized areas that exist in a specially grown crystalline material. It is currently in use by IBM and Texas Instruments computers.

Invented by Bell Labs, bubbles are considered to be a likely replacement for low cost storage devices like tape and floppy disk. It is nonvolatile and uses very little power with less heat radiation than other storage devices. A magnetic bubble device, the same size as an LSI memory, could store up to 70,000 bits of data.

The magnetic bubble memory shown in Figure 10-20 is available from Texas Instruments. It has a capacity of 92,304 bits and measures 2.54 cm. (1 in.) by 2.79 cm. (1.1 in.) by 1.02 cm. (0.4 in.). Expected applications are intelligent terminals, programmable calculators, word processing, voice storage, and disk storage replacement. The bubble chip is

Figure 10-19. Fairchild 7464 charged coupled memory. (*Courtesy of Fairchild Camera and Instrument Corporation*)

Figure 10-20. Texas Instrument 92K-bit bubble memory. (*Courtesy of Texas Instruments*)

composed of a gadolinium-gallium garnet substrate upon which a magnetic epitaxial film is grown. The diameter of the magnetic bubble domain is 5 microns.

Laser Holographic System

First built by RCA in 1972, the laser holographic system uses a laser beam passed through a multilayered film of cerium oxide on a glass substrate plate. The plate is called a random phase shifter; it disperses the laser beam as it passes through. This system has about 1000 times the storage density of semiconductor memory.

Virtual Storage

One problem plaguing programmers from the earliest computer application was making programs fit into the available storage space. It seems that no matter how large main storage was, someone would write a program that needed even more space. To solve this problem, a new technique, called virtual storage by some and virtual memory by others, was developed. Various interpretations of this method have been used by Burroughs, Univac, Control Data, and IBM.

The basic concept shown in Figure 10-21 extends the capacity of main storage (called real storage) by additional storage space on a direct access device (called virtual storage). A CPU with 500K of real storage might also use 500K of virtual storage. The program is divided into sections called pages, represented by the small squares in the diagram. A page is 2K in size on IBM computers. Some of the pages will be empty and others will contain program codes.

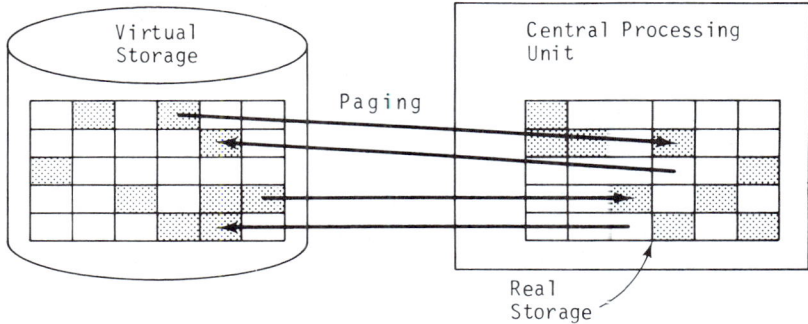

Figure 10-21. Virtual storage.

As the program is executed, inactive pages will be placed in virtual storage. This process is called page-out. When a page is to be executed, the CPU looks for it in real storage. If it is there, it can be executed; but if it is in virtual storage, it must first page-in to real storage prior to execution.

Although this system permits larger programs to be run, they also require longer to run because of the paging activity. When paging becomes a major activity, the system is said to be thrashing. In this situation, performance of the computer can deteriorate considerably. The solution is to reorganize the programs causing the excessive paging. The use of top down structured programming techniques often improves this situation. Failing this, it is necessary to order more real storage.

CHANNELS

Programs need to have access to input data for processing and in turn create a variety of outputs. The activity of the input and output devices used is controlled by a channel or I/O (input/output) processor. A channel is an electronic device connected between the CPU and input/output devices (Figure 10-22).

The channel acts like a small CPU and executes program instructions in a way similar to the main processor. In many cases, it is physically part of the box containing the CPU. When the channel has finished an operation, such as reading an input record, it interrupts the CPU to tell it the record is available. In this way, the channel frees the CPU from the task of performing I/O operations. This means the CPU is able to execute program instructions while the channel is busy processing I/O operations.

222 CENTRAL PROCESSING UNIT

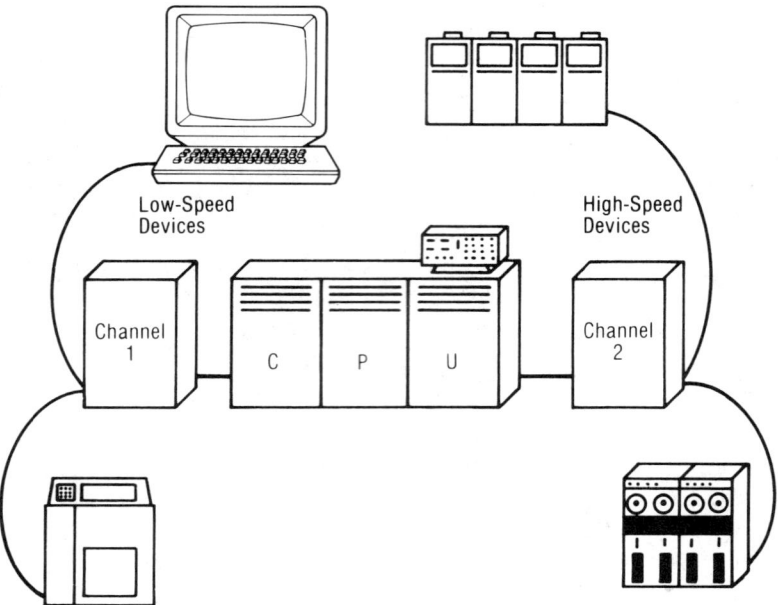

Figure 10-22. Channels.

This simultaneous operation is called Process I/O Overlap since both occur at the same time. When there are two or more channels on the system, several input and output operations may also be overlapped.

Figure 10-23 shows how Process I/O Overlap works. The first input record is read, and as record 1 is being processed, record 2 is read by the channel. During the next unit of time, the output for record 1 is produced. At this same time, record 2 is processed while record 3 is being read. This technique improves the efficiency of the computer because waiting time for I/O and processing of a record is minimized.

There are two basic types of channels. One, called a multiplexor channel, is used primarily for slow-speed devices. The other, a selector channel, is used on high-speed devices.

The multiplexor channel passes data one byte at a time from each low-speed device. This interleaving of bytes from each device gives the effect of all devices working simultaneously. If a high-speed device is attached to a multiplexor channel, an entire physical record is transferred from this device causing all slower devices to stop temporarily.

A selector channel is used primarily for magnetic devices such as tape, disk, and drum. It transfers physical records from a single device

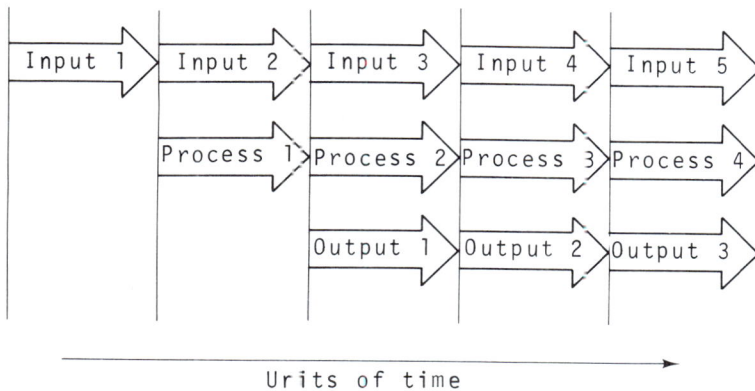

Figure 10-23. Process I/O overlap.

at one time. While one device is reading a record, all other devices on the channel with be inactive. Because of the higher speed, slower devices are not compatible with a selector channel.

CONTROL UNITS

Between the channel and the input/output device is a control unit (Figure 10-24). It is also called a data synchronizer or buffer. One of the functions of a control unit is for coding and decoding data from the I/O device. A device may operate in Hollerith, or ASCII, and needs to be recoded into EBCDIC or whatever code the CPU uses. The reverse is true when data flows from the CPU to the device.

When two or more devices are attached to the same control unit, the control unit determines the priority between devices. A higher priority device will have its requests for I/O serviced first while a lower priority one will have to wait.

The control unit also acts like a traffic routing officer. When data comes through the channel, the control unit directs the record to the correct device. Physically, the control unit is situated close to the I/O device and in some cases shares the same frame.

224 CENTRAL PROCESSING UNIT

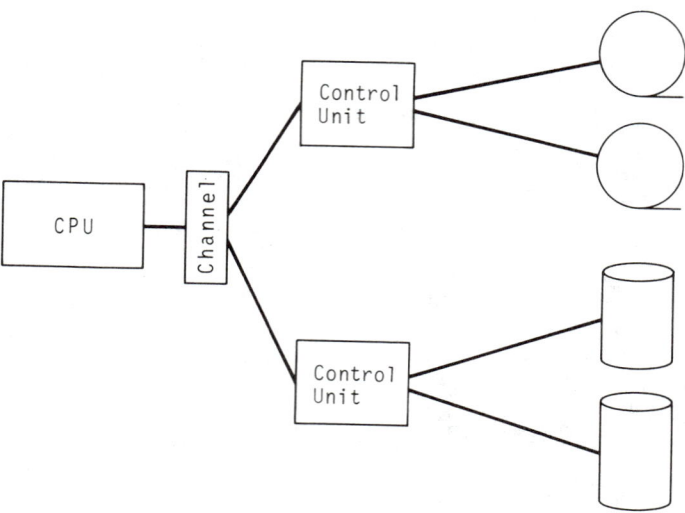

Figure 10-24. Location of control units.

TERMS TO STUDY

Arithmetic-Logic Unit
Central Processing Unit (CPU)
Channel
Charged Coupled Device (CCD)
Control Section
Control Unit
Cycle
Execution Cycle
Fixed Length Word
Instruction
Instruction Cycle
Laser Holographic
Machine Cycle
Magnetic Bubble

Main Storage
Non-Volatile
Operand
Operation
Paging
Plated Wire
Process I/O Overlap
Register
Semiconductor Memory
Thin Film
Thrashing
Variable Length Word
Virtual Storage
Volatile

QUESTIONS FOR REVIEW

1. Describe the physical structure of the CPU.
2. What is the difference between a general and special purpose computer?

3. What is an instruction, what does it do, and what are its components?
4. Describe a machine cycle.
5. Discuss the procedure followed by the CPU when two numbers are added together.
6. What are the two basic sections of the ALU? Describe their purpose.
7. What are registers? What kinds are there and what are they used for? Where are they located in the CPU?
8. What is the difference between main and auxiliary storage?
9. Discuss each of the types of main storage.
10. How is storage size measured?
11. What is the difference between volatile and non-volatile storage?
12. Compare the differences between fixed and variable length words.
13. Describe the function of virtual storage.
14. What is a channel and what is its purpose in a computer system?
15. Describe the concept of Process I/O Overlap.
16. What is the purpose of a control unit or data synchronizer?

QUESTIONS FOR RESEARCH AND DISCUSSION

1. Select a specific central processor. Perhaps the one used by your school. What main storage type is used? What type(s) of instruction format(s)? What is the memory cycle time? Does it do serial or parallel arithmetic or both? Does it use registers? What kind? Is storage addressed by words or bytes?
2. The IBM 4300 series uses five basic types of instruction formats. These are RR, RS, RX, SI, and SS. Find out the detail of these formats and discuss the meaning of each operand.

11

Minicomputers and Microcomputers

This chapter focuses on two types of computers that have made dramatic impacts on the computer industry. The "minis" and the "micros" are still essentially computers, and therefore the majority of the points in this book are directly related to them. However, it is the appearance of the machines and the markets that they have entered that make them different with respect to the large business computer. Two main sections will now follow: the first will discuss minicomputers, and the second will talk about microcomputers with references to such topics as background, components, and special markets.

MINICOMPUTERS

When one is asked to conjure up an image of the appearance of a typical computer room, the following characteristics usually emerge: false floor to hide the cables, special humidity and temperature controls, perhaps 1000 square feet to store the one and a half ton machine, transformers to generate the required voltage and so on . . . right? Well, if you were a minicomputer salesman in the late 1960s you would say emphatically . . . wrong! The reason is that your new product

1. Needs no special wiring.
2. Requires no special air-conditioning features.

3. Runs on standard 115-volt electric power.
4. Is a table-top size computer.
5. Is portable (weighing less than fifty pounds).

The prospective client would usually respond with a comment such as, "You are probably just selling a large calculator and are trying to capitalize on the word computer." The salesman could then come back with, "What about a calculator with 32K memory, 5-megabyte disk (fixed), floppy disks, 165 character/sec. printer, and two display screens, for a purchase price of approximately $100,000.00?"

And the battle was on. . . .

General Characteristics of the First Minis

The use of new storage techniques MOS (metal oxide semiconductor) and bipolar LSI (large scale integration) could generate integrated circuits that were small enough so that a central processing unit could be represented in a unit of hardware the size of a typewriter. Although a specific definition of a mini was almost impossible, it was generally described as a machine having the following:

1. A 16- to 32-bit word length with parallel processing.
2. A smaller instruction set than the larger machines.
3. A maximum of 64K main memory.
4. No special environmental considerations (as previously described).
5. Secondary storage on disk (usually floppies or diskettes although some units did have tape storage in cartridges and cassettes).
6. A purchase price ranging from $20,000.00 to $200,000.00 (even at the top end, the price was still a far cry from the cost of the larger computers).

The mini was originally intended for the Original Equipment Manufacturers (OEMs) who would incorporate them into their own products or systems. For example, a mini might be employed as a front-end machine to provide more sophistication in data-entry editing. In other words, a mini might receive all the data that was being entered into the main computer and perform all of the editing functions that might normally be performed by the large machine. In this way, a lot of "straightforward" tasks could be removed from the expensive main computer so that it could be "earning its keep" handling the more sophisticated update functions.

Uses for the Mini

When the main minicomputer CPU was combined with secondary storage devices and readers and printers, a system was born that could be acquired by users who at first did not think they had the system or volume of transactions to warrant the cost of electronic data processing. As such, minis soon started to turn up in libraries, pharmacies, small accounting offices, traffic control applications, instrumentation test and control systems, typesetting and photocomposition, and numerous other areas that took advantage of the economical but efficient machines. Many of these users were comparatively unsophisticated types who wanted a complete, inexpensive data processing system installed on a turnkey basis.

Branch offices, who before had to send all their data to the head office for computer processing, could now handle a large percentage of their work at the branch using a mini. The mini's acting in this role would communicate with the host headoffice computer via telecommunications for updating requirements. Another use of the mini was for companies that were already paying for a time-sharing service. These firms found that they could replace the service with a mini and have an associated cost savings and still have all the computing requirements they needed.

KEY CONCEPT

TURNKEY

A term to describe a computer system that is all set up with nothing for the user to do but "turn the key" and operate. All the programming is done, and the software is set up to guide the user through the system.

Minis in the 1970s

The minis at first were machines suited for a specific or pre-defined function and were weak in software support—for example, data-base concepts and alternative programming languages. Soon however, the full complement of high-level languages such as COBOL, RPG II, BASIC, and FORTRAN, as well as complete file-access techniques and report writing facilities, were developed.

The mini market grew tremendously over the decade of the 1970s, and predictions indicated no signs of decline as the 1980s approached. Figure 11-1 shows the growth in sales during the 1970s and indicates that a large percentage of sales was still to the Original Equipment Man-

"Well, let's see if the front office thinks THIS one is simple enough to operate!"
© *Creative Computing*

ufacturers. Mass production techniques and aggressive pricing strategies accounted for a lot of this success. Also, many companies that required an interactive system (i.e., terminals and on-line facilities with the CPU) found that the performance of some minis exceeded that of a mainframe machine. This point is based on the fact that the architecture itself of the CPU of a mini has always been directed towards interactivity rather than having software programs loaded in the CPU handle the interactive requirements. The Digital Equipment Organization with its PDP series of minicomputers took the lead in the market in the late 1960s and has not looked back since. Other entrants in the mini market are such firms as Data General, Hewlett-Packard, and Wang Laboratories.

Minis in the 1980s

In the first couple of years in the 1980s, the sales toppled the six billion barrier, e.g., 1981, $6.213 billion and 1982, $6.486 billion. (Note here that all statistics refer to the top 15 mini manufacturers and do not include IBM's minicomputer stats, which are roughly half of the totals presented.) However, things were not going well across the board. The average annual growth rate started to drop to 7 percent in an industry that had averaged 19 percent per year during the 70s. Some firms exited from the competition while others survived by introducing price cutting programs. Many customers were starting to consolidate their equipment selection to one vendor, i.e., if you have an IBM mainframe, then you will use an IBM mini.

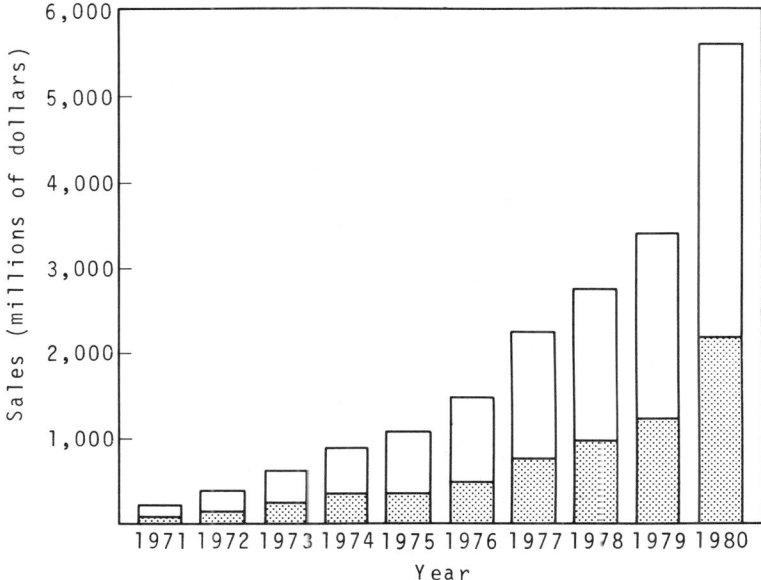

Figure 11-1. This bar chart shows minicomputer sales to firms using them as their main machine or one of their computers (white area) and to OEMs (shaded area).

Is there any one reason for this sudden drop in interest in minis? Yes, the continuing proliferation of the microcomputer. Many of the application areas typically created on a mini such as Inventory, Accounts Payable, etc., were now being developed and implemented on microcom-

Figure 11-2. The PDP-11 by D.E.C. (example of a minicomputer). (*Photo courtesy of Digital Equipment Corporation*)

Figure 11-3. The Data General NOVA 9. (*Courtesy of Data General Corporation*)

puters. So severe is the impact of the microcomputer to the mini market that many analysts are predicting long-term problems and minimal growth rates for the minis. Micros are starting to take over the distributed data processing requirements that were once the sole domain of the mini. The mini will certainly be around for a long time but perhaps will tend to slot into specialized functional areas such as office automation and engineering (Computer Aided Design) needs.

The next section will introduce the extremely popular machine—the microcomputer.

MICROCOMPUTERS

Background

As work progressed in the space program, various requirements for complex systems in both satellites and missiles (communication and control) were handled or solved by computers. The associated need to develop a unit that was small and compact led scientists to improve on the one main component of the computer—the transistor. This work resulted in the development of semiconductor integrated circuits. It became apparent that two of the main materials used in creating a transistor, germanium and silicon, had properties that could be used in the circuit design of a new "chip" (approximately the size of a dime) that could allow one chip to represent several hundred transistors. By using the resistance properties of the germanium and silicon, a series of transistors, resistors, and capacitors could all be stored on the one chip and the phrase "Integrated Circuit chip" was initiated. In fact, one very thin slice of silicon, measuring approximately 7.6 cm. in diameter, can produce over 200 chips. The slice or wafer of silicon can have impurities added to it, causing a deficiency of electrons that produces a "p-zone," or electrically positive zone. As well, a neighboring portion of the wafer can be "doped" with a surplus of electrons therefore creating an "n-zone," or negative zone. When an area of the wafer has two n-zones separated by a p-zone, the area acts as a transistor. To create the complete chip, the wafers of silicon are first exposed to steam in very hot ovens where they become covered by a thin electrically insulating layer of silicon dioxide to prevent short-circuiting. Next they are coated with an emulsion that is only sensitive to ultraviolet light. Then a scaled down photograph of the hundreds of patterns and circuits is placed over the wafer and exposed to ultraviolet light. The emulsion substance just remains soft (to be later washed away in an acid bath) except for the lines formed by the miniphoto that becomes hardened, thus forming the outline of the circuit. The wafer is then doped (i.e., impurities added to the silicon), coated with an aluminum conductor, and then sealed in plastic for delivery.

The refinements in the manufacturing of ICs allow several hundred circuits to be printed or produced on a single chip such that a complete CPU of a small digital computer can be stored (or represented) on a chip 3 cm. × 7 cm. These chips or microprocessors were used in the space program of course but were also used in automobile engines, microwave ovens, intelligent cash registers, and communication devices.

It was not until the mid-1970s that a firm named MITS (Micro Instrumentation and Telemetry Systems) decided to take one of the available microprocessors, the Intel 8008, and combine it with some memory, a clock timer, a keyboard for entry, a CRT for displays, and a board to link all the circuitry and store all the parts. The resulting microcomputer was called the Altair 8800. MITS had tremendous results in selling this product and, in effect, opened up a whole new market.

All the improvements in the chip-producing techniques provided a dramatic decrease in the cost of creating these components (witness a CPU on a chip for less than $10.00). As a result, more companies jumped on the microcomputer bandwagon. Although many firms were involved in this blossoming industry in the late 1970s, a group of companies emerged as leaders. Some of the members of this select group were the Apple Corporation with its Apple II; Tandy Radio Shack marketed its

Figure 11-4. The TRS-80 microcomputer system. (*Photo Courtesy of Radio Shack, A Division of Tandy Corporation*)

TRS-80 (Figure 11-4) line of micros; and Commodore Business Machines sold vast numbers of PETs (Personal Electronic Transactor, Figure 11-5). Even though the machines looked physically distinct and the companies had quite different marketing strategies, they were all basically made up of the following:

1. Microprocessor (on a chip)
2. Power source
3. A board to link all of the components together
4. Main memory chip(s)
5. Secondary memory (cassette tape recorder or diskette)
6. Clock timer and necessary circuits to synchronize all of the electrical operations together
7. Keyboard and display screen (CRT, monitor, or standard TV)

Figure 11-5. The PET by Commodore (a personal computer). (*Courtesy of Commodore Business Machines*)

As the 1980s started, there were literally hundreds of firms trying to cut a slice in the market for their microcomputer products. Several companies were quoting annual sales figures increasing at 1000 percent. Improved versions of existing machines were appearing as fast as Japanese car imports. Depending on whose survey you were examining, you would typically find that the Apple Corporation or Radio Shack was the number one company. Some surveys would quote sales, while others would reference amount of software available as the yardstick for comparison. In fact, the market was very geographical in that certain parts of the country "went Apple" while other areas "adopted Commodore." The success of an individual micro was based on aggressive marketing strategies adopted regionally.

There was one firm that was notable by its absence. IBM, the largest computer company, had not entered the market although rumors of a new "big blue" microcomputer were common at conferences and computer shows. Those rumors were ended in 1981 when the IBM PC (Personal Computer) was unveiled. The sales for that particular product sky-rocketed to the point where a couple of years later, IBM was shipping more of its micros than any other manufacturer. The pull of the IBM PC was so strong that many firms went into business making IBM look-a-likes. These clones could all run the programs for an IBM PC and were usually

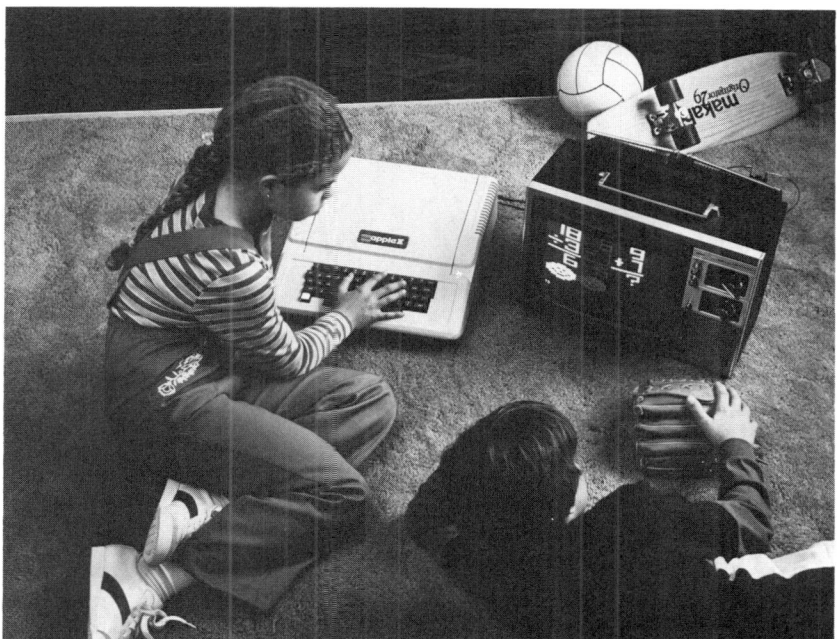

Figure 11-6. Enjoying the Apple II microcomputer. (*Courtesy of Apple Computer Incorporated*)

priced hundreds of dollars less than the real McCoy. IBM did something a little out of character in that they published the internal workings of their micro for anyone to access. In this way, even more firms entered the market as "Software Houses" to create programs for the IBM PC. The effect of the IBM product can further be shown as you start to read the sales brochures of its competitors and you see terms such as "IBM compatible" mentioned in prominent places. Many micro experts are predicting a shakedown in the industry as we enter the second half of the 1980s with the large corporations retaining large market shares and many small and intermediate-size firms dropping out. In fact, in 1983, firms such as Osborne, Atari, and Texas Instruments felt the pinch and made some major decisions in reducing their product line. The industry as a whole is still progressing in an exponential fashion as machines get faster, software becomes more sophisticated, prices come down, methods of communicating with a micro improve, and perhaps more importantly, different applications in many different environments become transferred to a microcomputer.

BREAKDOWN OF MAIN MICROCOMPUTER COMPONENTS

The next few pages will examine some of the basic components of a microcomputer that were just mentioned in the background section and will provide specific industry references where appropriate.

A Chip Off the Old Block— Microprocessors

One interesting observation is that even though there were hundreds of micros being created in laboratories, assembly plants, schools, and local basements and garages, there were really only a handful of microprocessors driving these systems. For example, the Z80 chip from the Zilog Corporation was at the heart of the popular North Star and TRS-80 micros; the 6502 chip from MOS technology could be found in the Atari 400, Apple II, and Commodore PET. These chips and many of the others found in the first wave of micros were known as 8-bit chips. As fast as microcomputers were, these 8-bit machines could only handle 8 bits (or one byte) at a time as data and instructions were passed from one part of the machine to another. The word size and architecture of their internal registers (the ones used when performing arithmetic operations or logical

Figure 11-7. Chip on a finger. (*Courtesy of Intel Corporation*)

comparisons between data fields) were set at 8 bits. A second wave of microcomputers in the early 1980s introduced 16-bit and even 32-bit microprocessors. The IBM PC has an Intel 8088 chip that can handle 16 bits or two bytes at a time while performing internal operations. It is interesting to note that while accessing data from an external storage device, the IBM PC used an 8-bit path thus deriving a 8/16-bit label for machines of this type. Others that were known as true 16-bit machines handled 16 bits at a time in all operations. The Motorola chip MC68000 found in the Apple Lisa and Macintosh could process 4 bytes or 32 bits at a time as it performed internal operations.

These faster chips also had about thirty more basic machine instructions stored in the main chip than the 8-bit machines that had to access a secondary chip to get at the full instruction set. Today it is not uncommon to have multiple chips in the same micro. Some are looking after the graphics functions of the machine; some are responsible for examining all the entries from the keyboard; while others contain a different CPU so that the owner can choose the type of system that he needs to have running the micro at a certain point in time.

The clock-timer located in each micro to synchronize activities is measured in megahertz, or cycles per second. The early micros ran close to one megahertz and subsequently improved to about four megahertz, e.g., Z80 chip at 4.0 and the Intel 8088 at 4.77 megahertz. This speed factor will continue to increase as refinements are made by the chip manufacturers. Some of the new Radio Shack equipment is working at almost 8.0 megahertz.

All Aboard the Data Bus—or How is Everything Linked Together?

The three major components, the CPU, the internal memory, and the input/output routines are connected by a set of "buses." The buses (or carriers of information) are of a standard size and might be circuit wires etched on a printed circuit board. Otherwise, they may be soldered wires between connectors that the various circuit board modules and subsystems are plugged into in order that the three main parts can communicate with each other.

The types of buses that generally would be found in a typical microcomputer are:

1. Address bus—Specifies the correct I/O port from which the data is being transferred.
2. Control bus—Looks after the addressing and data transfer.
3. Data bus—The data itself travels across these lines.
4. Power bus—Allows the power from the power source to be distributed to the various sybsystems.

A Trip Down Memory Lane

There are two very common expressions that are used when describing the memory in a microcomputer—RAM (random access memory) and ROM (read only memory). The following paragraphs explain the difference between the two terms.

The RAM memory involves storage that is temporary in nature in that it is not required after a specific use. For example, a user program would be stored in RAM, but when a second user program is required, it would go right over top of the first program thereby destroying the first program. A blackboard and a chalk brush can form a good analogy to a RAM that can be used over and over again after being wiped clean. In fact, when the power is removed from the micro, the contents of any RAM are lost. A static RAM stores each bit of information in a format such that the information is held as long as power is supplied to the circuit. However, dynamic RAMs represent information in the form of an electric charge that requires refreshing (recharging capacitance) at certain intervals. Also, a dynamic RAM requires fewer parts to represent a bit (e.g., 3 or 4 transistors as opposed to 6 or 8), therefore more bits can be stored on an integrated circuit. Dynamic RAMs are faster than static RAMs and consume less energy when at rest. The refresh circuitry is often an external add-on circuit, and therefore dynamic RAMs are cheaper when used in large memories. Static RAMs are generally less expensive for the small memories but as more of the refresh circuitry becomes built into the integrated circuit, more RAMs will be dynamic in format.

The ROM (read only memory), as the name implies, cannot be used by a programmer to store information. The contents of a ROM are fixed and cannot be changed, even if the power source is removed. Therefore any control routines, such as a supervisor, sort utility, compiler, or file management program could be stored in ROM. A PROM (programmable read only memory) offers the micro user an opportunity to create some routine or program and store it in a ROM so it can be used repeatedly as would a purchased ROM. Many computer stores have the facilities for "burning" or "etching" programs into a PROM. One further extension to a ROM is an EPROM (erasable programmable read only memory) that offers the chance to create a ROM, and then alter memory at a later date to create something new in the ROM.

The early micros were equipped with anywhere from 4K to 16K of RAM with 8K being a standard size. If you had an 8K machine, you were able to store some 8000 characters at one time in the computer's memory. (Remember K = 1024 bytes or characters.) This size of machine allowed you to perform all sorts of programming activities at the low end, but you were restricted to acquiring software that could fit in this space. However, software of this nature was not very sophisticated. Soon expansion boards and new micros were increasing the internal memory size to 32K, then 64K. With this size memory, programs such as word processing, graphics packages, and file management systems could fit in and

Figure 11-8. Intel's Ultraviolet EPROM, the 16,384-bit model 2716. (*Courtesy of Intel Corporation*)

Figure 11-9. The IBM PC is a 16-bit microcomputer in common use by today's business. (*Courtesy of IBM Corporation*)

therefore be used by the micro owner. As mentioned earlier, most of the first wave of micros were 8-bit machines. As they were constructed, sixteen lines were set aside for the address bus. This meant that 64K was the upper limit for RAM as 2^{16} evaluated to 64,000 (approximately) unique addresses. Some firms increased the limits by switching from one bank of 64K RAM chips to another 64K bank under special software control.

As the 16- and 32-bit machines came into the market, they were equipped with twenty address lines thereby accommodating up to one million characters of uniquely addressable main memory. In actual fact, sizes of 128K, 256K, and 512K became quite commonplace, especially for the business environment. Originators of software were now stating rec-

Figure 11-10. The DEC Rainbow microcomputer. (*Photo courtesy of Digital Equipment Corporation*)

ommended minimum RAM sizes for successful performance of their products. One of the most popular programs in the early 1980s, LOTUS 1-2-3, required 192K and VISI-ON from VisiCorp suggested 512K. Obviously, as you shop for a software program to meet a specific application that you have, you must check the RAM size needed to store and run your program.

How to Disk Connect—Or a Look at Secondary Storage

The first storage device sold with a microcomputer was a cassette tape recorder. Some companies built the tape recorder right into the front part of the micro so that everything was self-contained. Others offered it as an option that would simply plug into a connection on the micro. Whatever the method, the observation was the same—it was very slow! The activity of storing and accessing either programs or data contained on a cassette tape was a slow process. It was also reasonably inexpensive and thus for selected markets was accepted and still in use today. The other alternative was to use a floppy disk (or diskette) to retain work and programs. Diskettes have been discussed in an earlier chapter and it suffices to say here that for many years that 5¼-inch diskette became a standard size. Different storage techniques allowed increasingly larger capacities on the diskettes. There are discussions going on in the industry with respect to adopting a new standard size of 3 inches because there are 3-inch diskettes now able to store a million characters. Some micros are available with a 10-megabyte fixed disk as a standard part, e.g., IBM XT. For certain applications, this increased storage may be necessary to handle large files. For comparisons sake, a 10-megabyte disk can hold approximately 5,120 double-spaced 8½ × 11 typed pages while a 5¼-inch diskette can retain about 184 pages.

Has Anyone Seen My Pet Mouse?—Or Talking to Your Micro

The keyboard that used to communicate your requests to a micro has gone through some interesting changes. There are some that are multi-colored, some half-typewriter size, some with numeric keypads, and others with function keys that can be set by the software that is running in the micro. The Atari 400 had a "membrane-like" keyboard similar in operation to cash registers at restaurants. This type of keyboard could be wiped clean very easily and most spills could not get under any key to ruin the contacts.

The keyboards on many machines are fixed to the micro itself therefore making it very awkward to move the keyboard around. Other manufacturers allow the keyboard to be plugged into the micro with a phone-like extension cord so that keying can be done from a table or from a lap position.

Still another way of communicating something to the micro is via a joystick. This device is very popular when playing games but can also be used by graphics artists to create a design on the screen or by anyone who wants to move the cursor to a specific position on the screen.

Another alternative is the *mouse*. A mouse is a small box that is linked to the micro and rests on a tabletop beside the micro. You can hold this device in one hand and roll it around the table on a small wheel that extends out of the bottom of the box. As you roll the mouse up and down or back and forth, the cursor on the screen moves in a similar direction. When you have arrived at the spot on the screen that you were going to, you can push a small button on the mouse to indicate some type of activity. (See the picture of the Apple Macintosh, Figure 11-11). A similar idea is to build a trackball into the side of the keyboard itself. Then place the palm of your hand over the trackball and roll the cursor to whatever position you want.

The software packages are starting to use small diagrams or Icons to represent actions on the screen. The user can now just get the cursor over to the Icon he wants and then push a button. The activity represented by that Icon would then be carried out, activities such as storing a file, or printing a report.

Other micro owners are using graphics tablets to "paint" pictures and create designs by drawing on the special slate that is connected by cord to the micro. The cursor can also be moved around for selection purposes with a graphics tablet as in the case of a mouse system.

Another interesting trend is towards portability. There are microcomputers that combine all the standard components that have been discussed, including diskette drives, and package them into a lightweight transportable unit. These machines, such as the IBM® PCC, Compaq™, Kaypro®, and HYPERION™, are extremely handy for those who want to take a micro home to complete a certain activity. Salesmen and others who are on the road can have their computer with them at all times for inquiring or posting data. The screens are small, in the five-inch range, but there is a link out to a TV set or monitor for viewing. Some versions such as the Radio Shack Model 100 Portable Computer use a Liquid Crystal Display (LCD) to generate eight lines of viewing data. Some of these

Figure 11-11. The Macintosh microcomputer from Apple. (*Photo courtesy of Apple Computer Corporation*)

machines are equipped with nickel cadmium batteries to keep the RAM "alive" so that the contents of the RAM are not destroyed when the unit is switched off. An AC adapter charges the batteries. Calculators have gone from bulky handheld devices to wafer-thin pocket units; if the portability trend follows along, we will soon have wallet and purse-size micros.

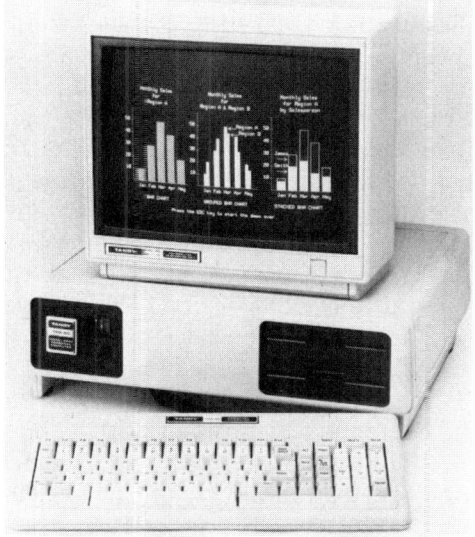

Figure 11-12. The Tandy Model 2000 Personal Computer. (*Photo courtesy of Radio Shack, a Division of Tandy Corporation*)

Software

Besides the growth and improvements in the microcomputer field, perhaps the most dramatic changes have been in the area of software. In fact, whereas good reliable hardware has been available for a variety of business and educational applications for a number of years now, solid responsive software is finally just now starting to emerge. For a time at the beginning of the micro, an owner could just use BASIC for his programs; could select a limited word processing package; play some games; and use a restricted set of mathematical programs. Today, however, there is a full-blown software industry that now offers an owner:

1. A full set of programming languages from COBOL to C
2. A choice of many word processing programs
3. Three-dimensional games with sound input and output
4. Proper data-base programs as well as numerous file management routines
5. Sophisticated modeling and statistical programs
6. Advanced graphics design options
7. Educational programs using creative simulation programs

Although the microcomputer industry is plagued by a lack of standards, there have been a few Operating Systems that can be labelled as "standards." The people at Digital Research were not happy with the basic Operating System that was available with microcomputers as you purchased them from a retail store. They wrote their own and called it CP/M, or Control Program for Microcomputers. It ran on the Z80 family of chips and became so successful that there was more software written for this Operating System than any other. Owners of machines that were not Z80 based would buy an expansion board that contained a Z80 chip and insert it into their micros so that they could take advantage of the abundance of CP/M compatible software. Another firm, Microsoft, released a popular Operating System called MSDOS or Microsoft Disk Operating System. They in fact released it to IBM in July of 1981 as PCDOS. Therefore, the Operating System on one of the leading (and driving) microcomputers was produced by Microsoft. The Digital Research group produced a version of CP/M for the 16-bit machines, CP/M-86 that now goes head-to-head against MSDOS. They, however, are both single-user, single-tasking Operating Systems and are running up against a multi-tasking Operating System known as UNIX. This product, developed by Bell Laboratories, is touted by some as the Operating System of the 1980s. It looks as if there is a "good fight" brewing between these three firms as they all develop and refine multi-tasking systems for the advanced microcomputers.

MARKETS—OR WHO IS BUYING MICROCOMPUTERS?

The following pages will introduce three main market areas: Business, Education, and Home.

Business Market

The business arena has been gobbling up micros at a fantastic rate with no end in sight. What are businessmen using the micros for? The next list contains the common application areas that micros have been used for.

1. Modeling and Forecasting.
   Anyone who is involved with budgets, sales plans, cost analyses, investment schedules, bid proposals, profit and loss projections, etc., can probably gain from one of the many spread-sheet programs available. When VisiCalc was released in the late 1970s by Software Arts Corp. (now called VisiCorp) a revolutionary tool became available to all those who work with paper and pencil doing spread-sheet calculations. An electronic spread-sheet allowed "what if?" questions with instantaneous results. The software program kept track of all the calculations and updated them when new or different parameters were introduced to the pro-

Figure 11-13. The Lisa microcomputer from Apple. (*Photo courtesy of Apple Computer Corporation*)

gram. The "number crunching" aspect of a manager's time could be reduced and replaced by the more important feature of examining the data.

2. **Data-Base Management.**
Firms with data on 3 × 5 index cards, manilla folders, or catalogues can now transfer that data on to a micro and have all the updating, sorting, inquiring, and summarizing functions done in an automated way.

3. **Graphic Illustrations.**
A businessman can use the micro to generate business graphs, i.e., bar, pie, line, and Gantt charts so that the analysis and presentation of large quantities of data becomes more manageable. One of the reasons why the software program LOTUS 1-2-3 became such a hot seller was that it combined aspects of the first three points and offered spread-sheet analysis with graphic illustrations and file management techniques.

4. **Word Processing.**
Many companies are hooking a letter quality daisy wheel printer to their microcomputer. Then they are acquiring a word processing program to permit an operator to create, update, and store reports with a final command to print the documents at 50 characters per second.

5. **Accounting.**
The various sub-headings within the Accounting umbrella, i.e., General Ledger activities, Accounts Payable, Accounts Receivable, and Job Costing, can all be done on a micro with automatic generation of such forms as balance sheets, cash receipts journals, customer statements, payables checks, and job status reports.

6. **Inventory.**
Microcomputer programs are now used to log inventory information and offer the user such automatic extras as re-order level calculations and selected item reports.

7. **Communications.**
If the micro is equipped with a *modem*, the owner can take advantage of the many data banks available today that are maintained by other firms. The *modem* can be part of the micro and actually installed inside the cover of the machine, or it might be a device attached to the micro and sitting on the desk beside it. This unit translates the voltage signals used by the microcomputer into a format that can be sent through telephone lines to another micro or large mainframe computer system. The owner can extract data from the various stock exchanges around the

country or link into popular business magazines, books, and daily newspapers. As well, a connection can be made to his own corporate mainframe computer so that data can be transmitted from the micro to the large computer or vice versa.

There are certainly other uses of the micro in a business environment and, in fact, the potential is just starting to be tapped. One interesting point to state is that the uses just listed are not new from the perspective of Data Processing, i.e., systems for those various application areas have been produced before. However, the difference is that the price of the micro software packages necessary to perform the functions listed above is in the "hundreds of dollars" range. Many firms that are currently using a time-sharing service to satisfy a data processing need are finding that one year's payments can buy them a complete micro system that can perform the same functions.

Education Market

Microcomputers are finding their way into the classroom. Almost every discipline today is trying to get a micro introduced somewhere in the curriculum. What has basically been holding educators back is the lack of software—i.e., pedagogically sound software that is placed at the right grade level. Witness such attempts as a program designed to teach the alphabet to pre-schoolers that requires them to respond to the prompt "Enter continue to go on!" If these children could read, they would not be learning about the alphabet.

But whether the school has three or four micros centered in a library (or learning resource center), or has a "traveling micro" that visits classrooms on a regular (albeit infrequent) basis, more and more students are getting exposure to microcomputers. Computers clubs are popular in many schools and compete for scarce budget dollars along with the science, chess, and glee clubs. At the college and university level, virtually all students receive an Introduction to Microcomputers course no matter what program they are enrolled in. Interestingly enough, some universities issue a microcomputer to the students as part of their registration fee in a similar fashion to a chemistry student paying for lab fees. Other universities require that registering students have their own micros for certain courses. The well-established firms such as IBM and Apple have been involved in some very interesting programs whereby they have given computers to school boards for use in the classroom. Other firms aware of the huge potential future market have offered attractive purchasing arrangements to the school boards to help get their machines installed.

"Either this goes or I go!"
© *Creative Computing*

It is becoming quite a challenge to higher learning institutes to structure their programs to deal with situations where one class member is a senior who has never worked on a micro and right beside him is a nineteen year old who has written more programs than the teacher!

Home Market—Home Computers or Will the Hobbyists Take Over?

A shopping list of the 1980s might contain the following entries:

- a loaf of bread
- package of cigarettes
- 1 64K RAM expansion board
- 2 cans of tomato soup

Hold it now! Is this suggesting that microcomputer components will be available at your neighborhood grocery store? . . . or that 64K of RAM will be as cheap as a can of soup? Well, it is a little dramatic to picture RAM boards hanging between the flashcubes and the batteries, but it is certainly correct to picture micros and parts for micros available through many different retail outlets. For example, there are specialized stores that sell micros and associated peripherals, and many of the large com-

Figure 11-14. The Commodore 64 microcomputer. (*Photo courtesy of Commodore Electronics Limited*)

that sell micros and associated peripherals, and many of the large commercial retail chains now have sections that concentrate on micros. A consumer can usually find such items as micro components, manuals, magazines, microprocessors, expansion boards, software, etc. As for the point about the RAM board and the tomato soup . . . well, it is probably a toss-up!

The impact and use of the microcomputer has extended past the firm that has converted its Inventory or Accounts Receivable systems over to a micro for a few thousand dollars. A home market is alive and booming! Perhaps in the past, consumers were using programmable calculators with magnetic card storage, but now they are using microcomputers. The price of a micro is so low that almost every home can afford to have one. There are two basic groups that have formed over time: one group that consists of those people who want to buy a computer, take it home, plug it in and play games with it right away. They will probably do some programming with it, but they do not want to fiddle around having to create software or interfaces before their unit will function. The other group appears to be the "do-it-yourself" type who wants to buy a chip (microprocessor), some RAM, a circuit board to store all the electrical components, and a keyboard and then create their own version of a micro.

Both of these groups can take advantage of the large amounts of software that are coming on the scene every day. Many micro owners are joining "users groups" that are perhaps meeting in local high schools and are able to share experiences as well as software in a number of instances. There appear to be four components to the home market that could be specified as follows:

1. Education.
   Many students are using micros at home for math drills, spelling bees, creative sessions using graphics tablets, and programming activities. Essays and reports are being produced using word processing packages at home rather than with the standard typewriter. The student of the future will be like a fish without water if he does not have access to a computer in the house.

2. Entertainment.
   Game after game is being produced, stored on cartridges, cassettes or diskettes, and sold at stores for a nominal amount. Blackjack, biorhythms, tic tac toe, moon landings, Star Trek— the list goes on. Libraries will start to stock computer games and loan them out as they do books and records. A visit to a friend's house will soon be characterized by an evening at the keyboard as opposed to ping-pong or cards. Some families are mixing education and entertainment by programming some logic into their home computers to prohibit any entries into the entertainment programs until three or four education drills have been done. Imagine having to learn how to convert some fractions to deci-

Figure 11-15. The VIC 20 microcomputer. (*Photo courtesy of Commodore Electronics Limited*)

mals before becoming Captain Kirk for the evening! An interesting option available for the micro is the music synthesizer chip that, when used in conjunction with an external speaker and some type of digital to analog converter, can allow the micro to function as a musical instrument.

3. Environment.
   The home computer can easily control thermostats, lights, and electrical outlets and can therefore offer a great deal of flexibility and control for the homeowner. As well, the owner of a small firm or warehouse can become more "energy conscious" by using a micro to control the environment-end of his business.

4. Small Personal Tasks
   There are numerous software packages available for the homeowner to help him balance his books, monitor his car maintenance, help in income tax preparation, or keep the records for the local church group. As well, standard graphics programs and electronic spread-sheet programs are dropping in price and becoming easier to use so many home micro owners are designing their own tailored applications.

The description of the home computer market and specifically the use of the micro at home is just the tip of the iceberg and will probably only be bound by the imagination of the micro's owner. The microprocessor's impact on life in general will probably be as great as the impact and effect of the small electric motor.

FUTURE TRENDS

If the current trends in micros continue we will see more integrated software, i.e., programs that have multi-functions. These programs can ship data from one part of the package, e.g., Word Processing component, to a another part (or function in the package) such as the data-base component and therefore offer the user lots of flexibility within the one purchased program.

There will be more work done on the "user-interface" question. In other words, how can you dialog with your micro in an improved fashion. For example, the IBM PCjr uses a cordless infrared keyboard to permit the user to sit basically where he pleases. The HP 150 is utilizing a touch sensitive screen to allow the user to point to selected areas on the screen to indicate an activity. The chapter has already talked about trackballs and mouse attachments as easier methods of cursor movement. Icon-driven software and multi-layered windows will also give the user better control of the activities in the micro. The whole area of direct voice input will become more developed and soon will be just another expansion board to insert.

TERMS TO STUDY

Bus
Chip
CP/M
Electronic Spreadsheet
EPROM
LSI
Microprocessor
Minicomputer
MOS
Mouse
MSDOS
PROM
RAM
ROM
Trackball
UNIX
8-Bit, 16-Bit, 32-Bit

QUESTIONS FOR REVIEW

1. List ten characteristics of a minicomputer.
2. Describe the original purpose of the minicomputer and then list eight application areas that it soon found its way into.
3. Explain the background leading up to the development of a microprocessor.
4. Explain how a thin wafer of silicon can store a whole central processing unit.
5. Describe the basic parts of any microcomputer.
6. What are some differences between MOS and Bipolar LSI?
7. Differentiate between static RAM and dynamic RAM.
8. What is the difference between ROM, PROM, and EPROM?
9. What are the four main types of buses?
10. Describe some alternative methods to keyboarding in order to communicate with a micro.
11. List seven application areas that a micro might be used for in a business.
12. Explain the different sections of the home computer market.

PROBLEMS FOR RESEARCH AND DISCUSSION

1. Does the fact that a minicomputer is portable and thus can be used anywhere pose a security problem to the manager of data processing?
2. List some advantages and disadvantages of having a computer at the head office, processing data from a series of branch offices, as opposed to a system whereby minicomputers are installed at the branches.
3. Determine three different uses for a microcomputer under the following headings: (a) appliances, (b) cars, (c) schools.
4. Describe the difference between a mini and a micro.
5. What effect will the micro have on education in the future?
6. Where will it all end? "Good things come in small packages," but just how small will they be?
7. Direct voice input to a micro is hampered by such things as homonyms, ums, and ahs, etc. Supply three other problem areas that would influence the design of a voice input system before it could be marketed to the general public.

Computer Programming

12

Problem Solving

PROBLEM ANALYSIS

The design and implementation of the smallest computer application to the largest requires a methodical process from problem definition to the development of programs and procedures as the final product. This is true regardless of whether the application is a small payroll system for a company with 100 employees or a real-time management information system for a large corporation. The resulting system in each case is quite different. The complexities involved are disproportionate. The time and manpower requirements in the second case are much greater than the first. Regardless of these differences, both systems need a systematic approach in studying the initial problem and progressing to the final solution.

Each step taken during this process, whether by a systems analyst or a programmer, must be not only systematic but thorough. This is essential because even the smallest detail must be considered. Questions like where should the date be printed on a paycheck, or should overtime on a given day be paid at the regular rate of 1.5 times the regular rate must be asked. The purpose of this chapter is to show the process of progressing from an overall problem definition to the final solution. Basically, we will look at the methods for developing and describing the solution. These consist of flowcharts, decision tables, and top down design techniques.

Program Flowcharts

One of the major tools developed for problem solving is the flowchart. It provides a graphic means to describe a process or a solution to a problem. The flowchart is to the computer professional what a blueprint is to an engineer. It can be used to provide precise details for the solution of a given problem.

The flowchart communicates to the programmer the method for developing the program logic. If the flowchart is developed correctly and followed closely, the result will be a program that is logically correct.

To aid in the flowcharting processing, a template is used. An example of a template is shown in Figure 12-1. Each symbol has a specific meaning and is used to represent a process or operation.

To promote uniformity among data processors, standards for flowcharting have been established by several organizations. The most prominent of these are the United States of America Standards Institute (USASI) and the International Organization for Standardization (ISO). These standards, when followed, improve the clarity and understanding of flowcharts and aid in the communication of information between those involved in data processing projects. Another convention in general use is drawing the flowcharts so that they read from top to bottom and left to right. To avoid possible confusion, arrowheads and connectors may be used to indicate flow.

Flowchart Symbols. A program flowchart describes the steps to be taken when writing a computer program for a specific application. The purpose of the flowchart is to assist in the planning of the program and its logic without becoming too involved with the technical details of the language. The flowchart presents a visual means of developing program logic that is easy for the programmer to read and follow when coding the program. Program flowcharting also has a set of symbols that are for the most part different from those used in system flowcharting discussed in Section D. The following symbols are all you will need in preparing a flowchart.

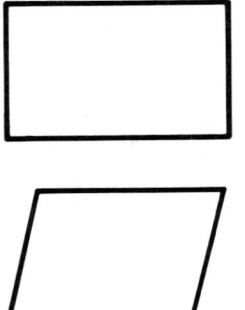

This is a process symbol. For programs, it is used for operations that cause a change in some value. Some processes are the arithmetic operations (add, subtract, multiply, divide), moves, or supplying an initial value.

This symbol describes an input or output operation. It is used whenever a read or write of a file is indicated. The operation may relate to any type of file such as cards, tape, disk, printer, or terminal.

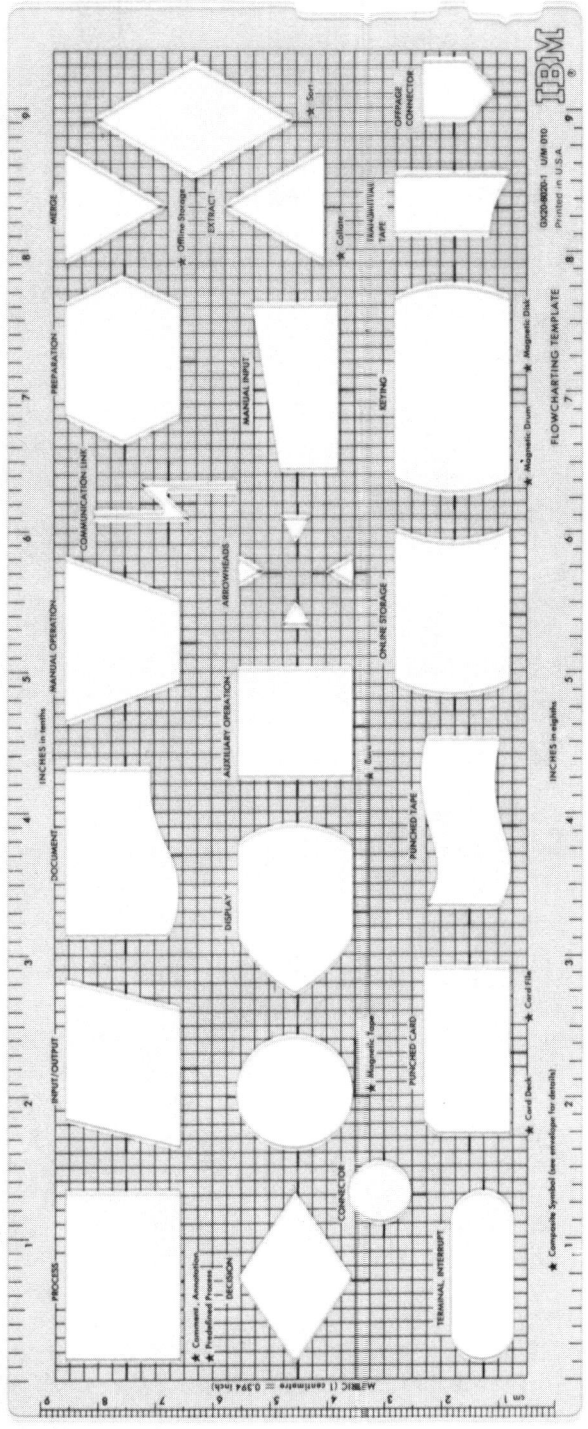

Figure 12-1. Flowcharting template.

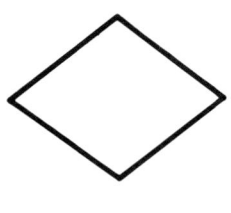
The decision symbol is used whenever a logical comparison is necessary. It always asks a question. Is A greater than B? Is Salary less than 10000? Is Number equal to 1? What is the relationship between Sum and Total? In the first three cases, the answer can only be True or False. (Some prefer to use Yes or No). In the last case there are three possibilities. Sum is less than Total, Sum is greater than Total, Sum is equal to Total. This symbol permits all three to be used.

This is a more advanced symbol called the predefined process. It is used to represent a relatively large segment of logic that has been defined elsewhere. An example might be—determine Income Tax. This is clearly not a simple step but involves several activities such as determining taxable income, looking up a tax table, calculating tax.

This is called a terminal symbol. It should not be confused with hardware terminals in a real-time system. Rather it represents the start and end of a program. In addition, it defines alternate entry and exit points to and from a program.

This is a connector. It is used for connecting separate parts of a flowchart. Usually it contains a number or letter to identify the connected points.

Problem 1—Read Cards and Write Data on Tape. The flowchart in Figure 12-2 shows a simple program that reads cards and places the data from the cards onto magnetic tape. To solve this relatively easy problem, we have used most of the flowchart symbols. This flowchart shows where the program begins (START) and where it ends (STOP). It shows step by step each action to be taken and the order in which it is taken. It is necessary to read a card before it can be moved to the tape area. It is important that a record is in the tape area before we attempt to write it on tape. So the flowchart shows not only what steps are taken by the program but also of equal importance, the order in which they are to be taken.

Problem 2—Print Report from a Disk File. The next flowchart in Figure 12-3 shows how a sequential disk file is read to produce a report. Since there will be many lines of output, headings are to be written at the top of each page. In addition, only a record type 3 is to be printed. All other record types are ignored.

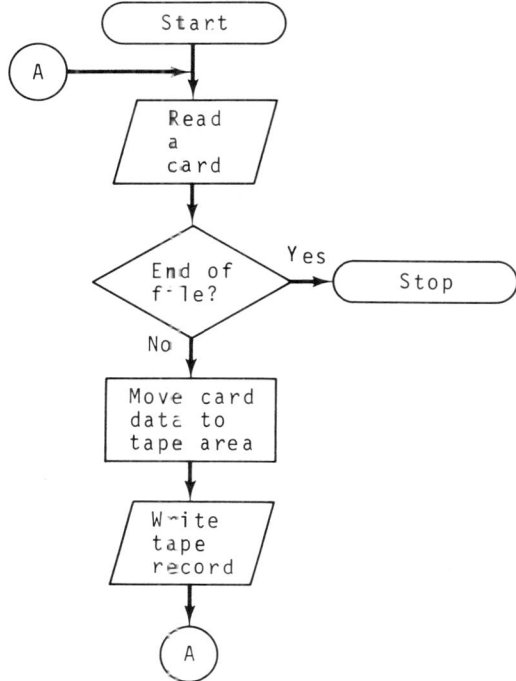

Figure 12-2. Program flowchart to write card records on tape.

As problems become more complex and there are more decisions and actions to be taken, the resulting flowchart will be different for each person who develops it. This is normal since each individual exercises his own creativity in developing program logic. Of course, the solution must still be precise and concise. Therefore several flowcharts may each solve the same problem, but one solution may be preferred over another.

Problem 3—Report with Totals and Page Overflow. A common data processing problem is to produce reports containing totals. Suppose we have a tape file containing payroll records. Each record contains an Employee Number, Gross Salary, and Deductions. A listing is required showing all of this data with totals at the end of Gross Salary and Deductions. In addition, a heading is required on the top of each page. A page can contain 40 detail lines. Figure 12-4 shows the flowchart to solve this problem.

Initially, the line counter and totals are set to zero and a heading is printed. Next, a record is read from the tape. For each record, Gross and Deductions are added to their respective totals, then a detail line is printed. A 1 is added to line count, which is then tested to see if 40 has been reached. Until this happens, the flowchart branches back to connector B to read another record. When line count does equal 40, the flow-

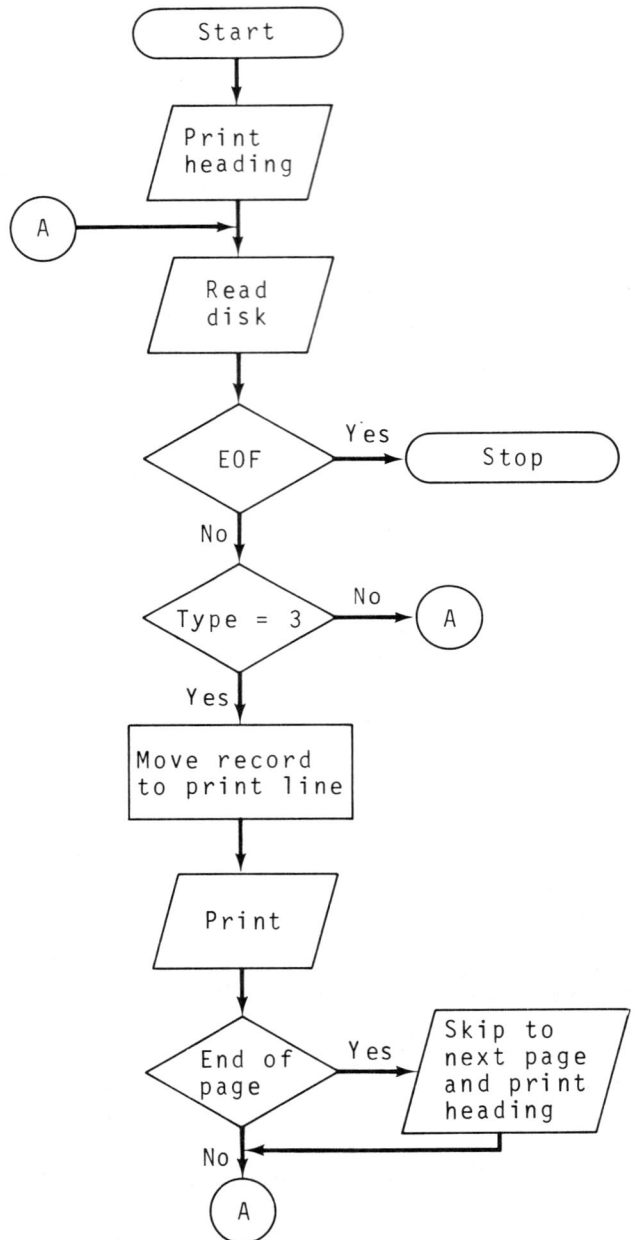

Figure 12-3. Program flowchart—print type 3 records from disk.

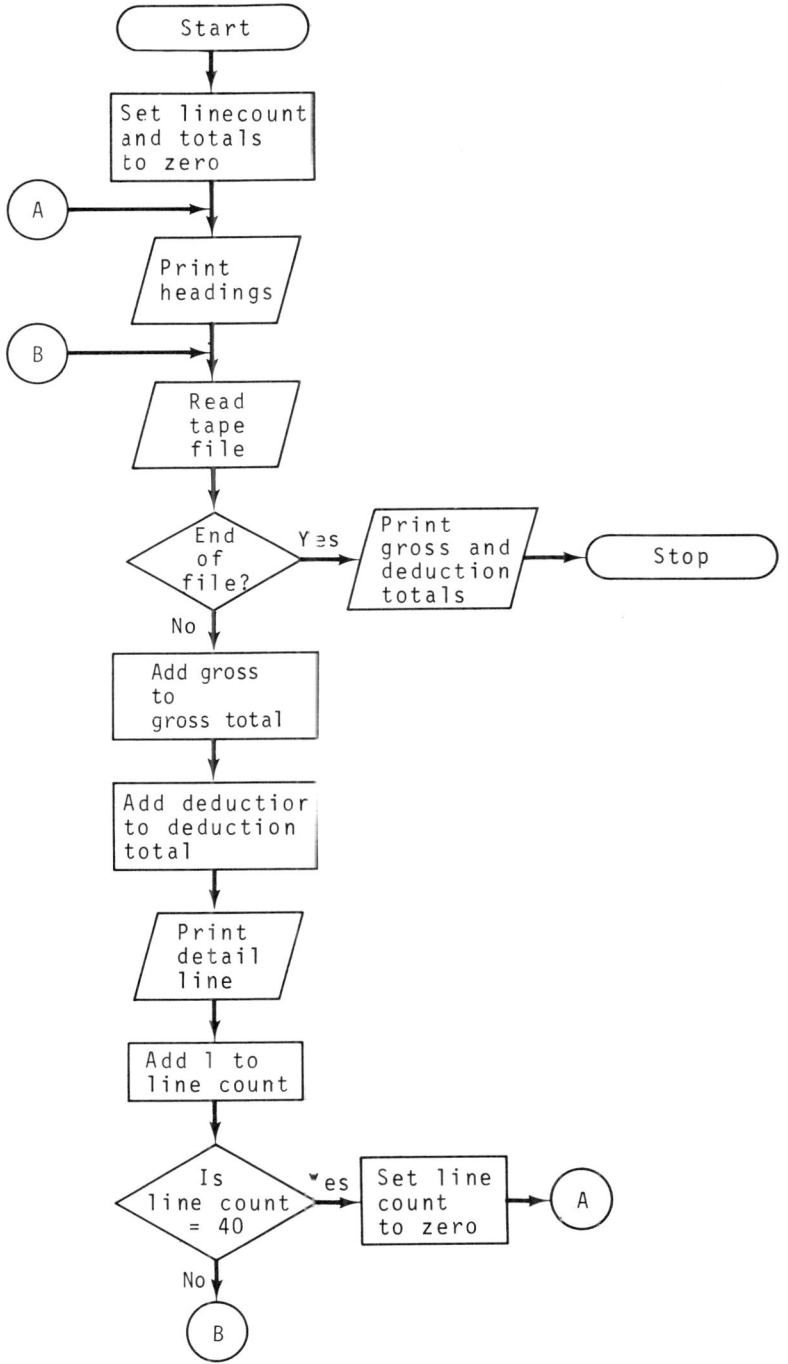

Figure 12-4. Report with totals and page overflow.

264 PROBLEM SOLVING

chart resets line count and branches to A, which prints a new heading prior to reading the next record. When end of file is reached on the tape, the totals are printed and the program terminates.

Problem 4—Report by Region with Totals. Another flowchart is shown in Figure 12-5 for a program that is to read cards containing a region number and an amount. The object is to print each record and, at the end of the region, print a total for that region. At the end of the report, a total for all records is required.

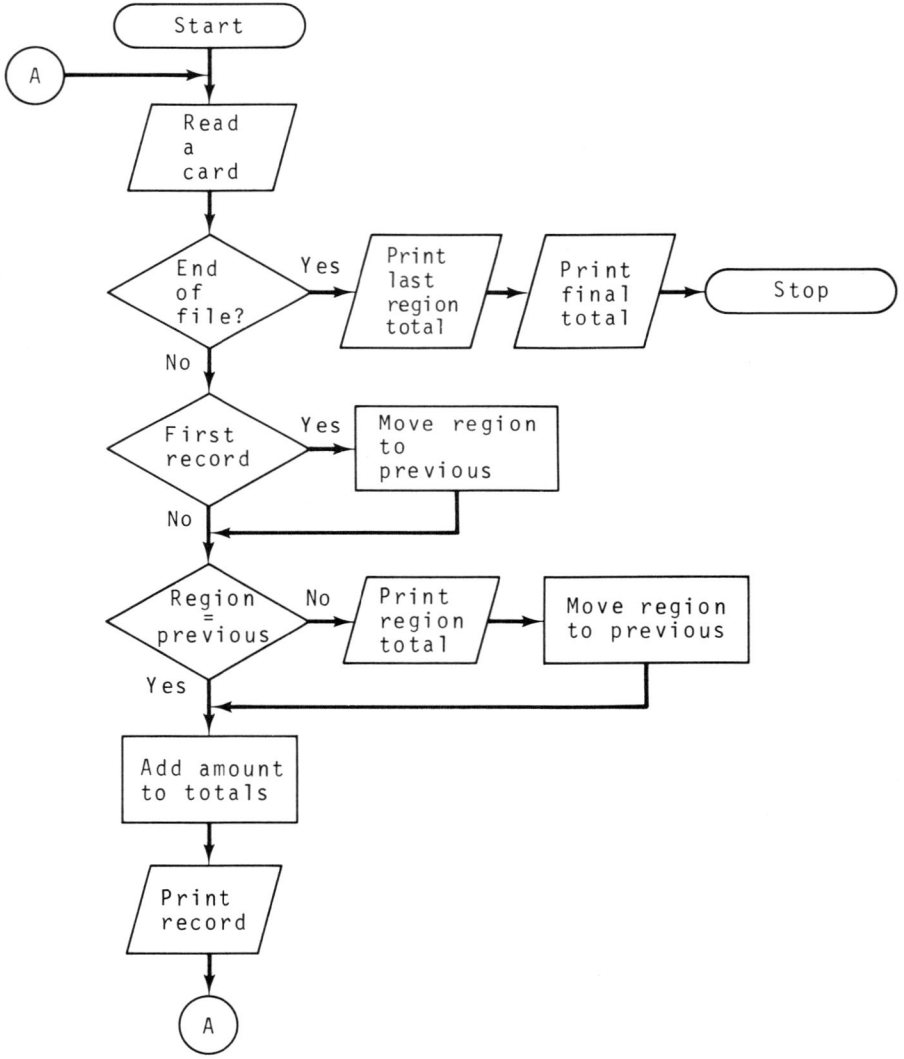

Figure 12-5. Program flowchart for report with region.

To solve this problem, the chart first reads a card. A check is made to determine if end-of-file has been reached. In this case, a card would not have been accessed, and therefore a region change could not have occurred for the last region processed. For this reason, the last region total is printed, followed by the final total before the program is terminated.

If end-of-file was not reached, we check for first card. This initiates the previous region field to the first region, otherwise a region change will have seemed to occur on this first card.

Next, the flowchart checks for a region change by comparing region to the previous. If a change occurs, the region's total is printed, and the region number from the present card is stored in previously. This now represents the next region to be processed. Finally, the amounts from the card are added to the totals, and the detail of the record is printed.

While flowcharts may seem to provide all the necessary tools for problem solving, they also have a few disadvantages. Because of the need for symbols and connecting lines, they are rather time-consuming to prepare. Once flowcharts are produced for a system or a program, they are difficult to change. Thus maintenance becomes a problem. Possibly the least of the problem areas is the amount of space needed to record relatively simple logic. As a result, data processors and computer scientists have been seeking more effective ways of developing and describing the solution to computer-related problems. One technique that closely followed the flowchart is the decision table.

Decision Tables

A decision table expresses a logical solution in a table format. They are sometimes used exclusively for program problem solving. In some cases, they are used as a supplement for flowcharting.

As the name implies, decision tables are particularly adapted to programs where many decisions are to be made. Since most program logic involves a great deal of decision making, decision tables have a widespread application. Some of the problems with flowcharting are reduced in significance here. Since preprinted forms may be used for a decision table, tables can be prepared in less time than flowcharts. They occupy less space on a page for equivalent logic, which improves readability. However, the maintenance factor is not much improved.

Components of a Decision Table. Figure 12-6 shows the general format for any decision table. There are basically four sections to the table:

1. Condition stub
2. Condition entry
3. Action stub
4. Action entry

266 PROBLEM SOLVING

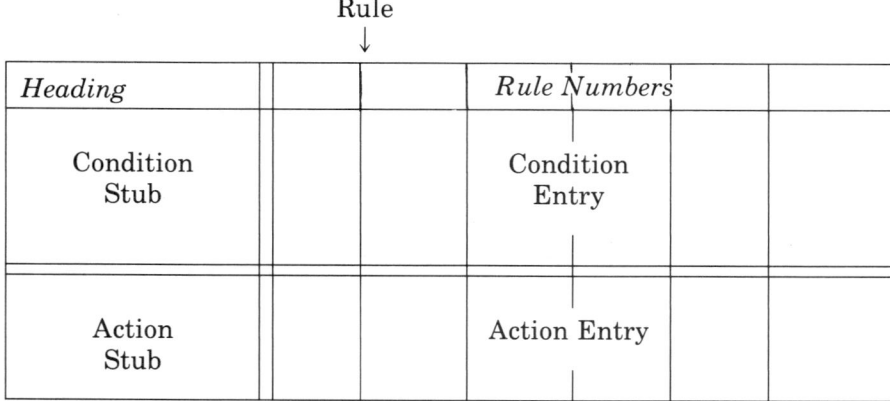

Figure 12-6. Decision table—general format.

There is a simple relationship between Conditions and Actions. The Condition specifies an IF characteristic and the Action a THEN property. If a given condition is present, THEN a specified action is to take place.

Each condition stub has a set of rules in the Condition Entry that determines the relationship between several conditions. These rules each have an Action Entry, which selects appropriate actions if a given condition occurs.

Limited Entry Table—Largest of Three Numbers. To demonstrate consider the following problem.

> Find the largest number of three numbers represented by the variable names A, B, and C. Assume no two numbers will be equal.

The first step in solving this is to write down all the conditions in the Condition Stub. This is shown in Figure 12-7. A certain amount of creativity is needed here to determine what the three conditions will be. One way to do this is to write down three possible values for A, B, and C and carefully examine your own procedure for finding the largest.

Next, write down the actions. In this case, they simply indicate which variable contains the largest number. Then we list the rules (1, 2, and 3) showing the various combinations of conditions we are using. Notice that mathematically we could have 2^3, or 8, different rules, if all possible combinations are used. It may be useful to consider all 8 rules to check for errors in our reasoning. On closer examination, we can determine that some of these 8 rules are redundant and thus unnecessary. By eliminating them, we find 3 rules that are essential to this problem.

Largest of 3 numbers	1	2	3
A greater than B	Y	N	
A greater than C	Y		N
B greater than C		Y	N
A is largest	X		
B is largest		X	
C is largest			X

Figure 12-7. Largest of three numbers.

Finally the actions to be taken are marked under the appropriate rule. Actions that are not checked are not applicable for that rule.

This decision table uses what is known as the limited entry condition. The limited entry is restricted to the use of Y or N for yes or no and T or F for true or false. Thus we could have also used the entry

	1	2
A greater than B	T	F

Extended Entry Table—An Order System Problem. An alternate method is the extended entry. This entry uses relational symbols such as > or <. An extended entry in our example would appear as follows:

	1	2
A compared to B	>	≤

The less-than-or-equal-to is used in rule 2 rather than simply less than. In this way it corresponds exactly to the original rule 2. However, since the problem definition rules out equal values, the less-than symbol would be correct here.

Consider the following problem. Before looking at the solution, it might be worthwhile preparing a decision table and then comparing your solution.

> An order system for electronic parts fills orders from stock shelves. If there are enough parts in stock, an invoice is prepared for the order quantity. This quantity is then supplied to the customer. In some cases there are parts in stock but not enough to fill the order. In this case, an

> invoice is prepared and the available quantity in stock is entered. The difference between the order and stock quantity is placed on a back-order. Finally, if there are no parts in stock, the entire order quantity is placed on back-order.

Now compare your solution with Figure 12-8. First notice the three conditions. This is the first step in preparing the table. Next examine the actions. This table uses six of them. Depending upon the approach taken and the wording of each action, there may be more actions than six and still be correct. It is also possible, but not as likely, to have fewer actions. If there are fewer, it may be due to an implied decision in the action. For instance, the action

Place Order Qty or Difference on Back-Order

combines the last two actions of Figure 12-8, but in doing so, it requires a choice between Order Qty and Difference. This involves a decision without directly saying so. Statements of this kind should be avoided. When a decision is to be made, however simple, it should be placed in the condition stub. Related actions will then be listed in the action stub.

Sales Commission Problem. Very often repetitive conditions and actions are necessary in a decision table. This is particularly important when the table is prepared to describe a computer program. Programs are usually repetitive in nature and require the ability to repeat a series of instructions until some condition is satisfied. This characteristic is demonstrated in the next problem.

It can be seen that this is a repetitive process because there are records for a number of salesmen. Each record is to be processed in the

	Order System	1	2	3
Conditions	Sufficient Quantity in Stock	Y	N	N
	Partial Quantity in Stock		Y	N
	Out of Stock			Y
Actions	Prepare Invoice	X	X	
	Enter Order Qty on Invoice	X		
	Enter Stock Qty on Invoice		X	
	Supply Invoice Qty to Customer	X	X	
	Place Difference on Back-Order		X	
	Place Order on Back-Order			X

Figure 12-8. Order system.

same way, and therefore the logic developed can be used again and again. Since this problem is somewhat larger than previous ones, it might be useful to break it into two parts. One part gives the general logic and the other the detail for computing the commission. This is exactly what has been done in Figure 12-9 for the solution.

A set of sales records are to be processed. Each record contains a Salesman Number, Sales Amount, and a Salary. The salesman is to be paid a Gross Salary, which is the sum of the Salary and a Commission. The amount of the Commission depends on the amount of the sales according to the following table.

Sales	Commission
Less than $10,000	5%
10,000 to 19,999	7%
20,000 to 29,999	10%
over 30,000	12%

The program is to print a report showing the input data as well as the amount of Commission and the Gross Salary. At the end of the file, an Overall Total is to be printed of all the Gross Salaries.

The table Sales Logic shows how the records are read and processed. Decisions here are quite simple. Is it the start of the problem, the end of the file, or neither? If it is the start, a record is read to get things going. Then the action

Go To Sales Logic

sends us back to the beginning of the table. If we have accessed a record, then rule 2 is followed. The first action is to compute the commission. Since this is rather involved, the action to

Perform Commission Table

is specified. This means that we go to a decision table of this name, follow its decisions and actions, and then finally return back and continue doing the actions in the table (Sales Logic). Notice that we continue with the actions in Sales Logic. Not the decisions. So we continue by adding Salary and Commission to give the Gross Salary. This Gross Salary is added to

Sales logic	1	2	3
Start	Y	N	N
EOF	N	N	Y
Perform commission table		X	
Add salary and commission giving gross salary		X	
Add gross salary to overall		X	
Print		X	
Read a record	X	X	
Go to sales logic	X	X	
Print overall			X
Stop			X

Commission table	1	2	3	4
Sales less than 10,000	Y			
Sales $10,000 to 19,999		Y		
Sales $20,000 to 29,999			Y	
Sales over 30,000				Y
Compute 5% commission	X			
Compute 7% commission		X		
Compute 10% commission			X	
Compute 12% commission				X
Return	X	X	X	X

Figure 12-9. Salesman commission problem.

the Overall, which is needed for the end of the report. Then the data is printed, a new record is read, and control branches back to Sales Logic. If another record had been accessed, the table is repeated.

Eventually, no more records remain to be read. At this point, rule 3 is followed. The overall total is printed and the repetition stops.

Although the Commission Table could have been included in the first table, it was not. By making it separate, each table is simplified and easier to manage. This reduces the possibility of error and increases the ability to read and understand the solution to the problem.

Difficulties with Decision Tables. If it would seem at this point that the decision table has replaced the flowchart as a problem solving and documentation tool, this impression must be corrected. Even though the decision table offers some improvements as suggested earlier, problem areas still exist. One outstanding problem is that the decision table does not present a flow of decisions and actions that can be directly translated by a programmer into computer language. In the table, a decision is completely separate from the related action. They belong in different stubs. However, in most programming languages, decisions and actions are closely related. So when it comes to writing the program, a flowchart is generally easier to follow than a decision table.

Secondly, the decision table has a very rigid format. It does not allow a great deal of flexibility or creativity. There is a limit here, of course, even in programming languages. However, many languages have less rigidity and allow a programmer greater freedom than decision tables. This may be an unnecessary limitation on the programmer and restrict the effectiveness of the solution.

Although the usefulness of the decision table still covers a broad spectrum of data processing needs, the acceptance of it has not been as widespread as the flowchart. Perhaps the very nature of the flowchart in that it presents a pictorial or graphic solution leads to a more general adoption. However in practice, it has been found that many programmers tend to write the program first and then follow this by drawing a flowchart or decision tables. Could they be saying that these tools do not really help in solving the problem originally as they were intended? For beginners these tools do work, there is no question of this; however, as expertise is increased, the need for this tool seems to diminish. Those who have studied this phenomenon have discovered that although a programmer may reject the flowchart or table, the programs do not necessarily become any better. So again the search was on for a tool that does assist in problem solving. It must be easy to use and understand. It must lend itself to the writing of a program directly from the solution. It must be flexible and suitable for systems as well as programming problems. The answer is found in Top Down Development techniques, which will be explained in the next section.

TOP DOWN DEVELOPMENT

The use of flowcharts and decision tables have been a part of traditional problem solving methods used by the data processor. These methods have been in use since the first computers were available to the general business population. Top Down Development, the third problem analysis method, will be discussed in this section. First let's consider why a new technique was needed.

Programmer Productivity

There has been a great deal of concern about programmer productivity and effectiveness. Studies showed that programmers averaged 5 to 10 debugged source language statements per day. What were they doing the rest of the time? Basically they were debugging programs of the errors introduced at the time the programs were written. These errors came from many sources:

1. Planning errors
2. Organizational errors
3. Lack of communication
4. Logic errors
5. Program language errors

Some of these problems could be overcome quite easily. For instance, Program Language Errors were usually detected by the diagnostic facilities of the compiler. However, errors in planning the needs of a system or in organizing the large quantities of information needed in a programming project were not easily overcome.

In fact, programmers were spending far more time correcting errors and debugging code that was written incorrectly the first time. This was considered a necessary part of the job, and to many it was an acceptable level of performance.

However, this began to change early in the 1970s. In 1972, Edsger Dijkstra made his classic ACM Turing Award Lecture. In this lecture he stated:

> Those who want really reliable software will discover that they must find means of avoiding the majority of bugs to start with, and as a result the program process will become cheaper.*

This search for reliability and reduced costs in computer programs led to the techniques of top down development, structured programming, and the chief programmer team.

Top Down Methods

Top down development involves a systematic procedure of problem solving. This method may be rather simply stated. It consists of specifying a solution to a problem in quite general terms. This is the top level. Then each top level statement is broken down into further detail. These statements are further broken down until no more detail is needed. This is the bottom level (Figure 12-10).

---

* E.W. Dijkstra, "The Humble Programmer," 1972 ACM Turing Award Lecture, *Communications of the ACM*, October 1972.

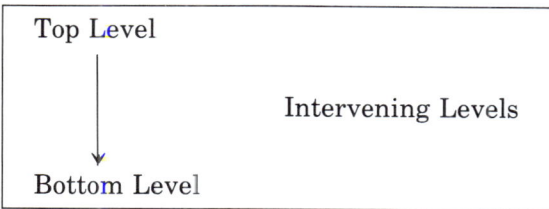

Figure 12-10. Top down development.

The method of progressing from the top level to the bottom level involves four basic steps (Figure 12-11). When these steps are applied, top down development becomes almost automatic.

To demonstrate this technique, let's take a simple problem of producing a product cost summary report from input data.

Product Cost Summary Report. The first step would involve analyzing the problem. The basic requirements might be that headings are needed, costs must be calculated, details and totals printed.

In the second step, the problem is divided into separate parts. This results in the following:

1. Print headings
2. Read data
3. Calculate costs
4. Print detail
5. Print total

Each entry made is quite simple and states in general terms what is to be done.

1. Analyze the problem in order to understand its basic requirements.
2. Divide the problem into easily understood and separate parts in a logical order.
3. Take each part that is not totally defined and break it into even smaller parts.
4. Repeat step 3 until all parts are totally defined.

Figure 12-11. Four basic steps of top down development.

274 PROBLEM SOLVING

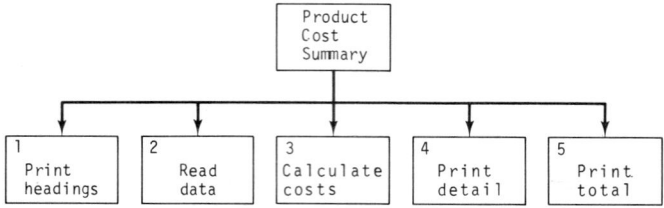

Figure 12-12. Top level and second level blocks.

Expressed in chart form, this development appears in Figure 12-12 where the progression from top level (Product Cost Summary) to the second level is clear. Some of the second level entries are not fully defined and need to be divided into smaller parts. Steps 1 and 3 are now developed to a more detailed level.

1.1 Print Heading Line 1
1.2 Print Heading Line 2
1.3 Print Heading Line 3
3.1 Labor Cost is Hours times Labor Rate
3.2 Overhead Cost is Hours times Overhead Rate
3.3 Total Cost is Material Cost plus Labor Cost plus Overhead Cost

If these details are added to the chart, we now have the representation in Figure 12-13.

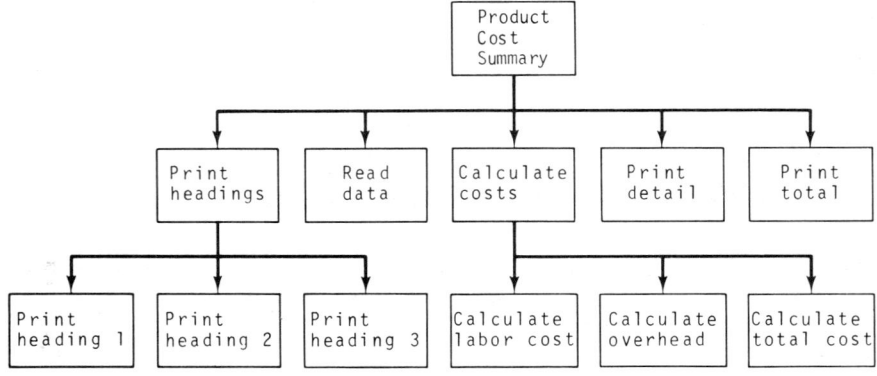

Figure 12-13. Top down with third level included.

In this example, only the headings and the calculations needed a more detailed development. They have been expanded to a third level, while the others remain at the second level. The more complex the problem, the more levels of development are needed. Finally, the logic for each of these steps is combined into a completed top down development of the solution:

> 1 Print Headings
>   1.1 Print Heading Line 1
>   1.2 Print Heading Line 2
>   1.3 Print Heading Line 3
> 2 Read Data
> 3 Calculate Costs
>   3.1 Labor Cost is Hours times Labor Rate
>   3.2 Overhead Cost is Hours times Overhead Rate
>   3.3 Total Cost is Material Cost plus Labor Cost plus Overhead Cost
> 4 Print Detail
> 5 Print Total

This solution may now be used to write a structured program. The steps shown represent statements needed in the programming language. If these steps are followed carefully, a logically correct program will be written. This of course depends on the top down being prepared correctly.

Structured Programming

The search for more effective methods of problem solving led not only to top down development, but also to structured programming concepts in the use of programming languages. The two are so closely related in concept that they form a unified approach to program design and coding.

The essence of structured programming was well described by Dijkstra when he suggested that due to the disastrous effects of the GO TO statement it should be completely abolished from high-level languages.

Although the languages have retained the GO TO, most structured programs do not use it. Instead they use three basic control structures. These control structures, when used properly, result in programs with certain positive characteristics as follows:

1. Easy to read and understand
2. Program modularity ensured
3. The program contains fewer errors
4. Programs are easier to debug
5. Program maintenance is simplified

Sequence Control Structure. The first control structure (Figure 12-14) represents a sequence of processing steps to be executed by the program in the order written.

These steps can be arithmetic operations, input/output commands, assignments, etc. A basic property of a control structure is that it has only one point at which it is entered and one point where it exits. Thus a sequence always begins at the first statement and ends at the last statement of the sequence.

An example of a sequence control structure in COBOL is

```
MOVE INPUT-RECORD TO STORAGE.
ADD ONE TO RECORD-COUNT.
MULTIPLY QUANTITY BY UNIT-COST GIVING TOTAL-COST.
```

This sequence consists of a move, an add, and a multiply. The sequence always begins at the move and ends at the multiply. This never changes since no decisions or branching occurs.

If-Then-Else Control Structure. Figure 12-15 shows the concepts of an If-Then-Else control structure. Again there is only one entry and one exit point. The crucial part here is the decision (If), which evaluates a condition and then chooses one of the actions. If the condition was true, the Then action is executed. However, if the condition was false, the Else action will be executed. A Then action may, if necessary, be a sequence control structure when a number of actions need to be taken. This also applies to the Else action.

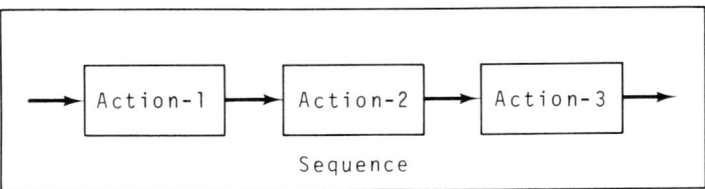

Figure 12-14. Sequence control structure.

PROGRAMMER PRODUCTIVITY 277

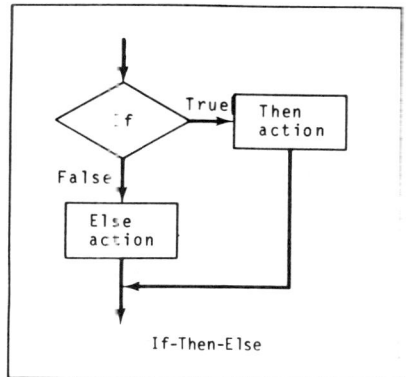

Figure 12-15. If-Then-Else control structure.

An example of this control structure may be a simple choice between adding or subtracting an amount to or from a balance. This may be expressed in COBOL as follows:

```
IF CODE = 1 THEN SUBTRACT AMOUNT FROM BALANCE
              ELSE ADD AMOUNT TO BALANCE.
```

This statement specifies the condition (IF CODE = 1), the action to be taken when true (THEN SUBTRACT AMOUNT FROM BALANCE), and the action when false (ELSE ADD AMOUNT TO BALANCE).

Perform-Until Control Structure. The Perform-Until control structure (Figure 12-16) shows a single input and output structure that permits

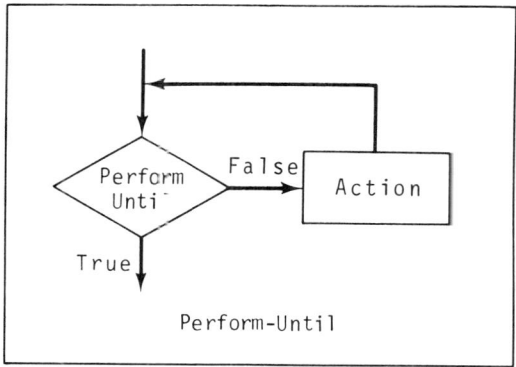

Figure 12-16. Perform-Until control structure.

iteration of actions. The Until is a decision that evaluates to true or false in a manner similar to the If. A false evaluation causes the action to be executed. As long as the condition evaluates false, the action will be repeated. When a true occurs, the sequence is completed, and control leaves by the exit. The action may consist of any other control structure as the need arises.

A simple example of the Perform-Until is a case of reading cards, calculating an amount, and printing the results.

> 1 Read initial card
> 2 Perform Until no more cards
>   2.1 Amount is quantity times cost
>   2.2 Print
>   2.3 Read next card
> 3 Stop

The Perform-Until consists of all step 2 statements. It indicates all statements at step 2 are to be executed until there are no more cards. When the supply of input cards is exhausted, step 3 stops the program. Notice that within the Perform Until, the statements are a sequence control structure.

The COBOL code for these statements is shown on the next page. In this program, a variable called NO-CARDS is initially given a value of zero (not shown here). When the end of the file is reached, this variable is set on to indicate no more cards are available. This causes the Perform to terminate. In COBOL, the performed statements are placed in a paragraph called PROCESS in this example.

Additional programs using structured principles will be found in the chapters on programming languages. These techniques are particularly valuable in high-level languages such as COBOL and PL/I. The methods may be applied to any language even though the essential control structures are not an inherent part of the language.

```
        READ CARD AT END MOVE 1 TO NO-CARDS.
        PERFORM PROCESS UNTIL NO-CARDS = 1.
        STOP RUN.

PROCESS.
        MULTIPLY QUANTITY TIMES COST GIVING
        AMOUNT.
        PRINT DETAIL AFTER 2 LINES.
        READ CARD AT END MOVE 1 TO NO-CARDS.
```

Chief Programmer Team

In 1969, a significant project was undertaken by IBM called the New York Times Project. This project was designed to automate the *New York Times* newspaper clipping file by placing abstracts on a large data base. This would allow users to browse through the file and then access original articles stored on microfiche. The system was developed over a period of 22 calendar months and consisted of approximately 83,000 source code lines.

F. Terry Baker, the team's chief programmer, reports that the file processing system passed a week of acceptance testing without error. It ran for 20 months before the first error was discovered. The chief programmer and back-up programmers produced code with only one detected error per man year. In comparison to most programming projects, the success of this venture is astounding. This success is based upon the chief programmer team concept.

The team approach combines several of the concepts already discussed. By including these factors together, an increase in productivity and reliability is achieved. These major factors are:

1. Top Down Design
2. Structured Programming
3. Chief Programmer Team

The first two areas have already been discussed in this chapter. In Top Down design, you begin with a high-level definition of a system and progress to lower levels by breaking the system into parts and sub-parts as detail is added. Structured programming uses the three basic control structures of Sequence, If-Then-Else, and Perform-Until.

The key to making the most effective use of these methods is the Chief Programmer Team. The team concept is essentially an organizational method for effectively using technical and clerical personnel. Team members consist of the following:

Chief Programmer Team Members

Chief Programmer
Back-up Programmer
Librarian

Each team member contributes specific skills and performs certain functional duties within the team. Depending on the size of the project, additional people are brought in to fill certain requirements. These people could be technicians, systems analysts, software experts, and procedure writers. The responsibilities of the team members are described in the following sections.

Chief Programmer. The chief programmer designs and codes the most critical parts of the project. Because of this primary role, he must be a highly skilled programmer. He also performs the critical tasks of system testing and implementation. In addition, he is the head administrator of the project, and all team members report to him.

Chief Programmer Functions

>Designs
>Codes
>Tests
>Administrates

Back-Up Programmer. The back-up programmer is also a highly skilled programmer whose primary responsibility is to provide support for the chief programmer. He designs parts of the system, codes and tests these parts, and assists with implementation. On a large project, he will be involved in some of the administrative duties as well. The back-up programmer must be ready to assume the role of chief programmer in the event that he quits, is reassigned to other duties, or for any other reason leaves the project. Thus he will be active in all phases of the system. Programmers at this level should be able to produce about 10,000 lines of code per year.

Back-up Programmer Functions

>Designs
>Codes
>Tests

Librarian. The librarian performs clerical and secretarial tasks in order to relieve the programmers of these nontechnical duties. Although this function is essentially not of a technical nature, its importance is not to be underestimated. A secretary with a small amount of training could qualify for this position.

Besides the obvious secretarial duties, a librarian supports the Programming Production Library. This library consists of two main components: an external and an internal file.

Librarian Functions

>Secretarial
>External File Maintenance
>Internal File Maintenance

The external file contains documents that are human readable. This includes design and implementation notes and letters, coding sheets, compilation listings, and test run results. All of these documents are filed, and a history is maintained of all activity. These records are basically public so that all team members have access to them and may benefit from them. This encourages the reading of code produced by each team member. Code reading in turn encourages the writing of programs that are easy to read, debug, and maintain.

The internal file is a machine-readable file. It consists of technical information needed for the operation of the system. Included are things like job control statements, source program statements, object programs, and test data. Changes to be made to this file are initiated by the programmer and submitted to the librarian. The librarian implements the change in the appropriate section of the internal file. New listings are then supplied to the programmer.

This kind of close knit organization is essential to any large project. The simulation system for Skylab produced by IBM required about 400,000 source statements. In order to produce a system of this scale, precise organizational techniques must be applied.

TERMS TO STUDY

Back-up Programmer
Chief Programmer
Chief Programmer Team
Decision Table
If-Then-Else Control Structure
Librarian
Perform-Until Control Structure

Processing
Program Flowchart
Program Production Library
Sequence Control Structure
Structured Programming
Top Down Development

QUESTIONS FOR REVIEW

1. Name and describe 6 different flowcharting symbols.
2. Draw a flowchart to read 10 cards, each containing a number. Find and print the sum and the average of these numbers.
3. Cards for payroll contain department, employee, rate per hour, and hours worked. Draw a flowchart showing how to produce a report showing each card and a gross salary. Print totals at the end of each department and at the end of the report. How would you produce a summary report showing only totals for each department without the employee detail?

4. What are some of the disadvantages of flowcharts?
5. Name the components of a decision table.
6. Create a decision table for problem 2.
7. A personnel card contains employee, status, age, and experience. Status consists of codes 1 to 6, representing different skill levels. Draw a decision table to select employees of status 5 or 6 who are over 30 and have more than 8 years of experience.
8. What is top down development? What are the four basic steps to follow when solving a problem?
9. Show the top down for problem 2.
10. Describe the three structured programming control structures.
11. Who are the members of the Chief Programmer Team? Name the responsibilities of each member.

13

Introduction to Programming

Developing a flowchart or top down is only a part of the solution to a specific problem. Although a solution to the problem has been organized, it is not in a form the computer can read. The next step is to code the solution in a specific computer language.

Several hundred languages are available, but only a handful are used for most business applications. The most common are COBOL, BASIC, FORTRAN, and PL/I. The objective of each of these is to translate the human solution into a form recognized by the computer. Each language has a translator, which translates the source program (COBOL, etc.) into the machine language of the computer. Translators come in two basic varieties: compilers and interpreters.

TRANSLATORS

Compilers

Most business languages use compilers. Compilers are programs that translate a source program to object (machine) language and then execute it under control of an operating system. A compiler takes each source statement and generates a series of machine statements that will effectively implement the solution. When object code is produced, the compiler no longer retains the source program that is not needed for execution. The source may be stored on a library for future reference if the programmer so decides.

"He's been wearing it ever since he single-handedly won that programming contest last week."

© *Creative Computing*

Compilers are usually large, complex programs. This is necessary for them to produce efficient and optimal object code. Some typical compilers are IBM's PL/I Optimizer, PL/I F and FORTRAN IV, Cornell's PL/C, Waterloo University's WATFOR, WATFIV, and WATFIV-S, as well as most COBOL translators.

Interpreters

Unlike a compiler, an interpreter takes each statement of source code, translates it, and executes it immediately. The interpreter progresses to the next statement and does the same. Translation does not usually use machine code but a pseudo-code, which is executed by the interpreter. If a statement in the source program is accessed a second time, the translation and execution process are repeated.

An interpreter is not as efficient as a compiler for large programs or programs used frequently. They are smaller than compilers and are often tailored to specific needs such as educational use where many small programs are translated. Some common interpreters are IBM's PL/I Checkout Compiler, University of Toronto's PLUTO, and most BASIC Translators.

Translator Types

Batch Translators. Programs can be run in either batch or interactive mode, depending on the type of computer hardware and translator in use. When batch mode is used, programs are written on coding forms by the programmer. The forms are keypunched on cards or key entered on tape or diskette. The program is then submitted to the computer for compilation and execution. The computer run results are returned to the programmer after a time delay of an hour, several hours, or even the next day.

When the programmer receives the results, errors are debugged and the program is corrected. The run is resubmitted and the process is repeated. This sequence of correction and resubmission recurs until the program is correct. The entire procedure may take weeks or even months to complete depending upon the program's size and complexity.

Interactive Translators. When a program is run in interactive mode, a CRT or teletypewriter terminal is used (Figure 13-1). The program is entered directly from the keyboard. Immediate response to errors is given by the interpreter, and they may be corrected immediately. Rather than wait for long turnaround times, programs are debugged immediately online to the computer. This method leads to greater programmer efficiency and can reduce the frustration often experienced when waiting long periods for computer runs. Programs are completed sooner than when a batch system is used, and greater job satisfaction is experienced by the programmer. However, the interactive approach uses more expensive hardware and software than a batch system.

PROGRAMMING LANGUAGES

Without a program, the computer would be a useless piece of electronic equipment. It is the program that provides the computer with the means for performing payroll operations, accounting, word processing, graphics, animation, and even music. Programs are required for the simplest of operations, such as adding two numbers together, to the most complex, such as an airline reservation system.

Figure 13-1. Interactive programming. (*Courtesy of Hewlett-Packard*)

What then is a program? We could say that a program is a set of instructions. These instructions are the directions that the computer must follow to do an operation such as payroll. But a computer program is not like directions that you or I would follow to do payroll. These would likely be written in English, and although they might be written as a series of steps to be followed, the English instructions could not be followed by a computer.

A computer program is written in a language the computer understands. Some widely used computer languages are shown in Figure 13-2. The instructions for the computer are written in one of these (or many other) languages by the computer programmer who has been trained to write in the computer language. But the computer may not directly understand this language and so it must be translated. As this diagram shows, a language such as BASIC or COBOL must first be passed through a translator before the computer can understand or follow the instructions.

Why, you may ask, don't we simply write the program in machine language? This is possible but it turns out that machine language is much more difficult to understand than, say, BASIC. Machine language is also much more error prone, or more accurately, the programmer is more error prone when writing programs in machine language.

BASIC

The name BASIC is an acronym of Beginners All-Purpose Symbolic Instruction Code. BASIC was developed by Dartmouth College for use in

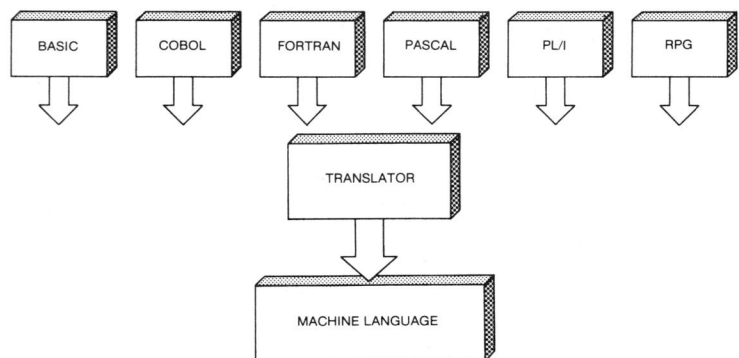

Figure 13-2. Computer programs are usually written in a high-level language such as BASIC before they are translated into the computer's machine language. Since each language has unique characteristics, each will have its own translator.

a time-sharing environment where each BASIC user works at his own typewriter or CRT terminal and interacts with the computer using the BASIC language as a problem-solving tool.

BASIC had been used primarily as an instructional language because of its inherent simplicity until the recent development of the microcomputer. Now the majority of microcomputers offer BASIC as the primary language for application programming.

One of the strongest features of BASIC is its ability to function interactively with the user of the program. This means the user can respond to questions from the program and then receive immediate results.

The sample BASIC program in Figure 13-3 interacts with a student by asking for input data consisting of name and number of subjects. The program then computes and displays the cost of tuition as shown in the output. Obviously, this program is oversimplified because many more factors may be involved in tuition costs.

COBOL

The name COBOL is derived from COmmon Business Oriented Language and is intended primarily for use in business-oriented applications. COBOL has been implemented by all major computer manufacturers including many of the larger microcomputers. The language arose when representatives from government and business met at the Pentagon in May 1959. They were looking for a high-level programming language to be used for general purpose business applications.

The first version of COBOL was released in December 1959 and was subsequently followed by several newer versions. In August 1968, the

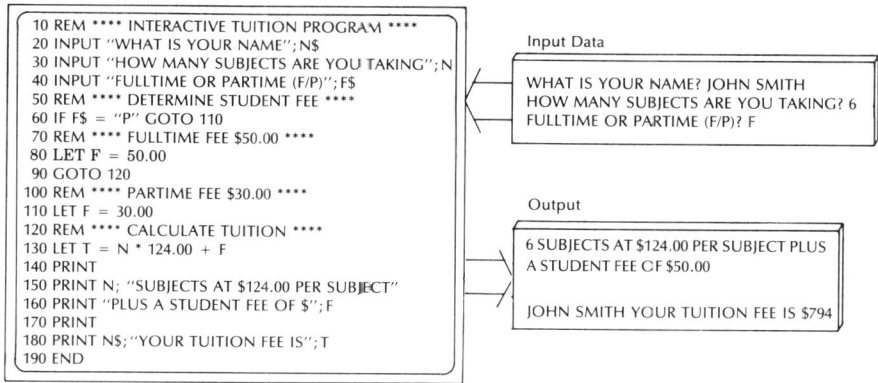

Figure 13-3. Interactive BASIC tuition program with sample input and output data.

first standard version was approved by the American National Standards Institute (ANSI). This was known as ANSI COBOL. Present versions of COBOL are based on the 1974 standards. The purpose of a standard is to allow a standard COBOL program to be machine independent. However, because of many manufacturer additions to the language, this independence is rarely true in real life.

Although COBOL is wordier than most languages, this feature generally renders it easier to read and understand. A major advantage of COBOL is its capability to handle files whether they be sequential, indexed sequential, or random. COBOL also has the capability to be linked with data-base languages for access to data-base files.

Figure 13-4 shows a short COBOL program, which prints one line of output. Although this is a relatively simple task (it could be done with

```
IDENTIFICATION DIVISION.
PROGRAM-ID.
   SAMPLE.
AUTHOR.
   DON CASSEL.

ENVIRONMENT DIVISION.
INPUT-OUTPUT SECTION.
FILE-CONTROL.
   SELECT REPORT-FILE ASSIGN TO UT-S-PRINTER.

DATA DIVISION.
FILE SECTION.
FD REPORT-FILE,
   RECORD CONTAINS 80 CHARACTERS,
   LABEL RECORDS OMITTED,
   DATA RECORD IS PRINT-LINE.
01  PRINT LINE.
    02   FILLER PIC X(40).
    02   LINE-A PIC X(93).

PROCEDURE DIVISION.
BEGIN-PROGRAM.
   OPEN OUTPUT REPORT-FILE.
   MOVE SPACES TO PRINT-LINE.
   MOVE 'FIRST TEST OF COBOL PROGRAM' TO LINE-A.
   WRITE PRINT-LINE AFTER ADVANCING 2 LINES.
END-OF-PROGRAM.
   CLOSE REPORT FILE.
   STOP RUN.
```

Figure 13-4. Sample COBOL program.

two statements in BASIC), COBOL requires substantial overhead to write the program.

All COBOL programs consist of four divisions: the Identification, Environment, Data, and Procedure divisions. The Identification Division indicates the name of the program and the programmer. The Environment Division selects the files and the device to be used by the program, such as a card reader and printer. The Data Division describes the logical characteristics of each file, such as the record size and format. Finally, the Procedure Division describes the logic or procedure to be used in solving the problem. This procedure may include opening files, reading and writing them, doing calculations, and decision making.

COBOL, unlike BASIC, has a predefined format for writing programs. Figure 13-5 shows a typical form used by a programmer when writing a COBOL program.

Statements that are division names, section names, or paragraph names begin in the A margin from columns 8 to 11. All other statement types begin in columns 12 to 72, which is called the B margin.

COBOL is a language with scores of rules and formats that need to be followed exactly. It is impossible in a short description to discuss all these requirements. However, it is a necessary process for anyone who wishes to write programs in COBOL.

FORTRAN

FORTRAN for many years has been a highly popular language among educators and the mathematical and scientific communities. The name is taken from FORmula TRANslation, which implies that its main use is for programming mathematical formulas. Its relative simplicity has led to a wide variety of uses. This widespread application has been encouraged because virtually every major computer manufacturer provides a FORTRAN compiler.

The most common compiler is FORTRAN IV. Many schools use WATFOR, WATFIV, or WATFIV-S, which are high-speed FORTRAN compilers written by the University of Waterloo in Canada. FORTRAN, like BASIC, lacks the essential statement types to promote good structured programming techniques. This deficiency has been somewhat improved by more recent compilers such as WATFIV-S and FORTRAN 77, which now have statements specifically tailored to encourage structured programming.

Figure 13-6 shows a FORTRAN program that reads a series of numbers and computes their average. If the data read consists of the numbers 78, 65, 83, and 54, the output showing the average of 70.0 percent is produced.

COBOL PROGRAM SHEET

System Cobol Description
Program Sample
Programmer Don Cassel Date 26/7/84

WRITTEN AS:	0	Ø	1	I	'	/	¢
PUNCH AS:	NUMBER	LETTER	NUMBER	LETTER	QUOTE	SLASH	12 PUNCH

Sheet 1 of 1
Identification 73 80

```
SEQUENCE
(PAGE)(SERIAL)
1  3 4  6 7 8   12  16  20  24  28  32  36  40  44  48  52  56  60  64  68  72
      010   IDENTIFICATIØN DIVISIØN.
      020   PRØGRAM-ID.
      030       SAMPLE.
      040   AUTHØR.
      050       DØN CASSEL.
      060   ENVIRØNMENT DIVISIØN.
      070   INPUT-ØUTPUT SECTIØN.
      080   FILE-CØNTRØL.
      090       SELECT REPØRT-FILE ASSIGN TO UT-S-PRINTER.
      100   DATA DIVISIØN.
      110   FILE SECTIØN.
      120   FD  REPØRT-FILE
      130       RECØRD CØNTAINS 133 CHARACTERS.
      140       LABEL RECØRDS ØMITTED,
      150       DATA RECØRD IS PRINT-LINE.
      160   01  PRINT-LINE.
      170       02 FILLER PIC X(40).
      180       02 LINE-A PIC X(93).
      190
      200
```

Figure 13-5. A COBOL coding sheet.

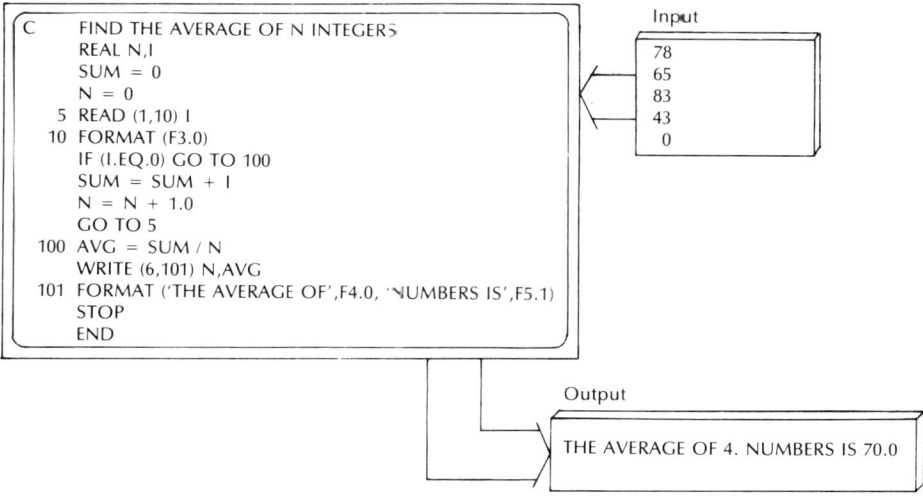

Figure 13-6. A FORTRAN program to compute the average of *N* numbers. In this case, the program will average four numbers; the fifth number (zero) identifies end of the data.

Although FORTRAN is an excellent "number cruncher," it lacks the flexibility to handle alphabetic strings and files effectively.

Pascal

The high-level language Pascal was developed by Nicklaus Wirth who intended it to be independent of the particular computer on which it is run and to take advantage of structured programming methodologies. Wirth's Pascal defines the Standard Pascal, which requires the programmer to use the structured techniques. Using structured programming results in more effective programs because they are easier to develop and debug, easier to maintain, and can be largely self-documenting.

Since Pascal has few language constructs, it is easy to learn (although not as easy as BASIC) and has been adopted by many schools as an introductory programming language. It is also in use by some industries for developing computer software and application programs. Although Pascal requires more memory than other languages, programs generally execute faster. This feature makes Pascal a natural for software development that previously used machine codes.

Pascal has been implemented on machines ranging from microcomputers to large-scale computer systems. Some standard Pascal compilers are USCD Pascal and Pascal 6000.

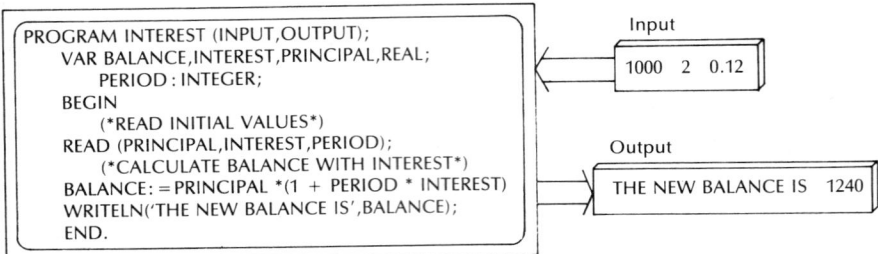

Figure 13-7. A Pascal program to calculate simple interest. Given a principal of $1000 invested for 2 years at a rate of 12 percent, the investment would be worth $1240 after applying simple interest.

PL/I

PL/I is one of the many high-level programming languages used for communicating with computers. It was originally developed by IBM for use with their System/360 series of computers. Today, most major computer companies offer PL/I as an application language for their medium- to large-scale computer systems.

When first announced, PL/I was said to combine the best features of FORTRAN and COBOL. Indeed, it had the excellent arithmetic capabilities of FORTRAN and the file-handling abilities of COBOL. In addition to these attributes, PL/I was based on the block structure of ALGOL, a scientific programming language, also used by Pascal. Although PL/I is widely used today, it never replaced FORTRAN or COBOL. The name PL/I comes from Programming Language One.

All PL/I programs consist of at least one procedure that contains the statements needed for the program. Figure 13-8 shows a sample PL/I program that consists of one main procedure called SAMPLE. The program reads values for a payroll number (NUM), HOURS, and rate of pay

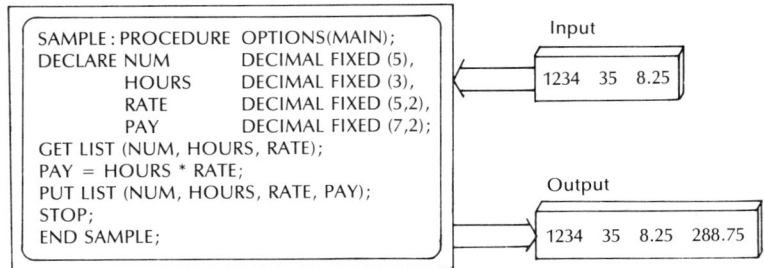

Figure 13-8. A sample PL/I program that calculates a gross salary for employee number 1234. With a 35-hour week and a rate of $8.25 per hour, the employee's gross earnings would be $288.75.

per hour (RATE). An arithmetic statement then calculates the PAY and the PUT LIST prints the results.

PL/I is as easy to learn as Pascal as a first language. However, PL/I has very extensive capabilities for arithmetic, logical operations, file processing up to and including data base, table handling, string manipulation, functions, list processing, and program pre-processing. It is fair to say that most programmers never exhaust the capabilities of the PL/I language.

RPG II

Many smaller companies have relatively routine data processing requirements and may not have a need for the complexity offered by languages like COBOL or PL/I. To meet these needs, RPG or Report Program Generator was developed.

RPG II, and a more recent enhanced version RPG III, is a language used primarily for business reports and routine file handling. It is typically used on minicomputer systems such as the IBM System/34, Burroughs B 1700, and the Sperry Univac System OS/3 for small- to medium-sized businesses. RPG is a problem-oriented language as compared to a procedure-oriented language such as COBOL. A problem-oriented language basically uses a coding system to define input, output, and processing requirements, while a procedure-oriented language uses statements and commands to solve a problem. Languages such as RPG are easier to learn and require less training to use effectively than a procedure-oriented language.

An RPG program is written by coding the pre-printed language specification forms shown in Figure 13-9. The program is then either punched into cards or keyed into a terminal. An RPG compiler takes these codes and translates them into a machine language program for computer execution.

The five commonly used RPG II coding forms are as follows:

1. File Description Specifications—Describes the input, output, and table files used by the RPG program. Computer system hardware is also defined on this form.
2. Extension and Line Counter Specifications—Defines tables, arrays, and disk processing information. The line counter section defines printer line spacing.
3. Input Specifications—Defines input record types including size, names, and fields type within each record in the input files.

294 INTRODUCTION TO PROGRAMMING

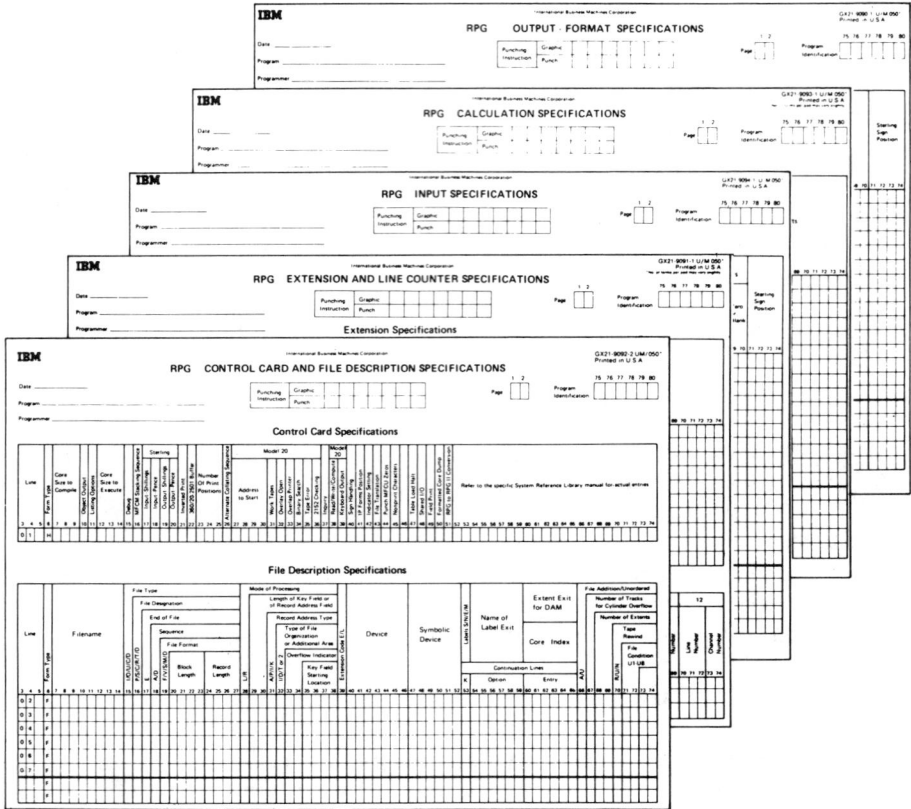

Figure 13-9. RPG II specification forms.

4. Calculation Specifications—Specifies all arithmetic operations, table lookup, and array handling.
5. Output-Format Specifications—Output formats such as the printer or disk files are specified on this form.

The forms are used by first entering a code in column 6 of each form to identify the form. These codes are F, E, I, C and O respectively. Then the appropriate information is coded into each form according to the rules for that form. Since each form is different, there will be five different sets of coding rules to learn, one per form.

In some cases, less than five forms will be needed, especially for simpler applications. But the average business application will have sufficient complexity to require all five.

FOURTH GENERATION LANGUAGES

In the 1980s, a whole new breed of languages erupted. Languages such as FOCUS, INTELLECT, NATURAL, RAMIS II, and TIS are contending for the leadership as fourth generation languages.

Compared to third generation languages such as COBOL and PL/I, this new breed represents a significantly reduced elapsed time from detailed user requirements to the implementation of an operational computer system. However, the fourth generation language (4th GL) provides functions that are significantly different from COBOL or PL/I so that a new way of thinking about programming is required. The fourth generation language typically represents a major reduction of the programmer's coding and testing time, and in many cases, 4th GLs are designed for use by users instead of programmers.

Computer applications may be classed as calculation—or information—intensive. 4th GLs are more effective for solving problems of an information-intensive nature. Also, 4th GLs encourage the development of transaction-oriented systems that are more applicable to an on-line interactive environment.

Another benefit of the fourth generation language is that it allows system designers to quickly produce a prototype of the system. This prototype highlights the essential features of a user's requirement, which leads to faster and more complete needs analysis.

A fourth generation language is characterized by being very high level, consisting of extremely powerful compact verbs. The language will usually integrate many of the features of an application language, query language, report writer, data dictionary, DBMS, and telecommunications into a single software product. 4th GLs are transaction oriented rather than batch oriented.

4th GLs are user friendly. The dialogue consists of commands that are easy to learn and remember. Keying syntax errors are often forgiven because the software has a degree of intelligence not found in the 3rd generation language. Menus are often used that hand hold the user, and prompts given are meaningful and easily interpreted.

Data structures used by 4th GLs are transparent to the user. The language function is independent of the operating system, so no other job control languages are needed. The fourth generation language represents a move away from the traditional programming solution toward a user-oriented product. This move represents a significant trend in software, which is perhaps comparable to the move to the miniaturization of components in hardware leading to widespread use of the computer in the 1970s.

LOW-LEVEL LANGUAGES

High-level languages like BASIC and COBOL make programming relatively easy to learn and programs easier and faster to write. But programs written in a high-level language do not produce very efficient machine code and they frequently use excessive amounts of memory. These problems can be partly reduced by using efficient compilers or optimizing compilers, but these are only partially effective. High-level languages, in order to be relatively easy to use, also restrict the programmer's access to special features available in the hardware.

While machine language resolves the above problems it is not easy to use, even for an experienced programmer. Instead, a symbolic language called Assembly language is used (Figure 13-10). Each type of computer will have an assembly language that is unique to that machine. An assembly language program written for an IBM 4341 would not be the same as the program written for a DEC VAX-11/70. After the program is written in assembly language, it is passed through an Assembler, which produces the machine code.

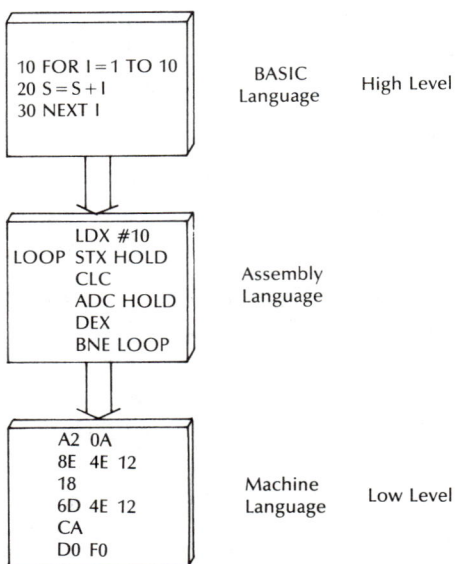

Figure 13-10. A small program that computes the sum of integers from 1 to 10 written in microcomputer (Apple or PET) BASIC, assembly language, and machine language. While the assembly language program appears to be slightly longer than the BASIC version, the assembly program will require less memory and execute about 40 times faster.

Assembler is most useful for programs that are for high volume applications and where computation and I/O speed is an essential characteristic of the program. Programs where memory size is a factor will also benefit from the use of low-level languages.

Most systems programs such as the operating system, compilers, and interpreters are written in a low-level language to minimize excessive use of memory and promote execution efficiency.

VISICALC: The First Spread-sheet

FOCUS

A new trend in computing is the development of user friendly software that does not require a programming background to use. Unlike most packaged software, VisiCalc is not designed for a specific application, but like BASIC or COBOL, it may be used for many applications. The major difference between VisiCalc and a programming language is the ease with which VisiCalc may be used.

VisiCalc was developed for microcomputer users and functions something like a large paper spread-sheet and electronic calculator combined. The computer's screen acts like a window onto the spread-sheet, which has 63 columns and 254 rows where information may be stored. Viewing the screen, you can see 20 rows of data and a number of columns, depending upon the width of the column and the width of the screen.

Learning VisiCalc is much easier than learning to use a programming language. Even after an hour's introduction, meaningful results may be produced. The VisiCalc program is loaded from disk, and it begins by displaying a section of the spread-sheet. Each column and row location is uniquely identified by a letter and a number. For instance, A1 identifies column A, row 1.

A large cursor may be moved to any location on the grid. At this location, either a number, formula, a function, or a label may be typed. The numeric data may represent a quantity, a cost, a test score, or anything the user wants. A function may describe an operation to be done—such as to sum a column of numbers—or compute an average.

One of the more powerful features of VisiCalc is its ability to automatically recalculate all values on the spread-sheet whenever a single value has been changed. For example, by entering a new tax deduction you can see immediately how this will affect your take-home pay.

If one window on the spread-sheet is not enough, then the screen may be split either vertically or horizontally to give two windows. Each window may be scrolled independently to give a view of different areas of the spread-sheet.

Another powerful feature is the ability to replicate a formula along a row or column rather than typing it in for each location. A few simple keystrokes will cause the formula to be replicated as many times as needed.

VisiCalc requires about 23K or more of RAM, depending upon the particular type of microcomputer. It costs around $150.00 and is considered to be one piece of software that has sold many microcomputers on the merit of the software alone.

CHARACTERISTICS OF A GOOD PROGRAM

In order to write good programs, we need to determine the elements that characterize "good" in terms of programming. A number of the traits associated with good programs are listed in Figure 13-11.

> *Characteristics of a Good Program*
>
> 1. The program works.
> 2. It is easy to read.
> 3. It is efficient.
> 4. It is well organized.
> 5. It is ready on time.

Figure 13-11.

Program Works

This may seem to be an obvious point, but no matter how well all of the other characteristics are implemented, the final result must be a working program. This can be further qualified by saying it must work according to the program specifications and do the job it was intended to do.

Easy to Read

Again this may seem obvious, but it is one area where many programmers fall short. Ease of readability is important not only for the programmer who originates the program, but even more so for the programmer who may eventually be responsible for its maintenance.

One simple solution is to use variable names which are meaningful to the reader. Instead of saying

$$V = L * W * D;$$

say

$$VOLUME = LENGTH * WIDTH * DEPTH;$$

This second form is quite clear and takes very little extra time on the part of the programmer.

Avoid using repetitive names like NUM1, NUM2, NUM3, etc. These do very little to explain the data being used. Even a variable like AC-COUNT-NUMBER is better than NUM or NUMBER.

When a name seems to be too long or there are compiler limitations, then meaningful abbreviations can be used. In this case, VOLUME could be VOL and still be understood. ACCOUNT-NUMBER could be ACT-NUM without loss of meaning.

Some languages such as BASIC have severe limitations on the names permitted by the translator. In this case the programmer will need to work within these limitations and use comments to give further explanation.

Comments are also a useful means of clarifying points of possible confusion in a program. They allow greater flexibility than the use of descriptive names. Comments are indicated in various ways, such as the /* */ in PL/I, REM statement in BASIC, an asterisk (*) in column 7 in COBOL and a letter C in the first position of the FORTRAN statement.

```
/* FIND THE SUM OF INTEGERS FROM 1 TO LIMIT */
DO COUNT = 1 TO LIMIT;
    SUM = SUM + COUNT;
END;
```

Efficient

There are extremes to program efficiency. Highly efficient programs such as widely used software are written with special care with major emphasis on efficiency. This is time consuming with sometimes as few as two or three source statements coded per day. While the average programmer may not aspire to this level of efficiency, a relatively efficient program is still a worthwhile goal.

A simple method to improve efficiency is to use as few statements as necessary to solve a specific problem. The statements

```
        IF AMOUNT > 100.00 THEN DO;
            TAX = AMOUNT * 0.07;
            GO TO X;
            END;
        TAX = 0;
X:
```

could have been written more simply as

```
        IF AMOUNT > 100.00 THEN
            TAX = AMOUNT * 0.07;
        ELSE TAX = 0;
```

or even

```
        TAX = 0;
        IF AMOUNT > 100.00 THEN
            TAX = AMOUNT * 0.07;
```

CHARACTERISTICS OF A GOOD PROGRAM 301

These examples in PL/I show how a program can be made more efficient with a little thought and time. This requires a thorough knowledge of the language as well as some ingenuity on the part of the programmer.

Well Organized

A program that is well organized is not only easier to read but also easier to debug. Good organization is promoted by top down development of program logic as well as the use of structured programming techniques. Programs written using the three basic constructs of structured programming limit the variations that lead to confusing program organization.

"Now if you will follow the simple logic of this subroutine - - "

Figure 13-12.

Structured programming also minimizes the use of GO TOs, which have a tendency to create program disorganization. In some languages, such as BASIC, structured programming may not be easily implemented. In this case the programmer needs to be especially careful about program organization.

Ready on Time

Most projects in the business world have schedules to keep if they are to succeed. Programming is no different. One of the main purposes of using a computer, and therefore in writing programs, is to save the company money. To save money, costs of program development must be predictable. These costs are for both hardware and the development of software. Unless programs are completed when they are scheduled, their costs will exceed the budget. In addition, the cost saving that the new system was to have generated will not be realized until the programs are implemented. So we lose in both additional development costs as well as a delay in the use of the new system.

PROGRAM CODING

The process of writing a program is called coding. This follows the step of preparing a flowchart or top down development of your solution. Figure 13-13 shows a structured COBOL program that might have been written from top down logic. COBOL has been used here since it is the most commonly used business language. It is also quite easy to read even for those without programming experience.

The business programmer has the option of many different languages besides COBOL. Sometimes the choice is based on which language is most suitable for the application. A mathematically oriented program might use PL/I or FORTRAN. A file-oriented program could use PL/I or COBOL or even RPG. A report program could use RPG, but COBOL or PL/I would also be effective, depending on the detail requirements.

A choice of language is often dependent upon the standards adopted by the programming shop rather than on machine capability. For ease of control, standardization, maintenance, and adaptability, many shops use only one or two languages. Thus in practice the programmer may not have a choice of language but must adhere to the shop standards.

Once the program is written, it must be tested for errors in syntax and logic. This step is as important as the program coding itself.

```
              OPEN INPUT INVOICE, OUTPUT SALES.
              READ INVOICE AT END MOVE 1 TO NO-MORE-SW.
              PERFORM PROCESS UNTIL NO-MORE-SW = 1.
              CLOSE INVOICE, SALES.
              STOP RUN.
       PROCESS.
              IF FIRST = 1 THEN MOVE REGION TO PREVIOUS
                           MOVE 0 TO FIRST.
              IF REGION NOT = PREVIOUS THEN MOVE REGION
                           TO PREVIOUS
                           WRITE REGION-TOTAL AFTER 2
                           LINES.
              ADD AMOUNT TO REGION-TOT.
              ADD AMOUNT TO FINAL-TOT.
              MOVE CORRESPONDING INPUT-REC TO DETAIL.
              WRITE DETAIL AFTER 1 LINE.
              READ INVOICE AT END MOVE 1 TO NO-MORE-SW.
```

Figure 13-13. COBOL program for report by region.

PROGRAM TEST AND DEBUG

There are two basic areas that the programmer concentrates upon in the debugging process. They are:

1. Program syntax
2. Program logic

Program Syntax

This is the first step in program debugging and for the experienced programmer is usually the easiest and least time consuming. Syntax refers to the correct use of the language. Missing commas, periods, brackets, operators, and such would constitute a syntax error. Other errors such as the misuse of symbols, or using a period where a semicolon should be are also in this category. Using variable names in the wrong place also constitutes a program error.

The intent here is not to list all possible errors in program syntax. Rather, the purpose is to create an awareness that each programming language has its own rules for use. Just as in English we have certain rules for using the language to ensure its ability to communicate, so each programming language has its own rules for use.

Although this may seem complex to a new programmer, we have a valuable aid in diagnosing program syntax. Each language has its own compiler or translator. One of the important functions of a compiler is to find improper uses of the language. In doing this, it produces a diagnostic report to aid the programmer in correcting program syntax.

Figure 13-14 shows a PL/I program with several syntax errors. Statement 3 is in error because the statement does not end with a semicolon—rather it has a period, which is invalid in PL/I. Secondly, statement 6 is missing a word that is essential to the correctness of the statement. The missing word is LIST. The corrections are shown in Figure 13-15.

Once the syntax is correct, we then move on to an even more important aspect of program debugging.

Program Logic

Although a program is syntactically correct, this does not mean it is logically correct. To follow through with the example in Figures 13-14 and 13-15, we can determine that although the program is now correct

```
TOTAL:PROCEDURE OPTIONS(MAIN);
NUM=0;
DO I=1 TO 10.
   NUM=NUM+1;
END;
PUT (NUM);
END TOTAL;




     3     1    1           DO I=1 TO 10.
       ERROR  IN  3  MISSING COMMA IN COLUMN 5 (SY06)
              FOR 3  PL/C USES DO I=1 TO 10.,NUM=NUM + 1;

     5     1    1              PUT(NUM);
       ERROR  IN  5  IMPROPER I/O PHRASE (SY22)
              FOR 5  PL/C USES   PUT LIST (NUM);
```

Figure 13-14. PL/I program with syntax errors, sum of 1 to 10.

```
TOTAL:PROCEDURE OPTIONS(MAIN);
NUM = 0
DO I = 1 TO 10;
    NUM = NUM + 1;
END;
PUT LIST(NUM);
END TOTAL:



10
```

Figure 13-15. PL/I program without syntax errors, sum of 1 to 10.

as far as the language is concerned, it still does not solve the problem, which is to find the sum of the numbers from 1 to 10. This sum should be 55. Instead, the result of the program in Figure 13-15 is the value 10. The debugging process involves examining the program to find out why an incorrect answer is given. Upon close examination, we find that statement 4 adds the value 1 to SUM rather than the value I. This accounts for the difference in the expected result and the actual result. Figure 13-16 shows the corrected logic of the program.

The point to consider here is that although the program in Figure 13-15 contained correct statements for PL/I, it did not contain correct statements for solving the problem. The error was found because we knew what to expect from the program. This is an important aspect of program

```
TOTAL:PROCEDURE OPTIONS(MAIN);
NUM = 0;
DO I = 1 TO 10;
    NUM = NUM + I;
END;
PUT LIST(NUM);
END TOTAL;



55
```

Figure 13-16. PL/I program with corrected logic, sum of 1 to 10.

testing. We must know what results to expect. You may wonder, "Why bother to write the program in this case if we know the result?" Suppose we really wish to find the sum of 1 to 1000. We obviously do not wish to manually add these numbers to find out what to expect. Instead we might first test our program using the sum of 1 to 10, which can be easily checked and once this works, apply the technique to the sum of 1 to 1000.

QUESTIONS FOR REVIEW

1. What is a compiler? Name some languages that use compilers.
2. What is the difference between a compiler and an interpreter?
3. What are the differences between programming using a batch translator and an interactive one?
4. Describe the basic characteristics of a good program.
5. After a program has been coded, what steps are necessary to ensure its validity?
6. What types of errors might be found in a program?
7. Why are there computer languages? Why not just tell the computer what you want it to do?
8. What is a program?

14

BASIC

The name BASIC is an acronym of Beginners All-Purpose Symbolic Instruction Code. BASIC was developed by Dartmouth College for use in a time-sharing environment. This is where each BASIC user works at his own typewriter or CRT terminal and interacts with the computer system using the BASIC language as a problem-solving tool. Since this development, BASIC has been used primarily as an instructional language on time-sharing systems; however, a number of batch translators are now in use. Since 1975 most mini- and microcomputers have offered BASIC as a primary language for application programming.

BASIC is similar to FORTRAN but is simpler and easier to use. It is a relatively easy language to learn because it consists of few syntax rules and a small number of statement types. BASIC can be used in a variety of applications ranging from business to computer science.

BASIC PROGRAMMING FUNDAMENTALS

Every statement in the BASIC language consists of some primary elements that apply to each statement. These elements are shown as follows:

      nnnnn   KEYWORD   PARAMETERS

A BASIC statement consists of (1) a line number represented by nnnnn, (2) a keyword that specifies the operation to be performed, and

(3) parameters that are usually variables, constants, or expressions. These parameters further direct the operation to be executed.

An example of a BASIC statement is

    10 LET N = 1

In this statement, 10 is the line number, the word LET is the keyword, and N = 1 are parameters.

Line Numbers

Every BASIC statement begins with a line number identifying the sequential location of that statement within the program. Each line number must be unique. A line number may be up to five digits in length, although it is usually more convenient to use fewer digits, particularly for smaller programs.

Spacing

Spaces are not required within BASIC programming statements. Thus, the statement

    20IFN=100THEN40

is a valid statement and can be recognized by the computer.

Even though this statement is valid, it is preferable to write BASIC statements with spaces to make them more readable. A better way to write the above statement would be

    20 IF N=100 THEN 40

Comments

Comments may be included in the BASIC language through the use of the REMARK statement. The format for this statement is

nnnnn REM comments

or

nnnnn REMARK comments

An example of a REMARK statement is

    100 REMARK COMPUTE TOTALS BY ITERATION

If a comment requires more than one line, a subsequent REMARK statement must be used. An example of this is

    50 REM THIS ROUTINE IS ONLY EXECUTED
    60 REM THE FIRST TIME INTO THE PROGRAM.
    70 REM SUBSEQUENT LOOPS CONTINUE AT
    80 REM STATEMENT NUMBER 230.

Liberal use of REMARK statements are particularly useful in a lengthy program where it is possible that complex routines may not be completely understood by the programmer unless some comments are included to explain how the logic works.

Names

Every program written in the BASIC language requires the use of variable names. These variable names usually represent some numeric value, and because this value is represented by a variable name, it can be changed in value at the direction of the program. For numeric values

© Creative Computing

in BASIC, a variable name is represented by a single letter or by a letter followed by a single digit. Thus, the following are considered valid variable names in the BASIC language:

A	B5
N	N1
K	D9
S	I0

Variables are assigned values in the LET, FOR, and READ statements, which will be discussed later.

Numeric Data

The major part of the processing in the BASIC language deals with the manipulation of numbers. These numbers can take the form of integers or fractional values in decimal form. Both of these can be positive or negative numbers of up to a maximum length depending on the computer in use. Some examples of valid BASIC numbers are:

235	$-.05$
37.5	-235
3.001	0
12345678901	.12345678901

Numbers such as these may appear in LET, FOR, and DATA statements.

Alphanumeric Data

In addition to the use of numeric data, many programs require that alphanumeric information be stored. This can be used for names, descriptions, addresses, codes, etc., which consist of alphabetic as well as, in some cases, numeric characters. A typical maximum size of an alphanumeric string is 132 characters. Variable names for string data consist of an alphabetic character followed by a dollar sign. Thus, for example,

A$

E$

Z$

are all valid alphanumeric names. Alphanumeric names can be assigned character strings through LET statements, INPUT statements, and READ statements. String data may be assigned from one string variable to another. It may be compared to another string variable or to another string constant, and it may be outputted as a string variable or a string constant.

STOP Statement

The STOP statement is a command in the BASIC language that instructs the computer to terminate the program. This may appear at more than one place in the program. Transferring control to the END statement would have the same effect as encountering a STOP statement.

END Statement

The END statement specifies the logical end of a program. No more BASIC statements may follow the END statement, which must have the highest line number of any statement in the program. If this statement is encountered during execution of the program either through a GO TO statement or during the sequential operation of the program, the program will be terminated at that point.

EXERCISES

1. (a) Why can't there be duplicate line numbers in BASIC?
   (b) What is the difference between a keyword and a parameter?
   (c) What effect do remarks have on the BASIC program?
2. Identify the valid variable names in the following:
   a. Z
   b. F7
   c. 3
   d. IN
   e. TOTAL
   f. #6
   g. AO
   h. READ
   i. AA
   j. I$
3. How can you recognize an invalid decimal number?
4. What statement must always be last in a BASIC program?

ARITHMETIC OPERATIONS

Arithmetic expressions appear in many forms, but the final result is the assignment of a constant, a variable, or some expression composed of constants and variables to some specified variable. This is accomplished in the BASIC language through the LET statement.

LET Statement

The LET statement is a statement that computes a mathematical formula and assigns the result of that computation to a variable. The general format for the LET statement is:

> nnnnn LET variable = formula

Assignment of Data. A common use for the LET statement is to assign some initial data to a variable, which is quite often used by other formulas within the program. Here are some examples:

```
100 LET N = 125
135 LET K1 = 23.775
170 LET P = 3.1416
200 LET A5 = K1
```

In the first example, statement 100 causes the value 125 to be assigned to the variable named N. This takes the place of any previous value which N may have had, and this value will never change unless N is used to the left of the equal sign in another LET statement or in a READ or INPUT statement. Thus, N may be used for comparison purposes in an IF statement or as part of a formula in another LET statement, and it will not change its value.

Similarly, in statement 135, the variable K1 is assigned the value 23.775; and in statement 170, the variable P is assigned the value 3.1416.

Statement 200 causes the contents of variable K1 to be assigned to the variable A5. If by the time the program reaches statement 200, K1 has not changed from the value established in statement 135, then the value 23.775 will also be assigned to A5. If, however, K1 has changed its value during the execution of the program, the present value of K1, when statement 200 is reached, will be assigned to variable A5.

Operations. The next major use of the LET statement is for the writing of formulas or arithmetic expressions that are to be computed by the computer. The resulting value is assigned to the variable specified by the LET statement. The arithmetic operators that may be used in the LET statement are:

+ addition
− subtraction
* multiplication
/ division
** or ↑ exponentiation

Each of these operators is applied to two variables or constants. The operation specified is applied to these two variables, and the result is either assigned to the variable in the LET statement or used further in the formula being computed. The only exception to this is when a term is negated. Negation is a variable name preceded by a minus sign causing the negative value of the variable to be computed.

Addition

Suppose two values V and A are to be added, and the result placed in a variable called T.

    10 LET V = 245.00
    20 LET A = 40.00
    30 LET T = V+A

	V	A	T
Before	245.00	40.00	0
After	245.00	40.00	285.00

In this example, we have assigned the values 245.00 and 40.00 to variables V and A, respectively. In statement 30, we instruct the computer to add the contents of V to the contents of A and store the result in T. After the operation, T contains 285.00, which is the sum of the values of V and A. V and A are unaffected by this operation and continue to retain the original values assigned to them.

Addition may also involve the use of a variable and a constant. For example, the expression

    100 LET N = N+1

causes whatever value is in N to be added to the constant value 1. The result of this is placed back into N. This has the effect of increasing N's value by one and is commonly called a counter in programming.

Subtraction

The subtraction operator is used in a similar way to addition.

```
10 LET V = 10
20 LET A = 0.5
30 LET D = V − A
```

	V	A	D
Before	10	0.5	0
After	10	0.5	9.5

In this example, V is assigned the value 10, and A the value 0.5. Statement 30 subtracts the value in A from the value in V and assigns the result to D. Thus, as the diagram shows, the resulting value in D will be 9.5.

The following statements

```
10 LET V = −10
20 LET A = 0.5
30 LET D = V − A
```

cause the result −10.5 to appear in the variable D. Here we can observe that the normal rules of algebra for signs have been applied and that the computer evaluates this expression in the same way that two negatives in mathematics would be evaluated.

Multiplication

In multiplication, two variables or constants are multiplied, and the result is placed in a variable specified in the LET statement. Here the values in A1 and Y are multiplied together by statement 120, and the result is assigned to variable P. This causes P to contain the value 7.035 after statement 120 has been executed.

```
100 LET A1 = 3.5
110 LET Y  = 2.01
120 LET P  = A1*Y
```

ARITHMETIC OPERATIONS   315

	A1	Y	P
Before	3.5	2.01	0
After	3.5	2.01	7.035

Division

```
75 LET X = 75
80 LET Y =  4
90 LET Z = X/Y
```

	X	Y	Z
Before	75	4	0
After	75	4	18.75

The value 75 is assigned to the variable X, and the value 4 is assigned to the variable Y. In statement 90, the value contained in Y is divided into the value in X. The result of this division is placed into Z. The diagram shows that the resulting value in Z is 18.75.

Hierarchy

It is sometimes necessary to combine two or more of the arithmetic operators into one formula: for instance, the expression

```
150 LET R = A + B/C
```

Supposing that the values in A, B, and C are 6, 4, and 2, respectively; then the question we are concerned with is, what is the result in R? This solution depends upon which part of the expression is evaluated first. Conflicts of this type are resolved by a hierarchal structure of arithmetic operators. This structure establishes a priority for these operations. This hierarchy is:

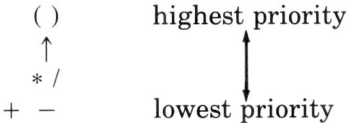

This shows that division has a higher priority than addition. Thus, the expression

150 LET R = A + B/C

requires that division be done first, and then the result of dividing B by C is added to A. This final result is then assigned to the variable R; therefore 8 is the solution to this particular statement. Some LET statements have several operations that utilize the same hierarchy. For example, the statement

25 LET K = A + L + R/A

has two operators at the same level of hierarchy, namely, the addition operators. In an expression of this kind, the operations of the highest level of hierarchy are done first. Therefore, R is divided by A. After this has been done, we then encounter two operators of the same level of hierarchy. In this case, execution proceeds from *left to right*, therefore, A + L will be the second operation computed; and the result will be added to the result of the division operation. The algebraic equivalent of this would be

$$k = a + l + \frac{r}{a}$$

Parentheses

Even though there is a predefined hierarchy of operations, there are some expressions that do not fit easily into this system of priorities. These can be dealt with by rearranging the priorities according to our own needs by using parentheses in appropriate places within the expression. For instance, if we were given the expression

10 LET R = A + B/C/D

this might appear to be a perfectly legitimate BASIC command, which in fact it is. Algebraically this represents

$$r = a + \frac{b/c}{d}$$

If this is the arithmetic expression that we wish to represent then all is well and good. However, if we had intended to represent the algebraic expression

$$r = \frac{a + b}{c/d}$$

then we do have problems. The easiest way to handle this is to use parentheses in the expression, which will then become the highest priority in the formula and force the addition to take place prior to division. Thus, the correct LET statement for this formula would be

10 LET R = (A+B)/(C/D)

Through the use of parentheses, we have established a new level of hierarchy.

ALPHANUMERIC OPERATIONS

Operations for alphanumeric fields are quite simple and are restricted to assigning data from either a constant to a variable or a variable to another variable. Thus, for example, the expression

10 LET A$ = "JOHN DOE"

causes the character string JOHN DOE to be assigned to the variable name A$. The expression

30 LET K$ = "3695 NORTH BLVD"

causes this address to be assigned to K$. The presence of numeric information in this string makes absolutely no difference to the operation. The expression

40 LET B$ = A$

causes the contents of the variable A$ to be assigned to B$. Following this operation, B$ and A$ will contain exactly the same characters.

SIMPLE INTEREST PROGRAM

The equation

$$b = p(1 + ni)$$

is used to calculate simple interest on a dollar amount invested at a particular interest rate for a predefined number of years. In this equation p   is the principal balance in the account at the beginning of the investment period

n   is the number of years over which the investment is made

i   represents the annual interest rate

b   is the account balance at the end of the investment period.

Suppose we are investing $2500.00 for 15 years at a rate of 8.5 percent. The following program shows how to implement the equation in the BASIC language.

```
10 LET P = 2500.00
20 LET N = 15
30 REM INTEREST I IS REPRESENTED IN FRACTIONAL FORM
40 LET I = .085
50 LET B = P*(1 + N*I)
60 LET R$ = "THE NEW BALANCE IS"
70 PRINT R$,B
80 END

READY
RUN

THE NEW BALANCE IS            5687.5
```

Statements 10, 20, and 40 assign the values for the problem to the appropriate variables. Variable names were chosen that closely represented the original formula. This is done for clarity and in no way influences the computer's analysis of the expression. The remark in statement 30 indicates that percent is entered in fractional form. Thus, 8.5 percent is entered as .085. Ten percent would have been entered as .10 or just .1.

Statement 50 is the formula for interest calculation. Notice that in the original formula, multiplication by p was implied. This is also the case for ni. In BASIC, we must use the asterisk to represent multiplication since implied multiplication is not permitted.

Statement 60 assigns a character string to variable R$. This will be used as a comment on the output generated by the program. The PRINT statement 70 instructs the computer to print the result of the calculation, which is $5687.50.

EXERCISES

1. Write a series of LET statements to assign the following data to the associated variable.

	Variable	Data
a.	N	000.00
b.	K2	2.5
c.	T1	1010
d.	N$	JACK SMITH
e.	Z	.00001

2. Given the following assignments, what is the result after each LET statement has been executed in the sequential order shown?

   ```
   10 LET A = 1.0
   20 LET B = 2.0
   30 LET N = 4
   40 LET X = A+B
   50 LET Y = A*B
   60 LET Z = A/B
   70 LET W = X+Y-Z
   80 LET X = X*Y ↑ B/N
   90 LET C = Y ↑ B ↑ 2
   100 LET C = (Y ↑ B) ↑ 2
   110 LET D = (((A*2.0*B)/N) ↑ 3) – 1.0
   120 LET K = –(N)
   130 LET N = –(K)*–(N)
   ```

3. Write equivalent BASIC statements for the following algebraic expressions ($\pi = 3.1416$).

   a. $h = a \cdot b$

   b. $a = b + c - d - 3$

   c. $c = \dfrac{a \cdot b}{e}$

   d. $x = \dfrac{y + z}{w \cdot v}$

   e. $j = \dfrac{k + (i/n)}{m}$

   f. $r = \pi r^2$

   g. $v = \dfrac{4}{3} \pi r^3$

   h. $a = \pi r \sqrt{r^2 + h^2}$

   i. $e = a^{n^i}$

PROGRAMMING PROBLEMS

1. Write a BASIC program that computes the area and the circumference of a circle given the radius.

$$A = \pi r^2$$
$$C = 2\pi r$$

2. Write a program to compute the volume and surface area of a sphere given the radius.

$$A = 4\pi r^2$$
$$V = \frac{4}{3}\pi r^3$$

3. The economic order quantity for a part is given by the formula

$$EOQ = \sqrt{\frac{2dc}{us}}$$

where
    d is the demand in units for a given time period
    c is the cost of placing an order
    u is the unit cost of the part
    s is the cost of sorting the item in stock.

Write a program to calculate EOQ using appropriate values for the data.

INPUT AND OUTPUT

In the previous section, the LET statement was used to assign data to a variable that was then used in the program. This approach was acceptable for programs where the data is known in advance of writing the program. However, in many cases, data values are not known in advance. For example, if we are writing a program to compute a class average, the grades to be used will not necessarily be known when the program is written but only when the end of the semester is reached. For situations like this the INPUT statement is useful.

INPUT Statement

nnnnn	INPUT	variable list
nnnnn	INPUT	"prompt";variable list

The INPUT statement, in the two forms defined above, lets the user of the program supply data for processing by the program. When an INPUT is encountered during program execution, the computer waits for the user to type in a value or values. When return is pressed, the values are entered into the program's variables and the program continues with these values.

Numeric Input. Numeric data may be accepted by the INPUT statement by using a numeric variable. For example,

```
100 INPUT N
110 PRINT N * N
RUN
```

? 25   Input data

625   Output printed

When this program is RUN, a question mark appears indicating the program is waiting for a value for N. If 25 is typed and the return key is pressed, the value 25 is now contained in the variable N and is used for the calculation in statement 110.

String Input. A character string may be accepted by the INPUT statement. This is defined by using a string variable for the input operation.

```
100 INPUT N$
110 PRINT N$
RUN
```

? DISKETTES   Input data

DISKETTES   Output

Entering Several Input Values. More than one value may be entered by separating them with commas. For instance:

```
100 INPUT A,B
110 PRINT A + B
RUN
```

? 12,25

37

expects two values to be entered, one for A and the second for B. These values must be entered with a comma between them as shown in the example.

Using a Prompt. One problem with the above examples is that the program's user may not know what is expected as input when the program is run. The second form of the INPUT statement defined above allows for a prompt string to be included in the statement. The prompt is a string that displays on the screen when the INPUT is executed by the computer. In the first example above we could have written

```
100 INPUT "ENTER A NUMBER";N
110 PRINT N * 2
RUN                                         Prompt

ENTER A NUMBER ? 12                         Input N

144                                         Print N
```

Notice the use of the semicolon in statement 100 to separate the string from the variable N. The semicolon is necessary to avoid a syntax error and it also lets the user type N's value directly following the message that asks for it.

Convert Fahrenheit to Celsius. The following program accepts a Fahrenheit temperature as input, calculates the equivalent in Celsius, and then prints the result with an appropriate message.

```
100 REM *****************************
110 REM * FAHRENHEIT TO CELSIUS    *
120 REM *                          *
130 REM * C - CELSIUS DEGREES      *
140 REM * F - FAHRENHEIT DEGREES   *
150 REM *****************************
160 REM
170 INPUT "ENTER FAHRENHEIT";F
180 C = (F - 32) * 5 / 9
190 PRINT "CELSIUS =",C
200 END

RUN
ENTER FAHRENHEIT ? 68
CELSIUS = 20
```

DATA Statement

The DATA statement is used to supply numeric or alphanumeric values to a program. The general format is:

nnnnn   DATA   data-list

As an example, the statement

500 DATA 23

is a DATA statement containing one integer number, the value 23. This value would be read into the program and placed in some variable name through the READ statement. The statement

600 DATA 36.5,7.01,0.95,155

contains four numeric values. The first value is the number 36.5, which is followed by a comma that separates it from 7.01, which is the second value. The decimal number 0.95 and the integer 155 are the third and fourth values, respectively. These values will be set up in a data block in the program, and each time a READ statement is executed, one value at a time will be taken from the data block for each variable specified in the READ statement.

Some programs require large amounts of data that cannot be placed in one DATA statement. For example

500 DATA 5,7,3,9,17,38,45,68
501 DATA 31,21,53,4,8,15,69,45
502 DATA 33,67,78,1,30,25,99

In this case, three DATA statements have been used to supply to the program all the data required. Since one DATA statement was not adequate to contain all the information necessary, we continued to a second DATA statement and then to a third statement.

READ Statement

The statement causing data to be transferred from the DATA statement to a variable within a program is the READ statement.

nnnnn   READ   variable-list

As an example, the statement

100 READ X1

causes an item of numeric information to be transferred from a DATA statement to the variable X1. Thus, if we had included the DATA statement,

    300 DATA 24.5

when the READ is executed, the value 24.5 would be assigned to the variable X1. If this were the only DATA statement in the program and we attempted to execute another READ, there would be no more data to be supplied to the variable. In this case, the program execution would be considered complete, and the job would be terminated. For some programs, we may require the inputting of more than one number at a given time. For example, we may have

    200 READ A,B,C

and a DATA statement

    500 DATA 26,48,19

In this example, when the READ statement is executed, the value 26 is assigned to the variable A, the value 48 is assigned to the variable B, and the value 19 to the variable C.

In another case, we may require the input of both numeric and alphanumeric data. Thus, the READ statement

    300 READ A,N$,Y$
    500 DATA 77.875,DIAL,"VERNIER 40:1"

Here the value 77.875 will be assigned to the variable A. The character string DIAL will be assigned to the variable N$, and the character string VERNIER 40:1 will be assigned to Y$.

In Figure 14-1, we see a simple program showing how the READ and DATA statements may be used. Statement 10 is used to read various data into the variables listed. Into N$ will be read the name of a student; into C$, the course in which he is enrolled; and into M1, M2, M3, M4, and M5, the marks for five courses he is taking. The calculation in statement 20 determines the average mark he has received in the five courses. In statement 30, we print out the name, the course, and the average.

```
10 READ N$,C$,M1,M2,M3,M4,M5
20 LET A=(M1+M2+M3+M4+M5)/5
30 PRINT N$,C$,A
40 DATA JOHN SMITH,COMPUTER SCIENCE 1,75,82,68,65,77
50 END

JOHN SMITH      COMPUTER SCIENCE 1        73.4
RUN
```

Figure 14-1. Simple program with READ and DATA statements.

Statement 40 contains the data for this particular student, whose name is John Smith, and his course, computer science. He has received 75 percent as a mark for course one, 82 percent for course two, and 68 percent, 65 percent, and 77 percent for courses three, four, and five, respectively. When the program is run, the output gives the name of the student and the course followed by the average calculated in the LET statement. From the output, we can see that this average is 73.4 percent.

PRINT Statement

The PRINT statement performs an important role in BASIC programming because it is through this statement that we are able to see the results of executing the program.

| nnnnn | PRINT | variable-list |

Data is placed on the typewriter in zones. This typewriter line is divided into five zones, or sections, consisting of 15 spaces each. As each data item is printed, it is allocated one zone; thus, if we had a number of five digits, it would occupy the first five digits of the first zone followed by ten spaces. The second number would then appear beginning in the second zone, etc. If our PRINT statement were

PRINT A,B,C

the contents of the variable A would be printed in the first zone, the contents of the variable B in the second zone, and the contents of C in the third zone. If A, B, and C had values of 27.5, 46, and .005, respectively, the output would be

27.5   46   .005

A semicolon causes the length of each zone to be ignored; thus, if we had the statement

100 PRINT A;B;C

and assumed the same values for A, B, and C, the output would be

27.5 46 .005

Thus, the values are more compacted on the line, and we could actually place more data on one print line than if we had separated the data items with commas. If eventually the computer finds that there is inadequate space at the end of a line for a variable specified in the PRINT statement, that variable will then be placed on a succeeding line.

Sample PRINT Program. The program in Figure 14-2 is used to demonstrate how various aspects of the PRINT statement may be used.

This program reads a student number, the name of the student, followed by the number of courses in which he is enrolled, and, lastly, the amount of tuition for each course. These four data items are represented by the variable names N, N$, C, and A, respectively. The data is provided through a DATA statement, which is statement 100 in the program.

The data is read by the READ statement 10. Statement 20 computes T, which is the total cost of the student's tuition. This is accomplished by multiplying the number of courses times the amount per course. Statement 30 causes the input data to be printed along with the total tuition amount T.

```
10 READ N,N$,C,A
20 LET T=C*A
30 PRINT N,N$,C,A,T
100 DATA 256781,JOHN JONES,6,124.00
200 END

RUN

256781        JOHN JONES        6        124        744
```

Figure 14-2. Sample PRINT program.

```
10 READ N,N$,C,A
20 LET T=C*A
25 PRINT "STUDENT NO.", "NAME", "NO. OF COURSES",
   "AMOUNT", "TOTAL TUITION"
30 PRINT N,N$,C,A,T
100 DATA 256781,JOHN JONES,6,124.00
200 END

RUN
```

STUDENT NO.	NAME	NO. OF COURSES	AMOUNT	TOTAL TUITION
256781	JOHN JONES	6	124	744

Figure 14-3. Sample program with headings.

When the program is run, we see the output line, which is the last line in Figure 14-2. This shows the student number, name, number of courses, amount, and the total tuition in the one line. These five variables occupy five zones on this line. Each variable is small enough to fit within the 15 characters allocated to a zone.

PRINT Headings. Figure 14-3 demonstrates how a heading can be added to this program. We wish to print out certain heading values prior to the data being printed. If we enter a new PRINT statement 25 and cause this PRINT statement to print out headings, this output will appear prior to the data printed in statement 30. Statement 25 tells the computer to print certain character strings that identify each field of output. Since we have five fields to be printed, we specify five character strings (one per field).

LABELLED OUTPUT PROGRAM

In Figure 14-4, this same program is rewritten to produce an entirely different form of output. In the previous examples, we have always printed the output data across the page; however, there may be some circumstances where we wish to print down the page. In order to do this, we have used a separate print statement for each line of output.

Statement 30 prints first the STUDENT NO. character string followed by a variable name N, which identifies the student number.

Notice particularly in statement 30, that the two variables are separated by a semicolon and not a comma. This semicolon causes a single space to the left after the character string prior to printing the numeric field. Thus, on the output the result is

```
10 READ N,N$,C,A
20 LET T=C*A
30 PRINT "STUDENT NO.";N
35 PRINT
40 PRINT "NAME ";N$
45 PRINT
50 PRINT "NO. OF COURSES";C
55 PRINT
60 PRINT "AMOUNT";A
65 PRINT
70 PRINT "TOTAL TUITION";T
100 DATA 256781,JOHN JONES,6,124.00
200 END

RUN

STUDENT NO. 256781

NAME JOHN JONES

NO. OF COURSES 6

AMOUNT 124

TOTAL TUITION 744

STUDENT NUMBER 256781
```

Figure 14-4. Sample of vertical output.

Statement 35 issues a print command but does not supply any data. This causes the output to skip a line. This spacing is used to make the report more readable.

Statement 40 prints the NAME, followed by the character string JOHN JONES. Pay careful attention to the literal for NAME and notice that it contains one blank character following the E in NAME. The reason for this blank character is to provide spacing between NAME and JOHN. If this space had not been left, JOHN would be printed against the E like this

NAMEJOHN

In these examples, we have shown various types of output for the same program. No one type of output has a particular advantage over the other, although the last case is slightly more difficult to program. The reason for choosing between one type of output and another is based upon the requirements of the person or persons who will be reading the output. In some cases, a simple line of output is adequate. In other cases, this line of data should be preceded by a heading. In still other cases, it is preferable to print each line as a separate output.

PROGRAMMING PROBLEMS

1. The volume of the segment of a sphere is given by the equation

$$\text{Volume} = \pi h^2 \left[\frac{c^2 + 4h^2}{8h} - \frac{h}{3} \right]$$

where c is the length of the chord of the segment and h is the height of the segment. Write a program to compute the volume and print the result along with the values for c and h. Design your own output.

2. Compute and print the interest rate given the formula

$$P = 100 \cdot \left[\left(\frac{T}{A} \right)^{1/n} - 1 \right]$$

where T is the final amount, A is the deposited amount, and N is the number of years.

3. A salesman receives a basic income plus a commission based on 10 percent of his total sales. Read the salesman's name, amount of sales, basic salary, and income tax percent. Compute the commission, income tax, gross salary, and net salary. Print the following report.

```
PAYROLL REPORT FOR     xxxxxxxxxxxxxxxxxxxx

BASIC SALARY     xxx.xx
COMMISSION       xxx.xx
GROSS SALARY     xxx.xx
TAX DEDUCTED      xx.xx
NET SALARY       xxx.xx
```

PROGRAM CONTROL STATEMENTS

The CONTROL statements used in the BASIC language provide a great deal of flexibility in computer programming. Without control statements, programming would be time consuming, monotonous, and extremely inefficient.

GO TO Statement

The GO TO statement causes control to branch from the location of the statement in the BASIC program to some other location in the same program.

> nnnnn GO TO statement-number

If the statement

    50   GO TO 150

is encountered during program execution, control will branch from statement 50 to statement 150. No other action is taken, and control branches immediately to the new location in the BASIC program.

IF Statement

The IF statement permits branching in a program dependent upon the existence of certain conditions. This differs from the GO TO statement, which is an unconditional branch. The IF statement only branches when a specified condition is met. The general format for the IF statement is

> nnnnn IF relational-expression THEN statement-number

The relational operators available in the BASIC language are as follows:

=	Equal To
>	Greater Than
<	Less Than
>=	Greater Than or Equal To
<=	Less Than or Equal To
><	Not Equal To

The following BASIC statements show how to implement certain logical operations in the BASIC language.

```
20 IF A = B THEN 100
30 LET S = S + 1
      .
      .
      .
100 LET N = N + 1
110 GO TO 30
```

If A is equal to B, then 1 is to be added to N, and control is passed back so that the value one (1) is also added to S. However, if A is not equal to B, then only S should be increased by one in value. The IF statement causes control to branch to 100 if A is equal to B. At 100, the value one (1) is added to N; and then an unconditional GO TO branches back to statement 30, which causes 1 to be added to S. If, however, A was not equal to B in statement 20, control would continue at statement 30; and S would be increased by 1.

```
20 IF A <= B THEN 100
30 LET N = N - 1
40      .
        .
        .
100 LET N = N + 1
110 GO TO 40
```

In this example, if A is either less than or equal to B, 1 is added to N. If A is greater than B, then 1 is subtracted from N. Only one operation or the other is done, never both. To do this in BASIC, we make the comparison, and if A is less than or equal to B, control branches to statement 100 where N is increased by 1. Following this, we go to 40, which is the next sequential statement following the instruction to subtract 1 from N. Statement 30 is only executed if A is greater than B.

Quite often we wish to compare variables to constants; thus, we might have the expressions

```
40 IF C = 1 THEN 100

50 IF C = 2 THEN 200
```

Alphabetic fields may also be used in the IF statement; thus, the statement

100 IF A$ = B$ THEN 40

causes control to branch to statement 40 only if the variable A$ contains the same character string as the variable B$.

We can also check for alphanumeric constants; thus, the statement

200 IF K$ = "TEST" THEN 60

will cause control to branch to statement 60 if the variable K$ contains the character string TEST.

SALES COMMISSION PROGRAM

Some of the principles covered have been incorporated in the program shown in Figure 14-5. This program processes salesmen's data records, which contain the salesman's number, name, and the amount of his sales. The program analyzes the sales amount and computes a commission based upon the following table.

Sales Amount	Commission
less than $1000	5%
over $1000 but less than $2000	7%
over $2000 but less than $3000	10%
$3000 or over	12%

Since we are printing a large number of records on the screen, it may be desirable to repeat the heading after a certain number of lines have been displayed. Thus, a counter L has been set up to count the number of lines printed. In this problem, a new heading is printed for every ten lines of detail. Depending upon the needs of the assignment, as many as 30 or 40 lines may be printed before a new heading is printed. This is easily accomplished by modifying the value in statement 430, which tests for the limit of the counter. Output from this program is shown in Figure 14-6.

```
10 LET L=0
20 PRINT
25 PRINT
30 PRINT"SALES NO.", "NAME", "AMOUNT", "COMMISSION"
40 PRINT
50 READ S,N$,A
60 IF S=999 THEN 450
70 IF A<1000 THEN 200
80 IF A<2000 THEN 300
90 IF A<3000 THEN 400
100 LET C=A*.12
110 GO TO 410
200 LET C=A*.05
210 GO TO 410
300 LET C=A*.07
310 GO TO 410
400 LET C=A*.10
410 PRINT S,N$,A,C
420 LET L=L+1
430 IF L <= 10 THEN 50
435 INPUT "CONTINUE (YES/NO);R$
440 IF R$ = "YES" THEN 10
450 PRINT "END OF INPUT"
460 DATA 100,J ABEL,500
461 DATA 115,S BELL,1500
462 DATA 119,A CAVE,2300
463 DATA 225,C CHART,3100
464 DATA 226,Q CRUZ,1000
465 DATA 278,D DE LANE,2000
466 DATA 305,F FLIN,3000
467 DATA 330, FULTON,5000
468 DATA 365,A GRAY,2300
469 DATA 400,L HOBBS,1990
470 DATA 444,W LAKELAND,3300
471 DATA 470,N PARKER,1999
472 DATA 500,R MOORE,4000
473 DATA 554,F PRATT,3900
474 DATA 598,V SMITH,1400
475 DATA 999,LAST,0
500 END

RUN
```

Figure 14-5. Program to process salesman's data records.

SALES NO.	NAME	AMOUNT	COMMISSION
110	J ABEL	500	25.
115	S BELL	1500	105.
119	A CAVE	2300	230.
225	C CHART	3100	310.
226	Q CRUZ	1000	70.
278	D DE LANE	2000	200.
305	F FLIN	3000	300.
330	FULTON	5000	600.
365	A GRAY	2300	230.
400	L HOBBS	1990	139.3
444	W LAKELAND	3300	330.

CONTINUE (YES/NO) ? YES

SALES NO.	NAME	AMOUNT	COMMISSION
470	N PARKER	1999	139.93
500	R MOORE	4000	400.
554	F PRATT	3900	390.
598	V SMITH	1400	98.

END OF INPUT

Figure 14-6. Output from program.

FOR and NEXT Statements

The FOR and NEXT statements shown here are used together in a BASIC program to allow a statement or group of statements to be executed over and over again until a given condition has been reached. This process is called *iteration*. The FOR statement controls the number of iterations required by the program logic.

```
nnnnn FOR variable = value-1 TO value-2 STEP value-3
         .
         .
         .
nnnnn NEXT variable
```

Figure 14-7 is a program that demonstrates the use of the FOR statement. We wish to find the sum of all numbers from 1 through 100. The variable S is used to represent the sum and is set to zero in statement 10. Statement 20 is a FOR statement that sets the variable I to the initial value of one and says that we wish to increase I by one until it reaches the terminal value 100. The increasing of I will take place each time the NEXT statement is reached. Within the iterative loop is statement 30, which increases the value of S by I. Thus, the loop consists of statements 20, 30, and 40.

The first time the loop is executed, I will have the value 1, which will be added to S. The second time through the loop, I will have the value 2; the third time, 3, etc., until the value 100 has been reached in I. The loop will be executed while I has the value 100; but on this last time through, control will pass to statement 50 rather than returning to statement 20 as it did in the previous 100 loops. So, after adding the values from 1 to 100 to S, statement 50 prints this sum, shown as output from the program.

The basic advantage of using the FOR statement is the convenience it gives to the programmer. It is not really doing anything we cannot do ourselves by using a counter, an IF statement, and a GO TO statement; but the FOR statement makes it easier for the programmer to represent an iterative process.

Sum of the Cube of Digits. An interesting problem using nested loops is shown in Figure 14-8. In this problem, we are attempting to find those three-digit numbers whose value is equal to the sum of the cube of the digits. In this program, we have three nested FOR loops. The inner loop, containing variable N1, represents the units position of the number. The FOR loop containing the variable N2 represents the tens digit of the

```
10 LET S = 0
20 FOR I = 1 TO 100
30      S = S + I
40 NEXT I
50 PRINT S
60 END

RUN

5050
```

Figure 14-7. Program demonstrating FOR statement.

```
10 FOR N3=1 TO 9
20   FOR N2=0 TO 9
30     FOR N1=0 TO 9
40       IF N1↑3+N2↑3+N3↑3<>N1+N2*10+N3*100 THEN 60
50       PRINT N1↑3+N2↑3+N3↑3
60     NEXT N1
70   NEXT N2
80 NEXT N3
90 END

RUN

153
370
371
407
```

Figure 14-8. Finding three-digit numbers equal to the sum of the cube of the digits.

number; and the outer loop, containing N3 as a variable, represents the hundreds digit of the number.

In statement 40, the sum of the cube of the digits is calculated on the left of the equal sign. On the right of the equal sign, the three-digit number itself is computed. This is necessary because we do not have the number available in this program, only the digits of the number. If the number is equal to the sum of the cube of its digits, we go to statement 60, which prints out the number found. If, however, the comparison was not equal, we go to statement 70, which causes the program to progress to the next number in sequence. Note that the nested FOR loops actually create the number we wish to analyze. Note also that since N1 is the inner loop, it varies the fastest and causes the units position of the number to be incremented before the tens position, just as if we were manually counting the numbers from 100 to 999. The results of this program show that there are only four numbers that are equal to the sum of the cube of their digits.

PROGRAMMING PROBLEMS

1. A computer dating service wishes to produce a report of all single females between 19 and 21 inclusive who have blue eyes and blond hair. Examine the codes in the data records to produce this report.

Data Record Fields	Codes
Name	
Address	
Phone Number	
Age	
Sex	1 — Male
	2 — Female
Marital Status	1 — Single
	2 — Married
	3 — Divorced
	4 — Separated
Eye Color	1 — Brown
	2 — Green
	3 — Blue
Hair Color	1 — Blond
	2 — Brunette
	3 — Red

2. Using the data records for problem 1, determine the number of males and females in each marital status. Print these eight totals indicating the percentage each of them represent of the entire data.
3. The present population of Toronto is 2,100,000, and the population of Hamilton is 260,000. Assuming Toronto grows at a rate of 2 percent per year and Hamilton grows at a rate of 5 percent, in what year will they have an equal population? If your calculations go beyond the year 3000, stop the program and determine what is wrong with your logic.
4. A student plans to save $40.00 per month upon leaving school at 21 until he retires at age 65. Given an annual interest rate of 8 percent computed and compounded quarterly, what will his investment be worth upon his retirement?

LISTS AND TABLES

Many programming applications involve the use of repetitive data items such as lists and tables. Even though each item in a group or list could be dealt with individually within the program, programming in this way becomes very inefficient and awkward. For example, we may have a series of six marks representing the grades a student received in six different courses. If we wanted to find the average of these six marks, we could use a different variable name to represent each mark. These values would be summed, and the total divided by six to give the average. However, if we group these marks together into a list, we can use a name that generalizes and refers to all six marks. By specifying the dimension or position within the list, we can access a particular mark for processing.

DIM Statement

The DIM statement in BASIC is used to set aside storage space in the computer for a list of data. For example, the statement

10 DIM A(15)

specifies that we are dealing with a single-dimension list, and that this list can contain 15 items of data. The statement

10 DIM C(10,5)

says that we are dealing with a two-dimensional matrix or table, and that along one dimension of the table we can store ten items and along the other, five. Thus, this particular table is capable of storing 50 items of data.

Tables and lists may also be used to store character strings. The statement

20 DIM Z$(5)

specifies a list capable of storing five character strings.

Average for a Student. The program in Figure 14-9 shows the use of a single-dimensional list. This is a program that reads six grades for a particular student, averages those grades, and prints the result of calculating the average. To store the grades, we have set up a list called N with space for six items of data representing the six marks. Pictorially the list may be visualized as follows

65	75	83	69	78	70
(1)	(2)	(3)	(4)	(5)	(6)

The name N refers to the list in its entirety. Each element of the list is capable of receiving a value. These elements are numbered from one to six. Note that the element number is distinctly different from the contents of that element.

```
10 DIM N (6)
20 FOR I = 1 TO 6
30      READ N(I)
40 NEXT I
50 S = 0
60 FOR I = 1 TO 6
70      S = S + N(I)
80 NEXT I
90 A = S/6
100 PRINT "THE AVERAGE OF THE 6 GRADES IS "; A
130 DATA 65,75,83,69,78,70
140 END

RUN

THE AVERAGE OF THE 6 GRADES IS 73.3333
```

Figure 14-9. Use of a single-dimensional list.

In the program, the READ statement 30 is contained within a FOR loop. The first time through this loop, I is set to the value 1. Thus, the effect of the READ statement is

30 READ N(1)

This takes the first item from the data record and stores it in position 1 of N.

The variable I in statement 30 is called a *subscript*. A subscript specifies the location in the list to be accessed. The second time through, this FOR loop has the effect of the statement reading

30 READ N(2)

Thus, the second number 75 is read from the DATA statement and stored in the second position of N. Similarly, positions 3, 4, 5, and 6 of N receive values from the DATA statement. Thus, after six loops, the program proceeds on to statement 50 having completed storing six values in the list N.

The next step is to find the sum of the values within the list. To do this, another FOR loop is placed at statement 60, and again we vary I from one to six. When the second FOR loop has completed its iterations, all the values contained within N will have been added to S; and statement 90 divides S by 6 giving the average of the marks in variable A. This average is then printed by statement 100.

Average for a Class. As the previous program stands, it is not really all that useful since it only deals with a single student and the marks he has received. Thus, Figure 14-10 shows a program that deals with a given number of students. In this case there are ten students who have each received six marks on the six courses they have taken.

In addition to the six marks, the DATA statements also contain the students' names. The approach taken here is to set up two storage areas— N$, which is single-dimensional, will contain the names and G, which is two-dimensional. The first dimension of G represents each of the ten students, and the second dimension represents the six marks each student has received. This is represented pictorially as follows:

	1	2	3	4	5	6
1	55	65	77	68	76	80
2	65	75	57	66	88	69
3	78	99	89	88	78	61
4	55	65	58	60	69	66
5	88	90	50	55	67	77
6	73	38	55	49	66	70
7	70	70	75	75	80	80
8	59	68	75	76	55	67
9	87	85	65	76	46	46
10	77	58	79	74	57	74

Now, this involves reading not only a name for every student and storing it in the first array but also six marks for each student and storing them in the appropriate locations of the second array. For this purpose, statements 20 and 30 set J and I to the values of one to ten and six, respectively. J represents a particular student that is the first, second, third, and so on, student. I represents a particular one of the six marks.

Statement 25 reads the name for a given student. To begin, J will be one, so N$ stores the name (ABEL) of the first student in the first position of the array N$. The first time statement 40 is executed, J will be one, and I will be one. This causes the first mark to be stored in the first position of table G. Following this, I will be increased to two, while J remains at one. This causes the second mark to be stored in G and so on. I will increase from one to six causing each of the six marks to be

```
10 DIM N$(10),G(10,6)
15 LET C=0
20 FOR J=1 TO 10
25      READ N$(J)
30      FOR I=1 TO 6
40          READ G(J,I)
50      NEXT I
60 NEXT J
70 FOR J=1 TO 10
74      LET S=0
75      PRINT "THE AVERAGE OF THE GRADES FOR ";N$(J);" IS ";
80      FOR I=1 TO 6
90          LET S=S+G(J,I)
100     NEXT I
110     LET A=S/6
111     LET C=C+A
120     PRINT A
130 NEXT J
140 LET A=C/10
150 PRINT
160 PRINT"THE CLASS AVERAGE IS ";A
200 DATA ABEL,55,65,77,68,76,80
201 DATA BELL,65,75,57,66,88,69
202 DATA COOL,78,99,39,88,78,61
203 DATA EAST,55,65,58,60,69,66
204 DATA GRANT,88,90,55,55,67,77
205 DATA HELD,73,38,55,49,66,70
206 DATA JACK,70,70,75,75,80,80
207 DATA KING,59,68,75,76,55,67
208 DATA NEW,87,85,65,76,46,46
209 DATA SMIT,77,58,79,74,57,74
300 END

RUN

THE AVERAGE OF THE GRADES FOR ABEL IS 70.1667
THE AVERAGE OF THE GRADES FOR BELL IS 70
THE AVERAGE OF THE GRADES FOR COOL IS 82.1667
THE AVERAGE OF THE GRADES FOR EAST IS 62.1667
THE AVERAGE OF THE GRADES FOR GRANT IS 72
THE AVERAGE OF THE GRADES FOR HELD IS 58.5
THE AVERAGE OF THE GRADES FOR JACK IS 75
```

Figure 14-10. Program for averaging grades of ten students.

THE AVERAGE OF THE GRADES FOR KING IS 66.6667
THE AVERAGE OF THE GRADES FOR NEW IS 67.5
THE AVERAGE OF THE GRADES FOR SMIT IS 69.8333

THE CLASS AVERAGE IS 69.4

Figure 14-10. Program for averaging grades of ten students (continued)

stored in G for the first student. When I reaches the value 6, control passes to statement 60, which causes J to be incremented to two; and the process is repeated for the second student, and so on, until all ten student records have been read.

When control gets to statement 70, all ten data records will have been read for the ten students, and the matrices N$ and G will contain all of the information that we have about these students.

Now we wish to compute the average grade for each student. Thus, in statement 70, the variable J is varied from one to ten to represent each of the ten students. Statement 80 varies I from one to six to represent each of the six marks obtained by a particular student. These marks are added to S in statement 90 through the use of the subscripts J and I for table G. When this inner FOR loop has been completed, control will pass to statement 110, and the average calculated. Since we wish to know the class average for all students, the average is also added into the variable C at this point, and A is printed by statement 120.

Notice that part of the data for this line of output is printed back in statement 75. Pay careful attention to how this statement works. After the first student record has been processed, J is incremented by one because of statement 130, and the process continues for each of the ten students. Finally, when statement 140 is reached, the class average is computed by dividing C, which is the sum of all the averages, by ten; and this average is printed in statement 160.

PROGRAMMING PROBLEMS

1. Write a program to read n student records (maximum 40) containing six marks each. Compute and print each student's average and the average for each of the six courses.
2. Write a program similar to problem 1 except that each student has n marks (maximum six).

    Hint: Use a negative number to represent a nonapplicable mark.
3. Write a program to sort a maximum of 100 numbers, using a single list.
4. Write a program to generate a calendar for this year.

SUBROUTINES

A vital aspect of good programming is reflected by the organization of that program. Good organization is indicative of the programmer's ability to clearly define the solution to a programming problem. The modularity this achieves leads to easier debugging of the newly created program since each section of the program functions independently of other sections. Therefore, an error in one will not adversely affect the logic of the other. Good modularity also leads to easier program modification. Additions, revisions, or deletions may be made to the programming logic as the occasion demands. In BASIC, modularity can be achieved through the use of the GOSUB and RETURN statements.

GOSUB and RETURN Statements

The GOSUB statement is used in BASIC to cause control to branch from a location in the program to a subroutine at some other location in the same program. The RETURN statement is used in association with the GOSUB; it causes control to return back to the point at which the subroutine was initiated, that is, the statement following the GOSUB statement.

The following statements show how a subroutine may be referenced in a program.

```
100 GOSUB 300
105
    ⋮
150 GOSUB 300
160
    ⋮
300 LET N=N-1
310 LET J3=N**2
320 RETURN
    ⋮
```

In this example, as the program executes statement 100, control will branch to statement 300. At this point, statements 300 through 320 will be executed. When the RETURN statement at line 320 is reached, control will branch back to statement 105. The program will continue to execute sequentially until statement 150 is reached, at which time, control will again go to subroutine 300. This time when the RETURN is executed, control branches back to statement 160. Thus, the point to which control returns is dependent upon the location of the GOSUB that invoked the subroutine.

PROGRAMMING PROBLEMS

1. A company employs less than 200 employees in the data processing department. The ages of these employees are recorded on DATA statements. The first value read indicates the number of employees in the department. Using subroutines, find the average age, the median, and the mode. The median is the number found at the mid-point when the numbers are sequenced. The median of 21, 23, 23, 25, 28, 29, 30 is 25. The mode is the number that occurs most frequently. In this example the mode is 23.

2. A DATA statement contains a starting and ending time recorded by a time measurement analyst. Each time consists of hours, minutes, and seconds. For instance

    1000 DATA   09,15,48,11,02,53

    represents a job starting at 9 hours, 15 minutes, and 48 seconds. It ends at 11 hours, 2 minutes, and 53 seconds. Write a program to calculate the amount of time taken to complete the job.

Systems Analysis
and Design

15

Concepts of a System

DERIVING A DEFINITION

... Doctor, his respiratory system is back to normal! ... Do you think the coach's new system of defense will help the team tonight? ... We need a better system of invoicing! ... The life-support system is failing, Commander. ...

The above sentences are taken from a wide range of examples, yet all employ a common word. What is the meaning of this overworked word, "system"? How does it apply to data processing?

In order to answer these questions and to lead into a description of the functions of a Systems Analyst, it is appropriate to provide an idea of what a system is comprised of and also to see if there are any standard characteristics of any given system.

In general, a system can be thought of as "a set of procedures used to accomplish a specified task." The set of procedures usually has some form of input and generates an output giving the basic block diagram shown in Figure 15-1.

Some examples of the general format fit the pattern in the following (Figure 15-2) way.

One special output that is generated by most systems is feedback. Whether it is in the form of reports, peoples' opinions and attitudes, pressure within the pipe, heartbeat, elevation, etc., this unique type of output can then be turned around and used as input, back into the system. The system can process this new input and in fact possibly turn out a new

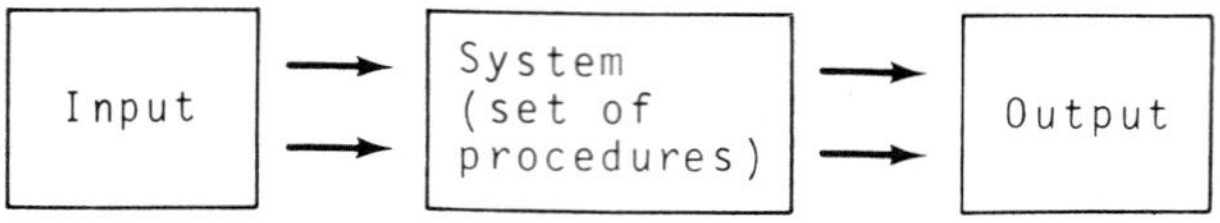
Input
System
(set of
procedures)
Output

Figure 15-1. Basic block diagram.

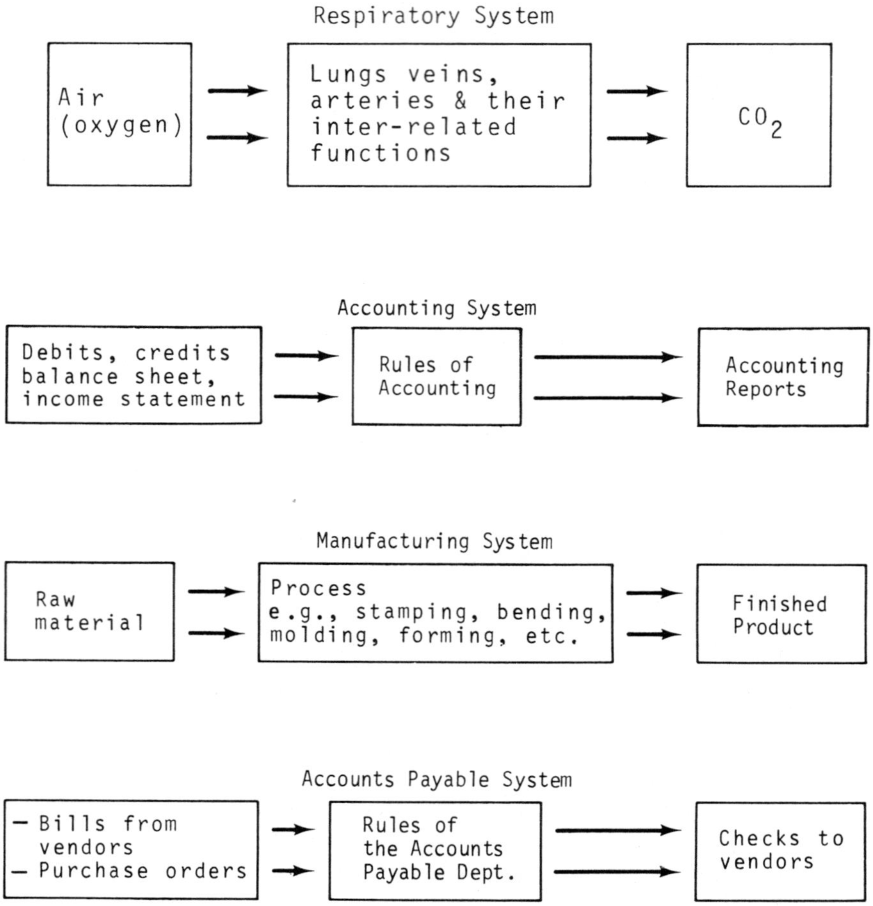
Respiratory System
Air
(oxygen)
Lungs veins,
arteries & their
inter-related
functions
CO_2
Accounting System
Debits, credits
balance sheet,
income statement
Rules of
Accounting
Accounting
Reports
Manufacturing System
Raw
material
Process
e.g., stamping, bending,
molding, forming, etc.
Finished
Product
Accounts Payable System
– Bills from
vendors
– Purchase orders
Rules of
the Accounts
Payable Dept.
Checks to
vendors

Figure 15-2. Examples of basic block in use.

set of outputs. Many systems use this technique to monitor themselves and automatically re-input the feedback. Other systems generate feedback but do nothing with it, leaving the system such that it has not gained from the feedback.

An example of this last point might be the time when a new registration system is installed at a college or university. Amid the many outputs will be viewpoints, complaints, and compliments that are felt by the students and faculty—i.e., feedback. If nothing is done to "tap this source," the system can continue for several registrations leaving people frustrated and isolated because the same problems exist. A well-designed system would have planned for this (and in fact searched out attitudes, etc.) and would have fed them back into the system so that it might be improved. (More of this type of technique will be discussed in a later chapter.)

A general block diagram might now appear as shown in Figure 15-3.

Within the organization, there are many "systems" that are functioning on a daily basis—some related, still others quite independent. The collection or set of these systems could be equated with the company's total operations or "How the firm operates its business." One extension to the idea that a system is simply "a set of procedures used to accomplish a specified task" is that within the business environment, there is an important requirement. This need is that the manner in which a job is performed should be consistent, uniform, or standard. In other words, what is performed at the Head Office in the Purchasing Department on a Monday will be the same as the set of procedures done on a Tuesday, or any other working day. The purchase order itself requires the same fields of information for all vendors (although the actual data will vary). The set of rules and regulations at one branch's operations should be identical to another branch's operations. Business, then, has a requirement for its systems to be standard, thus giving an extended idea of a system as "a set of standard procedures used to accomplish a specified task."

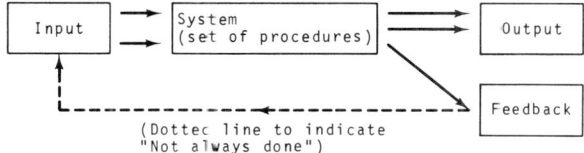

Figure 15-3. General block diagram.

THE FOUR STAGES OF A SYSTEM

Any given system can basically be divided into four stages: analysis, design, implementation, and operating and modification.

Stage 1: Analysis

The key point in this stage is defining (a) exactly what the problem is and (b) the requirements of the system that must be understood before any changes or improvements can be made. If an analyst is asked to design a better way of handling payments at a self-serve gas station, he must first examine all the needs, physical locations, equipment available, etc., before he would start to design in earnest. Or, if he has been presented with a specific problem such as, "Some customers are receiving incorrect statements each month," he must do some digging to formulate a "Problem Definition" that explains the root of the problem. Even in the case where nothing previously existed, as in space exploration or in the marketing of a brand new product, a lot of effort is expended researching before the design can begin. Analysis then, is characterized by a lot of hunting for information, and this "Data Gathering" requirement can be very important to the overall success of a new system.

Stage 2: Design

This term defines the stage where the new system or method of doing the job is created. This phase is characterized by

1. Engaging in lots of thought
2. Creating new forms, reports, codes, ideas, conventions, machines, etc.
3. Building in controls to ensure the integrity of the new system
4. Evaluating hardware-software

Throughout all of the work, it is important to try to involve the owners of the new system. In other words, it is the people who will run the new system who will dictate whether the new system is successful; therefore, they should not be ignored during this stage.

KEY CONCEPT

> **SOFTWARE**
>
> Software is the word to describe the programs that can be used by a computer. In a more general way, it is information or data as opposed to the machine itself (i.e., hardware).

Stage 3: Implementation

This stage describes the process of taking the new system and installing it in the department, firm, league, branch, etc., and bringing it to a working state. A phrase that is often heard is, "It works on paper, now let's make it work for real."

Stage 4: Operating and Modification

The day-to-day activities involved in the system are included in this stage. Small alterations and changes under control of the department (and not the analyst) are perhaps being effected to optimize the system or to make it more efficient.

Most systems are in Stage 4 when an analyst deals with them. It is infrequent that an analyst or an employee gets assigned the task of designing something "from the ground up." Although the bulk of the work is on an existing system, it should be pointed out the system did at one point pass through the first three stages. An analyst worth his salt realizes that not every system received the required amount of treatment during each stage. For example, a system might have had enough work done during Stage 1; also had adequate efforts expended in Stage 2; but, received minimal or no work during Stage 3. This might result in a system that is in Stage 4, but is neither a successful nor a workable system. An analyst who is asked to solve the problems that the new system has created can recognize that Stage 3 was poorly done. In this way, he might not spend any time on Analysis or Design, but concentrate on a better method of Implementation so that the employees, players, branch workers, etc., accept and support the new changes.

Although each of the first three stages are different and unique techniques and work habits belong to each one, the analyst must try to remember that if any stage receives shoddy treatment, the chance of an unsuccessful system increases. While an analyst can be involved in all four stages, he is, generally speaking, connected with the first three. The last phase, Operation and Modification, is left to the people, department, or company running the system.

Although there are different types of analysts (Figure 15-4), the job done by all occupations is basically the same as follows:

1. Be presented with a problem, weakness, or new goal or objective
2. Research the background involved with the part, student, customer, account, etc.
3. Think of a better way of handling the task (i.e., solve the problem)
4. Explain the new method and have it accepted by management
5. Supervise the installation of the improved or changed method of doing the job

Therefore, although there are specialized problem areas related to each field, many of the job skills required are the same for all analysts. The analyst's responsibilities will be demonstrated over the next few sections (as the stages are described showing many of the duties and points

Figure 15-4. Different types of analysts.

related to all analysts). There will be an emphasis on the computer systems analyst under the topics of Design (when a design of a new payroll system will be discussed) and Implementation (when a discussion of computer manufacturers and equipment selection will be covered).

TERMS TO STUDY

Feedback   System

QUESTIONS FOR REVIEW

1. Supply a definition for the word *system*.
2. Explain how feedback can be both an input and an output in a system.
3. What are the four main stages of a system?
4. How are the jobs of (a) Sales Analyst, (b) Financial Analyst, and (c) Computer Systems Analyst related?

QUESTIONS FOR RESEARCH AND DISCUSSION

1. Describe three systems that do take advantage of feedback, and then mention three that do not take advantage of processing feedback.
2. Choose a given system that already exists (for example, a school registration system, income tax, payroll system) and discuss the effect on the system if
   a. Analysis had been done poorly
   b. Design had been weak
   c. Implementation had been poorly handled
3. Establish some examples of systems that have a large number of inputs but few outputs. In contrast, think of some systems that have few inputs but many outputs.

16

Analysis

STAGE 1: ANALYSIS

This first stage, Analysis, is really a mixture of several possible requirements that must be resolved before the second stage, Design, is entered. These requirements range from acquiring a knowledge of the present system, to finding out the needs of a new system (i.e., management's objectives and plans for the future), and finally to determining the specific cause of a certain problem that exists within a company.

The chapter will be divided into three parts:

PART 1 will examine data-gathering techniques that will enable an analyst to better acquaint himself with the workings of an existing system. In the general model (Figure 16-1), the part, SYSTEM, requires a lot of explanation.

PART 2 will describe the various types of constraints, policies, and requirements that an analyst might have to deal with.

PART 3 will look at the difference between the symptoms of a problem and the cause of a problem.

PART 1: DATA-GATHERING TECHNIQUES

Perhaps an analyst has been given the task of increasing the efficiency of a department's operations. He would not want to arrive in the Design stage without understanding the way that the current system functions.

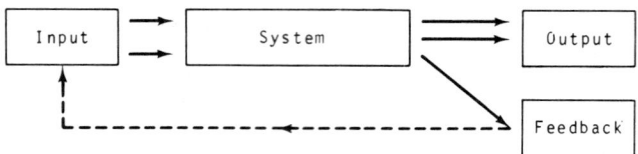

Figure 16-1. General model.

If, by error, this situation does happen, then design work might be done covering areas that are not the existing system's responsibility; or design might be wasted because it does not fit within the goals and objectives of the system.

Picture yourself being assigned the task of finding out how a certain system functions. For example: What system does your local library use for loaning books? How are the elections conducted in your area? What method does the neighborhood tennis club employ for assigning court time? How does the local clothing store process its sales receipts?

What would you do? How would you approach the job? Usually, after thinking about the task, people will say well, "I'll talk to someone in charge; or read some articles or magazines; or perhaps watch during a workday."

There are several techniques of investigation available to the analyst, and he chooses the ones that seem suitable to the situation at hand. He does not know at first what goes on in that area although he may have some idea of what occurs in a typical Accounts Payable Department. He cannot assume anything, however, and therefore, starts off his analysis with an open mind. The basic techniques of Data Gathering available are:

1. Examining procedure manuals
2. Interviews
3. Questionnaires
4. Forms analysis
5. Observation

Examining Procedure Manuals

A first step that the analyst can take during this data-gathering stage is to look at the company's (or department's) procedure manuals. In this way, he can start to familiarize himself with the functions that are being performed in the area he is studying. It should be noted that the manuals tend to be out-of-date in that first they do not reflect any short-cuts or "on-the-job improvements" that are performed by workers, and second, they are not always updated when a new machine or technique is utilized in the department. They do, however, provide the analyst with the following positive gains.

The analyst can generate a meaningful set of interview questions and prepare himself in general for talking to people. Instead of using very general (and sometimes useless) questions such as "What do you do here?" or "How is your job done?", questions that tend to put someone off who is being interviewed, the analyst can formulate more relative and specific points such as "Why do you phone for a credit limit check, after the sales slip has been filled out?" or "Is there any special reason why a back-ordered part receives special priority on unloading?"

KEY CONCEPT

PROCEDURE MANUALS

Those manuals written at a company to describe the responsibilities and actions of each clerk in the department. New employees are often asked during their orientation to sit and read the manual to acquire a picture of the job that they will be doing.

In this manner the analyst finds that any interviews or conversations will tend to go better since he does have some background; he also comes across as someone who knows a little about the area and interviewees tend to respect someone who has worked at learning about their section.

A second gain is that the analyst gets his first taste of the buzzwords, lingo, or terms used in the area. No matter where you work, there always seems to be a special terminology that means something very specific within its environment and yet perhaps means nothing outside. These are the types of words that are used so matter of factly by people that they are even unaware that they are using them. When a stranger (the analyst) enters a new department and hears the employees talking about S-4s and RN-40s, he of course finds it difficult to figure out what is being discussed. If during an interview, he must constantly interrupt the person he is talking to and ask, "What is that form?" or "What does that stand for?", the interview becomes chopped up and generally does not proceed very well. If, however, the analyst can read the procedure manuals (where for example an S-4 is described as the quarterly sales report by branch) and get accustomed to the new phraseology, the talk or meeting will flow more smoothly without interruptions. Hopefully, this will result in an overall quicker understanding of the system and its complex ideas (as well as building some confidence into the analyst).

Interviews

This particular technique of analysis is the most informative and the one most widely used. The two-way communication generated fosters a greater understanding in a shorter time.

The method used to conduct a proper data-gathering interview is to divide the task into three parts:

1. The pre-interview
2. The interview itself
3. The post-interview

Careful attention spent on all three parts will usually end up in a successful data-gathering episode. A description of the points to remember in each of the three parts will now be explained.

The Pre-Interview. The analyst should familiarize himself with the interviewee's area (department, branch, company), perhaps by reading a procedure manual.

He should arrange for the interview to be held in the interviewee's area. People generally feel more relaxed and comfortable in their own environment.

He should learn about the person's responsibilities and accountabilities. There is little sense questioning or probing into areas that are out of the interviewee's jurisdiction.

He should prepare any references or examples that he might want to use during the interview, for example: a list of questions; photocopies of checks, purchase orders, registration forms, etc.; sales figures, accounting reports.

He should inquire if it is all right to use a tape recorder. He should obtain permission from the correct manager or supervisor to talk to clerks, agents, secretaries, etc. If, for example, the analyst is studying a retail store, the first person to speak to would not be the sales clerk stocking the displays. Protocol suggests a reference to the store general manager at first (for approval) before working down the lines of the organization chart.

The Interview Itself. There are many general guidelines to follow when conducting an interview such as, do not be nervous, act as if you are in command, etc. Also there are various psychological considerations: do not be late (or be late if it's appropriate), chair position within the interview, type of clothes, tone of voice, etc. Although the author feels that most of these intangibles come with experience, a reference to the many behavioral books written on this subject would be a good idea because these types of discussions are not the concern here. Quite important, however, are the following three fundamental points.

First, the analyst should try to establish a good rapport because he will probably have to go back again. If not himself, perhaps someone else from his department (another analyst) will be required to interview the same person again. It is hard enough sometimes to get started, let alone having to try to undo someone else's bad feelings that were left from a previous interview. During analysis, it is very common to find that the analyst might speak to the same two or three people every week for the duration of the data gathering.

Second, the analyst should not use language that is brimming with words, acronyms, or phrases peculiar to his field. This point can apply to a representative from any industry, but computer systems analysts have been especially guilty of using language couched in computerese in discussions with workers from other departments, or "user reps."

When an assistant supervisor from an inventory department hears an analyst during the first interview state: "Well, as you know, we now have a partition freed up in main storage where we hope to have a multi-tasking on-line package directing requests through a concentrator connected via a 9600 baud line going to a CRT located on your desk, . . ." what do you say?

> **USER REP**
>
> The representative from the department that is either having Data Processing equipment installed or maintaining a previously installed system. Usually chosen by the affected department, the user rep. is their liaison with the Data Processing Department.

KEY CONCEPT

You know what he says (or at least thinks), "another winner from the systems department!" Has the analyst really gained anything from this sort of talk? No! In fact the distaste and confusion left in the mind of the inventory representative might require an investment of several weeks to change his feelings.

Third, the analyst should try to write down as little as possible. Although many managers and executives appreciate and understand that some of the conversation must go down on paper, they still do not like to wait while the analyst scribbles madly on his notebook. A good analyst, however, has his questions worded in such a way that all he has to add to his clipboard is a checkmark, a tick (beside possible answers), or an amount. He has already worded his questions such that they might be verbose and even occupy a full paragraph in his notes. The entry beside the questions (from the interview) is all then that is required.

Using a tape recorder would benefit the analyst because he can concentrate fully on the interview knowing that he can summarize it later in its entirety. However, the majority of people do not like to be interviewed in this way. Therefore, the analyst should clear the use of the tape recorder prior to the interview.

The Post Interview. The main point to remember during this part is to document the interview with respect to (a) information and (b) interesting or unusual characteristics of the interviewee or area he works in.

A good analyst realizes that during a half-hour conversation, there might be some figures misinterpreted, or items not heard correctly. Since the analyst has to document the information gained for his own records, he might send a copy or memo back to the person he has just talked to (Figure 16-2).

The interviewee then has the opportunity to clear up any misconceptions; he has a permanent record for his files; and he has an image of a prompt, courteous, on-the-ball representative from the systems department.

Any special features of the area or person should be noted. For example: The manager developed the manual system a long time ago and has guided it into its present status. The supervisor is someone who has a "bad taste in his mouth" concerning Data Processing systems because one failed in a department he once worked for. This department is termed a "guinea-pig" department and as such if the system is successful, it will be used in other branches and departments. The people feel very threatened in the department because a neighboring department reduced its staff when a new Data Processing system was installed last fall.

These characteristics might influence the structure, tone, or direction of the next interview, resulting in a more successful data-gathering period.

Forms Analysis

Another approach that is used by analysts who are trying to acquaint themselves with the workings of a section of a firm is to use the existing forms as a focal point for a series of questions.

1. Where does the form originate, and where does it go?
2. How is the form produced: typed, photocopy, spirit master copy, computer-generated report, off-line printer, etc.?
3. Are all the data you require for the decision or action you must make present on the form?
4. Where is the form stored?
5. What would happen if the employee did not receive a copy of the form at all?

> INTERDEPARTMENTAL CORRESPONDENCE
>
> To: Mr. S. Slater (Purchasing Manager)
>
> From: Mr. K. MacGregor (Systems Analyst)
>
> Date: Today
>
> Subject: Interview held earlier this morning
>   . . .

Figure 16-2.

This technique is employed because just about every type of business has at least one kind of form. Also the questions are tangible and not terribly deep and are therefore easily answered. Also, the questions can be directed to almost anyone in the department.

NOTE: At this stage the forms are not being checked for completeness, esthetics, or ease of use, etc., but rather they are used as a tool to provide a quick overview for the analyst.

Questionnaires

This technique is generally used when dealing with large groups of people who are needed to provide input to the study, but the analyst just does not have the time or the ability to get to all the physical locations where these people are (branch offices across the country, government agencies in each area, etc.).

In general, most questionnaires (marketing surveys, consumer questionnaires, work reports, government questionnaires) radiate the following impressions:

1. People do not like to answer them; they feel that the questionnaires are a nuisance or an inconvenience.
2. People tend to put off answering them.
3. An honest effort at answering is not always evident.

Given these three fairly powerful points it would appear that the use of questionnaires would be sketchy and perhaps a last resort type of move. There are, however, three situations that do warrant the use of questionnaires as a reasonable route to go:

1. The analyst requires a little bit of information from a lot of people.
2. The questions center on a day-to-day common activity (not something performed quarterly or annually).
3. The analyst wishes to derive a sub-group of people to further extend the data-gathering via interviewing.

The following points should be remembered when a questionnaire is decided upon:

1. Keep it short and concise.
2. Avoid using questions that could generate bias and misunderstanding.
3. Where applicable, build in techniques for ease in subsequent processing, e.g., keypunch field numbers, mark sense locations, use colored forms and envelopes, etc.
4. Include an accompanying explanation of the purpose of the questionnaire.
5. Make certain a location for return is described and provide as early a completion date as is reasonably possible.
6. Make use of CRTs instead of paper (hard copy). The analyst might arrange to have the questions stored in a computer file and then displayed on a CRT. The persons answering the questions can input their answers into the terminal (via the keyboard), and a program loaded in the computer can examine all the responses and choose the selected or desired group to provide the analyst with exactly what he requires. This process eliminates the need for handling paper, storing and filing paper responses, and delivery time. Also, the novelty of the exercise tends to increase the number of "answered questionnaires."

Observation

This term describes the activity of actually spending some time in the department that the analyst is studying and observing the daily procedures that the employees go through. An analyst can be a "silent observer," a term coined to describe someone present in the department, perhaps sitting in the corner or in the back of the department, taking notes that will provide questions to be answered during an interview. An "active observer" is introduced to the workers and might even be assigned to one worker's station or desk to follow through the job with that worker.

This approach allows the analyst to interrupt and question a procedure as it happens, therefore receiving an up-to-date, current answer.

A discussion concerning which technique is more valuable (silent or active) would have to include variables such as: attitude of employees, ability of the analyst, characteristics of the department supervisor, and background of the department in question (i.e., previous systems installed).

PART 2: CONSTRAINTS, POLICIES, AND REQUIREMENTS

As the analyst is progressing through the data gathering (Part 1), besides familiarizing himself with the procedures that are performed in the area he is examining, he is also trying to look out for any constraints, policies, or requirements that will influence the design of a new system.

There is no sense in designing a new method of doing a job if any one of the above mentioned factors has been omitted or forgotten. The new system will simply not be approved by management, and a lot of design effort will have been wasted. It is imperative to determine any entries under the three headings as soon as possible.

Constraints

A constraint is simply a factor that the system must accommodate—no questions asked—just work with it! The five main types of constraints that a system might be under are: equipment, legal, financial, physical location, and time.

Equipment Constraints. The firm has already decided on a certain hardware configuration that might have been purchased outright, and any changes that the analyst brings about must be within the framework of the equipment.

For example, the computer systems analyst working with a retail store with many branches knows that the many ordering problems could be resolved with the installation of a series of microcomputers with one per branch, with the store manager responsible for his stock . . . and so on. However, the store has made a corporate decision to acquire a large head-office computer with all files stored there as well. The analyst must scrap his distributed processing ideas and concentrate on improved telecommunications facilities.

A second example: A warehouse employing pallets (skids) and tow-motors could perhaps fill orders more efficiently using computer-controlled trucks that snake up and down tracks automatically selecting goods for shipment. Again the equipment in this example might be fixed, and any improvements to the system must use the tow-motor approach.

> **KEY CONCEPT**
>
> **DISTRIBUTED PROCESSING**
>
> The concept of giving the branch offices more computer power by actually installing small computers at each branch to process their data. This is different from the traditional idea of sending all data to Head Office for processing on one, huge, company computer.

Legal Constraints. In Canada, some firms are crown corporations or state enterprises and as such are actually administering Acts of Parliament (or state legislation). In the United States, there are governmental, quasi-governmental, and government contract firms. When an analyst is working in this environment, he must be careful not to mix up the company's rules and regulations with the legal regulations the firm is adhering to in its treatment of claims, people, products, or students.

Other firms are obliged to send forms in to the government at selected and fixed times throughout the year. Think of the annual income tax forms that are generated (by law) by a company for its employees (one copy for the government). The analyst has no influence over the content or format of the form, or over the time when it is required. Any changes he designs must allow for the production of the exact form.

Financial Constraints. Once the department's annual budget has been defined, the analyst must then tailor his new method of doing the job to those figures. While he might be aware of other more efficient and expensive improvements, he must put them aside if he is delivered a smaller dollar figure to work within.

The study itself might be limited by a budget. Even though the analyst might like to include all branches in his preliminary study, perhaps the funds are just not available within his framework for "across-the-country" travelling.

Physical Location Constraint. Sometimes a solution to a problem might involve the relocation of some of the buildings operated by the firm. For example, if the analyst could have the warehouse attached to the back of the retail outlet, he might resolve a lot of the paperwork and delivery problems of a certain store. However, the warehouse is located across the city (or across the country) and, as stated by management, "it must remain there."

Time Constraint. The major factor under this heading is the deadline, or the date, when the company requires the new system to be operating.

There are occasions when an analyst can foresee a very efficient system as a solution to the difficulties at hand. However, as a result, a long extensive analysis period would be required—perhaps lasting eight months. The firm he is working for wants an improved method of doing the job installed and working by next June (six months away). The analyst must abandon his plan and concentrate on an alternate solution that meets the deadline.

NOTE: Many design and ideas that violate constraints are presented to management for their consideration, and some of these submissions result in changes to the constraints.

Policies

Policies (or objectives, goals) are those statements made by management (or the owners of the system), and not by the analyst, that direct or guide the functioning and direction and attitude of the company. They influence what type of work must be done.

Policy examples: "Our store does not process a refund unless the original sales slip is shown." "Our guideline, at Preferential Life Insurance, is to be able to process any claim within five days of receipt of the initial letter." "Our goal, here at R-E-V-Auto Parts, is to be able to inquire on our huge inventory file and receive a description of the status of any item we carry within two to four seconds." "Due to our commitment to the environment, we will use recycled paper to package our goods."

The intent or message of the policies obviously have an effect on the design that will be started as well as influence the amount of money for the project. If immediate access to information is required to meet a goal (be it inventory, marketing, airline reservations), then a system involving computer equipment that can handle the fast transfer of data would be needed (disk, drum, large CPU storage capacity, sophisticated software, etc.).

If management states that the new computer system with its terminals located throughout the company should be accessible to everyone, then the subsequent design must reflect that directive. In other words, explanations describing the method of using the terminal must be avail-

---

KEY CONCEPT

LOGGING ROUTINE

A term used to describe a computer program whose function it is to store data entered through terminals on a storage device (usually magnetic tape) before or after the data updates a master file. In this way, a record of all the transactions is available at any time.

able on-call for a first-time user of the system. Also, a thorough logging routine should be developed to help trace back transactions (updates or inquiries) to their source.

Requirements

Closely related to the objectives of a system are the requirements. The requirements are those items that the analyst must make sure the system handles or performs (or in the case of future requirements, allows for). These needs are associated with day-to-day work and can be thought of as those things that must be done to achieve the goals and objectives set by the department or company.

Examples of the System Requirements:

1. The accounts are closed on the fifteenth of the month and therefore all purchases up to that time must be available on the sixteenth.
2. Fees must be paid before a college registration will be accepted.
3. The accounts payable department must have a copy of the original purchase order before they release any money to a vendor for a delivery received by the firm.
4. Information from people who have left the company during the year must be saved for income tax purposes.

The future needs of the firm should also be described in the report that will be used by the designers in Stage 2. Growth patterns, new product lines, expansion, etc., are examples of very important points that should influence any new system. A system that is only workable for one year and then requires massive changes due to a "future need" now realized could be termed a poorly planned system. Again in this instance, the analyst must get these points from management. He is not the one to provide the necessary information.

PART 3: DETERMINING WHAT THE PROBLEM IS!

Although an analyst might find himself assigned to a department to generally "improve the efficiency of the current system," he more often than not has been presented with a specific problem that he must resolve.

For example:

1. The books do not balance!
2. Why are we always out of stock?
3. The paychecks are incorrect again this week.
4. It takes too long to service a customer during peak periods.
5. We are accepting goods at the receiving docks that we do not need.

During Analysis, the analyst must strive to make sure he finds or locates the source of the problem. If perhaps he is working with example (5), he must think of some of the problem areas: Was the initial purchase order filled out incorrectly? Was the initial request for merchandise not specified correctly? Did the receiver mix shipments up? Did the vendor make a shipping error?

Now even within the first possibility (of an incorrectly filled Purchase Order) there are several possibilities: missing data fields, items put in wrong columns, and new Purchasing Agent.

He may take it even one step further and ask why were some items of information omitted. Possibly, the instructions describing how to handle a "Rush Order" had not been updated since the new version of the "purchase order form" had come into use. It is of course only *after* some digging that the analyst can report or state that the problem in the system

Okay . . . but except for that, when have I ever made a bad mistake?"

© *Creative Computing*

is poorly worded documentation (on Rush Orders) located in the Purchasing Department. This point is certainly more informative than hearing people complain that "Goods we unloaded are not even needed by the firm."

In other words, he has delved into the root of the problem and has not allowed the symptoms of the problem to cloud the issue. He wants the cause of the problem; and when it is established, it is then and *only then* that an appropriate design can begin. In the example just discussed, a solution or design might center on an improved set of notes or guidelines written for the Purchasing Agents and describing such points as the correct filling out of forms for normal, rush, and special orders.

TERMS TO STUDY

Active Observer
Constraints
Distributed Systems
Logging Routine

Policies
Procedure Manuals
Questionnaires
Requirements
Silent Observer

QUESTIONS FOR REVIEW

1. Develop a chart describing the good and bad features of the various data-gathering techniques.
2. List three activities that should be accomplished during the main stages of interviewing.
3. Give five design considerations when formulating a questionnaire, and supply a rationale for each of your answers.
4. Give an example of how each of the major constraints can affect the design of a system.

QUESTIONS FOR RESEARCH AND DISCUSSION

1, For each data-gathering technique, think of a situation where that technique would be appropriate or suitable.

2. Choose a form in your school and apply the forms analysis questions to it and see how much detail about the system that the form is part of would be generated.
3. Supply some examples of buzzwords, lingo, etc., from various work environments.
4. Discuss the use of a tape recorder during an interview.
5. Given the following situations or symptoms:

   a set of paychecks incorrectly generated

   some students receive a grade for a course that they did not take

   a credit card user gets an invalid entry on his account

   Derive three possible causes of the problem for each of the above.

17

Design

INTRODUCTION

Imagine the following scene:

Patient:	I haven't been feeling very well lately, Doctor.
(Systems Analyst) *Doctor:*	Have you been doing anything different?
Patient:	Well, I have been assigned to work out a new system design at my firm, and I'm getting a lot of headaches.
Doctor:	Well then, let me prescribe for you the following: a pill containing 3 grains of creativity, mixed with 2 grains of patience, plus 4 grains of hindsight, to be taken once a day or when required.

If it were only that easy! The Design stage is that part of the life cycle of a system that analysts generally like because it gives them a chance to explore, to be creative, and to be inventive. It is also a very difficult stage! Difficult because the solution or design must be all things to all people—it must satisfy all levels of management, the employees, the financial concern, customers, students, vendors, etc. When the analyst finds that his new method of doing a job is not being accepted by everyone, he must learn to make compromises within his own design work. In addition, he must often provide alternative system designs and have management select the one that they feel will offer the most workable solution.

A common misconception is that design is as simple as replacing people with a machine to increase efficiency within the department (be it a computer, lathe, printing press, etc.). In fact, that type of design-solution accounts for a very small percentage of all the design work being done. A solution to a problem can range all the way from one new form being created for a department, to a complete reorganization of the internal structure of a company.

This chapter cannot teach creativity, per se, but will offer many thoughts and guidelines concerning some of the more common aspects of design work.

CODING

The seven most commonly used words in the 1980s, next, of course, to "Big Mac, fries, and a Coke please" might well be contained in the phrase: "May I have your account number, please."

It appears as if everything connected with computers must have an accompanying code. Fields such as name, address, and even sex are not important anymore but are secondary to requested (and often mandatory) code numbers: charge no., student no., customer no., vendor no., part no., ... the list seems endless. This section will explain some of the widely used codes as well as show how many codes can be constructed.

Background

The abundance of codes is due to a number of reasons: First, with punch cards being limited or bound by a set number of card columns (usually 80), it is more desirable to allot one column for a month code (0, 1, 2, ... 9, A, B) rather than needing nine to represent "September." In this way, more information can be stored on one card. Both keytape records and diskette records offer the same problem even though some of the record lengths are up to 120 characters.

Second, the central processing units and secondary storage devices (tape and disk) are so quick that the time required to look up in a disk file to determine the contents of a given code does not offer a serious overhead with respect to overall processing speeds.

Fourth, a unique identification for each person, product, student, etc., reduces the time it takes to search and locate that particular record. There may be three or four pages of J. SMITHs in the telephone book, but there is only one customer 056431.

When a code is established, the coder should try to satisfy the following criteria: it should be (a) expandable, (b) convenient (i.e., easy to use and remember), (c) meaningful, and (d) precise.

The rest of this chapter will be devoted to the various kinds of codes that are available to the system designer.

Types of Codes

Sequence or Serial Coding. This technique simply assigns consecutive numbers (normally starting at one) as each subsequent item is to be coded.

Example: The sales force currently employs 20 salesmen with codes as follows:

                01   Arsenault
                02   Bridges
                 .
                 .
                 .
                20   Thompson

As the 21st salesman is hired, he will be code no. 21, even though his name might be Jenkins. In other words, the list can only be in alphabetical order when it is first generated. Also, there is no way of determining groups within the list (e.g., all the salesmen who work the east coast). This technique is used basically for numbering such things as checks, invoices, or purchase orders.

Block Coding. The weakness of sequence coding can be remedied in block coding by at least reserving a group or block of numbers for certain codes.

Example: In an inventory system, the part numbers might be assigned as follows:

Part No.	Description
01	21″ Toshiba Color
02	21″ RCA Color
03	21″ Sony Color
04	21″ Sony B & W
05	26″ Phillips
06	26″ Zenith
07	12″ Panasonic
08	12″ Sony
09	12″ RCA

In this way, at least a test can be performed on the codes to generate a desired group: for example, all codes less than 05 could be selected with the result being all 21″ TVs.

Group Classification Codes. An extension of block coding assigns a specific digit to represent the required group. The assigned digit can be in the first position to allow for a major grouping and could also be in secondary positions within the code to represent still other groupings.

Example: If the regions are assigned in the following manner: 1-East Coast, 2-North, 3-South, 4-Mid-West, 5-West Coast, then a salesman's code might be generated as follows:

101 Adams	201 Aaron	301 Butcher	401 Charles	501 Anson
102 Bilsky	202 Comeau	302 David	402 Ester	502 Hastings
.	.	.	.	.
.	.	.	.	.
199	299	399	499	599

Example: The Canadian Postal Code offers an example of an alphabetic entry used for a group classification. In the postal code M9R 1T4, the first position represents one of the geographical areas within Canada: M-Toronto, C-Prince Edward Island, V-British Columbia.

Further subdividing of the code provides both digits and alphabetic characters that allow the code to produce a reference to either a rural postal station *or* series of street numbers on a specific street—anywhere in Canada.

Final Digit Codes. This label refers to the concept of adding a suffix (usually one digit) to a given code to extend the classifications.

Example: Final Digit Values for a product might be:

1. Manufactured Product
2. Purchased Product
3. Assembled Product

Therefore, if part no. 54320 were a purchased item, its complete code number would be 54320-2.

Significant-Digit Codes. This approach uses some dimension of the object being described (distance, weight, size, capacity, and so on) and creates the code with that particular characteristic embedded within it. This technique allows for easy creation of a code for new items as well as providing a quick and easy visual identification of existing items.

Example:

Head Office	Branch Office	Code	
Toronto		001	
	Orangeville	060	Number of miles from head office
	Welland	070	
	London	100	
	North Bay	205	
	Smith's Falls	210	

Example:

Stereo Amplifiers

the 101 part stands for a certain manufacturer, say Marantz	10120 10125 10140 10160 10180	the 20, 25 . . . 80 are the R.M.S. power ratings of the amplifier

Phonetic Codes. Many times, names are taken down over the phone and then records created (either on paper or on computer secondary storage devices), and the information is filed away. Subsequently, when an inquiry is directed to the file, no matching record can be found. The reason for this is that Mr. BOWMAN who filed the claim, was talking to a clerk who recorded the claimant as Mr. BOUGHMEN. Due to this type of problem, some firms are switching to a phonetic code to represent names so that an inquiry to the file will generate all names that are the same and sound the same as the requesting name. All possibilities are returned to the clerk to help him find the desired record.

The following list is an example of a set of rules used to institute a phonetic coding routine:

Letters	Code
B, P, F, V	01
C, G, J, K, Q, S, X, Z	02
D, T	03
L	04
M, N	05
R	06
A, E, I, O, U, W, H, Y	ignored

e.g., Johnson 02050205
　　　Jonsen 02050205

e.g., Christal 0206020304
　　　Kristle 0206020304

NOTE: This technique is not 100 percent accurate because there are similar sounding names that will not generate to the same matching code (witness poor Mr. BOUGHMEN). However, these exceptions can be handled by the phonetic coding routine by reference to a special table created for these cases.

Check Digit Codes. Whenever important fields such as customer no., student no., etc., are being processed by a computer system, there should be an extra effort to ensure the accuracy of these types of data fields. A check digit code answers this requirement. When a student no. is issued, it is perhaps taken from a serial coding system consisting of five digits. Therefore, if 54321 were the last issued no., then 54322 is simply chosen as the next consecutive no. However, before issuing this number, a series of calculations are performed on the digits 54322 in order to derive a new digit. Many different algorithms can be used but the following technique will be discussed:

5	4	3	2	2
leave alone	×2	leave alone	×2	leave alone
5	8	3	4	2

Leave every alternate digit intact and then double the remaining digits,* producing a new set of digits 58342 that add up to 22. The units digit, in this case 2, is then subtracted from 10 giving 8. The no. 8 is called the check digit and is added on to the original number so that the issued student no. is 543228. This number is perceived as a six-digit figure and is used as such.

---

* If any digit to be doubled is greater than 4, add the digits of the doubled answer, e.g.,

$$\begin{array}{r} 6 \\ \times 2 \\ \hline 12 \end{array} \quad 1 + 2 = 3$$

Now, whenever this number enters into a computer program, the same set of calculations previously performed when the code was derived is performed again (at computer speeds of $1/1{,}000{,}000$ sec. per calculation, this check is not considered as extra or wasted time). If the computer program finds an error condition, then this transaction can be rejected and printed out on an error list. In this way, invalid data can be prevented from entering the system.

Example: If a data entry operator makes an error so that the student no. 543228 is entered as 534282, the calculations performed by the program would show as follows:

```
5       3      4      8     2    [8]  ← Check digit
↓      ×2      ↓     ×2     ↓                          not equal,
5  +   6  +   4  +   7  +  2 = 2 [4]                   therefore error
                                                       condition
                    Subtract the units
                    digit (4) from ten = 6
```

NOTE: This code is not foolproof because two or three errors could occur in the field such that the sum of the digits would still work out the same as the original. Many of the popular code numbers (Social Insurance No., Social Security No., charge account no.) all employ a check digit.

Date and Time Codes. Instead of using a six-position field to store a date—as in 11 10 85—many firms are using codes to save a position in their storage files as well as to provide a better storage format for performing calculations on date fields. For example, it is sometimes required to know how many days have elapsed since 3 June 1985 and 14 December 1985.

As an alternative to DDMMYR, e.g., 101185, a Julian representation would appear as 85344 where 85 stands for the current year and 344 represents the days since 1 January 1985. Or, in another method, 10 November 1985 would be stored as 31628, a number that represents the number of days since 1 January 1900. Again, it is the computer that actually determines the code based on tables supplied via computer programs.

As for time codes, instead of having four positions reserved for 08:45 and then needing another position to indicate a.m. or p.m., the European or Military clock can be followed such that 08:45 is a.m. and 20:45 is p.m.

FORMS DESIGN

If the following two statements are examined, an interesting point about business forms should be evident.

"One individual form costs, on the average, a fraction of a cent."

"For every dollar spent on purchasing forms, business in general estimates that it costs about $25.00 to process a form."

The important point is that poorly designed business forms are going to cost a firm money! An individual form might have to be ripped up and a new one started due to poor instructions concerning the way the form is to be filled out. At a ¼¢ per form, the paper cost is not the relevant feature. However, it is the time lost in misfilings, the extra time taken to prepare a form, and the wasted time having to reference a form a second time because the data is poorly recorded that accumulate to lost dollars. Therefore one of the main objectives of Forms Design should center on reducing the errors associated with the handling of forms.

Trends

With the speed of the current computer printer (an average of 1500 lines of 132 characters each, every minute), there has been a trend to generate massive amounts of paper and reports and distribute them back to requesting departments. However, are they looked at or used? Well not always! In fact many 100-page reports sit in an Inventory Department gathering dust, while the analyst (or generally the Data Processing Department) sits thinking that their work is done and that the Inventory Department has been serviced adequately. As each department in a firm becomes more aware of Data Processing features, this trend will be replaced by another that will have reports containing only the needed data.

Two other trends concerning forms are almost running a contradictory pattern. On one hand, there are more forms being created for devices that can process the form and send an input directly into the computer (e.g., optical character documents, bar-coded forms) in order to cut down the data-entry time. On the other hand, more and more visual display terminals are being installed and used for on-line entry of data—thereby eliminating the need for a form.

This part of the chapter will describe some of the more straightforward considerations of forms design such as paper color, size, weight, etc., and then provide a checklist of guidelines for the actual design of the form. A section on the "computer-generated" form will also be covered with references to printer spacing charts.

Standard Paper Sizes

Designation	Size in mm	Suggested Use
A0	841 × 1189	
A1	594 × 841	Posters
A2	420 × 594	Calendars, Maps
A3	297 × 420	Calendars, Maps
A4	210 × 297	Letterheads, Catalogs
A5	148 × 210	Text Books, Memos
A6	105 × 148	Postcards, Card Indexes
A7	74 × 105	Card Indexes
A8	52 × 74	Business Cards
A9	37 × 52	Passport Photos
A10	26 × 37	ID Card Photos

Figure 17-1.

Form Design Considerations

Size. The straightforward point in this section is simply to remember to try to match any new forms with the existing form sizes that are already in use. If forms are of random sizes, then of course all the filing cabinets, holding devices, manilla folders, binders, etc., all have to change as well. So whether the firm uses 8½" × 11", 8½" × 8½", etc., or if they have shifted to metric classifications A4, A5, etc., pick a size suitable to your application from the standard size charts (see Figure 17-1).

Weights of Paper. Another physical feature of a form is its weight. Forms are available all the way from onionskin (tissue paper used to separate carbons) that weigh about 10 pounds per 1000 sheets of 8½" × 11" pages to tag stock (used in warehouses to tag heavy machinery) weighing over 120 pounds for the same number of forms. The point to remember is again to match the requirements of the form to the available paper weights. A form that is going to be used only a couple of times and then discarded doesn't have to be tag stock weight. Also, a document such as a general ledger that will be consulted again and again should not be made out of flimsy, onionskin paper. An analyst should investigate the life expectancy of the forms because some are required in business for 10, 15, 20 years, while others such as life insurance documents, wills, etc., are to be considered as permanent records.

Colors. In general, colored papers or colored inks are going to improve the attractiveness of a given form but are going to increase the cost of producing that form. Some thoughts concerning colors are as follow:

1. Certain departments may have been assigned a color sales—green, accounting—pink, etc., so if a new form has multiple parts, make sure that the colors of the various parts coincide with the established standards of the company.
2. Some blues do not photocopy.
3. Use red for important financial messages: STOP PAYMENT, CREDIT MEMO, N.S.F. checks, and so on.
4. Watch the use of reds and greens because these two colors cause colorblind people a lot of trouble.
5. For extreme clarity, use combinations such as black ink on a yellow background or green on white.

Margins or Spacing. The rules to be concerned about here center on keeping an adequate space left blank, or open, on the form for specialized considerations.

Example:

1. ½" for loose leaf binders
2. 1½" for post binders
3. ½" for the "gripper edge" that is held and snapped to remove the carbon from multiple-part forms
4. ⅝" should be reserved for any magnetic ink coding requirements
5. ¼" should be left for each line when there is going to be a handwritten entry
6. ⅙" reserved for each line printed via a typewriter or computer printer.

Carbons. Whenever transfer of data from one page to another is desired (at the time of producing the form, not later as in Xeroxing), there are four basic types of carbon to type from.

1. One-time carbons—as the name implies, they are used just once and then thrown away. Examples of this type are the carbons used in multipart forms.
2. Block or split carbons—are similar to one-time except that they only cover a portion of the carbon page therefore allowing only selected information to pass. If, for example, an invoice was being produced with many copies required, full one-time carbons could be inserted to produce the output. However, the carbon just before the Bill of Lading would be split or blocked so that none of the

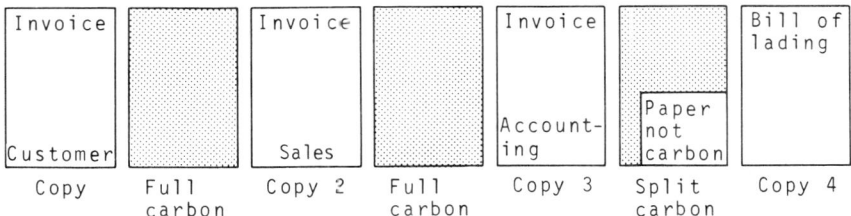

Figure 17-2. Example of block or split carbons.

pricing information would be transferred to the page that will accompany the shipment via a trucking line (see Figure 17-2).

3. Carbon-backed paper—in this case the carbon is actually affixed to the back of the form itself and is not a separate sheet to be disposed of. Many complex mailing sets generate the name and address on subsequent pages by using the carbon-backed paper.

4. N.C.R. (no carbon required) paper allows the passage of information to subsequent pages by chemically coating the sheets so that the pressure of a sharp object, usually a ball-point pen, will force the image to appear. There are of course no bulky carbon papers to dispose of in this case; however, care must be taken not to fold the forms (creases will mark subsequent pages); write a memo with these forms underneath as they will pick up an imprint from any source; or make unnecessary marks (fingernail lines).

NOTE: Even though N.C.R. paper and carbon-backed pages are more expensive, sometimes the situation warrants their use. For example, a shipper or receiver who must add additional information to a "produced multipart form" does not want to be concerned with carbons slipping or falling out as he carries the invoice around on his clipboard. Therefore in conditions where possible slippage is important, the more expensive carbons should be investigated.

Design Guidelines.

1. In general, a form should be easy to read, easy to work with, add to, expand, and dispose of (if necessary).
2. Every form should be labeled as to the type of form it represents, e.g., if the form is a "payroll coding sheet," then those words should be somewhere on the form.
3. If the form is to be used internally (e.g., an error list from the computer room to be delivered to the Accounts Receivable De-

partment), it is permissible to leave off the company name. If, however, the form is destined to go outside the firm (to a vendor, customer), the name should be prominently displayed.

4. Try to put the field, by which the form is to be sequenced, in the top right (or left) corner for easier filing and selecting.
5. Provide the person who is filling out the form choices via boxes rather than written comments to reduce preparation time.

Example:

Poor   *Better*

| SEX _____ | | MALE ☐   Please |
| | | FEMALE ☐ check one |

6. Along with guideline no. 5 is the idea to preprint as much information as possible with the intent to cut down the writing required by the person filling out the form.
7. Any headings should be to the top or to the side of the required entry for reduced typing problems.

Example:

Poor

NAME	
Date of Birth	Phone No.

Better

NAME	
Date of Birth	Phone No.

8. The use of abbreviations should be avoided on the preprinted headings. A label "P-No" might be clear to you as a purchase order no., but to someone else it could be considered a part no., product no., etc. There are a few widely accepted exceptions to this rule such as "no., ltd., and co."
9. Use meaningful headings to eliminate any possible confusion in the mind of the person filling out the form or of the person using the form.

Example:

Blank Application Form

```
DATE:    /   /
NAME:
_____
```

Form Filled Out

```
DATE:  01 / 03 / 85
NAME:
   Lloyd Thomas
```

Confusion: Is it the 3rd of January or the 1st of March?
Is the person's last name Thomas or Lloyd?

Better Approach

```
DATE:  DD  MM  YR
        /   /
─────────────────────
Surname,    Given Names
```

Even if the extra printing eliminates confusion in only a few cases, it is well worth any small additional expense at the time of creating the form.

10. Forms being sent down to the Data Entry Department should have starting field numbers printed on the form to help the data entry clerks.

Example:

```
        APPLICATION FOR EMPLOYMENT

                             DD MM YR
                   DATE:      /   /
                             30
 Surname,  Given Names
 _____

 1                           DD MM YR
               Date of Birth: /   /
                             37
               Phone No.:
                             43
```

Starting Field Numbers (1, 30, 37, 43) indicate where the data should be located in the input record.

11. To eliminate confusion with amount fields that may contain decimal places, use shading, dotted lines or a preprinted decimal.

Example:

Poor	*Better*	*Better*	*Better*
Amount Due	Amount Due $ ¢	Amount Due	Amount Due
1 5 0	1 5 0	1.5 0	1 5 0

12. If an explanation of a set of codes is required, then have the legend printed right on the form either at the bottom or on the back of the page.

Computer-Generated Output

When designing a form that is to be produced by a computer printer, a printer spacing chart (Figure 17-3) should be consulted. This chart conforms to automated printers in that it allots 6 lines/inch down the page, and 10 characters/inch across each line. Although most printers have a switch or clutch mechanism to generate 8 lines/inch, the industry standard is basically 6 lines/inch. Besides the columnar rulings, preprinted

---

KEY CONCEPT

COMPLEX MAILING SET

A term to describe a document that contains an envelope for mailing to a customer, a letter to the customer, a receipt for the customer's file, a return addressed envelope, and a slip to be returned with the payment—all in one form.

headings, colors, etc., that the analyst wants to record on the spacing chart, he can also show the location of the data to be printed by the computer printer. Established conventions suggest the use of 9's for numeric fields, and X's for alphabetic and alphanumeric fields (see Figure 17-3). Note that the maximum field sizes are accounted for to insure adequate spacing in the form design. When using a printer spacing chart remember:

1. To leave room for possible expansion.

Example:

Poor   *Better*

Quantity	Unit Price
9 9 9	

Quantity	Unit Price
9 9 9	

2. To allow for an extra ½" on each side for the pinfeed holes. A guideline suggests that if the form is to be delivered outside the company, then perforations should be built into the form to eliminate the pinfeed holes before delivery. An internal form can maintain the holes.

3. Sometimes forms are required that are small enough and as such do not occupy the full print line (whether it be 120 or 132). In this case, if the forms can be printed "two up" with a middle perforation for bursting, then valuable print cycles can be saved.

Example:

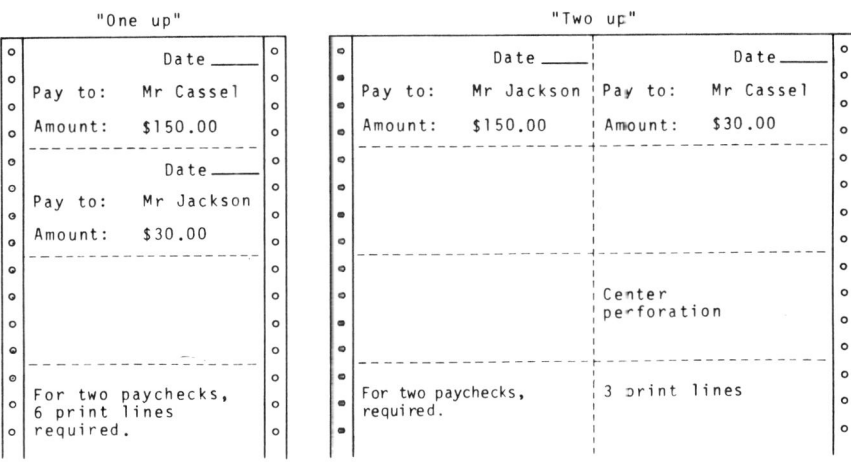

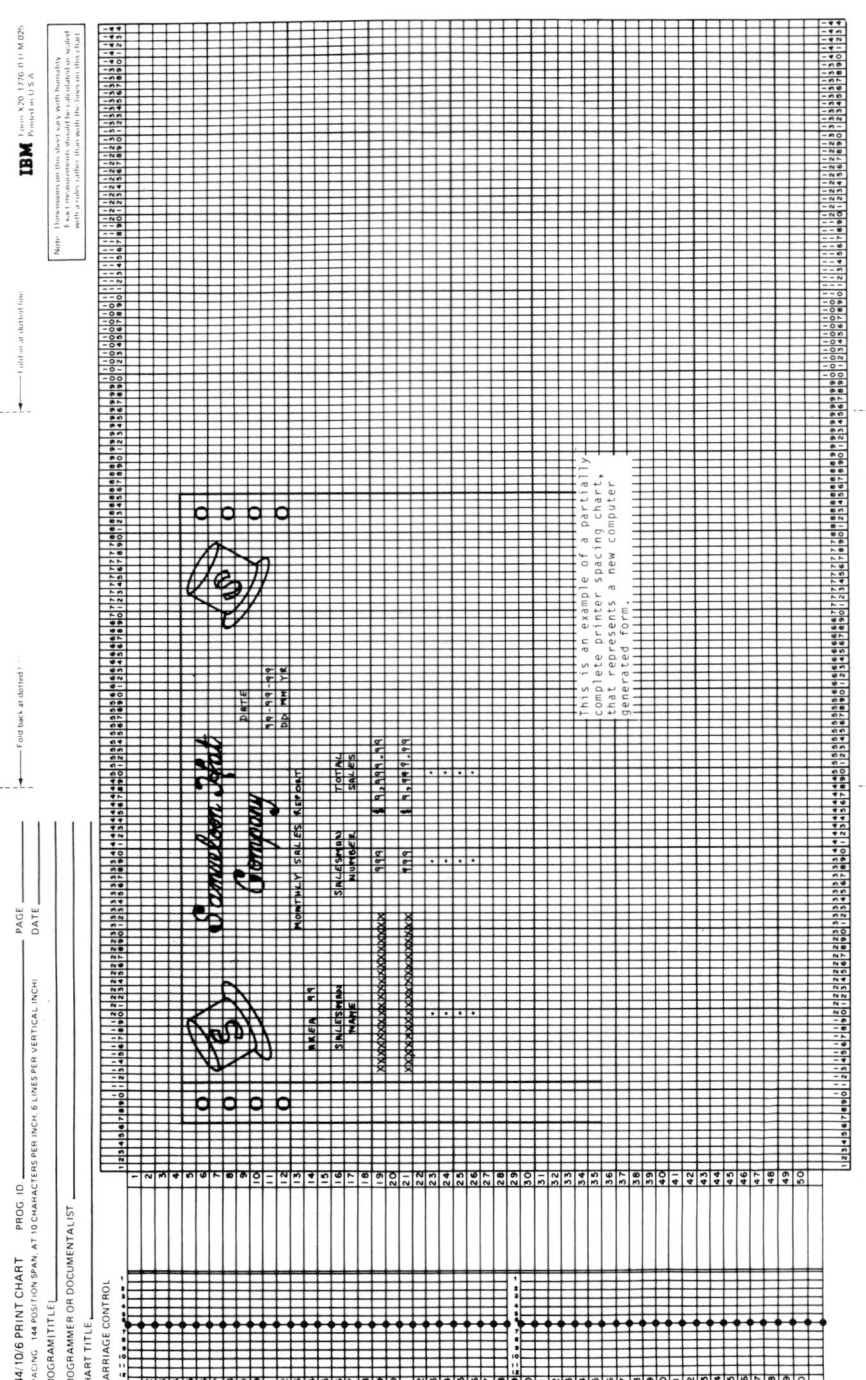

Figure 17-3.

For 300 employees paid weekly, quite a saving in print time is possible.

NOTE: Where applicable, THREE-UP and even FOUR-UP techniques can be applied.

DATA CONTROL

There are many and varied types of controls that can be incorporated into the design of a system, ranging from a required second authorization on a customer's check to a complicated voice pattern confirmation required by some computer systems to validate all users. The important statement to remember about controls is that "generally speaking, the more controls that a given system has, the greater the chance that it is a successful system" (successful in this sense can be equated with accepted, workable, or accurate).

The following sections will describe different controls that can be considered when working with the various stages of design work. For existing systems, the sections can provide a checklist to determine if the current system is adequately controlled. While it is not mandatory for a new system to have all the controls that will be described, the more that can be "built-in," the less chance of system failure, fraud, or embezzlement.

Eight Control Sections

Input Controls. The heading "Input Controls" refers to those control techniques that can be used with respect to data being delivered to the Data Processing Department. Whatever the firm, the source of data is still found in the user departments (Inventory, Sales, Accounts Receivable), and that information must get transferred to the Data Entry section so it can be prepared for processing by the computer. How does the system protect against (a) an invalid time card from the warehouse that contains eighty regular weekly hours for an employee, or (b) two time cards submitted for the same staff member, or (c) an unauthorized purchase order that might generate an extra color TV and have it delivered to a fictitious address?

Many firms have established a control section within the Data Processing Department to receive all documents coming in from user departments and to make sure a match is made with the outputs produced by the computer before sending them off to the correct department. In addition, the first program that processes any data is usually an "Edit Program." This type of program is responsible for checking for errors in the data and printing out these invalid transactions on an error list to be returned to the originating department for correction. The accepted data is allowed to continue on in the system and update files, generate invoices, etc.

A list of suggestions concerning improved control over the "inputting of data" is as follows.

1. Try to limit the number of people who can originate data. In other words, appoint one clerk who is responsible for creating the inputs to the computer in order to prevent just anyone from filling out a coding sheet or entering data through a terminal. Also, the analyst should establish some sort of identification (probably a code) that must be entered along with the regular data, so that the transaction can be traced back to the originating person.

2. When an error list is returned to an originating department, the errors should be brought to the attention of the clerk who was responsible for sending the data. Many systems simply return the list to a central point in the department where a different clerk might correct the error and resubmit it. The clerk who coded the error in the first place does not get a chance to learn from his mistake and might continue entering data incorrectly.

3. Use prenumbered documents so starting and ending numbers can be used to verify that all inputs have been accounted for. For example, if on a given day the first invoice no. happened to be 00541 and the last one 00637, then a check can be done to ensure that 96 outputs are generated from the computer.

4. Use check digits to allow a check to be performed on each record such that an invalid record can be rejected. (For details on check digits see the Coding section in this chapter.)

5. Batch totals can be employed to make certain that individual transactions are not misplaced or lost and to protect against someone inserting extra, fraudulent transactions. When a series of time cards is about to be delivered to the Data Entry section, the input clerk will create a batch-control slip that contains information such as date, batch no., clerk's identification, the number of transactions in that particular batch, and most importantly, a special total that represents the sum of the pay amounts from each time card (see Figure 17-4).

In actual fact, there would probably be approximately 50 transactions per batch. So if on a given day the input clerk received 160 time cards to process, he would create four batch slips

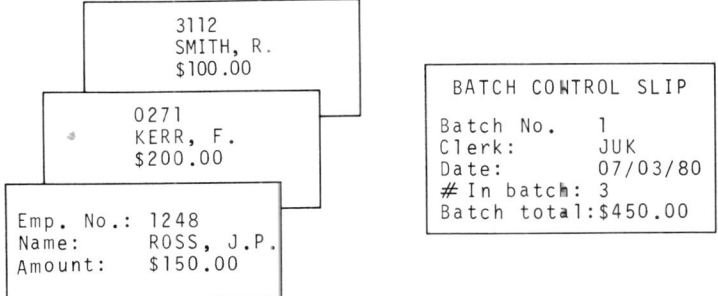

Figure 17-4. Example of batch control slip.

that would accompany the transactions to the Data Entry section where a record would be created for each of the four batch control slips.

Then as the data is being processed by a computer program, the program checks the total from the batch record and matches it against another total that it derives from adding the amounts from the time card records (as the input clerk once totaled). If the totals are not equal, then a transaction has been lost, not entered, or a new one has been supplied. At this point, the whole batch must be rejected and printed on an error list because it is impossible to tell where the actual error is.

If a set of transactions does not have an obvious field to generate a total for (such as a group of registration forms), a field such as phone number can be chosen, and even though the resulting total is not really meaningful, it fulfills the purpose of the batch total check. Totals of this nature are often referred to as "Hash Totals."

6. Another step to take is to ensure that the Data Entry instructions (i.e., what fields to enter and where to enter them) are clear and well documented. The check is simply to prevent a new Data Entry clerk from possibly misinterpreting some entering instructions and generating a series of error filled transactions.

7. Another concern is to make certain that there is at least a plan for the retention of the original source documents. After data has been entered into a computer system, there is a tendency to rely on the computer's version of the data whether it be stored on magnetic disk or tape. If, however, something goes wrong with the main files, it might be necessary to recreate the file. If the original source document is available (even a copy on microfilm), then a set of files can be restored.

Output Controls.

1. When reports are produced from a Data Processing Department, they should be delivered as soon as possible to the requesting department to eliminate the possibility of information being left sitting for operators, programmers, etc., to inspect.
2. Check to see that all error reports contain meaningful error messages that will not allow the clerk to be confused regarding the correction of the error.
3. When most companies use an Edit Program, the rejected errors are usually just listed on the hard-copy error list. Perhaps an extension of this is to also create a record of each error on magnetic tape. Then when the errors are reentered (in their corrected format), they can be matched to the "error tape" by a computer program so that the system can check to see if all of the errors are in fact being looked at. If after a period of time (say, for example, 2–3 weeks), there are still transactions on the error tape that have not been matched with reentered data, then these unmatched records can be printed out for immediate attention.

Hardware Controls. The ideal for an adequate back-up system with respect to hardware is to have two versions of each hardware device: two CPUs or two card readers. This setup is probably unrealistic from a financial point of view. There are however, a few guidelines that should be adhered to.

1. A regular preventive maintenance program should be followed.
2. The room housing the computer should be free of dust, smoke, excessive heat, and moisture.
3. Detection devices that monitor possible defective parts in magnetic tapes and magnetic disks should be investigated and acquired if possible.
4. When acquiring new hardware, check to see if it offers error retry routines, parity tracks, and even duplicate circuitry.
5. Any punch card files should be kept under pressure to protect against warping, and those files that are used frequently should be duplicated at various intervals.
6. Copies of master files should be stored in a remote location as a secure back-up for damage that might occur in the main computer room.

KEY CONCEPT

> **PREVENTIVE MAINTENANCE**
>
> A representative from the computer manufacturer visits on a regular basis to (a) clean tape drives, (b) clean and check the printer, and (c) run a special diagnostic program that alerts him to errors in the system.

Programming Controls. When a computer program is written, many different types of checks can be incorporated into the logic in order to ensure correct data. Some main methods are:

1. Sequence checking—if someone is tampering with input data (i.e., trying to insert a specially created transaction), the program can perform a sequence check on the input records and if a sequence error is found, can either stop processing or reject the record out of sequence.

2. Limit checks—for most numeric fields there is a limit as to the value that the field can contain. For example, a six-position field representing a net pay has the capacity to store the value $9,999.99. However, after a little questionning and investigating, the analyst can determine that, for example, $2,000.00 is the highest pay amount that should be generated for that firm. He would therefore ask the programmer to do a limit check on that pay field whenever it is to be used, and if ever it contains a figure greater than $2,000.00, print out a message alerting someone to the possible error. Similar limit amounts can be determined for fields such as quantity, total returned, fee amount, or unit price.

3. Another type of check involves the number of transactions for the same item. If during an examination of the habits of banking customers, it was found that the maximum amount of times that any one account was used during a given day was six times, then the analyst can request a check on the occurrence of a particular account number. If any account no. shows up as active more than six times on a certain day, then those transactions that used that account no. should be searched and printed out to provide any answer for the unusually high activity.

   This logic can also apply to the number of courses taken by one student in a semester, the number of orders by a customer in one day, or the number of entries on a single purchase order.

In general there should be no changes allowed for existing programs unless some sort of AUTHORIZATION FOR CHANGE memo is filled out. In this way, documentation can be kept and examined. Many companies have a separate group of programmers (usually known as maintenance programmers) who make changes to existing programs. The idea is that if the person who wrote the program initially is different from the person who is changing it, an environment is created that is less prone to the "fixing" of computer programs to do something other than what they were originally intended to do.

Operation Controls. In the computer room itself, the analyst can check for the presence of operating schedules. He should inquire to see if labels and checkpoint records are being extensively used. He should also find out what happens to the logs, or console listings. Since the logs contain a description of all activity in the computer, they can be checked to see if any programs are submitted and run that were not on the operating schedule. Does the supervisor of the machine room have any job-accounting statistics at his disposal? If not, he might be missing out on information that would show an excessive amount of time for a particular program or a large number of re-runs for a certain application.

KEY CONCEPT

> **LOGS, OR CONSOLE LISTINGS**
>
> Refer to the hard-copy printout of the activity that is occurring in the system, e.g., operator inputs and system messages.

Separation of Activities. Within the Data Processing Department, there should be an effort to separate many of the functions that must be performed. The main reasons being to reduce the risk of fraud or collusion in running programs and to reduce the chance of incorrectly tested programs being allowed to be run on the company's computer. The group that operates and selects the programs to be run should be different than the group who designs and writes the programs. If someone writing a program attempts something fraudulent, he probably requires access to the program when it is actually run on the computer. With a separation of activity, another party would then have to be part of the plan.

Many firms have a separate group of programmers to test programs so that a programmer would have to submit his program for independent testing by the test group before the program is allowed to be delivered to the computer room for operation.

There often is either a tape librarian or program librarian apart from all other groups who issues data files or programs to operators or programmers, only after they have displayed the proper authorization.

Auditing Controls. The auditor, dealing with the Data Processing Department, has a different set of concerns than when he works with the other departments in a company, such as:

1. There is the possibility of a loss of hard-copy forms (i.e., ledgers, sales requests, original order forms) because they have been replaced with tape or disk computer records.

2. Since the computer can centralize decision making, one clerk is now all that is required to complete an order. Before, decisions were required from different departments—a credit approval from Accounts Receivable, control of stock from the Inventory section, billing from yet another area, and so on. In this way, many different people would be required for a plan of deception. The same is not true with the one clerk and the computer configuration.

3. The auditing profession in general has closed its eyes to the computer industry mainly because of the buzzwords, slang, computerese-type language, and strangeness of the computer, and in many instances has taken a lot of things for granted. It is only recently that a class of auditors with special training in Data Processing Fundamentals has emerged to deal with the systems on a company's computer.

The key in this situation is auditor involvement at the beginning of the design of a new system. After a system has been developed and is actually running, many Data Processing Departments accommodate the auditor by simply running a program twice and then giving him the results of both runs to verify that they are identical.

Other auditors look at the inputs and outputs of a program, and if they correspond, then the auditors assume that all the in-between processing steps are correct.

An auditor should be able to test any program that will be run on the computer, with perhaps his own set of data independent of anything developed at the firm. When he is involved at the design stage of a system, he can help build in audit trails, to allow any record to be traced through the system (frontwards or backwards) even if the record is stored on a magnetic disk where it is obviously not visible. After each processing step, totals or record counts can be generated on paper to ensure that no bonus records have been inserted and that the original input group can be accounted for.

On-Line Controls. In an on-line system where transactions are entered directly from a terminal to a computer system where a master file on disk is updated, a problem exists because there may be no way of keeping track of the input transactions.

If a certain master record is changed three times in one day, there would be no record of the first two transactions because the updated master would only reflect the status of the last transaction. One control technique that can be implemented is to write a copy of the input transaction on a magnetic tape as it is being processed by the computer. In this way, all the transactions that were handled by the system are available if required at the end of the day.

Since it is the computer (and not a person who can use sight identification) that must determine if the input transaction was authorized in the first place, some different checks must be developed. Many firms simply use a password type of identification that would only be known to those in the department who are allowed to enter data. This password can be changed daily or more frequently if required. Other more advanced techniques that are being explored (and used in certain applications) are voice patterns, hand geometry, and thumb print analyzing.

DESIGN OF A PAYROLL SYSTEM

In order to summarize the points that the last few sections have provided, this part of the chapter follows the analyst as he creates an automated version of a Payroll system for a fictitious firm. The steps that he takes and the thinking processes that he goes through and the problems he has to overcome can in general be applied to many application areas. At the end of the chapter, a checklist is provided that describes the common things that must be done to fulfill the requirements of converting to a Data Processing system. Although the analyst does have an option of using an existing software package, this section will concentrate on the activities involved in specifying a customized system. In other words, instead of going to the marketplace and buying a "universal payroll program" that would force the users to adhere to a pre-determined set of functions, the analyst will specify a system that is tailored to the firm he is working for.

Design of a Payroll System

Background of a Company

Two years ago, a firm decided to rent a computer system to handle its Accounts Receivables, and things have generally worked out well. Now another department, the Payroll Department, has been given approval to use the computer and automate its system. (It does not matter here exactly what reason the Payroll area has for computerizing but typical reasons are: (1) an excessive number of errors in the paycheck amounts, (2) overtime required every week to get the checks prepared, and (3) a lack of statistics available to the Payroll manager.)

The Payroll system is completely manual for the 498 employees and is responsible for the following requirements:

1. Process the time cards from the 320 hourly workers from the warehouse and generate weekly paychecks for them.
2. Pay the 150 salaried office staff every week.
3. Prepare checks for senior management twice a month.
4. Produce personal income tax statements and all necessary tax information at year end.
5. Produce statistics each quarter concerning the breakdown of the labor cost distribution (currently many man-hours are being expended on this requirement and any reports that are generated are very late).

Beginning of the Design

Because nothing exists at this point for the Payroll Department (with respect to Data Processing), the first consideration will probably center on files, i.e., "What type of file is required?" and "How should a file be created?" A Data Processing system cannot be implemented without some sort of file for computer programs to process. It is important to say here that it is not so much the medium or type of file, but the contents of the file that is the major concern. In other words, at one point the analyst may have to make a decision on whether a tape file or a disk file should be the appropriate choice for storing the Payroll data. However, he should be thinking about the records and the associated data items or fields that he will need in the system, right at the beginning. After some data gathering and some thinking, he will probably determine that the following fields are required for each Payroll record that will be stored by the computer system:

1. Employee no.—Provides a unique reference.
2. Employee name—Used for printing on the paycheck.
3. Deductions—There are many entries for this heading but just one label will be used for this example.
4. Year-to-date totals—So that annual information can be generated.
5. Date of birth—More identifying information.
6. Date of employment—Used to check length of employment. For example, if an employee has been at the firm for longer than six months, he is entitled to a shift bonus.
7. Department—For statistical breakdowns.
8. Pay Amount—There is a requirement to accommodate hourly paid workers, weekly paid workers, and salaried management (twice a month).

It might appear that three fields are required, such as:

PAY-FIELD 1 (hourly)   PAY-FIELD 2 (weekly)   PAY-FIELD 3 (salaried)

If each field needed six positions, then it seems that eighteen positions are required just to store the "pay amount" data. However, since an employee can only be one of these three pay types (at any one point in time), the analyst would create one pay amount field and a one position field that would contain say, H, W, or S. In this way, only seven positions are needed to store the required information. The value in the pay code field dictates what figure is represented in the pay amount field.

Developing Field Sizes. When the fields have been selected, he would continue to develop field sizes until he could sum up and state a record length. Summarizing then, the following list has been determined (the field size is in parentheses):

EMPLOYEE NO. (4)—There are 498 people at the firm, and the analyst has determined that a dramatic increase is in the works because there are plans to amalgamate with a subsidiary on the East Coast. The forecast that he has been given suggests a complement of about 1500 employees.

EMPLOYEE NAME (25)—This widely used standard should hold the largest name.

DEDUCTIONS (60)—Just an arbitrary figure for the purpose of the example.

YEAR-TO-DATE TOTALS (70)—Again seventy just supplied to complete the example.

DEPARTMENT (2)—Probably a code used to represent the various departments.

DATE-OF-BIRTH (6)

DATE-OF-EMPLOYMENT (6)

PAY AMOUNT (6)

PAY CODE (1)

TOTAL: 177 positions

Input and Output Design. At this early stage, the analyst can create the following chart (a disk symbol is used here to represent the master file):

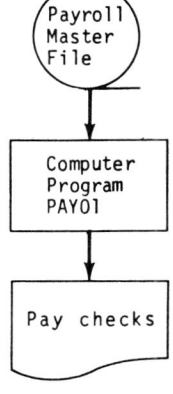

—A disk with 1500 records, each 177 positions in length, sorted in employee no. order

—A program will be needed to process or read the records on the file and produce the paychecks

—A series of paychecks will have to be designed and ordered from a forms supplier so that they can be put in the computer printer when an operator wants to run program PAY01

Figure 17-5. Chart representing master file.

```
Fred Arkin #014
Shipping Department
Pay period - Nov. 2 - Nov. 9
              In          Out
```

	In	Out
Mon.		
Tues.		
Wed.		
Thurs.		
Fri.		
	Total	

Authorization _____

SAMPLE TIME CARD

(Field) Available:

1. Name
2. Employee No.
3. Department
4. Pay period
5. Times In and Out
6. Total hours
7. Signature for authorization

Figure 17-6. Sample time card.

Although things are starting to take shape, one main missing element is data for the hourly worker. Once the Payroll Master File is created, pay amounts for the weekly and salaried workers are available but not for the group of hourly paid employees. The missing information is the time card data. How many hours did an employee work in a given week? His hourly rate is on a file, but the hours worked is also required.

The analyst knows that time cards are available, but he is also aware that the computer cannot process the time cards directly in their current format. He must arrange to have them gathered, probably batched, and delivered to the Data Entry clerk who is already responsible for the Accounts Receivable data. He must now develop a new set of data entry instructions for the clerk (and as well make sure that a format for verification will be followed). With this in mind, he may examine the contents of a typical time card (see Figure 17-6).

At first glance, it should be noted that not all the fields on the time card are required since some of them are already stored and available on the Payroll Master File (name, department); others are not relevant for this application (times in and out, signature).

So at a minimum, it appears as if only the employee no. and total hours fields are required. If the analyst requests the Data Entry clerks to enter only these two fields, the processing chart now changes to that shown in Figure 17-7.

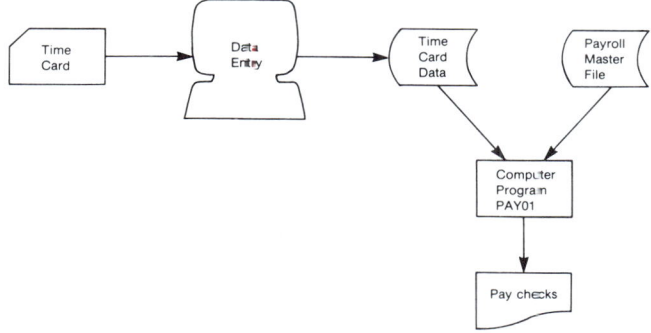

Figure 17-7. Amended processing chart.

However, a system that allows such an important match to occur only on one field would be very weak; therefore the analyst would realize he needs more than just the employee number to confirm a "hit." If a program is going to generate a paycheck for an hourly paid employee, the analyst wants to ensure that the correct record is located on the Payroll Master File. The name field looks like an obvious choice, and some companies would enter the name field as well as the employee number so that the name is verified after the program has found the corresponding master record with the input transaction. Other firms use only the first three or five positions of the name field as a secondary identifier to cut down on keying time by the Data Entry clerks.

KEY CONCEPT

SECONDARY IDENTIFIER

Describes a data field, other than the main key field, that helps match a transaction record to a master record. It is usually a relatively unique field such as name or date of birth.

Besides finding errors happening in this manner, a limit check might locate a pay amount of over $2500.00. In other words, errors might be found when processing the data. An extended chart now appears as shown in Figure 17-8.

The requirements of the system are now starting to emerge. The "system" that the analyst has created so far appears adequate for generating paychecks; however, he realizes that he has made no provision for allowing any changes to the Master File—for example, employee num-

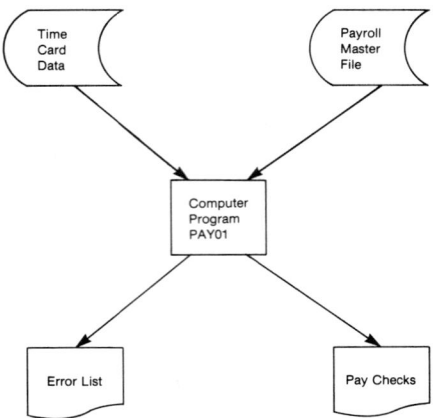

Figure 17-8. Extended processing chart.

ber 251 quits; John Larsen receives a pay raise of $25.00/week; Gale Pearson gets married and wants her new surname to appear on the checks.

These updates are going to originate from the operating departments and instead of having each department send its own version of an advice of change memo to the Data Processing Department, the analyst would probably design a new PAYROLL CODING SHEET. In this way, the operating departments can communicate their updates to the Payroll area where a standardized CODING SHEET would be filled out and sent to the Data Entry section. There, records are created that would update the Payroll Master File via a second computer program. Pictorially this can be represented as shown in Figure 17-9.

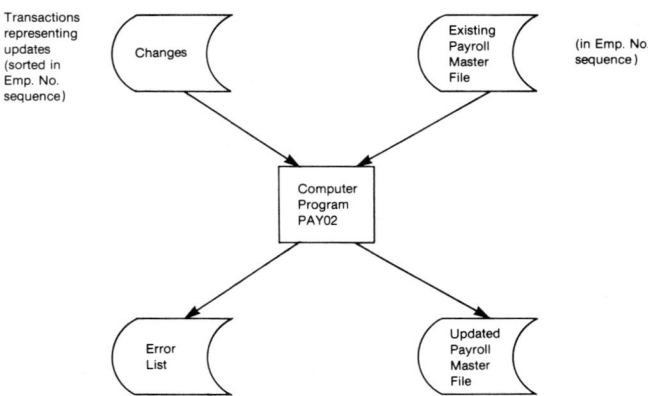

Figure 17-9. Updating the Payroll Master File.

DESIGN OF A PAYROLL SYSTEM 401

	PAYROLL CODING SHEET				
	Date _____				
Name	Department	Pay Code	Pay Amount	Date of Employment	Deductions

Figure 17-10. Payroll Coding Sheet

The analyst has now defined the need for two different computer programs. It is his job to prepare some documentation that describes what each program must do. These descriptions can then be forwarded to the programming department for action. The analyst would also be the one to communicate the "run instructions" to the Operations Department. In this case, it is important to run program PAY02 (the update program) prior to PAY01 (the check producing program).

Now the design of the PAYROLL CODING SHEET that is required in the various departments may appear at first glance as a straightforward task with a sample answer as shown in Figure 17-10.

However, when the analyst gets a chance to don his "forms design hat," he starts to remember the many guidelines for solid forms design (as discussed earlier in the chapter). As such, a more thorough form similar to the one in Figure 17-11 would emerge.

Once the PAYROLL CODING SHEET has been developed, it can be used to help create the initial file. The analyst would have to arrange for all the existing hard-copy files to be assembled and information from the files transferred onto the coding sheets. The current work force of 498 employees would all be "adds." These entries would then be processed by program PAY02 to create the first Payroll Master File.

Although there are many other features that the analyst must consider, this simplified Payroll example has demonstrated many of the main concerns from a Data Processing point of view. In summary then, a list of points to be looked at by an analyst when designing a computerized system includes the following:

PAYROLL CODING SHEET

Please print carefully

Date _____ DD MM YR

Clerk identification _____

Update code A-D-C	Employee number	Name Surname, Given	Dept.	Pay code H-W-S	Pay amount	Date of birth DD MM YR	Date of employment DD MM YR	Deductions (not described for this example)
1	2	5	30	32	33	39	45	51
		. . . .		.				. . . .
				.				
				.				

KEY
A - ADD - all fields must be entered
D - DELETE - only shaded fields required
C - CHANGE - fill out the shaded fields plus the required change field(s).

Pay code
H - Hourly
W - Weekly
S - Semi-monthly

Department
01 Sales   02 Accounting
03 Inventory 04 Payroll

Figure 17-11. Sample Payroll Coding Sheet.

1. Design fields and records for the main files
2. Decide on the type of file that will hold the information
3. Specify programming requirements or examine existing software
4. Design forms, e.g., coding sheets, computer generated outputs
5. Build in controls where appropriate
6. Arrange for conversion
7. Specify instructions and transportation guidelines necessary to allow the new system to function

MAKING MORE USE OF A TERMINAL

One interesting design that may be developed by the analyst for this Payroll application could use the terminal for more than just data entry. More and more systems developed today are in an interactive on-line mode; therefore, the terminal could also handle inquiries to the Payroll file and provide a way of generating the necessary commands to print the paychecks. One common way to present these choices to the owners of such a system is to offer a series of options in a "menu" format.

It is possible that the Data Entry operator (either working in the Data Processing Department or the user department) would see something similar to the screen in Figure 17-12.

The following paragraphs will explain the six options. When option 1 is entered, the screen shown in Figure 17-13 is returned.

This screen would contain a series of prompts that the Data Entry operator would fill in, so that complete information for new employees could be captured.

Option 2 would respond with the screen shown in Figure 17-14.

The first screen would ask for some identification information for the employee that needs to be changed. Then a second screen would display all the data for that particular employee. The operator could then change the necessary data, and the computer program would update the record on the disk file.

Option 3 would generate the screen shown in Figure 17-15.

After the operator enters the identification information, the program might return a "double-check" screen and ask the operator "Are You Sure? Answer Yes or No." In this way, after receiving confirmation, the program will delete that particular employee from the files.

Option 4 has already been discussed earlier in this section as the operator would be entering Emp. No., Hours Worked, and the first three or five characters of the employee's name.

```
PAYROLL DEPARTMENT

    1. Add new employee
    2. Modify existing employee
    3. Delete existing employee
    4. Process time cards
    5. Produce checks
    6. Inquire on status of an employee
    7. Finish Payroll Activities

Please enter the appropriate no.  _____
```

Figure 17-12. Payroll menu.

```
ADDING NEW EMPLOYEE

        Emp. No.      _____
        Emp. Name     _____
        Department    _____
        Birthdate     _____
        Salary        _____
        Pay Code      _____
```

Figure 17-13. Option 1 of Payroll menu.

```
MODIFYING EXISTING EMPLOYEES

    Emp. No.     _____
    Emp. Name    _____
```

Figure 17-14. Option 2 of Payroll menu.

```
DELETING EXISTING EMPLOYEES

    Emp. No.     _____
    Emp. Name    _____
```

Figure 17-15. Option 3 of Payroll menu.

```
┌─────────────────────────────────────────────────────────┐
│                    GENERATE PAYCHECKS                    │
│                                                          │
│   Enter Password       _____  │
│   Starting Check No.   _____  │
│   Run Date             _____  │
│                                                          │
└─────────────────────────────────────────────────────────┘
```

Figure 17-16. Option 5 of Payroll menu.

Option 5 could produce the screen shown in Figure 17-16.

It is possible that the order for the check-producing program to run could be issued from the terminal. Obviously, password protection is extremely important for this option. Many systems would feel that this facility is just too risky and therefore would just not have it in the menu.

Option 6 for inquiries would create the prompts shown in Figure 17-17.

Selected portions of an employee's record could then be displayed for the operator to view.

Option 7, the last option, simply permits the operator to finish the Payroll activities and return to some other system. Each of the first six options would have a facility to return to the main menu when the operator needed to perform another function. In addition, all the options could have a password protection feature as did option 5. Some systems also provide the operator with the ability to produce a hard copy of the data that is being displayed on the screen. This feature is very useful for inquiries.

TERMS TO STUDY

Audit Trail
Batch Control Slip
Block Classification Codes
Check Digit
Console Listing
Final Digit Code
Group Classification Code

Julian Date Representation
Limit Check
Phonetic Code
Preventive Maintenance
Secondary Identifier
Serial Coding
Significant Digit Code
Two-Up Printing

```
┌─────────────────────────────────────────────────────────┐
│                  INQUIRIES INTO THE FILE                 │
│                                                          │
│   Emp. No.       _____  │
│   Emp. Name      _____  │
│                                                          │
└─────────────────────────────────────────────────────────┘
```

Figure 17-17. Option 6 of Payroll menu.

QUESTIONS FOR REVIEW

1. What are some desirable characteristics of a coding system?
2. Why are codes heavily used in Data Processing?
3. For the block classification code example used in the chapter, can you spot an improvement by arranging things differently to gain more from the code?
4. For each of the following codes: serial, block, group classification, final digit, significant digit, give an example other than the one used in the chapter.
5. Describe the four major types of carbons.
6. Using the design considerations explained in the chapter and a printer spacing chart, design a new invoice for the Saywell Shoe Company. The information coming from the disk file consists of the following fields:

    —customer name & address (four lines of 25 positions each)
    —date of sale (size up to the analyst)
    —billing date (size up to the analyst)
    —terms of sale (13 positions)
    —unit price (5 positions)
    —quantity (4 positions)
    —description (20 positions)
    —extended amount (7 positions)
    —total invoice amount (9 positions)

    NOTE: one customer can have multiple entries on one invoice

    Also include the points that (a) invoice number is preprinted on the form and (b) the Marketing Manager has just developed a new slogan, "You'll lose your blues, wearing Saywell shoes," and he wants it to appear on the new form.

7. Name five things that can be done to control inputs to the computer. List six other control areas, and give two examples for each one.
8. Why have there been problems with Auditors and Data Processing?
9. List seven main areas that the analyst is responsible for when designing a computer system.
10. In the last topic for the chapter, option 5 was the only one with a password restriction. Choose two other options and explain why a password might be appropriate.

QUESTIONS FOR RESEARCH AND DISCUSSION

1. Pick a form that is currently in use in your school and see if you can spot any weaknesses in the design of the form.
2. Think of three applications where a split carbon could be used effectively.
3. Show how the new Payroll System (as designed in the chapter) is more readily adaptable to statistical reports than the old manual method.
4. Given that the new Payroll System (described in the chapter) uses a match of employee number (as the key field) and name (as a secondary identifier) to confirm a "hit" with the master file, how would the Payroll Coding Sheet handle changes to an existing employee's name or employee number? Supply two answers (a) leaving the suggested coding sheet as it is and (b) adding a new field to the sheet.
5. Discuss with your teacher the restrictions that can be encountered when a firm decides to buy a pre-written software application package, e.g., a Payroll package.

18

Implementation, Operation, and Modification

The purpose of this chapter is to try to really hit home with the point that the work on a new system is not finished when all the design has been completed. A very important consideration remains—"How well will the new system be accepted by the people who have to run it?" There has unfortunately been too many times when an employee has arrived at work to find a new purchase order to fill out, or a different machine to operate, or a new set of procedures to follow to obtain tools from the tool crib, . . . without any prior warning about the change to his job! Many analysts appear blind to the fact that the system must be thoroughly understood and supported by the employees using it in order for that system to be successful. It is this very point that should (a) influence or set the tone for any implementation method that is chosen and (b) explain why training and feedback sessions are important.

The first part of the chapter will describe different techniques for implementing new sets of work procedures; the second part is specifically concerned with dealing with computer manufacturers during implementation; and the third part concerns the general day-to-day running of the system.

PART 1: IMPLEMENTATION TECHNIQUES

Pilot Study

Sometimes one part of a company is selected to run the new system for a period of time. This "pilot," or "test," section is watched very closely, and any errors are documented and then fixed because this one area operates fully under the requirements of the new system. For example, a car insurance company might route all claim numbers ending in a "0" to a section within the Claims Department where the claim is processed using a new on-line system—all other claims go through the normal, existing, manual methods. Or, a chain of retail stores might choose one branch and convert the whole store over to a new method of marketing its products (new signs, displays, music).

The factor behind the pilot study approach as a desirable technique is that the errors that are discovered at one branch will not likely be any different from those that would be found at another location. Therefore, by correcting the system during its pilot operation, a very sound new system will be implemented throughout the entire firm after the pilot site has pointed out required changes. And, if there happens to be a major problem with the new system that shows up during the pilot study, the firm is not at a complete loss because the other branches, sections, or departments can be used as temporary substitutes.

Running in Parallel

This method involves running the new system and the old system together for a while until the new system is working to everyone's satisfaction. At that point, the old system is disbanded and everything functions via the new system. This technique involves extra time and effort on the part of the employees because, for example, two different order forms might have to be filled out for one customer order—one to satisfy the existing manual system and one to go to the new Data Processing version. Although this approach is costly (due to the inherent double cost involved), proponents of this method argue that if there is a serious unforeseen malfunction with the new system, then the firm can at least use the old method as back-up; and also it tends to create confidence in the operators of the new system because they can enter a transaction (e.g., an inquiry) through both systems and compare the results (e.g., response time) and therefore prove to themselves that the new system works. The more confident the employees are, the more supportive they will be of the new system.

Gradual Phase-In

As the title suggests, the new system is gradually introduced into the department perhaps in the following format: 10 percent the first month, 20 percent the second month, 50 percent the third month, and 20 percent the fourth. In this way, the employees get a taste of some of the new facets of the new system in stages. In some instances, a successive month's changes will not be done until the first month's prove successful. So a system might run for a period of time with just a small percentage of the new system in operation, and after it has checked out completely, the next phase is started.

Training

No matter what method of implementation is chosen, a critical aspect of any new system is adequate training. This term does not simply mean helping an employee who is having some difficulty operating the new system and while helping him, explaining how the system operates (to many analysts, this is training!). What the term should mean, however, is active participation by the users of a new system before it is fully operative. An analyst should make an extra effort to ensure that any new typewriters, presses, terminals, forms, etc., are inspected and used by the employees prior to complete conversion.

Perhaps an analyst and a new machine might travel from branch to branch and meet with the employees in a training session to explain the use of the new machine. Some analysts try to have a new terminal installed for a week at a time with some test programs that will simulate how the new system will work. Then an invitation is extended to the employees to try out the terminal at their convenience to familiarize themselves with its workings. In this way, the sometimes awkward environment of twenty people in a room listening to a demonstration can be avoided.

When a situation arises where it is required to have a new set of regulations or guidelines created (e.g., a new set of data entry instructions or new methods for processing overdue accounts), the employees should see the suggested samples and give the final nod that "Yes—they seem clear and meaningful."

Feedback

When any new system is implemented, feedback is generated! It might be in the form of two employees riding home in a car pool discussing the new method of calculating a salesman's commission, or a group of workers having a coffee break and talking about the new way of clocking in and out. The existence of feedback (i.e., comments, feelings, observations, criticisms) need not be contested. However, what the alert analyst should realize is that if he can capture some of the feedback, he might be able to put it to good use in the form of improvements to the system.

He can basically take the following steps in order to gain from the feedback:

1. He can ask for all the users of the new system to meet with him (for example every Friday morning for a month or so) and discuss any comments about the new system.
2. He could talk with the operators (as opposed to a group session) to obtain individual responses.
3. He could leave questionnnaires to be filled out, that he would gather after a period of time to analyze. Instead of having a survey after a month or so that would generate subjective, overview feelings such as, "Yes, generally I like it," or "It seems to work," the analyst might consider the idea of using a trouble report. This report is a form left beside the new piece of equipment; and each time something occurs that does not seem right, the operator can note the time, date, and type of error. The analyst would then collect these forms (perhaps even daily) and try to gain from these more objective points about the new system.

PART 2: DEALING WITH COMPUTER MANUFACTURERS

If a decision to acquire a computer has been made, then the next decision must be which manufacturer to choose. The various vendors should be investigated with regards to:

1. Speed of central processing unit
2. Speed of I/O devices (disks, tapes, printers)
3. Expandability of the machine
4. Compatibility with other hardware and software
5. Cost of hardware and software

PART 2: DEALING WITH COMPUTER MANUFACTURERS   413

"Gosh! How can you afford to sell a computer at that price?!"

© *Creative Computing*

6. Educational support
7. Maintenance support
8. Test centers available
9. Reputation of vendor
10. Languages available (COBOL, RPG, etc.)

Even with this list of factors, companies have generally made their selection via two basic approaches. First, they pick a preferred or established vendor who can offer educational support (books, manuals, films, courses) as well as systems support. This technique is particularly popular with first time users. The second approach is to analyze statistics of stated performances of various computers. The interested firm can produce a sample test program, indicative of the type of work the computer will be doing, and run it on various competitive machines and compare the results. These benchmark programs can be very instrumental in making a final choice of a computer vendor.

After a selection has been made, there could be a wait time for the equipment of anywhere from one month to a year. There is, however, a series of activities that can be accomplished to ready the firm for the new system. These are:

1. The room to house the computer can be constructed.
2. A new department (Data Processing) may have to be set up and staffed.
3. New forms can be finalized and ordered.

4. Perhaps the manufacturer will allow some test time that the firm can take advantage of. When a contract is signed, some vendors will assign a certain number of hours to the firm for use on a model similar to the ordered computer. In this way, programmers can test their logic and their programs before their actual machine is installed.
5. If there is no test time available, a firm can use time-sharing facilities in order to pre-test their computer programs.
6. The creation of computer master files can be started. This conversion process should not be taken lightly because it can be a very time-consuming process as well as a very expensive one. At some point, all the existing information stored in filing cabinets, folders, ledgers, and receipt books must be gathered and converted from its present hard-copy format to a computer file. Picture an insurance company with a quarter of a million policy holders all with records in four or five floors at head office! Think of the problems involved, and you start to realize why some conversions can take six months to complete and can cost from 20 percent to 80 percent of the total cost of the new equipment.

PART 3: "WE'RE UP AND RUNNING"

Basically when the system is "up and running," the analyst's job has finished and he can be assigned to a new project. Sometimes, though, there are some checks that can be performed on the new system as it is being run by its new owners. For example, there may have been a set of predicted results from either management or the manufacturer of the installed equipment that should be verified. A firm's management may state that the objective of the new system is to process all priority orders by eleven o'clock a.m. and have the delivery trucks on their way by one p.m. Well, is the new system really meeting this goal? It worked well in theory but perhaps real-life constraints will have a bigger influence than anticipated. The analyst then can be involved in designing some comparison techniques between the old and new systems or may simply be the one assigned to summarize and document the new system's performance. These requirements may take some time since the system might have to pass through a business cycle to ensure that quarterly reports, inventory counts, or billings will be accomplished in the manner that they were designed.

Another check that might be done is to compare the new system with industry standards. Perhaps there are enough firms in the same industry so that a society or organization representing that industry might publish reports or newspapers that quote such things as:

1. Average number of cars produced in one day
2. Percentage of inventory on hand vs. requested orders
3. Number of sales of a certain article during a week
4. Average installation time for a new muffler and shock absorbers

The analyst might be subsequently retained to help determine where the new firm "sits" with respect to its competitors and to the industry averages. If management is not particularly pleased with its current position, then perhaps some changes are needed.

This last point leads towards the very start of the section of analysis where a discussion was introduced concerning "What is a system?" and "What is the problem?" It seems that a system's requirements for improvements or changes are never ending. They might be silenced or subdued for a while, but then they surface again, and the whole procedure of analysis-design-implementation-operation and modification starts once more.

Perhaps this fact is a rationale for saying that although programmers, operators, users, and even management may come and go, there will always be a need for an analyst because there appears to be no such thing as a "perfect system."

TERMS TO STUDY

Benchmark
Conversion
Feedback
Gradual Phase-In

Pilot Study
Running in Parallel
Training
Trouble Report

QUESTIONS FOR REVIEW

1. One method of conversion to a new system is to start right off on a given day using the complete new system. Point out the weaknesses of such an approach and suggest some alternative methods.
2. There are many considerations concerning the acquisition of computer facilities, one of which is, "Which manufacturer do I buy

from?" List eight points to think about when analyzing computer manufacturers.
3. Explain what a firm can do while waiting for data processing equipment.
4. When a new system is installed at a company, feedback will be generated. Explain how the analyst can trap some of the feedback.
5. List three areas of comparison that an analyst might use when trying to determine if a new system is successful.

QUESTIONS FOR RESEARCH AND DISCUSSION

1. Think of four systems that have been developed and are running but might have failed as a direct result of poor implementation methods.
2. Select three examples of companies (or situations) where conversion would be a major factor, perhaps even taking two or three months. Also try to think of a new system that would involve little conversion.
3. What are some examples of real-life problems that might show up when a system is running that could not be determined when the system was tested?
4. Pick as an example an Airline Reservation System and show how implementation might have worked using (a) a pilot study, (b) running in parallel, and (c) a gradual phase-in.
5. When trying to gather feedback, the analyst can arrange for a group meeting with some clerks, or he can talk to them individually. Discuss the pros and cons of the group method as opposed to the individual method.

19

Tools of the Trade

Whether an analyst is involved with all of the four portions of the life cycle of a system, or whether he is assigned to help complete only one phase (e.g., Design), he more than likely is going to have to document or record most of his work. This might take many formats: a statement of requirements report, suggested design techniques, new training documents, data entry instructions, a problem definition report. The analyst, however, does not necessarily always have to record his work in a narrative format. There are other methods or techniques for documenting work, analyzing situations, or marking progress; and this chapter will offer descriptions of several of the major alternatives.

SYSTEMS FLOWCHARTING

When an overview of a series of steps is required or a pictorial representation of a procedure is needed, the analyst can use Systems Flowcharting. This approach involves choosing from a list of universally accepted symbols and linking the chosen symbols by means of a line and an arrowhead to show direction. Figure 19-1 (see also Chapter 12) shows a list of standard symbols as endorsed by ANSI (American National Standards Institute) and ISO (International Organization for Standardization).

The start of an Order-Entry procedure might be illustrated with a Systems Flowchart as in Figure 19-2.

SYSTEMS FLOWCHARTING SYMBOLS

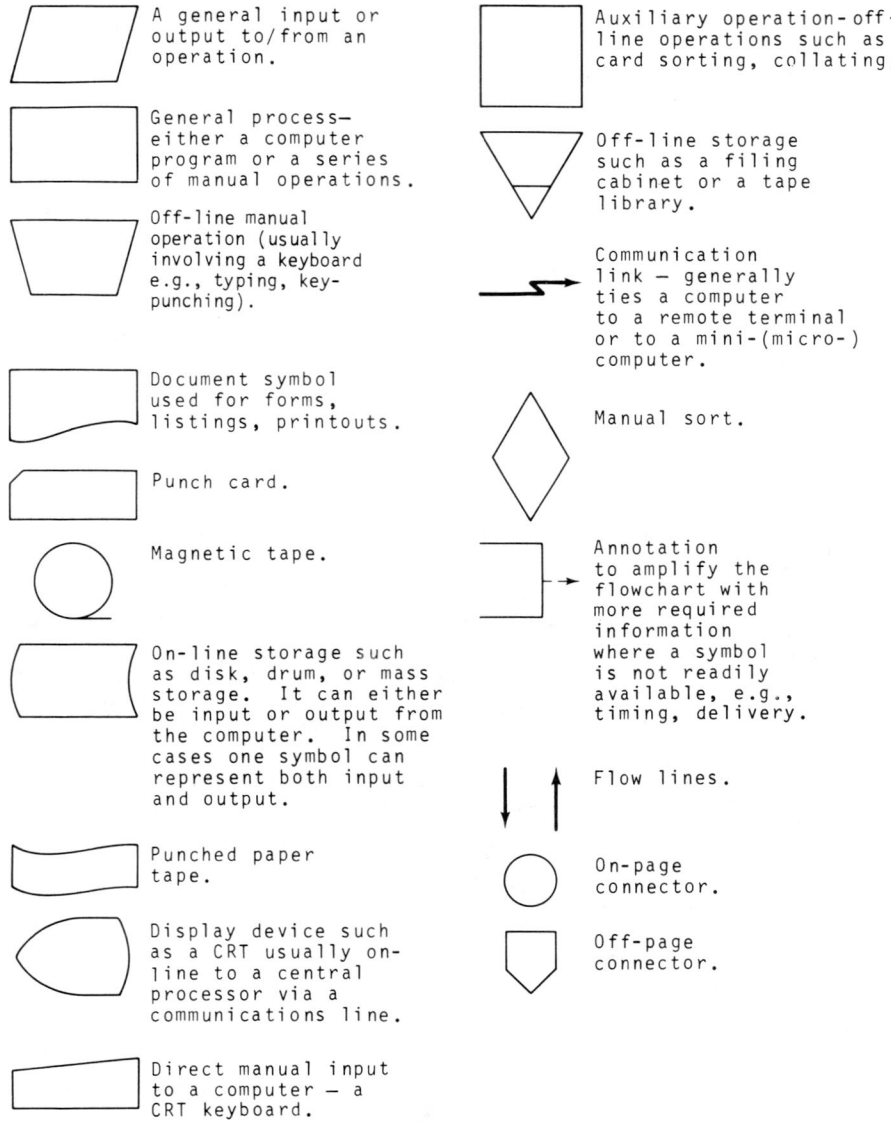

Figure 19-1. Systems Flowcharting Symbols.

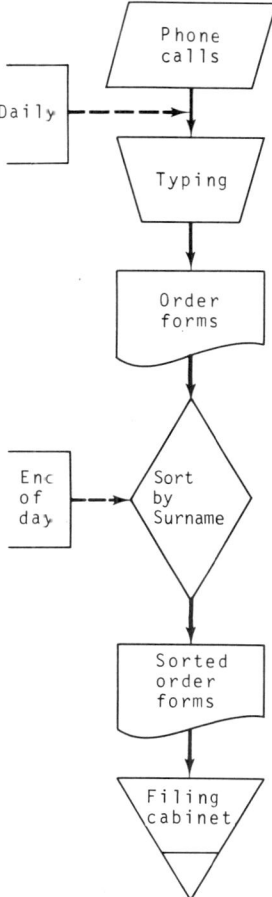

Figure 19-2. Example of a Systems Flowchart.

In this example, phone calls are handled each day by the telephone response clerks who type up an order form representing the customers' requests. At the end of the day, the orders are sorted into customer surname order and then put in a filing cabinet for future reference. Notice that each symbol is labelled with an appropriate or meaningful heading inside the symbol. The annotations were used to make the chart a little more representative, especially in places where a specific symbol is not available (e.g., the timing information "at the end of the day"). The flow in the charts is such that the symbols should work down the page or from left to right. In fact, pure Systems Flowcharting would probably leave off the arrowheads and direction would be assumed. Templates are available to the analyst (or the student) to help him construct his charts.

Flowcharts can be used to document existing procedures; to communicate with programmers to show where a specific program is required in a series of operations; and to demonstrate proposed new Design solutions. To demonstrate the last point, picture an analyst arriving at a meeting to explain the workings of a new suggested on-line banking system to a group of executives or branch managers. Now the last thing that the people at this meeting want is a fifty-page written report dumped in their laps describing the new system. They would probably be expected to read through the report (complete with buzzwords, acronyms, and the kitchen sink) and then comment with their opinions. Here then is a suitable place for a Systems Flowchart to give a representation of the new system—details to come later. The analyst might use a flowchart as drawn in Figure 19-3 to explain the basics of the new system.

This flowchart shows that data is transferred from remote terminals (tellers) and collected on a disk file known as the Accounts Master. The transactions are stored on a log tape for back-up purposes in the event of a system failure. Any inquiries coming in from the branches concerning the status of any current accounts are handled by program 1 (by searching through the Accounts Master) and returned to the user who originated the request. A listing covering the activity during a given day is produced along with an exception report that may contain information such as accounts that withdrew over $5,000.00 in a single transaction, or an account that has been used an excessive number of times.

The chart also shows that program 2 is run every week to produce the required set of financial statements. Programs 3 and 4 are used at month-end to generate first a magnetic disk file containing customer statement information, and then a second disk file with the same information but sorted in branch sequence, and last the set of statements to be delivered to each branch.

DECISION TABLES

Another standard form of communication is the Decision Table; it is generally found in the following situations:

1. Complex problem-solving areas
2. Research & Development and Operations Research Departments
3. Communications from an analyst to a programmer
4. Documentation of a program by a programmer
5. Training new employees (in place of boring procedure manuals).

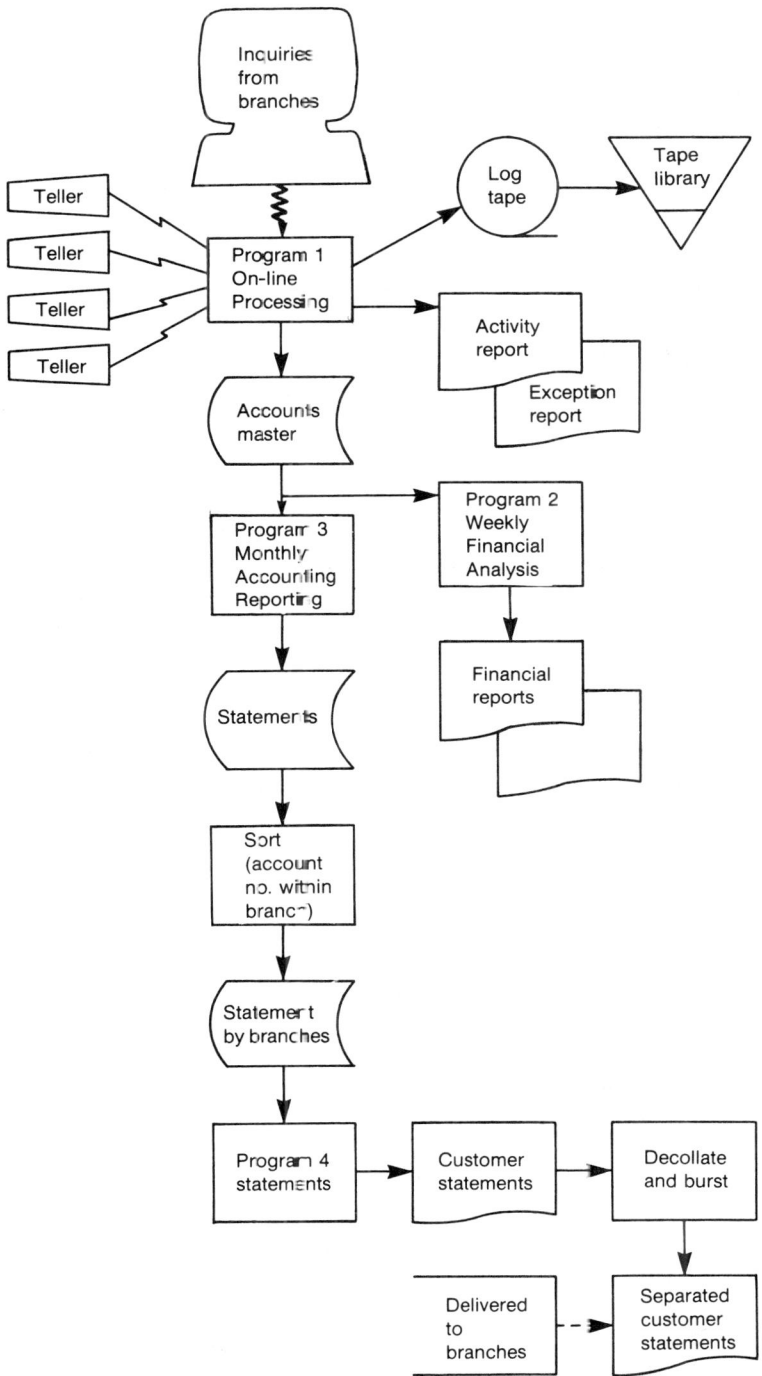

Figure 19-3. Systems Flowchart for banking change.

The format of a decision table, the mechanics of its use, and the rules covering the entries have already been discussed before in Chapter 12, under the topic of programming. It is appropriate here to show a sample decision table specified by an analyst (outside of the programming department) that can be consulted by users. Consider the following example that might be found in a typical receiving department (see Figure 19-4).

The first entry in the simplified example table is the norm situation and accounts for the majority of incoming shipments (i.e., nothing is missing, and it's all in good shape—send it to the warehouse). The next two entries are exceptions, but do occur sometimes. When a shipment is incomplete, an I-4 form is to be filled out before transferring the goods to the warehouse. If anything is damaged, the goods are to be held in an inspection area and D-21 report noted. Now, keeping in mind that the idea with a decision table is to get all possible combinations present, the analyst allows for the rare-bird case whereby the shipment was not all present, and what was received was damaged. If this decision table were taped on the receiver's desk, or on the back of a clipboard, or tagged to the wall, a new employee who has not experienced that particular situation can check the chart (quickly) and make a decision without having to track down a supervisor for help. The more complex the situation, the faster a result can be determined with a decision table than with a manual containing written explanations of job situations. Besides solving the problem at hand, the employee also gains some confidence in himself because he has acted independently of his supervisor.

STRUCTURED SYSTEMS ANALYSIS

One of the techniques or tools that an analyst can use in his work is an approach to problem solving and design known as Structured Systems Analysis. This technique represents a total approach to analysis and design that centers on developing an overall logical data flow of a new system and then refining the overall picture to various detailed levels to create a modular picture of the new system. The main chart in this "structured" approach is the Data Flow Diagram that basically employs only four symbols. These symbols are shown in Figure 19-5. These four symbols may appear together as in Figure 19-6 where a Data Flow Diagram is showing an overview of the basic flow of data in a typical college registration system.

The chart is readable and easy to understand by users because it is void of Data Processing jargon. At the next level, the box "Process Applications" would be further broken down into other Data Flow Dia-

Decision Table. Date:
Chart name:
Analyst:

Rules				
Shipment complete	Y	Y	N	N
Shipment damaged	N	Y	N	Y
Actions				
Send goods to warehouse	X		X	
Hold goods for inspection		X		X
Fill out D-21 report		X		X
Fill out I-4 incomplete form			X	X

Figure 19-4. Decision table for a receiving department.

grams, and this process would continue until the system was accounted for. This top down development that has proven successful as a technique for writing and organizing computer programs is becoming a very popular approach for systems work. Proponents of Structure Systems Analysis argue that

1. Users tend to be involved more often because the charts used (the Data Flow Diagram) are easy to read, use, and create. Also, the user appears more confident that he understands what exactly is being developed for his area.
2. The requirements of the user seem to be better described and demonstrated.
3. Errors that might occur in the new system's operation are being detected at an earlier point (i.e., during the Design stage and not the Implementation stage).
4. The analyst does not tend to get as bogged down in details as is usually the case at the beginning of both the Analysis and Design stages. He starts from an overview, and he is in control of deciding when he wants to get more detailed in his work.

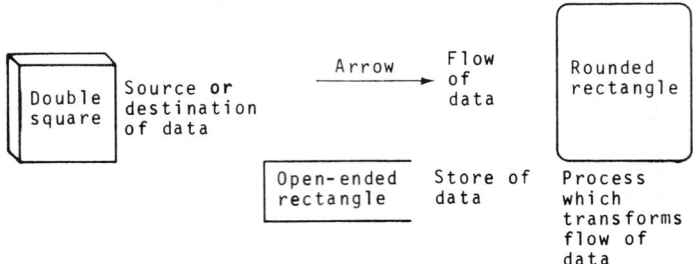

Figure 19-5. Symbols for Data Flow Diagram.

5. The charts used are superior to systems flowcharts. The reason is that the Data Flow Diagram does not commit itself to specific symbols as does systems flowcharting, (e.g., a punchcard symbol or a CRT symbol). Therefore, the charts do not condition a designer to think in terms of hardware but rather in terms of data flow.
6. Any new changes in design are easier to implement in a structured environment because of its modular nature.

Including this topic in this chapter was intended to demonstrate another type of charting technique available to an analyst. However, it should be emphasized that Structured Systems Analysis is more than just using a different chart. It is a philosophy, or way of performing the work, and therefore a reference to books on this subject, such as the Chris Gane and Trish Sarson book, *Structured Systems Analysis* (Prentice-Hall Inc., 1979), is heartily recommended to acquire a complete picture of this topic.

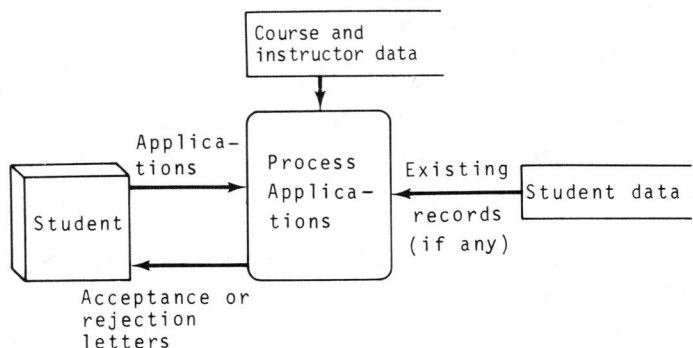

Figure 19-6. Overview of a college registration system.

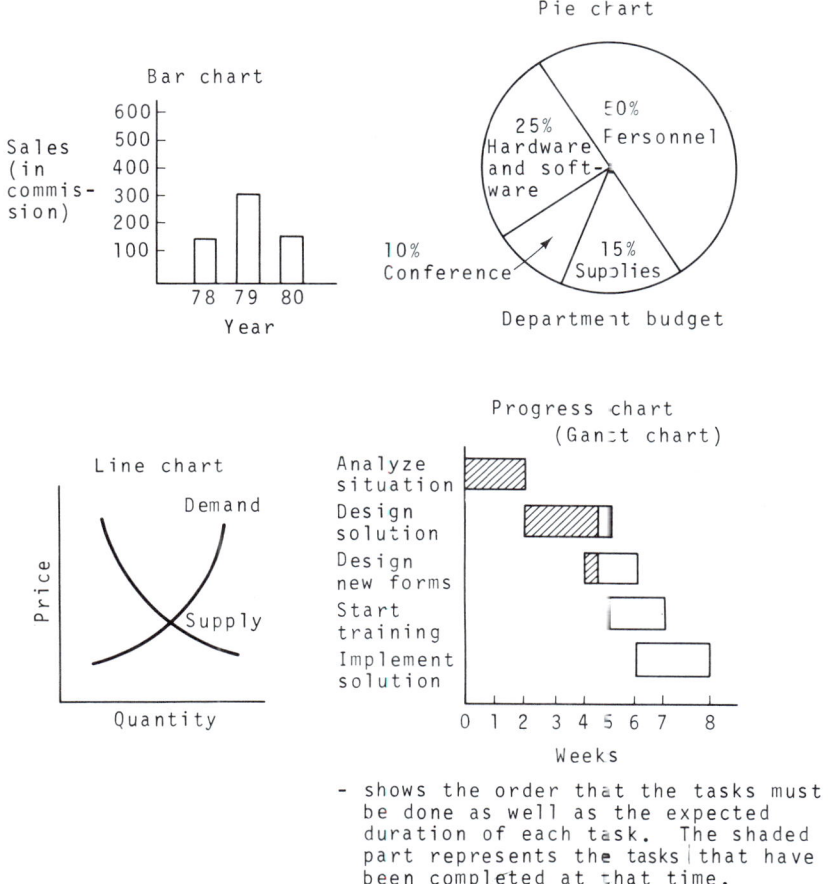

Figure 19-7. Examples of other charts.

Other Charts

Figure 19-7 shows a series of charts that can be used when a visual point (usually for emphasis) is required.

PRESENTATION ABILITIES

The analyst will be called upon many times to present new designs, new instructions, changes, etc., to various groups within the firm. Although the length, environment, and importance of different presentations will vary, the following is a list of points to remember when conducting any presentation:

1. If you have been given a time guideline, do a trial run to make certain that the presentation is neither too short nor too long. There have been occasions when a speaker has set up the format of his presentation with all the key points at the end for effect but was cut off before he got to them because he exceeded his time.
2. Explain what you are saying rather than read from a set of notes. The use of prompt cards or key words is a good idea.
3. Talk to the audience, not the projector or blackboard.
4. Explain, at the beginning, how you want to handle questions—"Please save any questions till the end" or "Feel free to interrupt when you wish."
5. Use visual aids where appropriate. A presentation with too many visual aids is just as bad as one with too few. Visual aids cover writing on the blackboard, overheads, slides, films, flip charts, handouts, music, etc. Make certain that the visuals can be seen by displaying (say) an overhead and then sitting in the furthest corner prior to the presentation, if possible, to test visibility.
6. Explain, at the beginning, the errors or situation that existed so that after you have explained your new solution, it is evident that the problems have in fact been resolved. Do not start right in with a solution without previously establishing the framework.
7. Many times you are in fact selling the new system; therefore appear enthusiastic and interested.

SUMMARY

From the past few chapters it should be very evident that an analysis has many hats and must possess a collection of different abilities in order to function successfully in his role. What does an employer look for then when hiring an analyst? What characteristics should be present in someone that might guarantee a successful performance in the role of an analyst? Well there is not any crystal ball answer, but there are a few points that a company can check out when considering someone to fill the position of Systems Analyst. These are:

1. Must have excellent communication skills (both oral and written).
2. Must be someone who can be very organized and thorough in his work habits.
3. Should possess some cost-accounting background for feasibility studies and for helping to rank projects with respect to cost-savings figures.
4. Should be patient, as the successes or rewards are very long term in nature. This would be different than say a programmer who could be "up and down" during the day depending on the nature of a program he is working on.
5. Must have an understanding of human behavior and the way that people react to change and/or new systems, a point that must be appreciated and built into implementation techniques.

TERMS TO STUDY

Bar Chart
Data Flow Diagram
Decision Tables
Line Charts
Pie Charts
Progress Charts
Structured Systems Analysis
Systems Flowchart

QUESTIONS FOR REVIEW

1. Each week, sales reports from the various sales regions are received at Head Office, grouped together by product type and then delivered to the Data Entry Department. There data from the reports are keyed-to-tape, and the resulting sales information plus last week's sales history file (on magnetic disk) are processed by computer program SA12. An updated sales history file is produced and then stored back in the disk library. Also, a listing of weekly sales by region is generated and sent to the assistant marketing manager. Draw a systems flowchart of the above procedure.

2. A clerk, working in a mailroom for a firm with branches the world over, generally handles the out-going mail and puts a 60¢ stamp on for airmail letters, 45¢ for bulk postage, and 30¢ for normal mail. Some letters are pre-paid as indicated by the envelope and of course do not require a stamp. Also, if the letter is going to a branch office, he affixes a special company seal (different from the stamp). All letters are finally placed in an out-going mailbag. Create a decision table to represent the above procedure.

3. Where are (a) systems flowcharts and (b) decision tables used in business?
4. List five desirable characteristics of a systems analyst and supply a rationale for each characteristic.
5. Explain six points to remember when getting ready for a presentation.

QUESTIONS FOR RESEARCH AND DISCUSSION

1. Draw a decision table representing whether you will do some homework on a given night. Create your own situations and actions and fill in the chart.
2. Think of a meeting or a presentation where the speaker was dynamic or energetic. What did the effect of the exhibited energy have on the outcome or success of the session?

20

Applications

The last five chapters have provided information giving a picture of the type of work done by a Systems Analyst. An Analyst works through Analysis, Design, and Implementation to produce a successful system for a firm or a department within a company. This chapter is devoted to looking at some of the systems that have been developed and in fact are available to a company for use with their computer. In other words, instead of showing possible uses or applications of the computer (that list is virtually endless), the sections to follow will first of all specify the typical requirements of some of the major areas within a company and secondly describe some of the existing systems that do meet the requirements. In all cases when a reference to "program" is made, the inference should be that the code already exists and can be purchased (or rented) from a computer manufacturer or other firm that sells software packages. The point to remember is that although firms are different in their products, people, location, goals, etc., they still all have Inventory-type problems, Payroll-type problems, and Accounting-type problems that are common to all of them. A good analyst can recognize a common-type problem and perhaps, instead of specifying new programs and procedures (that might take months or years to produce), might order a prepackaged solution in program form, that even after adjusting to that particular firm's needs, will be up and running in a fraction of the time.

There will be no attempt to cost justify any of the examples since a complete set of data would be required for an analysis of dollars and savings. Also, the scope of this chapter is to supply information on software packages and how they might be used at a company.

ACCOUNTS RECEIVABLE

Five of the major objectives of an Accounts Receivable system might be listed as follows:

1. Maintain a correct set of customer records
2. Collect and process payments
3. Bill customers at set intervals
4. Handle customer inquiries to the file
5. Produce statistics from the file concerning customers and their buying habits.

When a given firm had only a thousand or so credit card holders, these five goals could be met using only a manual system. Although a lot of paperwork, file folders, and clerks might have been required, the work would have been completed. However, as the application expands to twenty or thirty thousand customers, the usual problems related to a high volume application start to surface. As for the five objectives, the last one rarely gets done; the fourth one gets handled with a fair degree of confusion, but the response to a customer might take a half a day; and the first three are performed but more and more mathematical errors (interest calculations) occur and the dollars (payments) seem to get a little delayed thereby hurting the cash-flow picture.

If the firm already has a computer, then a new Accounts Receivable system can be designed to meet the climbing volumes. Of course if there is no Data Processing equipment existing in the firm, the company can acquire hardware and software, but this example will cover the former situation.

One of the early tasks will be to create an Accounts Receivable Master File. Now this is no easy task because it might involve pulling all the hard-copy files for the existing customers and entering the information required via a terminal, a key-to-tape unit, or a key-to-disk device. The layout for each customer record would have to be carefully designed by the analyst in conjunction with the Accounts Receivable staff and perhaps would appear as in Figure 20-1.

Account No.	Name	Address	Amount Due	Phone No.	Credit Limit	Date of Last Payment	Statement Date	Interest From Last Billing	....

Figure 20-1. Layout for a customer record.

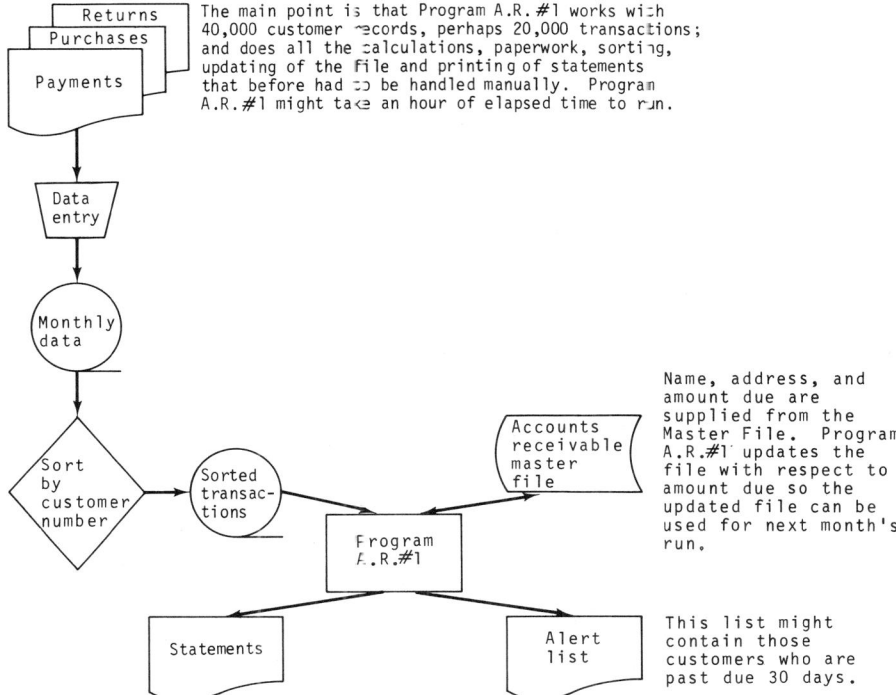

Figure 20-2. Processing transactions.

Once the Master File has been created (usually on disk), the transactions can be processed. Some clerks will probably be assigned the function of grouping or coding all of the payments, purchases (sales slips), and credit returns that have accrued since the last billing and see that they are delivered to the Data Processing department for processing. A pictorial representation of the procedure is shown in Figure 20-2.

If an inquiry comes in from one of the forty thousand customers, a clerk can use a terminal located in the department and enter the Account no., have it be processed by program A.R.#2 (Figure 20-3), access the Master File, and have a response displayed on the terminal in a matter of seconds. Also, any changes to the Customer Master File such as new address, updated credit limit, or new phone no. might be handled through a similar terminal setup so that the Master File will be up-to-date almost upon receipt of such a notification. At a minimum, the File will be ready for program A.R.#1 when it is requested to be run.

Program A.R.#3 (Figure 20-4) might be run periodically (weekly, monthly) at the department's discretion to produce a listing of those customers who have not used their cards during the past year, or to produce

432   APPLICATIONS

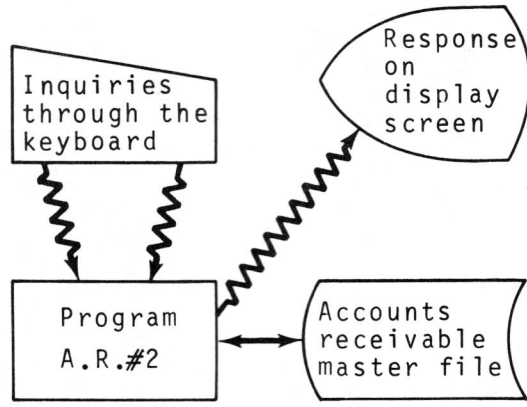

Figure 20-3. Processing a customer query through a terminal.

a percentage breakdown of those customers using their cards for purchases between $0–$10.00 or $10.01–$20.00, etc. A fourth program, A.R.#4 (Figure 20-5), could be used on a daily basis to produce a backup tape file for remote storage. In addition, every six months or so the program could perform a purge to delete the Master File of any customers that are no longer needed.

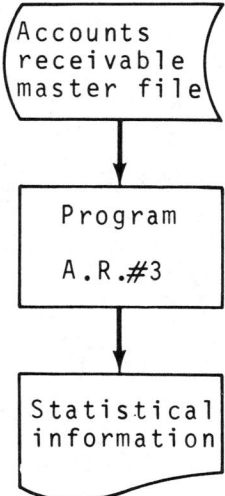

Figure 20-4. Program to provide statistical information.

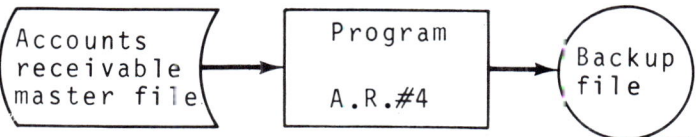

Figure 20-5. Producing a back-up file.

INVENTORY

A conversation with a manager of an Inventory Department on the subject of problems or weaknesses with his Inventory system might produce the following comments: "Our stock levels are never at the proper level; we seem to be ordering too late." "We cannot determine a picture of stock on hand quickly and accurately." "It would be great to know about those goods that have not moved much in the past six months or those that are fast moving items."

Although the Inventory components (i.e., goods, size of warehouse, staff complement) are certainly different from one firm to the next, most managers would probably echo the three comments. Numerous software houses have marketed standard Inventory programs that can be implemented on a firm's computer with the main intent of resolving these three concerns. As in most applications, some tailoring will be necessary to accommodate specific and unique problems at each firm.

KEY CONCEPT

SOFTWARE HOUSE

A phrase to describe a company that is in business with software programs as its product. Generally a firm of this nature stays out of the hardware manufacturing end of the Data Processing Industry but rather prefers to market general purpose programs that can run on most machines.

In order to implement a software package, a conversion would have to take place to create an Inventory Master File. That is, the hard-copy records of the inventory would have to be accessed in order to get the information necessary for the new computer record that will represent the status of the goods. For example, a typical Inventory master record for one product might contain the fields shown in Figure 20-6.

434 APPLICATIONS

Part No.	Description	Qty. on Hand	Date Item First Stocked	Location #1	Location #2 (Alternate)	Re-order Quantity	...

Figure 20-6. Fields in a typical Inventory master record.

Once the Master file has been created, the updating of the file can be controlled by terminals located at the entrance and exit areas of the warehouse (Figure 20-7).

After goods have been received and inspected, they are ready to go into stock (i.e., into the warehouse). However the rules of the new system would dictate that the goods would not be allowed into the warehouse until a terminal operator has updated the Master File with information about the goods. If they are re-order goods, the updating might just be as simple as changing the quantity-on-hand field or noting the date received. The location for the goods can be seen on the terminal as derived from the Master File record. If the goods are new items, the operator will have to enter more information in order to create a new record. In some systems, the computer program that the operator is interacting with can return a suggested location for the new stock based on a table of new locations developed by the Inventory manager for such cases. When goods are removed from the warehouse, either for a delivery to a customer or for delivery to the sales floor, another terminal operator must enter a transaction to update the file and keep it correct. If the firm feels that immediate updating is necessary, then the two terminals can update the Master File on a real-time basis. The first part of the software package can be represented pictorially as in Figure 20-8.

If a one-day delay is allowed or acceptable at a given firm (such that the file is always accurate at the start of a working day), then Inventory

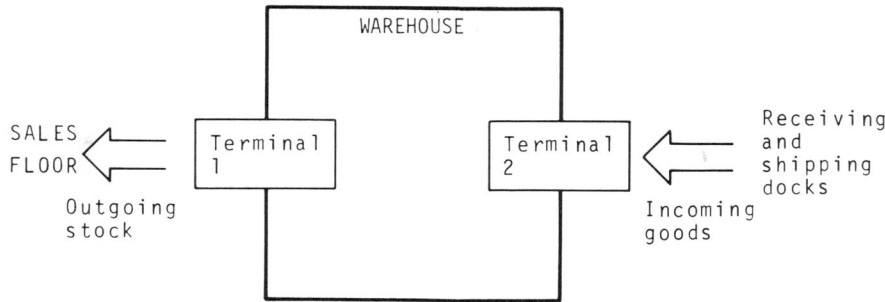

Figure 20-7. Updating the Inventory Master File with terminals at the warehouse.

INVENTORY 435

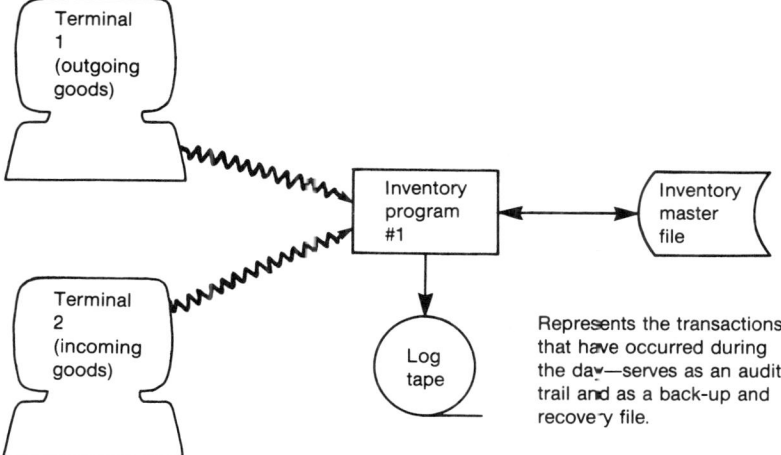

Figure 20-8. Program for immediate updating of Inventory Master File.

Program #1 can be altered to provide a different method of handling the transactions as shown in the next flowchart (Figure 20-9).

As the file is being updated, Inventory Program #1 can produce another file containing the records of all goods that have met or dropped below their re-order point quantity field. The figure in the re-order point field was established as the file was created and represents a signal that it is time to re-order that particular item because a limited number remain in stock. The quantity-on-hand field might have been reduced as a result of a transaction, and if the value in the field is equal to or below the value in the re-order field, then that product would be "written" on a Re-Order File. Figure 20-9 becomes extended to the chart in Figure 20-10.

Two other standard Inquiry-type Programs are usually available in a system of this nature. One program reads the Inventory Master File to produce statistics such as:

1. Those goods that have not moved over certain period of time
2. Those items that have had a great deal of activity over the past week (month or quarter)

If the system is working as designed, the user (probably the Inventory supervisor) will have control over Inventory Program #2 (see Figure 20-11) in that he can specify what he wants to analyze, over what time period, and when he wants the Data Processing Department to run the program.

If on-line inquiries are needed so that a picture of the Inventory can be supplied at any point in time, Inventory Program #3 can be accessed

436   APPLICATIONS

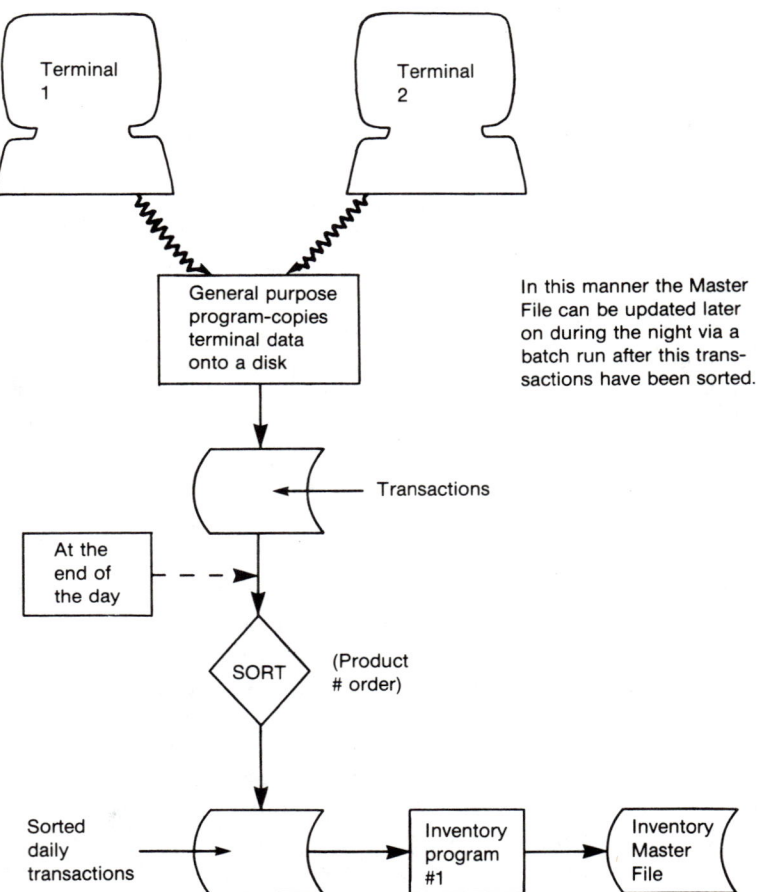

Figure 20-9. Altering the program to allow updating to be done later.

via terminals and can produce immediate responses. In this way then, a CRT could be located in the Manager's office, one on the sales floor, and perhaps one in the Purchasing Department, all producing soft-copy outputs. If a hard copy is required (e.g., for reference purposes to give to a customer), a printer-terminal could be hooked up to the system where required (see Figure 20-12).

ACCOUNTS PAYABLE

An Accounts Payable Department can be generally described as that part of the company that pays the bills received from vendors, suppliers, or manufacturers. Of course this Department only wants to pay for mer-

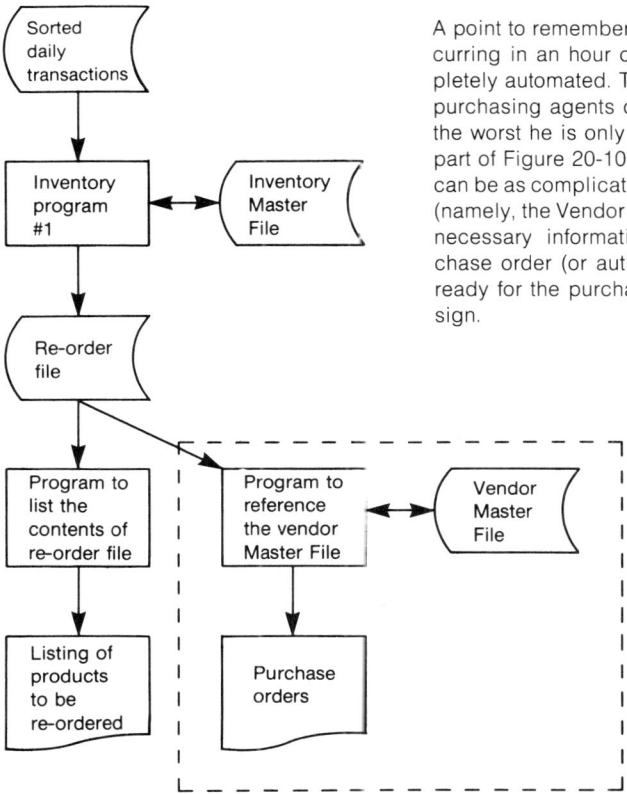

A point to remember is that this process is occurring in an hour or so at night and is completely automated. The reports should be on a purchasing agents desk in the morning, so at the worst he is only a day behind. The dotted part of Figure 20-10 shows that some systems can be as complicated to reference another file (namely, the Vendor Master File) and select the necessary information to generate the purchase order (or authorization to buy form) all ready for the purchasing agent to review and sign.

Figure 20-10. Procedure for re-orders.

chandise that has in fact been received by the firm and was not damaged in shipping. Therefore some indication from the Receiving Department about the status of the received goods is needed in the Accounts Payable area. Also, a copy of the purchase order that was originally sent out to a vendor should be available to verify that what was ordered, was actually received.

Besides the matching-up process with respect to purchase orders, vendor invoices, and receiving reports in order to verify and generate a payment, the clerks in this Department are also involved in trying to take advantage of any vendor discounts. A vendor might offer a discount of 1 percent on the total price of the shipment if the bill is paid within twenty days (sometimes this type of agreement will be written as 1N20). Therefore a 2N10 discount would suggest that if the firm issues a check for the goods within ten days of receipt of the invoice, a 2 percent factor can be discounted from the total price. If the payables checks are prepared once a month, it is therefore going to be very hard to take optimum advantage of all the vendor discounts. Generating the checks weekly

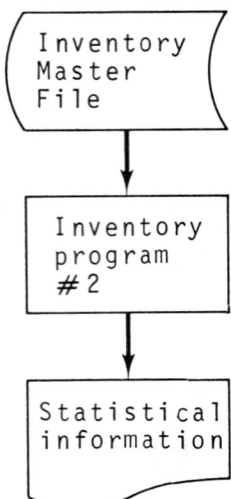

Figure 20-11. Using Inventory Program #2 to get statistical information.

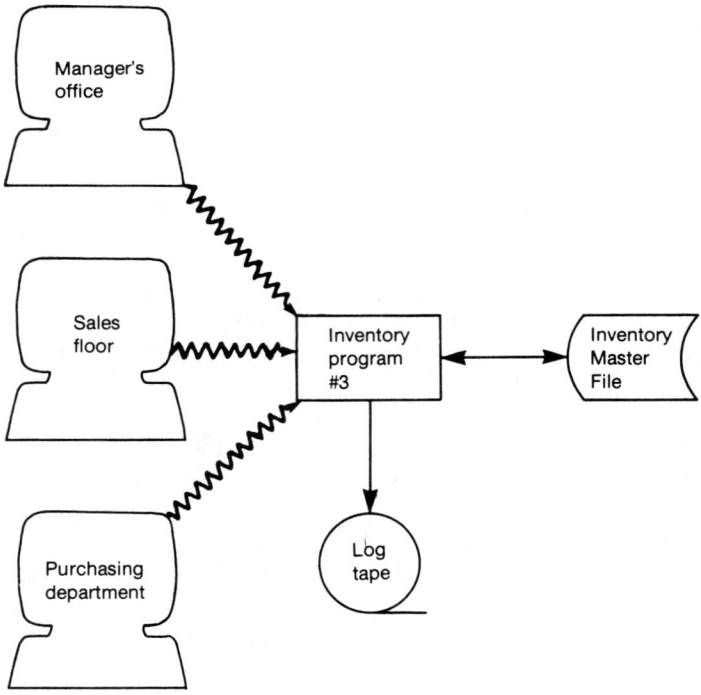

Figure 20-12. On-line inquiries via terminals.

might seem to be a reasonable solution, but that would involve an enormous manual effort to achieve that sort of deadline (given a large number of vendors and invoices). Also, the clerks are involved in checking other types of discounts concerning the quantities of the article purchased. For example:

1–5 Tractors	$20,000.00	each
6–10 Tractors	$18,000.00	each
11–20 Tractors	$15,000.00	each

However, if the data from the various forms can be entered into an Accounts Payable computer system (either on-line or batch), then possibly the software can take over and perform the matching and verifying and can determine optimum pay dates to take advantage of any discounts. The next series of charts (Figure 20-13) will show how such a system might be set up and operated.

As the purchase order is created, information from the form can be entered through a terminal into a program (A.P.#1) that is loaded into the computer and resides there all the working day. If on-line is not appropriate, the fourth copy of the purchase order can be batched and delivered to the Data Entry Department so that later that evening a file of pending purchase orders could be created.

The records on the Pending Purchases File would probably be sorted in vendor number sequence and contain such fields as vendor name, item, unit cost, date ordered, date expected, description.

Once the Pending Purchases File is created, a receiving clerk (see Figure 20-14) can enter information about the shipment he has unloaded, through a terminal located in the Receiving Department. The terminal

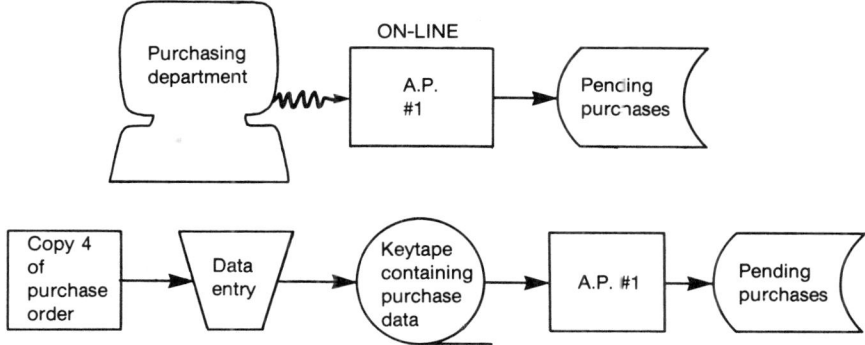

Figure 20-13. Program for Accounts Payable Department.

440 APPLICATIONS

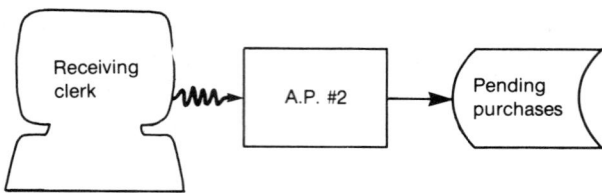

Figure 20-14. Entering information about a shipment that has been received.

would display the pending orders and then allow the clerk to enter data indicating which orders have been received, what was damaged in the order, and what came in on time.

To complement the Pending Purchases File, a Vendor Name and Address Master File would have to be created and would contain such fields as shown in Figure 20-15.

Now when vendor invoices are received in the Accounts Payable Department, the flowchart as described in Figure 20-16 is followed.

As data from the invoices enters the system each night, an edit program (A.P.#3) would reject any transactions in error (e.g., a missing vendor number, date incorrectly specified, etc.) and sort the valid cases onto a disk file in vendor number order. Then program A.P.#4 would read the transaction file, the Pending Purchases File (that has already been verified by the receiving clerk during the day), and the Vendor N & A file and generate those orders that are to be paid. If a vendor offered 3N20 on a shipment and the firm still had several days to go before twenty days had elapsed, then this account would not be generated as one to pay. Decisions can be made as to exactly when to issue a check (or notification of an order to be paid) by the individual firm. This system could be run daily or weekly and could even go so far as to have another program, A.P.#5, produce a payables check for a vendor, listing the detail information concerning the orders that the total on the check covers, on the stub of the check. If the system allows the software to generate checks, the firm is perhaps making a big assumption about its cash-on-hand account. Therefore it might prove advantageous to generate a listing of orders to be paid from program A.P.#4 and have the clerk decide which ones to issue checks on.

Vendor Number	Name & Address	Phone No.	Time Discounts	Volume Discounts	Credits	

Figure 20-15. Vendor Name and Address Master File.

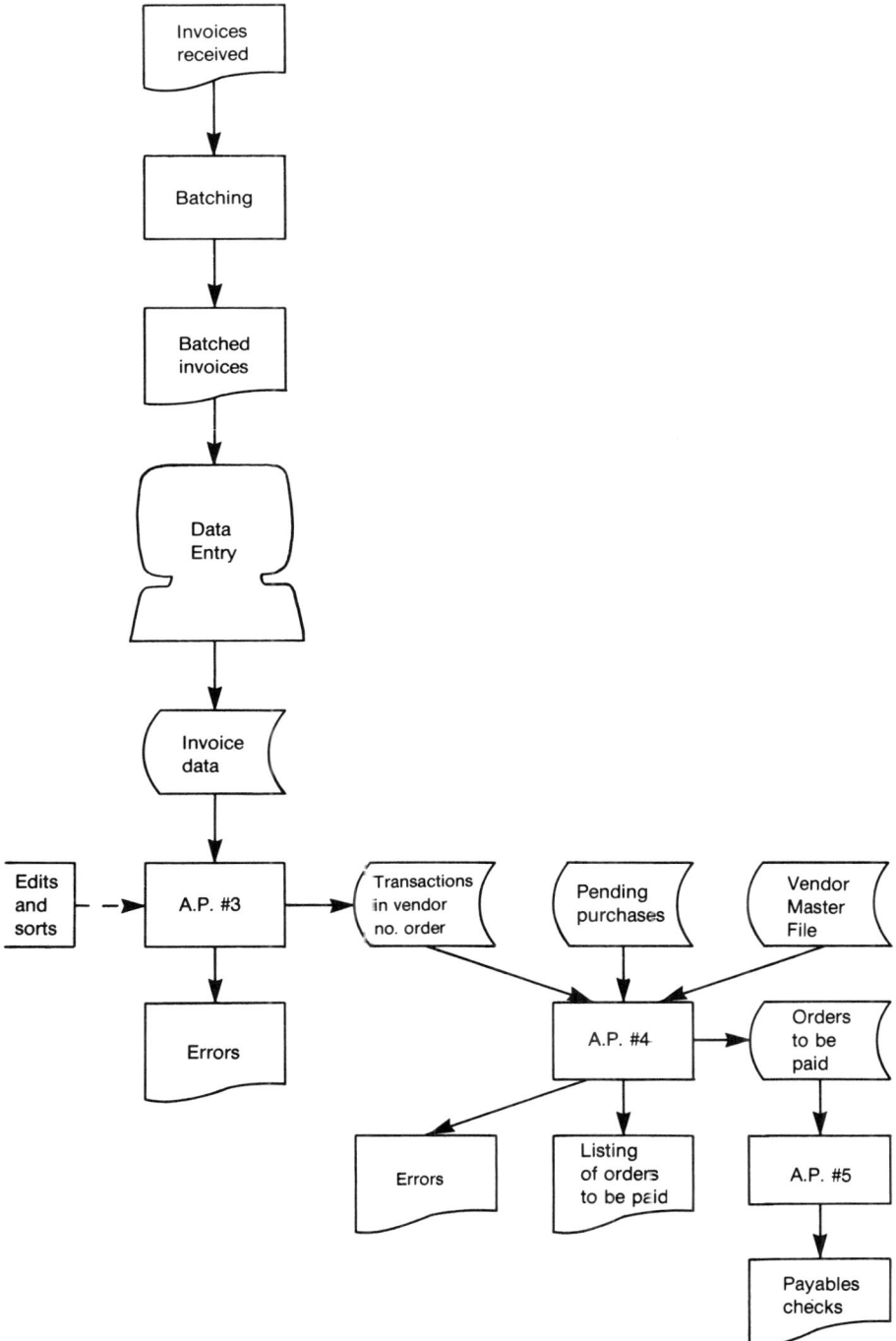

Figure 20-16. Processing vendor invoices.

02/28/80   CUSTOMER AGED TRIAL BALANCE   PAGE 001

CUST NO	NAME TEL NO	LAST PAYMENT	BALANCE	FINANCE TO-DAY	CHARGES TO-DATE	UNAPPLIED CREDITS	CURRENT	30 DAYS	60 DAYS	70 DAYS	120 & over
1235	COMSTOCK AND MATHEWS 213-278-4142	12/14/80	4115.34	12.48	13.82	.00	2275.00	994.85	742.67	89.00	.00
1236	DRUMBRIDGE AND FOSTER 301-465-2897	02/03/80	4001.27	3.90	3.90	.00	2757.65	979.72	.00	260.00	.00
1237	DURABLE OUTDOOR CORP 404-746-2864	01/18/80	2806.39	.00	.00	.00	2806.39	.00	.00	.00	.00
1238	KANTOR AND LEVINE 516-485-2332	02/24/80	2294.92	3.02	3.02	.00	1323.60	764.20	201.40	.00	.00
1240	NORTHERN STAR CORP 513-568-4268	01/11/80	979.21	1.13	3.39	50.00	468.22	382.40	.00	.00	75.20
1241	MERGIN FURNITURE CORP 312-894-6060	01/27/80	2682.00	.00	.00	.00	1421.80	1260.20	.00	.00	.00
	SUB-TOTALS		16879.13*	20.53*	26.83*	50.00*	11052.66*	4381.37*	944.07*	349.00*	75.20*

02/28/80   VENDOR AGED TRIAL BALANCE   PAGE 001

VEND NO	VENDOR NAME	CAT	BALANCE	CURR + O/DUE	NEXT PER	PERIOD 3	PERIOD 4	FUTURE	PURCH-YTD	DISC-YTD
1002	ACCURATE MANUFACTURING	1	25500.70	5500.70	5000.00	5000.00	5000.00	5000.00	25501	
1005	ALL-PURPOSE OFFICE SUPP	3	546.96		546.96				2028	15
2417	BENNETT TRANSPORT	2	2115.27		2115.27				5261	
2815	BURGESS MFG CO	1	15310.25	4125.00	4230.07	6955.18			15310	200
3115	CAPITAL EQUIPMENT CORP	1	295.00	295.00					4510	
3915	CURTIS EQUIPMENT MFG	1	1712.71			1712.71			2498	
11216	KLEIN PACKAGING CO	5	6115.10		3780.00		2335.10		18625	250
14700	NATIONAL TELEPHONE	7	1250.75		1250.75				2633	
16310	POWER TOOLS INC	4	911.55	911.55					2501	84
	SUB-TOTALS*		53758.29*	10832.25*	16923.05*	13667.89*	7335.10*	5000.00*	78867*	549*

02/28/80   GENERAL JOURNAL   PAGE 001

REF	DEBIT	CREDIT	ACCT NO	NAME	DEBIT	CREDIT	BALANCE
191156	1000.00		58121	INVENTORY LOSS	1000.00		1000.00
191156		1000.00	58111	ASSEMBLY INVENTORY		1000.00	48856.98
615	2750.00		61001	EQUIPMENT DEPREC. EXPENSE	2750.00		125685.50-
615		2750.00	61000	ACCUM DEPREC. EQUIP		2750.00	710500.70
1500	1418.16		24150	BANK LOAN INTEREST EXP.	1418.16		9416.12
1500		1418.16	10000	INTEREST PAYABLE		1418.16	39617.75
				SUB TOTALS	5168.16*	5168.16*	
				GRAND TOTALS	5168.16*	5168.16*	

02/28/80   INVENTORY STATUS REPORT   PAGE 001

PROD NO	NAME	WEIGHT	QTY ON HAND	COST PRICE	VALUE ON HAND	MTD QTY SOLD	YTD QTY SOLD	YTD SALES	YTD COST	PROFIT	PRFT %
2001	ARGO STEEL SCREWDRIVER	0.25	112.00	1.800	201.60	96.00	268	724	482	242	33.43%
2002	REGENT CROSS-CUT HAND SAW	1.25	42.00	3.900	163.80	143.00	480	2856	1872	984	34.45%
2003	HARDWIN PHILIPS SCREWDRIVER	0.20	413.00	1.650	681.45	112.00	361	884	596	288	32.58%
2004	ARGO ONE-PIECE STEEL HAMMER	1.00	269.00	2.550	685.95	138.00	297	1440	757	683	47.43%
2005	NOBILITY 3-IN WOOD PLANE	1.25	248.00	2.800	694.40	119.00	304	1414	851	563	39.82%
2006	WORK-MATE STEEL CHISEL ½"	0.20	217.00	1.650	358.05	186.00	359	1131	592	539	47.66%
	TOTALS*				2785.25*			8449*	5150*	3299*	39.05%

02/28/80   INVENTORY MOVEMENT REPORT

PROD NO	NAME	GRP	QUANTITIES/VALUES OPENING	RCVD	SOLD	ADJUST	CLOSING	COST PRICE	YTD SALES	YTD COST	PRFT %
2001	ARGO STEEL SCREWDRIVER	02	200.00	200.00	426.00	.00	12.00	1.800	724	482	33.43%
			428.40	360.00	766.80	.00	21.60				
2002	REGENT CROSS-CUT HAND SAW	02	139.00	200.00	143.00	.00	196.00	3.900	2856	1872	34.45%
			542.10	780.00	557.70	.00	764.40				
	GROUP 02 TOTAL*		970.50*				786.00*		3580*	2354*	34.25%
3001	ROGERS STEEL RULE-200 FT	03	247.00	600.00	536.00	2.00	313.00	2.600	2744	1399	49.02%
			642.20	1560.00	1393.60	5.20	813.80				
3002	VIKING PINCER PLIERS-½	03	258.00	400.00	460.00	.00	198.00	2.050	1591	959	39.72%
			528.90	820.00	943.00	.00	405.90				
	GROUP 03 TOTAL*		1171.10*				1219.70*		4335*	2358*	45.61%
	GRAND TOTAL**		2141.60**				2005.70**		7915**	4712**	40.47%

Figure 20-17. These reports are examples of the types of outputs that are produced automatically from various software packages. (*Courtesy of Philips Data Systems*)

WORD PROCESSING

Another application of the computer can be found in the area of Word Processing. Now the concept of automating a typing procedure is in itself, not new. There are applications where many copies of the same letter, or advertising brochure, or product announcement are required with just changes in name or address. A typist working with a sophisticated typewriter, such as the IBM Selectric II, can load a magnetic card into the unit and have the machine read the data from the magnetic card and automatically print the required report. Then all the operator would have to do is to enter, via the keyboard, the changed items (such as the name) in order to update the magnetic card. Next, the unit would produce the same required report, but this time using the updated name. Some obvious gains would be as follows: (a) the time for typing has been reduced, (b) mistakes are minimized as the majority of the report stays constant, and (c) a personal touch is created by producing specific letters for a customer instead of a photocopy with a name insert. In other words, just as tape and disk provided mediums for data to be stored and processed by a computer, the magnetic card provided the same features for a typewriter.

Figure 20-18. An IBM word processing system. (*Courtesy of IBM Corporation*)

Today, the computer industry has evolved so that this word processing concept is available through word processing software written for specific computer systems. In other words, a firm can acquire a small computer from such companies as AES, Micom, Wang, or IBM and get a dedicated machine to perform word processing. Alternatively (as mentioned in the chapter on microcomputers), there is an abundant supply of word processing software for microcomputers so that micro owners can also take advantage of this approach to "typing."

Now just what are the differences and gains. Well, instead of the typewriter and the magnetic card, an operator with a CRT display screen and keyboard would enter data onto disk (either a diskette or a fixed disk), and the report writing would be done by the printer attached to the system. In fact, as each operator enters data to be printed, a visual verification on the screen is presented so that errors can be detected and corrected. Once the data is "clean," or correct, the operator instructs the system to store the contents of the screen on a diskette. The software controlling this function in the computer's memory provides many automatic features to increase the efficiency of the operator. Some options include such things as right and left margin justification, automatic top and bottom margin information, automatic page numbering, page endings, decimal alignment, automatic centering, and different fonts for printing such as bold face, Essay, Arcadia, 10 or 12 pitch lines.

An operator can also ask the system to search through the data on a diskette and every time a certain word appears, replace it with another word. For example, the word "customer" is used many times in a four-page letter, and perhaps the word "consumer" is considered to be more appropriate. With one instruction and one keying, the operator can have the system generate the entire four pages with the word "consumer" appearing in the right location. Some word processing systems allow a glossary or dictionary of widely used words so that an operator need only key in the first two or three letters of the word and the system will automatically expand it on the screen to the full word. For example, the word "corporation" might be used very often and would be placed in the glossary so the system might accept "cor" from the operator and complete the word.

When there is a requirement to insert a new paragraph into the middle of a six-page report, the software will accept the change and insert it in the proper place and then realign everything following to the end of the report (i.e., indentations, new page numbers).

Many of the word processing packages have a "spelling check" feature. The operator can request the software to parse through all of the text and compare each word to a table of 25,000 correctly spelled words. Any word not found in the table is highlighted for inspection by the operator. There is usually a way for firms to enter their own unique set of acronyms into the table so that these expressions will be considered correct. Some packages also have a "grammar check" option so that the basic syntax of a sentence can be examined and obvious errors reported.

Another standard feature is the ability to process a previously established file of names and addresses. In this way, another file can be merged in when required in order to pick up a name, or an address, and have it inserted in the correct place in the document that is being prepared.

With the ever increasing speeds in the computer industry—i.e., accessing disk storage, faster printers, internal software performances—it is not difficult to see why traditional "typing pools" are being replaced in many companies by "word processing centers."

Another interesting advantage to the word processing format is that a telecommunications line can be added so that the word processing machines can transmit reports, memos, catalogues, etc., to the company's main computer system. A system set up in this manner can make use of the fast printer connected to the main computer.

Terminal-to-terminal communication is also available within the same word processing work station. Even further than this, the idea of Electronic Document Distribution (EDD) becomes a natural progression. Data can be transmitted from a computer-based location in one part of the country to the main head-office computer center where it would then be sent to a word processing center in still another part of the country for "typing" and then delivery to the appropriate party at that end. The paper handling and the Post Office have been eliminated in this procedure—a fact many people consider desirable.

Some examples of word processing systems in action are:

1. The Albuquerque National Bank generates 13,000 letters each month under the general umbrella of promotional advertising to new residents, newlyweds, new borns, and graduates.
2. A school system can produce letters to students (i.e., advice of acceptance or rejection into the program), as well as create the course outlines that are needed each year or semester. Also, the important letters to prospective employers concerning on-campus interview dates can be issued with a more professional appearance.
3. Law firms have found a use for word processing systems because many of the documents used are very repetitious in content with basically only the client's name and address and data information varying from one form to the next.
4. Most of the common forms found in a business environment can be produced—e.g., standard memos, past due account letters, pol-

Figure 20-19.

icy renewals, stockholder's correspondence, customer response forms, etc.

TERMS TO STUDY

E.D.D.
Log Tape
Re-Order Point

Software House
Vendor Discounts
Word Processing

QUESTIONS FOR REVIEW

1. List the main objectives of a typical Accounts Receivable Department.
2. What are three problems common to most (a) Inventory Departments and (b) Accounts Payable Departments?
3. Explain three gains from a mag card approach to typing problems.

4. Describe four new gains from a word processing environment using diskettes and CRTs.

QUESTIONS FOR RESEARCH AND DISCUSSION

1. Describe some problems that are not common or related to a given department, for example, what are some concerns that are unique to a certain Inventory, Accounts Receivable, or Accounts Payable department?
2. Discuss possible security problems posed by a word processing station under the general guidelines of (a) entering data via terminals and (b) working on confidential documents such as contracts, agreements, or annual reports.
3. Design some of the display-screen layouts for Inquiry-type programs such as A.R.#2 or Inv. Program #3.
4. What other statistics can be generated from a program such as A.R.#3?
5. What are some of the differences in performance between word processing on a dedicated computer—i.e., a machine just equipped for word processing—and word processing on a microcomputer?

Advanced Concepts

21

Operating Systems

In the later stages of the second generation and into the third, computers became increasingly complex. So much so that it became virtually impossible to write programs and run them without some software support. This software came in the form of programs called an operating system control program, or *monitor*. Today the operating system is a major component of all computer systems except for the very smallest. Regardless of whether you have an IBM mainframe or Personal Computer or Hewlett-Packard, DEC or NCR, an operating system will be necessary for its successful operation. This chapter discusses operating systems from the perspective of the IBM mainframes, but the concepts apply to most systems.

FUNCTIONS OF AN OPERATING SYSTEM

Increase Throughput

One of the management's primary concerns with a computer system is to utilize the hardware as efficiently as possible. In order to maximize the return on their investment, there is a need to optimize the throughput on the CPU in relation to the I/O devices. An operating system acts to improve the effectiveness of the hardware. It relieves much of the op-

Figure 21-1. An IBM 3032 uses the OS/MVS operating system. (*Courtesy of IBM Corporation*)

erational decision making from the human operator and performs these decisions at microsecond speed. This relieves the operator of routine matters such as when to read input, compile a program, load a module, and execute it.

KEY CONCEPT

THROUGHPUT

This term is used to express a measurement of the amount of work moving through the computer in a given time period. Another way of expressing it is the time interval between the input of data to the computer and the availability of results.

Reduce Job Set-up Time

To run a given program, the operator must load some cards into a reader, place the proper paper in the printer, mount tape and disk files, and type in any needed control information such as run date. Finally the program is ready to run, and the operator enters the ready command. The problem is that all this set-up takes time, time during which the computer is sitting idle.

FUNCTIONS OF AN OPERATING SYSTEM

> **Functions of an Operating System**
>
> Increase throughout
> Reduce job set-up time
> Job scheduling
> Interrupt handling
> Spooling
> Checkpoint/restart

Figure 21-2. Overview of mission of an operating system.

This may be reduced by placing programs using similar devices together. The operating system will control the initiating of each program and provides any needed control information. The effect of this action is shown in Figure 21-3. Notice that the number of jobs set-ups is reduced as well as the time taken for set-up. The overall effect is to use less computer time.

An important factor in reducing job set-up time is the use of stacked job processing. This technique allows one job or job step to progress to the next without operator intervention. A job stream or batch may appear as shown in Figure 21-4 where two jobs, each consisting of several job steps, are ready for processing. Some of these job steps may be source programs and require compilation and linking. Others may be object modules or utility programs. In each case, the step is processed without operator intervention except when a peripheral device needs attention.

Job Scheduling

Scheduling of computer runs may be done through a system of job classifications. This may categorize jobs on the basis of test runs, compila-

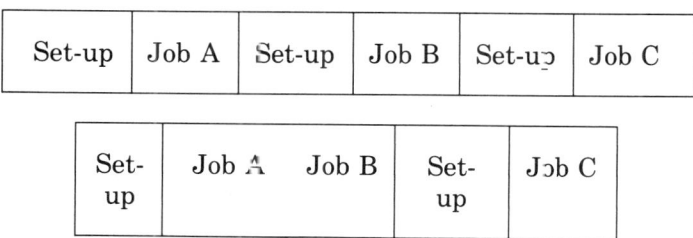

Figure 21-3. Effect of reducing job setup time.

454 OPERATING SYSTEMS

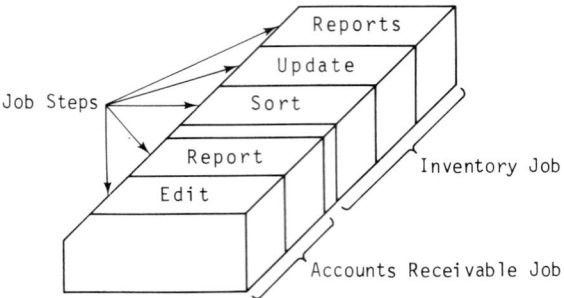

Figure 21-4. Stacked jobs.

tions, and production runs of application programs. Other types of categories may include jobs using the card reader and printer, jobs needing magnetic tape, others using disk, and on-line programs. These classifications are coded on a job identification card, which is supplied with the job. Jobs may then be scheduled on the basis of their classification to minimize set-up time and run time.

Jobs may also be scheduled on the basis of priority. This allows certain jobs to take precedence over others. For instance, jobs that are reruns may be needed urgently. Certain reports may be required by a specific time while others can wait. Higher priority jobs will be done first even at the expense of job set-up time.

We will discuss multiprogramming later in the chapter, but job scheduling also has a role to play here. In a multiprogramming environment, the CPU can process several programs simultaneously. Figure 21-5

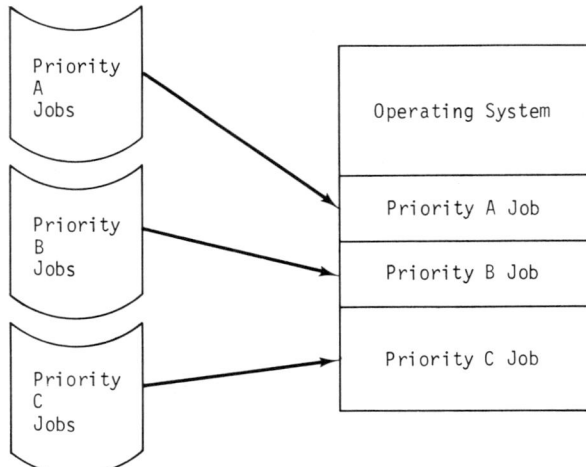

Figure 21-5. Job scheduling in a multiprogramming environment.

shows programs of three different priorities waiting to be run. As a space (partition) becomes available in the CPU, a job of that priority is brought into main storage and processing begins. Priority A jobs will be given more computer time than priority B jobs.

Another factor the scheduler considers is the size of the program contending for space in the CPU. If 60K of storage is available for a B priority job and the next B job requires 80K, then the second job must wait. In the meantime, a smaller B priority job will be scheduled to run. Thus no computer time is lost.

Interrupt Handling

Earlier in the book we discussed the concept of process and I/O overlap. This technique was used to allow processing and input or output to be done concurrently. The result was increased utilization of available processing time. When overlapping is used in a computer, the operating system must know when an input unit has finished sending its data to the CPU or when an output device has received the complete record. This information is supplied to the operating system in the form of a signal called an interrupt.

During the execution of an application program, as in Figure 21-6, an I/O device may complete an input operation. At this time the interrupt occurs and the operating system temporarily halts the execution of the

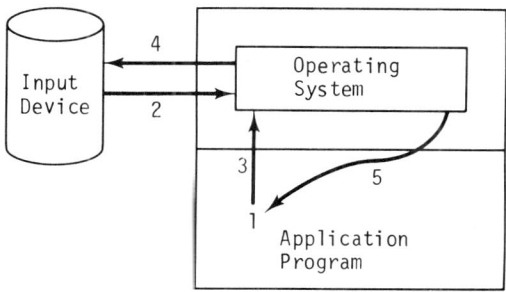

1. Application program is executing
2. Interrupt occurs from I/O device
3. Control is passed to the operating system
4. Operating system initiates action
5. Control is returned to the Application program

Figure 21-6. Interrupt handling.

interrupts. These are shown in Figure 21-7 and fall into the two general areas of interrupts (1) from an application program and (2) those from outside the CPU.

An external interrupt can come from the operator's console when the operator requests attention in order to make an entry to the CPU. It can also come from the timing device and in the case of a multiprocessing system, from another CPU.

The supervisor call (SVC) is an interrupt from an active program. This occurs when the program has a need for an operation such as Open or Close in COBOL to be handled by the operating system. The SVC also occurs when a Read or Write command is encountered in the application program.

Program interrupts occur as the result of a programming error. These result from problems familiar to most programmers. Things like zero divide, arithmetic overflow, invalid data, and addressing errors all cause a program interrupt.

Machine checks are caused by various types of hardware failure. This interrupt takes place when an I/O device malfunctions due to a component breakdown, which renders the device ineffective.

The input/output interrupt is a signal from the channel to the CPU. This indicates an I/O operation has been completed, and the channel is now free for other activity.

Spooling

In the quest for improved efficiency, a technique called spooling has emerged to reduce the impact of slow devices like the MICR and the printer on computer time. This name comes from SPOOL which is an acronym for Simultaneous Peripheral Operations On-Line (Figure 21-8).

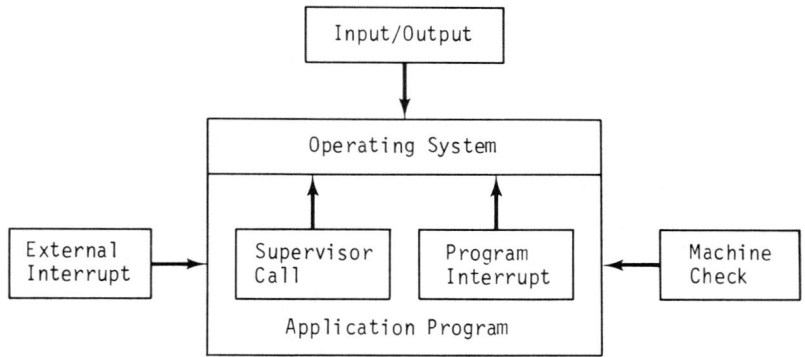

Figure 21-7. Types of interrupts.

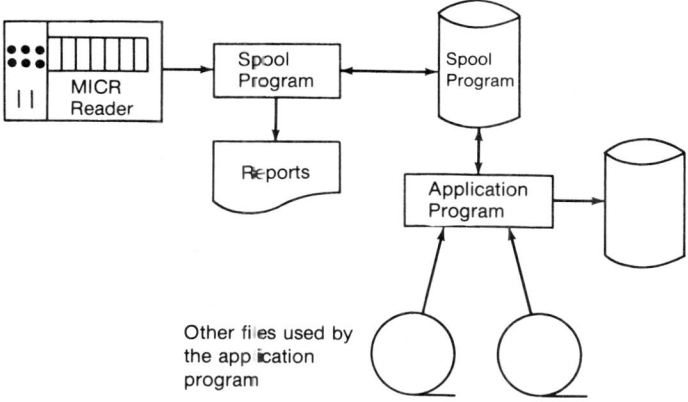

Figure 21-8. Simultaneous peripheral operations on-line, SPOOL.

The method involves reading data prior to the job in which they are used. These data are placed on a high-speed disk or tape. When the scheduled job is run, the data are now read from disk, and the job executes faster since no MICR reader is involved. In the same way, output destined for the printer is written on disk by the creating program. Later this disk is printed—often on a smaller computer.

From the programmer's viewpoint, nothing has changed. The program is still written for the printer. The operating system takes over the added responsibility of using a spool file in place of the slower device.

Checkpoint/Restart

Another problem facing the user of a computer is that of the unsuccessful completion of lengthy runs. A program that requires several hours to run may occasionally terminate due to a program error, machine failure, or power failure. In this case, a complete rerun would be necessary even if only 15 minutes remained on a three-hour job. This obviously wastes a great deal of computer time.

Operating systems solve this problem by providing a routine called checkpoint/restart. With this routine, the contents of the program are dumped on disk every 15 minutes. This interval may be adjusted according to the needs of a specific system. At this checkpoint, a test is made to ensure the correctness of the run at this time. If there are no problems, the run continues. However, if an error occurs at any time, the program and files may be restored to the position of the last checkpoint. This will be less than 15 minutes ago. The program is then restarted at this point, and no more than 15 minutes of computer time is lost.

Data Management

Prior to the development of operating systems, the programmer was responsible for all file processing commands. This included the activities program. The operating system will then take any necessary action for that device and initiate a further input operation if it is required. Control is then passed back to the application program at the point where the interrupt occurred. In the IBM System, there are five separate types of associated with Open and Close as well as the Read and Write. These are complex operations and consume a great deal of the programmer's time. Operating systems provide modules that take care of these activities and release the programmer for more productive work.

Under an operating system, an Open is processed prior to file use. The Open activity sends a message to the operator to mount the file and checks that the proper file has been supplied. On input files, the header label is checked for identification and sequence. For output files, a header label is created as a result of the Open. The Close, which is given after a file has been used, takes care of end-of-file activities. On input files, this means a check of the block count and also a determination of whether there is another volume in this file. Output files receive an end-of-file marker at this time and a trailer label is written with a block count and volume information.

Input/Output Control Systems (IOCS)

The Input/Output Control System is a component of the data management package that relieves the programmer of complex I/O commands. This includes coding for channel scheduling, error detection and retry, blocking and unblocking of records, and data buffering. In short, it promotes the efficient use of I/O without placing a heavy burden on the application programmer. Two sections of IOCS are Physical IOCS and Logical IOCS shown in Figure 21-9.

Physical Input/Output Control System (PIOCS). The main purpose of PIOCS is to initiate input/output operations on a device through a channel. A channel controls the activity between the CPU and the devices attached to the channel. In effect, the channel is like a small computer that has its own set of instructions. This is called a channel program. This program consists of channel command words (CCW). The CCW is the instruction in the channel program. To initiate the channel program, a CCB macro is coded. This command control block (CCB) contains information such as the symbolic name of the I/O device to be read, the address of the first CCW in the channel program, and a set of flags or switches to indicate the status of the I/O operation.

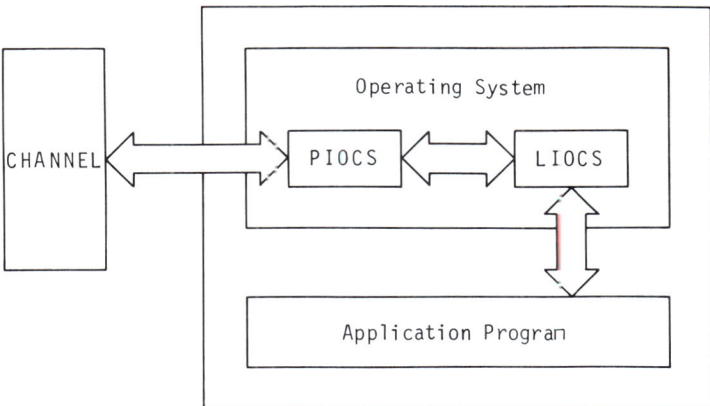

Figure 21-9. Input/output control systems.

KEY CONCEPT

MACRO

A macro is a statement that may be coded in a program to represent a series of operations. The programmer codes a simple keyword such as OPEN or GET. The compiler or assembler then generates a sequence of machine language statements in the place of this keyword.

Logical Input/Output Control System (LIOCS). Programmers generally don't write the commands for PIOCS. Rather LIOCS does this for them. As shown in Figure 21-9, LIOCS goes between the application program and PIOCS. This further simplifies the programmer's I/O responsibilities. LIOCS defines the logical characteristics of the file. This includes logical record size, block size, whether records are fixed or variable, and it also blocks and unblocks the records. As a result, the program sees only individual logical records.

Figure 21-10 shows blocked records being provided to an application program. To improve I/O efficiency, LIOCS uses two buffers. Initially a command is sent to PIOCS from LIOCS requesting a record from the device. The first physical record is brought into storage and placed in buffer 1. Now two things happen simultaneously. PIOCS begins to bring the next physical record into buffer 2. While this is happening, LIOCS takes the first logical record from buffer 1 and transfers it to the application program. This all happens as a result of a READ or GET statement written by the programmer. When the logical record has been transferred, control is returned to the program. The program then processes this single

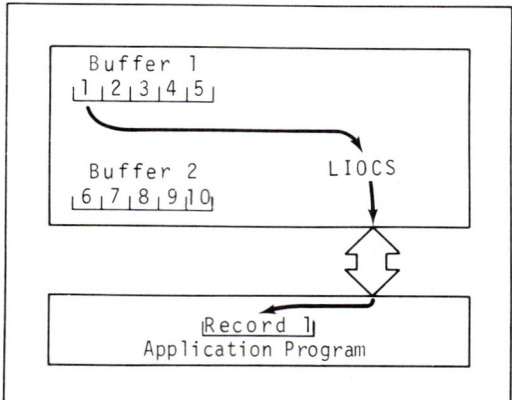

Figure 21-10. LIOCS unblocking a record.

In addition to blocking and unblocking, LIOCS provides addressing information for direct files and index data for indexed files. In either case, there may be a need in an application program to access a specific record directly. The programmer will supply the key that uniquely identifies the record required. The key is usually provided with the Read statement. LIOCS takes the key and creates the file address for finding the record. The record is then transferred to the application program. If a record was not found, the LIOCS module signals the program to take appropriate action.

OPERATING SYSTEM COMPONENTS

An operating system consists of a number of program modules located on a disk called the system resident device. The specific modules on this pack are determined at the time a computer system is installed. At this time, the programmers and the computer sales representative determine the needs of the installation. This includes consideration for the types of compilers needed, whether multiprogramming will be used, and if the system is to be batch or interactive. Based on these and other factors, an operating system is generated to satisfy the needs of this particular company. There are, however, a number of general components used by all installations (Figure 21-11).

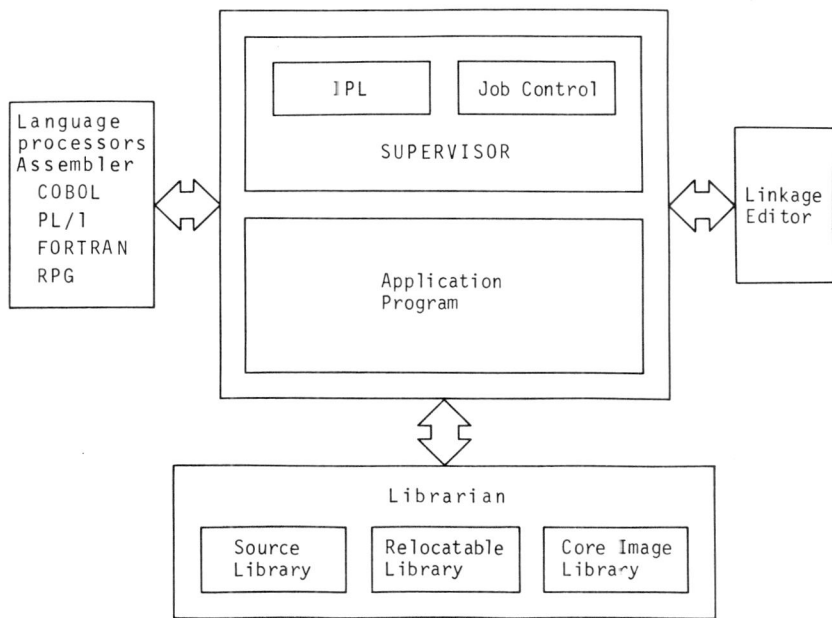

Figure 21-11. Operating system components.

Initial Program Load (IPL)

When the power to a computer system is first turned on, the operating system is resident on disk. To bring the supervisor into main storage, the Initial Program Load (IPL) module is used. The procedure followed by the operator is this: The resident disk on the system contains the IPL module. By entering a command on the operator's console, a program in read-only memory is activated. This process causes the IPL module to load the supervisor into a predefined location in main storage. At this point control is passed to the supervisor.

Supervisor

The supervisor is a program responsible for controlling all the activities within the CPU. Control of the system always begins with the supervisor and is passed to other modules to handle various needs and is then returned to the supervisor for additional direction. The supervisor calls compilers into storage to compile source programs into object modules, the linkage editor to relocate object modules into load modules, and service programs to provide for sorting activities. These actions are taken as a result of information supplied by the job control module.

Interrupt handling is also a function of the supervisor. When an interrupt occurs, control always passes to the supervisor. The correct module needed to handle the specific type of interrupt is initiated. When the interrupt has been processed, the supervisor passes control back to the point at which the interrupt occurred.

In a multiprogramming system, the supervisor selects the partition to be given control on the basis of priority. This ensures that high priority programs are given the maximum CPU time for efficient performance. The supervisor also allocates programs to the appropriate partition for execution.

The supervisor is a resident program—which means it resides in main storage at all times while the computer is running. It also has a storage area called a transient area. This is a part of main storage. The supervisor will call transient routines from disk as needed. These routines are also part of the operating system but are not required in storage at all times. As a transient is brought into storage, it replaces the transient routine that was there previously. This is called an overlay. The purpose of this procedure is to minimize the amount of storage needed for the operating system. This releases more storage to be used by application programs and contributes to efficient utilization of main storage.

Figure 21-12 shows the sequence of events followed when a source program written in COBOL is to be compiled and executed. First the supervisor passes control to the job control module. Job control reads the JCL (job control language) statements, which identify the compiler to be used. At this time, the COBOL compiler is brought into storage from disk. The COBOL compiler reads the source program, compiles it, and creates a relocatable object module on the relocatable library.

Next, the control passes to the supervisor which through job control brings into storage the linkage editor. The linkage editor reads the object module and adjusts its addresses to follow the supervisor in storage. This procedure determines the final address where the program will be located in main storage. The linkage editor creates a load module of the program, which is placed on the core image library.

Finally the supervisor brings the load module into storage and passes control to it. It is at this time that the application program, now in machine language form, is executed.

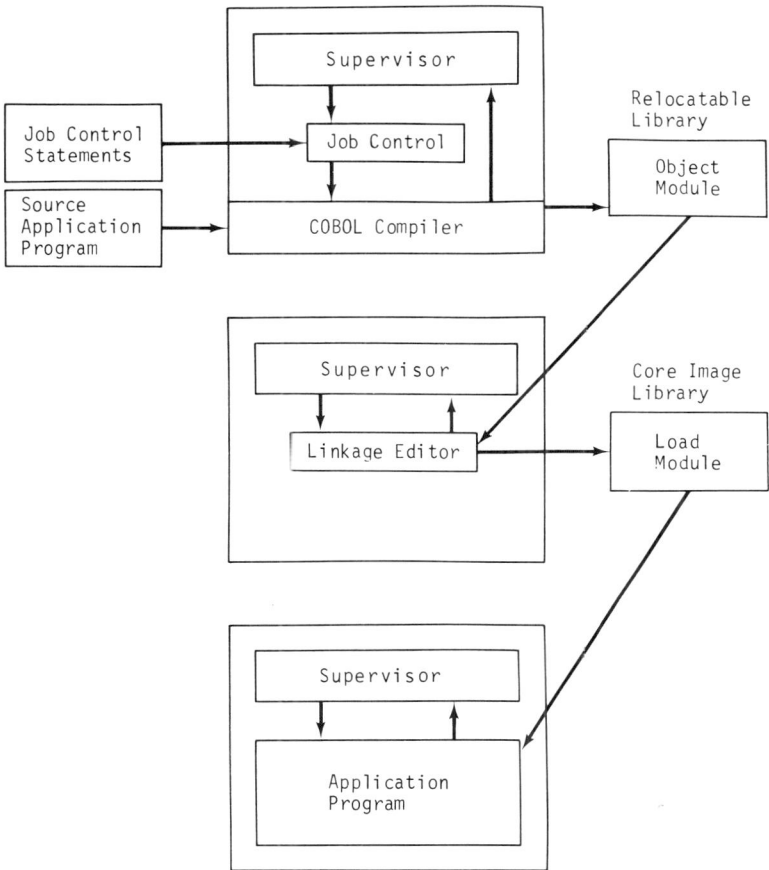

Figure 21-12. Supervisor functions when compiling and executing an application program.

Job Control

Programmers need a means of communication with the operating system. This is done with a series of control statements called a job control language (JCL). These statements define the beginning and end of a job as well as each of the job steps such as compiling, linking, and executing. Job control is a component of the operating system that reads and interprets the JCL statements. Each computer manufacturer has its own JCL; these languages vary from being quite simple to attaining a complexity on the level of a programming language.

Some of these JCL records shown in Figure 21-13 demonstrate a sequence of events typically controlled by job control. The JOB statement identifies the beginning of the job and gives it the name FINA for a financial application. EXEC PL/I causes the PL/I compiler to be called, which then reads and compiles the source program.

EXEC LNKEDT causes the linkage editor to be brought in for execution. After each step, control passes to the supervisor, which then calls on the job control module to access the next JCL statement. EXEC FINA executes the application program as discussed earlier. The DD statements provide a data definition for the Program FINA. These statements provide a definition of the physical device used for a specific file or data set. Finally the END statement identifies the end of the job, and control again returns to the supervisor. By now it should be clear that running programs is a very dynamic process. Yet the programmer is generally not responsible for all these activities.

Language Processors

Most programmers write in high-level languages such as COBOL, PL/I, FORTRAN, RPG, or APL. These are discussed in more detail in another chapter, but none of these languages is in a form the CPU understands. For this purpose, compilers or interpreters are used to translate the program into a machine language equivalent. A compiler generates machine language statements for each high-level statement. Each high-level statement may result in several machine language statements.

In the case of an Assembly language, each symbolic statement results in one machine statement. This is done by an Assembler, which is the equivalent of a compiler for a low-level symbolic language.

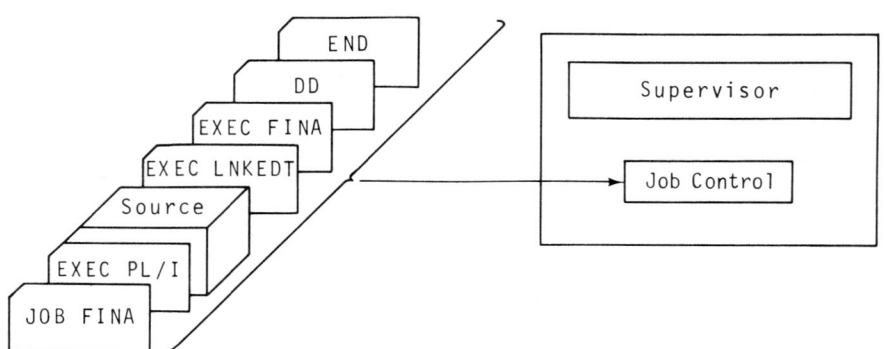

Figure 21-13. Job control language statements.

The appropriate language processor is called from disk, where it resides, by means of a JCL statement. This statement identifies the particular compiler required. The compiler is placed in main storage where it reads the source program and produces machine language code. This code is allocated temporary addresses and placed on the relocatable library. Figure 21-14 shows this process.

Also during the compile, macros or source program modules may be brought from the source statement library. For instance, a programmer may need a large structure to describe an input record for use in a COBOL program. Instead of writing the code for this structure a COPY statement may be used. This causes the structure that has been stored on the source library to be included in the program. This reduces the programmer's workload.

Linkage Editor

The linkage editor accesses object modules from the relocatable library. These modules have temporary addresses that are not suitable for purposes of execution in the CPU. The linkage editor adjusts these addresses to absolute form beginning with the first available address above the resident supervisor. In a multiprogramming system, the address is adjusted to the beginning address of the partition in which the program is to be run.

At this time, space is also added to the object module for I/O buffers. Storage is reserved for file label processing. The editor also accesses data management modules from the relocatable library and adds them to the object module.

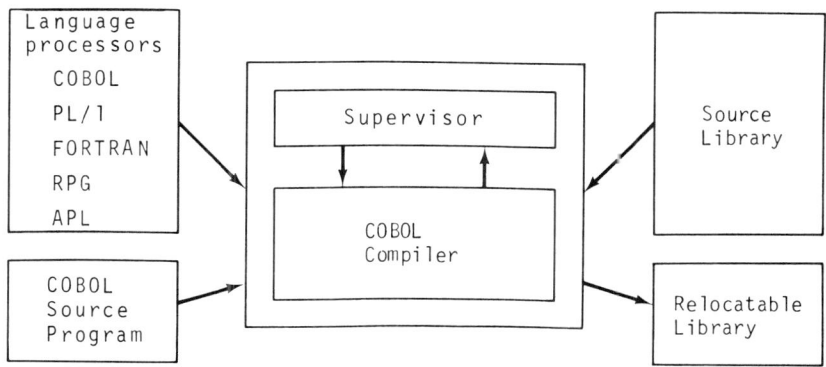

Figure 21-14. Compiling a source program.

Figure 21-15. A multiprogramming system permits several users to use the computer simultaneously. (*Courtesy of Sperry-Univac Corp.*)

The result of all this processing is a load module. This load module is now in a form that can be executed by the CPU. It is then placed on the core image library where it can be accessed for execution.

Librarian

As seen back in Figure 21-11, there are three basic types of libraries in the operating system. These are the source, relocatable, and core image libraries. The librarian is a routine that catalogues program modules into the library, provides for modification to existing modules, and deletes modules when required.

The use of libraries can reduce run time for jobs by providing object modules instead of source, thus eliminating compiling. It can supply modules, which have been pre-coded, for programmers, thus reducing programming time.

The source library in IBM's Disk Operating System (DOS) stores source programs, source modules, and macros. These are all in the source language used by the application such as COBOL or Assembler. These modules may be accessed by a JCL statement or a command in another source program.

Object modules are located in the relocatable library. These are modules created as a result of compiling, data management modules used by

OPERATING SYSTEM COMPONENTS   467

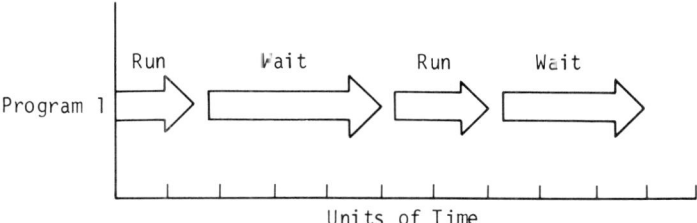

Figure 21-16. CPU waiting time for one program.

the operating system, and checkpoint/restart logic. These modules do not need compiling but are processed by the linkage editor to produce a load module.

A core image library holds the load modules. These modules are ready to be loaded into main storage for execution. In addition to application programs, the core image library will contain compilers and utility programs such as a sort/merge.

Multiprogramming

We discovered earlier that CPU speeds are much greater than the speed of I/O devices. This leads to an interesting problem. Figure 21-16 shows what happens to processing time during the execution of a program on a high-speed computer. In most business applications, processing time is a small percentage of the total computer time. Most of this time is spent waiting for I/O operations. This leaves the CPU idle for a major portion of the processing time available. As a result, the computer user is paying for computer power that is never used.

To resolve this problem, multiprogramming uses this wait state to run another program. Figure 21-17 shows the effect of running two programs simultaneously on the same computer. During the time when the

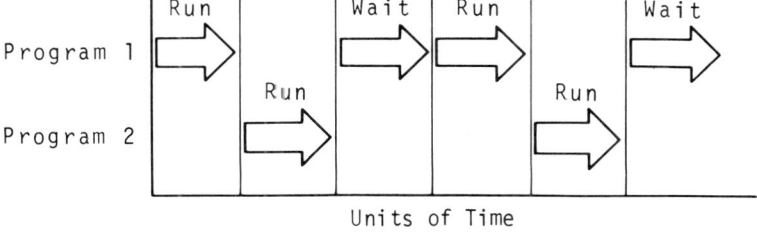

Figure 21-17. Multiprogramming with two programs.

CPU would normally be waiting for work, control is passed to a second program. This program is in main storage simultaneously with program one. Now program two uses some CPU time while I/O operations go on for the first program. When program two is finished processing, there is still some wait time, but it is less than in the first case. This wait time could be used to run a third program. Each program is run concurrently. This means that only one program executes at one time, but each is given a portion of CPU time. This is called concurrent processing.

The number of programs that can be processed concurrently in a multiprogramming system are determined by the capacity and speed of the CPU as well as the operating system in use. Main storage is organized into a number of partitions as shown in Figure 21-18. This system shows three partitions called background, foreground-one, and foreground-two. The foreground partitions are high priority and the background, low priority. Programs that are assigned to a foreground partition will be allocated more CPU time for faster processing.

Depending upon the type of computer and operating system in use, partitions vary from a fixed number with a fixed size for each partition to systems with a variable number of partitions each varying in size according to the needs of the system.

Storage protection is also an important aspect of multiprogramming. What happens if a program error in one partition causes a modification to a program in another partition? This would certainly degrade the integrity of the entire system. As a result, each program is protected from another by a storage protection feature of the supervisor. When one program attempts to address the storage area reserved for another, a system error occurs and the action is inhibited to prevent damage to the other program.

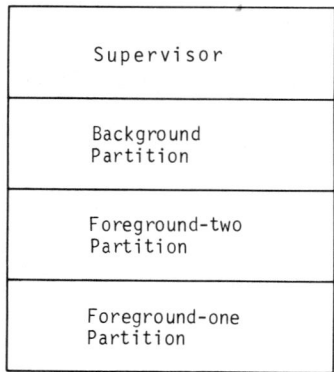

Figure 21-18. Multiprogramming partitions.

When several programs are run concurrently, there can be a conflict of needs for I/O. This can occur when JCL comes from the same device for every program, when each program needs data from the device, or if they all use the printer for some of their output. While it is possible to have a printer for each partition, it is not economically practical. Instead the JCL or data for each job is read and placed in a queue for each job on a direct access device (Figure 21-19). Each partition has its own queue so that when a program in that partition is executing, the data or JCL is read from the queue. To the program, it appears that data is coming from the reader when in fact it is coming from disk. The same approach is used for output. Each program writes its output on an output queue. Each queue is then separately written on the printer.

Multiprocessing

While multiprogramming runs several programs concurrently, a multiprocessing system is capable of processing several programs simultaneously. This type of system uses several processors (Figure 21-20) instead of the single processor used in a multiprogramming system. In some cases, these are two central processors attached together such as the twin Univac 1108 system. In other cases, one computer has several processors such as the Control Data Corporation's Series 70 computers.

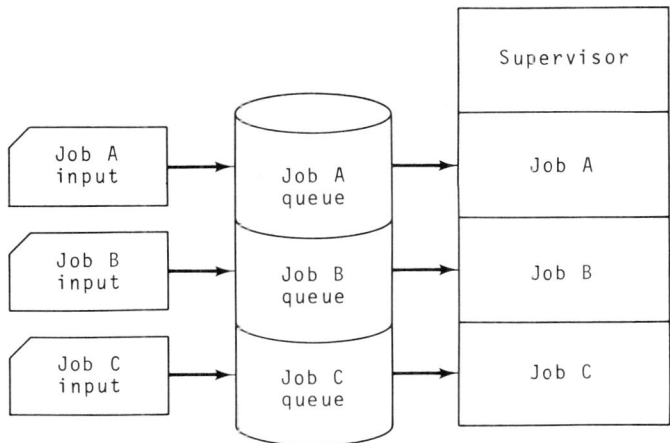

Figure 21-19. Multiprogramming job queues.

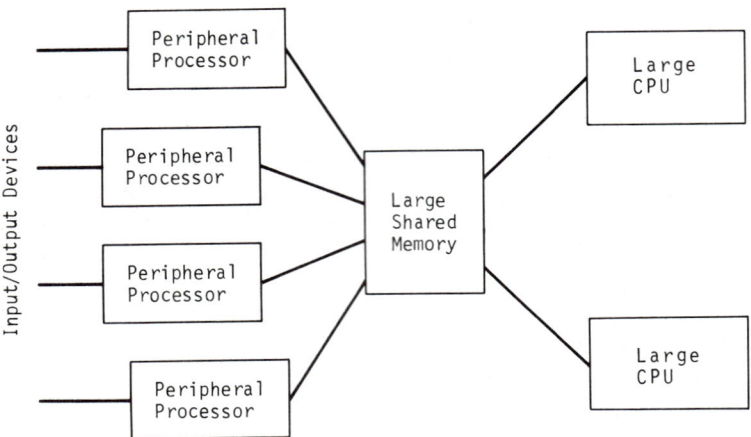

Figure 21-20. Control Data's multiprocessing system.

TERMS TO STUDY

Buffer
Checkpoint
Compiling
Concurrent Processing
Control Program
Interrupt
IOCS
IPL
JCL
Job
Job Step
Language Processor
Library
Linking
LIOCS
Load Module
Macro

Multiprocessing
Multiprogramming
Object Module
Operating System
Partition
PIOCS
Priority
Queue
Restart
Scheduling
Set-up Time
Spooling
Storage Protection
Supervisor
Throughput
Wait State

QUESTIONS FOR REVIEW

1. Describe the six primary functions of an operating system.
2. How does the term *throughput* relate to operating systems?

QUESTIONS FOR REVIEW 471

"I've found the trouble. The other computers are passing the work to number 12."

© *Creative Computing*

3. Describe the difference between a job and a job step. What steps are involved in job set-up?
4. What are the various considerations needed for job scheduling?
5. Describe an interrupt. What steps are followed when processing an interrupt? What are the five types of interrupts used on the IBM Systems?
6. Two major components of data management are PIOCS and LIOCS. What are these two components, what is their purpose, and how do they function?
7. What is the function of IPL in an operating system? When is it used by the operator?
8. The major component of an operating system is the supervisor. What are its responsibilities? Where does it usually reside?
9. Describe the sequence of events that are necessary to compile and execute a COBOL source program.
10. What role does JCL play in a computer system?

11. Would it be necessary for every computer system to have all of the language processors listed in this chapter? If not, why?
12. What kinds of libraries might be found in an operating system?
13. Discuss the inefficiencies leading to the development of multiprogramming.
14. Describe the concept of concurrent processing.
15. What is the essential difference between multiprogramming and multiprocessing?

PROBLEMS FOR RESEARCH AND DISCUSSION

1. The IBM DOS and OS operating systems were the basis for most of this chapter. What operating systems are used by other computer manufacturers? What are some of their characteristics?
2. What job set-up procedures are used in your computer system?
3. If your computer is not an IBM system, find out the type of interrupts used by the CPU.
4. What job control languages are used by the major computer manufacturers?
5. Choose a job control language and describe the major types of statements used in the language.

22

Data Communication Systems

A very powerful contribution to the effectiveness of computer data processing has been the development of data communication to areas remote from the computer. In a batch system, data must be physically transported to the computer for processing. Results are then physically carried back to the user. However, with data communication facilities, things are different. Data may be read from a remote location, processed immediately, and the results transmitted back to the person who needs the information. Most computers have the capability to use data communication concepts. Exactly how this is implemented depends on the systems' needs. In general, three kinds of data communication systems may be used. These are on-line systems, real-time systems, and time-sharing systems.

TYPES OF SYSTEMS

On-Line Systems

This is a term frequently used to describe a communications oriented system. An on-line (Figure 22-1) system is one that receives input directly from the environment creating it. This might be a terminal in an agent's office connected to an airline reservation system or a teller's terminal in

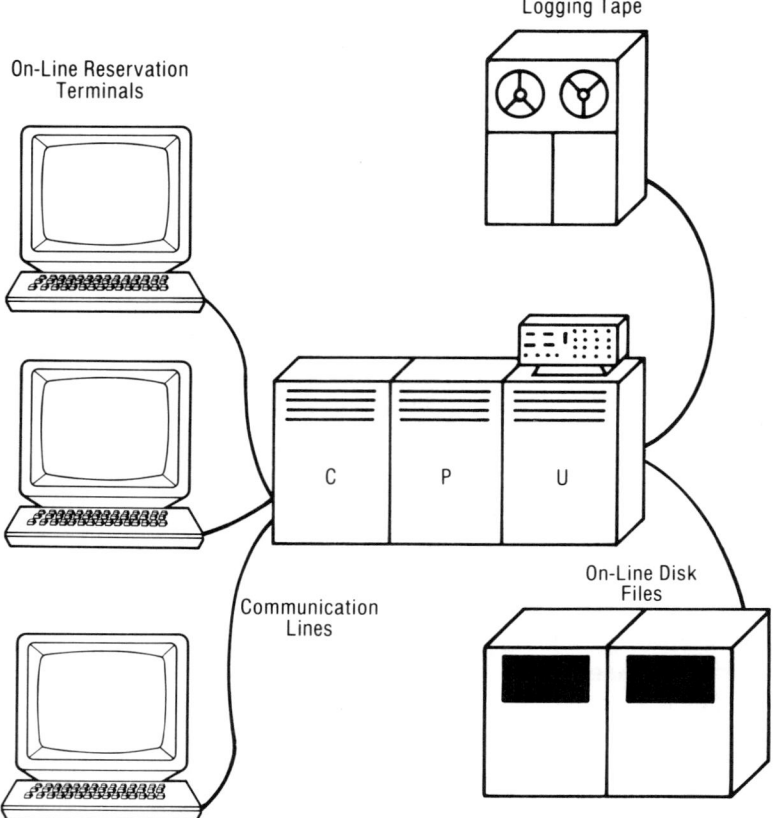

Figure 22-1. On-line system.

an on-line banking system. The output from an on-line system goes directly to the area using it. In the banking system, the output immediately updates the customer's passbook.

Terminals used with an on-line system are usually remote from the central computer, often across the country. Files containing the data to be referenced must be on-line for immediate access (more on files later). On-line systems are people oriented, and terminals are typically typewriters and display screens.

Real-Time Systems

Often confused with an on-line system is the real-time (Figure 22-2) system. In fact, the dividing line between them is rather vague as we shall see. A definition given by James Martin is, "A real-time computer system

TYPES OF SYSTEMS   475

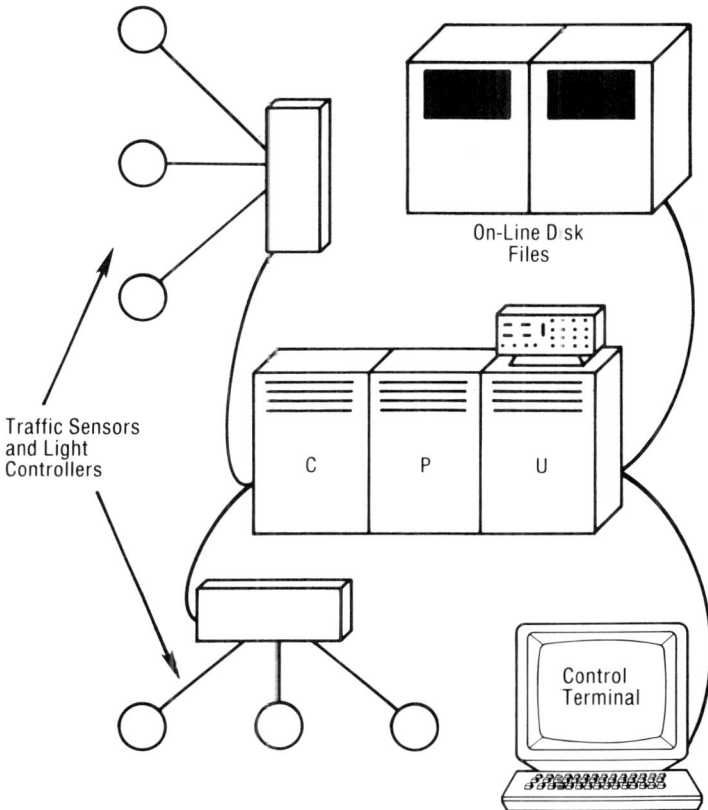

Figure 22-2. Real-time system.

may be defined as one which controls an environment by receiving data, processing them, and taking action or returning results sufficiently quickly to affect the functioning of the environment at that time."* The key here is the expression "sufficiently quickly." This is what is called response time. A real-time system usually has a response time measured in seconds or even milliseconds. This response time is crucial in some systems such as traffic control where the computer receives data on traffic flow and adjusts traffic signals to ensure optimum flow of traffic through each intersection. This can also be critical if the system is controlling a nuclear power generating system. In these cases the reason for quick response is self-evident.

The problem of precise definition occurs when we begin to change the response time. If this time becomes 15 seconds or 1 minute or 15

---

* James Martin, *Design of Real-Time Computer Systems* (Englewood Cliffs, N.J.: Prentice-Hall, Inc., 1967), p. 5.

minutes, at what point does the system become on-line instead of real-time? Unfortunately there is no definite answer to this question. In reality, it probably makes little difference since each system is designed with an appropriate response time for the particular application.

Timesharing Systems

A timesharing system is one that allows a number of different users to share the system for a number of different applications. For example, a number of automotive engineers may each be working at separate terminals. One may be designing a new fuel injection system, another may be simulating a test of aerodynamics, and a third may be doing a cost analysis of a new part.

Timesharing is accomplished by scheduling the central processor so that small time slots are available for each user. These time slots may be only a few microseconds. By quickly alternating between many users with each receiving a small amount of time, it appears that each is being given constant attention by the processor. Response time is important for timesharing systems also. As the number of users increases, the time available for each one decreases. When this happens, performance degrades and users will need to wait longer for a response from the computer.

Multiprogramming

Most data communication systems require a processor capable of multiprogramming. Regardless of whether the system is on-line, real-time, or timesharing, it usually has the requirement to handle multiple tasks. In the multiprogramming environment, one partition may process batch jobs, another may handle on-line inquiries for a management information system, and yet another provides a timesharing capability for programmers doing program development.

TYPES OF TERMINALS

A wide variety of terminals are available to satisfy a profusion of needs. Many of these are the same devices discussed in the section on computer hardware. Included in the ever-changing terminal market is the CRT display for digital or graphic applications (Figure 22-4). Specialized terminals are available for banking systems (Figure 22-5), reservation sys-

TYPES OF TERMINALS 477

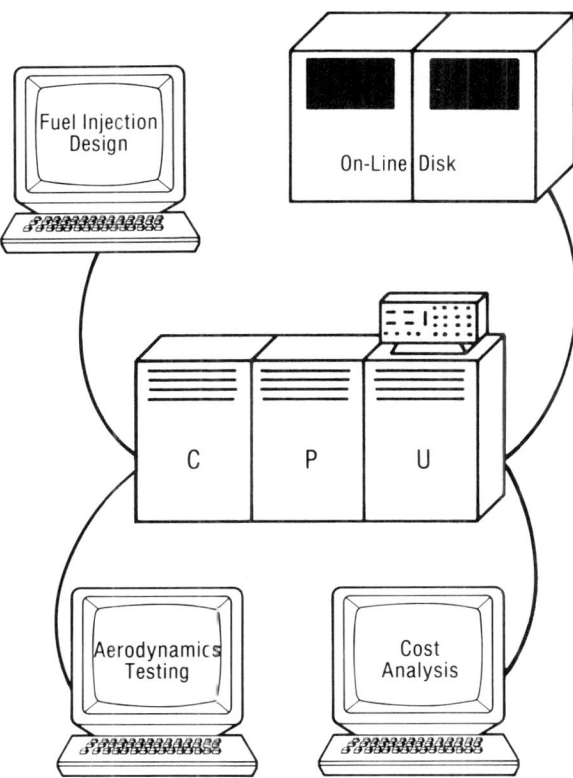

Figure 22-3. A time-sharing system using a multiprogramming capability. In this system, a variety of users may simultaneously use the system for quite different tasks.

Figure 22-4. Univac UTS 400 TE CRT terminal. (*Courtesy of Sperry-Univac*)

Figure 22-5. NCR financial modular terminal system. (*Courtesy of NCR Corporation*)

tems, and stock brokers (Figure 22-6). Texas Instruments even sells a portable terminal (Figure 22-7), which can be used from a phone booth or taken home for the evening or weekend. A more recent development is the intelligent terminal (Figure 22-8), which contains a programmable microprocessor. This built-in computer can do some of the editing and formatting of data formerly done by the central processor. This relieves the main computer of some of the workload, thus letting it function more efficiently.

Choosing a Terminal

A number of considerations are necessary when deciding what type of terminal to use in a data communication system. Proper selection will minimize cost and maximize efficiency. The major factors to consider are:

1. Speed
2. Reliability
3. Noise level
4. Security
5. Polling capability
6. Ability to use a voice grade line
7. Code compatibility

Now we will consider each of these in turn and discuss why these factors are important.

Speed. The speed of a terminal is dictated by the speed of the transmission line. The two must be carefully matched. Speed is measured in terms of baud, which means bits per second. A rate of 2400 baud is equiv-

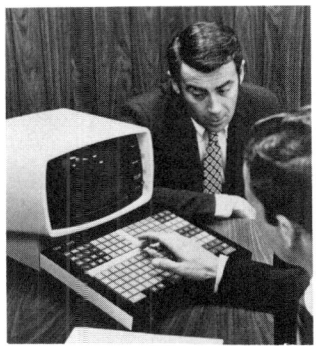

Figure 22-6. IBM 3670 brokerage system terminal. (*Courtesy of IBM Corporation*)

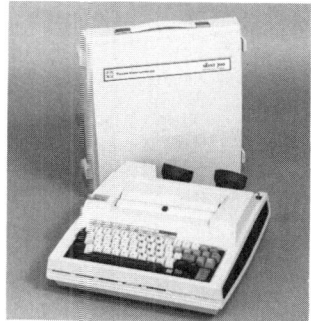

Figure 22-7. Texas Instrument Silent 700 portable terminal with bubble memory. (*Courtesy of Texas Instruments*)

Figure 22-8. Texas Instrument Model 770 intelligent data terminal. (*Courtesy of Texas Instruments*)

alent to 2400 bits per second. In some cases, the speed of a terminal is expressed in characters per second (cps). To relate this to baud it is necessary to know the number of bits per character, including any parity or check bits. Speeds range from typewriter terminals of 10 to 30 cps to CRTs of 1200 to 48,000 baud.

Reliability. This is a natural requirement when selecting a terminal. No one wants the device to be breaking down when it is most needed. For this reason, terminals may often be manufactured as either light duty or heavy duty. A light duty terminal should not be used more than 100 hours per month. A heavy duty unit could handle continuous use without excessive failure rates.

Noise Level. Most terminals are used in an environment where quiet operation is essential. Terminals used in a bank, library, reservation system, or for computer-assisted instruction are all in environments where noise levels should be kept to a minimum. This would not necessarily apply to terminals in a manufacturing plant where the general noise level is high. In this case, a quietly operating terminal is not essential and there may be a cost saving here by buying noisier models, which are cheaper.

Security. In many systems, it is desirable that only authorized persons have access to the computer through the terminal. Some method of identifying the user is needed. This can be solved by using a badge reader, which reads a credit card-like badge. Other systems may have a fingerprint reader or a voice print recognition device. However, these are mainly experimental and rather costly. The simplest and most widely used method is the security code or password. The user simply memorizes a code such as ZEBRA1, or whatever, and enters this code when about to use the terminal. To maintain security, most terminals have a feature that allows the code to be entered without it being displayed or printed.

Polling Capability. Some terminals gain access to the computer by sending an interrupt when they have a message to send. Others use a polling system. With this method, the processor polls each terminal at regular intervals asking if there is any message to send. Whether the terminal interrupts or is polled will influence the type of software needed to support the system.

Ability to Use a Voice Grade Line. Voice grade lines are the least expensive and the most plentiful on the North American continent. This is because voice grades are simply telephone lines. To minimize cost for lines, this is the way to go. Other specialized lines, which may be faster and cleaner (less noise), are more expensive and may need to be installed, thus leading to a long waiting period.

Code Compatibility. A terminal should use the same kind of transmission code as the rest of the system. A commonly used code is ASCII, which we discussed in Chapter 3. If different codes are used, then costly converters are needed—which will increase the system cost. Another aspect of compatibility is the mixing of several terminals of different types on the same line. Since each terminal may have different speeds of operation and various polling techniques, it may be difficult to match them. The best solution is to use the same type of terminal on a given communication line.

Communication Lines and Facilities

Lines are used to attach the remote terminal to the central processor. This can be a simple matter of stringing some wires from the computer center in one room to another room in the same building where the terminals are located. For more distant communication, existing lines may be leased from a common carrier such as AT&T or the Bell System. These may involve telephone lines or cables, microwave transmission, and even satellite communication. Lines are described in terms of several characteristics: directional capability, speed, and modulation.

Directional Capability. This refers to the direction a line is capable of communicating data. The three types shown in Figure 22-9 are simplex, half duplex, and full duplex.

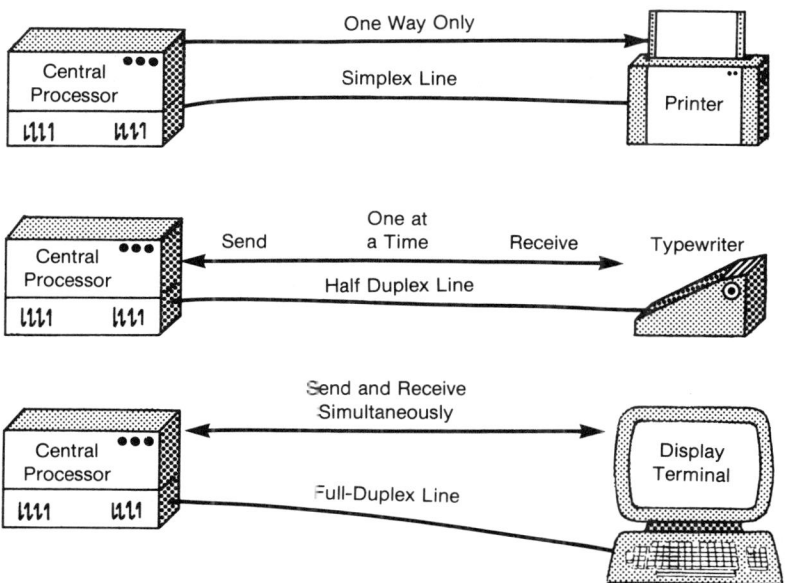

Figure 22-9. Directional capability of communication lines.

Simplex is a line that can transmit in one direction only. This line type would be used with a terminal that can only transmit, but not receive. A card reader or paper-tape reader is an example of this. The reader can send data to the processor but is not capable of receiving data. A printer, which is also in the simplex category, can receive data but not send it.

Half duplex can communicate in both directions, but only one direction at a time. Most terminals have this need. A typewriter or CRT with a keyboard both transmits and receives data. If a half-duplex line is used, data can be sent to the processor or received, but not simultaneously. Full duplex can send and receive simultaneously. While data is being transmitted to the processor, the processor may also be sending data to the terminal. Some terminals have a switch to select either half or full duplex, depending on line availability.

Line Speeds. The speed of a line will determine the kind of terminal that can be attached. Terminal speed and line speed must be carefully matched for successful operation. Line speeds are measured in bauds as are terminals. Line speeds are in different grade categories as follows:

Sub-voice Grade	75, 150, 300 baud
Voice Grade	1200, 2400, 4800, 9600 baud
Broadband	above 9600 baud

Speeds given above are typical, although others within the range are available. Broadband are specialized lines and may be matched to the customer's requirements.

Modulation. A detailed discussion of modulation techniques is beyond the scope of this book. It is sufficient to say that modulation refers to the type of analog signal that is used to represent the digital data transmitted over the line. Three basic types of modulation are used:

Amplitude Modulation (AM)
Frequency Modulation (FM)
Phase Shift Modulation

Modems and Data Sets. Terminals and computers generally operate with digital signals, whereas lines operate with analog signals. In order to convert signals from digital to analog, or vice versa, a modem is used. The name is derived from the expression *modulate-demodulate*. The modem, or data set as it is sometimes called, takes the digital signal from the terminal, converts it to analog, and sends this signal over the communication line. Often the data set has the appearance of a modified tel-

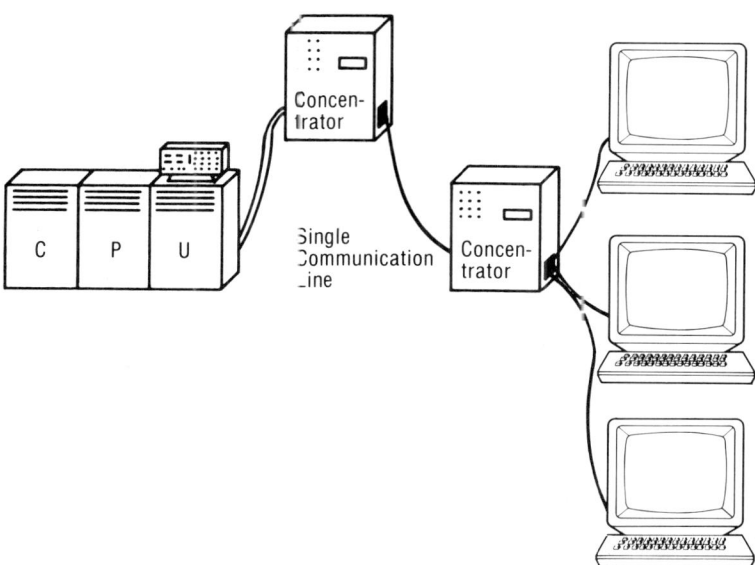

Figure 22-10. Using a concentrator for fewer communication lines.

ephone. Here the data set has a telephone dial and hand-set for calling the central computer. Once the computer is attached, identified by a tone or whistle on the phone, the data button is pressed, and communication can begin. Other modems are permanently attached, thus it is not necessary to dial the computer's number.

Concentrators. To save on line costs and reduce the number of lines necessary for several terminals at a remote location, a device called a multiplexor, or concentrator, is used. This attaches several terminals to a single line as Figure 22-10 shows. A concentrator can be used when several slow speed devices are attached to a higher speed line. Often it is used for terminals used in small time segments such as in computer-assisted instruction (CAI). A person using this terminal cannot type responses at line speed. Instead, most people using CAI type very slowly, thus leaving times when the line is not in use. The concentrator then will transmit data from another terminal thus interleaving data from several terminals on the one line.

In the opposite direction, the computer is sending data for display on the screen. When the screen is filled, the operator will take some time to read all of the information presented. During this time the processor may send data to other terminals selected by the concentrator.

484   DATA COMMUNICATION SYSTEMS

Figure 22-11. Datapoint 1800 Dispersed Processor using interactive COBOL and 60K bytes of user memory. (*Courtesy of Datapoint Corporation*)

FOCUS

LANs, LOCAL AREA NETWORKS

A typical company has installed a number of microcomputers but has discovered that communication between these computers is relatively difficult to achieve. On to the scene marches the local area network (LAN) with the solution.

A LAN provides the means for attaching your computers together from distances as short as a few feet to a mile or more. Using the LAN gives the company greater control over the communication channel than is the case with the phone company, and it is as easy to use as dialing a phone number.

Micros attached together on a local network are linked with a series of lines that can vary from twisted wire pairs at about $300 to $500 per connection. Speed ranges up to 9600 baud when used with standard modems. Broadband

> lines can cost up to $4250, with an average of $1200 per connection. Specialized broadband LANs can cost up to $40,000, with speeds to 100 million bits per second.
>
> A variety of LANs are available for satisfying different user needs. Although there are bus networks, ring networks, and star networks, the choice is best left to an expert. Then there is the data carrying capacity of baseband and broadband. One difference is that baseband can carry only a single transmission at a time while broadband splits the band into channels for carrying several transmissions.
>
> For example, a baseband may connect several micros locally in an office while a broadband may be used to connect them all to a remote mainframe computer.
>
> We are just beginning to use personal computers as communication devices and will no doubt see major developments in the use of networks with personal computing.

FILES

Data Communication Systems have unique needs when it comes to selecting a file organization. Because of the nature of remote data entry and retrieval, consideration of the file type for a specific application is critical. Improper selection can lead to poor response times or excessive costs in hardware and software.

Sequential Versus Direct Access

This is a very basic consideration in file choice. An on-line system may be designed so that data is collected for processing at a later time. In this case, it may be feasible to use sequential files. However, most systems are a variation of real time—which in general has a need for fast response times. To achieve acceptable response time, these systems will use some form of a directly accessible file. This could be a random, indexed, or virtual file, or even a data-base.

File Activity

James Martin expresses the activity of records processed in a file in terms of a ratio. The file activity ratio is

$$\frac{\text{Number of records read and processed in a run}}{\text{Number of records read in that run}}$$

For instance, if 575 accounts were processed in a run but 42,568 records were read sequentially to do the processing, the file activity ratio is

$$\frac{575}{42,568} = 0.013 \text{ or } 1.3\%$$

A low ratio such as this would indicate that a directly accessible file would function far more efficiently than a sequential one.

Frequency of Reference

In many types of files, certain records are used more frequently than others. For instance, in a file of bank accounts, only a small percentage of the customers will make the majority of deposits and withdrawals. Five percent may represent 95 percent of the activity against the file. This situation occurs in many types of files such as reservation systems, inventory files, and accounting files.

To optimize the access time, data records that are frequently used are placed on a high-speed device such as a head per track disk, while the less frequently accessed records will be on a slower and less expensive disk.

Addressing Methods

When a choice has been made to use a direct access method of file organization, the next consideration is the type of addressing scheme to be used to retrieve the records. Essentially four different methods are possible.

1. Direct addressing—With this method the key is identical to the actual address of the record on the direct access device. This is the fastest method.
2. Randomizing—In this method, the key is used as input to a randomizing formula, which derives the address of the record.
3. Index—This is used in indexed sequential files or their equivalent. An index acts as a pointer, which indicates the location of the record on the file.
4. Linked lists—This system uses pointers to form list, ring, or tree structures. Data-base systems commonly use this approach.

Expandability

Data communication systems are notorious for growing in size. It is an almost certain bet that any real-time or on-line system will grow in succeeding years. This means that the file requirements will increase as well. In the initial design, it is essential that files be developed with expansion in mind. If this is not considered, serious financial consequences will most certainly be the result when further growth occurs.

Reliability

What will happen to the system if the device containing a file breaks down? In a reservation system will this mean a loss of business? In an inventory system will this mean extra overtime to enter data? If the answer to questions like these is yes, then alternatives are needed. One solution is to duplicate the file on a separate device. Then if one file fails, the other is available and processing can continue.

DISTRIBUTED PROCESSING SYSTEMS

In many of today's communication systems, the workload on the main processor had become so great that performance begins to suffer. The traditional response to this has been to install a larger and faster processor or even shared multiprocessors. Since the introduction of the mini- and microcomputers and intelligent terminals, a new and creative solution has been devised. This involves placing a processor at the terminal (Figure 22-12), which does all of the initial processing before data is transmitted to the central processor. This remote processor is a minicomputer to which several terminals are attached. The initial processing may involve editing of data, formatting of records, and printing of reports. More complex tasks such as accessing the data-base are handled by the main computer. Not all systems use a mini. Some may have a microprocessor built into each terminal.

    Figure 22-13 shows a local intelligent terminal as part of a distributed processing system. It contains several display terminals attached to a microprocessor. Each terminal at this station has access to a local data-base stored on a floppy disk. The disk provides access to local data and programs necessary for the operation of the local office. Accumulated data from the day's business is also stored on the disk. At the end of the day, the processor transmits the data to the central computer. The intelligent terminal can also produce reports using the attached printer.

488   DATA COMMUNICATION SYSTEMS

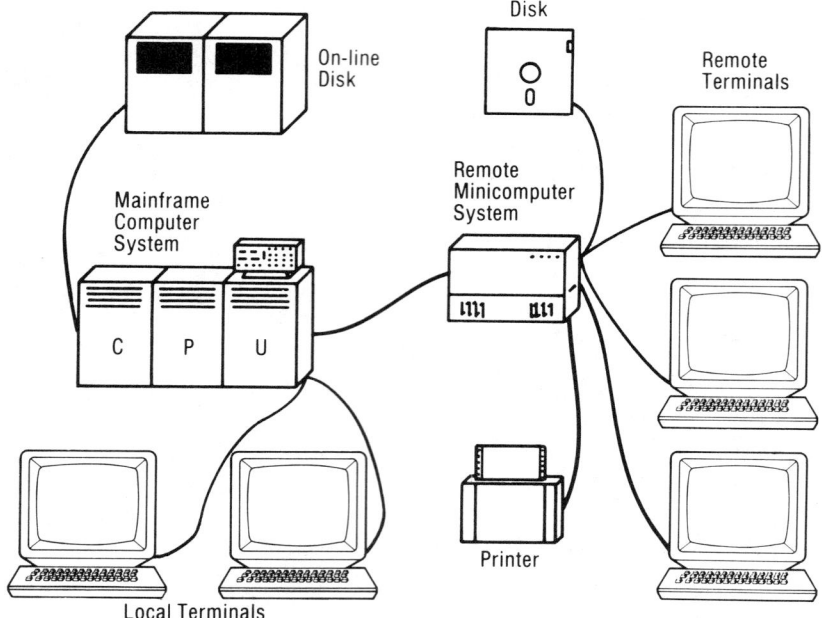

Figure 22-12. Distributed processing system.

Like the main computer, a distributed processor needs the flexibility to meet the changing demands of business. Therefore most terminals provide expansion capabilities. Additional printers, terminals, floppy disks, and even hard disks may be attached as the business expands.

Figure 22-13. Distributed processing local terminal. (*Courtesy of Texas Instruments*)

TERMS TO STUDY

Baud
Compatibility
Concentrator
Data Set
Distributed Processing
Expandability
File Activity Ratio
Frequency of Reference
Full Duplex
Half Duplex
Heavy Duty

Modem
Modulation
On-Line
Polling
Real time
Reliability
Response Time
Simplex
Timesharing
Voice Grade

QUESTIONS FOR REVIEW

1. What are the three main types of data communication systems? How do they differ? How are they alike?
2. A major motel chain uses a system with terminals in each motel connected to a central computer. Reservations may be made from any motel for any other motel by checking a central file containing all current reservations and room availability. Which of the three types of communication systems is this?
3. Why is multiprogramming necessary for most data communication systems?
4. Name some types of terminals that might be used on a real-time system. What types of I/O devices would not be used? Why not?
5. What factors need to be considered when choosing a terminal?
6. What considerations might you make when choosing a terminal for the motel reservation system described in question 2?
7. What are the directional capabilities of communication lines? If you were choosing a line for a terminal used for CAI course in mathematics, what kind of line would be appropriate?
8. What is a concentrator? Would a concentrator be appropriate for the terminals in the reservation system described above? Why or why not?

9. What considerations would be made for the choice of files in the reservation system?
10. What is a distributed processing system? Would the motel reservation system be a distributed processing system?

PROBLEMS FOR RESEARCH AND DISCUSSION

1. Locate a data communication system in your school or community. Describe this system in terms of type, terminals used, response time characteristics, lines, file access methods, and emergency back-up.
2. Describe a hypothetical system for on-line banking, student registration, or computer-assisted instruction. Discuss in depth the kinds of files used and their access method, the type(s) of terminals used and the rationale for your choice, and the characteristics of the communication lines used by your system.
3. Distributed processing is quite a new application of data communication systems. Do some research in this area and present a report on the current status of distributed processing systems.

23

Data-Base

Until third generation computers were firmly established, data file organization and design were based on the traditional concept of independent files. These files, designed for a specific application such as payroll or inventory, were used primarily by the programs related to each file in the system. When changes to the file were required, such as including a new deduction category, all programs accessing that file had to be modified to correspond to the change regardless of whether they used the deduction information or not. This made what appeared to be a simple change quite costly in terms of program maintenance.

The lack of compatibility of traditional files also creates problems when files from several different systems are needed to produce information. For instance, a manufacturer who is designing a new stereo system may wish to do an analysis of the files to identify existing components that may be suitable for use in the new product. A search for compatible components may be made on an engineering history file, but today's specifications may be metric while the file contains English measurements. This is only the beginning. To determine the availability of the part, the order file needs to be consulted. Then to evaluate the impact on production and inventory, the production control file and inventory files are used. Unfortunately, the part numbers used on the engineering file are not the same as on the order, production, and inventory files. It turns out to be cheaper to redesign a new part rather than to find an existing one. Had the file been designed with this purpose in mind, the analysis might have been quite routine.

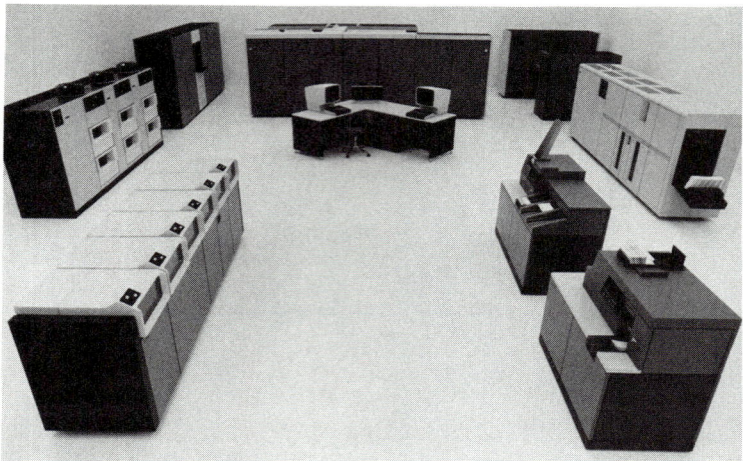

Figure 23-1. An IBM computer system using a data-base. (*Courtesy of IBM Corporation*)

If today's systems are to be truly Management Information Systems (MIS), then a coherent and orderly approach to file design is expected. In most large companies, data is a key resource that must not be designed or manipulated in a haphazard fashion. It must be subjected to careful planning as with any other resource. It is to these problems that data-base addresses itself.

DATA-BASE CONCEPTS

A data-base is a collection of data in a single location designed to be used by different programmers for a variety of applications. The data-base is intended to serve as many people as is possible by permitting the selection of data for various needs as well as the updating and modifying of the data as changes occur.

When a programmer needs data for a particular job, he codes a statement describing the fields needed from the data-base such as PART NUMBER, ORDER QUANTITY, SUPPLIER, and UNIT COST. Although the data-base may include many other items, it supplies the programmer with only these four. In fact, the programmer may never be aware that the file contains other data. If a new field called ENGINEERING is added to the data-base, this particular programmer would not need to change his program since it does not use ENGINEERING. Another program may never need SUPPLIER; therefore this field is never mentioned in this program. In data-base, the program is independent of the file. This characteristic makes changes to the data-base simpler with little impact on most programs.

Since the data is integrated into one place rather than on many independent files, compatibility improves. The same part number would be used for each application because the data-base contains only one part number, thus eliminating redundancy. This field may be used by the engineers or production control as the need arises.

A major problem with redundancy is maintaining a high level of integrity in the file. When data is duplicated it may be updated in one file but not in the other. This results in conflicting information and a reduced reliability of the file Data-base eliminates this difficulty.

Any changes to the data-base relating to data organization or the addition or deletion of the fields is the responsibility of a data-base administrator rather than the individual programmer. This minimizes the impact of change on the system and ensures continued compatibility between seemingly unrelated application areas. The following list outlines some of the objectives of a data-base organization:

Data-Base Objectives

1. Reduce or eliminate redundant data
2. Integrate existing files
3. Share data among users
4. Incorporate changes easily
5. Simplify file use
6. Lower the cost of storage and retrieval
7. Improve accuracy and consistency
8. Prevent unauthorized use of data
9. Exercise control over standards

In case it appears that data-base solves all of our problems, there are some disadvantages. One is the cost. Data-base software is expensive and usually requires larger and faster hardware. This leads to higher costs for the CPU and I/O as well as software. In addition, programmers and analysts who are competent in a data-base system must be highly trained. This leads to higher personnel costs.

Because of the greater complexity of a data-base system, a failure can be more difficult to solve. Since more people will use a data-base, a problem with it can have far-reaching consequences. Instead of one department being affected by a program error, many departments may be influenced. Greater integrity and reliability is therefore necessary in a data-base environment.

DATA STRUCTURES

Traditionally, files have consisted of records containing the same kinds of data items. Usually these records were in some sequence based on a key contained in the record. In a data-base, there can be a variety of ways to view the data, depending upon the needs of the user. For this reason, a data-base not only stores the data but shows the relationships between the various data items. This of necessity leads to a more complex organization than found in the file organizations discussed earlier in the book.

Figure 23-2 shows some of the relationships between the data items discussed at the beginning of the chapter. The lines connecting the various blocks show how one area of the file depends upon information available in another area. PRODUCTION PLANNING depends on data from ENGINEERING to give information on each PART#. INVENTORY also uses this data and in turn is connected to PURCHASING, where orders are placed for parts needed by INVENTORY. PURCHASING needs to know the individual parts to be ordered and their price and quantity, so a line connects the COMPONENTS information. Of course, a live application such as this is far more complex and shows many more data items and relationships than this example.

Trees

Basic Tree Structure. Data structures such as that used in Figure 23-2 are based on a file structure called a tree. A tree is represented in Figure

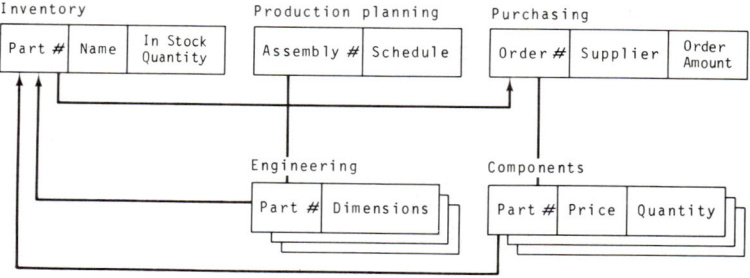

Figure 23-2. Data relationships.

DATA STRUCTURES 495

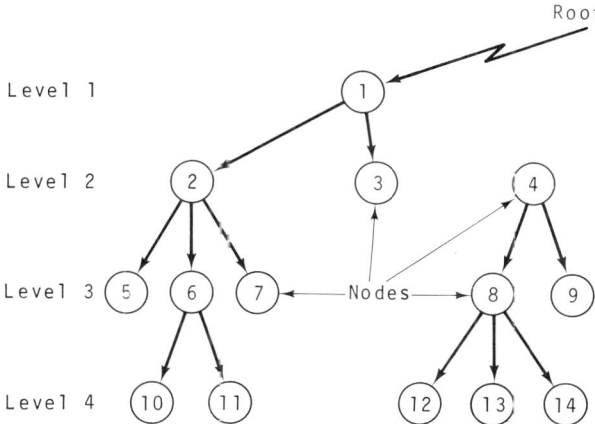

Figure 23-3. Tree structure.

23-3 with its root at the top. Each circle shown in the tree is called a node. Each node can be related to another at a higher level. A node that branches into several higher level nodes is called a parent. For instance, node 2 is the parent of nodes 5, 6, and 7, which are children. A child may also be a parent as in the case of node 6, which is the parent of nodes 11 and 12.

A student record file in Figure 23-4 shows how a data-base may be organized using a basic tree structure. In this example, the root is the General Student Record containing the basic information about the student. From here, branches are taken pointing to either the records containing present courses or to the education history. Since each student will have a different background and be taking a variety of present courses, several records, differing in number for each student, will be included at this level.

Simple Hierarchical Structure. When a tree has nodes with more than one parent, it is called a network, or hierarchical structure. This also can

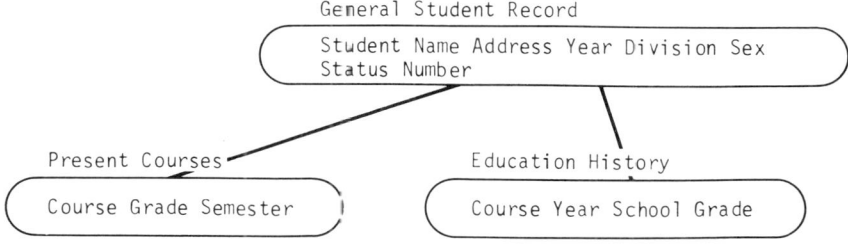

Figure 23-4. Student records using a basic tree structure.

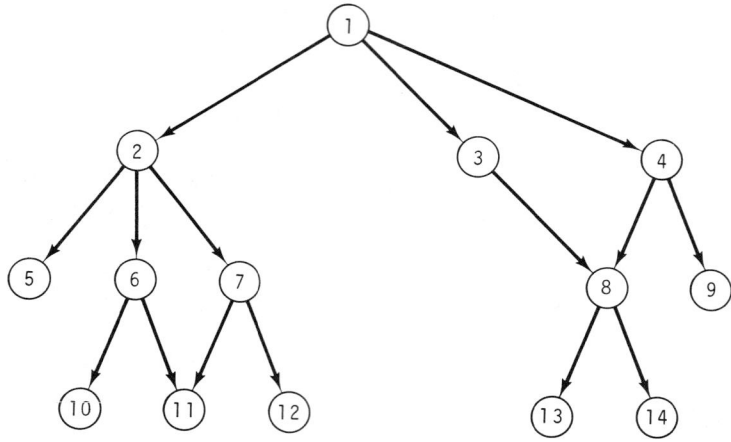

Figure 23-5. Simple hierarchical structure.

be thought of in terms of parents and children, but some children may have more than one parent. When the lines between the nodes still go in only one direction, the tree is a simple hierarchical structure as shown in Figure 23-5. In this diagram, node 11 has both nodes 6 and 7 as parents. A child may also be a parent in a simple structure. This is seen at node 8. In this case, 8 has both nodes 3 and 4 as parents, making it a hierarchical structure. But 8 is also a parent of nodes 13 and 14. Thus 13 and 14 are related to nodes 3 and 4.

The example in Figure 23-6 shows an Employee Records Data-Base that combines Personnel and Payroll using a simple hierarchical structure. In this structure, personnel and payroll could each be roots or may be children of a higher level parent. In either case, they are both parents of the Job History records containing both personnel and payroll historical information. This data may be needed by either department. However, year-to-date is only related to the payroll department's function. Therefore payroll is its only parent. With this structure, personnel may

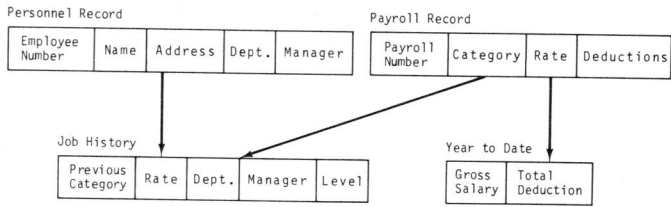

Figure 23-6. Employee records using a simple hierarchical structure.

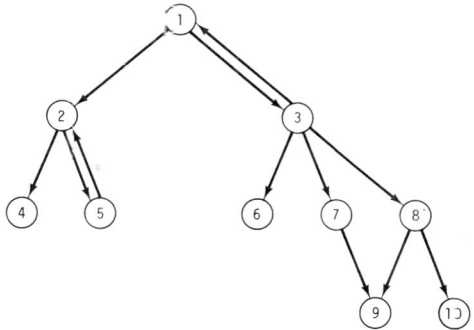

Figure 23-7. Complex hierarchical structure.

never be aware of the year-to-date information. A programmer using personnel data would not need to write any code for payroll or year-to-date data. Only personnel data would be used.

Complex Hierarchical Structure. In some cases, the connecting arrows run in both directions between nodes. Figure 23-7 demonstrates this. In the case of connecting arrows running in both directions, the tree is called a complex hierarchical structure. Some data-base software can handle simple structures but not the complex variety. Others are capable of handling both kinds. The software chosen will depend upon the type of application for which the data-base is used.

An application for a complex hierarchical structure is in a production environment. Here bills of material are used to record the various components used in the assembly of a product such as a toaster or a bicycle. As shown in Figure 23-8, a bill of material may itself contain another bill of material. In the example of a bicycle, a component is the

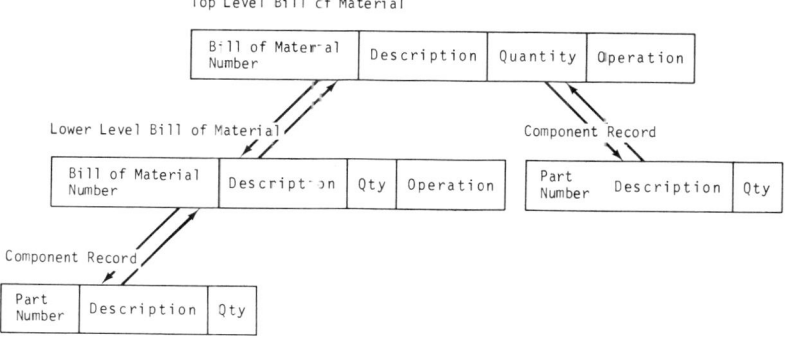

Figure 23-8. Bill of material and components using a complex hierarchical structure.

wheel. But the wheel is itself an assembly of a hub, spokes, rim, and tire. This is a lower level bill of material containing the several components listed.

The arrows in this diagram also point in the reverse direction, making this a complex hierarchical structure. If the part number of a single component such as a rim were available, the reverse pointers would tell us where the rim was used—in the wheel assembly and also in the specific bicycle identified by the top level bill of material.

DATA-BASE FILES

Design Considerations

When considering the organization of records in a data-base, thought must be given to a variety of factors. First we want to utilize the available storage space as effectively as possible. This is not always an easy accomplishment since records are seldom stored in a sequential order on the file.

Second, we want to minimize redundancy. This can be done if duplication of fields and records are avoided. This is largely a design problem. In a case where duplication is unavoidable, coding and compacting the fields can be a real improvement.

Next is whether the fields are to be processed sequentially or randomly. With the preponderance of real-time systems, most files would require random access capabilities. This is particularly true of a data-base that is frequently used in this environment.

Another consideration is the frequency of processing. This determines the placement of the records and the type of device used for storage. Some files, such as inventory, may have 90 percent of their records accessed only 10 percent of the time. These do not need to be stored in prime locations or on very high speed devices. Factors such as these will influence the time required to access the data, which may be of particular importance to a terminal user.

A final consideration relates to personnel rather than the data-base itself. In most cases, implementing a data-base means converting an existing system to a data-base environment. This requires a readiness in management, who must understand the basic concept of a data-base and be prepared with a long range plan for its implementation. Technical people such as analysts and programmers must be upgraded to handle the complexities of data-base. This may mean learning a new language such as CODASYL or DL/1 and new design techniques such as structured design.

FOCUS

PUBLIC DATA-BASES

With the widespread availability of inexpensive microcomputers, computer terminals, and modems, it was inevitable that information of interest to a broad spectrum of the public would be made available from centralized data-bases. Since the early 1980s, a number of companies have begun to offer information services to subscribers on an interactive basis. All that the customer with a microcomputer requires is a modem for from $100 to $1000 and a program costing between $30 and $100. There is an annual subscription fee, which is usually quite low, and then there are line costs based on the length of time the service is used and the time of day or week it is in use. Late night times and weekends are much cheaper than connect time during prime time.

One of the popular public data-bases is The Source, which operates in over 250 U.S. cities and offers over 1000 information services. The Source uses the United Press International (UPI) as their primary data source to offer news, stock quotations, almanacs, and even games. Other services available to subscribers are an electronic bulletin board for clubs and sale notices, travel and restaurant information, electronic mail for sending letters between subscribers, and even a chat mode where two or more people can communicate directly through the system.

Micronet is another data-base that also offers a bulletin board and electronic mail service. But a unique feature of Micronet is a downloading feature where a subscriber may

> purchase a program and download it from the data-base into the home-based personal computer. Programs include games, educational, business, and home application software.
>
> Another service is offered by CompuServe® Information Service, which as the name implies provides information on a broad range of topics from home finance to weather forecasts, coffee futures to book reviews and food preparation to accounting.

Even new positions may be created when a data-base is to be designed. One in particular is the job of data-base administrator (DBA). This may be one person or a team of individuals whose responsibility is to coordinate and plan the development of the data-base. The DBA may also establish standards and performance criteria and provide training for those who will use the data-base. In effect the administrator controls a resource needed by many different users. Requests for service and information will be directed from the user to the data-base administrator.

Physical Versus Logical Organization

So far we have considered only the logical organization of a data-base. This was particularly true in the section on trees. To form a particular logical sequence, records are interconnected by pointers. Pointers are in effect addresses that form a link between records. These links create a chain or list, which when followed gives the logical sequence of records desired from a data-base.

Figure 23-9 shows a chain of records organized on a disk file. Each record contains a pointer that directs to the next logical record. This may be on a different physical track or cylinder. Record A is equivalent to the root of a tree structure. The other records are the nodes at various levels. Depending on the type of structure, a record may have several pointers. A parent node with three children would be a record with three pointers.

The beginning of the chain may be found in an index, or all chains could begin at a common root. The end of each chain is identified by a null pointer. This is a pointer containing a special indicator identifying the end of a chain.

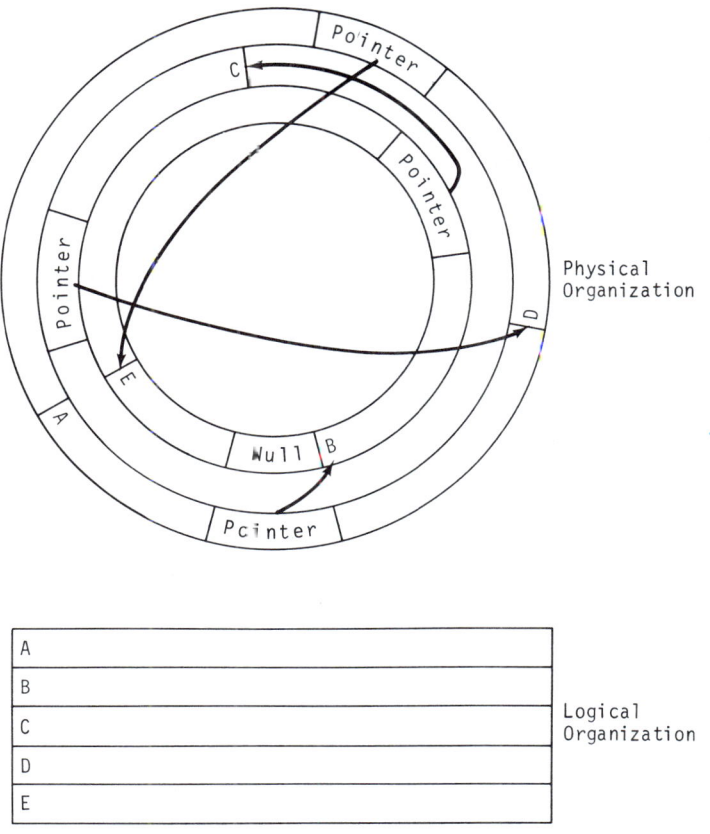

Figure 23-9. Difference between physical and logical organization.

DATA-BASE LANGUAGES

Language Attributes

Languages or data-base are available from most major computer manufacturers as well as a number of independent software houses. These languages, which must describe the data structure completely and precisely, have the following attributes:

1. The language identifies each data item, record, each subdivision of a record (segment) and each file uniquely.

2. It will specify which data items are used as keys. A key, also called a search argument, is used when selecting a specific element of the data-base.
3. The language specifies the relationship between segments to form the kinds of tree structures discussed previously such as parent-child relationships.
4. Pointers connecting segments are defined.
5. Privacy restrictions may be specified in some data-base languages. This determines who has access to specific information.

Data-Base Perspectives

The data-base language describes the data-base from three different perspectives: from the global viewpoint, the application programmer's viewpoint, and the physical organization. The first of these two represents the logical data-base that may be seen from Figure 23-10. In this diagram, the global viewpoint, or schema, describes the entire logical data-base. All of the data items, records, and files are described. Languages for describing the schema are called data description languages and are different from other programming languages. Two languages in use here are CODASYL and IBM's Data Language/1 or DL/1. DL/1 is used by IBM's Information Management System (IMS) and describes the schema or logical data-base description (logical DBD) and the physical data-base description (physical DBD).

The application programmer's viewpoint is called the subschema (Figure 23-10). Each programmer looks at different parts of the data-base and needs access to only a sub-portion of the entire data-base. For this use the programmer describes his specific requirements in an application language such as COBOL or PL/I. This is not much different than accessing a sequential or indexed sequential file.

CODASYL Data Description Language

The Conference on Data Description Languages has been active in striving for an industry standard in data-base languages. CODASYL, a result of this activity, is a language similar to COBOL and is used to describe the schema. Regardless of its COBOL-like appearance, it functions independently of other languages.

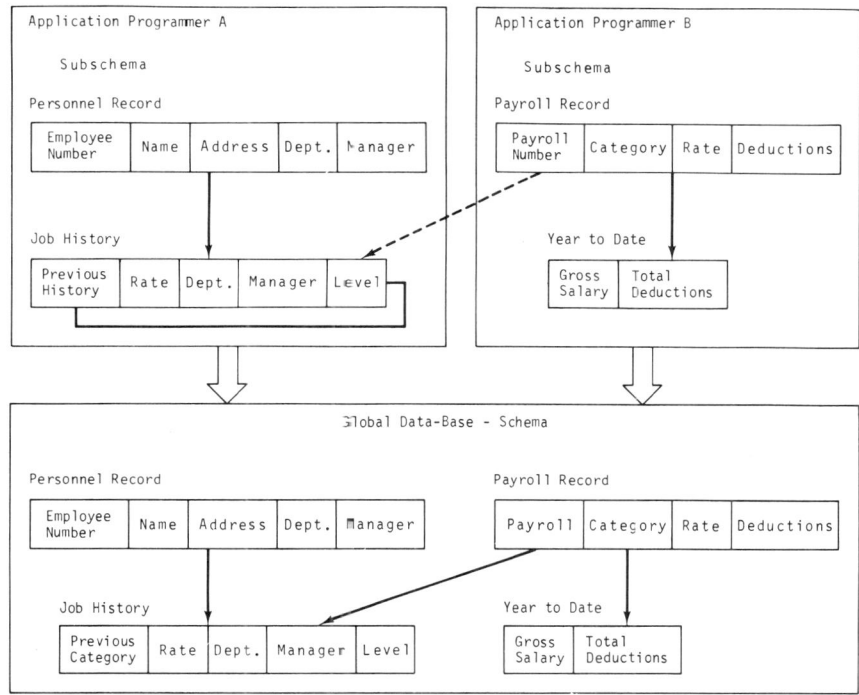

Figure 23-10. Schema and subschemas of the logical data-base organization.

Although a full description of CODASYL is beyond the range of this book a brief record entry is given to show the ease of reading CODASYL.

```
RECORD NAME IS PAYROLL
   01 PAYROLLNO PICTURE "9(7)"
   01 CATEGORY
      02 PAYPERIOD    PICTURE "9"
      02 PAYTYPE      PICTURE "A"
   01 RATE     PICTURE "9(3)V99"
   01 DEDUCTIONS OCCURS 5 TIMES
      02 TYPE PICTURE "9"
      02 AMOUNT PICTURE "9(5)V99"
```

In this record description entry, the record is uniquely identified as PAYROLL. The following entries specify data items or aggregates (a group of data items). PAYROLLNO is the payroll number, which is described by the picture as containing seven digits. A 9 represents a single digit position. CATEGORY is an aggregate consisting of a one digit PAY-PERIOD code and an alphabetic PAYTYPE code. The V in the picture for RATE represents the presence of an assumed decimal point.

The OCCURS clause on DEDUCTIONS represents an aggregate of five groups of TYPE and AMOUNT. Each of the five types is a single digit. Each amount is seven digits including two decimal positions. Other entries in CODASYL describe the schema name, privacy codes, sequence, and data structure relationships.

Data Language/1

The data description language (DL/1) used by IBM is an outgrowth of a development project by IBM and North American Aviation. It is currently used in their Information Management System (IMS) and the Customer Information Control System (CICS). DL/1 describes the schema, or logical data base, and the physical organization. It is independent of other languages.

DL/1 consists of a collection of trees laid out physically on the file unit. Records can be accessed in one of four ways:

1. Hierarchical Sequential Access Method (HSAM)
2. Hierarchical Index Sequential Access Method (HISAM)
3. Hierarchical Indexed Direct Access Method (HIDAM)
4. Hierarchical Direct Access Method (HDAM)

The term *hierarchical* refers to the tree structure. In DL/1, a tree can have up to 15 levels. An example of a DL/1 record description follows:

```
SEGM NAME = STUDENT,BYTES = 80,FREQ = 50
FIELD NAME = STUDENTNAME,BYTES = 30,START = 1,TYPE = C
FIELD NAME = ADDRESS,BYTES = 45,START = 31,TYPE = C
FIELD NAME = TUITION,BYTES = 4,START = 76,TYPE = P
FIELD NAME = SEMESTER,BYTES = 1,START = 80,TYPE = P
```

This code describes a record or segment (SEGM) called STUDENT, which could be used as a parent for another segment. This particular segment is 80 bytes in length and has a frequency of up to 50 occurrences in the data-base. Each FIELD is a further description of this segment. Entries are used to define the name of the data item, the number of bytes occupied in the physical data-base, and the starting location (START) of the data item in the segment. TYPE defines whether the data item is character information (C) or packed (P).

FOCUS

DATA-BASE SOFTWARE FOR MICROCOMPUTERS

With disk based storage capacities for the microcomputer ranging up to 10 million bytes or more, it was inevitable that data-base software for micros would emerge. Two such data-base packages, DB Master for the Apple and The Manager for Commodore CBM computers, are representative of many such programs now available.

These data-base programs are "relational" in the sense that the user of the computer designs his own application by telling the computer about the type of file needed, its fields, and access methods. These programs are "user friendly" so that a minimum of experience is needed to use them. In most cases, a programmer is not required to develop the application.

Applications are developed by defining fields such as name, address, city, state, zip code, order number, etc., directly on the screen in a page format using a form filling technique. Larger applications can even use multiple pages of definition. Data is then entered for each field and the data-base is created on disk as a permanent record.

As activity occurs against the data-base, such as a new order or a payment received, the record may be retrieved by defining a search key such as the customer's number. Updating to the record may be done directly on the screen and the record then rewritten onto the data-base.

One particular benefit of the data-base is the ability to define, at will, search keys to provide specific information from the data-base. For example, a search key to access all records for a single state like NY with orders over $500.00 could be specified and the program would quickly accumulate this information from the data-base. Databases also permit wild card searches for partial values. For instance, a search key for AB on name could access all records that contain an AB in the name field including ABEL, ABELL, ABLE, ABELTON, etc.

The data-base also provides a report generator that can define the format of printed outputs. With this feature, the

> results of a search can be listed with totals and subtotals or summarized in practically any desired format.
>
> Software such as this can make the power of the computer available to many people without the need for specialized training in computer technology.

Although this is a very brief example, it is evident that CODASYL and DL/1 are completely different languages. Yet their essential function of defining a data-base is the same.

Other Data-Base Languages

Other data-base systems available commercially include ADABAS, SYSTEM 2000, TOTAL, and IDMS. ADABAS, or Adaptable Data-Base System, is available from Software AG of North America. ADABAS is unique since it uses a data compression technique. Fields that contain leading zeros, trailing blanks, or are empty are deleted from the data-base resulting in a significant saving of storage space.

SYSTEM 2000 is marketed by MRI Systems Corporation and maintains a data-base on a group of fixed length records on a direct access file. Passwords are used to promote the security of the data-base, and access to any item of data is permitted only when a valid password is supplied. TOTAL is marketed by CINCOM Systems. It allows the database administrator more flexibility in determining how the data is stored physically, which is not the case with the other data-bases. Lastly, IDMS for Integrated Data Management System by Cullinane Corporation is based on the CODASYL data-base model. Its data is stored on direct access files.

FOCUS

dBASE II

dBASE II is a popular relational Data-Base Management program for use on microcomputer systems. It was developed in 1977 by Wayne Ratcliff, then a systems designer working at Jet Propulsion Laboratory (JPL). His original objective was to develop a data-base program for his home computer, an IMSAI 8080.

By 1979, Ratcliff had a workable program and began to advertise it for sale under the name of Vulcan, named after

Star Trek's Mr. Spock's home planet. By 1980, the program was improved and revised for use on a wider variety of computers. It was then renamed dBASE II for marketing reasons, and the program quickly became one of the sales successes of the 1980s.

To use dBASE II, you first define the structure of the file that will hold your data. The file consists of a collection of records and each record is made up of a group of fields. dBASE II permits you to use up to 32 fields per record; a field may contain up to 254 characters with a maximum of 1000 characters per record. As the file is defined, an entry form for entering the data is also developed directly on the screen.

After defining the file, data is entered from the keyboard and added to the disk. Any new data entered is appended to the end of existing data.

Each record stored on the disk has a serial number to uniquely identify it. Using this number will let you have immediate access to the record without taking the time to read other records on the file. If you don't know the number of the record you want, a browse command will let you scan through the data-base until you find it.

A number of commands are available to the dBASE II user to suit various needs. One of these is the Edit command. Edit permits you to make changes to existing records and then store the new information on disk for later access.

The Sort command will let you define a sequence you want for a file, and a new file will be created in this sequence by dBASE II. Since sorting can be time consuming, dBASE II uses an index method if only one or two fields are to be sorted. Using an index for the file allows direct access to records in the file without a physical rearranging of the data on disk.

Finally, the Report command is available to create reports from any data that is on the data-base. This command formats a report, including headings, details, and totals and also selects the required data from the disk to produce the desired report.

TERMS TO STUDY

Child
CODASYL
Complex Hierarchical Structure
Data-Base
Data-Base Administrator
Data Description Language
Data Language/1
Data Structure
Global
Independent Files
Integration

Level
Logical Organization
Node
Parent
Physical Organization
Redundancy
Root
Schema
Simple Hierarchical Structure
Subschema
Tree

QUESTIONS FOR REVIEW

1. What factors led to the development of the data-base concept?
2. Define the term data-base. What are its essential objectives?
3. What is the difference between the organization of a traditional sequential, or direct access file, and the structure of a data-base file?
4. Describe each of the three types of tree structures.
5. A college system is developing a data-base containing faculty records. These records will contain information relating to payroll, areas of teaching assignments, past history of both teaching and education, and a section on publications written by the faculty member. Design an appropriate tree structure to include this information. Supply your own data items for each record.
6. In your answer to question 5, what is the schema? Describe several subschemas that might be used in your data-base.
7. What are the four major considerations we should review when designing a data-base file?
8. Which file organization is the most like a date-base organization? Sequential, random, indexed, or virtual? Why?
9. What is the function of COBOL or PL/I in a data-base environment? How does this usage differ from CODASYL or DL/1?
10. A data-base contains a student record as a parent. This record contains a 9-digit student number, a 2-character count code, a 2-character state or province code, and provision for 7 course

entries each containing a course number (5 digits), description (20 characters), and grade (3 digits). Lastly is a tuition entry, which allows for a maximum of 6 digits including dollars and cents. Write a CODASYL record description entry for this record.

PROBLEMS FOR RESEARCH AND DISCUSSION

1. Write a program to demonstrate the use of pointers that connect the nodes of a basic tree structure. This can be done using one-dimensional arrays.
2. Study a data-base system, such as TOTAL, and determine the type of hierarchical structure used. Identify some of the commands used in the language you have chosen.

24

Computers in Society

As you have seen throughout the book, advances in technology have led to decreased cost and widespread use of the computer in all areas of society. Applications today go far beyond the traditional data processing of business information. The benefits of computer use have impacted such diverse occupations as law enforcement, space travel, medicine, weather forecasting, politics, and education.

The computer is one device upon which our society is becoming increasingly dependent, and the benefits are enormous. Many of the benefits in society that we take for granted are the result of computerized systems. Some of these benefits are immediate inquiry into large data banks by banking, the utilities, and the leisure industry in the form of reservation systems; increased human productivity when a person uses a computer as a professional tool; computer-related jobs for programmers, analysts, operators, and data entry and maintenance technicians; and shorter work weeks and increased leisure time. Of course, these are only some of the many benefits derived from computer use.

However, as with other inventions with immense potential such as the internal combustion engine or nuclear power, there are inherent dangers lurking beneath the surface. Although the computer can be and is a powerful force used for the good of society, it can also present some dangers. Next we will consider some of the additional benefits and dangers that the computer is creating for us.

PRIVACY

The use of computers has encouraged the standardization of identification numbers for individuals in our society; thus the widespread use of the Social Security Number in the United States, the Social Insurance Number in Canada, and other similar systems in most industrialized countries. These numbers are used by a variety of organizations such as government departments, educational institutes, hospitals, retail stores, and credit companies.

The use of a standard ID not only greatly simplifies processing data for each organization, but also makes it easier for them to exchange personal data among themselves. With this widely available data, access to information about our income, education, financial records, reading preferences, and credit status is available to any business willing to pay for it. Often decisions may be made on the basis of this data. If the data is not up-to-date or is in error, then invalid decisions may be made and these decisions can vary from causing minor inconveniences to causing major life-impacting actions.

As a result, a number of governments, usually on a state or provincial level, have passed legislation requiring companies to reveal to any individual the records kept about that person. If the person disagrees about the accuracy of the data, steps can then be taken to have it corrected. Of course, data that is correct but not enhancing to the individual, such as a poor credit rating, can only be changed by taking steps to improve the credit rating.

Some would question the right that companies have to sell the data they have collected to other organizations. There are also legal limitations here. Information of a private nature such as medical records is usually protected by government legislation. On the other side, if you subscribe to automotive magazines, these records are fair game to other magazines that may be looking for new customers. For instance, magazines specializing in vans, recreational vehicles, and even science may purchase the subscription list since an automotive reader is likely to be interested in these other topics.

There are no easy answers to the privacy question. We have two extremes of attitude and all shades of gray in between. One extreme suggests that all information should be available to anyone. This attitude is fast disappearing. At the other extreme it is suggested that any information an organization may collect is for use only by that organization and should be carefully guarded by them. Between these two extremes many interpretations and interests are represented. These are complex questions, and after thousands of hours of political debate, they have yet to be answered fully. Possibly, they never will be completely resolved.

ELECTRONIC FUNDS TRANSFER

We've all heard stories about the rich entrepreneur who has millions in assets but doesn't have sufficient cash on his person to pick up the bill for coffee at a restaurant. Of course today with credit cards such as Master Card and Visa, our affluent friend could simply say, "Charge it."

These cards are, of course, available to the majority of working people. Their widespread availability is only possible because of the computer. As transactions are made, the funds are transferred between the purchaser, bank, credit company, and retail store. In some cases, these funds are transferred electronically from computer to computer via a communications network.

Futurists suggest that the credit card is a forerunner of the cashless society in which all transactions will be done with a universal credit card and all cash will be transferred electronically. There will, in reality, be no actual cash. This future seems highly speculative at the moment. Although the cashless society might be practical even today for many of the large chain retail outlets, there are many small businesses that operate quite informally, such as the neighborhood flea market, where cash still is the best medium of exchange.

Regardless, there is still a strong movement in the direction of a cashless society. Later we will discuss some of the public computer systems such as Telidon and Prestel. But briefly they represent a computer system that is accessible from the home, usually through cable television or the telephone system. Some of these systems are designed to allow a consumer to shop at home by viewing goods on the television screen and then pressing a few buttons to order the item and to have its cost deducted directly from the bank account. These systems are in very limited use today but have great future potential.

The cashless society would have a number of benefits; some are reduced paperwork when processing transactions, a reduction in the number of errors made, and the existence of a complete record of a person's expenditures, which would be beneficial to personal budgeting.

On the negative side, an excessive dependence on credit is damaging to the nation's economy; a completely computer-controlled system could lead to complete government control and, therefore, could provide a danger to individual freedom. Usually these last two points are speculative, but a system of this capacity and control could present a major threat if in the wrong governmental hands.

UNEMPLOYMENT

For the last 15 years, there has been some social concern about the computer's role in producing unemployment. There have been some significant instances of this, such as typesetters who faced widespread unemployment in the 1970s. Other less significant cases (although they are not less significant to those involved) have occurred, but unemployment as a result of the computer has been overshadowed by the many new employment opportunities created by the computer industry. It is estimated that by the end of the 1980s over 50 percent of the workers in North America will be employed in computer-related jobs. The computer profession presents, in any case, one of the fastest growing employment opportunities of the 1980s.

The 1980s are bringing with it a new phenomenon: the industrial robot. These are not the typical science fiction humanoid robots, but are machines based on microelectronics. Industrial robots are programmed to perform manufacturing functions previously done by laborers. Jobs like spray painting, welding, picking up components, lubricating, and assembly are now possible functions of a robot.

The Society of Manufacturing Engineers predicts that within 15 years, 50 percent of the direct assembly of a car will be done by robots. Today robots cost around $50,000, which works out to $5.00 per hour of useful labor compared to a laborer at $15.00 per hour. But the robot receives no fringe benefits or annual increases, it won't go on strike, and it doesn't get sick.

Figure 24-1. "Laverne" and "Shirley" industrial robots. (*Courtesy of General Motors Canada*)

This type of solution to the high cost of labor produces conflicting results. On the positive side, the reduction of labor costs may help to reduce the inflationary effect on the prices of goods. On the negative side, job security is threatened as these machines displace workers. The burden is upon government and industry to find solutions such as retraining and relocating workers affected by this major industrial change.

ELECTRONIC MAIL

Electronic mail has been defined as the "delivery of messages from sender to receiver in some visual or digital form via electronic means." A variety of systems that fit this definition have been developed and marketed by IBM, Xerox, Burroughs, Exxon, and the U.S. Postal Service. There are basically three categories of electronic mail systems in use. These are:

1. Facsimile—Which uses some type of printer or page copier.
2. Communicating Word Processors—These are relatively expensive although costs are declining. Not all word processors have communications capability.
3. Computer-Based Message Systems—These are the most expensive systems. They are difficult to implement and require professional assistance.

The word processor with communication facilities is receiving the most attention today. Typically it begins as a small office word processor and then expands into a larger office management system with both interoffice and intraoffice communication ability. In addition to providing the efficient typing capability of work processing, the office management system permits memos to be sent at any time independent of postal service. These memos can be sent locally or around the world. Since electronic transmission is virtually instantaneous, the memo is received immediately (although this is not always the case; for instance, a central message forwarding computer may create a small delay of seconds or minutes). Also the receiver may only read the mail several times a day, but this is a major improvement over the postal service which may take days or weeks for letter delivery.

EDUCATION

Everyone goes to school for a significant portion of their lives, and because of this fact, the education system has become one of the main institutions

Figure 24-2. The HP 3000 Series 40 terminal is used for many areas of office management including electronic mail. (*Courtesy of Hewlett-Packard Company*)

providing computer literacy for the general public. In fact, education today is one of the largest computer users outside of the business community. For many years, the computer was used by education primarily to teach about the use of computers. The most common use was for Computer Science and Data Processing courses in universities and colleges.

Although the computer is still used extensively to teach about computers, it is now frequently being used to teach other subjects ranging from mathematics to English and flight simulation to medical diagnosis. In these cases, the computer uses a method known as Computer-Assisted Instruction, or CAI (Figure 24-3).

A CAI system frequently uses terminals attached to a central mainframe or minicomputer in a timesharing environment. In some cases, a microcomputer may be used for CAI but has been somewhat limited by its relatively small storage capacity. Regardless of the type of computer, the instructional program communicates with the student by displaying information and questions on the screen. The student then responds by typing an answer on the keyboard or in some cases by using a light pen or touch sensitive screen.

The procedure generally followed in a CAI system is to first present the student with some explanatory material. Depending upon the sophistication of the system, this material will range from English text to diagrams, graphics, and even animation. Some advanced systems will control a slide or movie projector, and recently, even video disks are being used for CAI.

EDUCATION 517

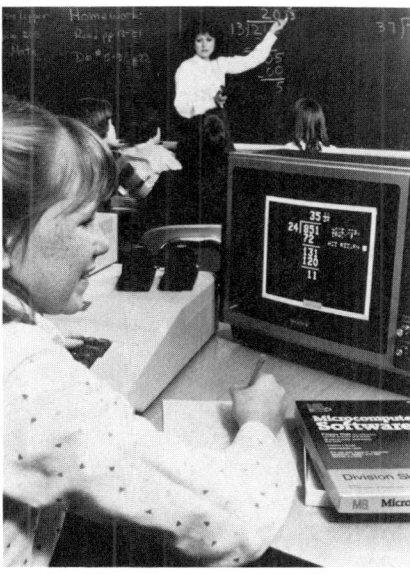

Figure 24-3. With the development of the microcomputer, educators at all levels are finding many uses for the computer in the classroom. (*Courtesy of Milton-Bradley*)

Next, the student is presented with a series of questions that require a response. The program evaluates the response and if necessary will give the student additional material to clarify problem areas. When understanding is apparent, the program proceeds to give instruction on the next topic within the lesson.

Finally, when a lesson has been completed, the CAI program evaluates the student's progress. A report is usually prepared for the instructor, and the student is directed to the next stage of instruction. If a student happens to be experiencing serious difficulty, the instructor is notified thus giving student and instructor an opportunity to correct the problem before progressing to the next lesson.

Three basic types of instruction used in CAI are:

1. Drill and practice—This method is used to drill students repetitively in basic skills such as elementary arithmetic. Many programs using a game format for instruction have been developed for use on the microcomputer making drill and practice fun and interesting unlike simple rote learning.
2. Tutorial—This is the traditional CAI approach, which presents the student with pre-programmed instruction and then requires the student to respond to questions on the material presented. A good program can anticipate the student's difficulties and give

corrective material. Tutorial programs generally let the students proceed at their own pace.

3. Simulation—Simulation techniques use graphics and animation to display a model of a real-life situation. Some computer games take this approach, but more serious applications simulate real life very carefully. Types of simulation programs include aircraft flight simulation, laboratory experimentation, and even business decision making. Simulation is often preferred to real life where mistakes can cause property damage or even result in the loss of life whereas the simulator avoids these serious difficulties.

CAI has an advantage over books and lectures because the programs interact directly with each student on an individual basis. The programs can use graphics, animation, and sound to promote interest in the subject. Unlike many humans, the computer has enormous patience and endurance.

On the down side there is considerable hardware and software cost associated with the CAI system. A good CAI program takes much longer to prepare than the time it takes an instructor to develop a course for a traditional classroom environment. And, in the final analysis, the computer lacks the creativity and spontaneity that can be present with human contact in the classroom.

HOSPITAL INFORMATION SYSTEMS (HIS)

Would you trust a computer for the care of your health? Although the computer is seldom used directly for health care, many hospitals do use the computer to automate hospital procedures and to maintain patient and employee records. In some cases, the patient records may be used by the computer to evaluate and diagnose illness.

Effective hospital computer systems decrease the cost of hospital operation, which is a major social concern in the 1980s. The computer can also help to improve on patient care by providing timely information on the patients' current status as well as evaluating their history of illness and health care.

What features should an effective centralized Hospital Information System include? While the list of needs is endless, the following list identifies some of the major components of a central HIS.

1. Accounts Receivable and Payable
2. Payroll

3. Personnel records
4. Patient admission and discharge data
5. Drug inventory and use
6. Laboratory data
7. General supplies inventory

Notice that this list includes many items required by the average business. Accounting, Payroll, and Personnel are all typical business applications that even a hospital requires. The other items in the list are specific needs that require specialized software for hospital use.

Other health care facilities may also make effective use of the computer in their operation. Many drug stores, for instance, are installing microcomputers or POS terminals attached remotely to a minicomputer. These computers are used for prescription handling, record keeping, drug inventory, and accounting.

Medical research institutes use mathematical models on the computer to simulate biological systems. These models can be used to predict how the body will respond to various stimuli. Another computer system for medical research is the Medical Library Data Base (MEDLARS) at the National Library of Medicine in Bethesda, Maryland. This library consists of more than 3½ million medical references that are used by universities, hospitals, and medical schools.

CAI systems are also used by students in medical school to practice patient treatment without endangering the lives of real patients. Other CAI systems are available for dieticians, pharmacists, and lab technicians.

TRANSPORTATION

As a nation, we are dependent upon efficient transportation systems for many aspects of daily life. Various forms of transportation methods are used to supply us with food and consumer items; we use the car or public transit to commute to our work; and the airlines are used for business and personal travel. Beyond these more common forms of transportation are the less used but still important trains and buses and the more exotic space travel. All of these transportation systems are familiar to us and to some degree they all make use of computer technology.

Airline Reservation Systems

One of the most widespread uses of the computer in transportation is for airline reservations. A computer terminal situated in an airline or travel agent's office can be used to give instant data on flight and seat availability.

When a customer calls the reservation office, an entry is made at the terminal indicating the date, airline, and destination. The computer responds, indicating the availability of the flight and seat, and the cost of the ticket. If the customer approves, the reservation is made immediately.

In some cases, however, there will not be a seat available for the particular flight the customer wants. Two alternatives may be presented. One is the waiting list, where the customer is placed until a seat becomes available due to cancellations or other changes. The second alternative is the possibility of an alternate flight. With the computer, other flights may quickly be examined and the customer is presented with an alternative flight that may satisfy his needs.

Reservation systems accept a variety of information. Of course, the most important is the customer's name, address, and telephone number, the flight number, and the number of seats reserved. In addition, many systems also provide special help for things like dietary restrictions and medical requirements as well as hotel and car reservations. Computerized reservation systems increase customer satisfaction and make the task of reserving a flight relatively easy and painless.

Air Traffic Control

In addition to making a reservation, air traffic safety is of vital importance to the travelling public. As air travel has become more complex for the pilot, and air traffic congestion has increased, it has become increasingly important to use partly automated systems to relieve the air traffic controllers of their complex task. This burden is increasingly falling upon computers as the Federal Aviation Agency (FAA) is converting to computer-based air traffic control systems.

Such systems are installed at major airports and other control centers around the country. A computerized traffic control system uses a computerized radar display. The computer, with input from the radar's signal, plots on the screen the plane's location, speed, and altitude, and a number that identifies the plane. This data is displayed next to the radar blip for the controller to observe. As the plane changes its flight path, altitude, or speed, these figures are constantly updated.

Systems such as this make airline travel one of the safest forms of travel there is today.

Vehicle Traffic Control

The science of traffic control is fast developing as an important tool that uses the computer to maximize traffic flow. A computerized traffic control system uses sensors implanted in the pavement or positioned above the traffic. These sensors act as input devices to the computer to provide information on traffic flow and congestion.

The computer analyzes this traffic data based on predetermined data, such as the time of day and traffic flow priorities. Then the traffic control computer sends signals to each intersection to control the lights to give the best traffic flow.

Another form of traffic control is controlled entry to expressways. In this type of system, a motorist is stopped at the entrance to the expressway by a red light under computer control. As the traffic flows by, sensors send information to the computer, which looks for a break in the flow. When this break occurs, the computer signals the motorist to proceed and merge with the expressway traffic.

Computer controlled sensors are also in use on sharp curves where excessive speed into the curve is a problem. As an automobile approaches the curve, the computer evaluates the vehicle's speed. If it is in excess of a safe speed for the curve, lights flash and a warning is given to SLOW DOWN to a safe speed.

LAW ENFORCEMENT

Centralized computer systems have added an information element to law enforcement that was only hoped for in the past. The computerized police information system provides both operational data and crime information. On the operational side, the computer can provide information on the units in the field, their location, and operational status. Units can be on traffic control, in pursuit of another vehicle, off for lunch, or officer needing help. With this information readily available from the computer, units that are available can be quickly identified and assigned to new duties.

The computer can also be used to provide criminal information in the form of stolen property records, wanted persons with descriptions, and criminal records. This data may be accessed by the police officer to help make decisions in the field more effective. In the more advanced systems, a communication device and computer terminal in the patrol car can display this data as requested by the officer. A routine traffic check can use the remote computer to give immediate data on the license number, owner's record, and identification of stolen cars or property.

In many cases where a computer terminal in the patrol car is not used, much of the same information is still available to the officer. By using the police radio to contact the information center, data can be dictated by radio from a control center that has the use of a computer information system. This approach reduces the cost of a system with terminals in each patrol car and yet suffers from only slightly reduced efficiency.

Where criminal activities are taking place, the computer can be a useful tool for helping identify the criminal. The investigating officer can enter the crime's MO (method of operation) into the computer's data-base. A program then analyzes the facts, including items such as the time and location of the crime, type of crime, special methods or tools used, and descriptions from the witnesses. This data may then be compared to existing cases to identify similarities. The computer can then identify similar cases and the person or persons who committed the former crime. Often this process leads to suspects who may eventually be convicted of their crimes.

Local law enforcement agencies also communicate with national systems such as the FBI's National Crime Information Center in Washington, D.C., or the R.C.M.P. in Ottawa, Canada. Since these national organizations use computerized information systems and because many crimes go beyond state or provincial boundaries, data flow between local and national agencies is vital to the success of crime fighting.

PUBLIC INFORMATION UTILITIES

A small but growing area of computer influence is the home interactive information retrieval system known as Videotex. This information utility would be piped into the home through existing telephone lines or television channels.

One such system provided by the British Post Office is called Prestel, which uses a modified TV set and Keypad to give subscribers access to data-bases via the telephone. Data received is displayed on the television screen. Prestel presently offers 200,000 pages of information provided by 200 organizations ranging from job vacancies to leisure activities to stock prices to business intelligence.

In Canada, the Telidon system is used in Ottawa, Montreal, and Toronto with 1,000 subscribers and a 100,000-page data-base. Telidon is attached to the television set with an adaptor and can be used to send electronic mail, read the news selectively, plan a vacation, or do electronic

Figure 24-4. The Telidon system. (*Courtesy of Government of Canada Department of Communications*)

shopping. In 1980, about 40 Telidon equipped television sets were placed in the Washington, D.C., area for a field trial. Also in 1980, 30 Telidon terminals were installed in storefront information centers in Caracas, Venezuela. These terminals will be used by people seeking government information about social services, education, statistics, health, and other services.

Other information utilities are being tested around the world, including Sweden, Finland, and France (Antiope system), and in the United States by AT&T (Electronic Information Service-EIS) and GTE (Viewdata).

CAREERS IN COMPUTERS

In 1978, the U.S. Department of Labor projected an increased need for programmers of 30 percent to 1990 and a 37 percent increase in the need for systems analysts. These figures represent an annual need for an additional 9,200 programmers and 7,900 systems analysts.

Since 1978, the demand for trained computer professionals has not changed substantially. Some analysts suggest that the need for computer people until the turn of the century will be greater than the supply of graduates from the colleges, universities, and private institutes.

In addition to the traditional programming and systems jobs are the needs for data entry and computer operators. New positions created by word processing and the microcomputer are also creating new demands for trained personnel.

Figure 24-5. Computer programming is one of the better known occupations created by the computer industry. (*Courtesy of Digital Equipment Corp. and Digital Equipment of Canada Limited*)

Career Opportunities

With the growth of computers expected to the end of the 20th century, a similar growth in career opportunities is expected. Jobs in the computer industry are widespread and varied with the majority being in data processing. As Figure 24-6 indicates, there are four general categories of occupations: data entry, computer operator, programmer, and systems analyst.

Generally higher levels of education are needed as you go from left to right on the chart. For data entry, only grades 10 and 12 are needed, while programmers and analysts require college or university education. Specific jobs within the categories may require different levels and types of training.

For example, a programmer working for a retail chain may perform adequately with a three-year college diploma. But a programmer who writes statistical programs for an insurance company may need a masters degree in mathematics.

Each position except systems analyst in Figure 24-6 accepts new employees at an entry level. Systems analysis normally requires a person to have had some experience in the company before moving into this career path.

Once an employee has gained experience and maybe additional training on or off of the job, advancement can lead to other positions of

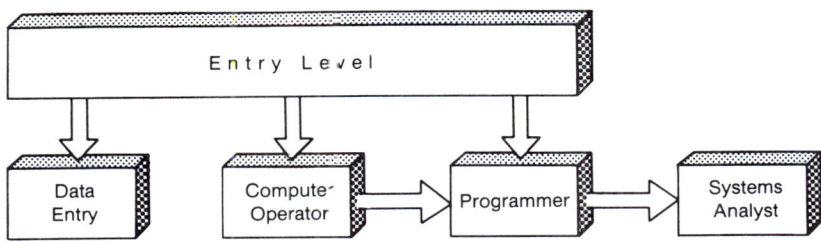

Figure 24-6. Major areas of computer career opportunities.

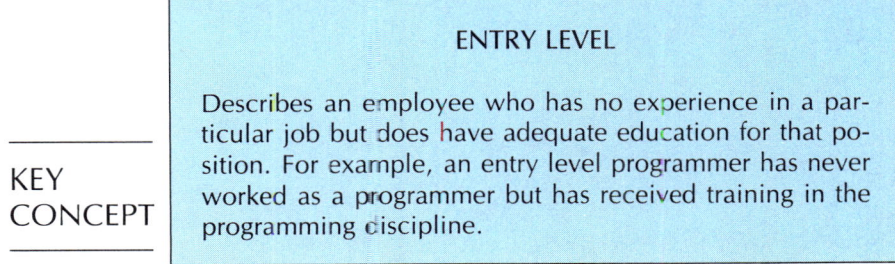

KEY CONCEPT

ENTRY LEVEL

Describes an employee who has no experience in a particular job but does have adequate education for that position. For example, an entry level programmer has never worked as a programmer but has received training in the programming discipline.

responsibility. One direction is to change career paths, such as moving from operations to programming or programming to systems analysis.

Another career move is up to higher levels of responsibility within the chosen career path. Figure 24-7 shows a number of potential career paths for a person employed in Data Processing.

As this chart indicates, there are many positions and career paths that an upwardly mobile person can follow. Although the diagram shows many of the paths that could be followed, there are many more that are less formally defined. This is due to the individuality and particular needs of each company. So depending on the company, there will be variations on the specific positions and career paths available.

Data Entry

A data entry operator is a person with typing or keying skills. The position involves the recording of source data from documents on a terminal, key entry device, or keypunch. When a terminal is used, it may be part of a distributed processing system or an input on a transaction oriented system. Terminals operate under software control, and thus verification of the data entered may be done on-line to ensure accuracy of the data.

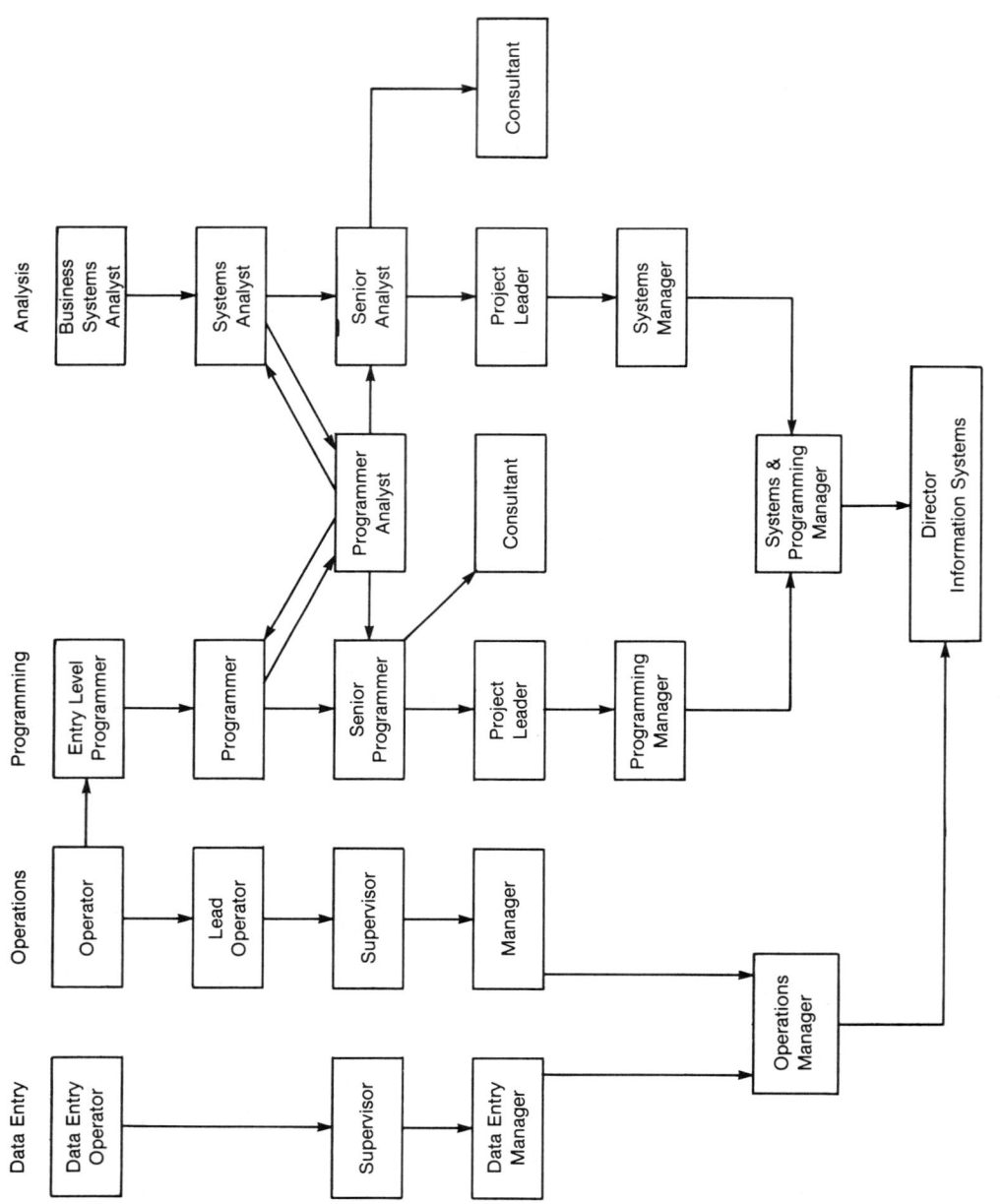

Figure 24.7 Career paths in data processing.

Key entry devices (tape or disk) may also provide for some data validation while a keypunch normally requires a separate verify operation. Key tape, disk, and cards are processed as batch input to the computer.

Computer Operations

A computer operator is responsible for the monitoring, control, and operation of computer hardware, including terminals, central processor, and peripheral devices. The job involves the mounting and dismounting of tapes and disk files, and loading card readers and printers. In addition, the operator calls up programs from disk into memory to perform specific functions.

As an operator is promoted into higher levels of responsibility, supervisor duties will become a part of the job. This may involve giving direction and training to new operators and monitoring of the operations department's production schedule.

Operations management has general responsibility for all personnel in operations and the control and preparation of work scheduling. An important component of the management's function is to ensure the quality and completeness of the computer output.

Programming

A computer programmer develops, codes, tests, and debugs application programs. Development of the program may involve interfacing with the user, and the systems and operations department to establish program requirements. Program development may require the use of flowcharts, structure charts, or pseudo-code to design the program structure and logic. In some cases, part or all of the design work is done by the systems analyst.

When design is complete, the programmer writes the program code in an appropriate language. The program is then compiled, debugged, and tested to ensure it is error free. When this process has been completed, live testing may be done with the user department taking part in the exercise. Finally the program is implemented and goes into regular use by the user.

Following implementation, changes to the program may be required. These changes are prompted by revised user requirements, changes in company policy, and even recently discovered errors in the program. Revising existing programs is called maintenance programming and is a very important function of the programming department. In many companies, more programmer time is spent on maintenance programming than on developing new applications.

In addition to programming responsibilities, programmers (such as a senior programmer or a consulting programmer) also review packaged software. Frequently a software package may be considered for purchase by the company instead of writing a new application program, thus saving thousands of dollars and hours of programming time.

The consulting programmer evaluates the appropriateness of the software and determines the extent of modifications needed to satisfy the company's requirements.

Systems Analysis

The systems analyst studies current operational procedures within the company and designs new procedures as solutions for specific operational problems. Design may involve new forms, documents, flow of information, screen formats, and so on. The design process results in flow diagrams showing the way data is to flow in the organization and the results of processing that data at various steps.

The analyst creates a link between the user departments and the programming staff. As a system is developed, the analyst presents a formal solution to the programmers who then develop the necessary programs to implement the system. Users will also need to adopt new procedures to interact with the computerized portion of the system. Implementation is guided by the analyst in cooperation with the programming department and user departments.

Computer Sales

The chart back in Figure 24-7 also overlooks other careers that are not specifically related to data processing. One such area is sales. Selling is primarily related to computer hardware, software, and related products. Although not as large as data processing, the marketing career is an important one. Usually a sales force is staffed by people with education in marketing or business administration.

Word Processing

Another career that is growing very rapidly is word processing. A word processing operator generally has secretarial training or experience with specific training on a word processing system. With modern offices looking for more effective ways of paper handling, word processing is becoming an important career opportunity.

Microcomputers

Beginning with the explosive growth of microcomputers from the early 1980s, new career opportunities have been created in this field. Jobs ranging from sales to servicing are widespread today. Many individuals have become successfully self-employed as programmers of microcomputers. These people have helped to spawn a new generation of software useable on the micro and needed for applications from accounting to music.

TERMS TO STUDY

CAI
Electronic Funds Transfer
Electronic Mail
Entry Level
HIS
Privacy

Programmer
Robot
Systems Analyst
Telidon
Videotex

PROBLEMS FOR RESEARCH AND DISCUSSION

1. What kinds of information about you should be kept private, and what kinds would you be willing to have on public file?
2. If the near future sees a computer terminal in every home, what benefits do you visualize? What dangers?
3. Choose a topic such as privacy, funds transfer, unemployment, information utility, etc., and write an in-depth paper on the subject. Most computer publications (see Appendix C) consider these problems and opportunities from time to time. Also, many newspapers have articles on these and other computer-related subjects.

25

The Future Is Now

Throughout the past 24 chapters, we have taken a look at the major areas of significance in the use of computers for information processing. We have seen many changes to the face of data processing in recent years. Much of this change is in the hardware, but we have also seen the impact of change on software and computer applications. Where is all of this leading?

If we were to take a predictive approach to this chapter and try to forecast the future of computers, we might suggest things like: public utility computer networks, transmission of computer data by satellite, home computers with access to large information networks, intelligent devices for consumer use, and so on. However, if we take another look at the current state of the art, it appears that all of these things are in the development stage and in many cases are already with us today. The availability of these applications is certainly limited, but nevertheless they do exist. So instead of trying to outguess the future let's consider the transition period through which we are now passing.

The single most influential development of the 1970s was the silicon microprocessor chip. The outcome has been personal computing, which is beginning to provide home education, record keeping, personal financial computation, educational and noneducational games, and home environment control. The trend in home computers has led to computer costs comparable to a black and white television. In fact a few computers are below this price range. Of limited availability, which no doubt will soon change, is a data communication facility for the home that provide a news service, telephone directory, computer assisted instruction (on a variety of topics at a reasonable price), library services, direct banking, electronic mail between individuals, and a data bank for shoppers supplying prices and suppliers of goods.

The microcomputer is impacting the small business to a much larger extent than the personal computing area. Computer power, which a decade ago was available only to the larger companies, is now an affordable tool for virtually all businesses. Many systems exist for less than $10,000 and are capable of handling accounts receivable, general ledger, inventory control, sales analysis, and word processing.

The microprocessor chip has also made available intelligent terminals and distributed processing networks for the business community. These developments are in their infancy and in the next few years will mature to the point where even the smallest department in every business will be using computer power. This means that a new type of literacy will be necessary for the business student. Virtually everyone who expects to be successful in the business world will need to be familiar with the computer and its potential. The computer as a business tool will become as common as the hand calculator for everyday use. In many cases the computer will be used without our being aware of it. For instance, cash registers and automatic cash dispensers are beginning to use the microprocessors in their operation.

The evolution of hardware technology is continuing to grow at a phenomenal rate. For instance, the Z-80 microprocessor chip contains 8,500 transistors in a module of 193 mils by 180 mils. In the 1980s, it is expected with very large scale integration that densities of one million components per chip will be commonplace.

This kind of compactness is expected to occur for memory devices based on solid state, magnetic bubble, and charged coupled device technology. When this happens, we can expect secondary storage devices such as disk to be replaced by these new memories. The real advantage, of course, is the elimination of seek time and rotational delay, which are time-consuming operations in today's direct access devices. Already magnetic bubble memory is being used in intelligent terminals for data storage. The advantages are their compact size and that data is retained even when the power is turned off.

Most of this discussion has centered on the small computer and individual user. This has certainly been an area of major impact; however, the large scale system is also going through a transition period. With the reduced cost of hardware and the use of microelectronics, there will be an increase in the use of parallel processors. These have formerly been available in only the very largest of computers. Today's technology is leading to widespread use of parallel processing. The microprocessor chip is also being used to store much of the operating system software (now called firmware) in the chip memory, instead of occupying space in the computer's main storage. This saves main storage space and permits much faster execution of software modules. Batch processing is gradually giving way to interactive processing as terminals decrease in price and data communication lines are readily available.

Software has not been untouched by these changes. Many user-oriented software packages have changed both the function and need for programmers. This change is particularly evident in the microcomputer where most users simply adopt one or more programs that are general purpose yet specific enough to satisy their requirements. On the mainframe, fourth generation is creating a change in the role of the programmer. Instead of writing programs, the technical specialist will become more of an advisor and trainer in the use of user-oriented software.

This is certainly an exciting phase in the development of computer technology. The next few years will no doubt lead to many new applications of the computer. New employment opportunities and career paths will open up and existing ones will certainly change. There will be plenty of challenges, in the computer and information processing field, for those who are prepared to meet them. We hope that this book has in some way made a contribution to those who wish to meet the challenge of the future.

Appendices

APPENDIX A
METRIC MEASUREMENT

The government of Canada and some areas of the United States are committed to conversion to the metric system. Already, highway signs in Canada have changed to kilometers and temperatures are being given in Celsius degrees by the media. In some industries, these changes may constitute a major expense while in others the effect may be minimal. However, to compete on world markets, a standard system of measurement is thought to outweigh the initial problems of conversion.

Abbreviations for Metric Measure

Linear Measure	Liquid and Dry Measure	Weight Measure
Millimeter—mm.	Milliliter—ml.	Milligram—mg.
Centimeter—cm.	Centiliter—cl.	Centigram—cg.
Decimeter—dm.	Deciliter—dl.	Decigram—dg.
Meter—m.	Liter—l.	Gram—g.
Decameter—dcm.	Decaliter—dcl.	Decagram—dcg.
Hectometer—hm.	Hectoliter—hl.	Hectogram—hg.
Kilometer—km.	Kiloliter—kl.	Kilogram—kg.
		Myriagram—myg.
		Quintal—q.
		Tonneau—t.

Conversions from the English System

Linear Measure

1 in.	= 2.54 cm.	1 mm.	= .03937 in.
1 ft.	= .3048 m.	1 cm.	= .3937 in.
1 yd.	= .9144 m.	1 dm.	= .3281 ft.
1 rd.	= 5.029 m.	1 m.	= 39.37 in.
1 mi.	= 1.6093 km.	1 m.	= 3.281 ft.
		1 m.	= 1.0936 yd.
		1 dcm.	= 1.9884 rd.
		1 km.	= .6214 mi.

Square Measure

1 sq. in.	= 6.452 sq. cm.	1 sq. mm.	= .00155 sq. in.
1 sq. ft.	= .0929 sq. m.	1 sq. dm.	= .1076 sq. ft.
1 sq. yd.	= .8361 sq. m.	1 acre	= 3.954 sq. rd.
1 sq. mi.	= 259 ha.	1 sq. km.	= .3861 sq. mi.
1 sq. rd.	= 25.293 sq. m.	1 sq. cm.	= .155 sq. in.
1 A.	= 40.47 ares (a.)	1 sq. m.	= 1.196 sq. yd.
		1 ha.	= 2.471 acre

Solid or Cubic Measure

1 cu. in.	= 16.3872 cu. cm.	1 cu. cm. (c.c.)	= .06102 cu. in.
1 cu. ft.	= .02832 cu. m.	1 cu. dm.	= .0353 cu. ft.
1 cu. yd.	= .7646 cu. m.	1 cu. m.	= 1.308 cu. yd.
1 cd.	= 3.624 steres (st.)	1 st.	= .2759 cd.

Liquid and Dry Measure

1 dry qt.	= 1.101 l.	1 l.	= .908 dry qt.
1 liquid qt.	= .9463 l.	1 l.	= 1.0567 liquid qt.
1 liquid gal.	= .3785 dcl.	1 dcl.	= 2.6417 liquid gal.
1 pk.	= 8.81 l.	1 dcl.	= 1.135 pk.
1 bu.	= .3524 hl.	1 hl.	= 2.8377 bu.

Weight Measure

1 gr. troy	= .0648 g.	1 g.	= 15.432 gr.troy
1 oz. troy	= 31.104 g.	1 g.	= .03215 oz. troy
1 oz. avoir.	= 28.35 g.	1 g.	= .03527 oz. avoir.
1 lb. troy	= .3732 kg.	1 kg.	= 2.679 lb. troy
1 lb. avoir.	= .4536 kg.	1 kg.	= 2.2046 lb. avoir.
1 T. (short)	= .9072 met. t.	1 met. t.	= 1.1023 T. (short)

Metric Measurements

Linear Measure

10 millimeters	= 1 centimeter
10 centimeters	= 1 decimeter
10 decimeters	= 1 meter
10 meters	= 1 decameter
10 decameters	= 1 hectometer
10 hectometers	= 1 kilometer
10 milometers	= 1 myriameter

Square Measure

100 square millimeters	= 1 square centimeter
100 square centimeters	= 1 square decimeter
100 square decimeters	= 1 square meter
100 square meters	= 1 square decameter
100 square decameters	= 1 square hectometer
100 square hectometers	= 1 square kilometer
100 square kilometers	= 1 square myriameter

Cubic Measure

1,000 cubic millimeters	= 1 cubic centimeter
1,000 cubic centimeters	= 1 cubic decimeter
1,000 cubic decimeters	= 1 cubic meter
1,000 cubic meters	= 1 cubic decameter
1,000 cubic decameters	= 1 cubic hectometer
1,000 cubic hectometers	= 1 cubic kilometer
1,000 cubic kilometers	= 1 cubic myriameter

Liquid and Dry Measure

10 milliliters	= 1 centiliter
10 centimeters	= 1 deciliter
10 deciliters	= 1 liter
10 liters	= 1 decaliter
10 decaliters	= 1 hectoliter
10 hectoliters	= 1 kiloliter
10 kiloliters	= 1 myrialiter

Weight Measure

10 milligrams	= 1 centigram
10 centigrams	= 1 decigram
10 decigrams	= 1 gram
10 grams	= 1 decagram
10 decagrams	= 1 hectogram
10 hectograms	= 1 kilogram
10 kilograms	= 1 myriagram
10 myriagrams	= 1 quintal
10 quintals	= 1 tonneau

APPENDIX B
CAREERS IN COMPUTERS

Career opportunities in data processing are many and varied. The list here shows many of the common positions available. Exact positions and job titles will vary from one company to another. Most categories of jobs use qualifiers to indicate specific responsibilities.

Manager—Is the person in charge of all activities within a department. This individual may personally supervise the work of the subordinates or direct senior staff who have this responsibility.

Senior —A person who is highly qualified for the specific activity. Usually works with minimal supervision and may also act in a supervisory role.

Trainee —Is a person who is new to the job and requires close supervision. Usually is assigned relatively simple tasks until technical ability is increased.

Each position also has a general category, which includes most of the employees. These are the positions such as systems analyst or applications programmer. This individual works under some supervision but is able to function independently a large part of the time. Figures in parentheses are average salary ranges.

Director of Data Processing
($34,200–$50,700)

This person is the administrator who has responsibility for all aspects of data processing. This position is usually seen in the larger organizations.

Systems Analysis

This career category is responsible for formulating new systems or revising existing ones. The work involves preparing system flowcharts, pseudo-code, and descriptions of systems, and working with user departments and the programming and operations staff. Job titles include:

>Manager of Systems Analysis ($33,300–$40,100)
>Senior Systems Analyst ($30,500–$33,700)
>Systems Analyst ($23,400–$28,000)
>Systems Analyst Trainee ($17,500–$21 400)

Applications Programming

This group produces program code that is debugged and documented. They work with program specifications prepared by the systems analysis group to produce new programs or maintain existing ones. In some installations the function of systems and programming are combined to create a position of programmer analyst. Common job titles are:

>Manager of Applications Programming ($33,500–$37,300)
>Senior Applications Programmer ($28,400–$29,500)
>Applications Programmer ($19,800–$28,200)
>Applications Programmer Trainee ($16,200–$17,500)

Systems Programming

This position is usually seen in the larger installations. Responsibility is for the operating system and software necessary for successful operation of the computer. Usually consisting of highly qualified programmers who provide consulting services, standards, performance evaluation, and troubleshooting. Job titles are:

>Manager of Systems Programming ($32,900–$35,500)
>Senior Systems Programmer ($23,800–$35,300)
>Systems Programmer ($19,100–$33,500)

Data-Base Administrator ($29,000–$39,200)

This is usually one person who coordinates design, file organization, and data dictionary creation of the data-base. Responsibilities also include establishing standards for data use and ensuring data security and integrity.

Computer Operations

This staff is responsible for the physical operation and running of the computer center. The job involves scheduling jobs, establishing priorities, routine maintenance, running programs, mounting and dismounting tapes, disks, and printer paper. In a small center, one or two people may do all of this while the larger installations will involve many people in its operation:

>Manager of Computer Operations ($22,500–$31,100)
>Senior Computer Operator ($15,000–$23,200)
>Computer Operator ($12,900–$19,300)
>Magnetic File Librarian ($18,700)

Production Control ($13,400–$22,400)

This position ensures that jobs to be run on the computer are set up with proper JCL and data. Mainly jobs that are batch are scheduled through production control. Detail functions include collecting data from user departments for processing, routing output back to the user, logging receipt of data, processing, and the output from the job.

Data Entry Operation
($13,400-$19,900)

Usually consists of a staff of people who enter data from documents onto a medium for computer input. This is generally a key entry function using devices such as key disk, key tape, data collection terminals, or keypunches.

NOTE: Because of space limitations this is a condensed treatment of career opportunities. For a full treatment, an excellent source is *Datamation's* Annual DP Salary Survey.

APPENDIX C
PERIODICALS OF INTEREST

Byte—The Small Systems Journal, P.O. Box 361, Arlington, Mass. 02174.
> A monthly journal with articles on hardware and software for microprocessors.

Canadian Datasystems, Box 9100, Postal Station A, Toronto, Ontario, Canada M5W 1V5.
> Monthly publication of articles relating to business data processing.

Communications of the ACM, Association for Computing Machinery, 1130 Avenue of the Americas, New York, N.Y. 10036.
> A monthly journal of technical and general interest in computer science.

Compute! P.O. Box 914, Farmingdale, N.Y. 11737.
> A monthly magazine of interest to personal computer users.

Computer Data—The Canadian Computer Magazine, Suite 2504, 2 Bloor Street West, Toronto, Ontario, Canada M4W 3G1.
> This magazine discusses current hardware and software developments and applications. Published monthly.

Computer Decisions, Hayden Publishing Co., Inc., P.O. Box 13802, Philadelphia, Pa. 19101.
> Includes articles on the application and administration of computers.

Computer Design, P.O. Box A, Winchester, Mass. 01890.
> Published monthly. Deals with various aspects of computer hardware circuitry.

Computer Education, P.O. Box 99, South Pasadena, Calif. 91030.
> A monthly publication with articles of interest to the educator in computer studies and data processing.

Computers and Automation, A monthly publication with articles on hardware, software and systems. Includes a computer census each month.

Computers and People, Berkeley Enterprises, Inc., 815 Washington St., Newtonville, Mass. 02160.

Computerworld, 129 Mt. Auburn St., Cambridge, Mass. 02138.
> A weekly publication in newspaper format covering items of interest to data processors.

Computing Canada, 211 Consumers Rd., Suite 106, Willowdale, Ontario, Canada M2J 4G8.
> Published weekly in newspaper format. Supplies current news on developments in hardware, software, and service organizations. Also contains articles of general interest.

Creative Computing, P.O. Box 789-M, Morristown, N.J. 07960.
> Published monthly; one-year subscription, $15. Of interest to the microcomputer user and especially the user of personal computers.

Data Management—Published monthly by Data Processing Management Association, 505 Busse Highway, Park Ridge, Ill. 60068.
> Articles of general interest to the business computer professional.

Datamation, P.O. Box 2000, Greenwich, Conn. 06830.
> Very complete monthly publication with articles covering state of the art, applications, politics, foreign computing, and general interest.

EDP Analyzer, 925 Anza Ave., Vista, Calif. 92083.
> In-depth monthly reports on specific topics.

Infosystems, Business Press International, Inc., 288 Park Ave., West Elmhurst, Ill. 60126.
> Monthly publication of interest to computer systems people.

Interface Age, P.O. Box 1234, Cerritos, Calif. 90701.

> A monthly magazine for personal and small business computing. Deals largely with hardware.

Journal of Systems Management, 24587 Bagley Rd., Cleveland, Ohio 44138.

> Monthly publication of ASM (Association for Systems Management).

PC Magazine, P.O. Box 2442, Boulder, Colo. 80321.

> A bi-weekly publication with articles of interest to users of the IBM Personal Computer.

Personal Computing, 167 Corey Road, Brookline, Mass. 02146.

> Published bimonthly. Contains articles relating to personal computing and small business applications.

Popular Computing, P.O. Box 307, Martinsville, N.J. 08836.

> Monthly magazine covers the entire range of developments in the personal computer field.

Language Supplement

COBOL

The name COBOL is derived from Common Business-Oriented Language and is intended primarily for use in business-oriented applications. COBOL has been implemented by all major computer manufacturers. The language was developed when representatives from government and business met in the Pentagon in May 1959. They were looking for a high-level programming language to be used for general purpose applications in business.

The first version of COBOL was released in December 1959 and was subsequently followed by several newer versions. In August 1968, the first standard version was approved by the American National Standards Institute (ANSI). This was known as ANSI COBOL. Present versions of COBOL are based on the 1974 standard. The programs in this book are based on the latest ANSI COBOL standards.

INTRODUCTION TO COBOL

Figure 1 shows an elementary COBOL program. Every COBOL program consists of 4 divisions: the IDENTIFICATION, ENVIRONMENT, DATA, and PROCEDURE Divisions. Each has a specific purpose. The IDENTIFICATION DIVISION indicates the name of the program and the programmer. The ENVIRONMENT DIVISION selects the files to be used by the program—such as the card reader or printer. The DATA DIVI-

```
IDENTIFICATION DIVISION.
PROGRAM-ID.
    SAMPLE.
AUTHOR.
    DON CASSEL.

ENVIRONMENT DIVISION.
INPUT-OUTPUT SECTION.
FILE-CONTROL.
    SELECT REPORT-FILE ASSIGN TO UT-S-PRINTER.

DATA DIVISION.
FILE SECTION.
FD  REPORT-FILE
    RECORD CONTAINS 80 CHARACTERS,
    LABEL RECORDS OMITTED,
    DATA RECORD IS PRINT-LINE.
01 PRINT-LINE.
    02 FILLER PIC X(40).
    02 LINE-A PIC X(93).

PROCEDURE DIVISION.
BEGIN-PROGRAM.
    OPEN OUTPUT REPORT-FILE.
    MOVE SPACES TO PRINT-LINE.
    MOVE 'FIRST TEST OF COBOL PROGRAM' TO LINE-A.
    WRITE PRINT-LINE AFTER ADVANCING 2 LINES.
END-OF-PROGRAM.
    CLOSE REPORT-FILE.
    STOP RUN.
```

Figure 1. Sample COBOL program.

SION describes the logical characteristics of each file in the file description (FD) and the format of each record in the structure (PRINT-LINE in this example) associated with the FD.

Finally, there is the PROCEDURE DIVISION. Its purpose is to open files, read and write them, and do calculations and decision making. This is usually the longest and most involved division of a COBOL program. In this program, the PROCEDURE begins by opening the REPORT-FILE in preparation for printing. This file has been assigned to the printer in the ENVIRONMENT DIVISION. The message 'FIRST TEST OF COBOL PROGRAM' is moved to the print line, which contains the identifier

LINE-A. The WRITE statement causes the message to be printed after moving the printer carriage down two lines. The REPORT-FILE is then closed and the program stops at the STOP RUN statement.

COBOL Coding Form

For coding COBOL programs and subsequent key entry, a coding form is used by most programmers. Figure 2 shows a typical form. The top portion of the page has space for descriptive information identifying the system to which the program belongs, the name of the program, programmer, and date.

The first 6 columns of the COBOL statement are used for a page and serial number. This is optional in most compilers, but if it is used, the compiler will check the sequence of the statements during compilation.

Column 7 is used to indicate when a literal is continued onto the next card. In this case a hyphen is entered in this column.

Beginning in column 8 is a field called the A margin. Only the following types of statements begin in the A margin:

> Division Names such as IDENTIFICATION DIVISION
> Section Names like INPUT-OUTPUT SECTION
> Paragraph Names like FILE-CONTROL or BEGIN-PROGRAM
> Level Numbers such as FD or 01

The A margin entry may begin from columns 8 to 11 and extend to column 72 if necessary.

All other statements in COBOL begin in the B margin, which includes all columns from 12 to 72. To allow for indentation, a statement may begin anywhere on this line. The remaining columns 73–80 (shown at the top of the form) are used for program identification. Usually some unique code is used to identify the program being written. This entry is also optional and not necessary for practice programs.

COBOL DIVISIONS

All COBOL programs have four divisions. We'll discuss the Identification and Environment Divisions in sufficient detail here for all programs in

COBOL PROGRAM SHEET

System: Cobol Description
Program: Sample
Programmer: Don Cassel
Date: 26/7/78
Sheet 1 of 1

Sequence		
010		IDENTIFICATION DIVISION.
020		PROGRAM-ID.
030		SAMPLE.
040		AUTHOR.
050		DON CASSEL.
060		ENVIRONMENT DIVISION.
070		INPUT-OUTPUT SECTION.
080		FILE-CONTROL.
090		SELECT REPORT-FILE ASSIGN TO UT-S-PRINTER.
100		DATA DIVISION.
110		FILE SECTION.
120	FD	REPORT-FILE
130		RECORD CONTAINS 133 CHARACTERS.
140		LABEL RECORDS OMITTED,
150		DATA RECORD IS PRINT-LINE.
160	01	PRINT-LINE.
170		02 FILLER PIC X(40).
180		02 LINE-A PIC X(93).
190		
200		

Figure 2. COBOL coding form with entries.

this book. Then some of the basics of the Data and Procedure Divisions will be discussed with additional detail introduced later as it is needed.

Identification Division

This is the first and easiest division to code. There are only a few entries to be made, and most of them are optional. These entries identify the program, programmer, and related information. Only the PROGRAM-ID with a program name is mandatory. The name is limited to 6 or 8 characters, depending on the compiler used. The remaining entries are treated as comments in most compilers and therefore offer flexibility of entry. Figure 3 is a complete Identification Division.

Environment Division

Configuration Section. In many report programs, control of the printer is needed to skip to the top of a page. This is required when headings are to be printed at the beginning of a report and after a page of output has been filled. Page control is done with a Write statement in the Procedure Division and a control code in the Configuration Section.

```
IDENTIFICATION DIVISION.
PROGRAM-ID.
    REPORTS.
AUTHOR.
    DON CASSEL.
INSTALLATION.
    HUMBER COLLEGE.
DATE-WRITTEN.
    23 JULY 1984.
DATE-COMPILED.
    27 JULY 1984.
SECURITY.
    NO-SECURITY-CODE.
REMARKS.
    THIS PROGRAM USED FOR DEMONSTRATION PURPOSES.
```

Figure 3. Complete Identification Division.

ENVIRONMENT DIVISION.
CONFIGURATION SECTION.
SPECIAL-NAMES.
    C01 IS TO-NEW-PAGE.

Figure 4. Moving to the top of a new page.

The code C01 is predefined in COBOL to indicate skipping to the top of a page on the printer. TO-NEW-PAGE is a name chosen by the programmer and used in a Write statement as follows:

WRITE ACT-REC AFTER ADVANCING TO-NEW-PAGE.

This statement is found in the Procedure Division at the place where a line is needed at the top of a new page. The page is first skipped, and then the contents of ACT-REC are printed on the first line of the page.
Input-Output Section. The INPUT-OUTPUT section describes the physical device associated with a file by using a SELECT clause.
The SELECT clause assigns the name of the file to be used in the program to the physical file. The file name such as ACT-REPORT is chosen by the programmer. The physical file is referenced by

UT-S-PRINTER.

The letters UT mean utility. This is used for a file assigned to any device, such as disk or printer (the device must be specified). This allows the programmer to use a printer for the file at one time and disk at another. The letter S means the file is sequential. PRINTER is the name used to represent the printer or disk. This is ultimately defined in the operating system through the job control language.

A complete Environmental Division appears as shown in Figure 6.

Data Division

The Data Division of COBOL contains the logical description of all files and records used in the program. This is done in two sections called the

ENVIRONMENT DIVISION.
INPUT-OUTPUT SECTION.
FILE-CONTROL.
    SELECT ACCOUNTS-FILE ASSIGN TO UT-S-CARDS.
    SELECT ACT-REPORT   ASSIGN TO UT-S-PRINTER.

Figure 5. INPUT-OUTPUT section.

```
ENVIRONMENT DIVISION.
CONFIGURATION SECTION.
SPECIAL-NAMES.
     C01 IS TO-NEW-PAGE.
INPUT-OUTPUT SECTION.
FILE-CONTROL.
     SELECT ACCOUNTS-FILE  ASSIGN TO UT-S-CARDS.
     SELECT ACT-REPORT     ASSIGN TO UT-S-PRINTER.
```

Figure 6. A complete Environmental Division.

FILE SECTION and the WORKING-STORAGE SECTION. The first of these describes all input and output files using a file description (FD) entry. Each FD in turn has a structure describing the record connected with that file. The WORKING-STORAGE SECTION contains data items used for processing in the program. Some of these may also be used in an input or output operation. This section will be discussed later.

File Section. The COBOL code in Figure 7 shows a FILE SECTION that describes a file for input records and a file for producing a report. The fact that these are the card reader and printer is not evident here; this is determined in the Environment Division. Each file used must have a separate FD and structure. The FD is used to describe the logical characteristics of the file. This includes the blocking factor, record length, and labels. The structure describes the format of the record and the type of each field—whether numeric or alphanumeric.

File Description (FD). The first FD in Figure 8 describes the ACCOUNTS-FILE, which is the file coming from the card reader. ACCOUNTS-FILE is the file name chosen by the programmer for this program. The next entry, BLOCK CONTAINS 1 RECORD, defines the blocking factor. Since a card reader is used, the factor must be 1. Tape or disk could use a higher blocking factor for greater efficiency. RECORD CONTAINS 80 CHARACTERS indicates the number of characters of bytes in a logical record. For a card reader this would usually be 80. The printer in the second FD uses 133. The first character is for a printer carriage control character, and the remaining 132 characters are the print line.

LABEL RECORDS ARE OMITTED says that header and trailer labels are not used on this file. These are generally used only for tape and disk files. In this case the entry LABEL RECORDS ARE STANDARD would be used in the FD.

The final entry in the FD indicates the name of the record (structure) to be used for this file. DATA RECORD IS ACT-INPUT means that the FD will be followed by a structure with a 01 level named ACT-INPUT.

Most entries in the FD are optional. When they are omitted, the COBOL compiler assumes certain characteristics. These are summarized

```
DATA DIVISION.
FILE SECTION.
FD  ACCOUNTS-FILE
    BLOCK CONTAINS 1 RECORD
    RECORD CONTAINS 80 CHARACTERS
    LABEL RECORDS ARE OMITTED
    DATA RECORD IS ACT-INPUT.

01  ACT-INPUT.
    02  ACT-NUMBER-1    PIC 9(7)
    02  NAME-1          PIC X(15).
    02  AMT-OWING-1     PIC 9(4)V99.
    02  FILLER          PIC X(52).

FD  ACT-REPORT
    BLOCK CONTAINS 1 RECORD
    RECORD CONTAINS 133 CHARACTERS
    LABEL RECORDS ARE OMITTED
    DATA RECORD IS ACT-OUTPUT.

01  ACT-OUTPUT.
    02  FILLER          PIC X(10).
    02  ACT-NUMBER-2    PIC 9(7).
    02  FILLER          PIC X(4).
    02  NAME-2          PIC X(15).
    02  FILLER          PIC X(6).
    02  AMT-OWING-2     PIC 9(4).99.
    02  FILLER          PIC X(84).
```

Figure 7. COBOL code with FILE SECTION.

FD Entry	Assumed Value When Omitted
BLOCK CONTAINS	1 RECORD
RECORD CONTAINS	Number of characters in the structure
LABEL RECORDS	STANDARD
DATA RECORD	The structure name following the FD

Figure 8. File description defaults.

in Figure 8. According to this summary, the FD used for ACCOUNTS-FILE in Figure 7 could have been written in the following condensed form:

FD ACCOUNTS-FILE

LABEL RECORDS ARE OMITTED.

Structures and Pictures. A structure is a form used to describe the fields of an input or output record. The structure ACT-INPUT in Figure 7 describes the layout of the card file. Each structure begins with a 01 level. This level contains a name, also called an identifier, which represents the entire record. Since this name is followed by higher level numbers, it is called a group item. A group item never contains a PIC, or PICTURE, entry. Rather, it is followed by several higher level entries that contain the PICTURE. These entries are elementary items.

Identifiers such as ACT-INPUT or ACT-NUMBER-1 are chosen by the programmer and may have from 1 to 30 characters. These characters may be numbers, letters, or hyphens. An identifier must contain at least one letter in it and may not begin or end with a hyphen. Any name may be used except for COBOL reserved words. A list of reserved words is shown in Figure 9. When an identifier is not expected to be referenced in the program, such as when it provides for space between two fields, the word FILLER may be used. This word may be used as often as needed.

The PIC clause on an elementary item is used to define the number of characters or digits in a field. This is done by specifying a picture character or characters to describe the exact format of each field. Figure 10 shows the basic picture characters and their meaning.

Picture characters 9, X, and A are written the number of times equal to the number of characters or digits in the field. For instance, a 3-digit number would use PIC 999 where each nine represents one of the digits in the field. This may also be written as PIC 9(3). The three in brackets is a repetition character indicating the number of nines in the picture.

Similarly, a 20-character address that has both alphabetic and numeric characters would use PIC X(20), which is equivalent to writing 20 X's. Although the data for this field may contain alphabetics, the A picture is not used because part of the field is numeric. These picture characters cannot be mixed.

The V is used for numeric fields containing an assumed decimal point. For instance, the number 37465 may actually represent 374.65, but without the decimal point. For this value, PIC 9(3)V99 would be used. The first three 9's represent the digit in front of the decimal. The V

ACCEPT	COPY	GIVING
ACCESS	CORR	GO
ACTUAL	CORRESPONDING	GREATER
ADD	CURRENCY	GROUP
ADDRESS		
ADVANCING	DATA	HEADING
AFTER	DATE-COMPILED	HIGH-VALUE
ALL	DATE-WRITTEN	HIGH-VALUES
ALPHABETIC	DE	
ALTER	DECIMAL-POINT	I-O
ALTERNATE	DECLARATIVES	I-O-CONTROL
AND	DEPENDING	IDENTIFICATION
ARE	DESCENDING	IF
AREA	DETAIL	IN
AREAS	DISPLAY	INDEX
ASCENDING	DIVIDE	INDEXED
ASSIGN	DIVISION	INDICATE
AT	DOWN	INITIATE
AUTHOR		INPUT
	ELSE	INPUT-OUTPUT
BEFORE	END	INSTALLATION
BEGINNING	ENDING	INTO
BLANK	ENTER	INVALID
BLOCK	ENVIRONMENT	IS
BY	EQUAL	
	ERROR	JUST
CALL	EVERY	JUSTIFIED
CF	EXAMINE	
CH	EXIT	KEY
CHARACTERS		
CLOCK-UNITS	FD	LABEL
CLOSE	FILE	LAST
COBOL	FILE-CONTROL	LEADING
CODE	FILE-LIMIT	LEFT
COLUMN	FILE-LIMITS	LESS
COMMA	FILLER	LIMIT
COMP	FINAL	LIMITS
COMPUTATIONAL	FIRST	LINE
COMPUTE	FOOTING	LINE-COUNTER
CONFIGURATION	FOR	LINES
CONTAINS	FROM	LOCK
CONTROL		LOW-VALUE
CONTROLS	GENERATE	LOW-VALUES

Figure 9. COBOL reserved words.

MEMORY	RANDOM	SPACE
MODE	RD	SPACES
MODULES	READ	SPECIAL-NAMES
MOVE	RECORD	STANDARD
MULTIPLE	RECORDS	STATUS
MULTIPLY	REDEFINES	STOP
	REEL	SUBTRACT
NEGATIVE	RELEASE	SUM
NEXT	REMAINDER	SYNC
NO	REMARKS	SYNCHRONIZED
NOT	RENAMES	
NOTE	REPLACING	TALLY
NUMBER	REPORT	TALLYING
NUMERIC	REPORTING	TAPE
	REPORTS	TERMINATE
OBJECT-COMPUTER	RERUN	THAN
OCCURS	RESERVE	THROUGH
OF	RESET	THRU
OFF	RETURN	TIMES
OMITTED	REVERSED	TO
ON	REWIND	TYPE
OPEN	RF	
OPTIONAL	RH	UNIT
OR	RIGHT	UNTIL
OUTPUT	ROUNDED	UP
	RUN	UPON
PAGE		USAGE
PAGE-COUNTER	SAME	USE
PERFORM	SD	USING
PF	SEARCH	
PH	SECTION	VALUE
PIC	SECURITY	VALUES
PICTURE	SEEK	VARYING
PLUS	SEGMENT-LIMIT	
POSITION	SELECT	WHEN
POSITIVE	SENTENCE	WITH
PROCEDURE	SEQUENTIAL	WORDS
PROCEED	SET	WORKING-STORAGE
PROCESSING	SIGN	WRITE
PROGRAM-ID	SIZE	
	SORT	ZERO
QUOTE	SOURCE	ZEROES
QUOTES	SOURCE-COMPUTER	ZEROS

Figure 9. (Continued)

Picture Character	Use
9	Numeric Digit
X	Alphanumeric Character
A	Alphabetic Character
V	Assumed Decimal Position
	Decimal Point (use only for printing)

Figure 10. Picture characters.

indicates the position of the assumed decimal, and then the two 9's represent the two digits following the decimal.

Figure 11 is a record format with a structure describing this record in the Data Division.

Procedure Division

The PROCEDURE DIVISION is the fourth and last division in a COBOL program. It provides the instructions for the computer to execute when solving the problem presented to it. This solution was originally prepared by the programmer in the form of a flowchart or through top down development. Now the instructions are coded in the COBOL language.

Figure 12 shows a PROCEDURE DIVISION for a program that reads an input card and prints a line containing the details found on the card. The identifiers referenced in the procedure are taken from the data division shown in Figure 7.

This program begins by opening the files and reading the initial record from ACCOUNTS-FILE. PERFORM PROCESS UNTIL END-OF-FILE = 1 is a statement that causes the paragraph PROCESS to be executed repetitively until the condition END-OF-FILE = 1 is true. This happens when the last card has been read and processed and an attempt is made to read the next (but nonexistent) card. At this time the files are closed, and the program is terminated at the STOP RUN.

PROCESS is executed once for each record read from ACCOUNTS-FILE. Each field from the record is moved to the print structure. When all fields are in this structure, it is written after advancing the printer 2 lines. The next record is read at the end of PROCESS, and if an end of file has not been encountered, PROCESS will repeat once more and proc-

```
              1-5   Customer Number
              6-20  Name
             21-35  Address
             36-38  Quantity
             39-43  Unit Cost
             44-49  Date
       01  CUSTOMER-RECORD.
           02  CUSTOMER-NUMBER  PIC 9(5).
           02  NAME             PIC X(15).
           02  ADDRESS          PIC X(15).
           02  QUANTITY         PIC 999.
           02  UNIT-COST        PIC 9(3)V99.
           02  DATE,
               03  DAY PIC 99.
               03  MONTH PIC 99.
               03  YEAR PIC 99.
           02  FILLER PIC X(31).
```

Figure 11. Record in Data Division.

ess this record. Now let's look at some of the basic statements used in the COBOL Procedure Division.

Open and Close. At the beginning of each program, an OPEN is used to make each file available for either input or output operations. The OPEN initiates certain technical operations in the operating system such as examination of the file header label for an input file or creating a label

```
PROCEDURE DIVISION.
BEGIN-PROGRAM.
       OPEN INPUT ACCOUNTS-FILE OUTPUT ACT-REPORT.
       READ ACCOUNTS-FILE AT END MOVE 1 TO END-OF FILE.
       PERFORM PROCESS UNTIL END-OF-FILE = 1.
       CLOSE ACCOUNTS-FILE ACT-REPORT.
       STOP RUN.
PROCESS.
       MOVE ACT-NUMBER-1 TO ACT-NUMBER-2.
       MOVE NAME-1 TO NAME-2.
       MOVE AMT-OWING-1 TO AMT-OWING-2.
       WRITE ACT-OUTPUT AFTER ADVANCING 2 LINES.
       READ ACCOUNTS-FILE AT END MOVE 1 TO END-OF-FILE.
```

Figure 12. Example of Procedure Division.

on an output file. A complete discussion of this is beyond the scope of this book. Examples of Opens are as follows:

OPEN OUTPUT PRINT-FILE RECORD-FILE.

OPEN INPUT MASTER TRANSACTION OUTPUT NEW-MASTER.

In the first OPEN, two output files are defined; these must be file names previously used in a SELECT clause and FD. This is true of all file names used in an OPEN or CLOSE statement.

The second OPEN specifies two input files MASTER and TRANSACTION and one output file NEW-MASTER. This same OPEN could have used two statements with identical results.

OPEN INPUT MASTER TRANSACTION.

OPEN OUTPUT NEW-MASTER.

There is no particular advantage in this approach, but some programmers prefer to group all inputs together and all outputs in a separate open statement.

The CLOSE is similar to the OPEN. It is used when a file is no longer needed by the program. The main difference is that no reference is made to input or output. The previous files would be closed as follows:

CLOSE PRINT-FILE RECORD-FILE.

CLOSE MASTER TRANSACTION NEW-MASTER.

Read Statement. A READ is used each time an input record is required from a given file. The READ always references the file named in the FD and causes a record to be transferred from the input device to the structure associated with the FD. Consider the code in Figure 13.
If we have this code in the Data Division and then use this READ in the Procedure Division

READ MASTER AT END MOVE 1 TO END-OF-FILE.

the record from a file called MASTER, probably a disk file, is transferred to the structure called MAST-RECORD. When the READ is finished and control passes to the next statement in the program, the individual fields in MAST-RECORD will each contain data that can now be used by the programmer.

```
FD   MASTER
     LABEL RECORDS ARE STANDARD
     DATA RECORD IS MAST-RECORD.
01   MAST-RECORD.
     02  PART-NUMBER PIC 9(6).
     02  DESCRIPTION PIC X(10).
     02  QUANTITY    PIC 9(5).
```

Figure 13. Transferring a record from the input device.

The AT END clause only takes effect when no more data exist to be read from the file. Until then it is essentially bypassed during the read operation. However, when a READ finally occurs and there is no more data to be read from this file, then the action specified in the AT END is executed. In this example, the value 1 is moved to an identifier called END-OF-FILE. The purpose of this is to indicate to the program that end-of-file has been reached and no more attempts should be made to read this file.

In some cases, more than one action is necessary in the AT END. This is accomplished by not writing the period until after all actions have been specified.

```
READ MASTER AT END MOVE 1 TO END-OF-FILE

                   PERFORM FINAL-TOTALS

                   MOVE ZEROS TO TOTAL-AMOUNT.
```

Write Statement. A major difference between a READ and WRITE is that the READ refers to the file name whereas the WRITE uses the name of the structure in the file description. Secondly, when the WRITE is referring to the printer, it uses the AFTER ADVANCING clause to control the printer carriage. Suppose we use the following file description and structure.

```
FD   PRINTER

     LABEL RECORDS ARE OMITTED

     DATA RECORD IS PRINT-LINE.

01   PRINT-LINE.

     02   PRINT-DETAILS PIC X(133).
```

The WRITE for this code could be

WRITE PRINT-LINE AFTER ADVANCING 2 LINES.

This statement causes the contents of PRINT-LINE to be written on file PRINTER. Prior to printing, the carriage is advanced 2 lines, and the data is printed on the second of these lines, leaving one blank line between this and the previous line printed. If only one line is to be advanced, the following is used:

WRITE PRINT-LINE AFTER ADVANCING 1 LINES.

Notice that the word LINES is still used, which may not be good English, but is good COBOL. A zero value may also be used if the programmer wishes to print again on the same line.

Another option in the AFTER ADVANCING clause is called a mnemonic-name and works with the Configuration Section of the Environment Division. Here we use an entry

C01 IS START-OF-PAGE.

The code C01 is predefined as the carriage control tape punch of 1, which is usually the first line of a page. The mnemonic-name START-OF-PAGE is defined by the programmer and would be used in a WRITE as follows:

WRITE PRINT-LINE AFTER ADVANCING START-OF-PAGE.

This will cause the printer to advance until the control tape mechanism senses the one punch and stops. The line defined in PRINT-LINE will be printed at that point on the page.

A COMPLETE COBOL PROGRAM

Now we will look at a complete COBOL program after we combine the four divisions discussed separately for the Accounts file. This complete program in Figure 14 includes a WORKING-STORAGE SECTION, which is necessary for the variable END-OF-FILE. It contains a value clause, which assigns an initial value to the identifier at the beginning of program execution. The program may subsequently change this value such as when the end-of-file condition occurs.

A second revision to the program are the two statements following the OPEN. The first of these moves spaces to the print line to clear it of

```
IDENTIFICATION DIVISION.
PROGRAM-ID.
    REPORTS
AUTHOR.
    DON CASSEL.
ENVIRONMENT DIVISION.
CONFIGURATION SECTION.
SPECIAL-NAMES.
    C01 IS TO-NEW-PAGE.
INPUT-OUTPUT SECTION.
FILE CONTROL.
    SELECT ACCOUNTS-FILE ASSIGN TO UT-S-CARDS.
    SELECT ACT-REPORT    ASSIGN TO UT-S-PRINTER
DATA DIVISION.
FILE SECTION.
FD  ACCOUNTS-FILE.
    LABEL RECORDS ARE OMITTED.
01  ACT-INPUT.
    02 ACT-NUMBER-1   PIC 9(7).
    02 NAME-1         PIC X(15).
    02 AMT-OWING-1    PIC 9(4)V99.
    02 FILLER         PIC X(52).
FD  ACT-REPORT
    LABEL RECORDS ARE OMITTED.
01  ACT-OUTPUT.
    02 FILLER         PIC X(10).
    02 ACT-NUMBER-2   PIC 9(7).
    02 FILLER         PIC X(4).
    02 NAME-2         PIC X(15).
    02 FILLER         PIC X(6).
    02 AMT-OWING-2    PIC 9(4).99.
    02 FILLER         PIC X(84).
WORKING-STORAGE SECTION.
77  END-OF-FILE       PIC 9 VALUE IS ZERO.
PROCEDURE DIVISION.
BEGIN-PROGRAM.
    OPEN INPUT ACCOUNTS-FILE OUTPUT ACT-REPORT.
    MOVE SPACES TO ACT-OUTPUT.
    WRITE ACT-OUTPUT AFTER ADVANCING TO-NEW-PAGE.
    READ ACCOUNTS-FILE AT END MOVE 1 TO END-OF-FILE.
    PERFORM PROCESS UNTIL END-OF-FILE = 1.
    CLOSE ACCOUNTS-FILE ACT-REPORT.
    STOP RUN.
```

Figure 14. Complete COBOL program.

PROCESS.
    MOVE ACT-NUMBER-1 TO ACT-NUMBER-2.
    MOVE NAME-1 TO NAME-2.
    MOVE AMT-OWING-1 TO AMT-OWING-2.
    WRITE ACT-OUTPUT AFTER ADVANCING 2 LINES.
    READ ACCOUNTS-FILE AT END MOVE 1 TO END-OF-FILE.

Figure 14. (Continued)

any extraneous characters. This blank line is then printed at the top of a new page to ensure that the following data begins on a new page. This concept will be discussed more fully in the next section of this chapter.

PROGRAMMING PROBLEMS

1. Write a program to read your name, address, and student number (or Social Security Number) from a card and print them on the printer.
2. Read a series of cards in the following format containing information relating to your courses:

        1–7   Course Number
        8–49 Name of Course
        50–69 Instructor

Print these cards one per line beginning at the top of a new page. Leave one space between each line. Leave 5 spaces between each field on the line.

WORKING-STORAGE

Most programs require more than input and output. They also do arithmetic operations on the data as well as prepare data for output by editing fields with decimal points, commas, dollar signs, and so on. In addition to this, headings are prepared for reports to give a more readable form to the output and create a more pleasing appearance. All of these activities make use of the WORKING-STORAGE SECTION. On the next few pages we will look at a number of the features of WORKING-STORAGE.

77 Items

Sometimes called independent items, these are identifiers that exist on their own in the program. They are not directly related to other variables, such as fields in the same structure are related. A 77 item can be used for the result of an arithmetic operation, such as creating a total, or it can be used as an indicator, such as we used for end-of-file in an earlier program. Here are some examples.

    77 GROSS-TOTAL   PIC 9(5)V99 VALUE IS ZERO.

    77 TAX-RATE   PIC V99   VALUE IS .07.

    77 DESCRIPTION   PIC X(10) VALUE IS 'CALCULATOR'.

In each case, 77's always appear in margin A and are the first items to be found in WORKING-STORAGE. Both numeric and alphanumeric pictures may be used depending on program requirements. Value clauses may also be used to give a starting value to the variable, although in some cases this is not necessary. Values may be constants such as in TAX-RATE or figurative constants as in GROSS-TOTAL. A figurative constant has a predefined value in COBOL. ZERO, ZEROS, or ZEROES used in a value clause will assign all zero digits to the identifier. SPACES is used for alphanumeric pictures and will assign all spaces (blanks) to the field.

PICTURE Characters

As we have already seen, each identifier at the elementary level in a structure or as a 77 item contains a PICTURE clause. This clause describes the type of contents a field may have. When this data is used for printing, it may not be desirable to print the numbers exactly as they appear in the program. For instance, the entry

    02 NUMBER PIC 9(5).99.

would print a value as

    00003.76

In most cases, we would prefer not to print the leading zeros, which would look like this

    3.76

If this represents a dollar amount, it might be better to print

    $ 3.76

or

    $3.76

All of these results are preferable to the first output we had. To accomplish any of these results requires a PICTURE character or characters to produce the desired format. Figure 15 lists some of the characters available in COBOL. When these characters are used, the picture is intended to be used for printing. It cannot be used in arithmetic operations—a common misunderstanding among beginning programmers. The editing of the data occurs when the data is moved to the edit picture from a source picture. For example, if we have the following:

    02 AMOUNT PIC 9(5)V99.

which contains the value

    0002340

and this field is moved to

    02 PRINT-AMOUNT PIC $Z(5).99.

with the statement

    MOVE AMOUNT TO PRINT-AMOUNT.

the result in PRINT-AMOUNT is

    $ 23.40

If calculations are necessary with this value, they must be done using the field AMOUNT. The purpose of PRINT-AMOUNT is only for printing and should be considered the final destination of the amount. Figure 16 shows how the picture characters work for a variety of data in a COBOL program.

PICTURE Character	PURPOSE
Z	Zero Suppression
$	Insert Leading Dollar Sign
$	Floating Dollar Sign
S	Numeric Sign
,	Comma Insert
−	Minus for Negative Values
+	Sign for Positive and Negative
CR	Credit
DB	Debit
*	Floating Check Protection
B	Blank Insert

Figure 15. Editing PICTURE characters.

ACCOUNT	NAME	AMOUNT OWING
230 6386	J.J. SMITH	$ 12.75
230 7398	K.L. BRIGHT	$345.90

Sending Field		Receiving Field	
Picture	Data	Picture	Data
9(5)	00012	Z(5)	12
9(5)	10000	Z(5)	10000
9(4)V99	001234	$Z(4).99	$ 12.34
9(4)V99	001234	$(5).99	$12.34
9(4)V99	000005	$(5).99	$.05
9(6)V99	00123456	$,$$$.$$$.99	1,234.56
9(6)V99	12345678	$,$$$,$$$.99	$123,456.78
S999	−123	−ZZZ	−123
S999	+123	−ZZZ	123
S999	−123	+ZZZ	−123
S999	+123	+ZZZ	+123
S9(5)V99	−0012345	***,***CR	****123.45CR
S9(5)V99	+1234567	***,***CR	*12,345.67
S9(5)V99	−0012345	***,***DB	****123.45DB
S9(5)V99	+1234567	***,***DB	*12,345.67
9(6)	141278	99B99B99	14 12 78

Figure 16. How picture characters work.

Print Structures

The program in Figure 14 printed lines of output without editing the data and without headings. This does not result in a very pleasing appearance. Rather, it would be difficult to read, and possibly it would cause the reader to misinterpret the results. This is improved if the following type of output is produced:

ACCOUNT	NAME	AMOUNT OWING
230 6386	J.J. SMITH	$ 12.75
230 7398	K.L. BRIGHT	$ 345.90

Two structures are required to produce these lines. One for the heading, which uses value clauses to set up the information, and a second for the detail line, which receives its data from MOVE statements in the Procedure Division. These two structures are shown in Figure 17, which contains the WORKING-STORAGE SECTION.

In both structures, FILLER's with VALUE SPACES are used between each field to ensure no garbage characters are present when printing the line. FILLER's are also used in HEADING-LINE for each heading item. This is possible since the data is supplied from the VALUE clause, and there is no need to reference the individual fields in the program.

```
WORKING-STORAGE SECTION.
    01  HEADING-LINE.
        02 FILLER          PIC X(6)  VALUE SPACES.
        02 FILLER          PIC X(7)  VALUE 'ACCOUNT'.
        02 FILLER          PIC X(14) VALUE SPACES.
        02 FILLER          PIC X(4)  VALUE 'NAME'
        02 FILLER          PIC X(12) VALUE SPACES.
        02 FILLER          PIC X(12) VALUE 'AMOUNT OWING'.
        02 FILLER          PIC X(82) VALUE SPACES.
    01  DETAIL-LINE.
        02 FILLER          PIC X(5)  VALUE SPACES.
        02 D-ACCOUNT       PIC 999B9999.
        02 FILLER          PIC X(10) VALUE SPACES.
        02 D-NAME          PIC X(15).
        02 FILLER          PIC X(5)  VALUE SPACES.
        02 D-AMOUNT        PIC $Z(4).99.
        02 FILLER          PIC X(81) VALUE SPACES.
```

Figure 17. Print structures in WORKING-STORAGE section.

When print structures are created in this way we handle the FD and WRITE statement differently from previous programs. For these two structures the FD would appear as follows:

```
FD   ACT-REPORT
     LABEL RECORDS ARE OMITTED.
01 ACT-OUTPUT.
   02 FILLER   PIC X(133).
```

The structure for this FD requires no detail since this has been defined in the WORKING-STORAGE. To WRITE from the heading structure, the following format is used in the WRITE statement:

```
WRITE ACT-OUTPUT FROM HEADING-LINE AFTER ADVANCING TO-NEW-PAGE.
```

The FROM clause has been added to the statement to allow writing from data in WORKING-STORAGE. Similarly the detail is written in this statement:

```
WRITE ACT-OUTPUT FROM DETAIL-LINE AFTER ADVANCING 2 LINES.
```

In this case, it is essential that data be moved to the fields D-ACCOUNT, D-NAME, and D-AMOUNT prior to writing the structure. Usually these moves immediately precede the WRITE statement and are used to transfer the data from an input structure to the structure used for printing.

PROGRAMMING PROBLEMS

1. Write a program to read a number of the following Product Summary Cards.

1–7	Product Number
8–14	Material Cost (3 decimal)
15–21	Labor Cost (2 decimal)
22–27	Overhead Cost (2 decimal)

    Produce a report in the format shown. Be certain to have the headings and detail align as indicated in the diagram. Test the program using a variety of values to ensure that the pictures produce the correct output.

Product Cost Summary

Product Number	Material Cost	Labor Cost	Overhead Cost
2361075	375.089	58.12	56.75
3679274	1,200.658	635.00	85.01
3875946	43.618	7.89	15.44

2. The economic order quantity for a part is given by the formula:

$$\text{EOQ} = \sqrt{\frac{2dc}{us}}$$

where

    d is the demand in units
    c is the cost of placing an order
    u is the unit cost of the part
    s is the cost of storing the item in stock

Write a program to calculate EOQ using this input format:

    1–3   Demand
    4–7   Order Cost
    8–12   Unit Cost
    13–16   Storage Cost

Print this output format:

DEMAND	ORDER COST	UNIT COST	STORAGE COST	EOQ
XXX	XX.XX	XXX.XX	XX.XX	XXX

The economic order quantity may be calculated in the COBOL Procedure Division using a statement of the form:

```
COMPUTE EOQ = ((2 * DEMAND * COST) / (UNIT * STORAGE))
** 0.5.
```

MORE ON THE PROCEDURE DIVISION

MOVE Statement

The MOVE takes data from a source field and moves it to a receiving field. Certain operations such as decimal alignment and editing may be done as a result of the move, depending on the type of pictures found in the fields involved. The number of rules relating to the MOVE are extensive, yet with a few of them the statement can be used quite successfully for a large variety of applications.

An informal rule to begin is to move only like pictures. Picture A to picture A, X to X, and 9 to 9 (or edited picture). This simple practice will avoid many of the pitfalls often faced by the beginning programmer. Consider the following:

```
77   A PIC A(5) VALUE 'COBOL'.
77   B PIC A(4).
77   C PIC A(6).
77   D PIC 999V99 VALUE 235.65.
77   E PIC 99V999.
77   F PIC 9999V9.
```

Move Statement	Result in Receiving Field
MOVE A TO B.	'COBO'
MOVE A TO C.	'COBOL'
MOVE D TO E.	35.650
MOVE D TO F.	0235.6

The first move takes A, a 5-byte field, and moves it to B, a 4-byte field. When the receiving field is shorter in a picture A, the data is left-justified and truncated on the right. In this case, the L is dropped.

Moving the same data to a longer field B causes an extra space to be appended to the right. The data is also left-adjusted in the field as a result of the move. The same rules discussed here apply to picture X fields. It is also possible to move data from a picture A to picture X since all alphabetic data are compatible with alphanumeric.

The moving of numeric data is demonstrated in the last two examples. When D is moved to E, the decimal positions are aligned according to the position of the V in the pictures. The digits of the field are moved to the digit positions on either side of the decimal point. E has only two digit positions on the left of the V while D had three. This causes the leading digit of D to be truncated. The three digits to the right of the decimal in E receive 650, containing the extra zero.

Moving to F gives an extra zero to the leftmost position of the field. To the right of the decimal, only one digit is moved, truncating the 5 digit.

Numeric pictures may be moved to edited pictures as we have already seen. Using the picture

    77   G PIC $ZZZ.ZZ.

would be valid for the move

    MOVE D TO G.

However, it would be incorrect to move G to any other field. An edited picture should be considered a final destination of the data.

Arithmetic Operations

Almost every program written in COBOL will require that some arithmetic be done to solve the problem. In most business applications this will not necessarily be complex but will use only the four basic arithmetic operations. There are two methods used for calculations in COBOL. One uses the ADD, SUBTRACT, MULTIPLY, and DIVIDE statements. The other method provides for all four operations plus exponentiation to be done in a single COMPUTE statement.

ADD Statement. The ADD causes two or more numbers to be added together with the result stored in place of one of the numbers or in a separate field. The following data will be used to demonstrate several formats of the ADD statement.

    77   A PIC 99 VALUE 12.
    77   B PIC 99 VALUE 5.
    77   C PIC 9V9 VALUE 2.7.
    77   D PIC 999V9 VALUE 0.

To add the contents of two fields, we could use the statement

    ADD A TO B.

This causes the 12 in A to be added to the 5 in B. The result 17 will be stored in B. If B's value is to be retained, the statement

    ADD A B GIVING D.

would give the same result except that the result is stored in D, and the 5 in B is intact. Here are some more examples showing the result after each operation.

Add Statement	Field	Result
ADD A B C GIVING D.	D	019.7
ADD B TO C.	C	7.7
ADD C TO D.	D	2.7
ADD 1 TO B.	B	6
ADD 25 B GIVING D.	D	30

SUBTRACT Statement. The SUBTRACT functions much like the ADD. It also has the two formats with or without the GIVING clause. Here are some examples of the subtract using the same values of A, B, C, and D defined in the previous section.

Subtract Statement	Field	Result
SUBTRACT B FROM A.	A	7
SUBTRACT 2 B FROM A.	A	5
SUBTRACT B FROM A GIVING D.	D	7
SUBTRACT A FROM 20 GIVING B.	B	8
SUBTRACT C FROM B GIVING D.	D	2.3

MULTIPLY Statement. The MULTIPLY follows quite naturally from the two previous arithmetic operations. Again two formats may be used. In the case of the MULTIPLY, the most common use is with the GIVING clause.

Multiply Statement	Field	Result
MULTIPLY A BY B.	B	60
MULTIPLY B BY C GIVING D.	D	13.5
MULTIPLY A BY 1.5 GIVING D.	D	18

The normal rules of mathematics apply to the MULTIPLY as well as to all arithmetic operations. A negative value multiplied by a positive will result in a negative result. In this case, a sign must be provided in the picture for the result field. Multiplying a number with 2 decimals by a number with 3 decimals results in an answer with 5 decimal positions. It is important that the result picture provide adequate space or truncation will occur.

DIVIDE Statement. The fourth arithmetic statement uses the usual rules of mathematics to divide one number into another. A separate option allows the remainder to be stored.

Divide Statement	Field	Result	Remainder
DIVIDE 2 INTO A.	A	6	
DIVIDE B INTO A GIVING D.	D	2.4	
DIVIDE B INTO A GIVING D REMAINDER E.	D	2.4	2
DIVIDE C INTO B GIVING D.	D	1.8	

COMPUTE Statement. The COMPUTE combines all of the operations of the previous statements into one. It does this with an arithmetic expression that is similar in concept to an algebraic expression. This expression uses symbols to represent the various arithmetic operations as shown

Operator	Use
+	Addition
−	Subtraction
*	Multiplication
/	Division
**	Exponentiation

These operators may be combined to represent any arithmetic statement or a combination of statements.

COMPUTE A = A + B.

This has the effect of adding the contents of field A to B.

COMPUTE A = N + 1.

This statement adds the value of N and 1 together placing the result in A.

COMPUTE B = C * D.
COMPUTE B = C * D + 55.

In this example, there are two operations necessary. COBOL uses a priority rule to determine which operation occurs first. This says that exponentiation comes first, multiplication and division next, and then addition and subtraction. In this example, C is multiplied by D, and then 55 is added to the result. This order may be changed by the use of brackets as follows:

COMPUTE B = C * (D + 55).

In this case, addition will go first followed by multiplication.

PERFORM Statement. The PERFORM is used in COBOL to aid in program organization and to permit sections or paragraphs of code to be executed repetitively without the need to write the code each time it is needed. There are several types of performs available. We will look at two of them here.

The most basic type of perform statement simply passes control to a paragraph, executes that paragraph, and then returns to the statement following the PERFORM. Consider these statements:

PERFORM HEADING.
———————
———————

HEADING.
———————
———————
———————

When the statement PERFORM HEADING is encountered during program execution, control is transferred unconditionally to the paragraph HEADING. Each statement in HEADING is executed until the end of the paragraph is reached. Control then returns to the statement following the perform. Another type of perform is the PERFORM UNTIL. This is a conditional statement that analyzes a condition clause before the paragraph named is performed. If the condition is false, the paragraph is performed until the condition becomes true. For example:

PERFORM READ-ROUTINE UNTIL NO-MORE = 1.
———————

READ-ROUTINE.
———————
———————
———————

When the PERFORM UNTIL is encountered, the condition NO-MORE = 1 is evaluated. If NO-MORE is not equal to one, then READ-

Symbolic Form	Descriptive Form
=	IS EQUAL TO
NOT =	IS NOT EQUAL TO
>	IS GREATER THAN
NOT >	IS NOT GREATER THAN
<	IS LESS THAN
NOT <	IS NOT LESS THAN

Figure 18. Conditional operators.

ROUTINE is executed. When the end of the paragraph is reached, the condition is again evaluated. If it is still false, READ-ROUTINE is executed again. This process continues until an evaluation is true. At this point, control continues at the statement following the perform.

Figure 18 shows the condition operators available in COBOL. These may be used in the PERFORM UNTIL as well as the IF statement to be discussed later. Each operator has a symbolic form as well as a descriptive one. Either may be used and is a matter of programmer preference.

Here are some more examples of PERFORM UNTIL statements with various conditions:

```
PERFORM CALCULATIONS UNTIL AMOUNT > 100.00.
PERFORM LINE-SPACE UNTIL COUNT NOT > 10.
PERFORM CHECK UNTIL ACCOUNT NOT = 2346539.
```

Payroll Program. Now let's apply these statements to a practical payroll problem in COBOL. For this program, cards are read indicating the number of hours worked each day for each employee. Also included are Saturday hours, which are paid overtime at 1½ times the regular rate. This is the card format:

```
1–20   Name
21–22  Monday Hours
23–24  Tuesday Hours
25–26  Wednesday Hours
27–28  Thursday Hours
29–30  Friday Hours
31–32  Saturday Hours
33–36  Rate Per Hour
```

A report is to be produced for these cards that summarizes the data in the following way:

Name	Overtime Hours	Regular Rate	Overtime Rate	Overtime Rate	Gross Salary
TOM BROWN	37	5	4.00	6.00	178.00
JANE SMITH	35	3	4.25	6.37	167.86
			TOTAL GROSS		345.86

The COBOL program for this output is shown in Figure 19. It can read an undetermined number of cards and print them, followed by a total of the Gross Salaries. WORKING-STORAGE is used extensively in this program both for the four print structures and a number of 77 items for the results of calculations done in the procedure division.

```
IDENTIFICATION DIVISION.
PROGRAM-ID.
      PAYROLL.
AUTHOR.
      DON CASSEL.
ENVIRONMENT DIVISION.
CONFIGURATION SECTION.
SPECIAL-NAMES.
      C01 IS TO-FIRST-LINE
INPUT-OUTPUT SECTION.
FILE-CONTROL.
      SELECT HOURS-CARD     ASSIGN TO UT-S-CARDS.
      SELECT PAYROLL-REPORT ASSIGN TO UT-S-PRINTER.
DATA DIVISION.
FILE SECTION.
FD    HOURS-CARD
      LABEL RECORDS ARE OMITTED.
01    HOURS-RECORD.
      02 NAME-1      PIC X(20)
      02 MON         PIC 99.
      02 TUES        PIC 99.
      02 WED         PIC 99.
```

Figure 19. Payroll report.

```
            02 THUR        PIC 99.
            02 FRI         PIC 99.
            02 SAT         PIC 99.
            02 RATE        PIC 99V99.
            02 FILLER      PIC X(44).
    FD  PAYROLL-REPORT.
        LABEL RECORDS ARE OMITTED.
    01  PRINT-LINE.
            02 FILLER      PIC X(133).
    WORKING-STORAGE SECTION.
    77  END-OF-FILE    PIC 9 VALUE 0.
    77  TOTAL-HOURS    PIC 999.
    77  REGULAR-AMT    PIC 999V99.
    77  OVERTIME-RATE  PIC 99V99.
    77  OVERTIME-AMT   PIC 999V99.
    77  GROSS          PIC 9(4)V99.
    77  TOTAL-GROSS    PIC 9(5)V99 VALUE ZERO.
    01  HEAD-1.
        02    FILLER PIC X(18) VALUE SPACES.
        02    FILLER PIC X(29) VALUE 'HOURS     OVERTIME
              REGULAR'
        02    FILLER PIC X(86) VALUE 'OVERTIME     GROSS'.
    01  HEAD-2.
        02    FILLER PIC X(38) VALUE 'NAME    WORKED'.
        02    FILLER PIC X(95) VALUE 'HOURS    RATE    RATE
              SALARY'.
    01  DETAIL-LINE.
        02    FILLER PIC X.
        02    NAME-2 PIC X(20).
        02    FILLER PIC X(8) VALUE SPACES.
        02    HOURS PIC ZZ9.
        02    FILLER PIC X(7) VALUE SPACES.
        02    OVERTIME-HOURS PIC Z9.
        02    FILLER PIC X(7) VALUE SPACES.
        02    RATE-2 PIC ZZ.99.
        02    FILLER PIC X(6) VALUE SPACES.
        02    OVERTIME-RATE-2 PIC ZZ.99.
        02    FILLER PIC X(4) VALUE SPACES.
        02    GROSS-2 PIC Z(4).99.
        02    FILLER PIC X(58) VALUE SPACES.
    01  TOTAL-LINE.
        02    FILLER PIC X(37) VALUE SPACES.
        02    FILLER PIC X(18) VALUE 'TOTAL GROSS'.
```

Figure 19. (Continued)

```
        02   TOTAL-GROSS-2 PIC ZZ,ZZZ.99.
        02   FILLER PIC X(69) VALUE SPACES.
PROCEDURE DIVISION.
TOP-LEVEL-LOGIC.
     OPEN INPUT HOURS-CARD, OUTPUT PAYROLL-REPORT.
     PERFORM HEADINGS.
     READ HOURS-CARD AT END MOVE 1 TO END-OF-FILE.
     PERFORM PROCESS UNTIL END-OF-FILE = 1.
     PERFORM PRINT-TOTAL.
     CLOSE HOURS-CARD PAYROLL-REPORT.
     STOP RUN.
HEADINGS.
     WRITE PRINT-LINE FROM HEAD-1 AFTER ADVANCING
     TO-FIRST-LINE.
     WRITE PRINT-LINE FROM HEAD-2 AFTER ADVANCING 1 LINES.
     MOVE SPACES TO PRINT-LINE.
     WRITE PRINT-LINE AFTER ADVANCING 2 LINES.
PROCESS.
     COMPUTE TOTAL-HOURS = MON + TUES + WED + THUR + FRI.
     MULTIPLY TOTAL-HOURS BY RATE GIVING REGULAR-AMOUNT.
     MULTIPLY RATE BY 1.5 GIVING OVERTIME-RATE.
     MULTIPLY SAT BY OVERTIME-RATE GIVING OVERTIME-AMT.
     COMPUTE GROSS = REGULAR-AMT + OVERTIME-AMT.
     ADD GROSS TO TOTAL-GROSS.
     MOVE NAME-1 TO NAME-2.
     MOVE TOTAL-HOURS TO HOURS.
     MOVE SAT TO OVERTIME-HOURS.
     MOVE RATE TO RATE-2.
     MOVE OVERTIME-RATE TO OVERTIME-RATE-2.
     MOVE GROSS TO GROSS-2.
     WRITE PRINT-LINE FROM DETAIL-LINE AFTER ADVANCING 1 LINES.
     READ HOURS-CARD AT END MOVE 1 TO END-OF-FILE.
PRINT-TOTAL.
     MOVE TOTAL-GROSS TO TOTAL-GROSS-2.
     WRITE PRINT-LINE FROM TOTAL-LINE AFTER ADVANCING 2 LINES.
```

Figure 19. (Continued)

Top down development was used to organize the logic for the program. This is evident upon examination of the procedure division. It begins with TOP-LEVEL-LOGIC, which controls the activities of all subsequent paragraphs. Both types of Performs discussed previously have been included to contribute to program modularity. Although HEADING and PRINT-TOTAL could have been written without separate paragraphs by including these statements in TOP-LEVEL-LOGIC, the program is much easier to read by using the separate paragraphs.

IF Statement

One of the most useful statements in COBOL is the IF statement. This statement lets the programmer make decisions and select alternate actions based on the result of the decision. Here is the general format of the IF:

```
IF   condition
        statement-1
ELSE
        statement-2.
```

The IF may be used with or without the ELSE portion depending on the needs of the program. The condition is the same as that described for the PERFORM UNTIL statement. The following are some possible IF statements:

```
IF TOTAL IS GREATER THAN 100
    MOVE AMOUNT TO AMOUNT-P.
IF CODE = 15
    ADD QUANTITY TO TOT-QUANTITY.
IF NAME NOT = 'JONES'
    ADD 1 TO NAME-COUNT.
```

In each of these cases, one action is taken if the condition specified is true. If it is false, execution continues at the statement following the period. Several actions may also be listed in the statement.

```
IF HOURS IS GREATER THAN 37.5
    ADD HOURS TO TOTAL-HOURS
    COMPUTE OVERTIME = HOURS - 37.5
    COMPUTE PAY = (OVERTIME * 1.5 + 37.5) * RATE.
```

In this example, all three actions will be taken consecutively if the condition is true. If it is false, all three actions will be bypassed and execution will continue after the period.

Another form of the IF uses the ELSE clause. This is necessary when there is a choice between two different actions or groups of actions.

```
IF AGE IS LESS THAN 65
    PERFORM EMPLOYED-CATEGORY
ELSE
    PERFORM RETIRED-CATEGORY.
```

In this case, the first action PERFORM EMPLOYED-CATEGORY is executed when AGE is less than 65. In this situation the ELSE is bypassed, and execution continues after the period. If AGE is greater than or equal to 65, only the ELSE action is taken.

For a final example, let's consider a case where data is being read that contains an item number (ITEM). Each time a new record is read, we want to check to ensure that it is in sequence by the item number. This is done in a performed paragraph called READ-CHECK. This is what it looks like:

```
READ-CHECK.
    READ PART-FILE AT END MOVE 1 TO END-OF-DATA.
    IF ITEM IS LESS THAN PREVIOUS-ITEM
        DISPLAY 'SEQUENCE ERROR IN - ', ITEM
        CLOSE PART-FILE REPORT-FILE
        STOP RUN.
    MOVE ITEM TO PREVIOUS-ITEM.
```

PREVIOUS-ITEM is a 77 item, which is given a value of zero to start. Each time a new item is read that is equal to or greater than the previous, that item is moved to PREVIOUS-ITEM, and then the next one is compared to it. If an item is read that is less than the previous, an error message is displayed, the files are closed, and the program is terminated.

PROGRAMMING PROBLEMS

1. Arnold's Autos accounting department needs a computer program to assist in the preparation of Trial Balances. This is used to verify the ledger balance at month-end. Input on cards is in the format shown consisting of debits and credits. The cards are read and printed to produce a Trial Balance Sheet. A trial balance

is correct if the total debits equal the total credits as indicated on the last output line.

    1   Code '1' Debit
                 '2' Credit
 2–25   Description
26–31   Amount

ARNOLD'S AUTO

TRIAL BALANCE

APRIL 30, 19__

DESCRIPTION	DEBIT	CREDIT
CASH	4,300	
ACCOUNTS RECEIVABLE	1,500	
BUILDING	12,500	
LAND	15,000	
OFFICE EQUIPMENT	5,600	
ACCOUNTS PAYABLE		6,100
ARNOLD BENSON, CAPITAL		32,800
	$38,900	$38,900

2. The Rollins Company requires a program to produce a Balance Sheet showing their assets and liabilities. Cards are available for input showing the following information:

    1   Code '1' Asset
                 '2' Liability
 2–25   Description
26–31   Amount

You are to write the program to read these cards and produce a Balance Sheet with all assets on the left and liabilities on the right. There may not be an equal number of each. At the end of the report, show a total for each column of figures. Your output will look something like this:

```
                    ROLLINS COMPANY
                     BALANCE SHEET
                    NOVEMBER 30, 19__

         ASSETS                        LIABILITIES

  CASH                  7,900    NOTES              17,900
                                 PAYABLE
  ACCOUNTS             11,200    ACCOUNTS            9,800
   RECEIVABLE                    PAYABLE
  BUILDINGS            76,000    OWNER'S            27,300
  LAND                 35,400    EQUITY
  OFFICE               23,200
   EQUIPMENT
                     --------                      --------
                     $153,700                      $55,000
```

3. Read data cards in the following format:

    1–2   Region Number
    3–10   Vendor Number
    11–17 Item Number
    18–30 Description
    31–37 Unit Cost (2 decimal)
    38–44 Quantity

Produce a Vendor Purchase Report in the format shown. There may be any number of cards per vendor, thus page overflow for headings is required. Page numbers begin at 1 for each region.

At the end of each vendor, print a total for all purchases from that vendor. A separate page is required at the end showing a total of each region and an overall total. There are a maximum of 10 regions.

```
              VENDOR PURCHASE REPORT

                                        PAGE 1
           REGION 01           VENDOR NUMBER 43012155

    ITEM                    UNIT                    TOTAL
   NUMBER   DESCRIPTION     COST    QUANTITY         COST
   0367815  CLAMP           1.50      100          150.00
   0428110  BRACKET         2.25       10           22.50
   0739337  FRAME          75.10       20         1502.00
                               VENDOR TOTAL       1674.50
```

Fortran

INTRODUCTION TO FORTRAN

FORTRAN is a highly popular language among educators and the mathematical and scientific communities. The name is taken from FORmula TRANslation—which implies its main use is for programming mathematical formulae. Its relative simplicity has led to a wide variety of uses. This widespread application has been encouraged because virtually every computer manufacturer provides a FORTRAN compiler. The most common compiler is FORTRAN IV. Many schools use either WATFOR, WATFIV, or WATFIV-S, which are high-speed FORTRAN compilers written by the University of Waterloo in Canada.

Sample Program

Figure 1 shows a sample FORTRAN program. This program reads a series of numbers and computes their average. If the data consists of the numbers 78, 65, 83, and 54, the following output is produced:

    THE AVERAGE OF 4. NUMBERS IS 70.0

The numbers are read into the program by the READ statement. Each number is examined for the value 0 in the IF statement, which indicates the end of the series of numbers. Each number read is represented by I

```
C         FIND THE AVERAGE OF N INTEGERS
          REAL N,I
          SUM=0
          N=0
    5     READ (1,10) I
   10     FORMAT (F3.0)
          IF (I.EQ.0) GO TO 100
          SUM=SUM+I
          N=N+1.0
          GO TO 5
  100     AVG=SUM/N
          WRITE (6,101)N,AVG
  101     FORMAT ('THE AVERAGE OF',F4.0,'NUMBERS IS',F5.1)
          STOP
          END
```

Figure 1. Program to compute the average of *n* numbers.

and is added to SUM. The letter N is used to count the number of values read. When all the numbers have been read, their average is calculated at statement 100 by dividing SUM by N and storing the answer in AVG. The following WRITE statement then prints the average and the numbers of values read.

FORTRAN STATEMENT FORMAT

Every statement in the FORTRAN language has a precise format that must be followed carefully if you want to write successful programs. First, there is a general format for all statements. Figure 2 shows this. The remainder of the chapter deals with the format and use of specific FORTRAN statements.

An example of a FORTRAN statement following this general format is:

1	5	6	7	72	73	80
	40		DEDUCT=TAX+HOSP+PENS			

In this example, 40 is the statement number. It may be from 1 to 5 digits and appear anywhere in columns 1 to 5 of the card. Not all statements require a statement number, although FORMAT and CONTINUE statements must have a statement number. Other statements use a statement number only if they are referenced by a GO TO statement.

Columns	Description of Use
1–5	Statement Number
6	Continuation Column
7–72	FORTRAN Statement
73–80	Not Used

Figure 2. Statement format.

The characters beginning in column 7 form the statement, which in this case does an arithmetic calculation.

Here is an example using the continuation column:

```
1    5 6 7                                              72 73 80
     10  FORMAT('THE VOLUME OF A SPHERE IS',
       - 8X,F7.3)
```

In this case, the actual statement would not have exceeded one card but is treated as though this length had occurred. To continue on a second card a hyphen (-) is punched in column 6 of the second card and the statement is continued in column 7.

COMMENT CARDS

For added clarity, it is often useful to include comments in a program. This is done with a comment card. Figure 3 shows the general format of a comment.

The comment card has a C in column 1 followed by alphanumeric characters, which form a descriptive comment. All remaining columns of the card may be used for the comment. Here are some examples:

```
1 2                                                           80
C   THIS PROGRAM COMPUTES STANDARD DEVIATION
C   CALCULATE THE SUM OF 20 NUMBERS
C   TEST FOR SALARY GREATER THAN 13595.99
```

NUMBERS IN FORTRAN

Programming generally uses a lot of numbers to solve problems suitable for computer applications. This is especially true of FORTRAN. In this

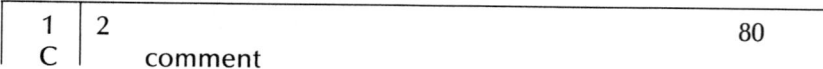

Figure 3. Comment card.

language, numbers fall into two categories—Integer and Real. Also available are Floating Point (an extension of real numbers) and Complex numbers, which are beyond the scope of this book.

Integer Constants

Integers are numbers that do not have a fractional part. They are whole numbers and may be positive or negative. These numbers may be used in FORTRAN statements as constants or may be read from a data card by a READ statement. Some integers are:

$$236 \quad 0 \quad -17 \quad +3785 \quad -13600$$

Real Constants

Real numbers do have a fractional part and may also be positive or negative. They may also be used in the program or read from data cards. Here are some examples:

$$1.5 \quad 2368.01 \quad .001 \quad -123.456 \quad +0.0$$

Mixed Mode

This refers to the mixing of two types of numbers in one expression. A calculation such as

$$35 + 14.7$$

mixes integer and real numbers while

$$10.5 - 5.0$$

does not. In FORTRAN, *mixed mode is not permitted* and if used, will lead to incorrect results in a calculation. The first expression above could be written as

$$35.0 + 14.7$$

By using 35.0, this changes the entire calculation to real and corrects the problem.

Variable Names

Numbers that may change in value during the execution of a program may be represented by variable names. These names may be from 1 to 6 characters in length. Some names may be

   RATE N AMOUNT SUM TOTAL I QUANT

Since there are two types of numbers, there are also two types of variable names. These are determined by the first letter of the name for implicit declaration. This means the name is simply used in the program when required.

Implicit Declaration:

First letter I–N   *integer variable* such as I NUM KOUNT
First letter A–H, O–Z *real variable* such as AMT TOTAL SUM

These statements used implicitly declared variables

```
AMT = 12.75
QTY = 15.0
VALUE = AMT*QTY
ITOT = NUM + ISUM
```

When you want to use a name such as TOTAL for an integer number, it must be explicitly declared. This overrides the first letter rule and lets the programmer choose the use of the name.

Explicit Declaration:

1	5	6	7	72	73	80
			REAL I,LEAST,NUM			
			INTEGER AMOUNT,QTY,TOTAL			

STOP and END Statements

The STOP statement is used to terminate the program when all processing is completed. It is simply the word STOP and begins in column 7.

1	5	6	7	72	73	80
			STOP			

The END statement must be the last statement in every FORTRAN program. It signals the end of the program statements to the FORTRAN compiler. Here is the format:

1	5	6	7	72	73	80
			END			

There may be several STOP statements in a program but only one END as the last statement of the program.

Arithmetic Statements

Calculations are done in FORTRAN with the arithmetic statement. The general format for this is:

nnnnn	variable = expression	

The variable may be any valid variable name used to represent the place where the result of the calculation is to be stored. An expression is a combination of variables, constants, and arithmetic operators to define the calculation required. FORTRAN arithmetic operators are:

      +   Addition
      −   Subtraction
      *   Multiplication
      /   Division
     **   Exponentiation

The hierarchy of operators is the same as most languages. The highest level is parentheses and proceeds as follows:

    ( )
    **
    * /
    + −

The following are some FORTRAN arithmetic statements that might be used in a program. Statements are executed as they are encountered in a program. When they are written with a statement number, they may also be branched to by a GO TO statement from another location in the program.

```
      KOUNT=KOUNT+1
      VOLUME=4.0/3.0*3.1416*RADIUS**2
50    XLEN=(CONST*(WAVE-0.05))/FREQ
```

Area of a Ring Formed between Two Concentric Circles

Now let's write a program using the statements we have learned so far. The problem we want to solve is to find the area of the ring formed between two concentric circles as visualized in Figure 4. This can be solved by finding the area enclosed by each ring and then calculating the difference. Figure 5 shows the FORTRAN program to solve this problem.

The radius r_1 is represented by RAD1 and r_2 by RAD2. They are assigned the values of 12.75 and 7.42, respectively. Next the program calculates the area of the outer circle using the formula πr^2. This uses the names known by the program. In the case of π, the actual value of 3.1416 is used since FORTRAN cannot use the symbol. The area of the outer circle is called AREA1 and the inner circle is calculated and stored in AREA2.

Finally, the area of the ring is computed by assigning to RING the difference between AREA1 and AREA2. The results are printed using the WRITE and FORMAT statements, which have not yet been discussed in this chapter. See the next section. The output of the program is

THE AREA OF THE RING BETWEEN CIRCLES OF RADIUS 12.75 AND 7.42 IS 337.74

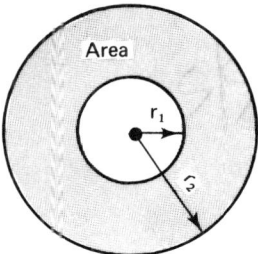

Figure 4. Area of ring formed by two concentric circles.

```
1  2                                                                          80
C  THIS PROGRAM COMPUTES STANDARD DEVIATION
C  CALCULATE THE SUM OF 20 NUMBERS
C  TEST FOR SALARY GREATER THAN 13595.99
```

```
C     CALCULATE AREA OF RING BETWEEN TWO CONCENTRIC CIRCLES
C     ASSIGN VALUES FOR EACH RADIUS
      RAD1 = 12.75
      RAD2 = 7.42
C     CALCULATE THE AREA OF THE OUTER CIRCLE
      AREA1 = 3.1416*RAD1**2
C     CALCULATE THE AREA OF THE INNER CIRCLE
      AREA2 = 3.1416*RAD2**2
C     THE AREA OF THE RING IS THE DIFFERENCE
      RING = AREA1 - AREA2
      WRITE(6,10)RAD1,RAD2,RING
   10 FORMAT ('AREA OF RING BETWEEN CIRCLES OF RADIUS',
     - F5.2,'AND',F5.2,'F7.2)
      STOP
      END
```

Figure 5. Program to compute area of ring.

PROGRAMMING PROBLEMS

1. Write a program to find and print the circumference (CIRC) and the area (AREA) of a circle with radius (RAD) of 4.7. The formulae are

$$c = 2\pi r$$

$$a = \pi r^2$$

Use the following statements to print your results:

```
      WRITE(6,50)RAD,CIRC,AREA
   50 FORMAT('RADIUS = ',F4.1, 'CIRCUMFERENCE = ',F6.2,
     'AREA = ',F6.2)
```

2. The following formula calculates the compound interest for an investment and shows the balance at the end of a time period.

$$b = p\left(1 + \frac{i}{m}\right)^{nm}$$

where

b is the account balance at the end of the period
p is the principal
n is number of years
m is number of times the interest is applied per year
i is the interest rate

Using appropriate names, write a program to compute and print an account balance.

3. The volume of the frustum of a right circular cone may be calculated by the formula

$$V = \frac{h}{3}(A_1 + A_2 + \sqrt{A_1 A_2})$$

Write a program to compute the volume given $r_1 = 5.2$ and $r_2 = 2.9$.

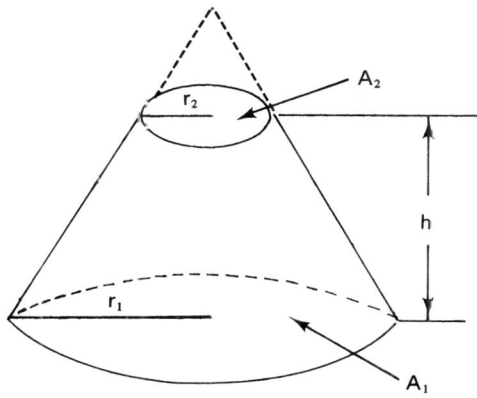

> READ, variable list
> READ n, variable list
> READ(u,n) variable list

Figure 6. READ general formats.

INPUT AND OUTPUT OPERATIONS

Reading Input Data

The programs we have discussed so far have assigned their data internally. Unfortunately, if the data changes, the program must be changed to use the new data. Instead of making continual changes to a program, data is read from an input device such as a card reader.

READ Statement. In FORTRAN, a READ statement is used to access data from an input device. Figure 6 shows the general format for the READ.

The availability of these statements depends on the compiler used. All formats are available with WATFIV. The first is called a format-free read since it makes no reference to the statement number of a format statement. Some examples of this read are:

    READ,NUM,I,AMOUNT
    READ,START

Data read by the format-free READ must be separated by blanks or commas. For example the data card for the first read above might be:

    | 15 267 23.75

Notice that real numbers are punched with the decimal point.

FORMAT Statement. The last two formats in Figure 6 use a format list referenced by a statement number (n) in the READ statement. The format is a statement describing the relative position of each field in the data card. The format for a FORMAT statement and the available format codes are shown in Figure 7.

The format is always used with a read statement in the following way:

            READ 10,NUM,AMOUNT
    10   FORMAT(I5,2X,F4.1)

| | nnnnn FORMAT (format list) | |

Format Code	General Format	Description
I	rIw	r integers each of field width w
F	rFw.d	r real numbers each of width w with a fractional part of d digits
E	rEw.d	floating point numbers
X	wX	w spaces or blank columns
A	rAw	r alphanumeric strings of width w
/	/	used to skip one card

Figure 7. Format statement and codes.

This refers to a card containing an integer of 5 digits called NUM, followed by 2 unused card columns, and then a 4-position real number with one fractional digit called AMOUNT.

The most widely available read format is the third one, which contains a unit number u as well as a format n. All programs in this book use this format of the read. Here is an example:

```
      READ(1,5)I,QTY,PRICE
    5 FORMAT(I3,F2.0,F4.2)
```

The number 1 in the READ refers to the device unit number. In FORTRAN, each input/output device is assigned a number. In my computer, the card reader is 1 and the printer is 6. Your computer system may use different numbers so it is important to find out the correct number.

This read uses format number 5 and reads three values from a card. I is a 3-digit integer, QTY a 2-digit real number with no fractional part, and PRICE a real number of 4 digits with 2 fractional positions. A card for this read may appear as follows:

100151298

The value assigned to I will be 100, to QTY the next two digits 15, and 1298 is understood as 12.98 and is assigned to PRICE.

> PRINT, variable list
> PRINT n, variable list
> WRITE(u,n) variable list

Figure 8. PRINT and WRITE general formats.

Writing Output Data

While the READ is used to read data from an input device, the PRINT and WRITE statements are used to place data on an output device. This device is usually the printer. Figure 8 shows the general formats available in WATFIV.

The first PRINT is format free and only requires a list of the variables to be printed.

    PRINT,I,SUM
    PRINT,FIRST,LAST,TOTAL

The other statements require a format list in a manner similar to the read statement. The formats for the PRINT and WRITE are shown in Figure 9.

> nnnnn FORMAT (format list)

Format Code	General Format	Description
I	rIw	r integers each of width w
F	rFw.d	r real numbers of width w and d fractional digits
E	rEw.d	r floating point numbers of width w and d fractional digits
H	wH	next w characters as a heading
X	wX	w spaces or blank print positions
A	rAw	r alphanumeric string of width w
/	/	advance one line

Figure 9. Format statement and codes for the PRINT and WRITE statements.

Now we can understand the WRITE and FORMAT used in the program in Figure 5. For convenience it is reproduced here.

```
    WRITE(6,10)RAD1,RAD2,RING
10  FORMAT('THE AREA OF THE RING BETWEEN CIRCLES OF
    RADIUS', - F5.2,'AND',F5.2,'IS',F7.2)
```

This WRITE uses device 6 (my printer) and prints three variables; RAD1, RAD2, and RING. Additional control of the printing is provided by the format in statement 10. The first entry of the format is a character string, which provides the title or heading for the data. An alternate way of printing this is:

46H THE AREA OF THE RING BETWEEN CIRCLES OF RADIUS

When the H format is used, the apostrophes are not required around the string. The F format is used for each of the values to be printed. It is important here to consider the entire length of the value to be printed including decimal points and a sign, if the number can be negative. A number like 123.01 would use a format of F6.2 in the FORMAT statement.

Now let's write another program using a READ and WRITE statement.

Area of a Trapezoid

A trapezoid (Figure 10) is a geometric plane with two parallel sides. To find the area of a trapezoid we use the formula

$$a = \frac{h}{2}(b + c)$$

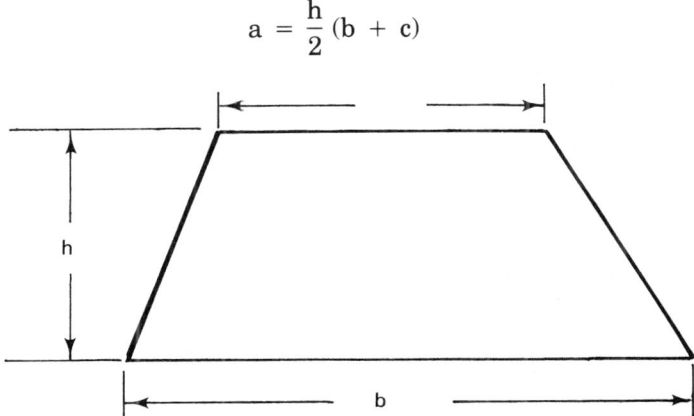

Figure 10. Trapezoid.

Figure 11 shows the FORTRAN program that reads values for H, B, and C and computes the area.

Using a data card containing the following

123171147

gives the following output:

```
THE AREA OF A TRAPEZOID GIVEN
                          H = 12.3
                          B = 17.1
                          C = 14.7
                          IS 195.6
```

Note in Figure 11 the use of the slash (/) to produce separate lines of output rather than one line.

CONTROL STATEMENTS

These statements are used in programming to allow for branching and decision making. With these additional capabilities, a programmer can solve a large variety of programming problems.

GO TO Statement

The most basic of these is the GO TO statement. Figure 12 shows the general format.

```
      C   FIND THE AREA OF A TRAPEZOID GIVEN H, B AND C
      C   WHERE H IS THE HEIGHT
              B IS THE LENGTH OF ONE PARALLEL SIDE
              C IS THE LENGTH OF THE OTHER PARALLEL SIDE
          READ(1,5)H,B,C
        5 FORMAT(3F3·1)
          AREA = H/2.0*(B + C)
          WRITE(6,10)H,B,C,AREA
       10 FORMAT('THE AREA OF A TRAPEZOID GIVEN',/
         -,26X,'H = ',F4.1,/,26X,
         - B = ',F4.1,/,26X,'C = ',F4.1,/,26X,'IS',F6.1)
          STOP
          END
```

Figure 11. Program to calculate the area of a trapezoid.

```
                ┌─────────────┐
                │   GO TO n   │
                └─────────────┘
```

Figure 12. GO TO general format.

This is called the unconditional GO TO because whenever it is encountered in the program, logic branching to statement n occurs immediately. Some examples are:

    GO TO 10
    GO TO 150

A GO TO may branch ahead in the program or back to an earlier statement. For example, the following program, which sums a set of numbers, uses both cases.

```
         SUM=0.0
    10   READ(1,15) VALUE
    15   FORMAT(F5.2)
         IF VALUE.EQ.0.0 GO TO 40
         SUM=SUM+VALUE
         GO TO 10
    40   WRITE(6,45)SUM
    45   FORMAT('THE SUM IS',F7.2)
         STOP
         END
```

Arithmetic IF Statement

The arithmetic IF allows the program to branch to one of three locations depending on whether an expression evaluates negative, zero, or positive. Figure 13 shows the general format and an explanation of the component parts.

Let's look at some examples:

    IF NUM 20,30,40

In this statement, if NUM contains a negative value, the program branches to statement number 20. If NUM is 0, branching goes to statement 30 and if greater than zero, to statement 40.

    IF AMT-SUM 10,150,330

```
IF e n₁,n₂,n₃
```

    e   represents an arithmetic expression or variable
    n_1 is the statement number branched to if the expression evaluates negative
    n_2 branches here if expression is zero
    n_3 branches here if expression is positive

Figure 13. IF general format.

In this case, a subtraction is done first, and then the result is evaluated. A negative answer causes branching to 10. If AMT and SUM are the same value, the result is zero and the program branches to 150. Otherwise it goes to 330. Here are a few more examples:

```
IF A+B*2    40,40,200
IF 100-T    30,70,30
IF CODE-2   90,50,50
```

Logical IF Statement

This form of the IF uses a logical expression that is evaluated for either true or false. Using a logical expression is often preferred by programmers since it states more explicitly the condition being examined. Figure 14 shows the general format for the IF. The types of logical expressions available in FORTRAN are shown in Figure 15.

Combining this information, we can use the logical IF with some of the following expressions and actions.

```
IF (SALARY.GE.250.00) TAX=0.27*SALARY
IF (CODE.EQ.1) GO TO 250
IF (LAST.GT.99) PRINT, 'LAST CARD'
IF (NUM.LT.IPREV) GO TO 1000
```

Tax Program. The program in Figure 16 demonstrates the use of the IF statement for determining income tax. This simplified tax program

> IF (logical-expression) action-if-true
> next-statement

logical-expression   This expression is evaluated for true or false. If true, the action-if-true is taken. If false, the program continues at the next-statement.

Action-if-true   May be any FORTRAN statement except IF, FORMAT, and END. Usually a GO TO or arithmetic statement is used.

Figure 14. Logical IF general format.

applies to taxable incomes in the range $10,000.00 to $34,000.00 based on the following schedule:

	up to		tax rate is	
		12,700.00		23%
		15,500.00		25%
		19,500.00		28%
		34,000.00		32%

The program reads cards containing Social Insurance Number, Taxable Income, and Tax Paid previously by payroll deduction. First the taxable income is checked to ensure it is in the correct range. If not, a branch is taken to statement 70 to where an error message is printed. Then each tax category is tested and the appropriate amount calculated and stored in TAX. Following this, the program continues at statement

Logical Operator	Logical Expression	Description
.EQ.	(N.EQ.1.0)	N is Equal to 1.0
.NE.	(A.NE.B)	A is not Equal to B
.LT.	(C.LT.D)	C is Less Than D
.LE.	(N.LE.100)	N is Less than or Equal to 100
.GT.	(S.GT.T)	S is Greater Than T
.GE.	(K.GE.L)	K is Greater than or Equal to L

Figure 15. Logical expressions.

```
      INTEGER SOC
    5 READ(1,10,END=99)SOC,TAXBLE,TPAID
   10 FORMAT (I9,F7.2,F6.2)
C  CHECK FOR PROPER RANGE OF TAXABLE INCOME
      IF (TAXBLE.LT.10000.00) GO TO 70
      IF (TAXBLE.GT.34000.00) GO TO 70
C  CALCULATE TAX AMOUNT
      IF (TAXBLE.GT.12700.00) GO TO 20
      TAX=TAXBLE*0.23)
      GO TO 50
   20 IF(TAXBLE.GT.15600.00) GO TO 30
      TAX=TAXBLE*0.25
      GO TO 50
   30 IF(TAXBLE.GT.19800.00) GO TO 40
      TAX=TAXBLE*0.28
      GO TO 50
   40 TAX=TAXBLE*0.32
   50 OWING=TPAID-TAX
      IF(OWING.GT.0.0) GO TO 65
   55 OWING=-OWING
      WRITE(6,56)SOC,TAXBLE,TPAID,TAX,OWING
   56 FORMAT(I9,2X,F8.2,2X,F7.2,2X,F7.2,2X,'YOU MUST STILL PAY'F7.2)
      GO TO 5
   65 WRITE(6,66)SOC,TAXBLE,TPAID,TAX,OWING
   66 FORMAT(I9,2X,F8.2,2X,F7.2,2X,F7.2,2X,'YOU ARE OVERPAID BY 'F7.2)
      GO TO 5
   70 WRITE(6,71)SOC,TAXBLE
   71 FORMAT(I9,2X,F8.2,2X,'TAXABLE INCOME EXCEEDS RANGE')
      GO TO 5
   99 STOP
      END
```

Figure 16. Tax program.

50 where the amount owed is determined. Positive amounts represent an overpayment, which are printed at statement 65. Negative amounts are made positive in statement 55 and printed in the following write as an amount still to be paid. In each case, the program goes back to statement 5 where the next card is read.

DO Statement

Many programs use logic that is iterative or repetitive in nature. Although this may be accomplished with arithmetic and IF statements, it

```
            DO n    i=m₁,m₂,m₃
                   .
                   .
                   .
     n      CONTINUE
```

n   defines the range of the DO and is the statement number of the CONTINUE.
i   is the variable used to control the looping of the DO statement
m_1 is the starting value of i
m_2 is the terminating value of i
m_3 is the increment by which i is increased after each pass through the loop. If it is not included it is assumed to be one.

Figure 17. DO general format.

is made much easier with the DO statement. The DO groups any numbers of statements together between the DO and a CONTINUE statement. These statements will be executed a number of times determined by the values given in the DO. Figure 17 shows the general format.

The following DO demonstrates how to find the sum of all positive integers from 1 to 100.

```
        DO 10 I = 1,100,1
           ISUM = ISUM + I
     10 CONTINUE
```

This starts I at 1 and causes I to be added to ISUM. At statement 10, I will be increased by 1 and checked to see if 100 has been exceeded. If not, the program loops back to the DO and 2 is now added to ISUM. This continues until all 100 values in I have been added to ISUM. At this time the loop is finished and processing continues after statement 10.

The next example shows how to print all of the even integers from 2 to 50.

```
        DO 30 N = 2,50,2
           WRITE(6,25)N
     25    FORMAT(3X,I2)
     30 CONTINUE
```

```
C   READ NO. OF YEARS, MONTHLY DEPOSIT AND RATE
        READ(1,5)N,DEPOST,RATE
      5 FORMAT(I2,F4.2,F3.3)
        SUM=0.0
        DO 20 IYEAR=1,N
          DO 10 MONTH=1,12
            SUM=SUM+DEPOST
     10   CONTINUE
          SUM=SUM*RATE+SUM
     20 CONTINUE
        WRITE(6,30)SUM
     30 FORMAT('FINAL AMOUNT OF INVESTMENT IS',F9.2)
        STOP
        END
```

Figure 18. Using nested DO loops

Value of an Investment Program. The entries m_1, m_2, m_3 may also use variables to give added flexibility to a program. This is used in the program in Figure 18, which computes the value of an investment. The program reads data from a card supplying the number of years in the investment, the amount of the monthly deposit, and the interest rate to be applied. The interest is calculated at the end of each year.

The program uses nested DO loops, which means one DO is inside the range of the other. The outer loop represents the years and the inner the months. In the inner loop, the deposit is added to the SUM. When 12 loops are completed, the inner loop ends and the interest is calculated. If the ending year has not been reached, the program loops back to the beginning of the outer loop to begin the next year. When all years are completed, the Write statement prints the final amount of SUM.

Using the data card

105000085

which represents an investment over 10 years of 500.00 dollars per month at a rate of 8½ percent (0.85), the following output is produced:

FINAL AMOUNT OF INVESTMENT IS 9657.63

PROGRAMMING PROBLEMS

1. Read cards containing 3-digit numbers in columns 1–3. Find and print the average of these numbers.

2. Using the same cards as problem 1, print only the numbers that are odd.
3. Read a card containing three numbers. Print the largest of these numbers.
4. Write a program that determines the number of ways change can be made for one dollar.
5. Aluminum doors are ordered on the basis of a product code

    1—Plain Color
    2—Plain Color Self-storing
    3—Black Self-storing
    4—Brown Self-storing
    5—White Self-storing

    Orders are placed on punched cards as follows:

    1   Product Code
    2–4   Quantity
    5–9   Unit Price

    Each card read is to be checked for a valid product code. Print a message to indicate an error. We have been advised by the manufacturer that plain self-storing doors are no longer available and cannot be ordered. Identify any of these orders. All other orders should be printed also including a product description based on the code, quantity, unit price, and total price.
6. Write a program to find all the prime numbers between 1 and 100.
7. Manhattan Island was purchased from the Indians in 1626 for $24.00. If the Indians had invested this money at an interest rate of 6 percent compounded annually, what would be the present value of the investment?

ARRAYS AND SUBSCRIPTS

Programmers are often required to write programs dealing with large quantities of similar data. For example, reading all the grades received by students in a class or the scores achieved on an aptitude or psychological test. These similar data items may be stored in an array for convenience in processing. An array may store numbers like any variable except that it may hold a series of them.

The FORTRAN statement DIMENSION defines an array. For example,

    DIMENSION MARK(40)

at the beginning of the program describes an array called MARK, which can hold 40 different marks. If MARK needed to be REAL, the array could have been defined

    REAL MARK(40)

which describes the same thing except MARK can store REAL numbers in this case.

Let's take a smaller array of 5 elements

    DIMENSION NUM(5)

Visually this looks like:

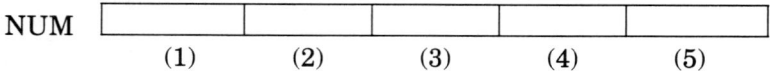

The numbers in parentheses are subscripts defining the location of NUM we want. The expression NUM(2) refers to the second position of NUM. NUM(5) is the fifth position.

If we want to store the numbers 3, 6, 9, 12, 15 in this array, we could write the following statements:

```
         N = 0
         DO 10 I = 3,15,3
           N = N + 1
           NUM(N) = 1
10       CONTINUE
```

Here N provides the subscript values from 1 to 5 while the DO generates the values to be stored in NUM. If these numbers had been punched on cards in columns 1–2 of each card, we would write the following statements to read the data and store it in

```
NUM
         DO 10 I = 1.5
           READ(1,5) NUM(I)
     5   FORMAT(I2)
    10   CONTINUE
```

```
C  CREATE THE FIRST 10 FIBONACCI NUMBERS
       INTEGER F(10)
       F(1) = 1
       F(2) = 1
       DO 1 I = 1,8
     1 F(I+2) = F(I+1) + F(I)
C  PRINT THE NUMBERS
       DO 5 J = 1,10
     5 WRITE(6,6)F(J)
     6 FORMAT(I10)
       STOP
       END
```

Figure 19. Creating an array of Fibonacci numbers.

Creating an Array of Fibonacci Numbers

Figure 19 is a program that creates the first 10 Fibonacci numbers and stores them in an array, F. The first two Fibonacci numbers are 0 and 1. The remaining numbers are the sum of the two preceding numbers. The first DO creates the third to tenth numbers in the array. The second DO is used to print the numbers.

The output from the program in Figure 19 is the following:

```
         1
         1
         2
         3
         5
         8
        13
        21
        34
        55
```

PROGRAMMING PROBLEMS

1. Read cards containing the temperature for each hour of the day and store in an array. Compute and print the average morning

and afternoon temperatures. Morning is from 0000 to 1100 hours and afternoon from 1200 to 2300 hours.

2. Read a set of n numbers from cards and store in an array of 100 elements. Print the numbers in the reverse order.
3. Read a set of n numbers into an array. Find and print the largest and smallest number with an appropriate message.
4. Read cards containing a student number and a mark. Place the student number in one array and the mark in another. Print the students and their marks in descending order of marks.
5. Read a set of n random numbers into an array. Sort them into ascending sequence and print them.

Pascal

The programming language Pascal is relatively new on the scene, although Nicklaus Wirth actually started developing this language in the late sixties and this work was then finalized during the early seventies.

Pascal tends to combine the features of BASIC and FORTRAN, thus producing a high-level language that is fairly easy to get started with, that provides the accuracy required with engineering and scientific problems, and that offers expressing language for business concerns. This extremely powerful language has come of age with the proliferation of microcomputers, and Pascal compilers seem to be appearing for most types of computers. Its format lends itself to many of the structured design techniques that are becoming so fundamental to programming in the eighties. Although there is no worldwide standard adopted for Pascal (at the time of this writing), there is a proposed ANSI standard currently being examined. The examples in this chapter should be correct for that proposed standard (being supplied by the British Standards Organization), and should work as well for the popular UCSD version (University of California—San Diego).

SAMPLE PROGRAM 1

Examining Sample Program 1

Before looking at each statement in Figure 1, it should be noted that the numbers 1 through 10 down the left side of the program are not Pascal numbers but rather just pointers in order to reference each statement in the paragraphs that follow.

The words *program, const, var, begin,* and *end* are Pascal words and are, in fact, found in programs in that very order. There will be other words of this kind that will be present in Pascal programs that are not commands or statements, but might be thought of as headings.

In line 1, the word "program" is required and signals the start of another Pascal program. The entry following "program" is the name of the program supplied by the programmer—i.e., PAYCHEQUE. This identifier should start with a letter and subsequently only have other letters or digits in its name. The "(input,output)" tells Pascal that during the program there will be a requirement to read (or to access) some data as well as to print (or write) some data on an output device (printer). The ";" immediately following "(input,output)" is required to separate this statement from the next since all the programmer wanted to say in the first line is finished.

In line 2, one of the heading entries, "const," is present to indicate that what follows are the *const*ants (numbers or character values) that will be used in the program. In this case, the data name "BONUS," found in line 3, is given the value of 10, and every time "BONUS" is referenced in the program, the computer will substitute the value 10. Again, the semicolon signals the end of a statement and, in this case, the end of the const part of the program.

```
1   program PAYCHEQUE (input,output);
2   const
3       BONUS = 10.00;
4   var
5       NUMBER, HOURS, RATE, PAY: real;
6   begin
7       READ(NUMBER, HOURS, RATE);
8       PAY := HOURS*RATE + BONUS;
9       WRITE(PAY :6:2)
10  end.
```

Figure 1. Pascal Sample Program 1.

Line 4 contains another heading, "var"; this indicates that following will be the data names or *var*iables that are to be used in the program. At this point no values have been assigned to the four entries "NUMBER, HOURS, RATE, PAY," but instead, the computer will reserve four areas in its memory representing these names. The word "real" following the ":" modifies the four data names in that for this program each of the variables can contain decimal values. More will be explained about this way of describing data names as the chapter gets into more detail.

In line 6, the "begin" heading is used to indicate the fact that all the defining and declaring of data names is finished and the instruction part of the program is about to start—i.e., following will be the commands that Pascal must obey. Line 7 has a Pascal command to read three values from an input device and assign those three values to the data names NUMBER, HOURS, and RATE. Notice the comma separating the variables and, once more, the semicolon terminating the command.

Line 8 is the Pascal method of determining the answer to a calculation and then storing or assigning the result in a specified variable (in this case, the answer will be stored in PAY). Thus, there can be many data names and calculation symbols on the right-hand side of the ": =" symbol, but only one variable on the left-hand side. Pascal would evaluate the expression on the right side and, when finished, would move the answer into the data name on the left side. The semicolon is present one more time. Note the use of the * to represent multiplication.

Line 9 is the command to output the contents of the data name PAY (just calculated in line 8) to an output device, such as a printer. The brackets are required, and if there were more variables to output, they would be separated by a comma within the one set of brackets. The ":6:2" that immediately follows the variable PAY is telling Pascal to use six print positions and two decimal places when printing the contents of the PAY field. Since this statement is the last one in the program, there is no need to employ a semicolon to end it.

Line 10, as it implies, signals the end of the program. In actual fact it indicates that the "begin" block (lines 6 through 10) has finished. That is to say, there may be more than one "begin" block and, therefore, more than one end statement in a program. Examples of programs with more than one begin–end combination will follow later in the chapter. Be aware of the period after the "end" heading. There will be only one "end" statement of this type in a program, and this is, in fact, the way that the real end of the program is indicated.

If the input values to this program happened to be 1011 (employee number), 40 (hours worked from the time card), and 7.50 (hourly rate), the program PAYCHEQUE would acquire these three values and store them in data names NUMBER, HOURS, and RATE from the command in line 7. Line 9 would ask Pascal to output the contents of the data name PAY. Thus, the value 300.00 would be produced on the output device, perhaps producing a hard copy or creating a soft copy visual display response.

Summary

To summarize, Pascal requires every program to have a "program" heading and at least one begin–end pair to signal the start and the end of the commands. Most programs would also use the "const" and "var" headings so that the programmer can introduce the constants and the variables that are to be used in the program. Pascal does allow the use of upper and lower case characters in order to create headings and data names. In Sample Program 1 (and in other samples found in the chapter), the heading entries are shown in lower case simply to help highlight the fact that they are required Pascal entries. The semicolon is a very important character (or delimiter) and should be used throughout a program to separate statements. Note that the headings "begin," "var," etc., do not need a semicolon. These words are special to Pascal and can be thought of as reserved words that are not available for the programmer to use as data names. Perhaps it is appropriate at this time to list the main set of words that constitute Pascal's reserved list (Figure 2).

If a programmer wishes to introduce a comment into the program, he may do so by enclosing the comment between a "(*" and a "*)." For example, in line 3 of sample program 1 a comment could have been placed as follows:

BONUS = 10.00; (* XMAS SPECIAL *)

If the system has the brace symbol, "{" and "}," they can be used instead.

and	array	begin	case	const	div
downto	do	else	end	file	for
function	goto	if	in	label	mod
nil	not	of	or	packed	procedure
program	record	repeat	set	then	to
type	until	var	while	with	

Figure 2. Pascal reserved list: main set.

DATA NAMES

A programmer can use data names that start with a letter and then use any combination of letters or numbers following. Even though he could formulate a data name of unlimited length—e.g.,

    var
        PRESIDENTIALCANDIDATEFORREPUBLICANS : real;

most Pascal compilers only recognize the first eight characters. Thus, if in the same program, a programmer chose another data name in the following manner:

    var
        PRESIDENTIALCANDIDATEFORDEMOCRATS : real;

a problem would arise: Pascal would believe that the two names are in fact the same. Therefore, in this chapter the data names will be kept to eight characters and will be meaningful where possible. As noted before, upper and lower case characters can be used to help make the data names easier to work with (if the printer connected to the computer system can handle the lower case characters). Figure 3 describes some different values for data names.

ENTRIES FOR THE VAR SECTION

When a programmer creates a data name, he must tell Pascal about his field by placing it in the "var" section of the program. At that time, he would also say what type of variable he would like it to represent. For example, he might define it as one of the following:

    integer, real, char, array, or boolean.

Valid and Meaningful	Invalid	Valid (but perhaps not so meaningful)	Better
PRICE	1STORDER	A17B3	PARTNO
SURNAME	TIME_OF_DAY	COSTOFGOODSSOLD	CostOfGoodsSold
PRODUCT50	STUDENT#3		
	NAME OF SCHOOL		

Figure 3. Some different values for data names.

At this point in learning Pascal, it is not imperative to discuss all the options. However the first three—integer, real, and char—are going to be used a lot and, therefore, will be explained in detail in subsequent pages.

Integer

If in a program, the following statements appeared:

    var
        TOTAL : integer;

Pascal would treat the data name TOTAL as being able to represent only integer values—e.g., $-47, 0, 3, 852$. In fact, any attempt to put any other type of value into TOTAL would be recognized as an error by the Pascal compiler. For example,

    TOTAL : = 42.32;

or

    TOTAL : = 'JANUARY';

would be incorrect assignments for the variable TOTAL defined as above. Often, there is a need in a program to use a data name as a counter or index or subscript that starts off with a value of 1, and changes by 1 until the end of a series of calculations has been reached. The integer option would therefore be appropriate for this type of variable.

Real

When more precision is required when storing a number, a programmer may write

    var
        SUM : real;

Any numeric value can be stored in SUM up to the maximum capacity of a location of the computer's memory. Fractions (e.g., .005, .25), mixed numbers (8.37, 165.444), and integers ($-5, 25$) are all handled by the label "real." Since there must be digits on both sides of the decimal point for a "real" field, the fraction values would be stored as 0.005 and

0.25 and the integers as -5.0 and 25.0. Pascal actually stores the number in a format that can be expressed as "mantissa E exponent." For example, another way of representing the number 500000 is, in fact, 5×10^5. The mantissa is the value in front of the "$\times$." The E stands for the "$\times 10$," and the exponent is the value after the 10. Therefore, the number 500000 would be represented internally in the computer as 5E5. Some other examples are:

Number	Represented As
2300	2.3E3 (or 2.3E+3)
.05401	4.501E−2
81200000	8.12E7 (or 81.2E6)

Numbers can be entered into "real" data fields using the E notation or simply with their regular values. See Figure 4.

Watch out for the following errors:

SUBTOT : =1,357.20;	—no commas allowed
SUM : =50.;	—must be at least one digit before and after the decimal point
FINALTOT : =3.8E2.3;	—the exponent must always be an integer

Char

If a data field requires character type values, it can be defined as

```
var
    FIELD : char;
```

Variables described as "char" represent a one-position field that can contain a letter (A through Z), a number (0 through 9), a space, or a special

```
var
    SUBTOT,SUM,FINALTOT:real;
    .
    .
    .
    .
    SUBTOT : =2537;
    SUM : =17E5;
    FINALTOT : =187E8;
```

Figure 4. Entering numbers into "real" data fields using E notation.

character (#, $, etc.). When supplying a value for a "char" field in a program, the value must be enclosed in quotes as in

TRUE := 'Y';
FALSE := 'F';

However, when supplying data via an input record that is to be stored in a "char" field, the data value must not have any quotes around it. For example:

```
program TEST1(input,output);
var
    INFIELD : char;
begin
    READ(INFIELD);
.
.
.
.
```

This data name description is extremely useful for solving problems that involve examining alphabetics (or special characters) to perhaps determine the occurrence of a certain character. For example, how many times does the letter "B" or a period appear in a data item? You will appreciate this point when you get into Pascal (or any other language) in greater depth. A discussion of how to handle headings and whole data items (other than one position) is reserved until the latter part of the chapter. At that point, some other facets of the language will have been discussed and, therefore, a more complete description will be appropriate then.

SAMPLE PROGRAM 2

Let us examine another sample program that will summarize some of the points presented so far. This program, perhaps of use in a communications field, computes the length of a long wire transmitting antenna based upon the frequency of the signal to be transmitted. The formula used is:

$$\text{length (feet)} = \frac{492(N - 0.05)}{\text{Frequency (megahertz)}}$$

where N is the number of half waves on the antenna. See Figure 5.

```
1    program ANTENNA(input,output);
2    const
3        CONSTANT = 492;
4    var
5        LENGTH,HALFWAVES,FREQUENCY : real;
6    begin
7        READ(FREQUENCY,HALFWAVES);
8        LENGTH := (CONSTANT*(HALFWAVES - 0.05))/
            FREQUENCY;
9        WRITE('THE REQUIRED LENGTH FOR', FREQUENCY:8:3,
10           'MEGAHERTZ IS',LENGTH:6:2,'FEET')
11   end.
```

Figure 5. Sample computational program (ANTENNA).

If the values from the input device (perhaps a terminal) were 14.210 and 2.0 (representing frequency and the number of half waves), then the above "program ANTENNA" would generate the following output:

THE REQUIRED LENGTH FOR 14.210 MEGAHERTZ IS 67.52 FEET

Analysis of Sample Program (ANTENNA)

In line 3, "program ANTENNA" defines or sets up a data field called "CONSTANT" that is assigned the value 492. This field is used in line 8 for the calculation of length. It is valid to omit the constant definition and simply use the amount 492 in line 8. If, however, during one program the value 492 was used, say five times, then this might be a good opportunity to use a constant type field as opposed to just the number value. In this way, if the value of 492 were to change, then only one program statement would have to be changed. Otherwise, five statements would need to be altered.

The write statement, line 9, shows that English can be printed by putting the desired output in quotes as in 'THE REQUIRED LENGTH FOR'. Note that the quote marks do not print; they are simply indicators of the beginning and ending of the English to be printed.

The two variables FREQUENCY and LENGTH are each printed in six positions, one with three places after the decimal and the other with two decimal positions. Again, this way of influencing how the field should be printed is due to the "real" reference in the definition of both data names FREQUENCY and LENGTH. Without any description such as :8:3 in the write statement, the two data fields would print as 1·4210E1 and 2·0E0.

Notice that when the printing requirements exceed one line in the Pascal program, the programmer can just drop down to the next line and continue until all the entries are complete (see lines 9 and 10).

EXERCISES

1. Which of the following are invalid Pascal data names?
   a. PRIMARYORDER
   b. 2ND NAME
   c. PAY-CHEQUE
   d. RUMPLESTILSKEN
   e. PRODUCT#
   f. C3P0
   g. LABEL

2. Given the following var section in a Pascal program:

   var
       FIELD1 : real;
       FIELD2 : integer;
       FIELD3 : char;

   which of the following assignments are correct?
   a. FIELD1 := 32.5;
   b. FIELD2 := 418.3;
   c. FIELD3 := 2.0E3;
   d. FIELD1 := .36;
   e. FIELD2 := 'HOT';
   f. FIELD3 := 'COLD';
   g. FIELD1 := 4.2E−3;
   h. FIELD2 := −8;
   i. FIELD3 := '15.0E10';

3. What would the output of the following Pascal program be?

   program EXERCISE11(input,output);
   const
       RATIO = 25;
   var
       VALUE1, VALUE2 : integer;
   begin
       VALUE1 := 32;
       VALUE1 := VALUE1 + RATIO;
       VALUE2 := VALUE1 * 2;
       WRITE(VALUE2)
   end.

4. Determine the output of EXERCISE12 :

```
program EXERCISE12(input,output);
var
    HEADING : char;
    SOMEVALUE : real;
    ANOTHERVALUE : integer;
begin
    READ(SOMEVALUE);
    ANOTHERVALUE : = 49;
    SOMEVALUE : = SOMEVALUE + ANOTHERVALUE;
    HEADING : = 'S'; (*S represents the sum *)
    WRITE(HEADING,SOMEVALUE)
end.
```

The input value is to be taken as 9.99E2.

ARITHMETIC EXPRESSIONS

A programmer must indicate to Pascal which arithmetic calculation he wants to perform, by using symbols to represent the various expressions. For example

addition	+
subtraction	−
multiplication	*
division	/ or DIV or MOD

The first three are fairly straightforward, but the division symbol requires some explanation because of the different options possible. Basically the / is used for division between real fields. The functions DIV and MOD are used with integer variables. For example, if A, B, and C were integer fields and the following occurred:

Contents Of Fields	Operation	Results
$\dfrac{A}{7} \dfrac{B}{9} \dfrac{C}{3}$	A := B DIV C;	$\dfrac{A}{3} \dfrac{B}{9} \dfrac{C}{3}$

then notice the change in A. Since they are all integer fields, there can be no decimal places; therefore, the DIV function produces the answer or quotient by truncating or eliminating the decimal place and everything to the right of the decimal (even if the value to the right of the decimal is .999). Check the next two examples to make sure you understand how the DIV works:

$\dfrac{A}{8}$ $\dfrac{B}{9}$ $\dfrac{C}{2}$	A := B DIV C;	$\dfrac{A}{4}$ $\dfrac{B}{9}$ $\dfrac{C}{2}$
$\dfrac{A}{3}$ $\dfrac{B}{9}$ $\dfrac{C}{10}$	A := B DIV C;	$\dfrac{A}{0}$ $\dfrac{B}{9}$ $\dfrac{C}{10}$

If a programmer just wants the remainder as a result of a division, he may use the MOD function. For example:

$\dfrac{A}{5}$ $\dfrac{B}{9}$ $\dfrac{C}{3}$	A := B MOD C	$\dfrac{A}{0}$ $\dfrac{B}{9}$ $\dfrac{C}{3}$
$\dfrac{A}{4}$ $\dfrac{B}{9}$ $\dfrac{C}{2}$	A := B MOD C	$\dfrac{A}{1}$ $\dfrac{B}{9}$ $\dfrac{C}{2}$
$\dfrac{A}{8}$ $\dfrac{B}{9}$ $\dfrac{C}{10}$	A := B MOD C	$\dfrac{A}{9}$ $\dfrac{B}{9}$ $\dfrac{C}{10}$

When the / symbol is used for division, the answer is created in the "real" format (e.g., 2.2E4) and, therefore, is not appropriate for any integer fields. If, however, it is required to use the / symbol with integer fields, Pascal offers a TRUNC and a ROUND function. The TRUNC option takes the integer part of the answer (to the left of the decimal) and assigns it to the data name on the left of the := sign. The ROUND version examines the values to the right of the decimal and rounds the integer value up by 1 if the decimal part is greater than 4. For example:

```
var
    X,Y,Z : integer;
begin
    X := 11;
    Y := 3;
    Z := ROUND(X/Y);        Z would be equal to 4
    .
    .
    Z := TRUNC(X/Y);        Z would be equal to 3
```

Order of Operations

Examine the following statements:

```
var
    W,X,Y,Z, :real;
begin
    W := 10;
    X := 20;
    Y := 5;
    Z := W + X/Y
```

What do you think would be generated if a WRITE(Z) statement were issued? Perhaps the value 6 or maybe 14? Well, the computer cannot guess, nor can it change its mind. Therefore, it must always be consistent when dealing with these assignment statements. The Pascal compiler follows the standard mathematical hierarchy that can be seen in Figure 6.

In other words, the computer will always do what is in brackets first, then either a multiplication or division, and finally an add or a subtract. Therefore, the answer to Z := W + X/Y would be 14. However, Z := (W + X)/Y would produce a 6 in Z. If two operators of equal priority are encountered, as in Z := W + X − Y, the computer simply performs the first one it meets starting from the equal sign and then continuing through the assignment statement.

PRINTING CONTROLS AND COMMANDS

When it is time to print some output—for example, some data, a heading, or some grand totals—the instruction that should be used is the WRITE command. There are two versions of this command as follows:

    WRITELN(   )   and   WRITE(   ).

The WRITELN (think of write a *line*) causes the printer to print the contents of whatever is inside the brackets and then perform a car-

( )	Highest Priority
*,/,MOD,DIV	Second Priority
+,−	Lowest Priority

Figure 6. Standard mathematical hierarchy.

riage return to ready itself at the start of a new line in preparation for the next print command. The WRITE alternative prints the contents of the brackets but does not indicate any movement of the carriage return. Figure 7 indicates the basic difference between the two commands.

If at any time a blank line is required, say to separate a heading line from a subheading, a WRITELN; can be used. Or, if the next item to be printed should be located at the top of a new page, the command PAGE; can be inserted where appropriate to tell the printer to skip to the top of a new page.

The entries in the parentheses after the command WRITE are either headings enclosed in quotes, variable names, numbers by themselves (referred to as numeric literals) or expressions. Figure 8 provides an example of these various options, without any concern about formatting the output.

The output from the program described in Figure 8 would appear as:

THE SUM OF   10AND   15IS   25

The program PRINTOUT shows that headings enclosed in quotes, such as 'THE SUM OF' and 'AND' and 'IS' can be handled. As well, the number 15 is simply referenced in the WRITELN statement and its value is generated on the output device. The value of variable FIELDA (which is 10) is printed and the expression FIELDA + 15 produces the 25 on the output line in Figure 8.

The integer variable FIELDA occupies 10 storage positions and, therefore, when printed would also require 10 print positions. This, of course, is not acceptable for a reasonable output. Also, the number 15 is

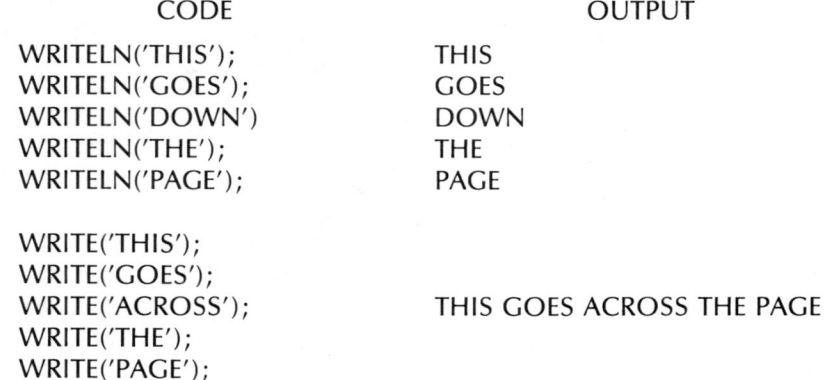

Figure 7. WRITELN contrasted with WRITE.

```
1    program PRINTOUT(input,output);
2    var
3        FIELDA:integer;
4    begin
5        FIELDA : = 10;
6        WRITELN('THE SUM OF',FIELDA, 'AND', 15,
             'IS',FIELDA+15);
7    end.
```

Figure 8. Examples of various entries.

sandwiched around the two words AND and IS because Pascal just prints the number of positions needed to represent the numeric literal, unless otherwise specified. Again, at the end of the printout the number 25 appears to be far away from the IS because ten positions are allocated for the result automatically by Pascal. In fact, if the answer to be printed happened to be in a "real" format, Pascal would set aside 20 print positions.

In order to tidy up this (and other) print lines, it is necessary to introduce a value after the item to be printed that in fact determines the number of print positions desired. This number is recognized by Pascal as being an indicator of print positions, and not just a number to be printed, by using a colon in the print statement. An alternative to line 6 in Figure 8 would be

WRITELN('THE SUM OF',FIELDA :3, 'AND' :4, 15:3, 'IS':3,
    FIELDA + 15 :3);

The output from the program in Figure 8 would appear as:

THE SUM OF 10 AND 15 IS 25

The value after the colon can be greater than the item to be printed and when that happens, spaces will be inserted to the left of the value of the item, up to the number of print positions specified. Examine Figure 9 and make certain that you understand the three alternate ways of generating the following output that was to be printed starting in column 16.

Earlier in this chapter, in two of the sample programs (see Figure 1 and Figure 5), the WRITE statements used a second colon for the printing of "real" fields. This second colon allows the programmer to indicate the number of decimal positions that he wishes, as well as to convert the "E" representation of the real field into decimal output. Figure 10 indi-

```
                    RADIO STATION                    DIAL POSITION
                         WCAL                             1050

           WRITELN'(' ':15,'RADIO STATION','DIAL POSITION':18);
           WRITELN(' ':19,'WCAL',' ':15,1050:4);
OR
           WRITELN('RADIO STATION              ':33,'DIAL POSITION');
           WRITELN('WCAL':23,1050:19);
OR
           WRITELN('RADIO STATION              DIAL POSITION':46);
           WRITELN('WCAL                       1050':42);
```

Figure 9. Alternate ways of generating output.

cates the different outputs that can be generated when working with a "real" field. Note the rounding operation in the third example. In the fourth example, the field length 7 is large enough to accommodate the sign if needed. If you specify too small a length, Pascal will not convert from the "real" to a decimal format.

PROCESSING MULTIPLE INPUT RECORDS

The discussion thus far in the chapter has used sample Pascal programs that basically access one data record, perform some calculating and printing functions, and then stop. It is very important to be able to handle many input records and, therefore, before detailing some of the control statements found in Pascal, a description of the method of reading many input records is appropriate. Just before you go through the program in Figure 11, let it be said that when Pascal reads a series of records, it raises a flag when it determines that there are no data records left. This flag or signal is called an EOF flag (end-of-file).

```
           var
             SAMPLE :real;
           begin                              OUTPUT
             SAMPLE : = 2·7245E + 02;
             WRITELN(SAMPLE);                 2·7245E + 02
             WRITELN(SAMPLE:8);               2·72E + 02
             WRITELN(SAMPLE:5);               3E + 02
             WRITELN(SAMPLE:7:2);             272·45
```

Figure 10. Different outputs from a "real" field.

```
1   program CUSTOMERS(input,output);
2   var
3     CUSTNO : integer;
4     UNITPRICE,QUANTITY,AMOUNT : real;
5   begin
6     WHILE NOT EOF DO
7       begin
8         READLN(CUSTNO,UNITPRICE,QUANTITY);
9         AMOUNT := UNITPRICE * QUANTITY;
10        WRITELN(CUSTNO,' ':3,AMOUNT:7:2);
11      end
12  end.
```

Figure 11. Method to read many records.

Analysis of Program Customers

There are many points to be detailed from "program CUSTOMERS," and the discussion will start from line 6 because the first five lines are not much different from programs earlier in the chapter.

Understanding the "WHILE NOT EOF DO". Line 6 can basically be translated in the following manner: while the EOF flag is not up (i.e., there is more data), do the instructions from the word "begin" in line 7 until an "end" statement is met (line 11) and then return to line 6 where the test for the EOF flag occurs again. Since, in this example, the flag is not raised, Pascal would cause a READLN to occur (line 8) and three values 0011, 1.80, and 15 would be read in and assigned to the fields CUSTNO, UNITPRICE, and QUANTITY. The READLN statement is similar to the READ statement except that after finding values for the data fields in the brackets, it causes a skip to the start of the next line. At this point, it is determined that there is still more data; therefore, the EOF switch remains off. A calculation for the AMOUNT is done (line 9) and a line containing the CUSTNO, and the AMOUNT is printed (line 10). The end statement (line 11) signifies the end of the statements for the WHILE NOT EOF DO and, therefore, control is returned to line 6. Since the EOF flag has not been raised, Pascal starts the "begin–end" loop once more. The values 0087, 2.50, and 30 are brought into the program, and a skip to the start of the next line indicates that the EOF flag should not be raised. A calculation for CUSTNO 0087 is performed, and a line is printed, and then the "end" statement returns control to line 6. Again, Pascal starts the begin–end pair because the EOF flag is not up, and this time the data values 1121, .95, and 10 are brought in; and when a skip to the next input line is done, Pascal realizes the EOF flag has to be raised. An amount is calculated for CUSTNO 1121, and a line printed. Then the "end" statement sends control back to line 6. Since the EOF flag is raised, the condition NOT EOF is false; therefore, control goes to the statement following the "end" (line 11). In this program it goes to line 12, the "end." statement that stops the program. Now line 12 could have been the start of another series of commands and does not necessarily have to be the "end." statement for the whole program as it was in this case. This program, CUSTOMERS, starts to show the "begin–end" blocks that are so fundamental to Pascal programming. The number of "begin–end" blocks within the one main "begin–end." pair is virtually unlimited and dependent on the programmer and his specific task.

EXERCISES

1. Translate the following formulas to Pascal assign commands:

$$A = \frac{B(R + C)}{C - \frac{D}{L}} \qquad X = Y^2 + \frac{R^3}{2} - T$$

2. Given the following three integer fields X, Y, Z and an operation involving them, determine the resulting values that would be stored in X, Y, and Z.

Starting Amounts			Operation	Results
X	Y	Z		X Y Z
4	10	5	X := Y DIV Z	
17	30	4	X := Y DIV Z	
19	8	40	X := Y MOD Z	
5	12	5	X := Y MOD Z	
101	4	7	X := Y DIV Z	
14	25	9	X := TRUNC(Y/Z)	
3	30	7	X := ROUND(Y/Z)	

3. Write a Pascal program(s) to generate the following outputs:
   a.

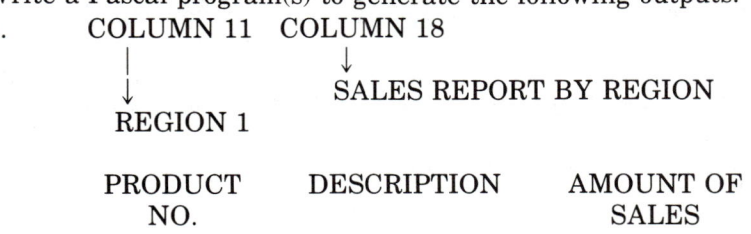

b.
```
              C
   B O U N    E
```

c.
```
   R            S
   I            T  L
   G            E     I
   H            P     D
   T A N G L E  S        E
```

4. The volume of a sphere is computed by the formula $\frac{4\pi R^3}{3}$, and the surface area calculated by $4\pi R^2$. Read R from a data card, and compute and print a volume and an area for that radius R in the following format:

   GIVEN THE RADIUS IS 13
   THE VOLUME IS 9202.77 AND
   THE AREA IS 2123.72

5. The economic re-order point for a series of articles in a warehouse is calculated at 10 percent of the starting inventory amount. Write a Pascal program to calculate the re-order point for a series of input records that each contain a product number, a starting inventory amount, and a current amount. The output should generally appear as follows:

INVENTORY RE-ORDER LISTING

PRODUCT NO	STARTING AMOUNT	CURRENT AMOUNT	REORDER AMOUNT
4410552	950	200	95

6. Write a program to read a series of records that represent a customer's balance in a bank. All these customers are to have 8 percent interest added to their balance; and after the last customer is printed, a total showing the amount from all of their new balances should be printed. Each input record just contains a customer account number and a balance. The format of the report should be as follows:

1ST NEVADA BRANCH

CUSTOMER ACCOUNT NO.	BALANCE	INTEREST	NEW BALANCE
101234	150.00	12.00	162.00
.			
.			
.			

GRAND TOTAL......

CONTROL STATEMENTS

IF Command

Many times during a computer program, a decision is needed to permit the logic set up by the programmer to work. In Pascal, a decision or test is handled by the IF command. A general format of the IF might be described as follows:

  IF condition   THEN
        statement;

Basically, if the condition is true, then the statement following the word THEN is performed. If the condition is false, then the program goes to the command following the statement for its next instruction. In the following example,

  IF AVERAGE >75 THEN
        WRITELN('HONORS');

the word HONORS will only be generated if the average exceeds 75.

When more than one item is to be done based on a condition being true, the commands are enclosed in a begin–end block.

In Figure 12, the word "honors" was to be printed if the average exceeded 75, and, as well, a field representing the number of honors was to be incremented by one. The statements located in the begin–end pair are done only if the result of the test is valid. Otherwise the program drops down to the command STUDENTS := STUDENTS + 1;. Notice that this field STUDENTS (perhaps representing the total number of students) is changed by one, independent of the result of the IF test.

```
IF AVERAGE > 75 THEN
   begin
      WRITELN('HONORS');
      HONORS := HONORS+1
   end
STUDENTS := STUDENTS+1;
```

Figure 12.

Compound Conditions

If more than one condition is to be satisfied before one or more operations are to be performed, a programmer can use a compound test in the IF test.

```
IF (WORKYEARS >5) AND (BILINGUAL = 'YES') THEN
   begin
      WRITELN ('RELOCATION POSSIBLE');
   end
```

Sometimes an "and" condition is not what is required, but rather an "or" situation is relevant. For example, a programmer wants to add one to a certain field if a player can dunk a basketball, or is taller than seven feet, or has a scoring average of over 20 points per game. He might code the statement in Figure 13.

ELSE Alternative

The IF statement can be extended to incorporate an ELSE condition that is performed only if the value of the IF test is false. For example:

```
IF GRACE >50 THEN
   WRITELN ('PASS')
ELSE
   WRITELN ('FAIL');
```

A more involved example should be examined in Figure 14.

```
IF (DUNK = 'YES') OR (HEIGHT > 7) OR
   (AVERAGE > 20) THEN
      STARTER := STARTER+1;
```

Figure 13. OR statements.

```
        IF SALES > 1000.00 THEN
          begin
            WRITELN ('BONUS');
            BONUS : = SALES * .1;
            WRITELN (BONUS:8:2)
          end
        ELSE
          begin
            WRITELN ('NOT THIS YEAR');
            AVGSALES : = AVGSALES + 1
          end
```

Figure 14.

IF and ELSE pairs can be used together to select certain conditions that are to be done if the result of one test is true but the result of another is false. In Figure 15, the program would output the value −4 if the values of the fields B and C were 5 and −5 respectively before the IF command was executed.

If B = 5 and C = 6, the answer would be 5. Finally, if B = −5 and C = 7, the answer that would be generated would be 7. The reason for this last answer is that if the original test in line 1 is false, then the next statement to be done is line 8. The ELSE in line 5 is only connected to the IF test in line 3.

FOR . . . DO

This command is very useful for problems that require solutions that are going to repeat themselves a fixed number of times. For example, if there was a need to generate the chart in Figure 16, the programmer knows that the output starts at 1 and goes to 10.

A program to handle this chart might be written as follows:

```
1   program CHART(input,output)
2   var     N,S : integer;
3   begin
4       WRITELN('NUMBERS', ':5,'SQUARES');
5       FOR N : = 1 TO 10 DO
6         begin
7             S : = N*N;
8             WRITE(N:4,' ':8, S:4)
9         end
10  end.
```

```
1    IF B >0 THEN
2       begin
3          IF C >0 THEN
4             C := C - 1
5          ELSE
6             C := C + 1
7       end
8    WRITELN(C);
```

Figure 15.

In line 5, Pascal would start N off with a value of 1 and perform all the instructions in the begin–end pair and return to the FOR statement. Here, the value 1 would be added to the current value of N, and if the derived value was greater than 10, then Pascal would drop down to the instruction after the "end" statement in the begin–end pair (in this case, it would drop to line 10). The data name after the word FOR (N in this case) must be previously defined as an integer field, and after the begin–end pair has been processed for the last time, the value of N is undefined. Therefore, care should be taken not to use the value of N afterwards. However, N can be set to any new value when required. The starting value of N, found after the := sign, could have been a number other than one—i.e., FOR N := 50 TO 100 DO.

NUMBERS	SQUARES
1	1
2	4
3	9
.	.
.	.
.	.
10	100

```
1    program CHART(input,output)
2    var    N,S : integer;
3    begin
4       WRITELN('NUMBERS',' ':5,'SQUARES');
5       FOR N: =1 TO 10 DO
6          begin
7             S := N*N;
8             WRITE(N:4,' ':8, S:4)
9          end
10   end.
```

Figure 16.

If there is a requirement to begin N at a value and then reduce it by one for a series of operations, Pascal allows the programmer to write

```
FOR N : = 100 DOWNTO 10 DO
   begin
       (SOME
       (STATEMENTS
   end
```

WHILE . . . DO

The WHILE . . . DO instruction is used to control the program to perform a series of commands while a certain condition is true. The commands are located in a begin–end pair, and when the condition specified in the WHILE . . . DO is false, Pascal proceeds to the statement following the "end."

The coding in Figure 17 would generate the numbers and their cubes from 1 to 10. The statements in the begin–end pair would be performed ten times, and when the condition R < 11 is evaluated to be false (at R = 11), the program would jump down to the statement following line 7. The condition that is placed between the words WHILE and DO can take many different forms as suggested by the table in Figure 18. The condition is actually evaluated before Pascal decides to go ahead and do what is described in the begin–end grouping. In Figure 19, the activities in the begin–end pair would not be evaluated at all as the test would prove false right at the beginning.

This type of program control was in fact described a little earlier in the chapter under the heading "Processing Multiple Input Records." In that section, a WHILE NOT EOF DO was referenced and that is the same automatic control that is being described at this point. Figure 20 demonstrates a full program with two WHILE . . . DO tests involved that generate the following output:

STUNO	SUM
101	92
138	391
194	130

This program was designed to add a series of marks for a student without knowing how many marks would be contained in the input record. The value 999, supplied as an "end of marks" indicator, would be present in each student record. Although this chapter has said little about program style and layout, you should intuitively recognize that the in-

```
1  R := 1;
2  WHILE R <11 DO
3    begin
4      C := R*R*R;
5      WRITELN(R,C);
6      R := R+1
7    end
```

Figure 17. WHILE . . . DO instruction.

CONDITION ENTRIES

A = B EQUAL
A > B GREATER THAN
A < B LESS THAN
A <> NOT EQUAL TO

A >= GREATER THAN OR EQUAL
A <= LESS THAN OR EQUAL

NOT, AND, OR (USED IN COMBINATION WITH THE OTHERS)

Figure 18.

```
COUNTER := 10;
WHILE COUNTER <5 DO
    begin
        (SOME
        (STATEMENTS
    end
```

Figure 19.

```
program STUSUM(input,output);
var
  STUNO,MARK,SUM:integer;
begin
  WRITELN('STUNO',' ':4,'SUM');
  SUM := 0;
  WHILE NOT EOF DO
    begin
      READ (STUNO, MARK):
      WHILE NOT (MARK=999) DO
        begin
          SUM := SUM + MARK;
          READ (MARK)
        end;
      WRITELN(STUNO:5,' ':4,SUM:3);
      SUM := 0
      READLN
    end
```

Input
101 14 78 999
138 300 90 1 999
194 130 999

Figure 20.

dentations make the program more manageable and easier to read. The indentations are not required by Pascal, but perhaps if you were to write the program out with every statement starting in the same column, you would appreciate the point.

REPEAT . . . UNTIL

The controlling command WHILE . . . DO has its place in many Pascal programs, but sometimes it can be replaced by an IF test or another control command, the REPEAT . . . UNTIL. This instruction says that the program will repeat the commands following the REPEAT statement up to the UNTIL, where a condition is evaluated. If the condition is met, then processing simply continues; if it is not met, the program returns to the statement following the REPEAT statement and goes through all the commands again. Figure 21 shows this command in operation generating the sum of the numbers from 1 to 100.

Although the REPEAT . . . UNTIL and the WHILE . . . DO are very similar in their respective effects on controlling a program, the REPEAT . . . UNTIL guarantees that the commands will be done at least once, as the test is evaluated after the commands are done (not so for the WHILE . . . DO).

CASE . . . END

This command is useful to help simplify the appearance of program coding that would normally be handled by a series of IF tests. For example, if a field called STATUS took on different values (representing a person's marital status) and certain print lines were to be generated based on these values, a programmer might handle the problem in either of the two ways described in Figure 22.

However, the CASE . . . END combination allows a fairly straightforward solution as follows:

```
CASE STATUS OF
    1 : WRITELN(MARITAL STATUS-MARRIED);
    2 : WRITELN(MARITAL STATUS-SINGLE);
    3 : WRITELN(MARITAL STATUS-DIVORCED);
    4 : WRITELN(MARITAL STATUS-SEPARATED);
    5 : WRITELN(MARITAL STATUS-WIDOWED);
end
```

```
    NO := 1;
    SUM := 0;
    REPEAT
      SUM := SUM+NO;
      NO := NO + 1;
    UNTIL NO > 100;
    WRITELN(SUM);
```

Figure 21. REPEAT . . . UNTIL program.

The command CASE is followed by the field to be examined. The word OF completes the start of the CASE command and introduces a series of values that the test field might contain. After each value is a colon and then the appropriate action to be done if the test field happens to be equal to that particular value. If the test field does not equal any of the suggested values, the program just continues on with no action having been done. The END statement signifies the end of the test field's possibilities. As in other END statements, the statement immediately

```
METHOD    IF STATUS = 1 THEN
  #1          WRITELN('MARITAL STATUS-MARRIED');
          IF STATUS = 2 THEN
              WRITELN('MARITAL STATUS-SINGLE');
          IF STATUS = 3 THEN
              WRITELN('MARITAL STATUS-DIVORCED');
          IF STATUS = 4 THEN
              WRITELN('MARITAL STATUS-SEPARATED');
          IF STATUS = 5 THEN
              WRITELN('MARITAL STATUS-WIDOWED');

METHOD    IF STATUS = 1 THEN
  #2          WRITELN('MARITAL STATUS-MARRIED')
          ELSE IF STATUS = 2 THEN
              WRITELN('MARITAL STATUS-SINGLE')
          ELSE IF STATUS = 3 THEN
              WRITELN('MARITAL STATUS-DIVORCED')
          ELSE IF STATUS = 4 THEN
              WRITELN('MARITAL STATUS-SEPARATED')
          ELSE IF STATUS = 5 THEN
              WRITELN('MARITAL STATUS-WIDOWED')
```

Figure 22.

before it does not require a semicolon. If the test field is a "char" field, the suggested values must be enclosed in quotes. For example:

```
CASE LANGUAGE OF
    'FRENCH' : NUMFR := NUMFR + 1;
    'ENGLISH' : NUMENG := NUMENG + 1;
    'SPANISH' : NUMSP := NUMSP + 1;
    'GERMAN' : NUMGER := NUMGER + 1
END
```

ARRAYS

Many programming applications involve repetitive data items such as lists and tables. Even though each data item in the group could be declared individually, this is an inefficient and awkward approach. For example, a group of student records might each be organized as follows:

DATA	*FIELDS*
12345	*Student Number*
73	Mark for Subject 1
81	Mark for Subject 2
65	Mark for Subject 3
78	Mark for Subject 4
85	Mark for Subject 5
68	Mark for Subject 6

To read this data and compute each student's average mark requires the declaration of 7 variables for the record plus one to total the marks and one to find the average.

Repetitive data of this type may be defined as a one-dimension array using the array attribute in Pascal. The var section for this program would be as follows:

```
var MARK: array [1 . . 6] of integer;
    NUMBER, I: integer;
    TOTAL,AVG : real;
```

MARK is a one-dimension array comprised of six elements, each capable of storing an integer number. Thus, all six of the marks from the record may be stored in the array. The next statements will read the data into the variables:

```
READ(NUMBER);
FOR I : = 1 TO 6 DO
    READ(MARK[I]);
```

First of all, the number is read into its variable name. This instruction is followed by the "FOR" loop which reads the six marks into the array, one number at a time.

To find the average, the numbers must first be accumulated and then divided by the number of marks. A "FOR" loop may be used to create a subscript that allows a reference to each value in MARK and then adds it to TOTAL. TOTAL is then divided by 6 to give the AVG.

```
TOTAL : = 0.0;
FOR I : = 1 TO 6 DO
    TOTAL : = TOTAL - MARK[I];
AVG : = TOTAL/6;
```

By combining this code, the following program emerges:

```
program GRADES(input,output);
var
    MARK : array [1 . . 6] of integer;
    NUMBER,I : integer;
    TOTAL,AVG : real;
begin
    READ(NUMBER);
    FOR I : = 1 TO 6 DO
        READ(MARK[I]);
    TOTAL : = 0.0;
    FOR I : = 1 TO 6 DO
        TOTAL : = TOTAL + MARK[I];
    AVG : = TOTAL/6;
    WRITELN(AVG : 6 : 1)
end.
```

Note the use of the square brackets "[ ]" to define the array and to reference any of the elements in the array.

ARRAYS INVOLVING CHARACTER VALUES

Sometimes a program reads a character value, perhaps examines it, and then reads another value right over top of the original, thus losing the first value. Instead of this procedure, it is often advantageous to read and store a series of characters in a program. Then a group of calculations (e.g., sorts, comparisons) can be performed on the respective values. A modification to the char definition in the var section can accommodate this point. For example:

```
var
    ITEM:array[1 . . 10] of char;
    .
    .
    .
    FOR N : = 1 TO 10 DO
        READ(ITEM[N]);
```

After the "FOR" loop has finished, ten characters would have been read into the data field ITEM. (Be careful of spaces in the input record as they are recognized as valid character values. Now ITEM[1] can be compared to ITEM[2] and so on. Under this format, the whole character string cannot be compared to another value and the array can only be printed out one character at a time. If, however, the array is described as follows:

```
var
    VALUE:packed array[1 . . 15] of char:
```

then more alternatives are available to the programmer. If a programmer wants to set up a heading in the field called VALUE, he may now do so by writing, for example, VALUE := 'REGION ANALYSIS'. Then, at some subsequent point, he might state WRITELN(VALUE), which would cause the full 15 position contents of VALUE to be printed. As well, the array VALUE could be compared to another array as long as both of them were the same length. Again, note the fact that the data from an input record must be read one character at a time.

READING CHARACTER DATA

If a programmer had three integer fields A, B, and C and put them in a READ command [e.g., READ(A,B,C);], he might keep returning to that READ(A,B,C); statement to pick up three more data fields from multiple input records. That is, if the data were

```
         1011  14  23
         1022  71  67
         1877  45  78
```

then A = 1011, B = 14, and C = 23 after the first READ. For the second READ, Pascal would start at the position immediately after the 23 and search along for a number. Eventually it would locate 1022 and that value would be stored in A. In other words, Pascal would not use all the spaces after the number 23.

However, if the program were working with character data as in Figure 23, a problem would occur.

After reading FRED into NAME, 61 into GRADE1, and 72 into GRADE2, the program would eventually try to read again. This time, although JOHN is probably wanted, the four spaces following the number 72 would be picked up and stored in NAME because spaces are legitimate values for a "char" field. Therefore, in order to get Pascal down to the start of a new line before the character data is referenced, a programmer would say READLN(GRADE1,GRADE2);. This command means that after reading and storing some values into the fields in the brackets of the READ statement, drop down to the start of the next input record. Then JOHN would be found for the NAME array.

EOLN

Sometimes it is required to read along an input record until the end of the record is encountered. For this problem, Pascal provides an au-

```
var
  NAME: packed array [1..4] of char;
  GRADE1,GRADE2:integer;
  .
  .
  .
begin
  FOR I: =1 TO 4 DO
    READ(NAME[I]);
    READ(GRADE1,GRADE2);
```

INPUT DATA

FRED 61 72
JOHN 84 74

Figure 23.

tomatic EOLN check (end-of-line) similar to the EOF check. A programmer may therefore write:

```
WHILE NOT EOLN DO
    begin
        I := I+1;
        READ(CONTENTS[I])
    end
```

This type of control reads data into an array called CONTENTS until an EOLN condition is established.

EXERCISES

1. Evaluate the outcome of the following partial program:

```
R := 1;
K := 3;
J := 9;
A := 5;
B := 6;
IF A = 5 THEN
    IF B = 6 THEN
        begin
            B := B + 1;
            A := A + 1
        end
    ELSE
        begin
            B := B + 2;
            A := A + 2
        end
ELSE
    begin
        A := A + 3;
        B := B + 3
    end
WRITELN(A,B);
FOR M := 1 TO 4 DO
    begin
        R := R + M * 2
```

```
    end
WRITELN(R);
REPEAT
    J := J - 2;
UNTIL J < 4
WRITELN(J);
CASE K OF
3 : WRITELN('CEST TOUT');
5 : WRITELN('FINIS');
7 : WRITELN('OVER');
9 : WRITELN('THATS ALL FOLKS');
```

2. Write a Pascal Program to read a series of data cards, each of which contains an account number, an account name, a status, and a balance. The following output should be generated for those customers who are "status three" and who have a negative balance in their account.

ACCOUNT NUMBER	OVERDRAWN ACCOUNTS NAME	BALANCE
123811	CARTER	-20.00
.	.	.
.	.	.
.	.	.

3. A student who leaves school at age 21 plans to save $40.00 per month until retiring at age 65. Given a constant interest rate of 9 percent per year computed monthly, what will this investment amount to upon retirement?

4. In the current year, the population of CALGARY is 1 million and the population of VANCOUVER is 2 million. Assume that CALGARY is growing at a constant rate of 6 percent per year and VANCOUVER grows at 2 percent per year. In how many years will CALGARY have more people than VANCOUVER?

5. A company requires a payroll report listing the earnings for each employee in each department. There is one input record per employee, and the records are in employee number within department number sequence. Each record should be checked for sequence on both fields and the program stopped if a sequence error occurs. One line of output is needed for each card, showing tax amount, gross salary, total deductions, and net salary. At the end of each department, print totals for tax amount, gross and total

deductions, and net. At the end of the report, show these totals again for all departments. The input record contains the following fields: employee number (5), department number (3), hours worked (3), hourly rate (4 positions, 2 decimals), tax percentage (3), savings deduction (4 positions, 2 decimals), and pension deduction (4 positions, 2 decimals). The numbers in brackets indicate the length of each field.

6. Determine the outcome of the following program:

```
program CONFUSE(input,output);
var      LSUM,XX,YY:integer;
         TT:packed array[1 . . 5] of integer;
begin
         LSUM := 0:
         YY := 3;
         FOR J := 1 TO 5 DO
             READ(TT[J]);
         FOR M := 1 TO 5 DO
             LSUM := LSUM + TT[M];
         WRITELN(LSUM:5);
     XX := TT[1] + TT[YY] * TT[5];
     WRITELN(XX:5)
end.                    DATA
                 23   45   456   23   7
```

7. Read n values (maximum 100) into an array. Find and print the smallest and largest numbers.

8. Read n values (maximum 100) into an array. Sort them into ascending sequence without using a second array. Print the sorted list.

Glossary

Abacus. An early computing device on which numbers are represented by the pattern of a series of beads on a number of rods.
Access arm. A part of a disk storage unit that is used to hold one or more reading and writing heads.
Access time. The time required for a computer to locate and transfer data to or from a storage medium.
Accounting machine. A machine that reads data from external storage media such as cards and automatically produces accounting records or tabulations, usually on continuous forms.
Accumulator. A storage area, called a register, that holds the results of computer processing operations.
Acoustic Coupler. The portion of a data set that holds the telephone receiver in a pair of rubber cups.
Acronym. A word formed from the first letter or letters of the words in a name, term, or phrase. For example, COBOL comes from Common Business-Oriented Language.
Address. A numerical location within memory, typically referring to a byte number or a word number.
Algorithm. A prescribed set of well-defined rules or processes for the solution of a problem in a finite number of steps, e.g., a full statement of an arithmetic procedure for evaluating sin x to a stated precision.
Alphabetic data. Data that is composed exclusively of letters of the alphabet and the blank character. Occasionally, the period and the comma are also used.

Alphanumeric data. Also called alphameric, is data consisting of alphabetic and numeric data.

American National Standards Institute (ANSI). A national organization with the purpose of establishing uniform standards within the United States.

American Standard Code for Information Interchange (ASCII). A commonly used internal code. ASCII is also accepted as an international code by the International Organization for Standardization (ISO).

Analog computer. A computer that simulates real time physical systems by measuring and processing signals that vary continuously with time.

Analysis. The methodical investigation of a problem and the separation of the problem into smaller related units for further detailed study.

ANSI. See American National Standards Institute.

Arithmetic and logical unit. The portion of a central processing unit in which arithmetic and logical operations are performed.

Artificial intelligence. Pertains to machines that possess reasoning, learning, and thinking capabilities that resemble those of humans.

ASCII. See American Standard Code for Information Interchange.

Assembler. A computer program that prepares a machine language program from an assembler language program.

Assembler language. The source language for a machine level language.

Asynchronous. A data transmission method without a regular time relationship.

Audio response unit. A device that responds to inquiries by using the voice. See Voice Response.

Audit trail. A system for tracing the flow of data through a computer or business system.

Auxiliary operation. See off-line.

Auxiliary storage. A storage that supplements other storage. Contrast with main storage.

Background partition. A partition in a multiprogramming system used to hold lower priority programs.

Back-up. A procedure, technique, or hardware intended to be used in an emergency to help recover lost or destroyed data or to keep a system running.

Bandwidth. The range of frequencies available for data transmission. The broader the bandwidth, the greater the volume of data transmission possible.

Base. A number that is multiplied by itself as many times as indicated by an exponent. Same as radix.

BASIC. Acronym for Beginners All-purpose Symbolic Instruction Code; a programming language.

Batch processing. (1) Pertaining to the technique of executing a set of computer programs such that each is completed before the next program of the set is started. (2) Pertaining to the sequential input of computer programs or data. (3) Loosely, the execution of computer programs serially.

Baud. A unit of measuring data transmission speed that is equivalent to one bit per second for binary values.

BCD. Binary Coded Decimal.

Benchmark. A representative program that will be tested on various computer manufacturers' machines in order to generate objective results concerning speed of processing.

Binary. A number system using base 2 and consisting of the digits 0 and 1.

Binary coded decimal. Positional notation in which the individual decimal digits expressing a number in decimal notation are each represented by a binary numeral.

Bit. An acronym for Binary Digit. A bit may be a 0 or 1.

Block. Another name for physical record. A collection of contiguous records recorded as a unit. Blocks are separated by interblock gaps, and each block may contain one or more logical records.

Block Diagram. A diagram similar to a flowchart, which represents the devices used in a computer system.

Block length. The number of bytes in a block.

Blocking factor. The number of logical records in a block.

Broadband. Pertains to a data communications system that handles high volumes of data, typically up to a million bits/second or more.

Buffer. A routine or storage used to compensate for a difference in rate of flow of data, or time of occurrence of events, when transmitting data from one device to another.

Buffered keypunch. A keypunch containing a buffer. In typical operation, data is keyed as rapidly as the operator can type into the buffer, and punched into the card from the buffer, thus allowing the operator to work at a pace somewhat faster than that imposed by the punch mechanism.

Bug. An error in a computer program.

Burst mode. Transferring data between a single high-speed I/O device and main memory.

Bus. A group of circuits that provides the communications paths between the elements of a digital computer system.

Business Data Processing. The systematic processing of data in a system. Usually the term is used to relate to computerized business systems.

Byte. A sequence of adjacent binary digits operated upon as a unit and usually shorter than a computer word.

Card punch. An output device that converts computer data into coded punches on a card.

Card reader. An input device that converts coded punches on a card into computer code.

Carriage control tape. A continuous loop paper tape in the printer that controls skipping and spacing of the paper.

Cassette. A compact self-contained tape used for data recording on data entry devices and microcomputers.

CCD. Charged-Coupled Device.

Central processing unit. A unit of a computer that includes the circuits controlling the interpretation and execution of instructions. Synonymous with mainframe.

Chain printer. A printer in which the type is carried by the links of a revolving chain.

Channel. (1) A path along which signals can be sent, e.g., data channel, output channel. (2) The portion of a storage medium that is accessible to a given reading or writing station, e.g., track, band. (3) In communication, a means of one-way transmission.

Character. A letter, digit, or other symbol that is used as part of the organization, control, or representation of data.

Character code. The representation of a character as a zone-and-digit combination. Common character codes include the Hollerith card code, EBCDIC, and ASCII.

Charged-Coupled Device. An electronic device using semiconductors for primary storage.

Checkpoint. A place in a routine where a check, or a recording of data for restart purposes, is performed.

Clock. A timer used to time cycles in the central processor.

COBOL. COmmon Business-Oriented Language. A high-level source language for business applications.

Coding. The process of writing computer instructions in a programming language.

Coding form. The form on which program instructions are written. Each programming language has its own unique coding forms.

Collating sequence. The sequence formed by characters in a particular coding system. Usually special characters are lower in value than alphabetic, which are lower than numeric.

Collator. A device used for collating sequences of punched cards.

COM. Computer Output Microfilm.

Common carrier. A communications company, such as AT&T or Bell, which provides voice and data transmission services.

Communications lines. The physical means of connecting one location to another for the purpose of transmitting and receiving data.

Communications Satellite Corporation (COMSAT). A privately owned company, chartered by the U.S. Congress for voice and television signal communication by satellite.

Compile. To prepare a machine language program from a computer program written in another programming language by making use of the overall logic structure of the program, or generating more than one machine instruction for each symbolic statement, or both, as well as performing the function of an assembler.
Compiler. A program that compiles.
Compute-bound. A program or a computer system that is restricted or limited by the speed of the CPU.
Computer. A data processor that can perform substantial computation, including numerous arithmetic or logic operations, without intervention by a human operator during the run.
Computer output microfilm. An output device that uses combined electronic, photo-optical, and electromechanical techniques to convert digital computer output to records that can be stored as rolls of microfilm or as frames of microfilm stored on cards called microfiche.
Computer system. The hardware and software components that must function together in order that a computer might actually process data into information.
COMSAT. Communications Satellite Corporation.
Concentrator. A device that allows a number of slow-speed devices to utilize a single high-speed line. Also called a multiplexor.
Concurrent. Pertaining to the occurrence of two or more events or activities within the same specified interval of time.
Connect time. The time interval from the initial connection to the final breaking of a communication.
Console. A typewriter or CRT terminal used by a computer operator to assist in operating the computer.
Console listing. A listing of activities that have occurred at the console.
Constant. A fixed value or data item that does not change in value.
Constraint. A condition, such as time or money, that limits the solutions to the problem that may be considered.
Continuous form. Paper that is a continuous length with pages that can be separated at a perforation.
Controls. Checks that should be built into a system to ensure the integrity and correctness of the procedures of that system.
Control program. An operating system program with the purpose of controlling the computer.
Control unit. An electronic device, intermediate between a computer and an I/O device, that performs such functions as buffering and standard interface.
Control unit portion of CPU (instruction control unit). In a digital computer, those parts that effect the retrieval of instructions in proper sequence, the interpretation of each instruction, and the application of

the proper signals to the arithmetic unit and other parts in accordance with this interpretation.

Conversion. The process of changing from an old system to a new one.

Core dump. See storage dump.

Core plane. Magnetic cores strung (wired) together in a plane in a pattern that enables combinations of cores to represent binary-coded characters.

Core storage. A form of high-speed storage using magnetic cores.

CPU. Central Processing Unit.

CRT. Cathode Ray Tube.

Cursor. A symbol on a CRT that indicates where the next character will be displayed.

Cycle stealing. Taking an occasional machine cycle from a CPU's regular activities in order to control such things as an input or output operation. Commonly used on minicomputers.

Cylinder. One position of a disk access arm, allowing access to a number of tracks.

Cylinder Index. An index used to reference the cylinder on an indexed sequential file.

Data. (1) A representation of facts, concepts, or instructions in a formalized manner suitable for communication, interpretation, or processing by humans or automatic means. (2) Any representations such as characters or analog quantities to which meaning is or might be assigned.

Data bank. A collection of data in one place (see data-base).

Data-base. A comprehensive collection of libraries of data.

Data cell. A mass storage device that utilizes strips of magnetic tape housed in a rotating cylinder.

Data collection. The act of bringing data from one or more points to a central point.

Data communication. The transmission of data from one point to another.

Data entry. Introducing data into a data processing or information processing system.

Data management. A general term that collectively describes those functions of the control program that provide access to data sets, enforce data storage conventions, and regulate the use of input/output devices.

Data processing. The execution of a systematic sequence of operations performed upon data. Synonymous with information processing.

Data set. A device that performs the modulation/demodulation and control functions necessary to provide compatibility between business machines and communications facilities.

Data transfer rate. Pertains to the rate at which data can be transferred from main memory to another medium on which data are recorded. For magnetic tape, the data transfer rate is equal to the product of the tape speed and the recording density.

DBMS. Data-Base Management System.

DDP. Distributed Data Processing.

Debugging. The process of finding and correcting bugs in a program.

Decimal number system. A number system with a base or radix of 10.

Decision table. A chart used to assist in developing program logic.

Demodulation. The process of retrieving intelligence (data) from a modulated carrier wave; the reverse of modulation.

Density. The number of bits in a single linear track measured per unit of length of the recording medium.

Detail file. See transaction file.

Detail line. A line of output (on a report) that contains detail information as opposed to a summary line.

Diagnostic. A message generated by a computer or interpreter to assist in program error correction.

Digit. A symbol that represents one of the non-negative integers smaller than the radix.

Digital computer. (1) A computer in which discrete representation of data is mainly used. (2) A computer that operates on discrete data by performing arithmetic and logic processes on these data.

Direct access. (1) Pertaining to the process of obtaining data from, or placing data into, storage where the time required for such access is independent of the location of the data most recently obtained or placed in storage. (2) Pertaining to a storage device in which the access time is effectively independent of the location of the data. (3) Synonymous with random access.

Disk, magnetic. A flat circular plate with a magnetic surface on which data can be stored by selective magnetization of portions of the flat surface.

Disk pack. A stack of magnetic disks in a single container.

Diskette. A small disk pack. Sometimes called a floppy disk.

Distributed data processing. Decentralized data processing.

Document Reader. An optical input device that is able to read documents printed in a special type font. The document content is, roughly, equal to a line on a punched card.

Documentation. (1) The creating, collecting, organizing, storing, citing, and disseminating of documents of the information recorded in documents. (2) A collection of documents or information on a given subject.

Doubleword. An entity of storage two words in length.

Drum printer. A line printer using a rotating cylindrical drum.

Dual density. A floppy disk with dual side recording capability.

Dump. See storage dump.

EAM. Electronic Accounting Machine.
EBCDIC. Extended Binary Coded Decimal Interchange Code.
EDD. Electronic Document Distribution. A technique for transmitting correspondence via a data communications system as opposed to using the mail system.
EFT. Electronic Funds Transfer.
Electronic checkout. A cash register that acts as a terminal or data collection device for a computer system.
Electrographic printer. A printer that uses laser and electrophotographic technology for high-speed page printing.
Emulate. A process whereby one computer is made to function like a different computer.
EPROM. Erasable Programmable Read-Only Memory. Is a type of PROM whose program can be erased and re-programmed when required.
Execution. The act of carrying out an instruction or performing a routine.
Feasibility study. An evaluation of alternative problem solutions in order to select the most cost-effective system, taking into account constraints that limit the solutions that may be considered.
Feedback. The process of feeding output from one area of a system back to an earlier process in the system.
Field. In a record, a specified area used for a particular category of data, e.g., a group of card columns used to represent a wage rate, a set of bit locations in a computer word used to express the address of the operand.
File. A collection of related records treated as a unit.
File layout. A document that describes the position and type of fields in records that constitute a file.
File maintenance. The act of maintaining or updating a file.
File protection ring. A small plastic ring that is inserted in the back of a tape reel to enable the writing process. When the ring is removed, only reading the tape is possible.
Firmware. A sequence of instructions (software) that is substituted for hardware. This sequence of instructions is stored in read-only memory (ROM).
First generation. A generation of computers characterized by the use of vacuum tubes.
Fixed-head magnetic disk. A magnetic disk system that eliminates the use of an access mechanism by distributing all the read/write heads over the disk surfaces.
Fixed length records. Records, contained in a file, that are identical in length.
Fixed word length. A measurement of a unit of addressable storage that is a standard length. For instance a word consisting of 4 bytes.

Floppy disk. A flexible magnetic disk used on mini- or microcomputer systems.
Flowchart. A graphical representation for the definition, analysis, or solution of a problem, in which symbols are used to represent operations, data flow, equipment, etc.
Foreground. The partition in a multiprogramming system containing the high-priority application program.
FORTRAN (FORmula TRANslating system). A language primarily used to express computer programs by arithmetic formulas.
Fourth generation language. A user oriented language requiring a minimum of programming skills to use.
Full duplex. In communications, pertaining to a simultaneous two-way independent transmission in both directions. Contrast with half duplex.
GIGO. Garbage In Garbage Out.
Graphic plotter. A computer output device that draws graphs by moving a pen between X and Y coordinates.
Half duplex. In communications, pertaining to an alternate, one way at a time, independent transmission. Contrast with full duplex.
Halfword. A measure of storage that is half the length of a word.
Handshaking. Exchange of predetermined signals when a connection is established between two data sets.
Hard copy. Refers to printed output or documents in general.
Hardware. Physical equipment, as opposed to the computer program or method of use, e.g., mechanical, magnetic, electrical, or electronic devices. Contrast with software.
Hexadecimal. A number system with a base, or radix, of 16. Its digits are 0 through F.
High-level language. Programming languages where a source statement may be translated into several object statements. Refers to language such as BASIC, COBOL, FORTRAN and PL/I.
High-order position. Is the left-most position of a field.
HIPO. Hierarchy plus Input, Process, and Output.
Hollerith code. A punch card code using zones and numerics invented by Herman Hollerith.
Hybrid computer. A computer that combines measuring capability of an analog computer and the counting capability of a digital computer.
Impact printer. A printer that forms characters by physically striking a ribbon and paper.
Implementation. The act of completing or installing a program or a system.
Indexed sequential. A file organization technique in which data are placed on a file in sequence and an index is maintained, thus allowing both sequential and direct access.

Information. The meaning that a human assigns to data by means of the known conventions used in their representation.

Input. Pertaining to a device, process, or channel involved in the insertion of data or states, or to the data or states involved.

Input device. A hardware device used for conveying data to the central processor.

Input/output control system. Software that assists the programmer in processing input or output files.

Inquiry. The process of requesting information at a terminal.

Instruction. A statement that specifies an operation and the values or locations of its operands.

Integrated circuit. Is a circuit design based on microminiaturization technology.

Intelligent terminal. A terminal with some logic ability used in a distributed processing system.

Interblock gap. A gap on tape or disk that separates blocks or physical records.

Interface. A shared boundary.

Internal storage. See Primary Storage.

Interpreter. (1) A computer program that transfers and executes each source language statement before translating and executing the next one. (2) A device that prints on a punched card the data already punched in the card.

Interrecord gap. Same as interblock gap.

Interrupt. To stop a process in such a way that it can be resumed.

I/O. An abbreviation for input/output.

I/O-bound. A program or computer system that is restricted or limited in processing speed by its I/O devices.

IOCS. Input/Output Control System.

IPL. Initial Program Load.

JCL. Job Control Language.

Job. A specified group of tasks prescribed as a unit of work for a computer. By extension, a job usually includes all necessary computer programs, linkages, files, and instructions to the operating system.

Job control statement. A statement in a job that is used in identifying the job or describing its requirements to the operating system.

K. Usually found in reference to storage capacity, 1024 in decimal notation or two to the tenth power.

Key. One or more characters within an item of data that are used to identify it or control its use.

Key field. A field within a data record that acts as the key, e.g., social security number, product number.

Key-to-disk. A method of data entry whereby an operator creates data on a small magnetic disk (usually referred to as a diskette) from a source document, using a standard keyboard.

Key-to-tape. A method of data entry whereby an operator creates data on a small magnetic tape from a source document, using a standard keyboard.

Keyboard terminal. This term describes a typewriterlike keyboard that allows data to be entered into a computer system.

Keypunch. A machine used to create a computer punch card. An operator enters data from a source document on a standard typewriterlike keyboard and the data is punched into the card.

Label record. A record on a file of magnetic tape that contains identifying information about that file, e.g., name of the file, expiry date.

LAN. Local Area Network.

Language processor. A program (such as an assembler, compiler or interpreter) that is used to translate source program instructions to object or machine language.

Laser-beam printer. See electrographic printer.

Layout. The format or arrangement of a series of data fields within a record.

Library. A collection of files or programs.

Light pen. An option with various CRT terminals to allow an operator to use a hand-held pen to (a) select from a series of choices offered on the screen or to (b) make changes to the data on the screen.

Line. See communications line.

Literal. Any data that is used exactly as it is defined, in a program.

Load point marker. A visible reflective strip placed on a magnetic tape (usually eight to ten feet from the beginning) that indicates the start of the area on the tape available for representing data.

Logging routine. A procedure that creates a record of all transactions (inquiries and updates) on a secondary storage device such as magnetic tape or magnetic disk. Usually found in telecommunications systems where there may be no original source document.

Logical record. A group of fields representing one individual record that is independent of its physical environment. It is usually a subset of a physical record.

Loop. A sequence of instructions (in a program or a flowchart) that is executed repeatedly until a certain condition occurs

Low-level language. A programming language requiring a translation on assembly into machine language before processing by the computer. The low-level languages require a greater understanding of the workings of the computer before they can be used effectively. This is in contrast to a high-level language such as COBOL or PL/I.

Low-order position. The right-most position in a data field.

LSI. Large Scale Integration refers to the process of putting large numbers of transistors and components on a very small chip thereby reducing the size of main memory storage.

Machine cycle. A reference to a procedure performed by the CPU whereby a single instruction is fetched, decoded, and executed.

Machine instruction. An instruction that a machine can understand and execute.

Machine language. A language that is used directly by a machine, therefore a program written in machine language would not require any translation process. A source language would have to be translated to machine language.

Macro. A single instruction (usually in an assembly language) that actually represents several assembler language instructions.

Mag card. A type of storage used with certain types of typewriters that allows the data entered through the keyboard to be stored on a magnetic card (about the size of a punch card). This card can then be reused at a later time to automatically produce a required report.

Magnetic bubble memory. An electronic storage device that uses the properties of certain materials, under applied magnetic fields, to represent binary 1's and 0's.

Magnetic core. A small ring of magnetic material that can be magnetized in either of two directions and thus can represent one binary digit.

Magnetic disk. A secondary storage device usually consisting of a series of flat, circular plates each of which can be magnetized. Data is thus stored on the disk by magnetizing various portions of the disk using a binary code. The magnetic disk is commonly found in large volume, high-speed applications.

Magnetic drum. A secondary storage device that consists of a magnetically coated cylinder with fixed reading and writing heads thereby making the drum work faster than most disks.

Magnetic tape. A secondary storage medium, about one-half inch wide that is coated with a material that allows the tape to be magnetized. Various binary codes represent the data on the tape.

Mainframe. A reference to the central processing unit of a computer system.

Main storage. See primary storage.

Maintenance. Any activity intended to eliminate faults or to keep hardware or programs in satisfactory working condition, including tests, measurements, replacements, adjustments and repairs.

Mark sensing. The electrical sensing of manually recorded conductive marks on a non-conductive surface.

Mass storage device. A hardware device capable of storing large volumes of data, e.g., magnetic drum on magnetic disk.

Master file. A file that is either relatively permanent or that is treated as an authority in a particular job.

Matrix printer. A printer that generates a character at a time using a print matrix of a 5 × 7 rectangle of print pins. Various combinations of the print pins represent the required characters.

Megabyte. One million bytes of storage.

Memory. The same as the term storage.

Merge. A merge describes combining two or more sets of records with similarly ordered sets into one set that is arranged in the same order.

MICR Magnetic Ink Character Recognition. Special characters constructed from magnetic ink that can be read by both humans and equipment. Used in high volume applications such as check handling procedures by banks.

Microcomputer. A small computer system usually consisting of a CPU (often on a single chip), some memory (random access memory and read-only memory), some storage (diskette on magnetic tape cassette), a keyboard (for data entry) and a CRT screen (for output results).

Microfiche. A unit of film (that is approximately four inches by six inches) that is divided into rectangles, each typically representing a page of information. Although the average microfiche contains about 250 pages of information, a large reduction ratio can generate up to 500 pages of information on a single card.

Microfilm. A photographed record of a source document in a reduced size stored in such mediums such as roll film, cartridge, aperture cards, microfiche.

Microprocessor. A chip of silicon that can actually have enough transistors and circuits imprinted on its surface so as to duplicate all the functions of a typical CPU.

Microsecond. One-millionth of a second.

Microwave. Any electromagnetic wave in the radio frequency spectrum above 890 megacycles. Used in Data Communications to transmit data from one source to another.

Millisecond. One-thousandth of a second.

Minicomputer. A small computer (usually thought of as a desk-top in size) that has most of the features of a standard computer system but does not require any special air-conditioning or wiring environment in order to process data.

MIS. Management Information System. An all-encompassing system designed to provide company information to those in management positions.

Modem. A device that MOdulates and DEModulates signals (from analog to digital and vice versa) transmitted over communications facilities.

Modulation. The encoding of data (usually in binary form) into an analog signal (either frequency modulation, amplitude modulation or phase modulation) for data transmission from one source to another.

Monitor. See supervisor.
MOS. Metal Oxide Semiconductor, a type of internal storage.
Multiplexing. The use of a device to allow two or more messages to be transmitted at one time over a single communications channel.
Multiplexor channel. A data channel that multiplexes or overlaps the operation of two or more low-speed I/O devices.
Multiprocessing. Two or more CPUs within the same computer system executing an instruction or a series of instructions (e.g., a program) at the same time.
Multiprogramming. This phrase describes the ability of the computer to actually run two or more programs concurrently. When one program requires an input or an output, another program can be performing calculations. In this manner (given the extremely fast internal speed of the machine), the computer gives the appearance of actually doing more than one program at once.
Nanosecond. One-billionth of a second.
Network. A series of stations interconnected by communication lines, terminals, or computers.
Non-impact printer. An output device that generates characters on a page using electronic or photoelectric techniques rather than having a mechanical device (e.g., a print hammer) strike the output paper.
Number system. Basically, a number system consists of a set of rules representing data. The rules are common throughout all the various systems, e.g., binary (base$_2$), octal (base$_8$), decimal (base$_{10}$).
Numeric field. A data item containing only numeric characters.
Object program. A program in machine language that has been generated from a compile or assembly (i.e., a translation) that can be executed by the computer without further translation.
OCR. See Optical Character Recognition.
Octal. A number system with the number eight (8) as its base.
OEM. See Original Equipment Manufacturer.
Off-line. A procedure using data processing machines or devices that is not under direct control of the central processing unit. Data entry would be an example of an off-line procedure.
OMR. See Optical Mark Reader.
On-line. Refers to a procedure under the direct control of the central processing unit. This condition usually allows for immediate processing of data as opposed to batch processing.
On-line storage. Secondary storage devices that are under direct control of the central processing unit (e.g., magnetic tape or magnetic disk) such that data is available immediately when required.
Operand. Represents an address of a unit of data to be operated upon.
Operating system. Software that controls the execution of computer programs and that may provide scheduling, debugging, input/output con-

trol, accounting, compilation, storage assignment, data management, and related services.

Operator. The character in a source language that represents an operation to be performed, e.g., + for addition (in most languages), or * for multiplication (in BASIC and COBOL).

Optical Character Recognition. A light sensitive device able to detect (and therefore read) upper and lower case alphabetic characters, numeric and special characters, and bar codes on many types of source documents.

Optical Mark Reader. An input device able to read and interpret marks (usually soft pencil marks) on special input documents.

Original Equipment Manufacturer. A manufacturer of computers who buys computer components (e.g., small microprocessors) for use in its own final product.

Output. The finished results of processing by a system. The output might be a printed report, a message over a communication line, or an updated disk file.

Output device. The device or collective set of devices used for conveying data out of another device. It is usually taking data from the computer and storing it in another format that is suitable for processing.

Overflow. The portion of the result of an operation that exceeds the capacity of the intended unit of storage.

Overlap. See Process I/O overlap.

Packed decimal. A technique of representing numbers in EBCDIC (a binary code) such that two numbers that normally would require two bytes to store their values could be "packed" into one byte.

Paging. In a virtual storage system, paging refers to the swapping of data (and programs) back and forth from real storage (primary storage to virtual storage (secondary storage).

Paper tape. An input/output medium that represents data via a pattern of punched holes along a continuous strip of paper.

Parallel run. A conversion technique, such that the old system and the new system are both run for a period of time until the new system is proven and accepted. Then the old system is discontinued.

Parity bit. A check (or extra) bit appended to an array of binary digits to make the sum of all the binary digits, including the check bit, always odd or always even.

Partition. In a multiprogramming environment, main storage is divided into areas or partitions such that each partition is thought of as a complete storage area and therefore each partition can process a computer program.

Peripheral equipment. In a data processing system, any unit of equipment, distinct from the central processing unit, which may provide the system with outside communication.

Personal computer. An inexpensive small computer (usually a microcomputer) designed for the home consumer.

Physical record. A block of data transferred between main memory and secondary storage. It may be divided into many logical records.

Picosecond. One trillionth of a second.

Pilot study. When a new system is being implemented, a branch of the business (on one section within a department) may be completely converted to the new system ahead of all areas within the firm. The results from the Pilot study would then be analyzed so that the determined errors will not be present when the system is fully implemented.

PL/I. Programming Language One is a high-level source language that many describe as a combination of COBOL and FORTRAN.

Plug compatible. A peripheral device that can function or work with another manufacturer's computer system by direct link-up as opposed to requiring connection modification (or an interface).

POS. A Point of Sale system employs terminals that double as cash registers and data collection devices for storing data on sales inventory. Also, the pricing data is usually generated by the terminal thereby decreasing keying time and keying errors for the cashier.

Polling. A technique by which each of the terminals sharing a communications line is periodically interrogated to determine whether it requires servicing (i.e., that particular line has some data to transmit).

Port. A connection point for a communication line.

Positional notation. A numeration system in which a number is represented by means of an ordered set of digits, such that the value contributed by each digit depends upon its position as well as upon its value.

Primary storage. It is that part of the central processing unit that data and programs must be loaded into in order for the programs to be processed by the computer. It is sometimes called main storage, or the storage unit.

Printer. A device in a computer system used to generate paper output (hard copy) from the coded (or internal format) of the data.

Printer spacing chart. A tool used by a systems analyst (or programmer) to draw an image of the form that is to be created through a computer program. The characteristics of the printer (e.g., 6 lines/inch and 10 characters/inch) would be indicated on the chart.

Printout. A document generated from a printer, synonymous with report, listing.

Problem definition. A report generated by a systems analyst after an analysis of a firm (or department) that describes the weaknesses or problems of the existing system.

Procedure manual. A manual that describes the job functions (by title) that are required in a certain department.

Process bound. A program (or system) that spends the majority of its execution time in calculations and operations rather than input or output procedures. Also known as compute bound.

Process I/O overlap. A method for overlapping processing operations and input/output operations.

Program. A series of instructions or statements in a form acceptable to a computer, prepared in order to achieve a certain result.

Programming language. A language used to create computer programs. The language could be a high-level language (such as COBOL or PL/I) or a low-level language (such as assembler).

PROM. Programmable Read-Only Memory is a type of memory available in many microcomputer systems such that data entered into a PROM is retained when the microcomputer is turned off.

Pseudo-code. A method used, just before the actual programming starts, that can show the control structures, in a structured programming environment.

Punch card. A card punched with a pattern of holes to represent data.

RAM. Random Access Memory is a type of memory available in a microcomputer for use over and over again. In fact, the contents of a RAM are lost when the microcomputer is turned off.

Random access. See direct access.

Read/write head. A mechanism found in a magnetic recording medium (e.g., tape or disk) that allows data to be written on the medium (by causing the surface to be magnetized) and read from the medium (by sensing the absence or presence of magnetized patterns).

Real memory. A computer's actual memory (i.e., internal storage) that is directly addressable by the central processing unit.

Realtime. A system that processes data fast enough such that the effects of the data (inquiry or update) can be examined right away and an associated decision can therefore be made.

Record. A collection of related fields of data, treated as a unit.

Record length. The size of the collection of related data fields within the record, usually measured in bytes or characters.

Redundancy. The repetition of data in more than one place, e.g., a product number appearing in eight different files.

Register. A unit within the central processing unit used for arithmetic calculations and for representing addresses of data and instructions within the storage unit. Often a register is big enough to accommodate four bytes of data.

Remote job entry. This term describes the entering of jobs from a terminal (remote from the main computer), having the job processed, and then having the results returned to that same terminal station.

Report Program Generator. It is a high-level business language that is suited for programs that require a lot of printed reports.

Reproducer. A piece of unit record equipment that could reproduce all or parts of the data on one punch card into another punch card.

Resident program. A program that resides permanently in the storage unit of the central processing unit (e.g., the supervisor, or monitor, program).

Response time. The elapsed time between the generation of a message or inquiry at a terminal and the receipt of the reply from the computer system.

Retention cycle. The length of time that a file is considered active. In most systems, three back-up copies of a given file are kept for restoration purposes. The three files are often known as the son-father-grandfather copies.

RJE. See remote job entry.

ROM. This type of memory, Read-Only Memory is found in microcomputers and as the name implies, stores data that can only be read or processed. New data cannot be entered into a ROM, and the contents of a ROM are retained when the microcomputer is turned off.

Rotational delay. The time needed for the read/write heads to find a given record once they have been positioned over the correct track on a disk or a drum.

Routine. A sequence of instructions that perform a specific procedure that is frequently needed.

RPG. See Report Program Generator.

Second generation. A group of computers (in the late 1950s and early 1960s) characterized by extensive use of transistors as their main component.

Secondary identifier. A name applied to a field used to confirm that a given record is in fact the one that was required. For example, an inquiry using a Social Security number as a key field might use the first five positions of the surname to check that the inquiry will find the correct record.

Secondary storage. Storage on devices such as magnetic tape, disk, or drum that must be accessed and have data read into main storage before the computer can act on that data. Also known as auxiliary storage.

Seek time. The time required to move the read/write mechanism of a direct access device to a desired track.

Selector channel. A data channel designed to connect several high-speed I/O devices (such as magnetic disk) to the central processing unit along a connected line and transmit data extremely quickly from one device at a time.

Semiconductor. Computer memory composed of integrated circuits.

Sequence. An arrangement of items (records, fields) in accordance with a given set of rules.

Sequential access. A method of processing required records from a file where the records are stored and accessed consecutively.

Service Bureau. A company that offers Data Processing services (consulting, programming, actual computer time) for a fee.

Simplex. A communications line that allows one-way transmission of data.

Simulation. A technique that involves creating a model to represent a real-life situation. The model can then be subjected to data, tests, changes, alternatives in order to (a) more fully understand the situation and to (b) be able to predict how the situation will perform in the future.

Soft copy. An output from a computer system on a device such as a visual display (CRT) or a voice response unit. If a hard copy is required, the output must also be directed to a printer.

Software. A set of computer programs, procedures, and possibly associated documentation concerned with the operation of a data processing system—e.g., compilers, library routines, manuals.

Sort. To segregate items into groups according to some definite rules.

Sorter. A unit record device that sorts punch cards into alphabetic or numeric sequence or selects cards with a specific punch in a certain column.

Source document. The original document containing the data that is required by the computer system. The Data Entry department usually receives the source documents (e.g., sales slips, application forms) and creates a new medium (punchcard, tape, or disk) containing the desired data in a machine readable format.

Source language. A computer programming language such as COBOL or Assembler that requires a translation into machine language before the computer can understand the instructions.

Source program. A computer program written in a source language. The point to remember is that a source program requires translation whereas an object program does not.

Special character. A character that is not a number, an alphabetic character, or a space. For example, a dollar sign, a period, and a comma are all examples of special characters.

Special purpose computer. A computer that is designed to handle a restricted class of problems.

Spooling. Data is moved from a slow I/O device (such as a card reader), to a fast I/O device (such as a magnetic disk) before that data is accessed by main storage. This technique helps to minimize the speed disparity between the internal speeds of the computer and the I/O devices. For an output procedure, the order of data movement is reversed.

Statement. In computer programming, a meaningful expression or generalized instruction in a source language.

Storage. Pertaining to a device into which data can be entered, in which they can be held, and from which they can be retrieved at a later time. Loosely, any device that can store data. Synonymous with memory.

Storage capacity. A measure of the amount of data that can be represented in a storage device, usually measured in characters or bytes.

Storage dump. A printout of the contents of the internal storage locations and registers for help in debugging computer programs. Also known as core dump.

Stored program. A series of commands loaded into the computer that in fact direct and control the operations within that computer.

Structured design. An approach to problem solving using a set of guidelines, techniques, and special symbols to determine a set of interconnected modules (or procedures), organized in a hierarchical fashion (as in top down development) that will resolve a certain problem.

Structured programming. A method of programming that uses top down development program design such that modules of program code are based on three basic control structures.

Subroutine. A routine that can be part of another routine.

Supervisor. This program, known as the supervisor, is part of the operating system and resides in the central processing unit. Its function is to control and direct the other parts of the central processing unit and to prepare the system for execution of programs. Also known as a monitor.

Synchronous. Occurring concurrently and with a regular or predictable time relationship.

Syntax. The grammatical correctness of a set of commands in a programming language. "Grammatical" with respect to the rules of that particular language.

System. A set of standardized procedures used to accomplish a specified task.

Systems Analysis. The analysis of an activity to determine precisely what must be accomplished and how to accomplish it.

Systems flowchart. A pictorial representation of a set of procedures using widely accepted symbols that are connected together on a page to show an overview of the processing steps in a system.

Tabulating equipment. See Unit Record equipment.

Tape. See magnetic tape or paper tape.

Tape drive. A device that allows the writing or reading of a magnetic tape by moving the tape across a read/write head. Also known as a tape transport.

Teletypewriter. A typewriterlike device using a keyboard for input and paper for output, often found as a component in a computer system.

Template. A piece of plastic with various shapes cut out for easier and more accurate drawing of common symbols, e.g., flowcharting template.
Terminal. A device in a telecommunications network that enters or receives data from the main computer.
Testing. The process of subjecting a computer program to representative sample data to assure that the logic in the program is correct and it in fact does solve the problem it was designed for.
Thermal printer. A dot matrix printer using heat-sensitive paper to form printed characters.
Third generation. A series of computers using integrated circuits and miniaturization as their main components.
Thrashing. In a virtual storage environment, an excessive amount of moving pages from secondary storage to the internal storage is sometimes referred to as thrashing.
Throughput. A measure of the efficiency of a computer system. It involves observing the amount of work done (or data processed) over a given period of time.
Timesharing. One company with a large central processing unit shares time on its computer with various other users (perhaps small firms who cannot afford their own machine). Although the computer is being used by several individuals, probably via terminals, each user is not aware of other users on the system.
Time slice. A period of time that is assigned to the various users in a timesharing environment when a particular user's programs are active in the computer.
Top down development. An approach to problem solving (either systems analysis or programming) that suggests starting at the top looking at the problem as a whole and then gradually introducing layers of details until the problem is solved.
Track. In general, a track is that portion of a moving storage medium, such as a drum, tape, or disk, that is accessible to a given reading head position. On magnetic tape, it is one of the seven or nine horizontal rows; on magnetic disk, it is one of several concentric circles.
Trailer label. A record at the end of a magnetic tape file that contains identifying information about that file—e.g., the number of records in the file.
Transaction. A single input record that could be an inquiry, an update, a delete, or an add to be applied to a given file.
Transaction file. A file containing information that changes with each transaction, e.g., amount of sale, quantity purchased.
Transfer rate. See data transfer rate.
Transmission. The sending of data from one location and the receiving of data in another location, usually leaving the source data unchanged.

Turnaround. The elapsed time between submission of a job to a computing center and the return of the results.

Turnkey system. A system (and its accompanying documentation) written in such a way that an untrained user can operate the system. The assumption is that the user simply wants to have to "turn the key" and have his computer function for him.

Unit record. A record such as a punch card that represents one unit of information. Prior to the sixties, unit record equipment stood for a series of devices (sorter, collater, interpreter, reproducer) that a firm would acquire to use with their punch cards in order to take advantage of electronic data processing.

Universal Product Code. An optical bar code placed on most grocery goods so that information such as name of product and price can be extracted from a computer file when the product is subjected to a bar reader by the cashier at the point-of-sale terminal.

User. A member of a department outside of the data processing department who has either some inputs or outputs connected with the computer system.

Utility program. Standard programs, usually within the operating system that perform standard routines such as sorts, card-to-tape programs, and disk-to-printer programs.

Variable. A storage area that can assume any of a given set of values.

Variable-length record. A file in which the records are of different lengths.

Verifier. A machine very similar to the keypunch that allows punch cards prepared on the keypunch to be checked for accuracy. Any cards found in error are returned to the keypunch for re-punching.

Verify. To determine whether a transcription of data or other operation has been accomplished accurately. To check the results of keypunching, key-to-tape entry or key-to-disk entry.

Video display. See CRT.

Virtual storage. A technique to maximize and optimize the storage available in a computer by using areas on secondary storage devices as extensions of internal storage. Pages of data are swapped back and forth from disk to storage unit as required. Also known as virtual memory.

Visual display. See CRT.

Voice grade line. A transmission line available for transmission of speech or data (in an analog form). The frequency range is 300 to 3000 cycles per second and the speed of data delivery is about 1200–9600 bits per second.

Voice recognition unit. A computer input device that converts spoken words into binary data.

Voice response unit. A terminal that generates output in a simulated voicelike response.

Wait state. An IBM phrase, as applied to tasks, that describes the condition of a task such that it is dependent on an event or events in order to enter a ready condition.

Word. A character string or bit string considered as an entity. Usually it is four bytes in length.

Word Processing. Instead of a typing pool with hard copy outputs created every time a typewriter is used, a word processing system employs terminals that allow operators to key in the required typing. They can change the data on the terminal and when it is finished and correct the operator can release the data for printing. The information can also be stored by the computer for future use to reduce the operator's keying time, the next time that report, letter, or contract is required.

Zoned decimal. The name of the format of storing digits in eight bits where the high-order four bits represent the zone, and the low-order four bits stand for the numeric part of the number.

Index

A

Abacus, 15, 643
Access arms, 163, 643
Access time, 167, 643
Accounting machine, 30, 643
Accounts payable, 436
Accounts receivable, 430
Accumulator, 213, 643
Acoustic coupler, 556, 643
Acronym, 643
Ada, 21
Address, 73, 207, 214, 643
Addressing, 486
Address register, 213
Airline reservation system, 519
Air traffic control, 520
Algorithm, 556, 643
Alphabetic, 94, 643
American National Standards Institute (ANSI), 547, 644
American Standard Code for Information Interchange (ASCII), 59, 149, 644
Analog computer, 11, 72, 644
Analysis, 350, 355, 644
Analytical Engine, 19
ANSI COBOL, 547
APL, 72
Apple, 36
Arithmetic and Logic Unit (ALU), 74, 205, 208, 644
Artificial Intelligence (AI), 644
Assembler, 644
Asynchronous, 644
Audit trail, 393, 644
Average rotational delay, 167
Average seek time, 167

B

Babbage, Charles P., 19
Back-up, 644
Back-up programmer, 280
Bandwidth, 482, 644
Bar code, 76, 116
Base, 41, 644
BASIC, 286, 307, 644
  arithmetic, 312
  arrays, 337
  DATA, 322
  DIM, 338
  END, 311
  FOR and NEXT, 334
  GOSUB, 343
  GOTO, 330
  IF, 330
  INPUT, 320
  iteration, 334
  LET, 312
  line number, 308
  lists, 337
  names, 309
  PRINT, 325
  READ, 323
  REM, 308
  RETURN, 343
  STOP, 311

BASIC (*Contd.*)
  subroutines, 343
  tables, 337
  variables, 309
Basic tree structure, 494
Batch processing, 89, 645
Batch total, 388
Batch translators, 284
Baud, 135, 478, 645
BCD (Binary Coded Decimal), 55, 645
Benchmark, 413, 645
Binary, 42, 645
Bit, 135, 150, 645
Block (*see* Physical record)
Block coding, 373
Block diagram, 348, 645
Blocking factor, 151, 645
Broadband, 478, 645
Buffer, 209, 645
Buffered keypunch, 98, 645
Bug, 271, 645
Burroughs, 21
Burst mode, 645
Bus, 238, 645
Byte, 70, 151, 167, 214, 645

C

CAI (Computer Assisted Instruction), 516
Calculator, 29
Carbons, 380
Card (*see* Punched card)
Card punch, 99, 645
Careers, 523, 538
Carriage control, 130, 646
Cash register, 115
Cassette, 102, 646
CCD (Charged Coupled Device), 218, 646
Central collection, 111
Central processing unit, 73, 205, 646
Chain printer, 123, 646
Channel, 221, 646
Channel Command Word (CCW), 458
Character, 102, 123, 646
Check digit coding, 376
Checkpoint, 457, 646
Chief programmer, 280
Chief programmer team, 279
Chip, 233
COBOL, 287, 547, 646
  A margin, 549
  arithmetic, 572
  B margin, 549
  CLOSE, 559
  coding, 549
  DATA DIVISION, 552
  COMPUTE, 574
  CONFIGURATION SECTION, 551
  ENVIRONMENT DIVISION, 551
  FD, 553
  FILE SECTION, 553
  IDENTIFICATION DIVISION, 551
  IF, 580
  INPUT-OUTPUT SECTION, 552
  MOVE, 571
  OPEN, 559
  PERFORM, 575
  PICTURE, 555, 565
  PROCEDURE DIVISION, 558, 571
  READ, 560
  SELECT, 552
  77 items, 565
  structures, 555, 559, 568
COBOL (*Contd.*)
  WORKING STORAGE, 564, 568
  WRITE, 561
CODASYL, 502
Coding, 549, 646
Collating sequence, 559, 646
Collator, 27, 646
COM (Computer Output Microfilm), 199, 645
Command Control Block (CCB), 458
Communication channel, 102, 111
Communication lines, 481, 646
Compilers, 283, 647
Complex hierarchical structure, 497
Computer number systems, 54
Computer revolution, 3
Computer system, 12, 647
Computerized checkout, 102
Concentrator, 483, 647
Concentric track, 163
Constraints, 363
Control area, 183
Control interval, 183
Control section, 75, 209
Control structures, 275
Control unit, 223
Core (*see* Magnetic core)
CPU (*see* Central processing unit)
CRT display, 133
Cursor, 108, 133–134, 648
Cycle, 208
Cylinder, 172, 648
Cylinder index, 180, 648

D

Daisy wheel, 123
Data, 67, 75, 648
Database, 491, 498, 648
Database
  Administrator (DBA), 500
Data communication, 473, 648
Data control
  auditing, 393
  hardware, 390
  input, 387
  on-line, 394
  operation, 392
  output, 390
  programming, 391
  separation of activity, 392
Data description languages, 502
Data entry, 93, 156, 174, 525, 648
Data flow diagram, 423
Data gathering techniques, 355
Data Language One (DL/I), 504
Data management, 458, 648
Data processing, 68, 648
Data rate, 151, 648
Data set, 482
Data structure, 494
Data and time codes, 377
dBASE II, 506
Debugging, 303, 649
Decimal, 40, 649
Decision table, 265, 420, 649
Density, 151, 649
Design
  coding, 372
  controls, 387
  forms, 378
  sample payroll, 394

Detail reports, 77, 84–85, 133
Difference Engine, 20
Digital computer, 10, 72, 649
Direct access files, 163, 175, 485, 649
Direct addressing, 486
Direct input, 76
Disk (*see* Magnetic disk)
Disk pack, 163, 649
Diskette, 241, 649
Display (*see* CRT display)
Distributed processing, 364, 487, 649
Document, 76
Dot matrix, 125
Drum plotter, 202
Drum printer, 124, 649

E

EBCDIC, 57, 149, 650
Education, 515
EDVAC, 24
Electrographic printer, 127, 650
Electronic components, 10
Electronic Document Distribution (EDD), 446, 650
Electronic Fund Transfer (EFT), 513, 650
Electronic mail, 515
End-of-reel marker, 147
ENIAC, 24
Entry level, 525
EPROM, 239, 650
Error reduction, 12
Exception reports, 88
Execution cycle, 208
Expandability, 487
Extended entry table, 267
External interrupt, 455

F

Feasibility, 650
Feedback, 349, 412, 650
Field 69–70, 396, 650
File, 70–71, 430, 485, 650
File activity ratio, 485
File maintenance, 180, 650
File protection, 145, 650
Final-digit coding, 374
Firmware, 650
First generation, 30, 650
Fixed head disk (*see* Head per track disk)
Fixed length record, 153, 650
Fixed length word, 216, 650
Floppy disk, 105, 651
Flowchart, 258, 417, 651
Font, 187
Foreground, 468, 651
Forms analysis (data gathering), 360
Forms control, 130–133
Forms design
  considerations, 379
  trends, 378
Forms filling, 139
FORTRAN, 289, 585, 651
  arithmetic, 590
  array, 605
  comments, 587
  DO, 602
  END, 589
  FORMAT, 594, 596
  GO TO, 598
  IF
    arithmetic, 599
    logical, 600
  integers, 588
  mixed mode, 588

FORTRAN (*Contd.*)
  numbers, 587
  PRINT, 596
  READ, 594
  real numbers, 588
  statement format, 586
  STOP, 589
  subscripts, 605
  variables, 589
  WRITE, 596
Fourth generation, 34, 295, 651
Frequency of processing, 498
Frequency of reference, 486
Full duplex, 481, 651

G

General-purpose, 11, 74
GIGO, 76, 651
Graphic display, 195
Group classification coding, 374
Group reports, 86

H

Half duplex, 481, 651
Hard copy, 77, 651
Hardware, 8, 390, 651
Header label, 154
Head per track disk, 167
Hexadecimal, 50, 651
Hierarchical structure, 495
High order, 41, 651
Hollerith, 22, 95, 651, (*see also* Punched card)
Hospital Information Systems (HIS), 518
Human-readable, 77
Hybrid computer, 72, 651

I

IC (Integrated circuit), 233
IF-THEN-ELSE control structure, 276
Impact printer, 122, 651
Implementation techniques, 410, 651
Index, 486
Indexed sequential, 177, 651
Index register, 213
Information, 67, 652
Information Management System (IMS)
Information processing, 68
Initial Program Load (IPL), 461
Ink-jet printer, 129
Input, 10, 75, 652
Input/Output Control System (IOCS), 458, 652
Input/Output interrupt, 455
Instruction, 207, 652
Instruction cycle, 208
Instruction register, 208, 213
Integrated Circuit (IC), 217, 652
Interactive translator, 285
Inter-block gap, 151, 652
Internal storage (*see* Main storage)
Interpreter, 29, 652
Interpreters, 284, 652
Inter-record gap, 151, 652
Interrupt, 455, 652
Interviewing, 358
Inquiry, 80, 136, 435, 438
Inventions, 15
Inventory system, 433

J

Jacquard, Joseph Marie, 19
JCL, 463, 652
Job control, 463
Job scheduling, 453
Job set-up, 452
Job step, 453

K

Key, 176, 652
Keyboard, 110
Keydisk, 105, 652
Keypunch, 97, 653
Keytape, 102, 653

L

LANs, 484, 653
Languages, 285, 464, 501
Laser holographic, 220
Laser printer, 127, 653
Law enforcement, 521
Least significant digit, 41
Librarian, 280, 466
Library, 466, 653
Limited entry table, 266
Linkage editor, 465
Linked list, 486
Loadpoint marker, 147
Local Area Network (LAN), 484, 653
Logging, 159, 174, 365, 653
Logical IOCS, 459
Logical record, 153, 168, 653
Low order, 41, 653
LSI (Large Scale Integrated Circuit), 228, 653

M

Machine check, 456
Machine language, 465, 654
Macro, 459, 654
Magnetic bubble, 219, 654
Magnetic core, 214, 654
Magnetic disk, 163, 654
Magnetic tape, 145, 654
Main storgage, 73, 211, 654
Management Information System (MIS), 492
Mark I, 23
Mark sensing, 191, 654
Mass storage, 198, 654
Master file, 70, 157, 431, 654
Master index, 180
Memory (see Main storage)
Menus, 139
Metric measurements, 535
MICR (Magnetic Ink Character Reader), 192, 655
Micro generation, 35
Microcomputer, 6, 232, 505, 529, 655
Microfiche, 199, 655
Microfilm, 199, 655
Microprocessor, 236, 655
Microsecond, 32, 655
Millisecond, 32, 655
Minicomputer, 227, 655
Modem, 482, 655
Modulation, 482, 655
MOS (Metal Oxide Semiconductor), 217, 228, 656
Mouse, 241
Multiplexor, 483
Multiplexor channel, 222, 656

Multiprocessing, 469, 656
Multiprogramming, 454, 467, 476, 656

N

Nanosecond, 32, 656
Napier's bones, 17
Network, 495, 656
Node, 494
Noise level, 480
Non-impact printer, 122, 656
Numbers, 39, 656
Numeric, 55–61

O

Object module, 453
Observation (data gathering), 362
OCR (Optical Character Recognition), 187, 656
Octal, 45, 656
Off-line, 159, 174
OMR (Optical Mark Recognition), 191
On-line, 438, 656
On-line system, 473
Operand, 207, 656
Operating system, 451, 460, 656
Operation, 207
Operator, 527, 657
Original Equipment Manufacturer (OEM), 228, 657
Output, 10, 77, 121, 657
Overflow track, 180

P

Page, 220
Paging, 220, 657
Parent, 494
Parity, 150, 657
Partition, 468, 657

Pascal, 291, 609
  arithmetic, 619
  arrays, 636
  BEGIN-END, 610
  CASE-END, 634
  CHAR, 615
  data names, 613
  DIV, 620
  EOLN, 639
  FOR-DO, 630
  IF, 628
  INTEGER, 614
  MOD, 620
  REAL, 614
  REPEAT UNTIL, 634
  reserved names, 613
  ROUND, 620
  TRUNC, 620
  VAR, 613
  VAR section, 613
  WHILE DO, 625, 632
  WRITE, 621
  WRITELN, 621
Pascal, Blaise, 18
Perform-until control structure, 277
Periodicals, 541
Personal computer, 6, 232, 658
Phonetic coding, 375
Physical IOCS, 458
Physical record, 153, 658
Picosecond, 32, 658
Pilot study, 410, 658
Plated wire, 216
PL/I, 292
Plotter, 202
Policies, 365
Polling, 480, 658
POS (Point Of Sale), 115, 658
Positional notation, 41–51, 658
Powers, James, 23
Presentation abilities, 425

INDEX

Primary Storage (*see* Main storage)
Printer, 121, 658
Privacy, 512
Problem analysis, 257
Problem solving, 257
Procedure manuals, 356, 658
Processing methods, 79
Program, 8, 283, 659
Program coding, 302
Program debugging, 303
Program flowchart, 258
Program interrupt, 455
Program logic, 304
Programmer, 527
Programmer productivity, 271
Programming production library, 280
PROM, 239, 659
Prompt, 139
Pseudo code, 274, 278, 659
Public databases, 499
Public information utilities, 522
Punch, 101
Punched card, 94, 659

Q

Questionnaires, 361
Queue, 94

R

RAM (Random Access Memory), 238, 659
Random files (*see* Direct access files)
Randomizing, 176, 486
Reader/punch, 101
Read/write head, 163, 659
Real storage, 220
Real time, 89, 474, 659
Record, 69–71, 659
Redundancy, 493, 659
Reel, 145
Reflective marker, 147
Register, 207, 213, 659
Reliability, 480
Relocatable library, 465
Remote batch, 89, 659
Report file, 158
Reporting, 77, 84, 87, 133
Reproducer, 28, 660
Requirements, 366
Response time, 475, 660
Restart, 457
Ritty, James, 21
ROM (Read Only Memory), 239, 660
Root, 494
Rotational delay, 167, 660
RPG II, 293, 660

S

Scanner, 188
Schema, 503
Second generation, 31, 660
Sector, 164
Seek time, 167, 660
Selector channel, 22, 660
Sequence control structure, 275
Sequence index set, 183
Sequential files, 172, 661
Serial code, 373
Serial operation, 167
Simple hierarchical structure, 495
Simplex, 481, 661
Significant-digit coding, 375
Society, 511
Soft-copy, 77, 661
Software, 8, 244, 661
Software house, 433
Sorter, 27, 661
Sorting, 83, 661
Source data, 75
Source document, 76, 661
Source library, 465
Source program, 453, 661
Special purpose computer, 74
Spooling, 456, 661
Spreadsheet, 297
Storage, 79, 662
Storage protection, 468
Storage register, 213
Stored program, 10, 25, 662
Structured design, 662
Structure programming, 275, 662
Structured systems analysis, 422
Subschema, 503
Summary reports, 87
Supervisor, 461, 662
Supervisor call (SVC), 455
System, 662
  definition, 347
  stages of a, 350
Systems analyst, 528, 662
Systems flowcharting, 417, 662
Syntax, 303

T

Tape (*see* Magnetic tape)
Tape drive, 147, 662
Tape speed, 151
Template, 259, 663
Terminal, 476, 663
Testing, 303, 663
Thin film, 216
Third generation, 33, 663
Throughput, 451, 663

Time-sharing, 90, 476, 663
Top down development, 271, 663
Track, 149, 663
Track index, 178
Track-to-track seek time, 167
Trailer label, 154, 663
Training, 411
Train printer, 123
Transactions, 70, 108, 431, 663
Translators, 284
Transmission speed, 135, 478
Transportation, 519
Tree, 494
Turnkey system, 229, 664
Typewriter printer, 127

U

Unemployment, 514
Unit record, 26, 664
Univac, 25
UPC (Universal Product Code), 116, 664
Updating, 81
User 359, 664

V

Variable length record, 154, 664
Variable length word, 216
Vehicle traffic control, 521
Verifier, 97, 664

Videotex, 522
Virtual files, 180
Virtual storage, 220, 664
VisiCalc, 297
Voice grade, 480, 482

W

Wand reader, 117
Wheel printer, 123
Wire matrix printer, 125
Word, 216, 665
Word processing, 444, 528, 665
Work file, 158, 174

Z

Zones, 55–61
Zoned decimal, 57, 149, 665